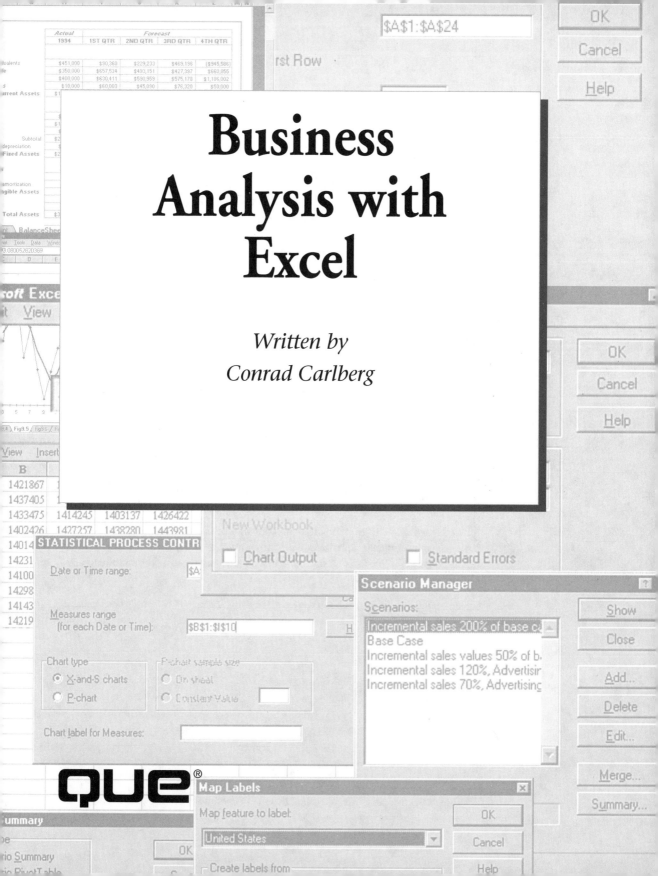

Business Analysis with Excel

Written by
Conrad Carlberg

Business Analysis with Excel

Copyright© 1995 by Que® Corporation

Library of Congress Catalog No.: 95-71465

ISBN: 0-7897-0382-3

97 96 95   5 4 3 2 1

Interpretation of the printing code: the rightmost double-digit number is the year of the book's printing; the rightmost single-digit number, the number of the book's printing. For example, a printing code of 95-1 shows that the first printing of the book occurred in 1995.

All terms mentioned in this book that are known to be trademarks or service marks have been appropriately capitalized. Que cannot attest to the accuracy of this information. Use of a term in this book should not be regarded as affecting the validity of any trademark or service mark.

Screen reproductions in this book were created using Collage Plus from Inner Media, Inc., Hollis, NH.

Composed in *Stone Serif* and *MCPdigital* by Que Corporation

Credits

President
Roland Elgey

Vice President and Publisher
Marie Butler-Knight

Associate Publisher
Don Roche, Jr.

Editorial Services Director
Elizabeth Keaffaber

Managing Editor
Michael Cunningham

Director of Marketing
Lynn E. Zingraf

Senior Series Editor
Chris Nelson

Acquisitions Editor
Deborah F. Abshier

Product Directors
Janice A. Snyder
Lisa D.Wagner

Production Editors
Linda Seifert
Lisa Gebken

Assistant Product Marketing Manager
Kim Margolius

Technical Editor
Roger D. Tedford

Technical Specialist
Cari Skaggs

Acquisitions Coordinator
Tracy Williams

Operations Coordinator
Patty Brooks

Editorial Assistant
Carmen Phelps

Book Designer
Ruth Harvey

Cover Designer
Dan Armstrong

Production Team
Angela D. Bannan
Brian Buschkill
Maxine Dillingham
Chad Dressler
Bryan Flores
Darren Jackson
Damon Jordan
Bob LaRoche
Michelle Lee
Julie Quinn
Bobbi Satterfield
Andy Stone
Michael Thomas
Colleen Williams

Indexer
Virginia Munroe

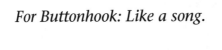

For Buttonhook: Like a song.

About the Author

Conrad Carlberg is president of Network Control Systems, Inc., a software development and consulting firm that specializes in the statistical forecasting of data network usage. He holds a Ph.D. in statistics from the University of Colorado, and is a three-time recipient of Microsoft Excel's Most Valuable Professional award. Mr. Carlberg resides near Denver, Colorado.

Acknowledgments

I would like to thank and acknowledge the following Que staff and associates for their energy and help, and especially for bearing with me during an over-long development: Debbie Abshier, Lisa Gebken, Linda Seifert, Jan Snyder, and Lisa Wagner.

Peter Kushar, Mark Randall, Jennifer Greenlee, and Diane Bartholomew, all of U S WEST Carrier Marketing, provided technical assistance and made substantial contributions to several chapters.

And Roger (not a sysop, not even close) Tedford for his technical editing. Really, I should be acknowledging him as a coauthor.

We'd Like to Hear from You!

As part of our continuing effort to produce books of the highest possible quality, Que would like to hear your comments. To stay competitive, we *really* want you, as a computer book reader and user, to let us know what you like or dislike most about this book or other Que products.

You can mail comments, ideas, or suggestions for improving future editions to the address below, or send us a fax at (317) 581-4663. For the online inclined, Macmillan Computer Publishing has a forum on CompuServe (type **GO QUEBOOKS** at any prompt) through which our staff and authors are available for questions and comments. The address of our Internet site is **http://www.mcp.com** (World Wide Web).

In addition to exploring our forum, please feel free to contact me personally to discuss your opinions of this book: I'm **74404,3307** on CompuServe, and **lwagner@que.mcp.com** on the Internet.

Thanks in advance—your comments will help us to continue publishing the best books available on computer topics in today's market.

Lisa D.Wagner
Product Development Specialist
Que Corporation
201 W. 103rd Street
Indianapolis, Indiana 46290
USA

Contents at a Glance

Financial Statements and Analysis

Financial Planning and Control

Investment Decisions

Sales and Marketing

Contents

3 Valuing Inventories for the Balance Sheet   57

4 Balance Sheet: Liabilities and Owner's Equity   87

5 Working Capital and Cash Flow Analysis   117

Introduction

Welcome to *Business Analysis with Excel*! This book is different from most others on Excel that you may have seen, because it focuses on a topic that is deeply important to all of us: Money.

Rex Stout once wrote, "The science of accounting has two main branches, one being addition, and the other being subtraction." I took these words to heart when I was casting about for a theme for this book. I wanted to write a book that would show people how to maximize profit, the result of the two branches Stout mentioned.

Profit, of course, is not revenue. I cannot teach you how to create revenue—that's more a matter for the heart, not the head—nor would I want to offer you MBA or CPA material. I did set out to write a book that any person engaged in any level of business could use as a refresher, from basic financial procedures such as General Ledgers and income statements, to operational tools such as quality control, to investment decisions such as business case-analysis.

I also wanted to structure the book around the most popular and sophisticated spreadsheet program available, Microsoft Excel. Therefore, each chapter in *Business Analysis with Excel* provides information about a different business task or procedure, and discusses how best to apply Excel to that situation.

You will find reference to many Excel functions and capabilities that you may already use in your business activities on a daily basis. But you will also find discussions of tools that you have never used, or that you might never have considered using in the context of business analysis.

After all, no one can be completely familiar with every option in an application like Excel. There is a forum on the CompuServe network that serves Excel users. A question appeared on that forum about how to enter a number in a worksheet cell so that Excel would treat the number as text (this is quite a basic operation). Surprisingly, the question was posted by one of the most experienced, best known, and creative Excel consultants in the country. This book's author thought that it was a put-on and responded in kind, but it turned out that the question was genuine.

So we all have gaps in our knowledge. The purpose here is to help fill in some of the gaps that may have penetrated your knowledge base since your last course in business, or since you first learned how to use a spreadsheet.

Business Analysis with Excel makes liberal use of case studies: that is, situations that are typical of decisions or problems that you might face on any given workday. These case studies discuss, first, the problem itself: why it represents a problem and how a solution can contribute to a company's profitability. Then the case studies demonstrate at least one possible solution that uses Excel as a tool. The intent is for you to mentally put yourself in the situation described, work through it, and then apply the solution to an actual situation that you face.

How This Book Is Organized

You can look in the table of contents or the index of *Business Analysis with Excel* whenever you encounter an unfamiliar or obscure situation, and read about how to solve it by means of the analysis tools in Excel. To make it easier to find related situations, the book is divided into four parts:

- **Financial Statements and Statement Analysis.** This section discusses fundamental financial concepts and tools such as income statements, balance sheets, cash flow, and ratio analysis.

- **Financial Planning and Control.** This section covers budgeting methods such as pro formas, forecasting trends, and quality control procedures including process measurement and defect analysis.

- **Investment Decisions.** You will find business case-analysis and profit planning in these chapters. Strategies for structuring and testing business cases are covered here, as well as ways to quantify the degree of risk involved in entering a new line of business. You will also find in this section a chapter on fixed assets, which normally account for the greatest portion of a company's capital investment.

- **Sales and Marketing.** Sales and marketing analysis, costing and pricing, and margin analysis are covered here. There is also a chapter that fully explains the structure and function of the Business Planner, a valuable template included with Excel 7.

Also included are a glossary that briefly defines many important terms, and an appendix that provides a full description of the files and utilities that you will find on the *Business Analysis with Excel* Companion disk.

As mentioned, you can dip into this book to find particular topics, and to make use of the information without necessarily reviewing everything that came before. Therefore, certain tips and recommendations on using Excel are (briefly) repeated from time to time. And in each chapter you will find full, step-by-step descriptions of how to accomplish a given task using Excel.

A disk accompanies this book. For your convenience, the disk contains Excel files that carry the data and formulas used in the tables and figures in *Business Analysis with Excel*. The disk also contains Visual Basic for Applications (VBA) code that you can use with Excel 5 or later to accomplish tasks such as forecasts and process control.

Two Special Skills: Names and Array Formulas

Have you ever had to interpret someone else's worksheet? Or have you ever had to use a worksheet that you constructed, months or perhaps years ago, and then been completely unable to figure out what you had in mind when you constructed it?

I bet you have.

The main difficulty with many otherwise useful worksheets is that their authors don't document them. Consider this cell formula:

```
=IF(AND(B12<3000,A12<5),C14*D14*.05,C14*D14*.075)
```

It would take you at least 10 or 15 *minutes* to figure out what that formula is up to, even if you know the worksheet's basic purpose. It would take you 10 or 15 *seconds* if the author had used this formula instead:

```
=IF(AND(YearToDateSales<3000,YearsSinceHired<5),Units*Price*
LowCommission, Units*Price*HiCommission)
```

It is not too difficult to infer that this formula says:

> "If this person's sales during this year are less than $3,000, and this person was hired less than 5 years ago, return the sales amount times a lower commission; otherwise return the sales amount times a higher commission."

So, to make your work self-documenting, I urge you in many instances to give names to Excel worksheet cells, ranges, and constants. Because you will find this approach taken throughout the book, review it here and, if you want to, in the Excel manual and online Help.

Assigning Names

To name a cell or range, begin by highlighting it on the worksheet. Then, choose Insert, Name, Define and type the name you want to use in the Names in Workbook edit box. Or, use this quicker method: after you have highlighted the cell or range, click in the Name box (immediately above the column header for column A and just to the left of the down-arrow), type the name, and press Enter.

To name a constant such as "LowCommission," choose Insert, Name, Define and type the name of the constant in the Names in Workbook edit box. Then, in the Refers to edit box, type the value that you want to assign to the constant. You cannot use the Name box to define a constant.

A side benefit of using names instead of cell or range addresses is that you can paste names into formulas as you are creating them. After you have started typing a formula, you can use Insert, Name, Paste and select the name you want to use from the Paste Name list box. This approach saves you keystrokes and helps prevent misspellings. Most important, you don't have to remember existing names: they're right there in the list box.

When you choose a name for a range or a constant, consider using both uppercase and lowercase letters: for example, "TotalLiabilities." Mixing uppercase and lowercase makes the name easier to read (compare with "totalliabilities." You should probably avoid using all uppercase letters. Excel's worksheet function names (for example, SUM and AVERAGE) use all uppercase letters, and you don't want to define a name that could be confused with a function.

Using Array Formulas

Many of the formulas that *Business Analysis with Excel* describes are a special type of Excel formula termed an *array formula*. An array formula contains an array of values, or a reference to an array of worksheet cells, such as:

```
=SUM(IF(MOD(ROW(SheetRange),2)=0,SheetRange))
```

which sums the values in the worksheet range named "SheetRange" if and only if they are in an even-numbered row. The formula requires a special keyboard sequence to enter it correctly. On a computer running Windows, the sequence is Ctrl+Shift+Enter: that is, simultaneously hold down the Ctrl and Shift keys as you press Enter.

To avoid confusion, this book provides emphasis in the instructions when any formulas that must be entered as array formulas are described, for example:

> ... *array* enter this formula:

You can tell that Excel has interpreted your formula as an array formula if you see curly (sometimes termed French) braces around it in the formula bar. For example, the formula shown previously appears in the formula bar like this:

```
{=SUM(IF(MOD(ROW(RANGE),2)=0,RANGE))}
```

Do not type the braces yourself. If you do so, Excel interprets the formula as text.

Conventions Used in This Book

Business Analysis with Excel uses a few typeface, terminology, and formatting conventions to denote special information:

- A sequence like this:

    Ctrl+Enter

    means that you should hold down the Ctrl key as you press Enter.

- When you should select a sequence of options from an Excel menu, you will see this:

    Choose Tools, Solver.

    This means that you should first select the Tools option in Excel's main menu, and then select Solver from the dropdown menu under Tools. The "hot" or "accelerator" keys associated with a menu item are underlined, indicating that you may use Alt+ the underscored letter to choose the command or option. If you want to use two hot keys consecutively (as in Tools, Solver), keep pressing the Alt key as you press T, then v. *Do not* use Alt+T, then Alt+v.

- Some Excel menu items have a submenu that appears to the right when you choose the main menu item. For example, when you select Insert, Name, you see a menu appear to the right of the Name menu item. This submenu is termed a "cascading" menu. You can identify the menu items that have cascading menus by the arrowhead that appears to their right.

- Data or formulas that you enter in an Excel worksheet cell are shown like this:

      =SUM(CumulativeNetIncome)/ProductLife

- New terms, or information that needs special emphasis, are shown in *italic*.

- Data that has to be typed in appears in **boldface**.

- Information about performing a task more efficiently or alternative ways to go about a task appears in tips. Tips are set apart from the main text like this:

> **Tip**
>
> To select a range of cells, even if it contains some blank cells, press Ctrl+*.

- Information that is related to the current topic, but that might not apply to it directly, is shown like this:

> **Note**
>
> You can find VBA code that automates this process on the disk that accompanies this book.

Part I
Financial Statements and Statement Analysis

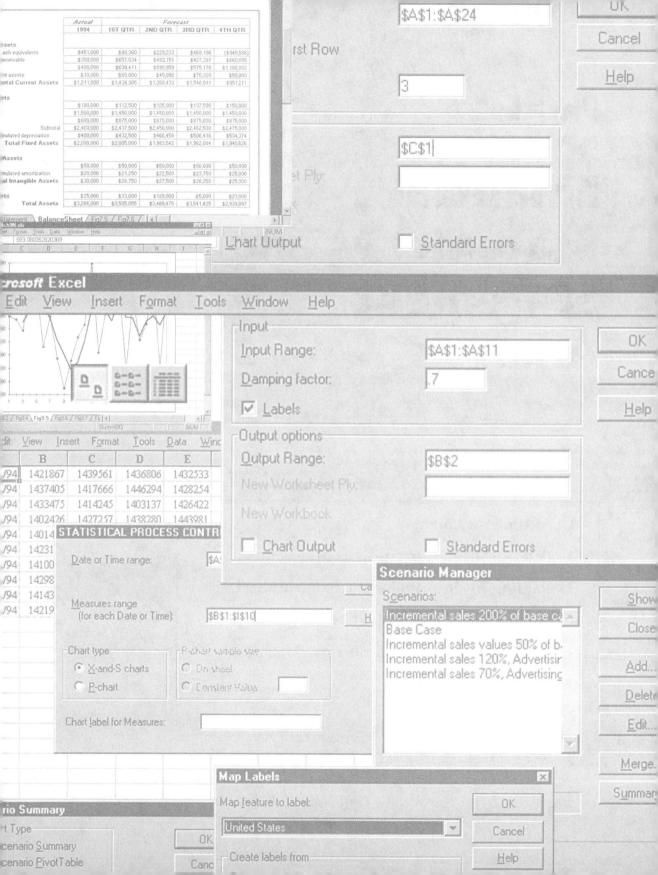

Accounting quantifies the everyday world of buying and selling. Would you buy something for more than you can sell it? Of course not—but many companies do exactly that every year. The annual number of small business failures continues to grow. Too often, businesses look at only the up-front costs, but ignore the related costs. The devil is in the details, and finance and accounting help keep the demons in their place. The point is that it is important to know the basics.

Choosing the Right Perspective

We all tend to think of accounting as an exact science, one that is fully governed by the rules of arithmetic, but the numbers generated are actually only best estimates. While the rules, procedures, and methods make the numbers appear to be absolute facts, they are not. However, the numbers can and do represent how well the managers are running the business. Balance sheets and income statements are not commandments, but rather guides, and are used by different users for different purposes.

This book classifies accounting information according to two categories of decision makers:

- *Management* accounting provides information to decision makers who are inside the company. If you want to bring a new product to the marketplace, you would analyze cost, price, and demand data to assess the product's potential. This is the management accounting information that's needed to manage the introduction of a new product. You make judgments about the product on the basis of the data you have available.

- *Financial* accounting provides information to decision makers outside the company, such as investors, creditors, and governments. Suppose that you wanted to raise funds by making your company a public corporation and issuing shares of stock to the investment community. Potential investors would demand detailed financial accounting information (and the law would require you to make it available). An investor wants to know that a set of rigid guidelines was used to create the information. Otherwise, there is no way to make an informed investment choice.

When you decide, for example, whether to introduce a new product, your analytical framework is defined less rigidly than when you are trying to raise capital in the investment community. You often need room to maneuver, and management accounting provides you with that room.

Both aspects of accounting are useful, and this book discusses financial accounting from time to time. However, the principal focus is on making information as useful as possible for internal decision-making purposes.

To use accounting information for routine decision making, it is not necessary to explore in-depth the nuances and technicalities of the accounting profession. But if you understand this information well enough to use it on a routine basis, you will be much better prepared to make good use of your accountant's time when a tricky decision *is* required.

Going for the Bottom Line

The income statement is a powerful tool for decision making. It portrays the flow of money and the relationship of revenues to expenses over a period of time. It tells us how much money was made in a year. The terms profit, net income, and earnings are commonly used to state the bottom line.

The income statement provides a starting point in the analysis of a business. The popular press frequently reports earnings and nothing more: "*Today, U.S. Widgets reported quarterly income of $240 million.*" This is positive, but there is more to the story.

Using the Income Statement

Businesses need to measure and report income. This sounds straightforward enough, but it gets complex in a hurry. Both measurement and reporting can, and are, complex enough to fill several texts. While it is not our purpose to go to that level of detail, this book provides highlights that simplify the process of measurement and reporting, and that enable you to make use of the results in day-to-day operational decisions.

Choosing a Reporting Method

The measurement of net income is an attempt to match the value generated by a business (its revenues) with the resources it consumes (its expenses). This sentence: "In 1994, we sold $200 million of products and services, at a cost of $175 million, for a profit of $25 million," quantifies the operation of the business over a one-year period. The business now has a track record: a place to begin the analysis of its operations.

However, to measure and report the net income in a generally accepted fashion, more is needed. Accountants use a series of conventions that strengthen the validity of the income statement report. If you read an income statement that you believe to have been prepared using these conventions, you generally have greater faith that the information is valid and credible. Perhaps the company is worth investing in. This is the world of debits and credits, Generally Accepted Accounting Principles, tax rules, and so on. These are rules of the game that make the measurement of the operation of the business valid for the purposes of an income statement.

There is no one way to format an income statement. Your choice will depend on the use you intend to make of the statment, and the picture that you want to present. The key is for the information to be useful in support of decision making. Your audience could be potential investors, creditors, or internal (sometimes, external) managers.

Some examples of commonly used income statement formats are shown in figures 1.1 through 1.4.

Case Study: Documentation for a Bank Loan

XYZ Products, Inc., wants to obtain a bank loan for the purchase of some new equipment. As XYZ's president, you oversee the preparation of an income statement that documents your company's financial position for the bank loan committee. The bank has little interest in the such matters as the amount of your variable costs relative to your earnings, or what your earnings are on a product-by-product basis.

The bank is, however, interested in your sales volume, your gross profit and your operating profit. You could use a format such as the one shown in figure 1.1 for the income statement that accompanies your loan application.

Figure 1.1 shows a typical format for an income statement used for external reporting purposes. It could also, for example, be used in an annual report. Notice that there are apparent math errors in the report, in rows 17 and 19. These are caused by the rounding that Excel applies when a currency format obscures significant digits. When, for purposes of space, you divide actual figures by, say, 1000 and indicate by a column header that the entries are in $1000's, it's best to use Excel's ROUND() function. For example:

```
=ROUND(4690/1000,0)
```

Had this been used in cell B16 of figure 1.1, instead of the actual entry of 4.69 (format-rounded to $5) then the result of the calculation in cell B17 would have been the correct value of $21 instead of $22. (You could also use Tools, Options, Precision as Displayed on the Calculation tab, but this is a risky procedure.)

There are many types of income statement formats and uses. The same firm might modify and adjust its report of income and costs, based on the type of business that it conducts and its purpose for the income statement.

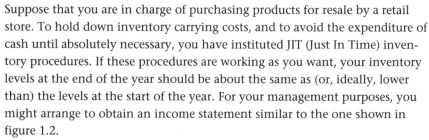

Fig. 1.1

An income statement format suitable for external reporting omits details such as inventory levels, but includes all categories that affect net income.

Case Study: Inventory Control in a Merchandising Firm

Suppose that you are in charge of purchasing products for resale by a retail store. To hold down inventory carrying costs, and to avoid the expenditure of cash until absolutely necessary, you have instituted JIT (Just In Time) inventory procedures. If these procedures are working as you want, your inventory levels at the end of the year should be about the same as (or, ideally, lower than) the levels at the start of the year. For your management purposes, you might arrange to obtain an income statement similar to the one shown in figure 1.2.

Another variation of an income statement format might be used by a manufacturing firm (see fig. 1.3). The major difference between the structure of the manufacturing firm's income statement and that of the merchandising firm is in the cost of goods sold. For the manufacturer, the cost of goods manufactured is added to the opening inventory. For the merchandiser, purchases from suppliers are added to the opening inventory. The manufacturer is likely to have various cost subcategories within the cost of goods manufactured, such as raw materials, factory overhead, and labor costs. These subcategories do not appear in the merchandiser's income statement: the cost of purchases is seldom broken down further.

Fig. 1.2
An income statement format suitable for certain management purposes in a merchandising firm might exclude dividend information but provide details on inventory levels.

Microsoft Excel - Pwxlch01.xls

A1 ABC Products, Inc.

	A	B	C
1	ABC Products, Inc.		
2	Income Statement		
3	For the year ended December 31, 1994		
4			
5		($ 000)	($ 000)
6			
7	Sales		$332
8	Less Cost of Goods Sold		
9	Opening Inventory	$43	
10	Add Purchases	$52	
11	Goods Available for Sale	$95	
12	Ending Inventory	$27	
13	Cost of Goods Sold		$68
14			
15	Gross Margin		$264
16			
17	Less Operating Expenses		
18	Administrative Expenses	$82	
19	Selling Expenses	$51	
20	Operating Expenses		$133
21			
22	Operating Income		$131
23			

Fig1.2 / Fig1.3 / Fig1.4 / Fig1.5 / Fig1.6 / Fig1.7-1.8

Fig. 1.3
An income statement for a manufacturing firm, formatted for planning purposes, often includes information about the cost of goods manufactured in a supplement.

Microsoft Excel - Pwxlch01.xls

A1 Clark Manufacturing, Inc.

	A	B	C
1	Clark Manufacturing, Inc.		
2	Income Statement		
3	For the year ended December 31, 1994		
4		($ 000)	($ 000)
5			
6	Sales		$223
7			
8	Less Cost of Goods Sold		
9	Opening Finished Goods Inventory	$58	
10	ost of Goods Manufactured (see supplement)	$127	
11	Goods Available for Sale	$185	
12	Ending Finished Goods Inventory	$62	
13	Cost of Goods Sold	$123	
14			
15	Gross Margin		$100
16			
17	Less Operating Expenses		
18	Administrative Expenses	$34	
19	Selling Expenses	$20	
20	Operating Expenses		$54
21			
22	Operating Income		$46
23			

Fig1.2 / Fig1.3 / Fig1.4 / Fig1.5 / Fig1.6 / Fig1.7-1.8

One type of income statement that deserves special mention targets the purpose of managing the business from the perspective of specific products and expenses. Figure 1.4 provides an example.

This income statement excludes such items as interest and amortization, and can be used for everyday operations. It provides a detailed look at revenue and expense, and is an example of the type of income statement a manager needs to guide a department.

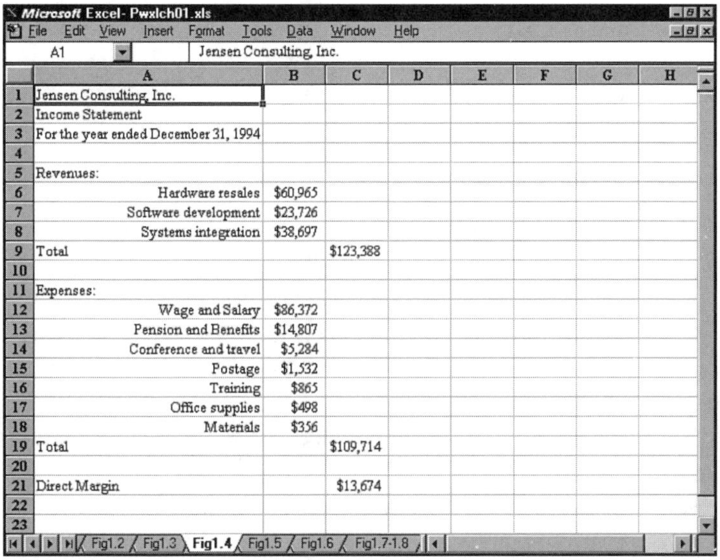

	A	B	C
1	Jensen Consulting, Inc.		
2	Income Statement		
3	For the year ended December 31, 1994		
4			
5	Revenues:		
6	Hardware resales	$60,965	
7	Software development	$23,726	
8	Systems integration	$38,697	
9	Total		$123,388
10			
11	Expenses:		
12	Wage and Salary	$86,372	
13	Pension and Benefits	$14,807	
14	Conference and travel	$5,284	
15	Postage	$1,532	
16	Training	$865	
17	Office supplies	$498	
18	Materials	$356	
19	Total		$109,714
20			
21	Direct Margin		$13,674
22			
23			

Fig. 1.4
An income statement format that is used for revenue and expense management purposes details the sources and uses of funds.

Ideally, you should tailor the income statement to a format that you and your managers can use daily. You can expand the level of detail shown in figures 1.1 through 1.4 to include the data that you need most often. It is here that judgment, as well as creativity, become critical. A simple reformat of data, or adding a detail line item, can enrich your insight into the way that your business operates.

For example, you could drive the behavior of your management team by means of a link between your bonus systems and a customized income statement. This link could take the form of the addition of a very specific measurement. Suppose that you want to push your sales force toward the creation of new accounts. Your income statement might show revenue figures both as sales to existing accounts and as new business, and might include cost figures for new business bonuses. This could help prod the sales force to concentrate on the more difficult process of new business sales.

As figures 1.1 through 1.4 imply, there are many possible ways to structure an income statement. Each one reflects a different set of circumstances, defined by the business's specific situation. There are guidelines, but there is also flexibility within those guidelines to tailor a statement to your particular needs. Your business and the way that you want to use the data set the direction for the type of income statement you would use.

Measuring the Operating and Non-operating Segments

An income statement records the flow of resources over time. Earnings, or net income, measures the extent to which revenues generated during the accounting period exceeded expenses incurred in producing the revenues. This measure tells whether the firm made money or not.

Income statements commonly divide this resource flow into operating and non-operating segments. The operating segment represents what occurred on a day-to-day basis. The non-operating segment represents the assets that the firm might have financed, and extraordinary occurrences such as a one-time sale of a company asset.

When you analyze a business, it is important to keep the two segments separate. If you were considering the expansion of your own business, you might first ask yourself whether the firm made money, and whether you can fund an expansion by means of the profits. Your focus would be on the numbers produced by your normal, everyday business operations. You would not want to base your decision on the effect of a one-time, unique event. You would take that event into consideration, but you would not rely on its effect on future earnings, because it is a one-time event.

An income statement's operating segment represents the results of the company's major, ongoing activities, while the non-operating segment represents all the company's secondary activities. The company needs to understand both segments so as to grasp the total picture, as well as to know how best to prepare for its future.

Moving from the General Journal to the Income Statement

It is typical for a business to record its daily transactions in a General Journal. This record keeps track of every individual transaction in every account, whether cash investments, cash paid, accounts receivable (for example, sales), accounts payable (purchase of materials), and so on.

Getting the General Journal into Excel

There are many different software programs available to help you record and store this information. Because some programs provide the user with such conveniences as a predefined chart of accounts, many people prefer to use software other than Excel to gather information on individual transactions.

(A chart of accounts is simply a list that associates account names with numbers that identify the account: for example, you might decide to identify Accounts Payable with the number 20.) Excel is, of course, a powerful and flexible means of entering, storing, and retrieving information about individual transactions. However, if you use Excel for this purpose, you will have to create your own categories for transactions.

On the other hand, if you enter and store individual transactions using software other than Excel, you may have difficulty importing files into Excel. Although most such programs have an option that allows you to export data in ASCII (text) format, the arrangement of the exported data might not be ideal for import into Excel. For example, some programs export each part of a record onto a different line of the ASCII file: one line for the account number, another line for the account name, another line for the transaction amount, and so on.

Certainly, you can import this type of structure into an Excel worksheet quite easily by choosing File, Open. However, after you have imported the information, you might find it necessary to move the account name and the transaction amount onto the same line as the account number. If you have many transactions to import, this cut-and-pasting can become tedious, and you should consider recording and then running an Excel macro to do the rearrangement for you.

Getting the Journal Data to the Ledger

Whether you enter the General Journal data directly into Excel or import it from another software application, the next step is usually to collect the transactions in their proper accounts within the General Ledger. Figure 1.5 shows an example of entries in a General Journal, and figure 1.6 shows how you could collect these entries in the General Ledger.

For ease in collecting the General Journal entries into the General Ledger, four range names are defined on the General Journal sheet: EntryDate (column A), AccountNumber (column C), JournalDebits (column D) and JournalCredits (column E). Each of these names, and their associated columns, refer to the General Journal worksheet in figure 1.5.

Two additional names are defined in the General Ledger: LedgerDate refers to cell $A$6, and GLAccount (short for General Ledger Account) refers to cell $D6. Notice that LedgerDate refers to an absolute reference, and GLAccount refers to a mixed reference. The effect of this referencing is explained in more detail later.

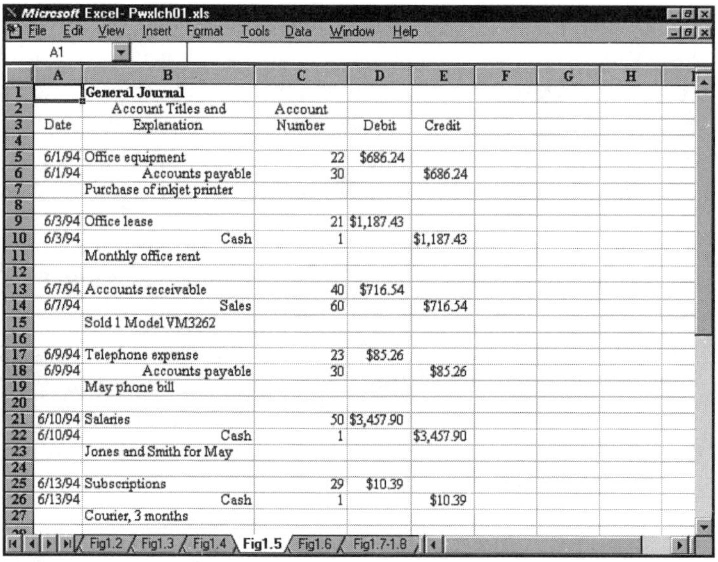

	A	B	C	D	E
1		General Journal			
2		Account Titles and	Account		
3	Date	Explanation	Number	Debit	Credit
4					
5	6/1/94	Office equipment	22	$686.24	
6	6/1/94	Accounts payable	30		$686.24
7		Purchase of inkjet printer			
8					
9	6/3/94	Office lease	21	$1,187.43	
10	6/3/94	Cash	1		$1,187.43
11		Monthly office rent			
12					
13	6/7/94	Accounts receivable	40	$716.54	
14	6/7/94	Sales	60		$716.54
15		Sold 1 Model VM3262			
16					
17	6/9/94	Telephone expense	23	$85.26	
18	6/9/94	Accounts payable	30		$85.26
19		May phone bill			
20					
21	6/10/94	Salaries	50	$3,457.90	
22	6/10/94	Cash	1		$3,457.90
23		Jones and Smith for May			
24					
25	6/13/94	Subscriptions	29	$10.39	
26	6/13/94	Cash	1		$10.39
27		Courier, 3 months			

Fig. 1.5
General Journal entries record individual transactions in chronological order as debits and credits.

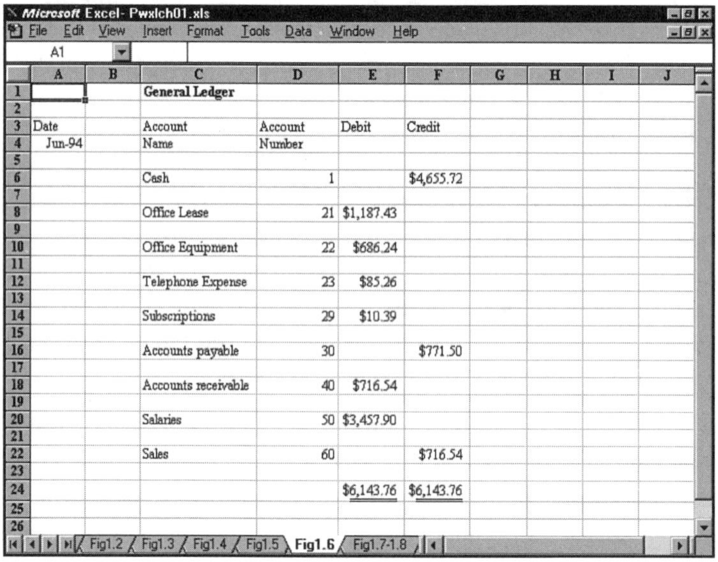

	A	B	C	D	E	F
1			General Ledger			
2						
3	Date		Account	Account	Debit	Credit
4	Jun-94		Name	Number		
5						
6			Cash	1		$4,655.72
7						
8			Office Lease	21	$1,187.43	
9						
10			Office Equipment	22	$686.24	
11						
12			Telephone Expense	23	$85.26	
13						
14			Subscriptions	29	$10.39	
15						
16			Accounts payable	30		$771.50
17						
18			Accounts receivable	40	$716.54	
19						
20			Salaries	50	$3,457.90	
21						
22			Sales	60		$716.54
23						
24					$6,143.76	$6,143.76
25						
26						

Fig. 1.6
General Ledger entries accumulate individual transactions from the General Journal into specific accounts.

On the General Ledger worksheet, the following formula in its Debit column accumulates the appropriate entries from the General Journal:

```
=SUM(IF(MONTH(EntryDate)=MONTH(LedgerDate),1,0)*IF(AccountNumber =
   GLAccount,1,0)*JournalDebits)
```

and this formula accumulates the appropriate credits:

```
=SUM(IF(MONTH(EntryDate)=MONTH(LedgerDate),1,0)*IF(AccountNumber =
    GLAccount,1,0)*JournalCredits)
```

> **Note**
>
> The two formulas shown here must be entered as *array formulas*. After typing the
> formula, but before pressing Enter, simultaneously hold down Ctrl+Shift. You will see
> a pair of curly (also known as French braces) braces around the formula. This indi-
> cates that Excel has accepted the formula as an array formula. Do not enter the
> braces yourself from the keyboard, or Excel will interpret the formula as text.

The formulas instruct Excel to do the following:

1. Evaluate each entry in the General Journal's EntryDate column. If the month of that date equals the date for the General Ledger, return 1; otherwise, return 0.

2. Evaluate each entry in the General Journal's AccountNumber column. If the account number is the same as the account number for the current General Ledger account, return 1; otherwise, return 0.

3. Multiply the result of step 1 by step 2. Only when both conditions are true will this step return a 1; otherwise, it will return 0.

4. Multiply the result of step 3 by the General Journal's entries in the JournalDebits range (or its JournalCredits range, in the second of the two formulas shown previously).

5. Return the sum of step 4.

Be sure that you understand the following aspects of the names used in these formulas. First, they assume that the General Journal and the General Ledger worksheets both belong to the same workbook. If the General Journal be- longed to a workbook named GJ.xls, then the definitions of the names in the formulas would have to be qualified by references to that workbook. For example:

```
='C:\EXCEL7\[GJ.xls]JournalSheet'!$A$4:$A$27
```

Second, consider the definitions of the names LedgerDate and GLAccount. LedgerDate refers to cell $A$6: because this is an absolute reference (note the two dollar signs), LedgerDate returns the same value regardless of the location of the cell where it is entered.

GLAccount, on the other hand, refers to cell $D6. This is a mixed reference: only the column is fixed, and the row can change depending on where a reference to GLAccount is entered.

Therefore, this formula:

```
=SUM(IF(MONTH(EntryDate)=MONTH(LedgerDate),1,0)*IF(AccountNumber =
    GLAccount,1,0)*JournalCredits)
```

if entered in cell F6 shown in figure 1.6, uses the value 1 (in cell D6) for GLAccount. But if the formula is entered in cell F8, it uses the value 21 (in cell D8). Because the name GLAccount refers to the mixed reference $D6, the name itself acts as a mixed reference.

By using these formulas, all the individual transactions from the General Journal are accumulated into the General Ledger, according to the account that they have been posted to and according to the correct date for the current General Ledger entry.

Getting the Ledger Data to the Income Statement

You can use a similar approach to accumulate the information in the General Ledger in your income statement.

The procedure suggested here makes use of a convention that you might use in defining your chart of accounts. Perhaps you have decided to number all accounts that pertain to fixed administrative expenses by means of the numbers 20 through 29. If you name the range in the General Ledger that contains the account numbers as LedgerAccounts, the range containing the credits as LedgerCredits, and the range containing the debits as LedgerDebits, then this array formula:

```
=SUM(IF(TRUNC(LedgerAccounts/10)=2,LedgerCredits-LedgerDebits,0))
```

returns the required information to the Income Statement's appropriate cell. (Remember to enter it as an array formula: use Ctrl+Shift before pressing Enter.)

The array formula first evaluates the elements in the range named Ledger-Accounts, and divides their values by 10. Then, if the integer portion of the result equals 2 (as it will if the account number is between 20 and 29 inclusive), it returns the sum of the difference between the accounts' debits and credits.

You could then use this formula to return the entry in your income statement that pertains to fixed administrative expenses. Similarly, if your chart

Chapter 1

Income Statements

In many ways, operating a business is like playing a game, and keeping track of your business is very similar to studying games such as baseball. Serious baseball fans know hundreds of statistics, such as batting averages and earned run averages. Similarly, if you are serious about your business, you need to be able to measure and understand the statistics that describe how your business operates. Accounting generally, and financial statements in particular, are the scorecards.

This chapter is not a treatise on accounting and finance, but it does describe tools that you can use to better understand certain financial aspects of operating your business. There are plenty of textbooks on the generally accepted practices of accounting and finance. This chapter highlights and demonstrates some practical techniques used in these disciplines.

Keeping Score

Accounting translates the actions that take place in the business world into a set of numbers that you can use to make informed decisions. It captures information on how well a company operates, the hundreds of obstacles that a company needs to overcome, and the company's prospects for the future.

Accounting rules enable you to compare your company with other companies and with other industries. These comparisons are important when you want to seek additional funds for expansion, such as by borrowing or by inviting capital investment. Following the rules can open opportunities to succeed and to receive equal treatment in a very rugged marketplace. But you don't need to be a CPA to use accounting for solid decision making. Often, it is as simple as subtracting your expenses from your revenues to determine your profits.

of accounts assigned all accounts pertaining to fixed production expenses to 2-digit numbers beginning with 3 (30, 31, ... , 39), you would use:

```
=SUM(IF(TRUNC(LedgerAccounts/10)=3,LedgerCredits-LedgerDebits,0))
```

> **Note**
>
> The procedures suggested here work most easily if you maintain your General Journal, General Ledger, and income statement all in the same workbook. However, Excel does not permit you to use the same local name more than once in the same workbook unless you qualify them with sheet names. Thus, you cannot use Debits, for example, as a local name on both the General Journal and the General Ledger in the same workbook. One option is to use names such as GeneralJournal!Debits, where GeneralJournal is the name of a sheet. Another option, used in the examples above, is to use the name JournalDebits to distinguish that range from LedgerDebits.

You can accumulate most of the entries on an income statement in a similar fashion, working from the General Journal to the General Ledger to the Income Statement. Two types of entries in particular, entries such as accounts payable and accounts receivable that involve accrual, and assets that are subject to depreciation, usually require special attention. Both affect the timing of your company's earnings. Accrual accounting is in the next section, and depreciation is covered in chapter 16, "Fixed Assests."

Managing with Accrual Accounting

Accrual accounting involves two steps: identifying the revenues for a given period, and matching the associated costs to those revenues. This is called the matching principle and is a basic concept that is used throughout the accounting process.

The notion of matching revenues to costs might seem obvious, but it has some subtle implications. Suppose that you purchase license plates for a company vehicle. You pay $400 for the plates in January. You write off the full $400 in January (that is, that you show it as a cost that you incurred fully during that month). You produce revenue or conduct business by using your vehicle both during January and during the next eleven months.

In this case, you have overstated your cost of doing business in January, understated it from February through December, and have failed to match the subsequent revenues with the initial expense. Accrual accounting allows you to spread the cost of the vehicle over the full twelve months, and to match the revenues the vehicle produces to the expense you incurred for the license plates.

Revenue is not the same as cash received, and expense is not the same as cash spent. You normally recognize revenue when the effort required to generate the sale is substantially complete, and there is reasonable certainty that you will receive payment. The accountant views the timing of the actual cash receipts, or the actual cash outlay, as only a technicality.

Another approach, termed the *cash method*, is sometimes used instead of the accrual method. Under the cash method, record revenue when the cash is received and costs or expenses when the cash is spent. Although the cash method is a less accurate means of associating revenues with costs and expenses, small businesses sometimes forego the accuracy of the accrual method for the simplicity of the cash method.

For credit sales, the accrual principle means that you recognize the revenue at the time of the sale, not when the customer makes payment. Suppose that you use your credit card to buy a new set of golf clubs at your local sporting goods store. The store recognizes the revenue when you sign the credit slip, but it does not receive cash until your credit card company sends them payment. The lag between recognition of revenue and cash payment can be significant. The fact that a company is profitable is no assurance that its cash flow will be sufficient to keep it solvent.

Income statements are necessary for a company's management to understand the relationship between the company's revenues and its expenses—its profitability—over a given period of time. Balance sheets, covered in chapters 2 through 4, are necessary for management to understand the relationship between the company's assets and its liabilities—its worth—at a given point in time. Cash flow statements, covered in detail in chapter 5, "Working Capital and Cash Flow Analysis," enable management to assess the company's solvency: whether sufficient working capital exists and will exist to continue business operation.

These three types of statements—income statements, balance sheets, and cash flow statements—are intimately related, even though they serve different purposes and provide different perspectives on a company's overall financial position. These relationships are determined in large measure by the principal of matching costs to revenues in the income statement via accrual.

For example, increases in revenues cause increases in the owner's equity on the credit side of the balance sheet, and increases in accrued expenses cause decreases in owner's equity on the debit side of the balance sheet.

Actual cash receipts and outlays, shown on cash flow statements, summarize the effects of increases and decreases in revenues and expenses on the amount of the company's working capital. The cash flow statements may or may not accurately reflect how the process of accrual apportions revenues and expenses during a given acccounting period.

The fact that cash flows might or might not reflect the accrual of revenues and expenses highlights the need for *adjusting entries*. When your company acquires an asset, such as an insurance policy, you might or might not use that asset up in order to create revenue during a particular accounting period.

Case Study: Adjusting Entries

Martin Consulting is a small business that provides assistance to its customers in assessing the quality of ground water. Figure 1.7 shows several examples of how Martin Consulting uses adjusting entries to record transactions via accrual.

Financial Statements and Statement Analysis

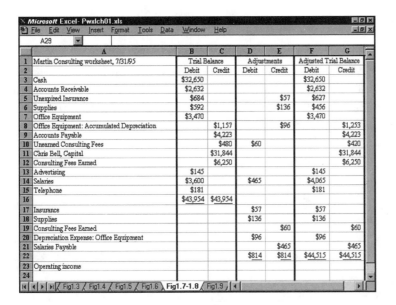

Fig. 1.7
Adjusting entries help to accrue revenues and expenses in the proper period.

	Trial Balance		Adjustments		Adjusted Trial Balance	
A — Martin Consulting worksheet, 7/31/95	Debit	Credit	Debit	Credit	Debit	Credit
3 Cash	$32,650				$32,650	
4 Accounts Receivable	$2,632				$2,632	
5 Unexpired Insurance	$684			$57	$627	
6 Supplies	$592			$136	$456	
7 Office Equipment	$3,470				$3,470	
8 Office Equipment: Accumulated Depreciation		$1,157		$96		$1,253
9 Accounts Payable		$4,223				$4,223
10 Unearned Consulting Fees		$480	$60			$420
11 Chris Bell, Capital		$31,844				$31,844
12 Consulting Fees Earned		$6,250				$6,250
13 Advertising	$145				$145	
14 Salaries	$3,600		$465		$4,065	
15 Telephone	$181				$181	
16	$43,954	$43,954				
17 Insurance			$57		$57	
18 Supplies			$136		$136	
19 Consulting Fees Earned				$60		$60
20 Depreciation Expense: Office Equipment			$96		$96	
21 Salaries Payable				$465		$465
22			$814	$814	$44,515	$44,515
23 Operating income						

At the end of July, Martin Consulting prepares this worksheet as the basis for its income statement and balance sheet. On July 1, an errors-and-omissions insurance policy was purchased in full to provide protection against any faulty advice given to the company's clients. The policy will remain in effect for 12 months. The cost of this policy is debited to an asset account in row 5, column B of the worksheet. When the worksheet is prepared at the end of the month, 1/12th of the value of the policy has expired: that value now becomes an expense incurred during the month of July. Row 5, column E contains $57 as an *adjusting credit entry*, reflecting that 1/12th of the policy's asset value has expired. Row 5, column F shows the remaining value of the asset, or $627. The *adjusting debit entry* appears in row 17, column D.

During the same period, Martin Consulting uses office supplies (stationery, photocopy toner, printing supplies, etc.) in the amount of $136 to support the production of its revenues. Another adjusting entry of $136 appears in row 6, column E, reflecting the decrease in the value of the original office supplies asset of $592, and applied against that amount in row 6, column F to show its remaining value of $456 at the end of the month. The adjusting debit entry appears in row 18, column D.

It is fairly easy to see the rationale for these adjusting entries. On July 1, the company owned twelve months of insurance, and owns eleven months worth of insurance on July 31. Similarly, it owns $592 in office supplies on July 1 and $456 on July 31. These amounts are directly measurable and Martin Consulting can easily enter, as adjusting debits and credits, the portions that expire or are used as expenses during the month of July.

But office equipment is another matter. At the beginning of July, the company owned equipment originally valued at $3470 (row 7, column B). How much of that $3470 was used up in the production of the month's revenues? The equipment is still there: the computer is still creating worksheets, the photocopier is still making copies, the telephone is still ringing. And yet some value was taken from the equipment in order to generate revenue.

Depreciation is the means used to account for the fact that the equipment provided value to the process of revenue generation. In contrast to counting the precise number of months that expire on an insurance policy, or the number of mailing envelopes that are used up, Martin must estimate the value of the office equipment "used" during the month of July.

Martin can use one of several methods of calculating depreciation to arrive at this estimate. These methods are covered in detail in chapter 16, "Fixed Assets." For now, suppose that Martin uses the straight-line method of depreciation. The assumption is that the office equipment has a useful life of three years. Then, for each month that passes, it is assumed that the value of the equipment declines by 1/36th of its original value: that is, the equipment depreciates each month by 1/36th, or $96. The adjusting credit entry is in row 8, column E, and the adjusting debit entry is shown in row 22, column D.

Tip

To avoid apparent errors in how your worksheet displays values when multiplication and division are involved, use the ROUND( ) function. For example:

=ROUND(3470/36,0)

By estimating the amount of monthly depreciation, Martin can assign an office equipment expense for the month. This makes it possible to associate the expense with the revenue, and to obtain a clearer picture of the month's income. Again, the matching principle holds that revenues should be matched with the expenses that helped to produce the revenues.

Adjusting entries are needed to accrue not only expenses but revenues. Suppose that toward the end of July, Martin has signed an agreement and accepted cash payment to perform eight hours of consulting at $60 per hour. The full amount of $480 is credited to an asset account called Unearned Consulting Fees. Before the end of the month Martin performs one of the eight contracted hours. Actually doing that work converts some of the unearned fees to an earned status. Adjusting entries, shown in row 10, column D and row 19, column E show how much—$60—of the unearned fee has been earned during July.

The four adjusting entries described above pertain to activities that both begin and end during an accounting period: for example, the use of $136 in office supplies began on July 1 and ended on July 31. An adjusting entry can also be used to record an activity that *spans* accounting periods. Suppose that Martin prepares an assistant's salary check, in payment for the prior two weeks, one week before the end of the month. The assistant then accrues one week of salary from July 25 through July 31. To show that this accrued salary is an expense attributable to July, rather than to August, Martin makes adjusting entries in row 14, column D. To show that it is a liability that will be met subsequently (probably, in August) it is also entered as a credit in row 21, column E.

Excel makes it simple to accumulate the trial balance and the adjusting entries into an adjusted trial balance. The actual formulas used in columns F and G of figure 1.7 (the adjusted debit and credit balances) are discussed in detail in chapter 5. For now, know that each adjusted debit entry is the sum of the trial balance and adjusting debits, less the sum of the trial balance and adjusting credits. Similarly, each adjusted credit entry is the sum of the trial balance and adjusting credits, less the sum of the trial balance and adjusting debits.

The totals of the adjusting entries and of the adjusted entries appear in row 22, columns D through G. The equality of the debit and credit totals *prove* that the entries are in balance.

> **Tip**
>
> Excel 7 provides several underline formats, including Single Accounting and Double Accounting. These are often used for, respectively, subtotals and totals. To access these formats, choose Format, Cells, and select the Font tab. Then, choose the Underline dropdown box.

Finally, it's time to move this information to an income statement (see fig. 1.8).

Rows 3 through 11 and 21 represent asset and liability accounts. They are copied from the adjusted trial balance to the balance sheet columns. Rows 12 through 20 represent revenue and expense accounts, and are copied to the income statement column. Then, in row 22 of columns H through K, the debits and credits are totalled. Notice that they are no longer in balance, nor should they be. The company's revenues for July exceeded its expenses, and

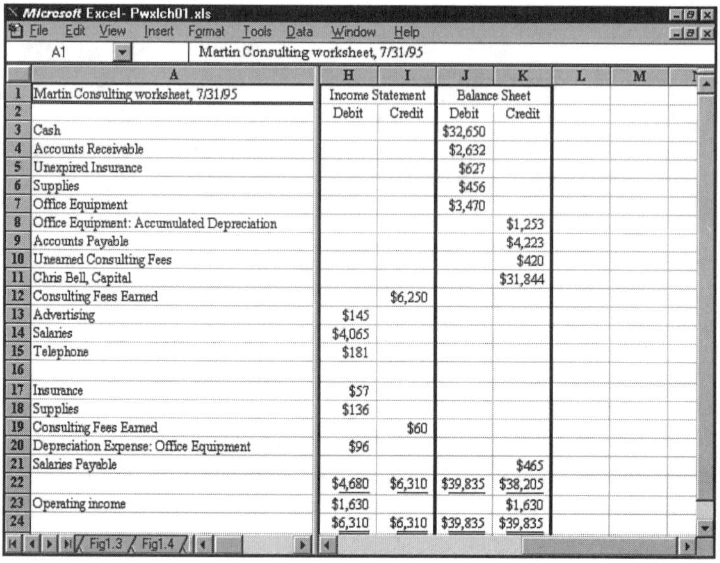

Fig. 1.8

Entries are copied from the adjusted trial balance columns to income statement and balance sheet columns.

	A	H	I	J	K	L	M
1	Martin Consulting worksheet, 7/31/95	Income Statement		Balance Sheet			
2		Debit	Credit	Debit	Credit		
3	Cash			$32,650			
4	Accounts Receivable			$2,632			
5	Unexpired Insurance			$627			
6	Supplies			$456			
7	Office Equipment			$3,470			
8	Office Equipment: Accumulated Depreciation				$1,253		
9	Accounts Payable				$4,223		
10	Unearned Consulting Fees				$420		
11	Chris Bell, Capital				$31,844		
12	Consulting Fees Earned		$6,250				
13	Advertising	$145					
14	Salaries	$4,065					
15	Telephone	$181					
16							
17	Insurance	$57					
18	Supplies	$136					
19	Consulting Fees Earned		$60				
20	Depreciation Expense: Office Equipment	$96					
21	Salaries Payable				$465		
22		$4,680	$6,310	$39,835	$38,205		
23	Operating income	$1,630			$1,630		
24		$6,310	$6,310	$39,835	$39,835		

the difference is its operating income. To arrive at this figure, subtract the total expenses of $4,680 in cell H22 from the total revenues in cell I22. The result, $1,630, appears in cell H23, and is the operating income for the month of July. Adding that to the total expenses of $4,680 results in $6,310, which equals the total revenues for the month.

A similar process is used to obtain the information for the balance sheet. Notice that this final step, copying information from the adjusted trial balance to the income statement and balance sheet, is merely a matter of segregating the revenue and expense data from the asset and liability data. The former go to the income statement; the latter to the balance sheet.

Organizing with Traditional versus Contribution Approaches

The traditional approach organizes income statements around the functions a business performs, such as production, administration, and sales. This functional method of cost classification does not allow for the examination of cost behavior. Traditional income statements are not set up to describe the cost drivers of the business.

There are no subcategories to analyze, or to use in the management of the behavior of costs within each classification. All costs are grouped without respect to whether they are fixed, variable, inherent or some other characteristic of cost behavior. When an income statement lumps everything together in this fashion, it is difficult to analyze, to make decisions and to offer recommendations.

The contribution format supplies answers to many additional questions. For example:

- What are the variable selling expenses for a given product?
- What percentage of total costs are represented by our fixed costs?
- New equipment will increase our fixed costs because it must be depreciated. Will it reduce our variable costs enough to result in lower *total* costs?

A manager needs more specific information than is available in the traditional income statement to answer questions like these.

This is not to say that there is no place for the traditional format: quite the contrary. Almost certainly, you would use a traditional format if you were applying for a business loan, considering the sale of your business, or preparing for an initial public stock offering.

In contrast, the contribution format is intended mainly for internal purposes, and is used by management for day-to-day, operational decisions. Consider the example shown in figure 1.9.

Fig. 1.9
The contribution format of an income statement focuses on data helpful for operational decisions.

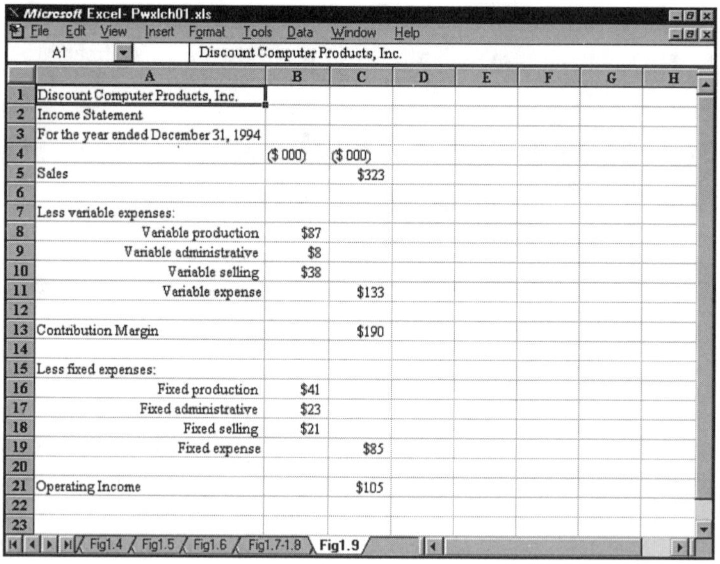

	A	B	C
1	Discount Computer Products, Inc.		
2	Income Statement		
3	For the year ended December 31, 1994		
4		($ 000)	($ 000)
5	Sales		$323
6			
7	Less variable expenses:		
8	Variable production	$87	
9	Variable administrative	$8	
10	Variable selling	$38	
11	Variable expense		$133
12			
13	Contribution Margin		$190
14			
15	Less fixed expenses:		
16	Fixed production	$41	
17	Fixed administrative	$23	
18	Fixed selling	$21	
19	Fixed expense		$85
20			
21	Operating Income		$105
22			
23			

In figure 1.9, variable expenses are deducted from sales to derive what is known as a contribution margin. See chapter 20 for more information, but note here that a contribution margin is the result of subtracting variable expenses from revenues. The contribution margin can then be used to meet fixed expenses, and to contribute toward a company's profit.

This information is critical for business decisions that pertain to products. For example, figure 1.9 shows that Discount Computer's largest cost category is Variable Production expenses. A *variable expense* is one that changes depending on the number of units sold. The more computer products that this firm sells, the larger its variable production expense.

The contribution format of the income statement in figure 1.9 directs a manager's attention to the costs involved in producing products. In the absence of this data, the manager who wants to cut costs might focus (perhaps inefficiently) on reducing *fixed* production costs.

The contribution approach is useful in making decisions about product profitability, product pricing, marketing channels and many situational decisions. It enables you to understand the contribution that each product brings to the bottom line, and how much to variable costs. It helps you to better understand the cost drivers of your business.

American business in the 1990s focuses on cost reduction, productivity, and total quality management. To sharpen that focus, it is necessary to understand the structure of the costs that reduce your profitability. You will see more on this matter in future chapters.

Summary

In this chapter, you have learned about different formats and different purposes for income statements. They can be structured very differently depending on their audience and which management functions they support.

You have also learned ways to use Excel to maintain a General Journal of transactions, and how to roll those transactions up into a General Ledger and an Income Statement.

You have also read about accrual accounting and the matching principle, under which costs are associated with the revenues that they help to produce. And you have worked with several different approaches to calculating depreciation costs.

The income statement is fundamental to an understanding of how your business operates. It has various uses and a virtually unlimited number of formats. The statement structure and format that you choose depends both on your audience and your purpose for a particular income statement.

There are guidelines for the construction of the statement, but you have broad latitude in selecting the data that you portray. You can measure and report income, but ultimately you have to make a business decision from the data. The key to making the best possible decision is to structure the statement so that it offers the most pertinent information available.

Chapter 2

Balance Sheet: Current Asset Management

The balance sheet is the second major type of financial statement that you need to keep track of your profitability. It is termed a *balance sheet* because its two major sections, Assets and Liabilities, must be in *balance*: that is, the total of the company's assets must equal the total of its liabilities and its owner's equity.

The balance sheet summarizes a company's financial position at the end of a given period. Whether that period is a month, a quarter, or a year, it tells you the value of the company's assets. It also describes the various classifications of liabilities, such as Accounts Payable, Debt and Equity, that have claims against the company's assets.

For example, suppose that your company has $5,000 worth of inventory in stock. That's an asset: you can, and presumably intend, to convert it into cash by selling it to your customers. Now suppose that your company acquired that inventory partly with $2,500 in cash and partly on credit.

Those amounts are liabilities. The company has assumed $2,500 in Accounts Payable, which is the credit portion of the purchase. The remaining $2,500 worth of inventory is part of the Owner's Equity, which is the portion of the company's Total Assets owned by its investors. Owner's Equity is grouped with liabilities such as Accounts Payable because it represents whatever difference exists between the assets and liabilities.

So, by showing the $5,000 worth of inventory once in Assets and once in Liabilities, the balance sheet keeps the company's holdings and obligations in balance. If this were all there is to a balance sheet, it wouldn't be of much interest. But as you will learn later in this book, the balance sheet is the starting point for a variety of analyses. Using Excel to analyze the balance sheet can give you insight into how a company is run, how well it manages its resources, and how it creates profit.

First, though, it's necessary to build the balance sheet. This chapter, along with chapters 3 and 4, describe that process.

Designing the Balance Sheet

In contrast to the income statement, discussed in Chapter 1, the balance sheet usually follows a fairly rigid format. Figure 2.1 shows a typical example.

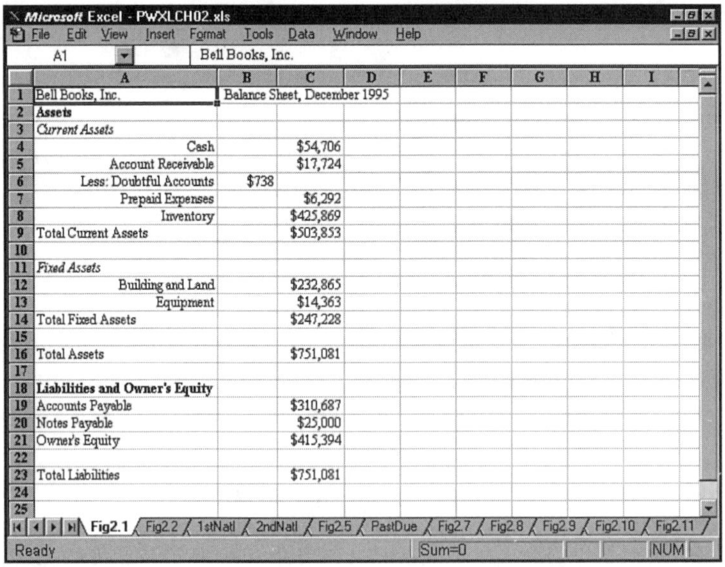

	A	B	C
1	Bell Books, Inc.	Balance Sheet, December 1995	
2	**Assets**		
3	*Current Assets*		
4	Cash		$54,706
5	Account Receivable		$17,724
6	Less: Doubtful Accounts	$738	
7	Prepaid Expenses		$6,292
8	Inventory		$425,869
9	Total Current Assets		$503,853
10			
11	*Fixed Assets*		
12	Building and Land		$232,865
13	Equipment		$14,363
14	Total Fixed Assets		$247,228
15			
16	Total Assets		$751,081
17			
18	**Liabilities and Owner's Equity**		
19	Accounts Payable		$310,687
20	Notes Payable		$25,000
21	Owner's Equity		$415,394
22			
23	Total Liabilities		$751,081
24			
25			

Fig. 2.1
The Balance Sheet for Bell Books, December 1995, demonstrates the equality of its assets with the total of its liabilities and its owner's equity.

The first part of the balance sheet describes the company's assets. These are usually classified as Current Assets, Fixed Assets, and Other Assets. The second part of the balance sheet summarizes the company's Liabilities and Owner's Equity.

Understanding Balance Sheet Accounts

The Current Assets classification is normally composed of Cash, Accounts Receivable, Prepaid Expenses, and Inventory. Because Inventory can require special techniques of management and analysis, this book discusses Inventory separately, in chapter 3. The remaining Current Asset classifications are discussed in this chapter, and Liabilities and Owner's Equity are covered in chapter 4.

> **Note**
>
> This chapter discusses a variety of accounts, such as Cash and Accounts Receivable. It does so in order to introduce certain concepts and terms that pertain to the measurement of profit. It does *not* describe where these accounts are found in Excel workbooks, or how they interact.
>
> Chapter 4 provides one suggested structure for two workbooks that contain these accounts and the ledgers and journals that underlie the balance sheet and income statement.
>
> In the meantime, keep in mind that understanding the structure of these workbooks is not necessary to an understanding of the purpose, usage, and structure of the balance sheet.

Fixed Assets normally include items such as Land, Buildings, and Equipment. The conceptual difference between Current Assets and Fixed Assets is that *Current Assets* can be converted into cash fairly quickly—usually, within a year or less—without disrupting the business's normal operating procedures.

So, if your company conducts its business in a particular building that it owns, located on land that it owns, you would regard both the building and the land as fixed assets. Even if you could sell them in a week, to do so would interfere with your normal business operations. In contrast, if your company owns a building and land, but conducts no business there, it might be right to regard them as current assets.

In the same way, liabilities are classified as current and long-term. A *current liability* is a debt that a business must pay within the same time period it uses to define its current assets: again, this is usually defined as a year or less. An example is a bank loan that must be repaid within 12 months. An example of a long-term liability is, say, a 10-year note used to acquire your place of business.

Understanding Debit and Credit Entries

You might question the reason that deposits to Bell Books' cash account worksheet are labeled Debits, and withdrawals from the account are labeled Credits (see fig. 2.2). It's mainly a matter of convention.

When you create an account in an Excel worksheet, you normally have two columns: one to record increases in the account balance, and one to record decreases in the account balance. This format is referred to as a *T-account*, because a horizontal line drawn beneath the column headers, and a vertical line drawn between the columns themselves, together resemble a "T."

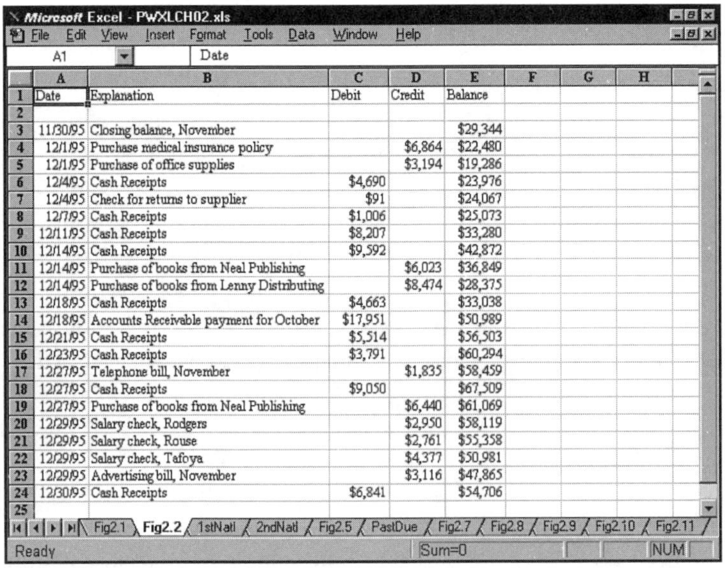

Date	Explanation	Debit	Credit	Balance
11/30/95	Closing balance, November			$29,344
12/1/95	Purchase medical insurance policy		$6,864	$22,480
12/1/95	Purchase of office supplies		$3,194	$19,286
12/4/95	Cash Receipts	$4,690		$23,976
12/4/95	Check for returns to supplier	$91		$24,067
12/7/95	Cash Receipts	$1,006		$25,073
12/11/95	Cash Receipts	$8,207		$33,280
12/14/95	Cash Receipts	$9,592		$42,872
12/14/95	Purchase of books from Neal Publishing		$6,023	$36,849
12/14/95	Purchase of books from Lenny Distributing		$8,474	$28,375
12/18/95	Cash Receipts	$4,663		$33,038
12/18/95	Accounts Receivable payment for October	$17,951		$50,989
12/21/95	Cash Receipts	$5,514		$56,503
12/23/95	Cash Receipts	$3,791		$60,294
12/27/95	Telephone bill, November		$1,835	$58,459
12/27/95	Cash Receipts	$9,050		$67,509
12/27/95	Purchase of books from Neal Publishing		$6,440	$61,069
12/29/95	Salary check, Rodgers		$2,950	$58,119
12/29/95	Salary check, Rouse		$2,761	$55,358
12/29/95	Salary check, Tafoya		$4,377	$50,981
12/29/95	Advertising bill, November		$3,116	$47,865
12/30/95	Cash Receipts	$6,841		$54,706

Fig. 2.2
The Cash worksheet for Bell Books records cash outlays as credits and cash receipts as debits.

In the context of your business's accounts, the words "debit" and "credit" do not carry the meanings that they have in everyday usage—that is, indebtedness versus resources. Instead, these terms refer to the left-hand (debit) and right-hand (credit) columns of a T-account. Accountants have four fundamental rules for entering amounts in these columns:

- If the account is an asset account, record an increase in the amount of the asset in the left-hand (debit) column.
- If the account is an asset account, record a decrease in the amount of the asset in the right-hand (credit) column.
- If the account is a liability or owner's equity account, record an increase in the liability in the right-hand (credit) column.
- If the account is a liability or owner's equity account, record a decrease in the liability in the left-hand (debit) column.

So, according to these rules, deposits to a cash account are recorded in the account's left-hand, or debit, column: cash is an asset account and a deposit increases its balance. Similarly, because writing a check reduces the cash account's balance, the amount of the check is recorded in the right-hand, or credit, column.

Keep in mind that, in this context, "debit" means left-hand column and "credit" means right-hand column.

Getting a Current Asset Cash Balance

In the Balance Sheet shown in figure 2.1, the Cash classification of Current Assets section contains this formula:

```
=NovemberEndCashBalance+SUM(DecemberCashDebits)-SUM(DecemberCashCredits)
```

The names in this formula refer to ranges in the Cash worksheet shown in figure 2.2.

In the worksheet shown in figure 2.2, there are three named ranges:

- NovemberEndCashBalance refers to cell E3. This amount is the closing Cash balance at the end of November, the prior month.

- DecemberCashDebits refers to cells C4:C24. This range contains all the deposits to Bell Books' corporate checking account that were made during December.

- DecemberCashCredits refers to cells D4:D24. This range contains all the withdrawals from Bell Books' corporate checking account that were made during December.

Cell E3, named NovemberEndCashBalance, contains the value $29,344. Cell E4 contains this formula:

```
=E3+C4-D4
```

Each entry in the Cash worksheet is either a debit or a credit: there are no entries that contain both a debit and a credit. Therefore, the formula in cell E4 either adds to the prior balance (cell E3) a debit figure from column C, or subtracts a credit figure from column D.

The formula is copied from cell E4 and is pasted into the range E5:E24. The process of copying and pasting the formula adjusts its relative cell references, so each balance depends on the prior balance as well as on the current debit or credit. Cell E24 contains the ending balance for the month of December, and this balance will be used as the beginning Cash balance when it comes time to create the Cash worksheet for January.

It would be possible, and perhaps preferable, to create the name DecemberEndCashBalance to represent cell E24 of figure 2.2. Then, the Cash classification in figure 2.1 could contain this formula:

```
=DecemberEndCashBalance
```

As the worksheets are constructed, the ending cash balance for December is calculated twice: once on the Cash worksheet and once on the Balance Sheet.

This construction is used partly for illustration, and partly to make the calculations explicit.

Getting a Cash Balance for Multiple Cash Accounts

It would be unusual for a company of any size to maintain only one bank account. More often, companies use several bank accounts, often for different purposes. In this case, a 3D reference would be useful, because you generally want a different worksheet for each cash account. You would use the 3D reference to sum the balance of the account in each worksheet (see figs. 2.3 and 2.4).

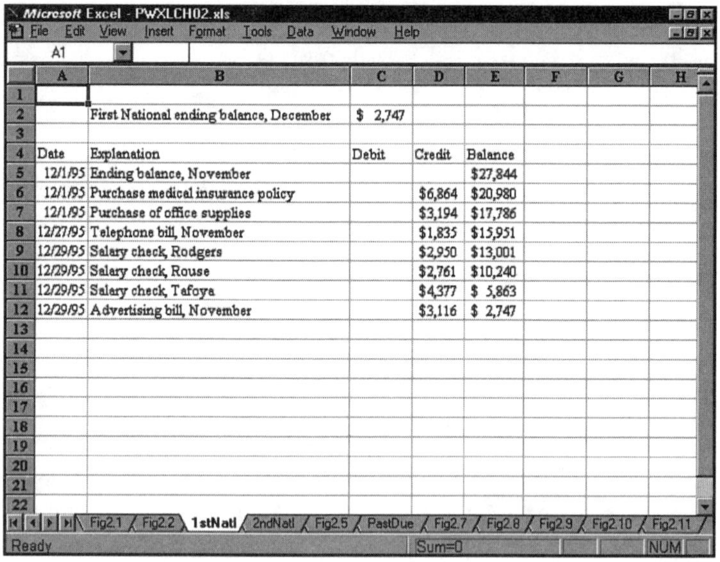

	A	B	C	D	E
1					
2		First National ending balance, December	$ 2,747		
3					
4	Date	Explanation	Debit	Credit	Balance
5	12/1/95	Ending balance, November			$27,844
6	12/1/95	Purchase medical insurance policy		$6,864	$20,980
7	12/1/95	Purchase of office supplies		$3,194	$17,786
8	12/27/95	Telephone bill, November		$1,835	$15,951
9	12/29/95	Salary check, Rodgers		$2,950	$13,001
10	12/29/95	Salary check, Rouse		$2,761	$10,240
11	12/29/95	Salary check, Tafoya		$4,377	$ 5,863
12	12/29/95	Advertising bill, November		$3,116	$ 2,747

Fig. 2.3
The Cash worksheet for First National account shows all operating expenses except those involving suppliers.

Suppose that Bell Books uses an account at the First National Bank to handle all cash transactions *except* cash receipts and purchases from inventory suppliers. Figure 2.3 shows these transactions, identical to those in figure 2.2, for the month of December.

Suppose further that Bell Books uses an account at the Second National Bank to handle all cash receipts and purchases from inventory suppliers. Figure 2.4 shows those transactions for the month of December.

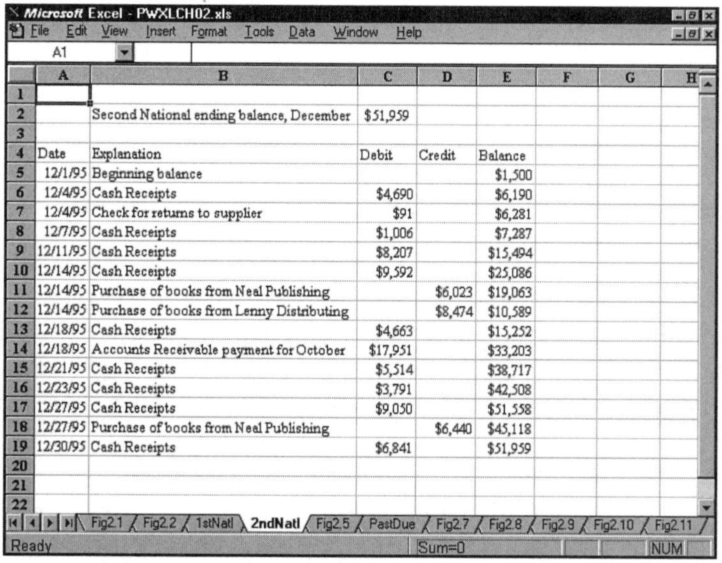

	A	B	C	D	E
1					
2		Second National ending balance, December	$51,959		
3					
4	Date	Explanation	Debit	Credit	Balance
5	12/1/95	Beginning balance			$1,500
6	12/4/95	Cash Receipts	$4,690		$6,190
7	12/4/95	Check for returns to supplier	$91		$6,281
8	12/7/95	Cash Receipts	$1,006		$7,287
9	12/11/95	Cash Receipts	$8,207		$15,494
10	12/14/95	Cash Receipts	$9,592		$25,086
11	12/14/95	Purchase of books from Neal Publishing		$6,023	$19,063
12	12/14/95	Purchase of books from Lenny Distributing		$8,474	$10,589
13	12/18/95	Cash Receipts	$4,663		$15,252
14	12/18/95	Accounts Receivable payment for October	$17,951		$33,203
15	12/21/95	Cash Receipts	$5,514		$38,717
16	12/23/95	Cash Receipts	$3,791		$42,508
17	12/27/95	Cash Receipts	$9,050		$51,558
18	12/27/95	Purchase of books from Neal Publishing		$6,440	$45,118
19	12/30/95	Cash Receipts	$6,841		$51,959

Fig. 2.4
The Cash worksheet for Second National account shows all cash receipts and those transactions that involve suppliers.

The worksheets shown in figures 2.3 and 2.4 make use of *local names.* The worksheet in figure 2.3 contains these local names:

- The name 1stNatl!Debits refers to the range '1stNatl'!C6:C12.
- The name 1stNatl!Credits refers to the range '1stNatl'!D6:D12.
- The name 1stNatl!BeginningBalance refers to the cell '1stNatl'!E5.

Notice two aspects of these range names: First, the name itself is qualified by the name of the worksheet, and separated from the name by an exclamation point. Second, the range is also qualified by the name of the worksheet and an exclamation point and, in the reference, single quotes enclose the worksheet's name.

Defining the names in this fashion makes them *local* names: that is, the name refers specifically to the sheet where the range exists. Unless it is qualified by the name of the sheet where it exists, the name is not accessible from any other sheet in the workbook. However, on the worksheet named 1stNatl, you can use the names Debits, Credits, and BeginningBalance without further qualification. For example, cell C2 in figure 2.3 contains this formula:

```
=BeginningBalance+SUM(Debits)-SUM(Credits)
```

which returns the ending balance in the First National account at the end of December.

Now consider figure 2.4. It contains these local names:

- The name 2ndNatl!Debits refers to the range '2nd Natl'!C6:C19.

- The name 2ndNatl!Credits refers to the range '2nd Natl'!D6:D19.

- The name 2ndNatl!BeginningBalance refers to the cell '2ndNatl'!E5.

and cell C2 in figure 2.4 contains this formula:

```
=BeginningBalance+SUM(Debits)-SUM(Credits)
```

which is identical to the formula in cell C2 of figure 2.3. However, because of the use of local names, *Debits* in figure 2.4 refers specifically to the name *Debits* on the worksheet named "2ndNatl". Similarly, *Debits* in figure 2.3 refers specifically to the name *Debits* on the worksheet named "1stNatl." Therefore, the arguments to the SUM functions represent different ranges and normally return different results.

Local names have some other effects. For example, suppose that you activate a worksheet other than 1stNatl or 2ndNatl, and choose Insert, Name, Define. The local names on the 1stNatl and 2ndNatl worksheets would not appear in the dialog box: they are *local* to their specific worksheets.

As another example, if you were to activate the 1stNatl worksheet, and activate the Name Box in the Formula Bar, you would see the names *BeginningBalance*, *Credits* and *Debits*. These range names would not be qualified by their sheet names, because the sheet where they exist is active.

Finally, note that there are single quote marks surrounding the sheet names in the definitions of the range names. This occurs because the sheet names begin with a numeral. If a sheet were named "SecondNatl" instead of "2ndNatl," for example, the local name *Debits* would appear in the Define Names dialog box as SecondNatl!Debits—without the single quote marks. A space in a sheet's name also makes the single quote marks necessary.

Tip

A quick way to determine if a sheet name, when used as a qualifier to a range name, requires surrounding quote marks is to examine the Insert, Name, Define dialog box. If the quote marks are needed, Excel shows them in the Refers To edit box.

Although this preliminary work might seem onerous, it helps to make your workbook formulas more self-documenting, and it leads to easier name usage.

For example, notice that the ending balance for each bank account in figures 2.3 and 2.4 is in cell C2 of each sheet. This allows you to create a 3D reference in the workbook, one that crosses multiple sheets. To do so, follow these steps:

1. Choose Insert, Name, Define.

2. In the Names in Workbook edit box, type **CashBalance**.

3. In the Refers To edit box, use your mouse pointer to drag across whatever reference is presently there.

4. Click the sheet tab named 1stNatl, hold down the Shift key, and then click the sheet tab named 2ndNatl. Both tabs are highlighted, and the Refers To edit box now contains: ='1stNatl:2ndNatl'!

5. The active sheet is the one whose tab you first clicked: in this example, that sheet is the one named 1stNatl. Click cell C2, which contains the ending balance for December.

6. Choose OK.

You will now have a 3D name: CashBalance refers to cell C2 in the worksheets named 1stNatl and 2ndNatl. Finally, you are in a position to use all these local and 3D names. In the Balance Sheet worksheet, cell C4 of figure 2.1, you can enter this formula:

```
=SUM(CashBalance)
```

which returns the sum of all the cells that compose the 3D name CashBalance. In this case, the formula adds the value in cell C2 of the 1stNatl worksheet ($2,747) to the value in cell C2 of the 2ndNatl worksheet ($51,959) to return the value $54,706. This is the total of Bell Books' current asset for its Cash accounts.

Tip

3D names do not appear in the Name box. The Name box displays only book-level names and sheet-level names that belong to the active sheet. Because a 3D name belongs to at least two sheets, but is not a book-level name, it does not conform to the rules for names that can appear in the Name box.

To review:

- The local names *Debits*, *Credits* and *BeginningBalance* are defined on each worksheet that contains a cash account.

- A cell that occupies the same position in each cash account worksheet contains this formula:

  ```
  =BeginningBalance+SUM(Debits)-SUM(Credits)
  ```

  and returns the ending balance for the cash account contained in that worksheet.

- A 3D name is created. It refers to the same cell in each worksheet that has a cash account ending balance. This is the balance created in step 2, above. The 3D range is given a name such as *CashBalance*.

- On the Balance Sheet, this formula:

  ```
  =SUM(CashBalance)
  ```

  returns the sum of the cells in the workbook that compose the CashBalance range.

Handling Restricted Cash Accounts

Because cash is the most liquid, and is therefore the most "current," of current assets, it's easy to think of all cash accounts as current assets. This is not necessarily true. Some of your cash accounts might be restricted, either as to their usage or as to the point in time that you can access them.

Suppose that your company builds houses. A new customer approaches you, asking you to build a custom house to particular specifications. You estimate that it will take about 18 months to complete the work, and you request that the customer pay you a substantial amount of the cost at the beginning of the project. This payment is to ensure that the customer will not simply walk away prior to making full payment.

Because you and the customer have not done business before, you mutually agree to put this preliminary payment in an escrow account. Neither party may access the account prior to the completion of construction. Although this account contains cash, it is not available to pay current liabilities, per the terms of your agreement with the customer. Therefore, you should not include it in a balance sheet as a current asset. Instead, you might include it as Unearned Revenue in an Other Assets classification on the balance sheet.

You might find that the interest rates on savings accounts that are denominated in a foreign currency are attractive. Or, you might anticipate that the value of the U.S. dollar will fall in relation to that currency. Having no other operational use for the funds, you invest $10,000 in a foreign savings account with a term of two years. Because you cannot withdraw these funds prior to completion of the term of the account, you cannot use them to pay current liabilities. Again, you would represent this investment as an asset on the balance sheet, but in a classification other than Current Assets.

Getting a Current Asset Accounts Receivable Balance

Credit sales are a fact of business life. If yours is a retail business with any appreciable degree of competition, you almost certainly must accept credit cards as a method of payment or risk losing business to your competitors. If your principal customers are themselves businesses, you must contend with the fact that they, like you, want to use their assets most efficiently. One way to do so is to use a good credit history to acquire more goods on credit.

The result is that you must temporarily show these credit sales as funds that you expect to receive at some point in the future. The matching principle, which was discussed in chapter 1, applies here: it requires that you match revenues to the expenses required to produce the revenues, in the same time period. Because you have not yet received payment for these credit sales in cash, it's necessary to record them as funds to be received: thus the term *accounts receivable*. Figure 2.5 shows an example of Accounts Receivable for Bell Books.

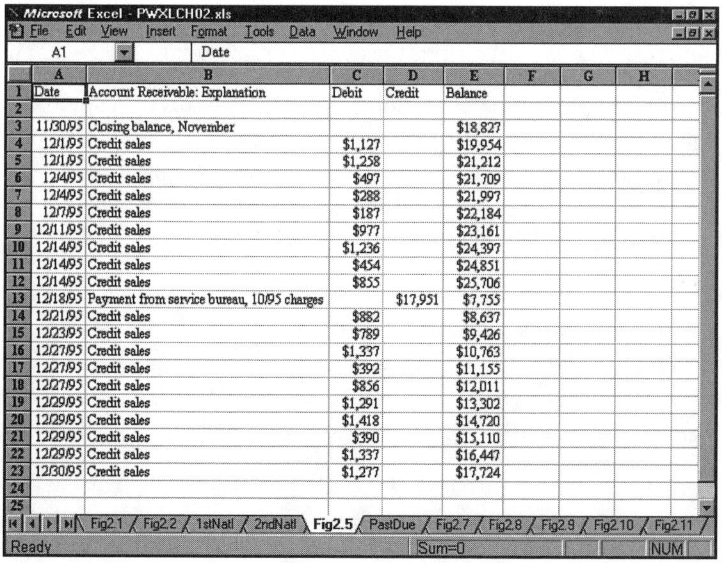

	A	B	C	D	E
1	Date	Account Receivable: Explanation	Debit	Credit	Balance
2					
3	11/30/95	Closing balance, November			$18,827
4	12/1/95	Credit sales	$1,127		$19,954
5	12/1/95	Credit sales	$1,258		$21,212
6	12/4/95	Credit sales	$497		$21,709
7	12/4/95	Credit sales	$288		$21,997
8	12/7/95	Credit sales	$187		$22,184
9	12/11/95	Credit sales	$977		$23,161
10	12/14/95	Credit sales	$1,236		$24,397
11	12/14/95	Credit sales	$454		$24,851
12	12/14/95	Credit sales	$855		$25,706
13	12/18/95	Payment from service bureau, 10/95 charges		$17,951	$7,755
14	12/21/95	Credit sales	$882		$8,637
15	12/23/95	Credit sales	$789		$9,426
16	12/27/95	Credit sales	$1,337		$10,763
17	12/27/95	Credit sales	$392		$11,155
18	12/27/95	Credit sales	$856		$12,011
19	12/29/95	Credit sales	$1,291		$13,302
20	12/29/95	Credit sales	$1,418		$14,720
21	12/29/95	Credit sales	$390		$15,110
22	12/29/95	Credit sales	$1,337		$16,447
23	12/30/95	Credit sales	$1,277		$17,724
24					
25					

Fig. 2.5
The Accounts Receivable worksheet for Bell Books details the credit sales made during December 1995.

Notice that the ending balance for Accounts Receivable, shown in cell E23 of figure 2.5, is identical to the Accounts Receivable balance shown in Bell Books' Balance Sheet (refer to fig. 2.1).

Roughly every third day during the month of December, Bell Books records new credit sales in the *debit* column of the Accounts Receivable account. This is according to the rule for recording increases to asset accounts: you record such increases in the asset account's debit column.

In figure 2.5, a credit entry appears in cell D13 for $17,951. This represents a payment to Bell Books by the credit card firm that Bell Books uses. This is according to the rule for recording decreases to asset accounts: you record decreases in the asset account's credit column. The amount of $17,951 also appears in figure 2.2, showing that Bell Books' cash account balance has increased per the deposit of the check in the bank.

That payment reduces the (debit) balance of Accounts Receivable for December, and increases the (debit) balance of Cash by an identical amount. Notice that this transaction has no net effect on Total Assets. It simply shifts the asset from Accounts Receivable to Cash, to reflect the fact that you have finally received payment for purchases that occurred in October.

Allowing for Doubtful Accounts

Unfortunately, not all credit purchases result in eventual, actual cash payment. Some business customers go bankrupt subsequent to making a purchase on credit; others simply disappear. Recognized credit cards such as MasterCard or American Express help to minimize this risk. In most cases, if you accept one of these cards as payment for a product or service, you can count on receiving payment from the credit card company.

In return for accepting the risk of non-payment (and for associated services) the credit card company charges you some percentage of the credit purchases from your business. For every $100 worth of sales, you might receive $97 from the credit card company. Many firms view this avoidance of risk as an additional benefit of accepting credit cards as payment.

Many businesses also extend credit terms directly to regular customers and clients, instead of (or in addition to) extending credit via an intermediary such as a credit card firm. In these cases, the business assumes the risk that it will never receive payment. Of course, the business avoids the payment of a service charge to a credit card firm in cases like these.

When you assume the risk of non-payment, you must anticipate that some customers will fail to pay you. Then, the matching principle requires that you estimate the amount of credit sales during a given period will eventually turn out to be uncollectible. In accordance with the principle, estimating uncollectible accounts reduces the revenue that is recorded for the period during which the sales occurred.

There are two basic approaches to estimating the amount of credit sales that will become uncollectible: the *aging approach* and the *percentage of sales approach*. Both depend on historic estimates of the percentage of credit sales that you will eventually have to write off.

Using the Aging Approach to Estimating Uncollectibles

The aging approach depends on an analysis of the aging of credit sales (see fig. 2.6).

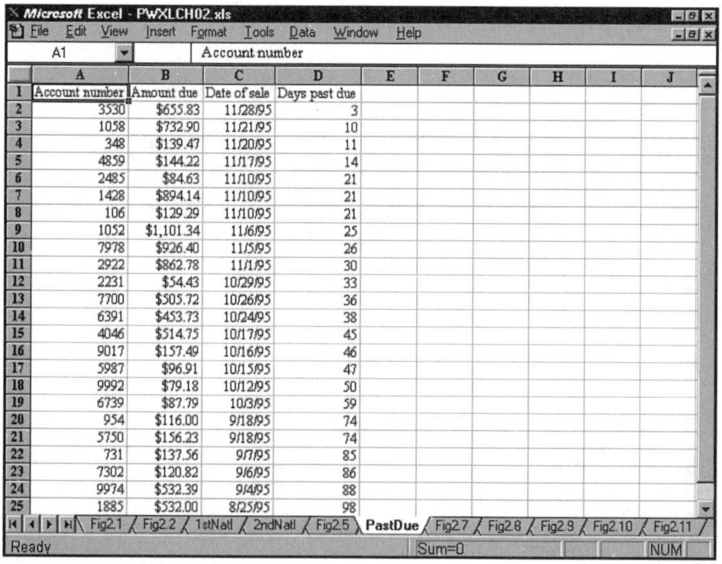

	A	B	C	D
1	Account number	Amount due	Date of sale	Days past due
2	3530	$655.83	11/28/95	3
3	1058	$732.90	11/21/95	10
4	348	$139.47	11/20/95	11
5	4859	$144.22	11/17/95	14
6	2485	$84.63	11/10/95	21
7	1428	$894.14	11/10/95	21
8	106	$129.29	11/10/95	21
9	1052	$1,101.34	11/6/95	25
10	7978	$926.40	11/5/95	26
11	2922	$862.78	11/1/95	30
12	2231	$54.43	10/29/95	33
13	7700	$505.72	10/26/95	36
14	6391	$453.73	10/24/95	38
15	4046	$514.75	10/17/95	45
16	9017	$157.49	10/16/95	46
17	5987	$96.91	10/15/95	47
18	9992	$79.18	10/12/95	50
19	6739	$87.79	10/3/95	59
20	954	$116.00	9/18/95	74
21	5750	$156.23	9/18/95	74
22	731	$137.56	9/7/95	85
23	7302	$120.82	9/6/95	86
24	9974	$532.39	9/4/95	88
25	1885	$532.00	8/25/95	98

Fig. 2.6
The PastDue worksheet details individual accounts receivable for Bell Books, that are past due as of December 31, 1995.

The worksheet shown in figure 2.6 details the purchases made by individual accounts, the sales amount, the date of sale, and the number of days past due for each purchase. The following formula returns the number of days that an account is past due, in cell D2 of figure 2.6:

```
=MAX(0,DATE(1995,12,31)-30-C2)
```

Bell Books extends a 30-day grace period to its customers, after which it considers the account past due. The formula uses the closing date for the Balance Sheet (12/31/95), subtracts the 30-day grace period, and then subtracts the date of the sale (the date value in cell C2). This results in the number of days past due for that sale. The formula is surrounded by the MAX function, to prevent it from returning a negative value if the date of sale was within 30 days of the closing date.

> **Note**
>
> Does it seem strange to subtract a number from a date? Excel keeps track of dates by means of a serial number system. By default, in Excel for Windows, January 1, 1900 is serial number 1, January 2, 1900 is serial number 2, and so on. The DATE function accepts a year, month, and day as its arguments and returns the serial number for that date. Even though a cell's format causes it to display, say, 12/31/1995, the actual value in the cell is the date's serial number. Therefore, the formula in cell D2 works out to:
>
> ```
> =35064-30-35031
> ```

The worksheet shown in figure 2.7 summarizes this information.

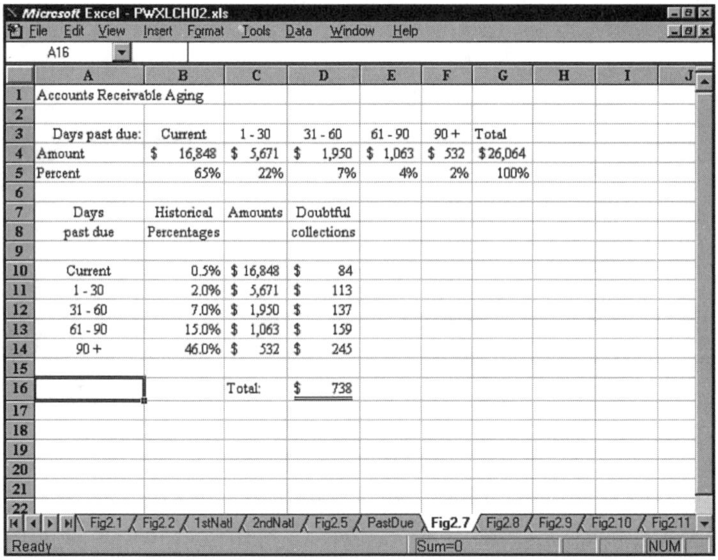

	A	B	C	D	E	F	G
1	Accounts Receivable Aging						
2							
3	Days past due:	Current	1 - 30	31 - 60	61 - 90	90 +	Total
4	Amount	$ 16,848	$ 5,671	$ 1,950	$ 1,063	$ 532	$26,064
5	Percent	65%	22%	7%	4%	2%	100%
6							
7	Days	Historical	Amounts	Doubtful			
8	past due	Percentages		collections			
9							
10	Current	0.5%	$ 16,848	$ 84			
11	1 - 30	2.0%	$ 5,671	$ 113			
12	31 - 60	7.0%	$ 1,950	$ 137			
13	61 - 90	15.0%	$ 1,063	$ 159			
14	90 +	46.0%	$ 532	$ 245			
15							
16			Total:	$ 738			

Fig. 2.7 The aging approach to analysis of accounts receivable for Bell Books, December 31, 1995, summarizes the amount receivable according to the length of time the payment is past due.

The amount of $16,848, in cell B4 of figure 2.7, is the total of all credit sales in Accounts Receivable that are current as of 12/31/95. The formula sums the values in DecemberARDebits (cells C3:C23 in figure 2.5):

```
=SUM(DecemberARDebits)
```

The value in cell C4, $5,671, is returned by this array formula:

```
=SUM((PastDue!$D$2:$D$25<31)*(PastDue!$B$2:$B$25))
```

(The worksheet named PastDue is shown in fig. 2.6). This array formula examines the values in the range $D$2:$D$25, and returns an array of TRUE (if the value is less than 31) or FALSE (if the value is not less than 31). Excel converts these TRUE and FALSE values to 1's and 0's, and then multiplies the 1's and 0's by the corresponding dollar amounts in the range $B$2:$B$25. Finally, Excel sums the results of the multiplication, to return the value of $5,671.

Similarly, the value in cell D4, $1,950, is returned by this array formula:

```
=SUM((PastDue!$D$2:$D$25>30)*(PastDue!$D$2:$D$25<61)*(PastDue!$B$2:$B$25))
```

The only differences between the two array formulas are:

- The first comparison restricts SUM function to accounts where the number of days past due is greater than 30.

- There is now a second comparison, which restricts the SUM function to accounts where the number of days past due is less than 61.

So, the array formula interprets the account shown on line 12 in figure 2.6 as follows:

- TRUE for the first condition, because 33 days past due is greater than 30

- TRUE for the second condition, because 33 days past due is less than 61

- $54.43 for the third term

and, as Excel interprets the array formula, TRUE * TRUE * $54.43 is equivalent to 1 * 1 * $54.43. Finally, the SUM function adds all the values (either the actual sale amount or 0, depending on whether both conditions are true for a given sale).

The percentage values shown in line 5 of figure 2.7 can be useful as a means of evaluating the store's credit policies. If they stray too far from percentages that management considers acceptable for a given aging period, it may be necessary to either tighten or relax the requirements for extending credit to a particular customer.

Cells B10:B14 contain historical information about the percentage of accounts that become uncollectible after a given period of time has elapsed. Bell Books' past experience has shown that 1/2 of 1 percent of all current credit sales go unpaid, 2 percent of credit sales from 1 to 30 days past due, and so on. These percentages are multiplied by the dollar amounts in each aging category. The results of these calculations consist of the values shown in cells D10:D14.

Their sum, $738, appears both in cell D16 of figure 2.7 and in cell B7 of figure 2.1. This is the amount that Bell Books estimates as uncollectible accounts receivable as of 12/31/95, the date of the Balance Sheet.

Using the Percentage of Sales Approach to Estimating Uncollectibles

A much simpler method of estimating uncollectible accounts receivable depends on historical information about the ratio of dollars lost due to nonpayment to sales dollars. If you know that some percentage of sales eventually becomes uncollectible, you can simply multiply that percentage by your sales dollars for a given period.

If you decide to use this method, it's best to calculate the historic percentage of uncollectibles as a ratio of credit sales. This is because a cash sale never becomes uncollectible, so it does not help to include cash sales in the calculation. Furthermore, the relationship between the total credit sales and total cash sales in a given period might be substantially different than their relationship during the basis period. In that case, you are likely to seriously misestimate the amounts that you will never collect.

The aging approach is usually more accurate than the percentage of sales approach, because it forces you to focus on the actual length of time that individual accounts are past due. The sad fact is that the longer an account is past due, the less likely that you will ever receive payment.

Additionally, the process of focusing on specific aging periods enables you to evaluate your policies for granting credit. For these reasons, the aging approach is usually the recommended procedure for estimating an allowance for doubtful accounts.

Getting a Prepaid Expenses Balance

The entries to the balance sheet that this chapter has discussed so far—Cash and Accounts Receivable—are both driven by transactions that occur during the period covered by the balance sheet. Another category of Current Assets covers a subset of a business's resources that span accounting periods. Transactions that occur during the period in question might, or might not, change the value of these assets. But whether such a transaction changes the value of the asset, it usually requires that you make an *adjusting entry*.

Suppose, for example, that your business uses a postage meter. From time to time, you take the meter to the post office, write a check for a few hundred dollars, and a clerk increases the amount of postage shown in the meter by that amount.

In effect, what you have done is *prepay* a few months of expenses by decreasing the value of one current asset, Cash. If you were to prepare an income statement and a balance sheet at the end of each month, you would show the amount of metered postage that you actually used during that month as an operating expense on the income statement. However much postage remains in the meter at the end of the month is a prepaid asset, one that you need to account for on the balance sheet.

In this way, you can associate the postage that you actually use during the month—the operating expense—with the revenues that the expense helped to generate. Doing so results in an accurate estimate of your profit for that period. Similarly, on the balance sheet, you can accurately estimate the (admittedly, small) contribution that the postage remaining in the meter makes to the worth of your company.

During the months that you are using the postage in the meter, no transaction with a customer occurs that triggers an entry in a journal, which would eventually show up in an income statement or balance sheet. Therefore, it's necessary to make an adjusting entry at the end of each period to accurately estimate the amounts in these categories. The process of making adjusting entries is discussed in more detail in chapter 6, "Statement Analysis," which covers the topic of adjusted trial balances.

While there are many types of prepaid expenses that your business might incur, there are two that nearly every company must deal with at some point: supplies and insurance.

Although the acquisition of office supplies is, formally, a prepaid expense, most businesses do not bother with recording it as such in their financial statements. Their position is that it is too much trouble to perform a physical count of office supplies at the end of every accounting period in order to determine the value of supplies used during that period. A large corporation might treat supplies as a prepaid expense in its financial statements. However, it is likely to use an estimate of the supplies used during the period in question, rather than taking a formal inventory of all the pencils, stationery, and staples in its possession.

Insurance, however, is another matter. It is relatively easy to quantify the amount of insurance that expires during a period of time, and its value is usually considerably higher than that of office supplies. The brief example that follows will clarify the treatment of insurance as a current asset.

Dealing with Insurance as a Prepaid Expense

Bell Books purchases a medical insurance policy for its employees on December 1, 1995. The policy will remain in force for one year, during which the company has the benefits provided by the insurance. Therefore, Bell Books can consider the cost of the policy a prepaid expense: an asset whose value declines over time and may require adjusting entries at the end of each accounting period. The purchase of the policy is recorded in the General Journal as shown in figure 2.8.

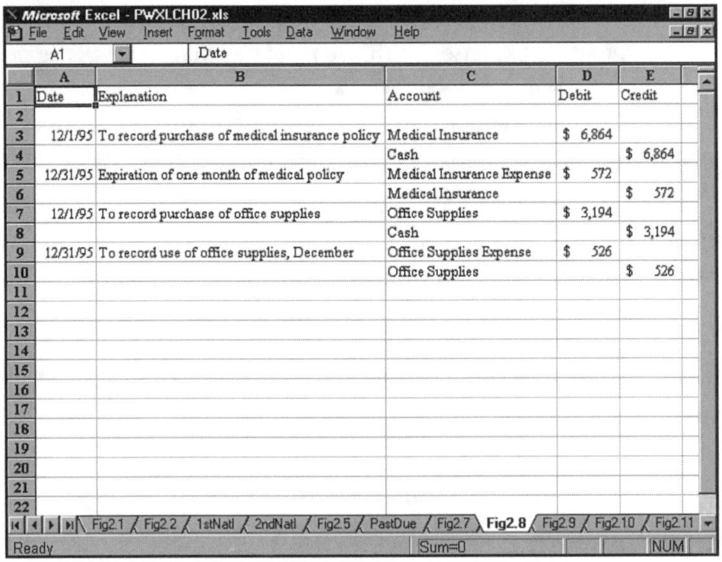

Date	Explanation	Account	Debit	Credit
12/1/95	To record purchase of medical insurance policy	Medical Insurance	$ 6,864	
		Cash		$ 6,864
12/31/95	Expiration of one month of medical policy	Medical Insurance Expense	$ 572	
		Medical Insurance		$ 572
12/1/95	To record purchase of office supplies	Office Supplies	$ 3,194	
		Cash		$ 3,194
12/31/95	To record use of office supplies, December	Office Supplies Expense	$ 526	
		Office Supplies		$ 526

Fig. 2.8
Both the original purchase of an asset such as insurance, and its periodic expiration, are recorded as journal entries.

Medical Insurance is an asset account: after purchasing the policy, the company has an additional asset in the form of insurance for its employees against the cost of medical treatment. According to the rules on debit entries and credit entries for asset accounts, an increase in the account's balance is recorded as a debit. Therefore, the amount of coverage provided by the policy shows up in both the General Journal and the Medical Insurance asset account (see fig. 2.9) as a debit.

After one month of coverage, on December 31 one twelfth of the period of the policy has expired, and the value of the asset therefore declines by one twelfth. Again, the rules for debits and credits in asset accounts state that a decline in the value of an asset is recorded as a credit. Therefore, on December 31, Bell Books makes credit entries in its General Journal and its General Ledger Medical Insurance accounts. These entries reflect the expiration of one twelfth of the value of the policy (see figs. 2.8 and 2.9).

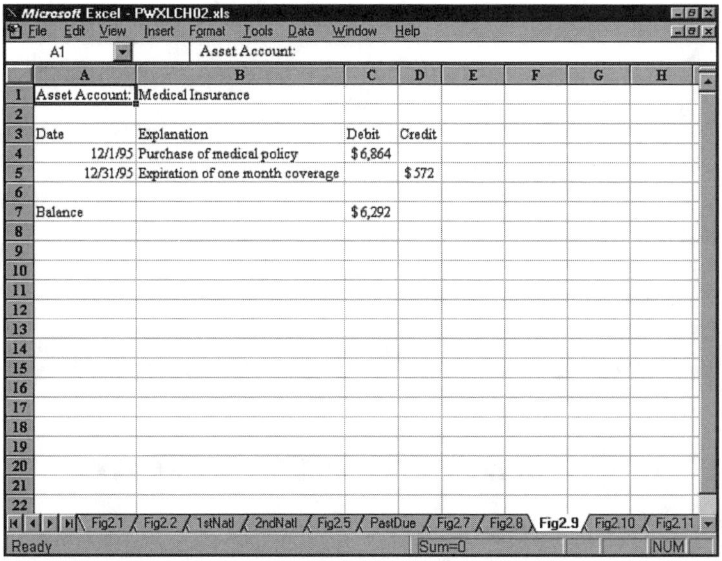

A	B	C	D
Asset Account:	Medical Insurance		
Date	Explanation	Debit	Credit
12/1/95	Purchase of medical policy	$6,864	
12/31/95	Expiration of one month coverage		$572
Balance		$6,292	

Fig. 2.9
The journal entries for the purchase and partial expiration of the Medical Insurance policy are also recorded as asset account ledger entries.

Because this is a prepaid *expense,* the expiration of the one month of coverage should also be recorded in an expense account. An expense results in a decrease in owner's equity, and according to the debit and credit rules a decrease in a liability or owner's equity account is recorded as a debit. Therefore, the expense incurred as a result of the expiration of one month of insurance coverage is recorded as a debit to the Medical Insurance account (see fig. 2.10).

There is one more place—the subject of this chapter—to record the prepaid expense: the balance sheet. At the end of the first month of coverage, the value of the policy has dropped by $572. During the remaining eleven months of coverage provided by the policy, this prepaid expense balance will continue to decline. If Bell Books prepares a Balance Sheet at the end of each of those eleven months, the prepaid expense asset will continue to decline until the asset has no value left.

Fig. 2.10

Debiting the
Medical Insurance
expense account
ledger entry offsets
the credit to the
Medical Insurance
asset account.

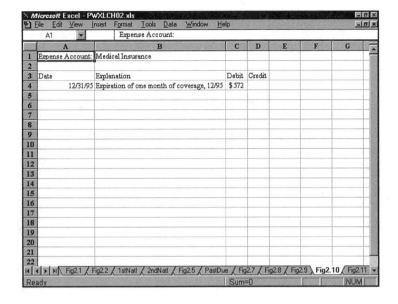

Getting a Current Asset Inventory Balance

Chapter 3 goes into considerable detail on the topic of valuing inventories. However, because a company's inventory is also a current asset, some of the mechanics of moving inventory asset amounts among various accounts as the balance sheet is being prepared are discussed here.

At the end of an accounting period, when you are preparing an income statement and a balance sheet, it is usual to bring the balances of the various revenue and expense accounts to zero. The reason for this is that the next time you prepare these statements, you want them to reflect the activity that takes place during the *next* period.

A starting value of zero allows you to accurately determine the profit that you earn during that period. If there are dollar amounts from a prior period remaining in the revenue and expense accounts, you will be unable to subtract the correct amount of expenses from the correct amount of revenues to arrive at an accurate earnings estimate.

The following four steps define the process of bringing the revenue and expense accounts to zero (also called *closing the accounts*):

1. For revenue accounts, which normally carry credit balances, make an offsetting debit entry in a revenue account to bring its balance to zero.

2. For expense accounts, which normally carry debit balances, make an offsetting credit entry to close them.

3. Also enter these closing entries in a special, temporary account in the General Journal, termed an Income Summary. The difference between the sum of the revenue entries and the sum of the expense entries is, of course, the earnings for the period that are attributable to operations.

4. Close the temporary Income Summary account by means of a debit entry in the amount of its balance, and place the same entry as a credit to Retained Earnings.

The result of this process is that the next period can begin afresh with zero amounts in the revenue and expense accounts. It also places the earnings from the current period (whether positive or negative) in the appropriate balance sheet account.

The procedure that you use for asset and liability accounts is different from the procedure for revenue and expense accounts. The dollar amounts in asset and liability accounts fluctuate over time, as resources grow and debts are paid. To arrange for an asset account to have a zero balance at the beginning of an accounting period would be to say that the company's assets somehow vanished at the end of the prior period.

One such asset account is Inventory. If your business produces products or resells them to retailers or consumers, you have inventory to account for. (If your business provides a service for its customers, you might well carry no inventory at all.)

Understanding the Inventory Flow

At the beginning of a period, you normally have some amount of goods in your inventory. During the period, you might purchase additional goods from your suppliers—these purchases have the effect of increasing the inventory. At the same time, you sell as many items from the inventory to your customers—these sales decrease your inventory. The result of these activities is your ending inventory: beginning inventory, plus purchases, minus the goods used in the sales that you make to your customers.

> **Note**
>
> By rearranging this equation, you can arrive at the Cost of Goods Sold (COGS). This is an important element in determining your company's gross profit, which is defined as Sales minus COGS. COGS is calculated by this equation:
>
> COGS = Beginning Inventory + Purchases – Ending Inventory
>
> The cost of goods available for sale is the sum of the beginning inventory and any purchases that were made. The difference between the cost of goods available for sale and the ending inventory is the cost of the goods that you actually sold to your customers.

Of course, many events can occur that complicate these basic relationships. You might have an arrangement with your suppliers that allows you to return to them, for any reason and for credit, some portion of the goods you purchase from them. It might be that some goods are damaged or otherwise unacceptable.

Your purchase terms might call for discounts if you make payment within a specified period. Adjusting entries or special accounts are sometimes necessary to quantify the effects of these occurrences. Nevertheless, they do not materially change the basic flow of starting inventory, through purchases and sales, to ending inventory—which becomes the starting inventory for the next accounting period.

Closing the Inventory Account

At the end of the period, a company often performs a physical count of the ending inventory. When it subsequently applies one of the valuation methods described in the next chapter, the result is the value of the inventory. This is the value that is used in the Current Assets section of the balance sheet.

This probably seems a little anticlimactic after all the discussion above about closing accounts, inventory flow, and Income Summaries. And in practice the process is more complex than simply performing an inventory count and entering the result on the balance sheet (see fig. 2.11).

Figure 2.11 contains seven sections, indicated by their bold borders. These sections could be maintained in separate Excel worksheets, but to conserve space, they are shown on one sheet.

	B	C	D	F	G	H
1	*Ledger accounts:*	Debits	Credits	*General journal:*	Debits	Credits
2	**Inventory**			Sales	$ 53,354	
3	Beginning balance (12/1)	$431,820		Purchases		$ 20,937
4	Ending balance (12/31)	$431,820		Advertising		$ 3,116
5	To close beginning inventory		$431,820	Telephone		$ 1,835
6	To close ending inventory	$425,869		Salaries		$ 10,088
7	Beginning balance (1/1)	$425,869		Income summary		$ 17,378
8	**Purchases**			To close revenue and expense accounts		
9	December purchases	$ 20,937				
10	To close		$ 20,937	Income summary	$431,820	
11	**Sales**			Inventory (12/31)		$431,820
12	Ending balance		$ 53,354	Close beginning inventory		
13	To close	$ 53,354				
14	**Advertising**			Inventory (1/1)	$425,869	
15	Ending balance	$ 3,116		Income summary		$425,869
16	To close		$ 3,116	Establish ending inventory		
17	**Telephone**					
18	Ending balance	$ 1,835		Income Summary	$ 11,427	
19	To close		$ 1,835	Owner's Equity		$ 11,427
20	**Salaries**					
21	Ending balance	$ 10,088				
22	To close		$ 10,088			

Fig. 2.11
Closing accounts at the end of a period takes revenue and expense accounts to a zero value, but normally leaves a value in asset and liability accounts.

The first section, labeled Inventory, shows the amount of inventory at the beginning of the period ($431,820), and the ending balance (also $431,820). Under a periodic inventory system (see chapter 3 for more information), no changes are made to the Inventory account during the period: purchases are recorded in their own account. A closing entry, equal to the ending balance, is made in the account's credit column. This amount is also entered in the General Journal's Income Summary (cell G10). A physical inventory count is taken, and entered as a debit ($425,869 in cell C6), and also to establish the beginning inventory for the next period (cell C7). The ending inventory is closed to cell G7 in the Income Summary.

Purchases made to inventory during the period are also closed out by a debit entry in the ledger (cell D10) and transferred to the Income Summary with a credit entry (cell H3).

This illustrates the process described earlier in this chapter, under which asset and liability accounts such as Inventory are *not* left with a zero balance at the end of an accounting period. In contrast, revenue and expense accounts such as Purchases *are* closed to leave them with a zero balance. For example, the Sales account is given a zero balance at the end of one period and, thus, at the beginning of the next. Its ending balance, $53,354, is entered twice at closing: once in the ledger account, to close it, and once in the Income Summary. The latter entry begins the process of moving revenue out of its ledger account and into the balance sheet.

The formula used in cell D12 to calculate Sales is an array formula:

```
=SUM(IF('2ndNatl'!B5:B19="Cash Receipts",
   '2ndNatl'!C5:C19,0))+SUM(IF(Fig2.5!B3:B23="Credit
   purchases",Fig2.5!C3:C23,0))
```

This array formula looks to a different worksheet, here named "2ndNatl," to find any values in cells B5:B19 that match the value "Cash Receipts." For any matching values, the formula sums the corresponding dollar amounts in cells C5:C19 (refer to fig. 2.4).

The same process is completed for the credit purchases, and the results of the two SUM functions are totaled to give the full amount of sales for the month. In practice, you would keep these two accounts separate, and add their closing balances together for the purpose of the Income Summary.

The next three sections in figure 2.11, labeled Advertising, Telephone and Salaries, each represent expenses incurred during the current period. The details of the activity in each account during the period have been omitted, and only the ending balance and the closing entry are shown.

Recall that at the end of the period, revenue and expense account balances are brought to zero by means of a closing entry. This entry also appears in the General Journal's temporary Income Summary account. Note that the values in cells D16, D19 and D22 are identical to the values in cells H4:H6 in the figure.

Notice also the value of $17,378 in cell H7 of figure 2.11. It is the result of subtracting the period's expenses (Purchasing, Advertising, Telephone and Salaries) from the period's sales revenue ($53,354). Cell G18 contains this formula:

```
=H7+(H15-G10)
```

which adds the difference between the ending inventory and the beginning inventory to the Income Summary. This amount, $11,427, represents the change in equity for the period: sales, less operating expenses, plus the change in the inventory valuation. Because the value of inventory dropped during the period, its effect is to reduce the amount that is added to Owner's Equity. Had the inventory grown, its effect would have been to increase the amount added to Owner's Equity.

Summary

In this chapter, you have learned about some of the preliminary aspects of balance sheets: their uses, their construction, their current asset components, and their relationships to underlying accounts. Changes over time in these accounts cause changes in your company's worth, and thus in its balance sheet. However, revenue and expense accounts are treated differently at the end of an accounting period than are asset and liability accounts.

While it is not this book's purpose to teach accountancy, the use of some accounting terminology is necessary in a discussion of the measurement of profit. As well, some discussion of certain rules used in double-entry accounting—such as recording an increase in an expense account as a debit entry—is necessary if you are to measure your profits in a way that others can understand.

The reason is that potential investors and creditors, as well as the accountants who will inevitably insist on examining your books, will insist that you follow accepted principles and practices in the creation of your financial statements. This chapter has introduced some of these concepts; more will be covered in subsequent chapters, but only to the extent necessary to help you create your financial statements.

Because the valuation of inventory is a somewhat complicated topic, chapter 3 covers it in detail. Choosing the appropriate method for valuing the items in your business's inventory is essential if you are to estimate the worth of your business properly. The measurement of your profits also depends on your choice of valuation method. After this excursion into the topic of inventory valuation, this book returns to the balance sheet with a consideration of Liabilities and Owner's Equity.

Chapter 3

Valuing Inventories for the Balance Sheet

Particularly for a line of business that manufactures or sells tangible goods, the size of the company's inventory exerts a powerful influence on its profitability. The inventory of goods is often the company's major current asset, and therefore contributes heavily to the calculation of the company's worth. Because the cost of goods sold is dependent on the valuation of the inventory, it also largely determines the company's gross profit (and, thus, its net income).

Due to the importance of inventory analysis to a company's worth and profitability, you have at your disposal a variety of methods to value an inventory and techniques to categorize it. Because you are expected to be consistent from year to year as to your inventory valuation and accounting methods, it's important to make sound choices early on. Using Excel's tools and capabilities properly helps you with these choices.

This chapter describes the different methods you can use to assign a value to your inventory, and the different ways available to account for it. You will learn how your choice of a technique to assign a value to your inventory affects both your profitability and your business's calculated worth.

Valuing Inventories

The basic principle of inventory valuation is that the value of a unit of inventory is its cost. For example, if your company purchases products at a wholesale cost and resells them to consumers at a retail price, then the value of your inventory of goods is determined by the amount you pay to acquire them.

On the other hand, if your company manufactures or otherwise produces goods, the situation is more complicated. In that case, there are typically three categories of inventory: raw materials, work in process, and finished goods. You would value each category differently. The value of the raw materials is simply their acquisition cost. The value of work in process is the cost of the raw materials plus any labor costs incurred to date. And the value of finished goods consists of the material cost plus all the labor costs involved in bringing the product to completion—including factory overhead.

There are three basic methods you can use to assign a value to your inventory:

- *Specific identification.* This method assigns the actual cost of acquiring each inventory unit to that unit. Historically, it has been companies that resell relatively few but relatively costly products that use specific identification. If your business sells expensive jewelry, you find it fairly easy to attach a specific acquisition cost to each unit. But if your company sells art supplies, you find it difficult to do so. It is much harder to keep track of the amount you paid for each of 100 paintbrushes.

- *Average cost.* This method is relatively simple to apply. The average cost per unit of inventory is just the total of your payments to suppliers, divided by the number of units in stock. Because the actual unit cost usually varies, due to changes in your supplier's pricing over time and to changing suppliers, this method can be less accurate than specific identification. But average cost is often a feasible method when specific identification is not.

- *FIFO* and *LIFO*. FIFO stands for first-in, first-out, and LIFO stands for last-in, first-out. These methods involve assumptions about when you acquired a unit of inventory and about when you sell it. Because your acquisition costs normally change over time, your cost of goods sold changes accordingly. Both your profitability and your total assets depend on whether you bought a unit for $50 and sell it for $75, or whether you bought an identical unit for $60 and sell it for $75.

The following sections in this chapter discuss each of these methods in detail.

Using Specific Identification

As mentioned previously, it is relatively easy to use specific identification as a means of valuing inventory if you have relatively few units to value. And as a practical matter, this has usually meant that those items are quite costly: a business that has just a few items to sell must either sell them at a substantial profit or cease operations for lack of cash.

In recent years, however, the proliferation of such technology as point-of-sale terminals at retail stores, the imprinting of serial numbers on many different kinds of electronic equipment, and the widespread use of computer-based support systems, has changed that situation—in the retail industry, at least. It is now much less onerous to track each and every unit from its acceptance into inventory through its eventual sale.

Although specific identification is probably the most intuitively satisfying of the valuation methods, it will become apparent that it is not always preferable to its alternatives—particularly from the profitability standpoint. Consider the case of a retail store that sells electronic equipment.

Case Study: Evans Electronics

Evans Electronics, a retail store located in a shopping mall, sells personal computers, data communications equipment, and ancillary products such as printers and disk drives. Making use of what it sells, Evans Electronics has put in place a small but sophisticated information system. This system enables the sales staff to enter into a database the serial number and product code of every item purchased from the store.

The system also maintains information about inventories. It keeps records of when a unit of stock was purchased, its cost, and its product code. Summary information on the starting inventory as of 4/1/95 and quantities purchased during the month is displayed in figure 3.1.

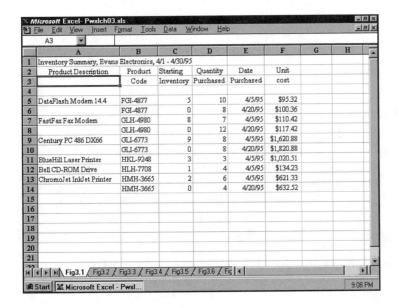

Fig. 3.1

Evans Electronics starting inventory and quantities purchased during April 1995 form the basis for valuation at the end of the period.

Evans' supplier raised its prices during April 1995: notice that identical products have entered the inventory at different times and at different costs. For example, Evans acquired seven fax modems on 4/5/95 at a unit cost of $110.42, and another 12 units of the same modem on 4/20/95 at a unit cost of $117.42.

The worksheet shown in figure 3.1 contains four named ranges that will become important later in this chapter:

- InventoryProductCode refers to the range B5:B14. It contains the identifier that distinguishes, say, a fax modem from a laser printer. Although this range uniquely identifies a product, it does not uniquely identify a product at a particular supplier cost.

- StartUnits refers to the range C5:C14. It contains data on the number of units of each product code *at a particular unit cost* that are in the inventory at the beginning of the period.

- PurchaseUnits refers to the range D5:D14. It shows how many units were purchased to the inventory during the period—again, at a particular unit cost.

- InventoryUnitCost refers to the range F5:F14. This is the cost of each product that was acquired from the supplier *at a particular time.*

The process of closing the books at the end of each month causes the information on products sold to flow from the sales database, a separate application, to an Excel worksheet. The worksheet for sales during April is shown in figure 3.2. Because the specific identification method is being used, each row contains information on the product code and serial number of each unit sold. Because this information uniquely identifies a particular unit, the sales database also contains, and passes to Excel, Evans Electronics' cost for that specific unit.

Although the unit costs for some products are different, Evans sold each product at the same price. As a new business, Evans made a tactical decision not to increase the sales price during the first month of operation. Clearly, Evans' decision to absorb the supplier's price increase, rather than to pass it on to its own customers, reduces its profitability. This is not an unusual decision, but the fact that the inventory contains identical units acquired at different costs has consequences both for the store's gross profit and for the balance sheet's asset evaluation.

Using the specific identification method of valuation, Evans can analyze its inventory for the month of April as shown in figure 3.3.

Fig. 3.2

The record of Evans Electronics product sales for April 1995 shows that some units that were sold had different acquisition costs.

	Description	Product Code	Serial Number	Unit Cost	Unit Sales
1	Description	Product	Serial	Unit	Unit
2		Code	Number	Cost	Sales
3	DataFlash Modem 14.4	FGI-4877	433158	$100.36	$127.02
4		FGI-4877	864596	$100.36	$127.02
5		FGI-4877	496061	$95.32	$127.02
6	FastFax Fax Modem	GLH-4980	816748	$110.42	$138.54
7		GLH-4980	531168	$110.42	$138.54
8		GLH-4980	668396	$117.42	$138.54
9		GLH-4980	328322	$117.42	$138.54
10	Century PC 486 DX66	GLI-6773	231352	$1,620.88	$2,130.42
11		GLI-6773	527035	$1,620.88	$2,130.42
12		GLI-6773	128837	$1,820.88	$2,130.42
13		GLI-6773	680652	$1,820.88	$2,130.42
14		GLI-6773	755851	$1,820.88	$2,130.42
15	BlueHill Laser Printer	HKL-9248	330711	$1,020.51	$1,298.31
16	Bell CD-ROM Drive	HLH-7708	370544	$134.23	$167.39
17		HLH-7708	531937	$134.23	$167.39
18	ChromoJet InkJet Printer	HMH-3665	568101	$621.33	$774.95
19		HMH-3665	888336	$621.33	$774.95
20		HMH-3665	849167	$621.33	$774.95
21		HMH-3665	614869	$632.52	$774.95
22		HMH-3665	900254	$632.52	$774.95
23					
24	Totals			$13,874.12	$17,095.16

Fig. 3.3

By matching product codes and costs to the sales database, Evans Electronics can tell how many units of each product were sold.

	Description	Product Code	Unit cost	Starting units	Purchases, units	Cost of goods available for sale	Units Sold	Ending inventory Units	Costs
1	Specific identification method								
2		Product	Unit cost	Starting	Purchases,	Cost of goods	Units	Ending inventory	
3	Description	Code		units	units	available	Sold	Units	Costs
4						for sale			
5									
6	DataFlash Modem 14.4	FGI-4877	$95.32	5	10	$1,429.80	1	14	$1,334.48
7		FGI-4877	$100.36	0	8	$802.88	2	6	$602.16
8	FastFax Fax Modem	GLH-4980	$110.42	8	7	$1,656.30	2	13	$1,435.46
9		GLH-4980	$117.42	0	12	$1,409.04	2	10	$1,174.20
10	Century PC 486 DX66	GLI-6773	$1,620.88	9	8	$27,554.96	2	15	$24,313.20
11		GLI-6773	$1,820.88	0	8	$14,567.04	3	5	$9,104.40
12	BlueHill Laser Printer	HKL-9248	$1,020.51	3	3	$6,123.06	1	5	$5,102.55
13	Bell CD-ROM Drive	HLH-7708	$134.23	1	4	$671.15	2	3	$402.69
14	ChromoJet InkJet Printer	HMH-3665	$621.33	2	6	$4,970.64	3	5	$3,106.65
15		HMH-3665	$632.52	0	4	$2,530.08	2	2	$1,265.04
16									
17	Totals				70	$61,714.95	20	78	$47,840.83
18									
19	Cost of goods sold:	$13,874.12							
20	Gross profit:	$3,221.04							
21									
22									
23									
24									

In figure 3.3, the columns for product description, product code, and unit cost contain the unique combinations of the variables from the worksheet in figure 3.2: for example, there are only two possible combinations of product code and unit cost for the DataFlash 14.4 modem. The number of units in the starting inventory is obtained from a physical count made at the end of

March, displayed in figure 3.1. The cost of each item available for sale is the product of the unit cost and the number of units.

The critical portion of figure 3.3 is in column G, Units Sold. Cell G6 contains this array-formula:

```
=SUM((B6=SalesProductCode)*(C6=SalesUnitCost))
```

which returns 2 as its value: 2 DataFlash 14.4 modems that were purchased for $100.36 each were sold during April. To understand how this formula works, examine its components.

There is a range named SalesProductCode, which occupies cells B3:B22 in figure 3.2. This fragment:

```
B6=SalesProductCode
```

evaluates to:

```
{TRUE;TRUE;TRUE;FALSE;FALSE; . . . ;FALSE}
```

and returns an array of values that are TRUE or FALSE. The logical value depends on whether the value in B6 (FGI–4877) equals any values in the SalesProductCode range. In this case, the first three values in the array are TRUE. The B6 value of FGI–4877 equals the first three elements in SalesProductCode (see cells B3:B5 in fig. 3.2).

This fragment:

```
C6=SalesUnitCost
```

evaluates to:

```
{TRUE;TRUE;FALSE;FALSE;FALSE; . . . ;FALSE}
```

and operates in much the same way. There is a range named SalesUnitCost, which occupies cells D3:D22 in figure 3.2. It also returns an array of logical, TRUE or FALSE values, depending on whether the unit cost in C6, $100.36, equals any unit costs in the SalesUnitCost range. In this case, only the first two values are TRUE (see cells D3:D4 in fig. 3.2).

Tip

You can see the arrays of TRUE or FALSE values—indeed, the results of any portion of an Excel formula—by highlighting a fragment in the Formula Bar and pressing the F9 key. When you have finished, be sure to press Esc or click the cancel box. Otherwise, the results replace the original fragment.

Excel can perform arithmetic operations on logical values. The rules are that TRUE*TRUE = 1, TRUE*FALSE = 0, and FALSE*FALSE = 0. So this fragment, which multiplies the first array of logical values times the second:

```
(B6=SalesProductCode)*(C6=SalesUnitCost)
```

evaluates to:

```
{1;1;0;0;0;0;0;0;0;0;0;0;0;0;0;0;0;0;0}
```

and returns an array of 1s and 0s. The first array contains TRUE in its first three elements, and the second array contains TRUE in its first two elements; the remaining elements in each array are FALSE. So, the result of this multiplication is an array whose first two elements are 1s and the remaining elements are 0s.

Finally, the full formula:

```
=SUM((B6=SalesProductCode)*(C6=SalesUnitCost))
```

returns the sum of the array of 1s and 0s. In this case, that sum equals 2: the number of sales of products whose product code is FGI-4877 and whose unit cost is $100.36.

The formula in cell G6 is then copied and pasted into the range G7:G15 in figure 3.3. The references to the product code and unit cost adjust accordingly, but the range names, being a sort of absolute reference, do not adjust. This results in a count of each unit that was sold during April at a given unit cost.

The units in the ending inventory for April (column H in fig. 3.3) are simply the result of subtracting the units sold from the starting inventory. And the cost for each product code at a given unit cost (column I in fig. 3.3) is the result of multiplying the number of units in the ending inventory by the associated unit cost.

By obtaining the total cost of the goods available for sale ($61,714.95), and subtracting from that figure the total cost of the ending inventory ($47,840.83), Evans can arrive at a cost of goods sold for the month of April of $13,874.12.

Therefore, Evans Electronics' income statement for April would show a gross profit of $3,221.04, the result of subtracting the cost of goods sold from its total sales revenue of $17,095.16. Its balance sheet for April would show ending inventory assets of $47,840.83.

Return to the number of units in the starting inventory (column D in fig. 3.3). Although these data are obtained from a physical count at the end of

March, there is no need to enter the information in both the inventory summary worksheet (refer to fig. 3.1) and in the worksheet shown in figure 3.3. The array formula in cell D6 references the inventory summary worksheet:

```
=SUM((B6=InventoryProductCode)*(C6=PurchaseUnitCost)*StartUnits)
```

This array formula employs the same concepts as does the formula that calculates the number of units sold. That is, it multiplies two arrays of logical TRUE/FALSE values times one another to return an array of 1s and 0s:

```
(B6=InventoryProductCode)*(C6=PurchaseUnitCost)
```

which returns this array:

```
{1;0;0;0;0;0;0;0;0}
```

Then, the latter array is multiplied by the array containing the number of units in the starting inventory (StartUnits, which represents the range D4:D13 in figure 3.1). The sole 1 in the above array, times the first element in StartUnits, returns 5; the remaining zero-values return 0 when multiplied by StartUnits. And the SUM function adds the 0s to the 5 to return the result.

Using Average Cost

Suppose that, as in the previous case study, Evans Electronics has in its starting inventory items that carry different costs of acquisition but are otherwise identical. What if the store had no means of knowing which specific item it sold? That is, suppose that when it sells a Century PC 486 DX66 computer, Evans does not know whether it is a unit that was purchased from the supplier for $1,620.88 or for $1,820.88.

In cases such as these, you would typically choose to use the *average cost* method of valuing your inventory. There can be other reasons to use this method. For example, if you had some means of recognizing whether a computer cost you $1,620.88 or $1,820.88, it would be possible for you to use the specific identification method—possible, although perhaps not feasible.

But if you use specific identification, your gross profit on a sale would depend in part on which of several identical computers your customer happened to choose. In this case, your gross profit should surely be irrelevant to the customer's purchasing choice. The average cost method recognizes this: it assigns a cost to each unit of inventory that is a weighted average of all the unit costs for a particular product. Figure 3.4 illustrates the average cost method as it might be used by Evans Electronics.

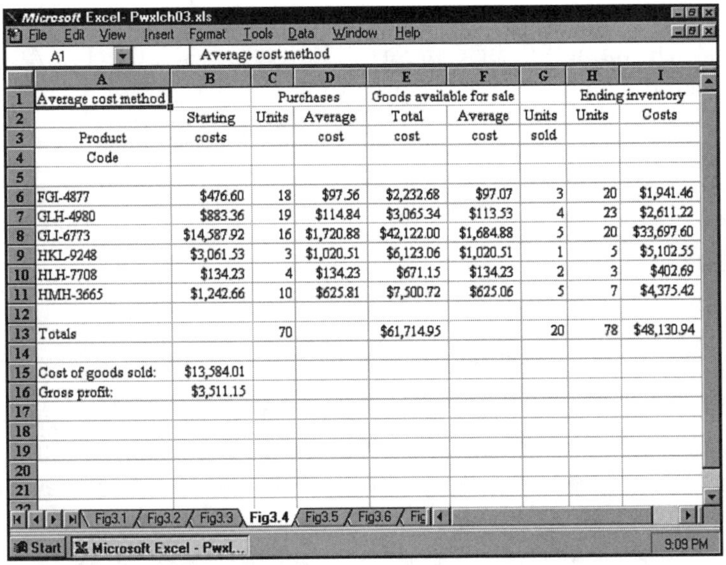

	A	B	C	D	E	F	G	H	I
1	Average cost method		Purchases		Goods available for sale			Ending inventory	
2		Starting	Units	Average	Total	Average	Units	Units	Costs
3	Product	costs		cost	cost	cost	sold		
4	Code								
5									
6	FGI-4877	$476.60	18	$97.56	$2,232.68	$97.07	3	20	$1,941.46
7	GLH-4980	$883.36	19	$114.84	$3,065.34	$113.53	4	23	$2,611.22
8	GLI-6773	$14,587.92	16	$1,720.88	$42,122.00	$1,684.88	5	20	$33,697.60
9	HKL-9248	$3,061.53	3	$1,020.51	$6,123.06	$1,020.51	1	5	$5,102.55
10	HLH-7708	$134.23	4	$134.23	$671.15	$134.23	2	3	$402.69
11	HMH-3665	$1,242.66	10	$625.81	$7,500.72	$625.06	5	7	$4,375.42
12									
13	Totals		70		$61,714.95		20	78	$48,130.94
14									
15	Cost of goods sold:	$13,584.01							
16	Gross profit:	$3,511.15							
17									
18									
19									
20									
21									

Fig. 3.4
Evans Electronics starting and ending inventory for April 1995 with the average cost method returns different results than with specific identification.

In contrast to figure 3.3, which shows ten combinations of product code by unit cost, figure 3.4 shows six product codes, each with just one unit cost. The average cost method derives a single unit cost for each product code, and therefore there is no need to represent the different actual costs for each product code on the inventory summary.

Column C of figure 3.4 shows the count of each product code in the starting inventory. Cell C6 calculates this with the array formula:

```
=SUM(IF(A6=InventoryProductCode,PurchaseUnits,0))
```

Notice that there is only one array of logical values in this formula, so no multiplication of logical values is involved. The fragment:

```
A6=InventoryProductCode
```

returns this array of TRUE/FALSE values:

```
{TRUE;TRUE;FALSE;FALSE;FALSE;FALSE;FALSE;FALSE;FALSE;FALSE}
```

Surrounding this fragment with the IF function and the reference to InventoryUnits converts the array to numeric values:

```
IF(A6=InventoryProductCode,PurchaseUnits,0)
```

which returns this numeric array:

```
{8;10;0;0;0;0;0;0;0;0}
```

Using this array as the argument to the SUM function returns 18, the total of the array. The formula is copied from cell C6 and pasted into cells C7:C11 to complete the count of the starting inventory.

Column D in figure 3.4 shows the average cost for each product code. It begins with cell D6, which contains this array formula:

```
=SUM(IF(A6=InventoryProductCode,PurchaseUnitCost*PurchaseUnits))/C6
```

Again, this fragment:

```
A6=InventoryProductCode
```

returns this array of logical values:

```
{TRUE;TRUE;FALSE;FALSE;FALSE;FALSE;FALSE;FALSE;FALSE}
```

which act as the criteria for the IF function. When the criterion is TRUE, Excel returns the product of the unit cost and the number of units; else, Excel returns FALSE. That is, this fragment:

```
IF(A6=InventoryProductCode,PurchaseUnitCost*PurchaseUnits)
```

returns:

```
{953.2;802.88;FALSE;FALSE;FALSE;FALSE;FALSE;FALSE;FALSE}
```

The SUM function adds 953.2 and 802.88, treating the FALSE values in the array as zeros. Finally, this sum is divided by the total number of units for that product code, which is the value in cell C6. Notice that this is a *weighted* average: each of the two unit costs ($95.32 and $100.36) is weighted by multiplying it times the number of units with that cost in the starting inventory. Thus, 10 units @ $95.32 cost $953.20, which is the first value in the array shown above. 8 units @ $100.36 cost $802.88, which is the second value in the array. $953.20 plus $802.88, or $1,756.08, is the total cost of this product in the starting inventory (see fig. 3.4 cell E6). Dividing by the total number of such units, 18, yields an average cost of $97.56 for this product.

This formula is copied from cell D6 and pasted into cells D7:D11 of figure 3.4 to get the average cost of each product code purchased to inventory during the month. Then, the product code's total cost is placed into E6:E11 by adding the starting cost to the product of the units purchased by their average cost. The result is the total cost of the goods available for sale: starting costs plus purchase costs.

Column F contains the average cost of the goods available for sale, on a unit basis. It is simply the result of dividing the amount in column E by the number of units in the starting inventory plus the number of units purchased.

Column G contains the number of units sold for each product code. It is considerably simpler than the corresponding calculation for the specific identification method. In this case, there is a single average unit cost associated with each product code, and the number of units sold can be retrieved by this formula:

```
=SUM((A6=SalesProductCode)*1)
```

The range named SalesProductCode is as shown in figure 3.2, cells B3:B22. It is necessary to multiply by 1 the array of logical values returned by testing the value in B6 against the SalesProductCode array to convert the TRUE values to a value of 1. Then, these values are summed to determine the number of units sold.

Column H, the ending inventory in units, is obtained by subtracting the units sold from the units in the starting inventory plus the units purchased. Column I, the total cost of each product line in the ending inventory, is the product of the number of units in the ending inventory times their average unit cost.

The cost of goods sold is the total cost of the starting inventory, plus the cost of purchases, less that of the ending inventory, just as it is using specific identification. However, the value of cost of goods sold is different. Under specific identification, the cost of goods sold is $13,874.12, whereas under average cost it is $13,584,01, about $300 less. This is because the average cost method results in a different unit cost than does specific identification. Although the total cost of the starting inventory is the same in both cases (because the cost of each unit is known), the cost of each unit sold is different for the two methods (because the actual cost of each unit sold is unknown, and the average cost is used in place of its actual cost).

The difference of $300 in cost of goods sold is small in this illustration, because there are roughly the same numbers of units carrying different average costs in the starting inventory. The difference would be larger if the starting inventory had one Century PC 486 DX66 computer at a cost of $1,620.88, and fifteen at a cost of $1,820.88.

Under the average cost method, Evans Electronics' income statement for April would show a gross profit of $3,511.15, the result of subtracting the cost of goods sold (the total cost of the goods available for sale less the total cost of the ending inventory) from its total sales revenue of $17,095.16. Its balance sheet for April would show inventory assets of $48,130.94. Thus, its gross profit is about $300 more, and its inventory assets about $300 less, than with specific identification.

> **Note**
>
> *This result is not a general rule about the relationship between the two valuation meth-ods.* The use of average cost could cause a gross profit either greater or less than specific identification, and the same is true of asset valuation. Both the direction and the size of the difference between the two methods depend on the difference in the number of units in the starting inventory that carry different actual unit costs. In fact, if the numbers of units are equal, the two methods return the same result.

Using FIFO

FIFO, or *first-in, first-out,* is a method of valuing inventory that, like specific identification, uses the actual cost of a unit of inventory. Unlike specific identification (but like average cost) FIFO makes an assumption about the cost of the unit that is actually sold.

The average cost method assumes that the cost of a sold unit is the weighted average of the costs of all such units in the starting inventory. In contrast, FIFO assumes that the first unit sold during the month has a cost equal to that of the first unit purchased to the starting inventory. Thus, first-in to inventory, first-out of inventory.

When, for the first time during April, a customer purchases a modem from Evans Electronics, it is not known whether the supplier charged Evans $95.32 or $100.36 for that specific modem. It is assumed, though, that the modem's cost is the same as that of the first modem purchased to the starting inventory: $95.32.

Figure 3.5 illustrates the FIFO valuation method.

The value of the ending inventory in figure 3.5 is determined by means of a user-defined function (UDF) named FIFO. This function is called in cell I6 of figure 3.5 with this entry:

```
=FIFO(B6,G6)
```

Its arguments, cells B6 and G6, contain the particular product code being analyzed and the number of units of that product that were sold during April. The FIFO function is written in Excel Visual Basic, Applications Edition (VBA) code, and is shown in figure 3.6.

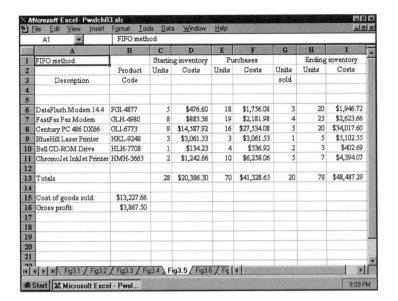

Fig. 3.5
Using FIFO, Evans Electronics assumes that the cost of a unit sold is the cost of the unit that entered its inventory the earliest.

Fig. 3.6
This VBA code calculates the value of ending inventory using the FIFO method.

The function works as described here. The first line of code:

```
Function FIFO(oProductCode As Object, oUnitsSold As Object) As Single
```

declares the function by giving it the name FIFO, specifies that its arguments are Excel objects, and that its degree of arithmetic precision is Single. Used in cell I6 of figure 3.5, the argument oProductCode represents cell B6, and the argument oUnitsSold represents cell G6. Single precision is precise enough for dollar amounts, and saves a very small amount of memory in contrast to double precision.

The function's next two statements:

```
Dim oStartCount As Object, oStartCost As Object, oStartProduct As Object
Dim oPurchaseUnits As Object
Dim Counter As Integer, RemainingUnits As Long, AccountedFor As Long
```

declare several variables:

- oStartCount is an object variable. (Some VBA programmers use the initial letter of a variable's name as a mnemonic to help them remember a variable's type. Here, the initial letter "o" stands for "object.") The FIFO function will use oStartCount to represent the range in the workbook that contains the number of units of each product that are in the starting inventory.

- oStartCost is an object variable. It is used to represent the workbook range that contains the unit cost of each product.

- oStartProduct is an object variable. It is used to represent the workbook range that contains the product codes in the starting inventory.

- oPurchaseUnits is an object variable. It is used to represent the workbook range that contains the number of units purchased during the month.

- Counter is an integer variable. It is used to control a loop in the FIFO function that examines each product in the starting inventory to see whether it should contribute to the product's valuation in the ending inventory.

- RemainingUnits, a Long variable, is used to determine how many inventory units are left in inventory after the units sold have been subtracted.

- AccountedFor, a Long variable, keeps track of the number of units sold that have been subtracted from the starting inventory to determine the ending inventory.

The next four statements:

```
Set oStartCount = Range("StartUnits")
Set oStartCost = Range("PurchaseUnitCost")
Set oStartProduct = Range("InventoryProductCode")
Set oPurchaseUnits = Range("PurchaseUnits")
```

point each object variable to its appropriate range in the workbook. The first of the four, for example, specifies that oStartCount is a Range object, and that the range it represents is the range named StartUnits.

Next, the FIFO function initializes the value of the Long variable AccountedFor to the number of units sold.

> **Tip**
>
> A Long variable is an Integer variable that can accommodate values as large as 2,147,483,647. It requires very slightly more memory than an Integer variable, which can accommodate values up to 32,767. The small premium in additional memory is often worth the variable's extra capacity.

The object variable oUnitsSold is the second argument to the FIFO function: in this example, it is cell G6 in figure 3.5, and the AccountedFor variable is set equal to that value:

```
AccountedFor = oUnitsSold.Value
```

Because E6 contains the value 3, AccountedFor starts life with the value of 3.

FIFO's For loop contains the meat of the function:

```
For Counter = 1 To oStartCount.Rows.Count
    If oProductCode.Value = oStartProduct(Counter, 1) Then
        RemainingUnits = Application.Max(0, oStartCount(Counter, 1) +
        ↪oPurchaseUnits(Counter,1) - AccountedFor)
        FIFO = FIFO + oStartCost(Counter, 1) * RemainingUnits
        AccountedFor = AccountedFor - (oStartCount(Counter, 1) +
        ↪oPurchaseUnits(Counter,1) - RemainingUnits)
    End If
Next Counter
```

The For and the Next statements cycle the loop through all the rows of the oStartCount range: that is, the loop executes once for each row in the range that is represented in the function by the oStartCount variable. oStartCount represents the range named StartUnits, which is contained in cells C5:C14of figure 3.1. That range has ten rows, so the loop will execute ten times as its control variable, Counter, progresses from 1 to 10.

Within the loop, the If . . . End If block tests whether the value of oProductCode equals the current value of the oStartProduct range. If it does, then the statements within the If block are executed; else, the For loop continues to the next value of Counter.

For example, suppose that oProductCode is equal to FGI-4877, as it is if cell B6 of figure 3.5 is passed to FIFO's first argument. The first time that the loop executes, Counter equals 1. Then, the expression:

```
oStartProduct(Counter, 1)
```

represents the first row of the first (and only) column of the oStartProduct range. That range is cells B5:B14 in figure 3.1. The first row, first column of that range contains FGI-4877. Therefore, oProductCode equals oStartProduct(Counter,1), and the statements within the If . . . End If block are executed.

In contrast, Counter equals 3 during the third time that the loop executes. oProductCode still equals FGI-4877: nothing that occurs in the loop changes that value. But now, the expression:

```
oStartProduct(Counter, 1)
```

refers to the *third* row of the range B5:B14in figure 3.1. That cell contains the value GLH-4980. Now, oProductCode no longer equals oStartProduct(Counter, 1). The statements within the If . . . End If block are skipped, the Next statement increments the Counter variable to 4, and the loop continues.

So, when Counter equals 1 and when Counter equals 2, the statements in the If . . . End If block are executed. Follow the logical flow of those statements:

```
RemainingUnits = Application.Max(0, oStartCount(Counter, 1) +
    oPurchaseUnits(Counter,1) - AccountedFor)
```

Application.Max invokes Excel's worksheet function MAX( ). Therefore, this statement returns the larger of 0, or the result of adding the number of units in the starting inventory, plus the number of units purchased, less the number of units AccountedFor so far. This is to prevent RemainingUnits from taking on a negative value if the number of units sold is greater than the number of units in the available inventory at a given unit cost.

oStartCount(Counter, 1) equals 5, and oPurchaseUnits(Counter,1) equals 10 when Counter equals 1 (see fig. 3.1 Cells C5 and D5). AccountedFor was initialized to oUnitsSold.Value, or 3, before the loop began. So RemainingUnits equals 5+10–3, or 12. This is the number of units remaining in inventory after accounting for the number that were sold.

```
FIFO = FIFO + oStartCost(Counter, 1) * RemainingUnits
```

FIFO starts life with a value of zero. So when Counter equals 1, this statement adds to zero the product of the unit cost times the number of units remaining in inventory. oStartCost(Counter, 1) equals 95.32 when Counter equals 1 (see cell F5 of fig. 3.1). RemainingUnits equals 12, so FIFO is set equal to 95.32 * 12, or 1143.84.

```
AccountedFor = AccountedFor - (oStartCount(Counter, 1) +
    oPurchaseUnits(Counter,1) - RemainingUnits)
```

Before this statement executes, AccountedFor equals 3 (it was set to that value before the loop began). oStartCount(Counter,1) equals 5, oPurchaseUnits(Counter,1) equals 10, and RemainingUnits equals 12. The statement resolves to:

```
AccountedFor = 3-(5+10-12) = 3-3 = 0
```

The If . . . End If block is now complete. The Next statement increments the value of Counter to 2. The If statement is tested again, and it passes the test because the second value in oStartProduct is still FGI-4877. Execute the statements in the If . . . End If block once again, with Counter equal to 2:

```
RemainingUnits = Application.Max(0, oStartCount(Counter, 1) +
    oPurchaseUnits(Counter,1)  - AccountedFor
```

At present, the value of AccountedFor is zero, so RemainingUnits is set equal to the value of the second row of oStartCount plus the second row of oPurchaseUnits. Those values are 0 and 8 (see cells C6 and D6 of fig. 3.1).

```
FIFO = FIFO + oStartCost(Counter, 1) * RemainingUnits
```

At present, FIFO equals 1143.84. To that value is added the product of the second row of oStartCost and RemainingUnits. oStartCost(2,1) equals 100.36 (see fig. 3.1 cell F6). RemainingUnits equals 8, so FIFO is set equal to 1143.84 + 100.36 * 8, or 1946.72.

Because there are only two instances of FGI-4877 in oStartProduct, the If . . . End If block will not execute again, and the final value of FIFO is 1946.72. This is the value returned to cell I6 in figure 3.5.

Conceptually, what the FIFO function has done is to look for every instance of FGI-4877 in the starting inventory. It subtracts the number of units sold from the first instance of FGI-4877, and adds to the value of FIFO the number of units remaining times their unit cost. In accordance with FIFO's basic assumption, the units sold are considered to be the first units to enter the inventory. The number of units sold is subtracted from the first units that FIFO encounters in its loop through the starting inventory.

You will find it a useful exercise to go through this same step-by-step progression by setting the number of units sold to a value greater than the first row of oStartCount. For example, try setting the value in cell G6 of figure 3.5 to 7. Doing so would cause FIFO to "use up" all the units of FGI-4877 in the starting inventory that cost $95.32, plus two of the units that cost $100.36, resulting in an ending inventory value for FGI-4877 of $1,565.44. In particular, watch what happens to RemainingUnits and AccountedFor as Counter changes from 1 to 2.

The cost of goods sold shown in figure 3.5 is the difference between the total cost of the starting inventory and that of the ending inventory, just as it is using specific identification and average cost. Under the average cost method, the cost of goods sold is $13,584.01, about $350 more than under the FIFO method ($13,227.66). This is because the average cost method uses the weighted average of all units in the starting inventory to calculate the cost of goods sold. In contrast, FIFO uses the costs of, say, the three units that entered the starting inventory first to calculate the cost of goods sold. Keep in mind that the earliest costs are used, even though the actual, physical units that were sold might be the ones that entered the starting inventory last.

Under FIFO, Evans Electronics' income statement for April would show a gross profit of $3,867.50, the result of subtracting the cost of goods sold from its total sales revenue of $17,095.16. Its balance sheet for April would show inventory assets of $48,487.29. Thus, its gross profit is about $350 more, and its inventory assets about $350 less, than with the average cost method.

Again, this is not a general rule about the relationship between the two valuation methods. FIFO's effect is different according to whether supplier prices are rising or falling over time. If supplier prices are rising, FIFO returns a lower cost of goods sold on the income statement, and a greater valuation of ending inventory on the balance sheet. This is because, when prices rise, units acquired earlier cost less than units acquired later, and FIFO assumes that the cost of goods sold are a function of the cost of goods acquired earlier.

In contrast, neither the specific identification nor the average cost method is sensitive to the timing of a purchase to starting inventory.

Using LIFO

LIFO, or *last-in, first-out*, works much as does FIFO. The difference, of course, is that the cost of a unit sold is assumed to be the cost of units that entered the starting inventory most recently, instead of the cost of the units that entered the starting inventory earliest.

Just as with FIFO, the effect of LIFO is dependent on whether your supplier costs are rising or falling—although the LIFO's effect is the reverse of FIFO's. If your unit costs are rising, then your cost of goods sold will rise, your gross profit will be smaller and your balance sheet assets will be smaller (because the cost of the units in ending inventory will be assigned the lower, earlier values). If your unit costs are falling, however, your cost of goods sold will be lower, your gross profit will be larger, as will your balance sheet assets. Therefore, your choice of a valuation method impacts your company's reported income (and, indirectly, its income taxes) as well as its worth as reported on the balance sheet.

Figure 3.7 illustrates the use of LIFO for Evans Electronics.

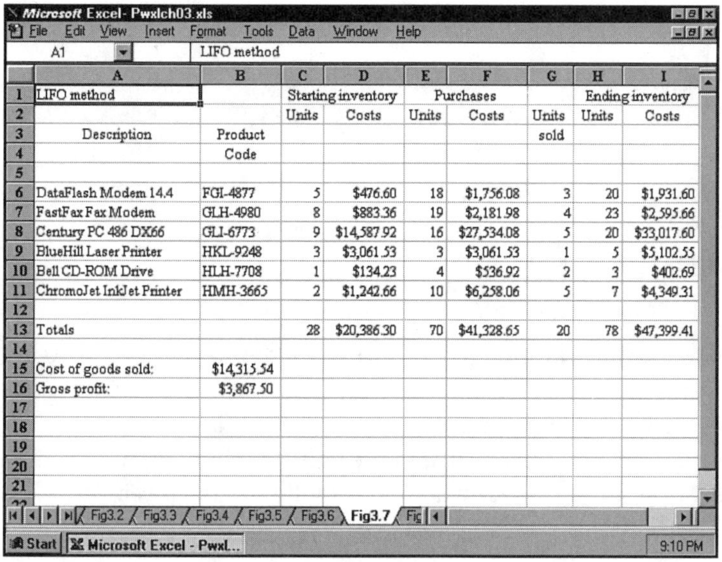

	A	B	C	D	E	F	G	H	I
1	LIFO method		Starting inventory		Purchases			Ending inventory	
2			Units	Costs	Units	Costs	Units	Units	Costs
3	Description	Product					sold		
4		Code							
5									
6	DataFlash Modem 14.4	FGI-4877	5	$476.60	18	$1,756.08	3	20	$1,931.60
7	FastFax Fax Modem	GLH-4980	8	$883.36	19	$2,181.98	4	23	$2,595.66
8	Century PC 486 DX66	GLI-6773	9	$14,587.92	16	$27,534.08	5	20	$33,017.60
9	BlueHill Laser Printer	HKL-9248	3	$3,061.53	3	$3,061.53	1	5	$5,102.55
10	Bell CD-ROM Drive	HLH-7708	1	$134.23	4	$536.92	2	3	$402.69
11	ChromoJet InkJet Printer	HMH-3665	2	$1,242.66	10	$6,258.06	5	7	$4,349.31
12									
13	Totals		28	$20,386.30	70	$41,328.65	20	78	$47,399.41
14									
15	Cost of goods sold:	$14,315.54							
16	Gross profit:	$3,867.50							
17									
18									
19									
20									
21									

Fig. 3.7
The LIFO method values inventory under the assumption that the most recently acquired goods are sold first; equivalently, the goods acquired earliest remain in inventory at the end of the period.

All the information in figure 3.7 is the same as in figure 3.5, except for the value of the ending inventory and the total cost of goods sold. The value of the ending inventory is determined by means of a UDF named LIFO. This function is called in cell I6 of figure 3.7 with this entry:

```
=LIFO(B6,G6)
```

The only difference between the entry in I6 of figure 3.7 and the entry in I6 of figure 3.5 is the call to LIFO instead of to FIFO. The VBA code for the user-defined LIFO function is shown in figure 3.8.

Fig. 3.8
This VBA code calculates the value of ending inventory using the LIFO method.

There is only one difference between the FIFO and LIFO UDFs: the loop that controls the progression through the starting inventory starts at the bottom of those ranges rather than at the top:

```
For Counter = oStartCount.Rows.Count To 1 Step -1
```

So, instead of progressing from 1 to 10, Counter progresses from 10 to 1 in increments of –1. Because the ranges that describe the starting inventory are sorted, top to bottom, in earlier to later order, this means that the more recent entries are examined first, and the units that have been sold are "removed" from the most recent additions to the starting inventory.

Therefore, items remaining in inventory at the end of the period are assigned the cost of those that entered the inventory first. This is in accordance with the last-in, first-out approach.

Notice, in figure 3.7, that the cost of goods sold is $14,315.54. Using the FIFO method, the cost of goods sold is $13,227.66 (refer to fig. 3.5). Therefore, choosing to use LIFO instead of FIFO increases the cost of goods sold by $1,087.88. LIFO reduces the gross profit just like FIFO, and increases the asset value of the ending inventory, by the same amount.

Comparing the Four Valuation Methods

As you might expect, each valuation method discussed in this chapter has both advantages and drawbacks:

- *Specific identification* is the most intuitively satisfying method, because it adjusts the ending inventory valuation according to the actual cost of the items that were sold during the period. It avoids the average cost method's assumption that all otherwise identical units bear the same acquisition cost, and it avoids the assumptions made by FIFO and LIFO that a unit was purchased at a particular time.

  However, specific identification enables the manipulation of cost of goods sold, gross profit and asset valuation. The person who chooses the actual unit that is provided to the customer controls the value of the unit that is leaving the inventory. Your company may not want its financial records to be under the direct control of a person who removes an item from stock. However, this would probably not constitute a problem if your business were, for example, the retail sale of custom jewelry. In this case, each item in your inventory might be unique, and the removal of a unit from inventory is left to the marketplace, not to a member of your staff.

  Furthermore, if a company has thousands of units in its inventory, specific identification makes recordkeeping virtually unmanageable.

- The *average cost* method treats each otherwise identical item in the inventory as though it had the same cost, regardless of its actual supplier price. It makes no assumption as to when an item was acquired, as do LIFO and FIFO. Furthermore, the item's assigned cost is not affected by the choice of which physical unit to deliver to the customer, as is the case with specific identification.

  But consider the effect of rising or falling supplier prices. If your costs of acquisition are changing substantially or swiftly, the current replacement cost of your inventory is changing to the same degree. Average cost combines the cost of older but functionally identical units with the cost of newer units. This can cause you to under- or over-value your inventory. And it can cause inaccurate pricing decisions if you base your selling price as a fixed percentage of your cost.

  On the other hand, if you manage your inventories according to Just-in-Time principles they will tend to be small relative to the amounts that you buy into stock and sell from stock. In that case, the current costs of acquisition will enter the average cost equation with a greater weight, and provide quite an accurate valuation.

- The *FIFO* method values the ending inventory according to the cost of the units that were most recently acquired. Therefore, the valuation of the inventory assets on the balance sheet tends to be more closely in accord with their current replacement cost. And, as a result, the value of the business on its balance sheet tends to be more accurate.

On the other hand, the time lag between the acquisition of older units and the sale of the merchandise is greater than the lag between the acquisition of the newer units and the sale of the merchandise. Therefore, from the standpoint of the income statement, FIFO is less accurate than LIFO. This is because the measurement of the gross profit is based on the revenues that derive from current market conditions and the costs that derive from earlier market conditions.

■ The *LIFO* method values the units sold during the period at the cost of the units that were most recently acquired. Therefore, the calculation of the gross profit is in closer accord with current market conditions, resulting in a more accurate income statement.

However, LIFO values the inventory at the end of the period according to the costs of the units that were acquired earliest. This can cause a mis-estimate of the current value of the inventory assets for the purpose of reporting the worth of the business on its balance sheet.

Because of changes in income tax laws, changes in market conditions such as rising and falling costs, and occasional changes in accounting standards, no one can offer broad-brush advice about which method of inventory valuation is best, even for a given company. Use the knowledge you have gained about inventory valuation to select the appropriate method in consultation with your accountant or tax lawyer, and implement that method in your daily operations.

Handling Purchase Discounts

It often happens that a supplier will offer a discount from cost in return for quick payment for goods. This purchase discount is not applied to the valuation of the inventory, but is recorded in a Purchase Discounts account. In turn, the entries in the Purchase Discounts account are used to adjust the income statement's Purchases account.

Note

Some companies handle purchase discounts as adjustments to their inventory accounts. However, because this complicates the process of valuing the inventory, most companies use the approach outlined here.

Is it to your advantage to pay a supplier promptly and thus obtain a purchase discount? As you might expect, that depends on the amount of the discount as well as the payment deadline.

Suppose that Evans Electronics orders two PCs from its supplier. The supplier offers Evans a $30 discount if payment is made within 30 days. Payment must be made within 60 days (see fig. 3.9).

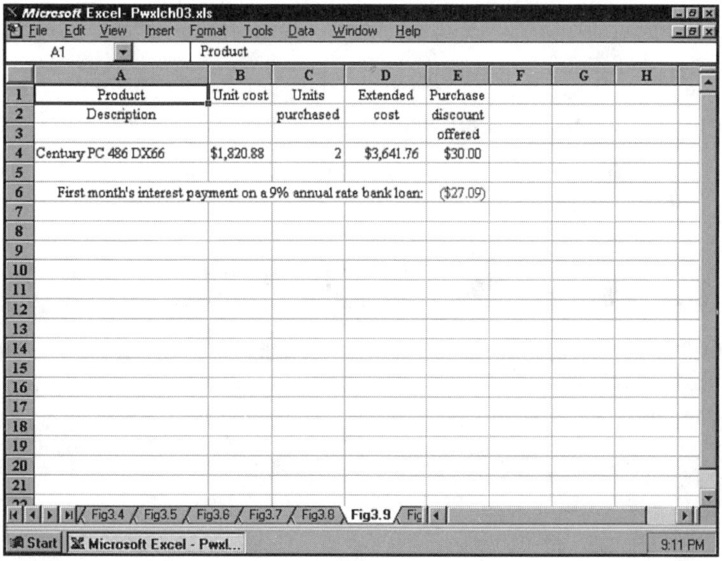

Fig. 3.9
Analyzing a purchase discount as though it were interest on a loan can help you decide whether to take the discount.

The extended cost (that is, the number of units times the unit cost) for the two PCs is $3,641.76. Evans' choices are to pay $3,611.76 (the extended cost less the purchase discount) within 30 days, or to pay the full extended cost within 60 days. This choice is tantamount to borrowing $3,611.76 for the 30 days between the discount deadline and the payment deadline: the interest to be paid on the "loan" would be the $30 discount that the supplier offers. Evans knows it is possible to obtain a bank loan at 9 percent annual interest. By entering the following formula in an Excel worksheet:

```
=IPMT(0.09/12,1,12,D4-30
```

Evans can compare the purchase discount to the cost of the money. The first month's interest on a bank loan would be ($27.09), as shown in cell E6 of figure 3.9. Therefore, it is to Evans' advantage to make payment on (but not much before) the discount deadline, because the discount obtained exceeds the cost of money for the same period.

This worksheet function, IPMT (*interest payment*), takes four required arguments:

- The interest rate per period. In the example, the annual interest rate is 9 percent or .09. Because the payment period is monthly, the interest rate is .09/12, or 0.75 percent.

- The period for which the payment amount is desired. In the example, 1 is used to return the first month's interest payment for a twelve-month loan.

- The number of payment periods in the loan. For monthly payments on a one-year loan, the example uses 12.

- The principal amount of the loan. The example shows D4 – 30, or $3,611.76, as this argument.

Tip

In Excel's annuity functions, including IPMT, the result of the function itself and any argument to the function are positive if they indicate a credit and negative if they indicate a debit. Because this example analyzes a loan, the function's fourth argument is entered as a positive value. Because Evans would pay out $27.09 in interest for the first month, the function returns a negative value.

Using Perpetual and Periodic Inventory Systems

As mentioned at the beginning of this chapter, businesses that deal in goods that carry a high value usually have an easier time tracking their inventories. A boat dealer, for example, tends to have fewer units in stock than does an office supply store. Other things being equal, it is easier for the boat dealer to do a physical count of the number of boats in the inventory than for the office supplier to count the number of reams of photocopy paper in stock.

The boat dealer can determine the cost of goods sold and the value of the ending inventory on a daily basis. It is simply a matter of counting the number of boats sold, shown on the sales receipts, and multiplying that number by the cost of each unit. The boat dealer might use any one of the four valuation methods discussed in the previous section to calculate the cost of goods sold.

Similarly, the boat dealer can value the ending inventory by performing a physical count of the boats in stock at the end of the day, and multiplying by their unit costs. Again, any method of valuation could be used.

This approach is termed a *perpetual inventory* system, so named because it is both possible and feasible to directly determine the inventory on any given day.

On the other hand, using traditional methods of tracking inventory, the office supply dealer would have great difficulty maintaining a perpetual inventory. There would be hundreds, perhaps thousands, of units to count, both in the sales records and on the shelves and storerooms at the end of the business day. Furthermore, the office supply dealer typically has many different categories of merchandise and several different brands within each category. This is far too much information to track by hand in a perpetual inventory system.

Of course, in recent years point-of-sale terminals and electronic recordkeeping have put a perpetual inventory system within the reach of many businesses. Still, these systems are not pervasive as yet, and the alternative to a perpetual system, the *periodic inventory* system, remains in widespread use.

Under the periodic inventory system, a business conducts a physical count of the items in inventory at the end of an accounting period—typically, at the end of the month or of the year. The count of each product is multiplied by that product's value, as determined by any one of the four valuation methods. (As a practical matter, it is unlikely that specific identification would be used. The same considerations that would lead a business to use a periodic inventory would normally preclude the use of specific identification.)

The total value of all products in stock at the end of the period has two uses: it becomes the value of the starting inventory for the next period, and it is used to determine the cost of goods sold during the period.

At the start of an accounting period, a business normally has units in stock: its starting inventory. During the period, the business normally acquires more units. The sum of the starting inventory and purchases made during the period is the *cost of goods available for sale*:

> Cost of Goods Available for Sale = Starting Inventory + Purchases

With this information, and with knowledge of the value of the ending inventory, the company can calculate its cost of goods sold:

> Cost of Goods Sold = Cost of Goods Available for Sale − Ending Inventory

For example, suppose that Evans Electronics could not record its sales on a daily basis. In that case, its inventory analysis and its figures for cost of goods sold and gross profit would be the same as shown in figures 3.3 through 3.7, depending on the method of valuation that Evans selected. However, the number of units sold would be determined not by the sales records but by subtracting the ending inventory (physical count) from the starting inventory plus any purchases made during the period.

Calculating Turns Ratios

A *turns ratio* is a measure of how often inventory is depleted: that is, how frequently it turns over. Calculating turns ratios helps you understand how well you are managing your inventory.

The longer that units are in inventory, the longer your assets are tied up in stock, and thus unavailable for other uses. Holding units in stock often involves carrying costs: the costs involved in storing the goods and, possibly, the costs involved in financing their purchase. And during the time that units are in stock, you are not earning a profit on them unless you are holding them in the expectation that their replacement value will increase. (The latter effect, termed *inventory profits*, is something you should discuss with an accountant.)

Therefore, the concept of Just-in-Time (JIT) inventory is one to which many companies subscribe. The notion is that you do not want to tie up assets in inventory until the goods are actually needed for operational or resale purposes. The turns ratio is one measure of your ability to keep your inventory as low as possible, given operational and sales demands.

The turns ratio is expressed in terms of a time period: usually, a year. For example, an annual turns ratio of 4.5 means that the inventory turns over 4.5 times per year. This means that sales have been brisk enough, and inventories low enough, that it is necessary to replenish the stock 4.5 times in a twelve-month period.

You can calculate a turns ratio in terms either of units or of costs (see fig. 3.10).

Rows 1 through 10 in figure 3.10 show a snapshot calculation of the turns ratios achieved by each product during the month. No purchases to inventory were made between 3/31/95 and 4/30/95.

The turns ratio for product code FGI-4877 is shown as 6.0 in cell G5. The formula in G5 is:

    =E5/C5*12

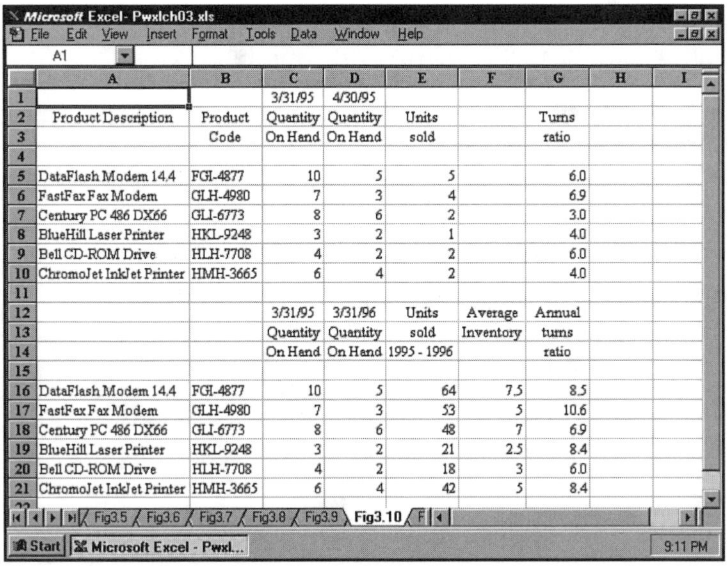

	A	B	C	D	E	F	G
1			3/31/95	4/30/95			
2	Product Description	Product	Quantity	Quantity	Units		Turns
3		Code	On Hand	On Hand	sold		ratio
4							
5	DataFlash Modem 14.4	FGI-4877	10	5	5		6.0
6	FastFax Fax Modem	GLH-4980	7	3	4		6.9
7	Century PC 486 DX66	GLI-6773	8	6	2		3.0
8	BlueHill Laser Printer	HKL-9248	3	2	1		4.0
9	Bell CD-ROM Drive	HLH-7708	4	2	2		6.0
10	ChromoJet InkJet Printer	HMH-3665	6	4	2		4.0
11							
12			3/31/95	3/31/96	Units	Average	Annual
13			Quantity	Quantity	sold	Inventory	turns
14			On Hand	On Hand	1995 - 1996		ratio
15							
16	DataFlash Modem 14.4	FGI-4877	10	5	64	7.5	8.5
17	FastFax Fax Modem	GLH-4980	7	3	53	5	10.6
18	Century PC 486 DX66	GLI-6773	8	6	48	7	6.9
19	BlueHill Laser Printer	HKL-9248	3	2	21	2.5	8.4
20	Bell CD-ROM Drive	HLH-7708	4	2	18	3	6.0
21	ChromoJet InkJet Printer	HMH-3665	6	4	42	5	8.4

Fig. 3.10
You can use actual units sold to calculate turns ratios, or use average inventory levels to estimate turns ratios.

This is the number of units sold during the month divided by the number on hand at the beginning of the month, multiplied by 12 so as to annualize the ratio. A ratio of 6.0 means that the inventory would have to be replenished six times during the year. Notice that five units were sold during the month. At this rate, the stock for this product would have to be replenished every two months, or six times (that is, its turns ratio) during the year.

Rows 12 through 21 illustrate a convenient way to examine the turns ratios for a full year. This represents a look back as of 3/31/96, rather than a look forward as of 4/30/95. The quantities on hand at the beginning and end of the year are shown in C16:D21. The units available for sale, E16:E21, are obtained from the sales records for the year. The average inventory, F15:F21, is estimated by means of averaging the quantity on hand at the beginning of the year and the quantity on hand at the end of the year. Finally, the annual turns ratio is the number of units sold divided by the average inventory.

Tip

Turns ratios in the range of 4 to 6 are normally regarded as quite good: the inventory is being managed well. A turns ratio of less than 1, indicating that it takes more than a year to turn the stock over, is terrible.

On a broader scale, it is also possible to calculate a turns ratio for an entire stock, rather than on a product-by-product basis (see fig. 3.11).

Fig. 3.11
A turns ratio can be calculated for an entire inventory, irrespective of product-by-product differences.

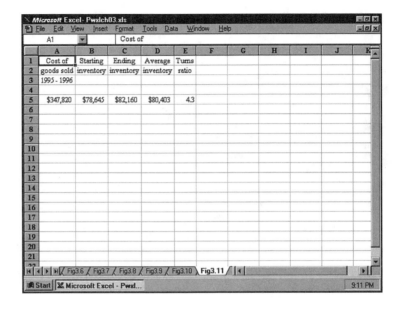

Figure 3.11 shows the cost of goods sold, the starting inventory and the ending inventory for the 12-month period. The average inventory is again the average of the starting and ending values. The turns ratio is the cost of goods sold, divided by the average inventory.

Note that a company's choice of method to value its inventory (specific identification, average cost, FIFO, or LIFO) impacts its turns ratios when they are based on cost data rather than units. Particularly using LIFO or FIFO, the total inventory valuation can be based on different costs at the beginning of the year than it is at the end of the year.

Normally, a purchasing manager will be interested in the turns ratios on a product-by-product basis. These can help guide purchasing decisions, as well as the minimum and maximum units that should be on hand at any given time.

An overall look at a company's turns ratio, such as is shown in figure 3.11, would normally be of greater interest to a principal in the company, or to an outside investor or creditor. Product-by-product turns ratios tend to be of little interest to those requiring an overall view of how a business manages its inventories, but are of great interest to those responsible for managing them.

Summary

In this chapter, you have learned about four methods of valuing inventory and how to implement them using Excel. Their effects on both the income statement (via the gross profit calculation) and on the balance sheet (via the amount of company assets in ending inventory) were discussed. You have seen how user-defined functions, such as LIFO and FIFO, can automate worksheet tasks in general and of valuing inventories in particular. And you have learned how to use different sorts of turns ratios to evaluate how well a company manages its assets.

The next chapter turns from a focus on a company's assets to a focus on its liabilities.

Chapter 4

Balance Sheet: Liabilities and Owner's Equity

Chapter 3 covered the topic of inventory valuation in some detail. The various methods discussed there are needed to properly complete the current assets section of the Balance Sheet. This chapter returns to a discussion of the Balance Sheet itself. The liabilities and owner's equity section of the Balance Sheet are discussed here.

To review the basic structure of a balance sheet:

- The Assets section consists of the company's current assets (typically including Cash, Accounts Receivable, Inventory, and Prepaid Expenses), fixed assets, and any other assets that do not correspond to the current and fixed classifications.

- The Liabilities and Owner's Equity section consists of the company's current and long-term liabilities. Typically, these include Accounts Payable, Short- and Long-term Notes Payable, and a few other types of liabilities that will vary according to a company's line of business.

- The difference between the company's Total Assets and its Liabilities represents its equity: that portion of the company's worth that belongs to its owner or owners.

The first three chapters of this book have introduced some fundamental concepts, such as accounts, revenues, assets, debits, and credits. They have also discussed some of the functional relationships among these concepts. This chapter introduces ways that you can use Excel to establish the *structural* relationships among such tools as accounts, journals, and ledgers: that is, how to support the flow of information about revenue, expenses, and profit by using Excel workbooks, worksheets, and Visual Basic for Applications (VBA) code. This chapter illustrates these techniques using both concepts already discussed in chapters 1 through 3, and new information on Liabilities and Owner's Equity.

Understanding Journals and Ledgers

The basic flow of information about business transactions follows this structure:

1. A business transaction, such as a sale, a purchase, a receipt of funds, or an expenditure of funds occurs.

2. Information about the transaction is recorded in a *journal*. The journal usually retains the information about the transactions in chronological order: so, one record might contain data on a sale, the next record might contain data on a purchase, the next data on a payment, and so on.

3. Information about the transactions is copied (or *posted*) from the journal to a *ledger*. This ledger has different sections: one for each type of account, such as Accounts Receivable or Notes Payable. Within each of these sections, information is usually recorded chronologically. The basic difference between the journal and the ledger is that the ledger disaggregates or categorizes the information in the journal into specific accounts.

4. Information in the ledger is summarized, to obtain a total for each account at the end of an accounting period. These totals are used to prepare financial statements such as an Income Statement and a Balance Sheet.

See figure 4.1 for an example of a General Journal.

Why qualify the term "journal" with the word "general"? Because keeping just one journal and just one ledger tends to become cumbersome. If you had only one journal, the task of posting information from the journal to the ledger could become too time-consuming. Furthermore, finding information about a specific sale or a specific payment to a creditor becomes less practical—even using Excel's lookup functions.

Notice, in figure 4.1, that there are only three transactions shown in the General Journal. These transactions pertain to three relatively infrequent events:

the return of some merchandise from a customer, the return of some inventory to a supplier, and the purchase of office equipment. All the remaining transactions during June are kept together in special journals.

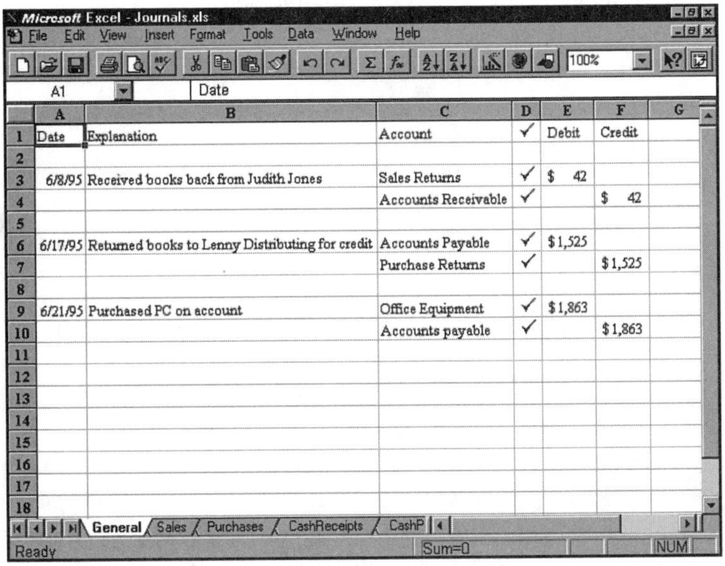

Date	Explanation	Account	✓	Debit	Credit
6/8/95	Received books back from Judith Jones	Sales Returns	✓	$ 42	
		Accounts Receivable	✓		$ 42
6/17/95	Returned books to Lenny Distributing for credit	Accounts Payable	✓	$1,525	
		Purchase Returns	✓		$1,525
6/21/95	Purchased PC on account	Office Equipment	✓	$1,863	
		Accounts payable	✓		$1,863

Fig. 4.1
The General Journal may be treated as a catchall for transactions that cannot be recorded in special journals.

Understanding Special Journals

Most companies use *special journals*, which are places to record information about particular types of transactions. In most cases, the most frequently occurring transactions are sales to customers and payments to creditors. Also, many companies do business with their customers and suppliers on both a cash basis and a credit basis. This implies the use of four special journals:

- A *Cash Receipts* journal contains information about payments that you receive from customers. These payments could take the form of either currency, as when a customer hands you $20 to purchase an item, or a check, as when you receive payment for a credit purchase. It also contains other information about cash that the company receives, such as capital investments that you make in the company or any funds that you borrow from, say, a bank.

- A *Cash Payments* journal contains information about payments that you make to creditors and suppliers. Normally, these payments are checks that you write, but of course they could also be payments made in currency. It also contains information about operating expenses that you pay in cash, such as salaries or a building lease.

- A *Sales* journal contains information about credit sales that you make. Together with sales information in the Cash Receipts journal, this accounts for all sales that your business makes.

- A *Purchases* journal contains information about credit purchases that you make from your suppliers. Together with cash purchase information in the Cash Payments journal, this accounts for all purchases from suppliers that your business makes.

There are, of course, many types of transactions other than those that go in these special journals. These remaining transactions are recorded in the General Journal, which then becomes a sort of catchall for miscellaneous transactions.

Your own business might conduct transactions that are both frequent and that do not fit into the structure outlined above. There is no special reason to adopt this structure for journals: any structure that has special journals for the most frequently occurring types of transactions will do. For example, suppose that you run a car rental agency. It is likely that the purchase of cars from suppliers is a relatively rare event, but that the maintenance of your cars by garages and body shops occurs frequently. In that case, you might dispense with a special Purchases journal, and use a special Repairs and Maintenance journal instead.

Figure 4.2 shows an example of a special Sales journal.

Fig. 4.2
The special Sales Journal for Bell Books records credit purchases by its customers.

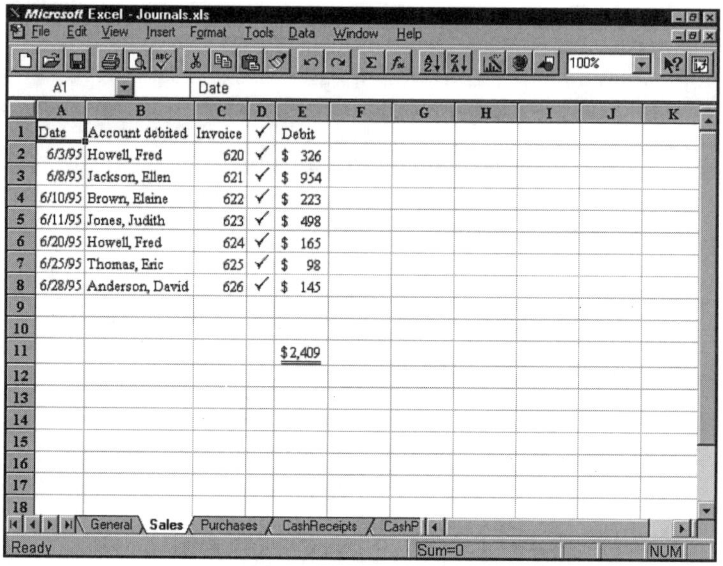

	A	B	C	D	E
1	Date	Account debited	Invoice	✓	Debit
2	6/3/95	Howell, Fred	620	✓	$ 326
3	6/8/95	Jackson, Ellen	621	✓	$ 954
4	6/10/95	Brown, Elaine	622	✓	$ 223
5	6/11/95	Jones, Judith	623	✓	$ 498
6	6/20/95	Howell, Fred	624	✓	$ 165
7	6/25/95	Thomas, Eric	625	✓	$ 98
8	6/28/95	Anderson, David	626	✓	$ 145
9					
10					
11					$2,409

There are several items to notice about this special journal:

- Each account has a different customer name (e.g., Fred Howell, Ellen Jackson, and so on). These accounts are also found in the Accounts Receivable ledger account, so that Bell Books can keep track of whether a customer owes money on an account (and if so, how much) or whether the account is paid up.

- Because a journal (the General Journal or a special journal such as Sales) contains transactions in chronological order, there can be—and often will be—several transactions for a particular account. For example, figure 4.2 shows that Fred Howell has made two purchases during June. This account is summarized, to obtain a current balance, in a ledger Accounts Receivable account. The accounts are not summarized in the Journal.

- There is no column headed "Credit" as there is in the General Journal shown in figure 4.1. This is because the only activities recorded in the Sales journal are non-cash sales, and the offsetting credit amounts are accumulated in the General Ledger's Sales account (see below).

- There is a column headed with a checkmark (✔). This checkmark indicates that a particular transaction has been posted from the Sales journal to the Sales account in the General Ledger.

Tip

You can show a variety of special characters in Excel by choosing a particular font. These characters can be the entire cell entry, or only a portion of the entry. For example, to show the checkmark in figure 4.2, the cells were formatted using the CommonBullets TrueType font. When formatted with this font, using the numeral 4 as the cell's value causes Excel to display a checkmark.

To find a particular symbol, you can use Edit, Fill, Series to enter a numeric series from 0 to 255 in, say, cells A1 to A256 of a worksheet. In cell B1, enter this formula:

```
=CHAR(A1)
```

and copy and paste this formula into the range B2:B256. Then, select B1:B256 and choose Format, Cells. Using the Font tab, assign the range a font such as Symbol. After choosing OK, you can examine the B1:B256 range to see whether it contains the symbol you want. After you have found it, you can use the combination of the value and the font to display the symbol. Note that you can assign different fonts to different characters in a text entry by highlighting the character and continuing exactly as you would to format a full cell.

Bell Books' special Purchases journal is shown in figure 4.3.

Fig. 4.3

The special Purchases Journal for Bell Books records credit purchases from its suppliers.

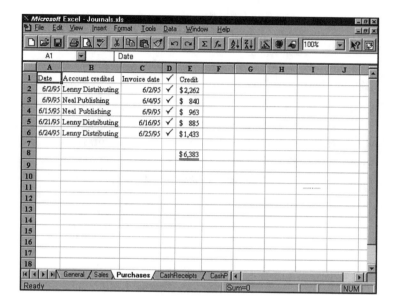

There is no structural difference between the Sales and Purchases journals. However, for tracking purposes, the Sales journal uses the invoice *number* in column C. In contrast, the Purchases journal uses the *date* of the supplier's invoice: this enables Bell Books to keep track of the length of time a payable invoice has been outstanding. Should the user want, of course, the supplier's invoice number can also be shown in the Purchases journal.

Another difference between the Sales and Purchases journals is that the amount of the purchase is shown as a credit, whereas the amount of a sale is shown as a debit. When a purchase is posted from the Purchases journal, it is posted as a credit to the ledger account Accounts Payable.

Again, there is no debit column because all entries in this journal are non-cash purchases. The offsetting debit entry is found in the ledger account Purchases.

These two special journals, taken together, account for all of Bell Books' non-cash transactions, and it remains to account for the cash receipt and cash payment transactions. Figure 4.4 shows the special Cash Receipts journal.

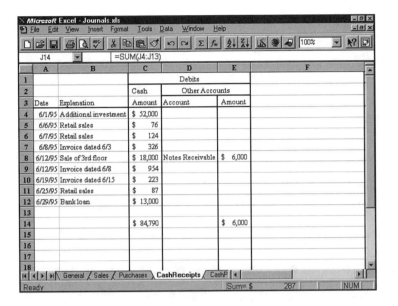

Fig. 4.4
Normally, the
Cash account
should be debited
for the receipt of
cash.

(Due to space limits, only the debits section of the Cash Receipts journal appears in figure 4.4. The credits section of the journal appears in fig. 4.5.)

The structure of the Cash Receipts journal is quite different from the structure of the Sales and Purchases journals. As explained above, *all* transactions entered in the Sales and Purchases journals are destined for one ledger account: either the Sales account or the Purchases account. However, cash transactions can be posted to a variety of accounts.

Usually, a transaction in the Cash Receipts journal is posted to the ledger account Cash. The total ($84,790) of all the transactions whose amounts appear in column C of figure 4.4 will be posted to the Cash account in the General Ledger. For example, the owner of Bell Books invests an additional $52,000 in the company on June 1 (see cell C4 of fig. 4.4). This investment comes in the form of cash, and consequently will be posted—as part of the total cash receipts in column C—as a debit to the General Ledger's Cash account.

Notice, however, that on June 12 Bell Books sells the third floor of its building to another company for $24,000. Bell Books receives $18,000 of the $24,000 in cash, and accepts a Note Payable from the buyer for the $6,000 remainder of the amount due. The $6,000 *could* have been entered in the General Journal instead of in the Cash Receipts journal; however, it's convenient to keep the two portions of the transaction together, so that the entire transaction can be seen in one place.

This is the purpose of the columns headed "Other Accounts," columns D and E of the worksheet. Column D contains the name of the ledger account where the transaction will be posted, and column E contains the debit amount that will be posted there.

So, the amounts in the debits section of the Cash Receipts journal are posted to the General Ledger as follows:

- The *total* of the receipts in column C is posted as one value to the General Ledger's Cash account.
- The *individual amounts* of any receipts in column E are posted in the General Ledger to the account that is named in column D.

Figure 4.5 shows the credits section of the Cash Receipts journal.

Fig. 4.5
The special Cash Receipts Journal (credits section) for Bell Books shows which accounts should be credited for the receipt of cash.

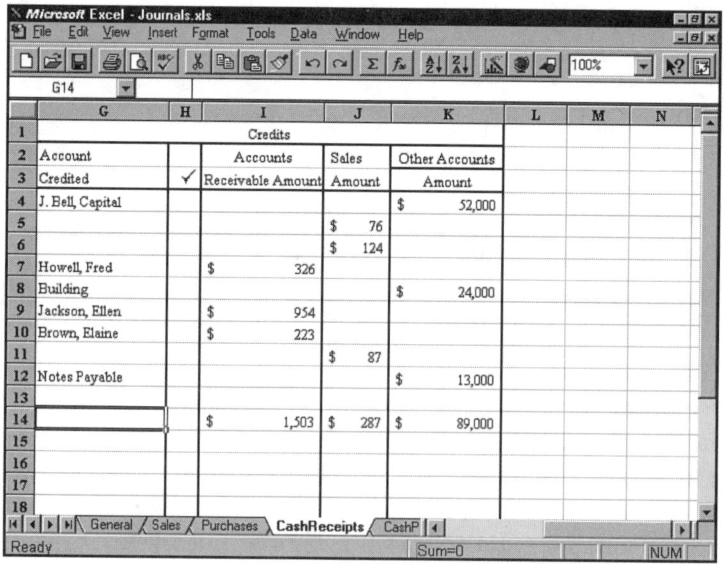

	G	H	I	J	K
1			Credits		
2	Account		Accounts	Sales	Other Accounts
3	Credited	✓	Receivable Amount	Amount	Amount
4	J. Bell, Capital				$ 52,000
5				$ 76	
6				$ 124	
7	Howell, Fred		$ 326		
8	Building				$ 24,000
9	Jackson, Ellen		$ 954		
10	Brown, Elaine		$ 223		
11				$ 87	
12	Notes Payable				$ 13,000
13					
14			$ 1,503	$ 287	$ 89,000

Figure 4.5 shows that the credits section of the Cash Receipts journal is similar in structure to the debits section. There are two main ledger accounts that are to be credited when transactions are posted from the Cash Receipts journal: Accounts Receivable (column I) and Sales (column J).

For example, Bell Books receives a check on 6/8/95 from Fred Howell. This check is payment for an invoice dated 6/3/95. The transaction is shown in row 7 of the Cash Receipts worksheet in figures 4.4 and 4.5, and results in the following actions:

1. An entry showing the amount of the check is made in cell C7, indicating that the General Ledger account Cash is to be debited by $326.

2. An entry showing the account that is to be credited is made in cell G7: Fred Howell's account will be credited by $326.

3. An entry showing the amount of the check is made in cell I7, indicating that the ledger account named Accounts Receivable is to be credited by $326.

4. When the amount of $326 is actually posted to Accounts Receivable, a checkmark is entered in cell H7, to indicate that the posting has been made.

The posting of $326 as a debit to Cash and as a credit to Accounts Receivable ensures that the amount is moved *into* Cash (an asset in hand) and *from* Accounts Receivable (an asset not yet in hand) at the point that the payment is received.

As another example, when a customer makes payment with $76 in currency on June 6 (see row 5 in figs. 4.4 and 4.5), this amount is entered in cell C5, to show that the General Ledger account named Cash is to be debited by that amount, and the same figure is entered in cell J5 to show that the ledger account named Sales is to be credited by $76.

The reason for entering the sale amount of $76 in both the Cash and the Sales ledger accounts is due to a concept that this book has, so far, assumed but not yet made explicit: *double-entry* accounting. Every business transaction must be entered as both a debit and a credit, and these entries must be made in different accounts. Among other benefits of the double-entry method is the result that the sum of all debit entries in the ledger must equal the sum of all credit entries, which helps prove that the business's accounts are in balance.

For example, consider the transaction shown in row 12 of figures 4.4 and 4.5. On June 29, Bell Books assumes a bank loan in the amount of $13,000. In return for signing the note, the bank writes a check to Bell Books for $13,000, and the company deposits it in a checking account. Therefore, Bell Books' cash assets have increased by $13,000. But the company has not suddenly become $13,000 richer by virtue of signing a note: eventually, it will have to repay the loan. Therefore, the company's liabilities have increased by $13,000, and to document this fact the account named Notes Payable is increased by the same amount.

The net effect, of course, is that the company's worth remains unchanged, because loans themselves do not contribute directly to profit. But when Bell Books sells a book to a customer for cash, four events occur:

1. Its Cash account (an asset account) is debited.
2. Its Sales account (a revenue account) is credited.
3. Its Inventory (an asset account) is eventually credited.
4. Its Cost of Goods Sold (a revenue account) is eventually debited.

If the amount involved in 1 and 2 is greater than the amount involved in 3 and 4, the company obtains a profit. Buy low and sell high.

Finally, notice that there is another column in the credits section of the Cash Receipts journal that indicates, by means of a checkmark, whether a receipt of funds has been posted. The only entries in this journal that are ever marked as posted are payments to Accounts Receivable. The reason is that the ledger account maintains detailed information about specific accounts (for example, Fred Howell's account, Ellen Jackson's account, etc.). Therefore, when funds are received in payment for a specific account, Bell Books posts the amount to a specific customer account. In contrast, the company can post a *total* amount for cash sales to the General Ledger's Sales account.

The last special journal discussed here is the Cash Payments journal. Its credits section is shown in figure 4.6.

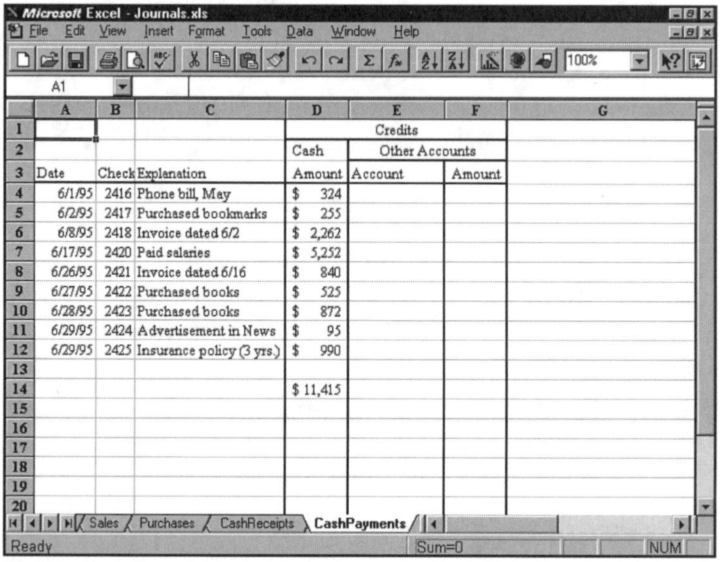

			Credits		
			Cash	Other Accounts	
Date	Check	Explanation	Amount	Account	Amount
6/1/95	2416	Phone bill, May	$ 324		
6/2/95	2417	Purchased bookmarks	$ 255		
6/8/95	2418	Invoice dated 6/2	$ 2,262		
6/17/95	2420	Paid salaries	$ 5,252		
6/26/95	2421	Invoice dated 6/16	$ 840		
6/27/95	2422	Purchased books	$ 525		
6/28/95	2423	Purchased books	$ 872		
6/29/95	2424	Advertisement in News	$ 95		
6/29/95	2425	Insurance policy (3 yrs.)	$ 990		
			$ 11,415		

Fig. 4.6 Normally, the Cash account is credited for cash payments.

The overall structure of this journal is the same as that of the Cash Receipts journal, with one major difference: the credits section is shown on the left, instead of on the right of the debits section. Normally, debits are shown to the left of credits, but in a special journal it's normal practice to allow the columns to be in any sequence.

It's more convenient to show the credits section to the left of the debits section in the Cash Payments journal because doing so places the Cash column on the left side of the worksheet, where it is easily accessible. The accessibility is important because, since these are Cash transaction journals, every transaction in each journal will contain a Cash entry.

Figure 4.7 shows the debits section of the Cash Payments journal.

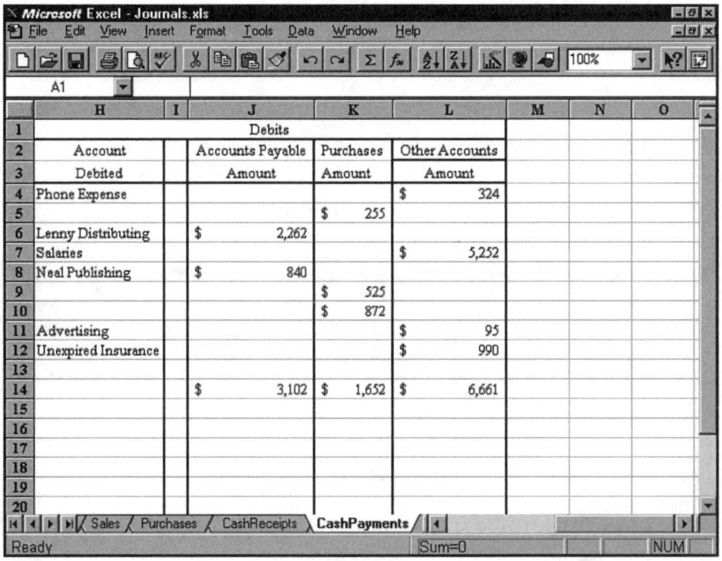

	H	I	J	K	L
1			Debits		
2	Account		Accounts Payable	Purchases	Other Accounts
3	Debited		Amount	Amount	Amount
4	Phone Expense				$ 324
5				$ 255	
6	Lenny Distributing		$ 2,262		
7	Salaries				$ 5,252
8	Neal Publishing		$ 840		
9				$ 525	
10				$ 872	
11	Advertising				$ 95
12	Unexpired Insurance				$ 990
13					
14			$ 3,102	$ 1,652	$ 6,661

Fig. 4.7
The debits section of the special Cash Payments journal shows which account is debited for each payment.

Notice in figure 4.7 that the specific ledger accounts referenced in columns J and K are Accounts Payable and Purchases, respectively. This is because these accounts are the accounts most frequently debited when a cash payment is made. Other accounts, such as salaries and telephone expenses, are typically debited only once a month, when checks are written to employees and to the phone company. Again, the way that your company does business should dictate which accounts you show as columns in the Cash Payments journal, and which ones you show as line items in the Other Accounts column (fig. 4.7, column L).

Understanding Subsidiary Ledgers

Your decision about what sorts of ledgers to maintain follows reasoning similar to the decision to maintain special journals. If you kept only one ledger, with detailed information about all accounts, it would lose much of its value as a summary document.

Therefore, it's normal to establish *subsidiary ledgers* that contain detailed information from the journals. You can then keep the detailed information about specific sales and specific purchases in the subsidiary ledgers, and transfer totals from them to a General Ledger. Because of the frequency of transactions involving sales and purchases, many businesses maintain an Accounts Receivable subsidiary ledger and an Accounts Payable subsidiary ledger.

Creating the General Ledger

By keeping detailed information from the journals in these subsidiary ledgers, it's easier to keep up with the status of your individual accounts with both creditors and customers, and at the same time to keep the General Ledger from becoming cluttered with detailed information about customers who owe you money, and about creditors who expect to be paid (see fig. 4.8, which displays the General Ledger's asset and liability accounts).

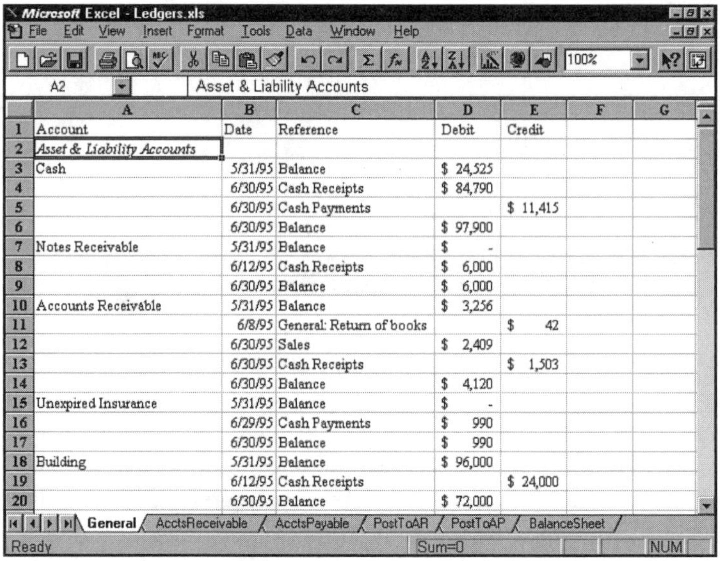

	A	B	C	D	E	F	G
1	Account	Date	Reference	Debit	Credit		
2	*Asset & Liability Accounts*						
3	Cash	5/31/95	Balance	$ 24,525			
4		6/30/95	Cash Receipts	$ 84,790			
5		6/30/95	Cash Payments		$ 11,415		
6		6/30/95	Balance	$ 97,900			
7	Notes Receivable	5/31/95	Balance	$ -			
8		6/12/95	Cash Receipts	$ 6,000			
9		6/30/95	Balance	$ 6,000			
10	Accounts Receivable	5/31/95	Balance	$ 3,256			
11		6/8/95	General: Return of books		$ 42		
12		6/30/95	Sales	$ 2,409			
13		6/30/95	Cash Receipts		$ 1,503		
14		6/30/95	Balance	$ 4,120			
15	Unexpired Insurance	5/31/95	Balance	$ -			
16		6/29/95	Cash Payments	$ 990			
17		6/30/95	Balance	$ 990			
18	Building	5/31/95	Balance	$ 96,000			
19		6/12/95	Cash Receipts		$ 24,000		
20		6/30/95	Balance	$ 72,000			

Fig. 4.8
The General Ledger should show the account, date, and journal reference for each debit and credit.

This example of a General Ledger is atypical and every dollar entry in this ledger either refers directly to an entry in a journal, or to a total of transactions in a journal. For example, the formula in cell D8 is:

```
=[Journals.xls]CashReceipts!$E$8
```

Figure 4.4 shows the debits section of the Cash Receipts journal. Notice that this value of $6,000 in the General Ledger is the single entry in the Cash Receipts journal that represents the note accepted by Bell Books in partial payment for the third floor of its building. In contrast, the formula in cell D4 of figure 4.8 is:

```
=[Journals.xls]CashReceipts!$C$14
```

Cell C14 of the Cash Receipts journal also appears in figure 4.4. Notice that the value of $84,790 is the total of all cash receipts during June. This illustrates how a ledger entry summarizes all the transactions in a given category that appear individually in a journal.

So, debits to the General Ledger's Cash account are based on the Cash Receipts journal. In contrast, credits to the General Ledger's Cash account are based on the Cash Payments journal. The formula in cell E5 of figure 4.8 is:

```
=[Journals.xls]CashPayments!$D$14
```

Figure 4.6 shows the credits section of the Cash Payments journal, and cell D14 is the sum ($11,415) of the cash payments made during the month. The outflow of cash is represented in the General Ledger by credits to its Cash account.

Consider the Accounts Receivable classification in figure 4.8. There are three figures: $42, $2,409, and $1,503. The $42 value represents the return of merchandise from a customer, and is taken from the General Journal. This formula returns the $2,409 value:

```
=SUM([Journals.xls]Sales!Amount)
```

which totals the values of credit sales in the Sales journal. There is a range in the Sales journal that is named Amount, and that refers to cells E2:E8 of that worksheet (compare with fig. 4.2). The $1,503 value is returned by this formula:

```
=[Journals.xls]CashReceipts!$I$14
```

which refers to the total of the credits to Accounts Receivable, from the credits section of the Cash Receipts journal (refer to fig. 4.5).

In this way, the activity in the Accounts Receivable account is summarized for the month. New purchases on credit are totaled in cell D12, and payments for purchases on credit are totaled in cell E13, both in the General Ledger. You will find it useful to open the Ledgers.xls file and inspect each of its entries to determine their sources in the journals. (If you do so, you will find that every value for June in the General Ledger refers to an entry in a journal.)

The Revenue and Expense section of the General Ledger is shown in figure 4.9.

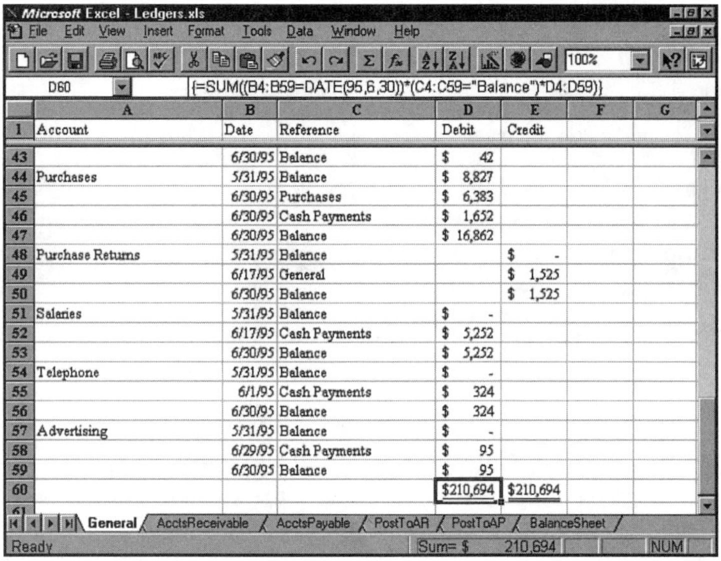

	A	B	C	D	E	F	G
1	Account	Date	Reference	Debit	Credit		
43		6/30/95	Balance	$ 42			
44	Purchases	5/31/95	Balance	$ 8,827			
45		6/30/95	Purchases	$ 6,383			
46		6/30/95	Cash Payments	$ 1,652			
47		6/30/95	Balance	$ 16,862			
48	Purchase Returns	5/31/95	Balance		$ -		
49		6/17/95	General		$ 1,525		
50		6/30/95	Balance		$ 1,525		
51	Salaries	5/31/95	Balance	$ -			
52		6/17/95	Cash Payments	$ 5,252			
53		6/30/95	Balance	$ 5,252			
54	Telephone	5/31/95	Balance	$ -			
55		6/1/95	Cash Payments	$ 324			
56		6/30/95	Balance	$ 324			
57	Advertising	5/31/95	Balance	$ -			
58		6/29/95	Cash Payments	$ 95			
59		6/30/95	Balance	$ 95			
60				$210,694	$210,694		

Fig. 4.9
General Ledger entries should all be linked to General Journal or special journal transactions.

The entries in this section follow the pattern established in the assets and liabilities section: that is, each entry comes from a journal, and is either a specific journal entry or the total of several journal entries that belong to the same account.

The values in cells D60 and E60 of figure 4.9, $210,694, help to demonstrate that the accounts are in balance. As noted above, the double-entry method is intended to ensure that the total of the debits for a given period equals the total of the credits for the same period. Each transaction that occurs exists as a debit to one account, and as a credit to another account. Cells D60 and E60 total the debit and credit account balances in the General Ledger, and are equal: this is evidence that accounts are in balance. The two cells' equality does not *prove* that all entries are accurate, because the possibility of, for example, compensating errors exists. But if the two amounts were unequal, that would demonstrate that at least one error existed somewhere.

Creating Subsidiary Ledgers

Bell Books uses two subsidiary ledgers: Accounts Receivable and Accounts Payable. The purpose of these ledgers is to help to keep tabs on accounts that customers have with Bell Books, and that Bell Books has with its suppliers. Figure 4.10 shows the Accounts Receivable ledger.

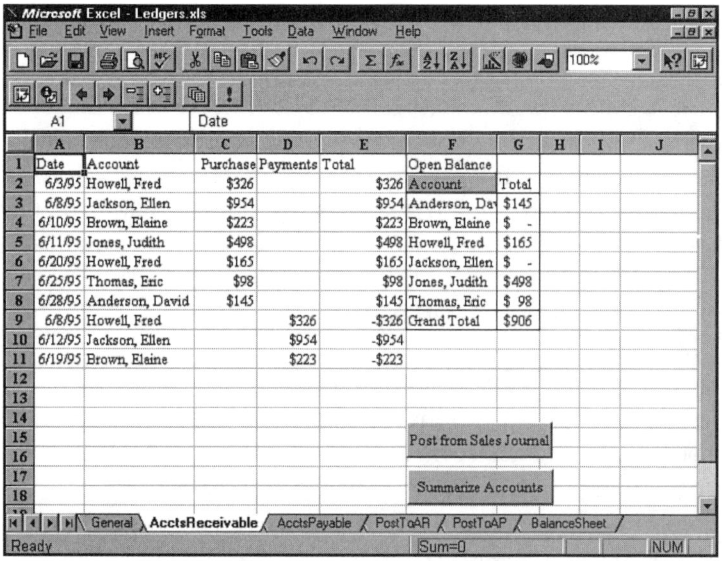

Fig. 4.10

The Accounts Receivable Ledger helps to track the status of individual accounts.

Neither the Accounts Receivable ledger nor the Accounts Payable ledger links to the General Ledger. Each simply replicates some of the information in the General Ledger: specifically, the Accounts Receivable ledger provides details about the individual accounts maintained by Bell Books' credit customers.

There are two worksheet buttons on the Accounts Receivable ledger. These are labeled "Post from Sales Journal" and "Summarize Accounts." The "Post" button is linked to VBA code that automatically posts information about non-cash sales from the Sales journal to the Accounts Receivable ledger. The "Summarize" button is linked to VBA code that creates the pivot table shown in figure 4.10. This pivot table provides the current balance for each of the accounts receivable.

The action of posting information from the Sales journal is not all that's necessary to complete the Accounts Receivable ledger. It's also necessary to post information about payments received from the customers who buy on credit. For example, cell D9 contains the value $326.

This represents the payment received from Fred Howell on June 8, and entered into the Cash Receipts journal (refer to cell I7 of figure 4.5). The value $326 is also entered in the General Ledger in cell D7, as part of the total of the credits to Accounts Receivable.

This illustrates that amounts which are posted to subsidiary ledgers must be posted twice: once to the General Ledger, and once to the subsidiary ledger.

Doing so ensures that the account as shown in the General Ledger equals the amount shown in the subsidiary ledger.

While the Accounts Receivable ledger has a worksheet button that automates the posting of information from the Sales journal, it makes no provision to automate the posting of information from the Cash Receipts journal or the General Journal. You might find it useful to place such a button on the ledger, and link it to code patterned on the code that posts from the Sales journal. The next section takes a look at the VBA code that is linked to the existing "Post from Sales Journal" button.

Automating the Posting Process

There are various types of buttons that you can use in Excel: buttons on worksheets, buttons on dialog boxes, and buttons on toolbars are examples. You can put a custom toolbar button on a worksheet by using View, Toolbars and choosing Customize. However, if you do so, that toolbar button will appear on all sheets in the workbook.

To place a button on a worksheet so that it appears on that sheet only, use the Drawing toolbar:

1. Choose View, Toolbars, and check the Drawing checkbox in the Toolbars list box. Then, choose OK.

2. The Drawing toolbar appears on the active worksheet. Click the Create Button button on the toolbar. The mouse pointer changes from an arrow to crosshairs.

3. Holding down the left mouse button, drag in the worksheet to indicate where you want the button to appear. Then, release the mouse button.

4. The Assign Macro dialog box appears. Unless you have already written a macro that you want to assign to the button, click Cancel. You will be able to assign a macro to the button later, by right-clicking the worksheet button you have created to bring up a shortcut menu.

5. The button has a default title, such as "Button 1," and should have handles on its borders and corners. When you move your mouse pointer over the default title, it will appear as a vertical bar. Then, hold down the mouse button and drag across the default title to highlight it, and type whatever text you want to appear on the button.

6. Deselect the button by clicking any worksheet cell.

The "Post from Sales Journal" button was created in this manner. It is linked to the VBA macro named PostFromSalesToAR, shown immediately below, which actually performs the posting. This macro can be found on the *Business Analysis with Excel* companion disk in the file named Ledgers.xls.

On the Disk

```
Option Explicit
Option Base 1
Sub PostFromSalesToAR()

Dim SalesDate As Range, Acct As Range, Posted As Range, SalesAmount As Range
Dim ThisTransaction As Integer, NewEntry As Integer

'Note: This requires that Journals.xls be open
Workbooks("Journals.xls").Activate
Sheets("Sales").Select

Set SalesDate = Range("Date")
Set Acct = Range("Account")
Set Posted = Range("Posted")
Set SalesAmount = Range("Amount")

For ThisTransaction = 1 To Acct.Rows.Count
    If Posted(ThisTransaction) <> 4 Then
        IncrementRangesAR NewEntry
        NewEntry = NewEntry - 1
        With ThisWorkbook.Sheets("AcctsReceivable")
            .Range("Date").Offset(NewEntry, 0).Resize(1, 1) =
SalesDate(ThisTransaction)
            .Range("AccountNames").Offset(NewEntry, 0).Resize(1, 1) =
Acct(ThisTransaction)
            .Range("Purchases").Offset(NewEntry, 0).Resize(1, 1) =
SalesAmount(ThisTransaction)
            .Range("Total").Offset(NewEntry, 0).Resize(1, 1).Formula = "=Purchases-
                Payments"
        End With
        Posted(ThisTransaction) = 4
    End If
Next ThisTransaction

End Sub
```

The first two lines of code set two general options. The first, Option Explicit, requires that all variables mentioned in the macro be explicitly declared. If this option were not set, new variables could be created on the fly—simply typing a variable name would create it. Because this approach tends to make the code much more difficult to trace and debug, it's wise to use Option Explicit and to specifically declare each variable (see the discussion of the Dim statements later in this section).

The second option, Option Base 1, requires that the first element of all VBA arrays be element number one. Omitting this Option causes Excel to treat the first element of an array as element number zero. Suppose that the first element of MyArray were "Fred Howell." Using Option Base 1, you would refer to this value as MyArray(1). Without Option Base 1, you would refer to it as MyArray(0). If you prefer to start counting at one, rather than at zero, use Option Base 1 in your VBA code.

The next line, Sub PostFromSalesToAR( ), simply gives the procedure a name. VBA subroutines always have a set of parentheses following the name itself. If the parentheses enclose a variable name or names, it means that those variables are being passed as arguments to the subroutine. In this case, no variables are being passed to the subroutine.

The next two lines are Dim (short for *dimension*) statements. In accordance with the use of Option Explicit, these statements declare the existence of several variables and define their types. The variable ThisTransaction, for example, is declared as type Integer. This means that the variable cannot take on a numeric value that has a fractional component, such as 3.1416.

The four variables that are declared as type Range will refer specifically to worksheet ranges. These ranges are subsequently assigned to the variables that represent them, by means of the Set statements. In this case, the variables are simply conveniences: the code can refer to the variable instead of having to make reference to the name of the range in the worksheet where it exists, in the workbook that contains the worksheet.

The next statements:

```
Workbooks("Journals.xls").Activate
Sheets("Sales").Select
```

cause Excel to make Journals.xls the active workbook, and to make the sheet named Sales in that workbook the active worksheet. The Sales worksheet, of course, contains the Sales journal. These two statements require that the Journals.xls workbook be open at the time that the statements are executed. Knowing the location of Journals.xls on your disk would allow you to also use a statement such as:

```
Workbooks.Open Filename:="xxx"
```

where xxx would be the fully qualified path to the file, as well as its name.

After the Sales journal is selected, the four Range variables are assigned to named ranges; for example:

```
Set SalesDate = Range("Date")
```

This causes the variable SalesDate to stand in for the range that is named "Date" in the Sales journal.

After these range variables are set, the main work of the procedure begins. This statement:

```
For ThisTransaction = 1 To Acct.Rows.Count
```

starts a loop that executes once for each row in the range represented by the Acct variable. The fragment "Acct.Rows.Count" works as follows:

- Acct is a worksheet object: specifically, a range object.

- A range has, among other methods, a method called Rows. This is simply the collection of the rows within the range.

- Many objects and methods have the Count property. The Count property is the number of items in a given collection.

Thus, Acct.Rows.Count returns a number that represents the number of rows in the range represented by the Acct variable, and the For loop will execute as many times as there are rows in that range.

The first statement in the loop is:

```
If Posted(ThisTransaction) <> 4 Then
```

This statement causes the statements that follow it to execute if its condition is satisfied. The condition is that a particular value does not equal 4. The particular value is the element in the Posted variable that corresponds to the current value of ThisTransaction. And the Posted variable refers to the range named Posted in the Sales journal.

So, the first time that the loop executes, ThisTransaction has a value of 1. Excel examines the 1st value in Posted, to see if it equals 4. If it does not, subsequent statements are executed; otherwise, they are skipped.

Why look for the value 4 in Posted? Recall that the checkmarks in the Sales journal are created by putting a 4 in their range, and formatting the range with the CommonBullets font. A checkmark means that the transaction has been posted from the Sales journal to the Accounts Receivable ledger. Therefore, if the current value in Posted contains a 4, that transaction has already been posted, and you do not want to post it again.

If, on the other hand, the current transaction has *not* yet been posted, the statements that follow the If should be executed—resulting in the posting of the transaction to Accounts Receivable.

The first statement following the If is:

```
IncrementRangesAR NewEntry
```

I

Financial Statements
and Statement Analysis

On the Disk

IncrementRangesAR is the name of another subroutine; AR stands for Accounts Receivable. This subroutine is shown immediately here and found on the companion disk in the file named Ledgers.xls:

```
Sub IncrementRangesAR(NewRow)
With ThisWorkbook
    NewRow = .Worksheets("AcctsReceivable").Range("AccountNames").Rows.Count + 1
    .Names.Add Name:="AcctsReceivable!Date", RefersTo:="=AcctsReceivable!" _
        & .Worksheets("AcctsReceivable").Range("Date").Resize(NewRow, 1).Address
    .Names.Add Name:="AcctsReceivable!AccountNames", RefersTo:="=AcctsReceivable!" _
        & .Worksheets("AcctsReceivable").Range("AccountNames").Resize(NewRow, 1).Address
    .Names.Add Name:="AcctsReceivable!Purchases", RèfersTo:="=AcctsReceivable!" _
        & .Worksheets("AcctsReceivable").Range("Purchases").Resize(NewRow, 1).Address
    .Names.Add Name:="AcctsReceivable!Payments", RefersTo:="=AcctsReceivable!" _
        & .Worksheets("AcctsReceivable").Range("Payments").Resize(NewRow, 1).Address
    .Names.Add Name:="AcctsReceivable!Total", RefersTo:="=AcctsReceivable!" _
        & .Worksheets("AcctsReceivable").Range("Total").Resize(NewRow, 1).Address
End With
End Sub
```

At the point that the loop calls the subroutine IncrementRangesAR, control passes to that subroutine. The subroutine takes an argument, NewEntry, which is an integer variable declared in the main subroutine. Note that the argument is *not* enclosed in parentheses when IncrementRangesAR is called. As will become evident, you want the main subroutine to have access to NewEntry's value after IncrementRangesAR is complete; the main sub would not have access to that value if the argument were enclosed in parentheses at the point that IncrementRangesAR is called.

> **Tip**
>
> It's not strictly needed here, but the ability to give an argument a new name in a called subroutine can be very useful. A called subroutine often uses the variable for a different purpose than does the calling subroutine, and in that case it's helpful to give it a name that describes that new purpose.

IncrementRangesAR, as noted above, takes an argument. The main subroutine refers to it as NewEntry, and IncrementRangesAR refers to it as NewRow. It is in fact the same variable as NewEntry; it is simply given a different name in IncrementRangesAR; the different name is established within the parentheses in the statement that defines the procedure:

```
Sub IncrementRangesAR(NewRow)
```

IncrementRangesAR begins by establishing a With block:

```
With ThisWorkbook
```

"ThisWorkbook" directs Excel's attention to the workbook that contains the VBA code—in this case, that is Ledgers.xls. Because the IncrementRangesAR subroutine works on Ledgers.xls, you want Excel to look for ranges that are in Ledgers.xls instead of ranges that are in the active workbook, which is Journals.xls.

> ### Tip
>
> The ThisWorkbook object is particularly useful when you display a dialog box. The workbook that contains the dialog box is frequently inactive at the time that the dialog box is displayed. In that case, it's important to be able to refer to dialog box controls with a statement such as this:
>
> ```
> ThisWorkbook.DialogSheets("Dialog1").EditBoxes(1).Text = ""
> ```
>
> Without the ThisWorkbook object, VBA might look for the dialog sheet named Dialog1 in the active workbook when it's actually in an inactive workbook.

The statements inside this With block all refer to the ThisWorkbook object, identified in the With statement. For example, this statement:

```
NewRow = .Worksheets("AcctsReceivable").Range("AccountNames").Rows.Count + 1
```

refers to the worksheet named AcctsReceivable. That worksheet belongs to ThisWorkbook (again, this is Ledgers.xls). If the With statement were omitted, the statement would have to read as follows:

```
NewRow = ThisWorkbook.Worksheets("AcctsReceivable").Range("AccountNames").Rows.Count + 1
```

That is, every reference to something that appears in ThisWorkbook would have to be qualified by the ThisWorkbook object. Using the With statement allows you to omit the object from references to other objects that belong to it.

The first statement in the With block calculates a new value for NewRow. Every time that the loop in the main subroutine calls the IncrementRangesAR subroutine, NewRow takes on the value of the number of rows in the range AccountNames in the AcctsReceivable worksheet in the Ledgers.xls workbook, *plus 1*. The reason is that every time the main loop posts a new transaction to Accounts Receivable, the code redefines the size of the ranges in the AcctsReceivable worksheet. These redefinitions are accomplished by the remaining statements in the With block. For example, this statement:

```
.Names.Add Name:="AcctsReceivable!Date", RefersTo:="=AcctsReceivable!"
&Worksheets("AcctsReceivable").Range("Date").Resize(NewRow, 1).Address
```

adds (really, redefines, because the name already exists) the range named Date. This is a range on the AcctsReceivable worksheet, and is local to that sheet, so its name is qualified by the name of its worksheet plus an exclamation point.

The RefersTo portion of the statement establishes a new address for the range. The new address is the same as its existing address, except that one row is added to it. The statement looks at the current Date range, and resizes that range according to the new number of rows (NewRow) but leaves it occupying one column. Finally, the RefersTo is set equal to the address (in A1 notation) of the resized range. After this statement executes, the range named Date in the AcctsReceivable worksheet is one row longer than it was before.

The same process is repeated for the other named ranges in the AcctsReceivable worksheet: AccountNames, Debits, Credits, and Balance. When the final statement in the With block has been executed, the statement:

```
End With
```

terminates the block, and the subroutine ends. Control is now returned to the loop in the main subroutine, at the statement immediately following the statement that calls IncrementRangesAR. Because NewEntry (known to IncrementRangesAR as NewRow) is used as an argument, its current value is returned to the main subroutine, where it is used to locate the position of the posted transaction in the AcctsReceivable worksheet.

Upon return of control to the main loop, the first statement to be executed is:

```
NewEntry = NewEntry - 1
```

The reason for decrementing the NewEntry variable will become apparent shortly, but it now contains the number of rows in the named ranges in the AcctsReceivable worksheet, less 1.

Next, another With block is initiated:

```
With ThisWorkbook.Sheets("AcctsReceivable")
```

All objects, methods, and properties referred to inside this With block are deemed to pertain to the sheet named AcctsReceivable, which in turn belongs to ThisWorkbook—the workbook that contains the VBA code.

Each statement inside the With block accomplishes the posting of a transaction from the Sales journal to the Accounts Receivable ledger. For example, this is the first statement inside the With block:

```
.Range("Date").Offset(NewEntry, 0).Resize(1, 1) = SalesDate(ThisTransaction)
```

Notice the following aspects of the statement:

■ The fragment .Range("Date"), by virtue of the With statement, is deemed to refer to the sheet named AcctsReceivable in ThisWorkbook.

■ The Offset fragment defines a range that is offset from the Date range. It is offset from the Date range by NewEntry rows and zero columns. This is the reason for decrementing NewEntry by 1 after the return of control from IncrementRangesAR. The (0,0) offset to the Date range refers to its first row, first column. Therefore, if NewEntry referred to the number of rows in the range, the offset would return the first cell below the end of the range, instead of the last cell in the range.

■ The Resize fragment defines, temporarily, the size of the range as containing one row and one column: thus, one cell.

■ This cell is set equal to the value in the Sales journal range, referred to by the variable SalesDate, for the current value of ThisTransaction— which is the transaction being posted.

This process is repeated in the remainder of the With block, so that the values of AccountName and Purchases are also posted. Finally, this statement:

```
.Range("Total").Offset(NewEntry, 0).Resize(1, 1).Formula = "=Purchases-Payments"
```

enters a formula in the Balance range of the Accounts Receivable worksheet, to subtract an amount in the Payments range from an amount in the Purchases range.

> **Tip**
>
> If you want the worksheet to be able to recalculate results, set a cell equal to a formula such as "=Purchases–Payments." If you want to prevent recalculation, you could perform the math in the VBA code and set the cell equal to the result. For example:
>
> ```
> Difference = Purchases-Payments
> Cells(1,1) = Difference
> ```

The With block is then terminated, and a checkmark is placed in the Posted range of the Sales journal by means of this statement:

```
Posted(ThisTransaction) = 4
```

Then, the If block is terminated with an End If (this marks the end of the statements that are executed if a transaction in the Sales journal has not yet been posted). The loop is terminated with:

```
Next ThisTransaction
```

Control returns to the beginning of the loop if the value of ThisTransaction does not yet exceed Accts.Rows.Count. When the loop has executed once for each row in the range named Account in the Sales Journal, the loop ends, as does the subroutine (End Sub). There are slightly more efficient ways to write this VBA code. For example, you could create more variables that, via Set statements, refer to worksheet ranges in the AcctsReceivable worksheet as well as in the Sales worksheet. However, the structure was chosen in order to illustrate a variety of VBA capabilities, including the With statement, the Offset and Resize methods, the automated redefinition of range addresses and names, and the passing of a value to and from another subroutine such that its new value is available to the calling subroutine.

On the Disk

The other button on the Accounts Receivable ledger worksheet creates a pivot table that provides a balance for each account. It is associated with the VBA code shown here, and can be found on the companion disk in the file named Ledgers.xls:

```
Sub SummarizeAR()
Dim OpenAccounts As Range

ThisWorkbook.Activate
Sheets("AcctsReceivable").Select
Set OpenAccounts = Union(Range("AccountNames"), Range("Purchases"),
Range("Payments"), Range("Total"))
ActiveSheet.PivotTableWizard SourceType:=xlDatabase, SourceData:= _
    OpenAccounts, TableDestination:="R1C6", TableName:="ARSummary"
With ActiveSheet.PivotTables("ARSummary")
    .AddFields RowFields:="Account"
    With .PivotFields("Total")
        .Orientation = xlDataField
        .Name = "Open Balance"
        .Function = xlSum
        .NumberFormat = "_($* #,##0_);_($* (#,##0);_($* ""-""_);_(@_)"
    End With
End With
End Sub
```

After reviewing the code required to post transactions from the Sales journal to the Accounts Receivable ledger, this code will be easy for you to follow. The first statement in Sub SummarizeAR is:

```
Dim OpenAccounts As Range
```

which declares a variable named OpenAccounts as a worksheet range type. Then, these statements:

```
ThisWorkbook.Activate
Sheets("AcctsReceivable").Select
```

activate the Ledgers.xls workbook and select the Accounts Receivable ledger worksheet. The next statement:

```
Set OpenAccounts = Union(Range("AccountNames"), Range("Purchases"),
Range("Payments"), Range("Total"))
```

assigns the *union* of all the ranges in AcctsReceivable to the OpenAccounts range variable. That is, the range variable now refers to a four-column range, consisting of the account names, their purchases, their payments, and their total.

The next statement:

```
ActiveSheet.PivotTableWizardSourceType:=xlDatabase,SourceData:=OpenAccounts,
TableDestination:="R1C6", TableName:="ARSummary"
```

automatically replies to the questions normally posed by the Pivot Table Wizard. That is:

- The type of data source is an Excel List or Database.

- The source data come from the range referred to by the OpenAccounts range variable.

- The pivot table itself will have its upper-left corner in cell F1, or, in R1C1 format, "R1C6."

- The table will be given the name ARSummary instead of the default name PivotTable1 or PivotTable2.

The next statement begins a With block:

```
With ActiveSheet.PivotTables("ARSummary")
```

which allows the subsequent code to refer to objects, properties, and methods belonging to the active sheet's pivot table, without referring to it explicitly. The pivot table's row field is defined as the range named Account:

```
.AddFields RowFields:="Account"
```

Then, a With block is nested inside the outer With block:

```
With .PivotFields("Total")
```

In combination with the outer With block, this statement provides further qualification for subsequent methods and properties. For example, the next statement:

```
.Orientation = xlDataField
```

defines the field named "Balance" as the pivot table's data field. In the absence of the inner With block, the statement would need to be:

```
.PivotFields("Balance").Orientation = xlDataField
```

and in the absence of the outer With block, the statement would need to be:

```
ActiveSheet.PivotTables("ARSummary").PivotFields("Total").Orientation = xlDataField
```

You can see that the statements that define the pivot table would be much longer and complex without the With blocks.

The remaining statements in the inner With block:

```
.Name = "Open Balance"
.Function = xlSum
.NumberFormat = "_($* #,##0_);_($* (#,##0);_($* ""-""_);_(@_)"
```

establish the name of the data field as "Open Balance," require that the balances be shown as a sum, and assign an accounting number format to the field. Then, the two With blocks are terminated and the subroutine is ended.

It is for the purpose of the pivot table that the Total field is used in the Accounts Receivable ledger worksheet. You cannot arrange for a pivot table to create a field that is computed from two existing variables: the computed field must already exist. As a result, the pivot table shows, as an account's balance, the difference between the charges made to the account and the payments made to an account.

On the Disk

These VBA subroutines, and their associated buttons, are replicated for the Accounts Payable ledger (see fig. 4.11). The subroutines can be found on the companion disk in the file named Ledgers.xls.

The main functional difference in the VBA code that posts to the Accounts Payable ledger is that a different journal is accessed (Accounts Payable instead of Accounts Receivable).

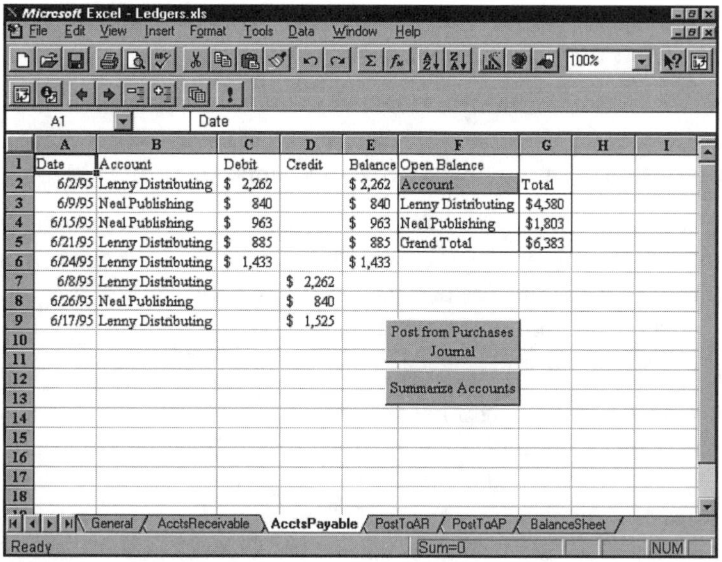

Fig. 4.11
The Accounts Payable Ledger details information about open accounts with the company's suppliers.

Getting a Current Liabilities Balance

Now that a structure for journals and ledgers has been defined, it is straight-forward to move amounts for liabilities into the Balance Sheet (see fig. 4.12).

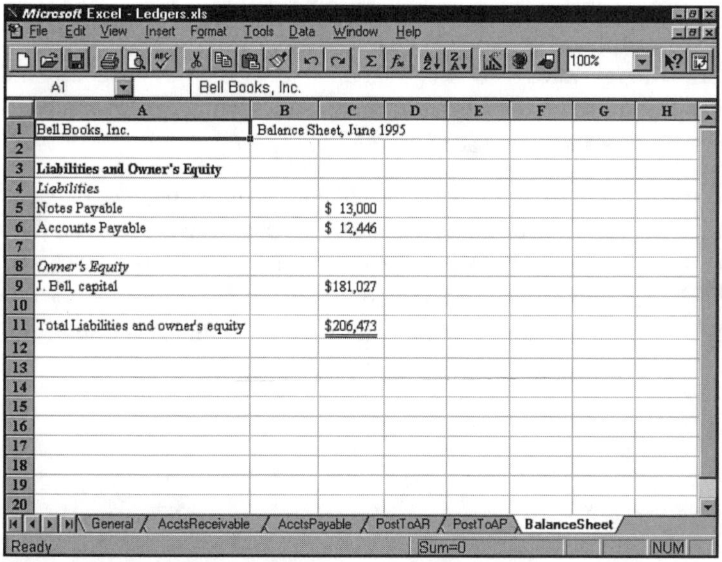

Fig. 4.12
The Balance Sheet for Bell Books, June 1995 (liabilities and owner's equity) links directly to the General Ledger's asset and liability accounts.

Both Notes Payable and Accounts Payable are copied from their General Ledger balances to the Balance Sheet.

Although this illustrative structure contains only two types of liability, Accounts Payable and Notes Payable, there are other types of liability that you might need to account for in your ledger accounts. These include:

- *Taxes payable.* You will often need to estimate the taxes that will be due on both income and salaries. You should consult an accountant or tax lawyer to determine the percentage rates to apply against your estimated income and estimated salaries. With these amounts, you can establish journal and ledger accounts that contain these estimates.

- *Salaries payable.* It might happen that you pay employees' salaries on a date prior to closing your books. In that case, the days that elapse after payment is made and before the books are closed usually result in the accrual of salary amounts that will have to be paid after closing the books. Journal and ledger accounts that accumulate these salaries help you keep track of these liabilities.

- *Interest payable.* Depending on whether a note is discounted, you might want to account for interest on the note on a periodic basis, rather than as of the date that the note is actually paid. An Interest Payable account will allow you to accrue this liability over time.

- *Unearned revenue.* Sometimes, a customer might pay you for a product or service that will not be delivered until after the books are closed. In that case, the revenue represents both an asset in the Cash account and a liability (until delivery has occurred), which you can account for with an Unearned Revenue account.

- *Long-term debt.* If you have acquired a loan whose payable date is longer than a year from the date that the books are closed, you should keep this amount separate from the Current Liabilities section of the Balance Sheet. Its amount would be listed in a separate account, perhaps named Long Term Debt, and listed in a long-term liabilities section of the Balance Sheet.

Summary

This chapter has demonstrated how you can use Excel to create an account structure in a workbook that contains both a General Journal and special journals, and in a workbook that contains both a General Ledger and subsidiary ledgers. As they occur, transactions are entered in the journals in chronological order. The transactions are then posted to the appropriate accounts in the ledger workbook. This accounts for the bulk of the work involved in creating both the Assets and the Liabilities sections of a Balance Sheet.

You have also learned some VBA techniques for automating the process of posting from journals to their associated ledger accounts, and how to use Excel's pivot table facility to determine the current outstanding balance of an account, whether receivable or payable.

Chapter 5, "Working Capital and Cash Flow Analysis," discusses an important technique for determining your company's financial position. While the accrual method of accounting is, for most companies, the most accurate way to match revenue and expenses so as to determine profit, it tends to obscure how the company handles its most liquid asset, cash. You will learn techniques for tracking the flow of cash and working capital in chapter 5.

Chapter 5

Working Capital and Cash Flow Analysis

Several other chapters of this book discuss the *matching principle*: the notion that revenue should be matched with whatever expenses or assets produce that revenue.

This notion leads inevitably to the *accrual method* of accounting. If you obtain the annual registration for a truck in January, and use that truck to deliver products to your customers for twelve months, you have paid for an item in January that helped you produce revenue all year long.

To record the entire amount of the expense in January causes you to overstate your costs, and understate your profitability, for that month. It also causes you to understate your costs, and overstate your profitability, for the remaining eleven months.

It is largely for this reason that the accrual method was developed. Using the accrual method, you would accrue 1/12th of the expense of the truck registration during each month of the year. Doing so enables you to measure your expenses against your revenues more accurately, and so to measure your profitability more accurately throughout the year.

Similarly, suppose that you sell a product to a customer on a credit basis: you might receive the payment for the product over a period of several months, or you might receive payment in a lump sum several months after the sale. Again, if you wait to record that income until you have received full payment, you will mis-measure your profit until the customer finishes paying you.

Some very small businesses—primarily sole proprietorships—use an alternative to accrual, called the *cash method* of accounting. They find it more convenient to record expenses and revenues during the period in which they were paid or received. An accrual basis is slightly more complicated than a cash basis, and requires slightly more effort to maintain. But it is a much more accurate way to keep track of your profits.

The main distinction between the two methods is that if you record revenue and expenses during the time period that you incurred them, you are using the accrual method. If you record them during the time period that you received or made payment, you are using the cash method.

As a brief example, consider figure 5.1.

Fig. 5.1
Marble Designs Income Statement: The cash basis understates income.

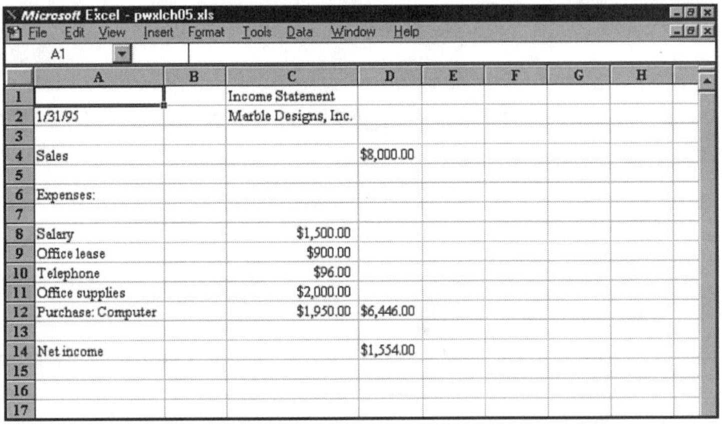

	A	B	C	D
1			Income Statement	
2	1/31/95		Marble Designs, Inc.	
3				
4	Sales			$8,000.00
5				
6	Expenses:			
7				
8	Salary		$1,500.00	
9	Office lease		$900.00	
10	Telephone		$96.00	
11	Office supplies		$2,000.00	
12	Purchase: Computer		$1,950.00	$6,446.00
13				
14	Net income			$1,554.00

Jean Marble starts a new firm, Marble Designs, in January. At the end of the first month of operations, she has made $8,000 in sales and paid various operating expenses: her salary, the office lease, phone costs, office supplies, and a computer. She was able to save 20 percent of the cost of office supplies by making a bulk purchase that she estimates will last the entire year. Recording all of these as expenses during the current period results in net income for the month of $1,554.

Contrast this result with figure 5.2.

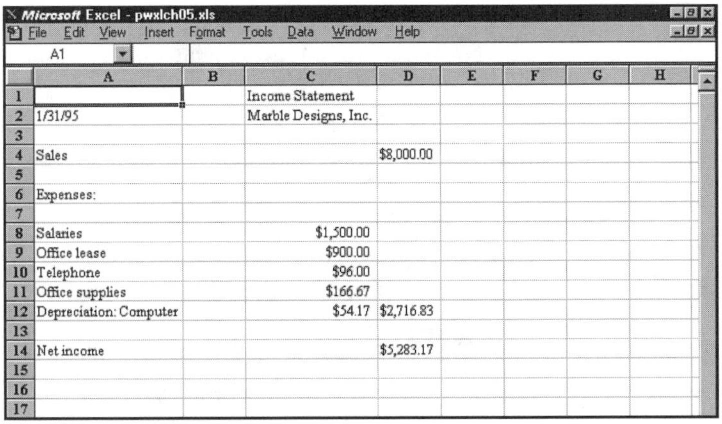

	A	B	C	D	E	F	G	H
1			Income Statement					
2	1/31/95		Marble Designs, Inc.					
3								
4	Sales			$8,000.00				
5								
6	Expenses:							
7								
8	Salaries		$1,500.00					
9	Office lease		$900.00					
10	Telephone		$96.00					
11	Office supplies		$166.67					
12	Depreciation: Computer		$54.17	$2,716.83				
13								
14	Net income			$5,283.17				
15								
16								
17								

Fig. 5.2
Marble Designs Income Statement: The accrual basis more accurately estimates income.

Here, Marble Designs records 1/12 of the cost of the office supplies during January: a reasonable decision since they are expected to last a full year. It also records 1/36th of the cost of the computer as depreciation: the assumption is that the computer's useful life is three years. Now, net income for January is $5,283: 3.4 times the net income recorded under the cash basis.

Net income of $5,283 is a much more realistic estimate for January than is $1,554. Both the office supplies and the computer will contribute to the creation of revenue far longer than one month. In contrast, the benefits of the salary, lease, and phone expenses pertain to that month only, and so it is appropriate to record the entire expense during January.

However, this analysis says nothing about how much cash Marble Designs has in the bank. Suppose that the company must pay off a major obligation in June. Under the accrual method, the income statement does not necessarily show whether Marble Designs is likely to have enough funds, or working capital, to be able to meet that obligation.

Furthermore, a balance sheet may not show whether Marble Designs has sufficient assets and equity to pay any large obligations that may come due. If its assets are not liquid, it may be difficult to convert them to cash quickly enough to pay a large debt.

Cash is the most liquid of all assets, so many managers are intensely interested in how much cash is available to a business at any given time. And because the flow of cash into and out of a business is mainly a matter of investing (purchasing assets) and dis-investing (disposing of assets), an analysis of cash flows can be a good measure of how well managers are performing their investing functions.

This chapter describes the process of accounting for and analyzing these cash flows. The cash flow statement is a useful adjunct to, although not a replacement for, income statements and balance sheets. Using tools that are available to you in the form of different functions and links, you will learn how to convert the information in a balance sheet and income statement to a cash flow statement.

Broadening the Definition: Cash versus Working Capital

So far, funds have been discussed in terms of cash only. A broader and more useful way of looking at the availability of funds involves the concept of *working capital*.

Consider the process your company uses to create income. If you manufacture a product, you use funds to purchase inventory, produce goods with that inventory, convert those goods into accounts receivable by selling them, and convert accounts receivable into funds when you receive payment. If yours is a merchandising firm, the process is basically the same, although you probably purchase finished goods rather than produce them.

During this process, each of its components is a current asset: that is, an asset that you can convert into cash in a relatively short period (usually, but not always, one year) as a result of your normal business operations. Inventory and accounts receivable, for example, are not as liquid as cash, but your business expects eventually to convert them to cash.

Current liabilities, on the other hand, are obligations that you must meet during the same relatively short time period that defines your current assets. Notes payable, accounts payable, and salaries are examples of current liabilities.

Determining the Amount of Working Capital

Working capital is the result of subtracting current liabilities from current assets. It is a measure of a company's solvency, of its capacity to make large purchases and realize bulk discounts, and of its ability to attract customers by offering advantageous credit terms.

Case Study: Marble Designs' Working Capital

To complicate, with one additional transaction, the activities of Marble Designs in January 1995, assume that it purchases $2,000 worth of inventory on January 1. The inventory is purchased on credit, and Marble Designs uses $500 of the inventory during January to deliver products to customers.

The cash transactions that occur during January are shown in figure 5.3.

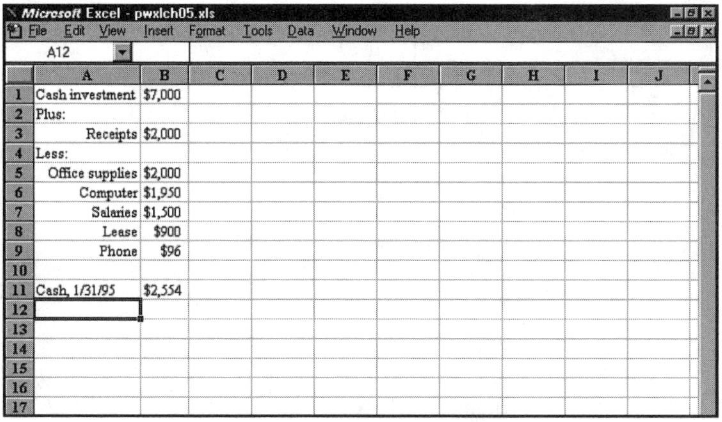

	A	B	C	D	E	F	G	H	I	J
1	Cash investment	$7,000								
2	Plus:									
3	Receipts	$2,000								
4	Less:									
5	Office supplies	$2,000								
6	Computer	$1,950								
7	Salaries	$1,500								
8	Lease	$900								
9	Phone	$96								
10										
11	Cash, 1/31/95	$2,554								

Fig. 5.3

The cash transactions undertaken by Marble Designs during January 1995 affect, but do not define, its working capital.

Jean Marble establishes capital for her new firm by investing $7,000 at the outset. Of the $8,000 in sales that she makes during the first month, she receives cash payment of $2,000: her cash account is now $9,000. Out of that $9,000, she makes payment for:

- $2,000 in office supplies

- $1,950 for a computer

- $1,500 for her salary

- $900 for the monthly office lease

- $96 for the telephone line

These transactions are shown in a format that helps you move to a Trial Balance, to an Adjusted Trial Balance (see fig. 5.4), and subsequently to the income statement and balance sheet.

Fig. 5.4
Marble Designs' Trial Balance, Adjustments and Adjusted Trial Balance begin to focus on the company's working capital.

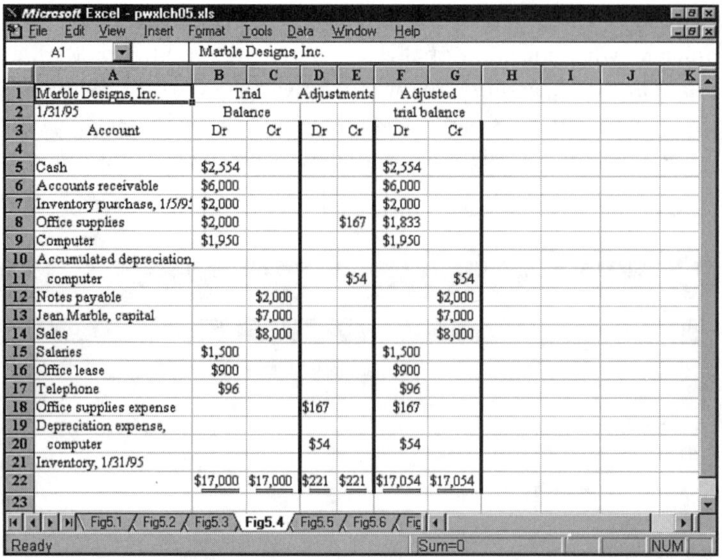

	A	B	C	D	E	F	G
1	Marble Designs, Inc.	Trial		Adjustments		Adjusted	
2	1/31/95	Balance				trial balance	
3	Account	Dr	Cr	Dr	Cr	Dr	Cr
4							
5	Cash	$2,554				$2,554	
6	Accounts receivable	$6,000				$6,000	
7	Inventory purchase, 1/5/9:	$2,000				$2,000	
8	Office supplies	$2,000			$167	$1,833	
9	Computer	$1,950				$1,950	
10	Accumulated depreciation,						
11	computer				$54		$54
12	Notes payable		$2,000				$2,000
13	Jean Marble, capital		$7,000				$7,000
14	Sales		$8,000				$8,000
15	Salaries	$1,500				$1,500	
16	Office lease	$900				$900	
17	Telephone	$96				$96	
18	Office supplies expense			$167		$167	
19	Depreciation expense,						
20	computer			$54		$54	
21	Inventory, 1/31/95						
22		$17,000	$17,000	$221	$221	$17,054	$17,054
23							

On the left hand, or debit, side of the Trial Balance are shown the ending cash balance of $2,554, the accounts receivable of $6,000 (recall that sales of $8,000 were made, and $2,000 in cash payments were received), the inventory purchased with the $2,000 loan, and the office supplies, computer, salary, lease, and telephone service paid for with cash.

On the right hand, or credit, side of the Trial Balance are shown Marble's initial capital investment into Cash (balancing the items paid for with cash plus the $554 cash remaining from the initial investment), the $8,000 in sales (balancing the $6,000 in accounts receivable plus the other $2,000 in cash), and the $2,000 borrowed to purchase the inventory.

The Adjustments to the Trial Balance include $54 in depreciation on the computer during the first of 36 months of its useful life, and the $167 worth of supplies consumed during the first month. The $54 in depreciation is found with this formula:

```
=SLN(B9,0,36)
```

This is the Excel function that returns straight-line depreciation. You will learn more about Excel's depreciation functions in chapter 16, "Fixed Assets," but this particular entry computes the monthly depreciation on the value in cell B9 ($1,950), assuming that its eventual salvage value is $0 and that its useful life is 36 months.

The value of the Office Supplies consumed during the month is $167: the value of $2,000 in cell B8 divided by 12.

These adjustments are added to (or in the case of the office supplies, subtracted from) the Trial Balance to arrive at the debit amounts in the Adjusted Trial Balance. The worksheet accomplishes this by means of this formula in cells F5:F21:

```
=IF(TrialDebits-TrialCredits+AdjustDebits-AdjustCredits>=0,
    TrialDebits-TrialCredits+AdjustDebits-AdjustCredits,0)
```

The formula makes use of four named ranges:

- TrialDebits refers to B5:B21, the debit amounts in the Trial Balance.

- TrialCredits refers to C5:C21 the credit amounts in the Trial Balance.

- AdjustDebits refers to D5:D21, the debit amounts in the Adjustments.

- AdjustCredits refers to E5:E21, the credit amounts in the Adjustments.

The first portion of the formula establishes the conditions under which the formula will return a computed value. It will do so if the combination of the trial balance debit or credit with the adjustment's debit or credit is greater than or equal to zero. In that case, the account has a debit balance.

Tip

Single-cell formulas usually require less memory than do array formulas. The formulas described here are entered as single-cell formulas, even though they evaluate arrays. As a rule of thumb, if an array already exists on a worksheet, a formula that uses the array need not be entered as an array formula.

The credit amounts in the Adjusted Trial Balance section are returned by this formula:

```
=IF(AdjustedDebits=0,TrialCredits-TrialDebits+AdjustCredits-
    AdjustDebits,0)
```

It makes use of the AdjustedDebits range, which occupies cells F5:F21. The formula simply checks to see if there is an entry in its row within the AdjustedDebits column, and if not, it combines the Trial Balance credit amounts with the Adjustment amounts. Again, the formula is initially entered into cell G5, and copied into cells G6:G21.

You might have noticed that these various formulas call for Excel to return a zero amount if a condition is not met. For example, the latter formula returns an AdjustedCredits amount when the condition is met, but a zero when it is not met. The figure does not show these zero amounts, primarily to avoid visual clutter.

> **Tip**
>
> You can suppress any zero amounts in a worksheet by choosing Tools, Options, selecting the View tab, and clearing the Zero Values checkbox.

With the cells in the Adjusted Trial Balance section completed, their revenue and expense information is carried over from the Adjusted Trial Balance to the Income Statement and Balance sheet (see fig. 5.5).

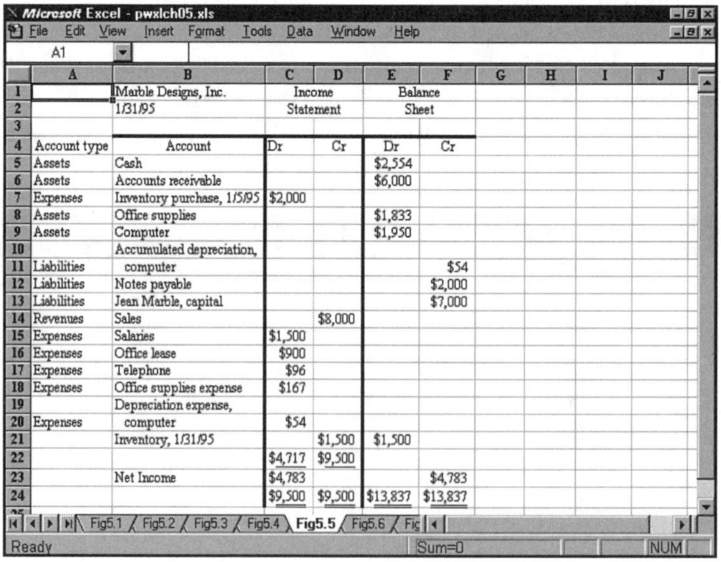

	A	B	C	D	E	F
1		Marble Designs, Inc.	Income		Balance	
2		1/31/95	Statement		Sheet	
3						
4	Account type	Account	Dr	Cr	Dr	Cr
5	Assets	Cash			$2,554	
6	Assets	Accounts receivable			$6,000	
7	Expenses	Inventory purchase, 1/5/95	$2,000			
8	Assets	Office supplies			$1,833	
9	Assets	Computer			$1,950	
10		Accumulated depreciation,				
11	Liabilities	computer				$54
12	Liabilities	Notes payable				$2,000
13	Liabilities	Jean Marble, capital				$7,000
14	Revenues	Sales		$8,000		
15	Expenses	Salaries	$1,500			
16	Expenses	Office lease	$900			
17	Expenses	Telephone	$96			
18	Expenses	Office supplies expense	$167			
19		Depreciation expense,				
20	Expenses	computer	$54			
21		Inventory, 1/31/95		$1,500	$1,500	
22			$4,717	$9,500		
23		Net Income	$4,783			$4,783
24			$9,500	$9,500	$13,837	$13,837

Fig. 5.5 Marble Designs Income Statement and Balance Sheet: the Balance Sheet enables you to determine Working Capital.

For the Income Statement, information on revenues and expenses are needed. The debit amounts are obtained by means of this formula:

```
=IF(OR(AccountType="Revenues",AccountType="Expenses"),AdjustedDebits,0)
```

The range named AccountType occupies cells A5:A20, and contains values that identify the type of account: revenue, expense, asset, or liability. The values in this range enable the formula to bring only the needed accounts into the Income Statement. Similarly, the credit amounts in the Income Statement are obtained by means of this formula:

```
=IF(OR(AccountType="Revenues",AccountType="Expenses"),AdjustedCredits,0)
```

(The AdjustedCredits range occupies cells G5:G21 in figure 5.4.)

There are two additional amounts required to bring the Income Statement into balance: Ending Inventory and Net Income. Both of these amounts are as of the statement date, 1/31/95.

Ending Inventory is included as a credit amount, to help balance the expense of the initial $2,000 purchase.

Net Income is included in the Debit Column, as the difference between the Income Statement's total Credits and its total Debits. The figure returned is $4,783. As a check, notice that this is the result of:

```
$8,000 (Gross Sales) - $500 (Cost of Goods Sold) - $2,717
(Total Operating Expenses) = $4,783
```

and the inclusion of the Ending Inventory and Net Income brings the Income Statement into balance.

Note

Recall that Cost of Goods Sold equals Beginning Inventory (here, $0) plus Purchases ($2,000) less Ending Inventory ($1,500).

Finally, the debit and credit columns of the Balance Sheet are obtained by formulas that are similar to those used for the Income Statement. The debit amounts are returned by this formula:

```
=IF(OR(AccountType="Assets",AccountType="Liabilities"),AdjustedDebits,0)
```

and the credit amounts are returned by:

```
=IF(OR(AccountType="Assets",AccountType="Liabilities"),AdjustedCredits,0)
```

At last, Marble is in a position to calculate her Working Capital. Recall that this is defined as the difference between Current Assets and Current Liabilities. As of 1/31/95, Marble's Current Assets are:

$2,554 (Cash)

$6,000 (Accounts Receivable)

$1,833 (Office Supplies, a pre-paid expense)

$1,500 (Ending Inventory)

for a total of $11,877. Her Current Liabilities include only the $2,000 note payable. Her Working Capital is therefore $9,877, or $11,877 – $2,000.

> **Note**
>
> Notice that the computer asset is not involved in computing Working Capital. This is because the computer is not a current asset: one that can quickly be converted to cash in the normal course of business operations.

Determining Changes in Working Capital

From a management perspective, it is important to understand how the amount of Working Capital changes over time. A comparative Balance Sheet is useful for this purpose. Figure 5.6 shows an Income Statement and a Balance Sheet for Marble Designs, in a more condensed format than the one used in figure 5.5.

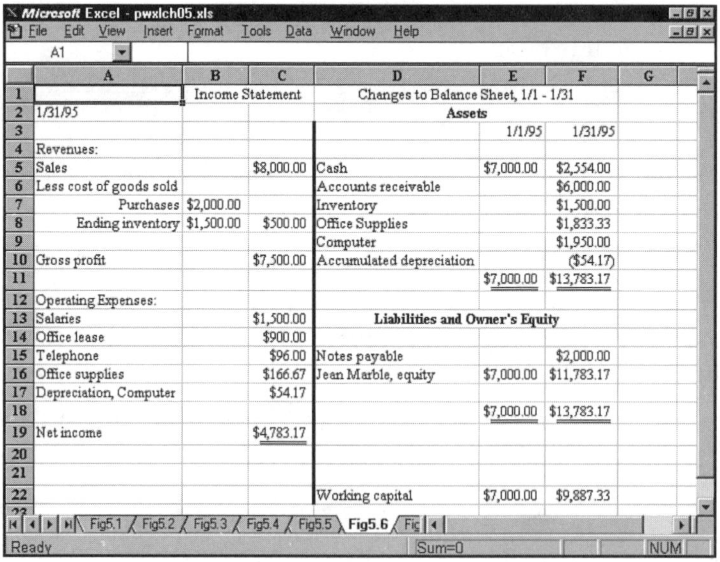

	A	B	C	D	E	F
1		Income Statement		Changes to Balance Sheet, 1/1 - 1/31		
2	1/31/95				Assets	
3					1/1/95	1/31/95
4	Revenues:					
5	Sales		$8,000.00	Cash	$7,000.00	$2,554.00
6	Less cost of goods sold			Accounts receivable		$6,000.00
7	Purchases	$2,000.00		Inventory		$1,500.00
8	Ending inventory	$1,500.00	$500.00	Office Supplies		$1,833.33
9				Computer		$1,950.00
10	Gross profit		$7,500.00	Accumulated depreciation		($54.17)
11					$7,000.00	$13,783.17
12	Operating Expenses:					
13	Salaries		$1,500.00	Liabilities and Owner's Equity		
14	Office lease		$900.00			
15	Telephone		$96.00	Notes payable		$2,000.00
16	Office supplies		$166.67	Jean Marble, equity	$7,000.00	$11,783.17
17	Depreciation, Computer		$54.17			
18					$7,000.00	$13,783.17
19	Net income		$4,783.17			
20						
21						
22				Working capital	$7,000.00	$9,887.33

Fig. 5.6 An income statement and comparative balance sheet can clarify how your financial position changes over time.

The Balance Sheet section of figure 5.6 lists Marble Designs' assets and liabilities. On 1/1/95, when the firm began operation, it had no liabilities and $7,000 in assets, consisting entirely of cash. Its working capital was therefore $7,000. By the end of the month, the sum of the firm's assets was $13,783 (as, of course, was the sum of its liabilities and owner's equity).

Not all of these assets and liabilities are *current*, however. The current assets include cash, accounts receivable, inventory, and office supplies, which total to $11,887. The sole current liability is the note for the purchase of the beginning inventory, for $2,000. The difference between the total of the current assets and the current liability is $9,887, which agrees with the amount arrived at via the information in figure 5.5.

So, the change in Working Capital from the beginning to the end of the month is $9,887 – $7,000, or $2,887.

There are several alternative ways to calculate changes in Working Capital. One way to do so is shown in figure 5.7.

Microsoft Excel - pwxlch05.xls

	A	B
1	Effect of transactions on working capital	
2		
3	Increases	
4	Gross profit ($8,000 - $500 COGS)	$7,500
5	Addition to inventory	$2,000
6		
7	Total increases	$9,500
8		
9	Decreases	
10	Note payable for purchase to inventory	$2,000
11	Purchase of computer from cash	$1,950
12	Payment of salary from cash	$1,500
13	Payment of lease from cash	$900
14	Payment of phone bill from cash	$96
15	Use of office supplies	$167
16		
17	Total decreases	$6,613
18		
19	Net increase in working capital	$2,887

Fig. 5.7
A laborious way to determine changes in Working Capital is by examining individual transactions.

During January, Working Capital was increased by selling products for more than their cost: the gross profit of $7,500. It was also increased by placing $2,000 worth of materials in inventory. These are both current assets, totaling $9,500.

Working Capital was decreased by acquiring an obligation of $2,000, the note payable that was used to purchase the inventory. Working Capital was also decreased by the payment of cash for the computer, for various operating expenses, and the use of office supplies. These are all current liabilities, totaling $6,613.

The net effect of the increase of $9,500 in working capital and the decrease of $6,613 in working capital is $2,887. During the month of January, Marble Designs was able to increase its working capital by this amount. Note that this is the same figure as was determined by the analysis in figure 5.6 ($9,887 – $7,000).

Normally, you would not determine changes in Working Capital by examining each transaction that occurred in a given period: there are quicker ways. Also, many transactions occur that affect current assets and current liabilities to the same degree, and therefore have no net effect on Working Capital.

For example, when you collect payment for a product or service, this transaction has no effect on Working Capital. So doing merely increases one current asset (cash) and decreases another current asset (accounts receivable) by identical amounts.

Therefore, the example shown in figure 5.7 could have ignored the transactions involved when Marble Designs acquired $2,000 in inventory. This transaction increased a current asset, inventory, and increased a current liability, notes payable, by identical amounts. In general, transactions that involve only current asset or current liability accounts *do* have an effect on Working Capital accounts, but they *do not* have a net effect on the amount of Working Capital.

As this chapter has emphasized, Working Capital is the difference between current assets and current liabilities. Similarly, the *change* in Working Capital is the combined effect of *changes* in current liabilities and in current assets. Figure 5.8 shows how you can quickly determine the change in Working Capital by examining changes to the accounts that comprise current assets and liabilities.

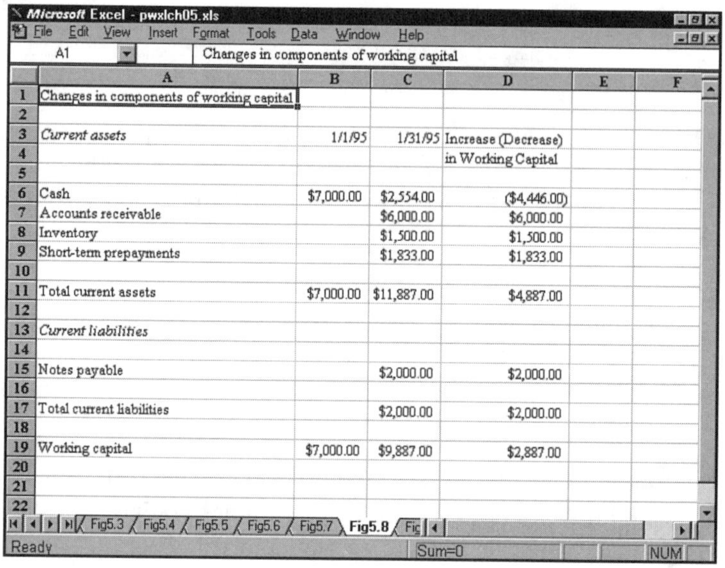

Fig. 5.8
You can determine changes in Working Capital by comparing changes in current assets and in current liabilities.

	A	B	C	D	E	F
1	Changes in components of working capital					
2						
3	Current assets		1/1/95	1/31/95	Increase (Decrease)	
4					in Working Capital	
5						
6	Cash		$7,000.00	$2,554.00	($4,446.00)	
7	Accounts receivable			$6,000.00	$6,000.00	
8	Inventory			$1,500.00	$1,500.00	
9	Short-term prepayments			$1,833.00	$1,833.00	
10						
11	Total current assets		$7,000.00	$11,887.00	$4,887.00	
12						
13	Current liabilities					
14						
15	Notes payable			$2,000.00	$2,000.00	
16						
17	Total current liabilities			$2,000.00	$2,000.00	
18						
19	Working capital		$7,000.00	$9,887.00	$2,887.00	
20						
21						
22						

As it happens, the only current asset that declines during January is the Cash account. All other current asset accounts increase in value. One current liability account, Notes Payable, increases. The change in Working Capital can then be determined by subtracting the net increase in current liabilities from the net increase in current assets: $4,887 – $2,000 = $2,887.

One additional means of determining changes in Working Capital is to compare its sources with its uses. Recall that transactions involving only current accounts have no net effect on Working Capital. The same is true of transactions that involve only non-current accounts. For example, when Marble records $54 as the month's depreciation on the computer, she adds $54 to a non-current account, with no effect on Working Capital.

However, a transaction that involves a current account and a non-current account does affect the amount of Working Capital. For example, suppose that Marble were to invest an additional $1,000 in her business, recording it in both the capital account (non-current) and the cash account (a current asset). This transaction would have the effect of increasing Working Capital by $1,000.

Therefore, when determining changes to Working Capital, it is often convenient to limit the analysis to transactions affecting only current accounts and non-current accounts (see fig. 5.9).

Microsoft Excel - pwxlch05.xls

	A	B
1	*Sources*	
2	Operating income	$4,783
3	Depreciation	$54
4	Total sources	$4,837
5	*Uses*	
6	Computer purchase	$1,950
7	Total uses	$1,950
8		
9	Increase in working capital	$2,887
10		
11		

Fig. 5.9
Another way to determine changes in Working Capital is to examine current and non-current accounts.

The sources of Working Capital, in this case, consist solely of Net Income. What is Depreciation doing there? Recall that depreciation is a non-cash expense that, for the purposes of the income statement, acts as an offset to gross profit in the calculation of net income. But no funds change hands as a result of recording depreciation. Therefore, when you use Net Income to calculate your sources of Working Capital, it is necessary to add depreciation back in: in other words, to reverse the effect of subtracting it on the income statement.

The cash portion of Net Income, a non-current account, is deposited in the cash account, a current asset. Therefore, in combination with the act of adding depreciation back in, it can be used to calculate the change in working capital.

The sole use of Working Capital shown in figure 5.9, the purchase of the computer, is also used to determine the change in Working Capital. Funds from the Cash account, a current asset, were used to purchase Equipment, a noncurrent asset.

The difference between the total sources of Working Capital and the total uses of Working Capital is, once again, $2,887, just as was found by means of the analyses in figures 5.6 through 5.8.

Analyzing Cash Flow

As noted above, there are various reasons that you would want to determine how a company uses its cash assets. The choice to use cash to acquire an asset, meet a liability, or retire a debt is a process of investment and dis-investment, and there are always choices, some smart and some maladroit, that a manager can make. It's important to keep track of how well a company's management is making these choices.

Furthermore, the accrual method of accounting, for all its usefulness in matching revenues with expenses, tends to obscure how cash flows through a firm. One of the purposes of cash flow analysis is to highlight differences between, say, net income and the actual acquisition of cash. For example, accounts receivable is one component of net income, but it will not show up as cash until the check makes it to the bank. A company may have a healthy net income, but if its customers do not pay it on a timely basis it might have difficulty meeting its obligations. Cash flow analysis can illuminate problems, even impending problems, such as this.

To illustrate this process, consider what might transpire in Marble Designs' financial structure over the period of a year.

Case Study: Marble Designs (Continued)

During the twelve months following the analyses shown in figures 5.1 through 5.9, Marble Designs enjoys successful operations, and engages in the following transactions:

■ Makes $90,000 in sales to customers, using $24,500 in inventory as part of those sales. As of January 31, 1996, $5,500 remains in accounts receivable.

■ Uses cash to purchase $25,000 in materials to supply its inventory.

■ Collects the $6,000 that remained in accounts receivable at the end of January 1995.

■ Pays $32,951 in cash to cover operating expenses.

■ Purchases a new computer in July for $2,320 in cash.

■ Buys $2,000 in additional office supplies.

■ Purchases office space in a new building for $30,000. Decides against occupying the space before construction of the building is complete, and sells the space for $35,000, making a $5,000 nonoperating profit.

■ Retires the $2,000 note acquired during January 1995, and obtains a new note for $3,000.

■ Depreciates the two computers, for a total of $1,037 from 1/31/95 through 1/31/96 (thus, taking into account the $54 depreciation during 1/95, a total of $1,091 from 1/1/95 through 1/31/96).

Some of these transactions are cash, some are transactions that pertain to normal operations, and some affect current assets and liabilities. Others are noncash, nonoperating, and long-term. To determine their effect on Marble Designs' cash flow, it's necessary to disaggregate them.

> **Note**
>
> This is a relatively simple situation to analyze, and because it is illustrative it omits many of the transactions that you would normally take into account. For example, it assumes that Marble Designs is an S-corporation, and therefore the treatment of its income taxes is deferred.

As a benchmark, against which the following analysis will be compared, figure 5.10 shows the actual cash transactions that occur as a result of Marble Designs' activities during the twelve-month period.

Fig. 5.10
Marble Designs' cash positions can be tracked by examining individual cash transactions.

	Deposits	Withdrawals	Balance
Beginning cash balance			$2,554
Plus revenue deposits	$84,500		$87,054
Less purchases to inventory		$25,000	$62,054
Plus payment from old accounts receivable	$6,000		$68,054
Less cash expenses		$32,951	$35,103
Less purchase of new computer		$2,320	$32,783
Less purchase of new supplies		$2,000	$30,783
Plus gain on sale of office	$5,000		$35,783
Less retirement of old note		$2,000	$33,783
Plus issuance of new note	$3,000		
Ending cash balance			$36,783
Increase in cash balance:			$34,229

Again, though, the information in figure 5.10 is simply a benchmark used below as a check on the cash flow analysis. You would almost never attempt to do a cash flow analysis using actual cash receipts and payments over any lengthy period of time: it's too time consuming and it's not as informative a way of going about the analysis.

Developing the Basic Information

Instead of beginning with a checkbook register, start with the standard financial reports: the Income Statement and Balance Sheet. Figure 5.11 shows the Income Statement for the period 1/31/95 through 1/31/96 for Marble Designs, as well as a comparative Balance Sheet showing assets, liabilities and equity at the beginning and end of that period.

Fig. 5.11
The Income Statement and Balance Sheet provide starting points for a cash flow analysis.

	Income Statement		Changes to Balance Sheet, 1/31/95 - 1/31/96		
1/31/96			Assets		
				1/31/95	1/31/96
Revenues:					
Sales		$90,000	Cash	$2,554	$36,783
Less cost of goods sold			Accounts receivable	$6,000	$5,500
Beginning Inventory	$1,500		Inventory	$1,500	$2,000
Purchases	$25,000		Office Supplies	$1,833	$2,000
Ending inventory	$2,000		Computer (486)	$1,950	$1,950
Cost of goods sold		$24,500	Computer (P5)		$2,320
Gross profit		$65,500	Accumulated depreciation	($54)	($1,091)
				$13,783	$49,462
Expenses:					
Salaries		$21,000	Liabilities and Owner's Equity		
Office lease		$10,800			
Telephone		$1,151	Notes payable	$2,000	$3,000
Office supplies		$1,833	Jean Marble, equity	$11,783	$46,462
Depreciation, Computers		$1,037			
				$13,783	$49,462
Gain on sale of office		$5,000			
Net income		$34,679			

The Income Statement shows that there was $1,500 worth of materials in inventory at the beginning of the period, an additional $25,000 worth was purchased during the period, and $2,000 remaining at the end. Therefore, $24,500 in materials was used in the completion of $90,000 in sales for the period, resulting in a gross profit of $65,500.

Against that gross profit, various operating expenses were incurred: salaries, the cost of the office lease, and the telephone expense. The $1,833 in office supplies that remained at the end of 1/31/95 were consumed: this was a pre-paid expense, because Marble purchased the entire stock of supplies at the beginning of January 1995.

The depreciation on the computers also appears in the Income Statement. This is, however, a noncash expense. The formula used in cell C18 of figure 5.11 is:

```
=SLN(1950,0,3)+SLN(2320,0,3)*0.5
```

It makes use of Excel's straight-line depreciation function, whose arguments are *cost, salvage value,* and *life.* The cost is simply the item's initial cost; its salvage value is the item's value at the end of its useful life—here, Marble estimates that value to be zero; its life is the number of periods that will expire before the item reaches its salvage value. The function returns the amount of depreciation that occurs during one period of the item's useful life. So, this fragment:

```
SLN(1950,0,3)
```

returns $650, the amount of depreciation in the value of the first computer purchased, during one year of its assumed three-year life.

The second computer cost $2,320, and was purchased in July of 1995, half-way through the period covered by the Income Statement. Therefore, the depreciation on that computer during the second half of the year, $387, is returned by this fragment:

```
SLN(2320,0,3)*0.5
```

Together, the $650 in depreciation over twelve months for the first computer, and the $387 in depreciation over six months for the second computer, result in a total equipment depreciation of $1,037.

Note

Expenditures, such as the purchase of the computer, that add to business assets are *capital expenditures.* They are recorded in asset accounts, which is why the cost of the computers does not appear in the income statement. Expenditures for repairs, maintenance, fuel and so on are *revenue expenditures,* and do appear in the income statement.

It's important to keep in mind that this depreciation does not constitute a cash expense such as a salary check or the payment of a monthly telephone bill. As noted above, no funds change hands when you record depreciation: it is merely a means of apportioning, or accruing, an earlier use of capital to a period in which the item contributes to the creation of revenue.

Lastly, the $5,000 profit from the acquisition (for $30,000) and subsequent sale (for $35,000) of the office space is recorded and added to obtain a total net income. Note that this $5,000 is nonoperating income: that is, it is profit created from an activity, the purchase and sale of property, that is not a part of Marble Designs' normal operations.

The Balance Sheet repeats from figure 5.6, in column E, Marble Designs' assets, liabilities, and equity at the end of 1/31/95. Column F also shows these figures as of 1/31/96. As noted previously, the transactions that occurred during the twelve-month period resulted in a substantial increase in cash, and minor changes to the remaining asset and liability categories. These entries are taken from ledger accounts; the exception is the owner's equity figure of $46,462. Just as explained in the discussion of the balance sheet shown in figure 5.6, the owner's equity in cell F17 of figure 5.11 is calculated as:

    =E17+C22

That is, the prior equity figure of $11,783 in cell E17, plus the net income of $34,679 for the period in cell C22.

Summarizing the Sources and Uses of Working Capital

Figure 5.12 shows the changes in working capital that occurred during the year, determined by analyzing the effect of noncurrent accounts. Sources of working capital include operations, the nonoperating profit realized from the purchase and sale of the office space, and borrowing on a new short-term note.

Uses of working capital include the purchase of the office space, the purchase of the new computer, and the retirement of the original short-term note. Again, the difference between the sources and the uses of working capital returns the change during the period in working capital, whether a decrease or, as in this case, an increase.

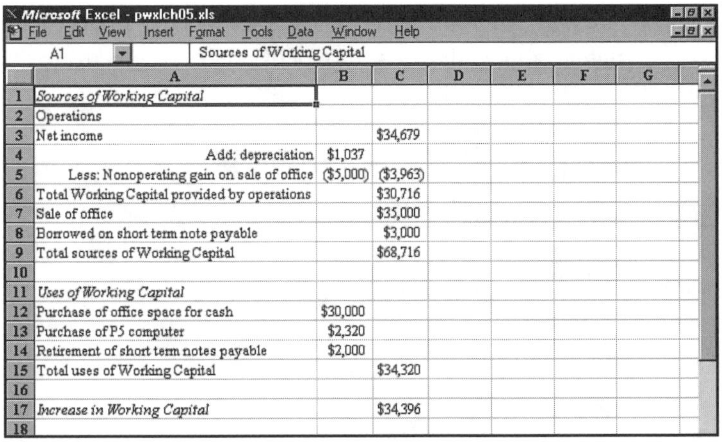

	A	B	C
1	*Sources of Working Capital*		
2	Operations		
3	Net income		$34,679
4	Add: depreciation	$1,037	
5	Less: Nonoperating gain on sale of office	($5,000)	($3,963)
6	Total Working Capital provided by operations		$30,716
7	Sale of office		$35,000
8	Borrowed on short term note payable		$3,000
9	Total sources of Working Capital		$68,716
10			
11	*Uses of Working Capital*		
12	Purchase of office space for cash	$30,000	
13	Purchase of P5 computer	$2,320	
14	Retirement of short term notes payable	$2,000	
15	Total uses of Working Capital		$34,320
16			
17	*Increase in Working Capital*		$34,396
18			

Fig. 5.12
Analyzing the sources and uses of working capital is often a useful indicator of how well a business is managing its resources.

There are three points to note about this analysis of sources and uses of working capital:

- You can *calculate* overall cash flow by determining the net change in the Cash account, but to *analyze* cash flow you need to examine all the changes in the balance sheet accounts—including working capital. The details and the overall effect of changes in working capital usually differ from those of cash transactions. Both the working capital and the cash impacts are important to an understanding of a company's financial position.

- Changes in working capital are not the same as changes in cash. In this particular example, the two are very close because a rather simple set of transactions is presented to illustrate the process. The difference between change in working capital and change in cash is only $167, due to the difference in the amount of prepaid office supplies on hand at the beginning and end of the period.

- Notice that the profit on the purchase and sale of the office space apparently has no effect on the increase in working capital. In fact, however, it does: the profit of $5,000 has already been included in net income. Figure 5.12 subtracts that profit from net income to provide a more accurate picture of operations as a source of working capital. Further, the transaction is shown both under sources and uses to show how capital has been generated and used, not simply to calculate the increase or the decrease over time.

Identifying Cash Flows Due to Operating Activities

The next step in analyzing cash flows is to focus on cash generated by and used in operations (see fig. 5.13).

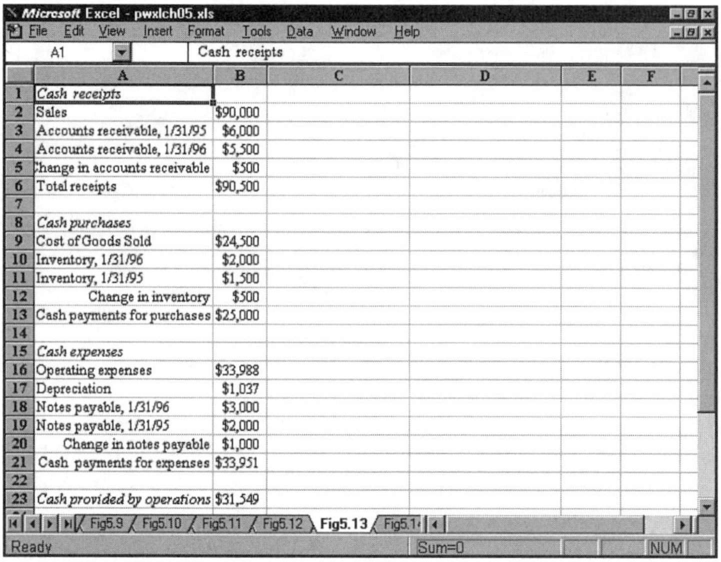

	A	B
1	*Cash receipts*	
2	Sales	$90,000
3	Accounts receivable, 1/31/95	$6,000
4	Accounts receivable, 1/31/96	$5,500
5	Change in accounts receivable	$500
6	Total receipts	$90,500
7		
8	*Cash purchases*	
9	Cost of Goods Sold	$24,500
10	Inventory, 1/31/96	$2,000
11	Inventory, 1/31/95	$1,500
12	Change in inventory	$500
13	Cash payments for purchases	$25,000
14		
15	*Cash expenses*	
16	Operating expenses	$33,988
17	Depreciation	$1,037
18	Notes payable, 1/31/96	$3,000
19	Notes payable, 1/31/95	$2,000
20	Change in notes payable	$1,000
21	Cash payments for expenses	$33,951
22		
23	*Cash provided by operations*	$31,549

Fig. 5.13
Determining cash flows from operating activities.

Generally, there are three sources or uses of cash that arise from operating activities:

- *Cash receipts from customers.* You can easily determine this amount by combining the value for sales (net of any discounts that may have been provided to customers) with changes in accounts receivable. That is, add accounts receivable at the end of the period to the sales figure, and then subtract accounts receivable at the end of the period. The logic is that if accounts receivable has declined during the period, you have collected more in receipts than you have accrued into accounts receivable; if it has increased, you have accrued more than you have collected in cash.

- *Cash outlays for purchases.* From the standpoint of operating activities, there is one use of cash for purchases: inventory. Therefore, to summarize cash flow for operating purchases, add to the cost of goods sold during the period the ending inventory level, and subtract the beginning inventory level.

  Additionally, you might have purchased inventory via a note or account payable to the suppliers of your inventory materials. In that case, you would add any decrease in these payables (because you would have used cash to decrease them) or subtract any increase in these payables (because you used credit, not cash, to acquire the materials).

- *Cash outlays for expenses.* These are easily determined from the operating expenses portion of the income statement. Combine the total operating expenses with any changes in prepayments and accrued liabilities, such as employee salaries earned, but as yet unpaid, at the end of the period.

In the case of Marble Designs, applying these steps as shown in figure 5.13 indicates that sales, increased by a reduction of $500 in accounts receivable, results in cash receipts of $90,500. Cost of goods sold, increased by the $500 change in inventory level, results in $25,000 cash purchases. And total operating expenses were (a) reduced by $1,037 in depreciation, a noncash, long-term prepayment, and (b) a change in the amount of notes payable, converted to cash and used to acquire office supplies.

This completes the process of converting information contained in the income statement, receipts and outlays represented as accruals, into a cash basis, represented as actual cash receipts and outlays occurring during the period in question.

Combining Cash from Operations with Cash from Nonoperating Transactions

The final step in developing the cash flow analysis is to combine the cash amounts used for normal operations with the cash transactions that apply to nonoperating activities. Figure 5.14 provides this summary.

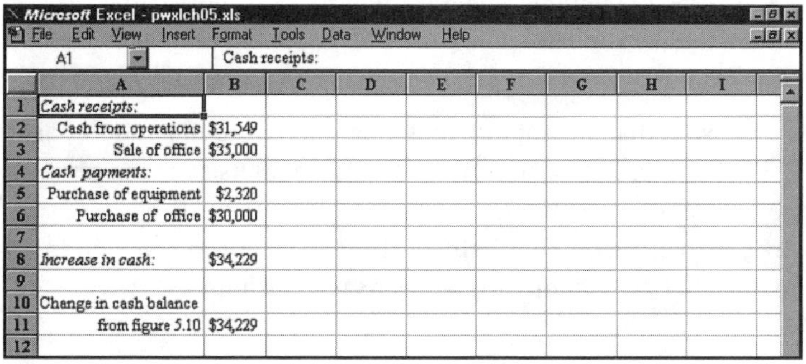

	A	B
1	*Cash receipts:*	
2	Cash from operations	$31,549
3	Sale of office	$35,000
4	*Cash payments:*	
5	Purchase of equipment	$2,320
6	Purchase of office	$30,000
7		
8	*Increase in cash:*	$34,229
9		
10	Change in cash balance	
11	from figure 5.10	$34,229
12		

Fig. 5.14
Marble Designs cash flow statement, 1/31/95–1/31/96.

Cash receipts, in this case, are comprised of cash from operations and cash received from selling the office space. Cash outlays are comprised of the purchase of the new computer and the office space. The difference between the two, $34,229, represents the amount of cash generated by Marble Designs during the twelve-month period, and should agree with the difference in the cash account between 1/31/95 and 1/31/96. Refer to figure 5.10: the difference between the ending balance of $36,783 and the beginning balance of $2,554 is $34,229, which agrees with the results of the cash flow analysis.

Remember, cash flow analysis is a much more complicated task than the relatively simple example provided here. There are many more transactions than are included in this example: the effect of taxes must be taken into account, accrued liabilities complicate the process, and such transactions as the issuance of stock, dividends, and long-term bonds affect the identification and calculation of cash flows. However, the example serves to illustrate the basic principles and the overall process of converting balance sheets and income statements into information about how a company creates and uses its cash resources.

Summary

In this chapter, you have learned how to analyze working capital, its sources and uses, to move beyond the information in the balance sheet and income statement. Working capital is an important gauge of a company's financial health, and it can be hidden by the accrual basis used by other analyses.

This chapter has also described how to analyze the flow of cash into, through, and out of a company as a result of its transactions. Because cash is the most liquid form of working capital, it is an important component of many financial ratios used by investors and potential creditors; you will learn more about these in chapter 7, "Ratio Analysis." Cash flow analysis is also an important means of understanding the difference between such items as net income and actual receipts.

Further, the ways that a company uses its working capital, and in particular its cash, is a good indicator of how well it manages its assets. It serves to highlight the choices of investments and disinvestments made every day by the company's management. Highlighted, those choices can give you insight into the way that management handles its responsibilities.

Chapter 6

Statement Analysis

Chapters 1 through 4 discussed the creation of income statements and balance sheets, and how to use them for reporting purposes. This chapter, as well as chapter 7 "Ratio Analysis," describes how you can use the information in income statements and balance sheets to improve your insight into business operations.

Neither a particular dollar amount in a financial report, nor the report itself, stands on its own. The knowledge that a company's total operating expenses during 1995 were $250,000 is not, by itself, very informative. To understand the meaning of that number, you have to know other figures such as gross profit and operating income. Similarly, although a balance sheet helps you estimate a company's current worth, it does not speak to questions such as these:

- Is the company's worth increasing or decreasing over time?

- How do the company's current assets relate to its current liabilities?

- How well does the company's management use its resources to create profit?

- How do the components of the company's assets change over time?

The processes of statement analysis and ratio analysis provide you the contexts to make judgments like these. There are close relationships between the two: *statement analysis* helps complete the picture of a company's operations and strategies, and *ratio analysis* helps fill in the details of why a company's profit is increasing or declining.

Fundamentally, statement analysis examines the relationships among all items on an income statement or a balance sheet, and how they change over time. Ratio analysis focuses on certain relationships between individual numbers on a financial report.

At its heart, statement analysis depends on *common sizing*, which converts the raw numbers to a common level of measurement.

Understanding a Report by Means of Common-sizing

To common-size a report, you typically divide every number in that report by the same number. It's conventional, for example, to common-size an income statement by dividing each entry by the total sales for the period covered by the statement. Doing so converts each dollar figure, from cost of goods sold to operating income to income taxes to operating expenses, to its percentage in terms of total sales.

Using Common-sized Income Statements

The rationale for common-sizing in terms of total sales is that most of a company's activities depend on its revenues. The more the company sells, the greater its cost of goods sold. In a well-managed firm, greater revenues result in greater profits. And, although there are exceptional cases, a higher level of sales tends to cause a higher level of salaries. Because total sales exerts an effect on so many of the items in an income statement, a common-sized statement is usually based on total sales.

Figures 6.1 and 6.2 provide an example.

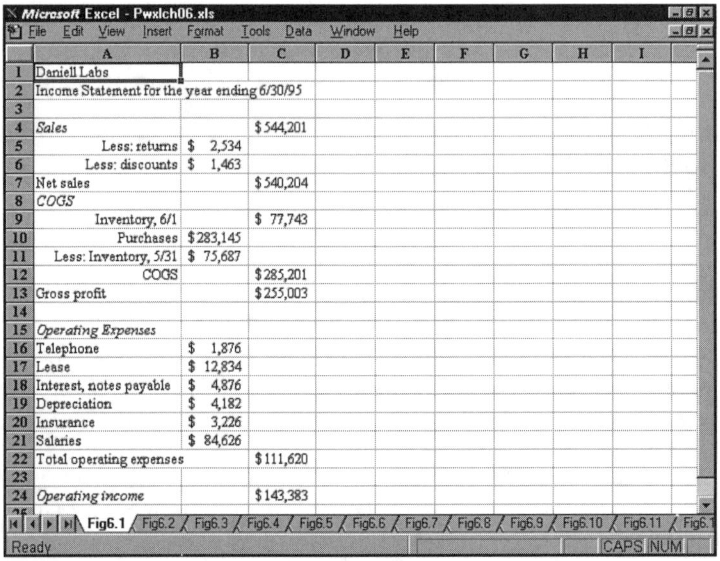

	A	B	C
1	Daniell Labs		
2	Income Statement for the year ending 6/30/95		
3			
4	*Sales*		$544,201
5	Less: returns	$ 2,534	
6	Less: discounts	$ 1,463	
7	Net sales		$540,204
8	*COGS*		
9	Inventory, 6/1		$ 77,743
10	Purchases	$283,145	
11	Less: Inventory, 5/31	$ 75,687	
12	COGS		$285,201
13	Gross profit		$255,003
14			
15	*Operating Expenses*		
16	Telephone	$ 1,876	
17	Lease	$ 12,834	
18	Interest, notes payable	$ 4,876	
19	Depreciation	$ 4,182	
20	Insurance	$ 3,226	
21	Salaries	$ 84,626	
22	Total operating expenses		$111,620
23			
24	*Operating income*		$143,383

Fig. 6.1
This Income Statement uses the regular dollar metric. It is not common-sized.

To convert the income statement shown in figure 6.1 to a common-sized income statement based on total sales, follow these steps:

1. Highlight the worksheet range containing the entire statement: in figure 6.1, this range is A1:C24.

2. Choose Edit, Copy.

3. Activate a new worksheet.

4. Choose Edit, Paste Special.

5. In the Paste Special dialog box, click Values in the Paste group box, and choose OK. This converts any formulas in the original income statement to values in the new worksheet.

6. Switch back to the original income statement. Highlight the cell that contains the value of total sales. In figure 6.1, this is cell C4.

7. Choose Edit, Copy. and switch back to the new worksheet.

8. Highlight the worksheet range containing the numbers in the entire statement; in figure 6.2, this range is B1:C24.

9. Choose Edit, Paste Special.

10. In the Paste Special dialog box, click Divide in the Operation group box, and choose OK. This divides all the values in the range by the value of the copied cell, Total Sales.

11. While the full range is still highlighted, choose Cells from the Format menu. In the Format Cells dialog box, click the Number tab. Select Percentage in the Category list box, adjust the number of Decimal Places, and choose OK.

Tip

You might want to clear any cells in the range B1:C24 that now contain zero values. (The Skip Blanks option in the Paste Special dialog box refers to blanks in the range you are copying from, not in the range to which you copy.) Or, and better, you can select Tools, Options, choose the View tab, and clear the Zero Values checkbox.

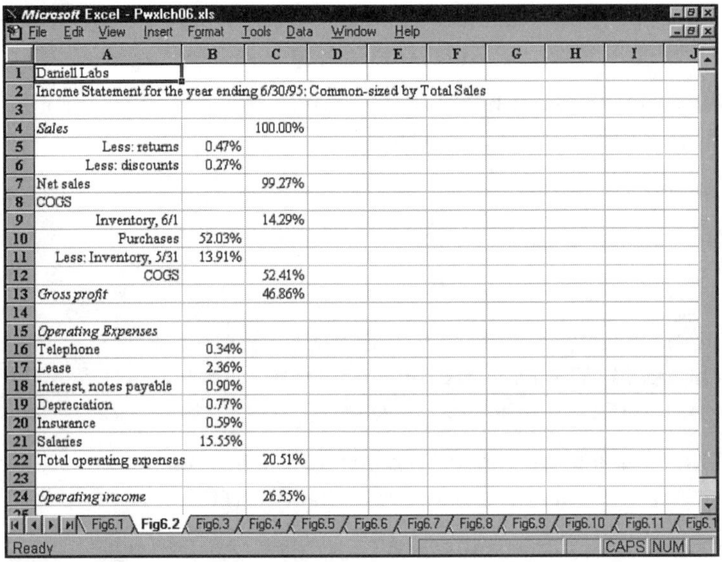

Fig. 6.2

This Income
Statement has
been common-
sized on the basis
of Total Sales.

	A	B	C	D	E	F	G	H	I	J
1	Daniell Labs									
2	Income Statement for the year ending 6/30/95: Common-sized by Total Sales									
3										
4	Sales		100.00%							
5	Less: returns	0.47%								
6	Less: discounts	0.27%								
7	Net sales		99.27%							
8	COGS									
9	Inventory, 6/1		14.29%							
10	Purchases	52.03%								
11	Less: Inventory, 5/31	13.91%								
12	COGS		52.41%							
13	Gross profit		46.86%							
14										
15	Operating Expenses									
16	Telephone	0.34%								
17	Lease	2.36%								
18	Interest, notes payable	0.90%								
19	Depreciation	0.77%								
20	Insurance	0.59%								
21	Salaries	15.55%								
22	Total operating expenses		20.51%							
23										
24	Operating income		26.35%							

Microsoft Excel - Pwxlch06.xls

File Edit View Insert Format Tools Data Window Help

Fig6.1 | **Fig6.2** | Fig6.3 | Fig6.4 | Fig6.5 | Fig6.6 | Fig6.7 | Fig6.8 | Fig6.9 | Fig6.10 | Fig6.11 | Fig6.1

Ready   CAPS NUM

> **Note**
>
> The reason that step 5 recommexnds that you convert formulas on the income
> statement to values is that the subsequent Divide operation in step 10 does not work
> as intended (here) on a formula. For example, cell C7 in figure 6.1 contains this
> formula:
>
>   =C4-B5-B6
>
> If you copied this formula, and subsequently divided it by Total Sales, this formula
> would result:
>
>   =(C4-B5-B6)/544201
>
> Because cells C4, B5, and B6 now contain percentages, this formula would return
> 0.00%, instead of the desired value of 99.27%.

Notice that, while the common-sized income statement in figure 6.2 does not
add any information to the raw dollar income statement, it makes it a little
easier to answer some questions. For example, it's easy to see that the greatest
cost incurred by Daniell Labs is its cost of goods sold (COGS). Although it's
by no means unusual to find that COGS are around 50 percent of total sales,
this alerts you that COGS is a good candidate for management attention in
the search for greater profits.

Furthermore, if you have developed a feel for what a percentage of total sales *should* be in your business, the common-sized income statement makes it very easy to identify categories of income and expenses that are out of line.

Using Common-sized Balance Sheets

You can do the same sort of analysis using a balance sheet. Figure 6.3 shows Daniell Labs' balance sheet, in both raw dollar format and common-sized by Total Assets.

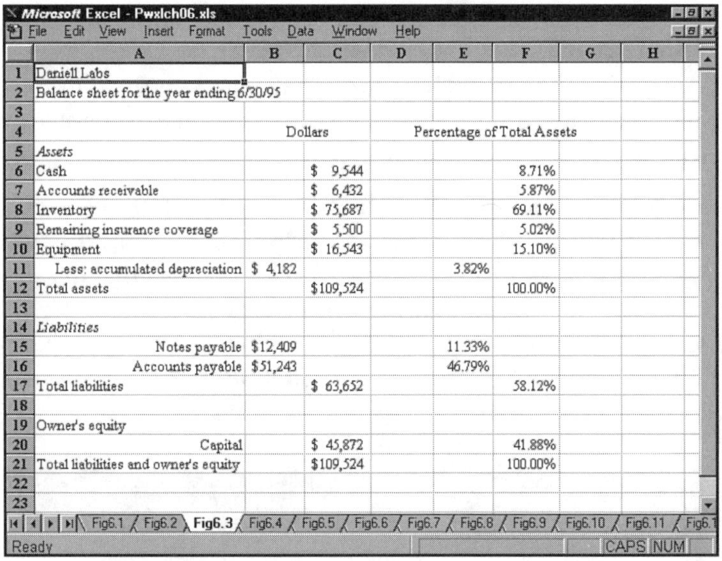

	A	B	C	D	E	F
1	Daniell Labs					
2	Balance sheet for the year ending 6/30/95					
3						
4		Dollars		Percentage of Total Assets		
5	*Assets*					
6	Cash		$ 9,544			8.71%
7	Accounts receivable		$ 6,432			5.87%
8	Inventory		$ 75,687			69.11%
9	Remaining insurance coverage		$ 5,500			5.02%
10	Equipment		$ 16,543			15.10%
11	Less: accumulated depreciation	$ 4,182			3.82%	
12	Total assets		$109,524			100.00%
13						
14	*Liabilities*					
15	Notes payable	$12,409			11.33%	
16	Accounts payable	$51,243			46.79%	
17	Total liabilities		$ 63,652			58.12%
18						
19	Owner's equity					
20	Capital		$ 45,872			41.88%
21	Total liabilities and owner's equity		$109,524			100.00%

Fig. 6.3
Balance sheets, as well as income statements, can be more informative when they have been common-sized.

Again, the use of component percentages in the common-sized balance sheet begins to answer some questions about how the company does business. You can immediately determine the relative importance of various assets and liabilities.

For example, figure 6.3 immediately makes it clear that a very large percentage, over 69%, of the company's assets are in its inventory. This knowledge would probably cause you to focus on the firm's inventory management procedures. In a case like this, when you begin to analyze specific ratios (see chapter 7, "Ratio Analysis"), you might well begin with a careful look at the firm's inventory turns ratios.

The situation would, of course, be very different if Daniell Labs' inventory represented only 40% of its total assets. The point is that by looking at the component percentages in a common-sized financial report you can direct your attention immediately to sources of existing and impending problems.

Examining a common-sized balance sheet often gives you insight into a company's procedures for raising capital. By comparing the component percentages for short-term liabilities such as Accounts Payable, long-term liabilities such as Notes Payable, and Retained Earnings, you can determine how the company focuses its efforts to obtain resources. A relatively large component percentage for long-term Notes Payable, for example, would indicate a reliance on debt financing. On the other hand, a relatively large component percentage for Retained Earnings would suggest that a company relies on operating income to provide its resources.

Using Comparative Financial Statements

The advantages of using common sizing become more apparent in comparative financial statements. Such statements display results side-by-side over time. Figure 6.4 shows a comparative income statement for Daniell Labs.

In figure 6.4, the annual income statement for 1994 appears in columns B and C, and for 1995 in columns D and E. Focusing only on the firm's ending inventory dollar amounts (cells B11 and D11), you can tell that the amount of inventory has increased from the end of 1994 to the end of 1995. Initially, this tends to confirm your suspicion (from viewing the common-sized balance sheet) that Daniell Labs needs to tighten its inventory management procedures.

Fig. 6.4 Comparative income statements, especially when common-sized, make it easier to assess year-to-year performance.

Microsoft Excel - Pwxlch06.xls

	A	B	C	D	E	F	G	H	I
1	Daniell Labs Comparative Income Statements								
2			Raw Dollars				Common Size (Total Sales)		
3		1994		1995		1994		1995	
4	*Sales*		$544,201		$583,478		100.00%		100.00%
5	Less: returns	$ 2,534		$ 2,663		0.47%		0.46%	
6	Less: discounts	$ 1,463		$ 1,588		0.27%		0.27%	
7	Net sales		$540,204		$579,227		99.27%		99.27%
8	*COGS*								
9	Inventory, 6/1		$ 77,743		$ 75,687		14.29%		12.97%
10	Purchases	$283,145		$287,896		52.03%		49.34%	
11	Less: Inventory, 5/31	$ 75,687		$ 77,589		13.91%		13.30%	
12	COGS		$285,201		$285,994		52.41%		49.02%
13	Gross profit		$255,003		$293,233		46.86%		50.26%
14									
15	*Operating Expenses*								
16	Telephone	$ 1,876		$ 1,954		0.34%		0.33%	
17	Lease	$ 12,834		$ 12,834		2.36%		2.20%	
18	Interest, notes payable	$ 4,876		$ 4,876		0.90%		0.84%	
19	Depreciation	$ 4,182		$ 4,182		0.77%		0.72%	
20	Insurance	$ 3,226		$ 3,226		0.59%		0.55%	
21	Salaries	$ 84,626		$ 87,925		15.55%		15.07%	
22	Total operating expenses		$111,620	$114,997		20.51%		19.71%	
23									
24	*Operating income*		$143,383		$178,236		26.35%		30.55%

Raw dollars

Common-sized by sales

However, the common-sized income statements in columns F through I present a somewhat different picture. At the end of 1994, inventory amounted to 13.9% of total sales, whereas at the end of 1995 it amounts to 13.3% of total sales. Although you might not regard 0.6% as a sizable difference, at least the ending inventory levels are moving in the right direction, *when viewed in terms of total sales*. As sales increase (as they do from 1994 to 1995), you normally expect that inventory levels will increase, because management must allow for more contingencies in customers' requirements. Figure 6.4, however, shows that—relative to total sales—inventory levels decreased from 1994 to 1995. Inventory might still require further management attention, but there is some evidence that management has been taking steps to bring it under control.

Figure 6.4 also makes it apparent that Daniell Labs has been managing its profit levels more efficiently in 1995 than in 1994. Notice (cells G12 and I12) that as component percentages the cost of goods sold decreased during the two-year period, even though the raw dollar amounts increased slightly (compare cell C12 with cell E12). The decrease in the COGS percentage occurs because, although the dollars spent were virtually identical, the amount of total sales increased. This finding points to one of two conclusions: either Daniell Labs has increased its unit sales price while holding its unit COGS constant, or it has obtained more favorable pricing from its suppliers (thus, its unit sales price could remain constant while its unit COGS decreases).

This effect also shows up in the company's gross profit margins (cells G13 and I13), which increase by 3.4% from 1994 to 1995. Nearly the entire increase can be attributed to the change in the COGS percentage. And the greater gross profit margin flows down to the company's operating income, which increases by roughly 4% from 1994 to 1995.

The difference between the growth in the gross profit margin and the growth in operating income is due to the fact that, as component percentages, operating expenses dropped while total sales increased. This effect emphasizes the importance of examining *both* the raw dollar statements *and* the common-sized statements. Even though operating expenses, measured as component percentages, drops from 1994 to 1995, the actual dollar amount expended increases during the same time period.

This would not be clear if you looked only at the common-sized statements. By examining the raw dollar statements as well, you can tell what happened to the basis (total sales) of the component percentages. Doing so helps you better understand the context in which changes over time occur.

On the basis of the comparative income statements, you might conclude that business is proceeding satisfactorily for Daniell Labs. Figure 6.5, however, presents a somewhat different picture.

Fig. 6.5

Daniell Labs Comparative Balance Sheets for 1994 and 1995 show some erosion in the company's worth.

		B	C	D	E	F	G	H	I
1	Daniell Labs Comparative Balance Sheets								
2				Raw Dollars			Common Size (Total Assets)		
3			1994		1995		1994		1995
4			6/30/94		6/30/95		6/30/94		6/30/95
5	*Assets*								
6	Cash		$ 9,544		$ 8,692		9%		8%
7	Accounts receivable		$ 6,432		$ 5,211		6%		5%
8	Inventory		$ 75,687		$ 77,589		69%		76%
9	Remaining insurance coverage		$ 5,500		$ 2,750		5%		3%
10	Equipment		$ 16,543		$ 16,543		15%		16%
11	Less: accumulated depreciation	$ 4,182		$ 8,364		4%		8%	
12	Total assets		$ 109,524		$ 102,421		100%		100%
13									
14	*Liabilities*								
15	Notes payable	$ 12,409		$ 6,733		11%		7%	
16	Accounts payable	$ 51,243		$ 58,946		47%		58%	
17	Total liabilities		$ 63,652		$ 65,679		58%		64%
18									
19	Owner's equity								
20	Capital		$ 45,872		$ 36,742		42%		36%
21	Total liabilities and owner's equity		$ 109,524		$ 102,421		100%		100%
22									
23									

From 1994 to 1995, Total Assets are declining, as is its Owner's Equity. At the same time, Accounts Payable is increasing. Two assets, Equipment and Remaining Insurance, are declining due to depreciation and the expiration of one year of prepaid insurance. These effects show up in both the raw dollar figures and in the common-sized balance sheet.

Particularly in view of the fact that operating income increased during the same period (refer to fig. 6.4), you should conclude that a working capital and cash flow analysis of the sort described in chapter 5 is in order, so as to determine the uses that Daniell Labs made of its assets during 1995.

Using Dollar and Percent Changes in Statement Analysis

Another way of viewing changes over time in income statements and balance sheets is by means of dollar changes and percentage changes (see fig. 6.6).

It's always satisfying for an owner to view changes in dollar amounts such as those shown in Cash and Accounts Receivable from 1993 to 1994. Column H, which contains the difference in each classification from the end of the first year to the end of the second, shows that the company's assets increased dramatically during that period.

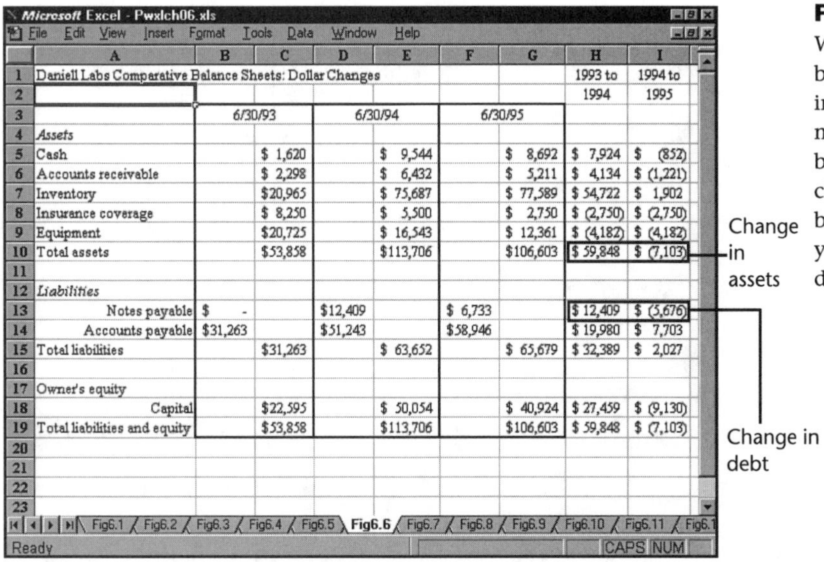

	A	B	C	D	E	F	G	H	I
1	Daniell Labs Comparative Balance Sheets: Dollar Changes							1993 to	1994 to
2								1994	1995
3		6/30/93		6/30/94		6/30/95			
4	*Assets*								
5	Cash		$ 1,620		$ 9,544		$ 8,692	$ 7,924	$ (852)
6	Accounts receivable		$ 2,298		$ 6,432		$ 5,211	$ 4,134	$ (1,221)
7	Inventory		$20,965		$ 75,687		$ 77,589	$ 54,722	$ 1,902
8	Insurance coverage		$ 8,250		$ 5,500		$ 2,750	$ (2,750)	$ (2,750)
9	Equipment		$20,725		$ 16,543		$ 12,361	$ (4,182)	$ (4,182)
10	Total assets		$53,858		$113,706		$106,603	$ 59,848	$ (7,103)
11									
12	*Liabilities*								
13	Notes payable	$ -		$12,409		$ 6,733		$ 12,409	$ (5,676)
14	Accounts payable	$31,263		$51,243		$58,946		$ 19,980	$ 7,703
15	Total liabilities		$31,263		$ 63,652		$ 65,679	$ 32,389	$ 2,027
16									
17	Owner's equity								
18	Capital		$22,595		$ 50,054		$ 40,924	$ 27,459	$ (9,130)
19	Total liabilities and equity		$53,858		$113,706		$106,603	$ 59,848	$ (7,103)
20									
21									
22									
23									

Fig. 6.6
With comparative balance sheets and income statements, you can better focus on changes over time by calculating year-to-year differences.

It is true that a major portion of the increase in assets was paid for by means of the acquisition of debt (Notes Payable and Accounts Payable), but it is also true that the amount of the increase in Total Assets is larger than the increase in debt.

Furthermore, including information about 1993 helps to put the changes from 1994 to 1995 (refer to fig. 6.5) in perspective. Viewed in the context of the large increases in assets and equity that occurred in 1994, the decreases in assets and increases in liabilities that occurred in 1995 (see column I of fig. 6.6) do not appear as threatening.

But a better understanding yet of Daniell Labs' business operations is available from an examination of percentage changes (see fig. 6.7).

In figure 6.7, the year-to-year changes in each statement classification are shown as percents, rather than as dollar amounts, in columns H and I. The percents are *not* simple ratios, such as Total Assets for 1994 divided by Total Assets for 1993. Instead, they are the difference between a comparison year's amount and a base year's amount, divided by the base year's amount.
For example, the formula in cell H5 of figure 6.7 is:

```
=(E5-C5)/C5
```

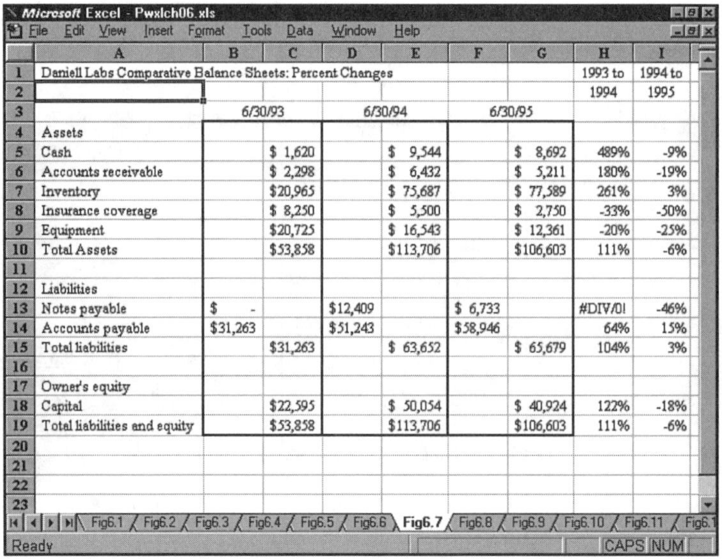

	A	B	C	D	E	F	G	H	I
1	Daniell Labs Comparative Balance Sheets: Percent Changes							1993 to 1994	1994 to 1995
2									
3		6/30/93		6/30/94		6/30/95			
4	Assets								
5	Cash		$ 1,620		$ 9,544		$ 8,692	489%	-9%
6	Accounts receivable		$ 2,298		$ 6,432		$ 5,211	180%	-19%
7	Inventory		$20,965		$ 75,687		$ 77,589	261%	3%
8	Insurance coverage		$ 8,250		$ 5,500		$ 2,750	-33%	-50%
9	Equipment		$20,725		$ 16,543		$ 12,361	-20%	-25%
10	Total Assets		$53,858		$113,706		$106,603	111%	-6%
11									
12	Liabilities								
13	Notes payable	$ -		$12,409		$ 6,733		#DIV/0!	-46%
14	Accounts payable	$31,263		$51,243		$58,946		64%	15%
15	Total liabilities		$31,263		$ 63,652		$ 65,679	104%	3%
16									
17	Owner's equity								
18	Capital		$22,595		$ 50,054		$ 40,924	122%	-18%
19	Total liabilities and equity		$53,858		$113,706		$106,603	111%	-6%

Fig. 6.7
You can obtain further perspective on changes in financial position by means of ratios that represent percentage of change.

This represents the difference between 1994's Cash account and 1993's Cash account, expressed as a percentage of 1993's Cash account.

Notice that each year's balance sheet information occupies two columns, while the information on percentage changes occupies one column for each pair of years. This means that once you have entered this formula:

```
=(E5-C5)/C5
```

in cell H5, you cannot simply copy and paste it into cell I5 to get the analogous percentage change from 1994 to 1995. If you did so, the relative references in the formula would show up in I5 as:

```
=(F5-D5)/D5
```

and would return the Excel error value #DIV/0!, because cell D5 is empty.

Tip

To overcome this relative referencing problem, copy the formula to the cell that will adjust the references properly. In this case, you could copy cell H5 to cell J5, so that the references would adjust to:

```
=(G5-E5)/E5
```

Then, use either Edit, Cut and Edit, Paste or use your mouse pointer to drag-and-drop the formula in J5 back into I5. Neither of these operations is sensitive to relative references in the way that either Edit, Copy and Edit, Paste or autofill is. Basically, this is a matter of first using Copy to adjust the references properly, and then using Cut to adjust the formula's location.

Also in figure 6.7, notice the Excel error value #DIV/0! in cell H13. Its formula is:

```
=(D13-B13)/B13
```

Because cell B13 is a zero value (there is no amount for Notes Payable in 1993), the formula results in an error due to the attempt to divide by zero. You can avoid this type of error by means of Excel's IF statement. For example, the formula you enter in H13 might be:

```
=IF(B13<>0,(D13-B13)/B13,"")
```

This formula would cause Excel to examine the value in cell B13. If it does not equal zero, the cell would display the appropriate percentage change. If B13 does equal zero, the cell would display nothing, as indicated by the null string defined by the pair of empty quotation marks.

Back to the discussion of the perspective that percentage changes can provide. Notice that in cells H9 and I9 of figure 6.6, the raw dollar changes from year to year are constant. This is because Daniell Labs is using straight-line depreciation on its equipment, and this method results in a constant depreciation figure from period to period. Therefore, the book value of the firm's equipment declines by a constant $4,182 during each year. (See chapter 16 for a full discussion of depreciation methods in Excel.)

However, cells H9 and I9 of figure 6.7 show that the decrease in the value of the equipment is accelerating from year to year, from a loss of 20% during 1993–1994 to a loss of 25% during 1994–1995. The reason for this, of course, is that each percentage difference uses a different base. As the size of that base decreases from 1993 to 1994, the formula's denominator decreases, and the size of the ratio increases.

In this case, the difference between a loss in value of –20% to –25% is not too large, especially considering the associated, and rather small, raw dollar differences. If you were to observe a very large decrease in equipment valuation, you might want to check into the depreciation methods being used. The company might employ a very aggressive, accelerated depreciation method, which would tend to reduce its taxable income markedly while the equipment was still fairly new.

Alternatively, such a decrease in equipment valuation might suggest that the company has sold or written off a significant portion of its equipment. Did it do so in the normal course of operations, because the equipment had become obsolete? In that case, was the equipment replaced? At a lower cost? Or did the company sell the equipment to raise needed cash?

Examining period-to-period changes in balance sheets and income statements, measured both in dollar amounts and as percentage changes, can provide you with useful information about how a company is going about the management of its operations and financial position.

Common-sizing for Variance Analysis

The term *variance analysis*, in the context of finance and accounting, means the examination of differences between one statement and another. For example, if your company's actual total salaries during the first quarter differ from its budgeted first quarter salaries, there is a variance between the budget and the actual results.

Common-sizing can help you do variance analysis more quickly and easily. Speed and facility in variance analysis are particularly important, because companies spend an enormous amount of time and effort examining the differences between their plans and their actual results and between prior and current results. Consider the following case study on New Way Tours, a travel agency.

Case Study: New Way Tours

New Way Tours is a small business with five employees, two of whom work part-time. It specializes in planning and arranging for ski vacations. Therefore, its business is highly seasonal, with the majority of its revenues occurring during the winter months.

New Way's owner, Gena Anderson, has prepared an operating budget for 1996, based on past information about revenues and operating expenses during the most recent five-year period (see fig. 6.8).

Figure 6.8 shows, for each month in 1996, Anderson's anticipated gross profit (its revenues less its sales discounts and any purchases subsequently canceled by its customers) based on average monthly results from 1991 through 1995.

Figure 6.8 also shows the operating expenses (abbreviated "OPEX" in cells A11 and A24) for each month. The major operating expense is Salaries, which is higher during the winter than during the summer and varies due to the variable number of hours worked by her two part-time employees. Payroll tax dollars vary with the monthly salaries. The cost of New Way's lease and insurance are expected to be constant throughout the year. Telephone expenses and office supplies are difficult to estimate on a monthly basis, and in any event are small enough in relation to gross profit that making a constant monthly estimate is a reasonable approach.

	A	B	C	D	E	F	G	H	I	J	K	L	M
1		Jan	Feb	Mar	Apr	May	Jun	Jul	Aug	Sep	Oct	Nov	Dec
2	Gross profit	$42,589	$53,765	$38,846	$15,214	$20,512	$21,213	$20,674	$12,698	$11,854	$12,779	$55,155	$52,702
3													
4	Salaries	$20,000	$20,000	$20,000	$17,500	$17,500	$17,500	$17,500	$17,500	$17,500	$17,500	$20,000	$20,000
5	Payroll taxes	$2,240	$2,240	$2,240	$1,960	$1,960	$1,960	$1,960	$1,960	$1,960	$1,960	$2,240	$2,240
6	Lease	$1,000	$1,000	$1,000	$1,000	$1,000	$1,000	$1,000	$1,000	$1,000	$1,000	$1,000	$1,000
7	Phone	$500	$500	$500	$500	$500	$500	$500	$500	$500	$500	$500	$500
8	Supplies	$200	$200	$200	$200	$200	$200	$200	$200	$200	$200	$200	$200
9	Insurance	$500	$500	$500	$500	$500	$500	$500	$500	$500	$500	$500	$500
10													
11	Total OPEX	$24,440	$24,440	$24,440	$21,660	$21,660	$21,660	$21,660	$21,660	$21,660	$21,660	$24,440	$24,440
12													
13	EBITDA	$18,149	$29,325	$14,406	($6,446)	($1,148)	($447)	($986)	($8,962)	($9,806)	($8,881)	$30,715	$28,262
14													
15	Gross profit	100%	100%	100%	100%	100%	100%	100%	100%	100%	100%	100%	100%
16													
17	Salaries	47%	37%	51%	115%	85%	82%	85%	138%	148%	137%	36%	38%
18	Payroll taxes	5%	4%	6%	13%	10%	9%	9%	15%	17%	15%	4%	4%
19	Lease	2%	2%	3%	7%	5%	5%	5%	8%	8%	8%	2%	2%
20	Phone	1%	1%	1%	3%	2%	2%	2%	4%	4%	4%	1%	1%
21	Supplies	0%	0%	1%	1%	1%	1%	1%	2%	2%	2%	0%	0%
22	Insurance	1%	1%	1%	3%	2%	2%	2%	4%	4%	4%	1%	1%
23													
24	Total OPEX	57%	45%	63%	142%	106%	102%	105%	171%	183%	169%	44%	46%
25													
26	EBITDA	43%	55%	37%	-42%	-6%	-2%	-5%	-71%	-83%	-69%	56%	54%

Fig. 6.8
New Way Tours operating budget for 1996.

Row 11 shows the total of the monthly operating expenses, and row 13 shows the anticipated Earnings Before Interest, Taxes, Depreciation, and Amortization (EBITDA).

Rows 15 through 26 show the budget, common-sized by Gross Profit: each entry in B15:M26 is the classification's percentage of that month's Gross Profit. Anderson can make some use of this common-sized information in isolation. For example, as noted previously, most of New Way's business occurs during the winter, and Anderson expects to lose money during the summer months. This expectation is reflected in the fact that, from April through October, the total budgeted operating expenses are greater than 100% of gross profit. Anderson has made the business decision that it is more important to keep three experienced employees year around than to reduce the staff further during her business's off months.

But it is the process of comparing the budgeted information with the actual results that helps to bring matters into focus (see fig. 6.9).

Figure 6.9 shows New Way Tours' actual financial results for the first two quarters of 1996. The budgeted, monthly EBITDA from figure 6.8 is shown as well. January has been a disastrous month. Besides a gross profit that is nearly $10,000 less than projected in the budget, Anderson has paid over $7,500 more in salaries than budgeted, in a failed attempt to increase revenues for the month. February is better, but the subsequent four months continue the pattern that began in January.

Fig. 6.9
New Way Tours actual financial results for 1996 are much worse than its budget anticipated.

Microsoft Excel - Pwxlch06.xls

	A	B	C	D	E	F	G
1		Jan	Feb	Mar	Apr	May	Jun
2	Gross profit	$32,845	$46,208	$21,710	$12,607	$18,938	$18,268
3							
4	Salaries	$27,520	$22,701	$25,984	$22,618	$16,761	$16,783
5	Payroll taxes	$3,082	$2,542	$2,910	$2,533	$1,877	$1,880
6	Lease	$1,000	$1,000	$1,000	$1,000	$1,000	$1,000
7	Phone	$562	$737	$608	$678	$486	$259
8	Supplies	$142	$263	$132	$299	$106	$158
9	Insurance	$500	$500	$500	$500	$500	$500
10							
11	Total OPEX	$32,807	$27,743	$31,134	$27,629	$20,730	$20,580
12							
13	EBITDA: Actual	$38	$18,465	($9,424)	($15,022)	($1,793)	($2,312)
14	EBITDA: Plan	$18,149	$29,325	$14,406	($6,446)	($1,148)	($447)
15							
16	Gross profit	100%	100%	100%	100%	100%	100%
17							
18	Salaries	84%	49%	120%	179%	89%	92%
19	Payroll taxes	9%	6%	13%	20%	10%	10%
20	Lease	3%	2%	5%	8%	5%	5%
21	Phone	2%	2%	3%	5%	3%	1%
22	Supplies	0%	1%	1%	2%	1%	1%
23	Insurance	2%	1%	2%	4%	3%	3%
24							
25	Total OPEX	100%	60%	143%	219%	109%	113%
26							
27	EBITDA: Actual	0%	40%	-43%	-119%	-9%	-13%
28	EBITDA: Plan	43%	55%	37%	-42%	-6%	-2%

Fig6.1 / Fig6.2 / Fig6.3 / Fig6.4 / Fig6.5 / Fig6.6 / Fig6.7 / Fig6.8 / **Fig6.9** / Fig6.10 / Fig6.11 / Fig6.1

Anderson can easily perform this variance analysis by checking the common-sized EBITDA values in rows 27 and 28 of figure 6.9. For January through June, EBITDA as a percentage of gross profit is less than budgeted, and if business does not turn around during the second half of the year New Way Tours will lose money for the year. Anderson will either have to find a way to increase gross profits or to decrease her operating expenses. Another way to view the actuals for the first six months of 1996, in the context of the 1996 budget, is to subtract the budgeted gross profit dollars from the actual gross profit dollars; the same can be done for budgeted and actual operating expenses. Anderson can also calculate the ratio of the actual to the budgeted figures (see fig. 6.10).

Notice that for each month, the dollar differences for Gross Profit are negative, and for operating expenses they are positive (the formulas subtract the budgeted figures from the actual figures). These dollar differences help Anderson understand how much money is being lost. The ratios (actuals divided by budgeted figures) put the losses into a percentage context. For example, the actual gross profit during January is 77% of the budgeted figure, and the actual salaries paid for January is 138% of the budgeted amount.

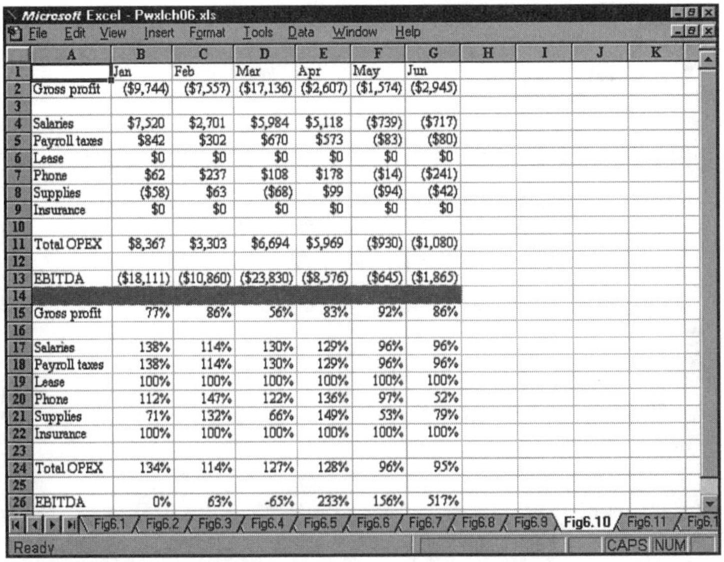

	A	B	C	D	E	F	G
1		Jan	Feb	Mar	Apr	May	Jun
2	Gross profit	($9,744)	($7,557)	($17,136)	($2,607)	($1,574)	($2,945)
3							
4	Salaries	$7,520	$2,701	$5,984	$5,118	($739)	($717)
5	Payroll taxes	$842	$302	$670	$573	($83)	($80)
6	Lease	$0	$0	$0	$0	$0	$0
7	Phone	$62	$237	$108	$178	($14)	($241)
8	Supplies	($58)	$63	($68)	$99	($94)	($42)
9	Insurance	$0	$0	$0	$0	$0	$0
10							
11	Total OPEX	$8,367	$3,303	$6,694	$5,969	($930)	($1,080)
12							
13	EBITDA	($18,111)	($10,860)	($23,830)	($8,576)	($645)	($1,865)
14							
15	Gross profit	77%	86%	56%	83%	92%	86%
16							
17	Salaries	138%	114%	130%	129%	96%	96%
18	Payroll taxes	138%	114%	130%	129%	96%	96%
19	Lease	100%	100%	100%	100%	100%	100%
20	Phone	112%	147%	122%	136%	97%	52%
21	Supplies	71%	132%	66%	149%	53%	79%
22	Insurance	100%	100%	100%	100%	100%	100%
23							
24	Total OPEX	134%	114%	127%	128%	96%	95%
25							
26	EBITDA	0%	63%	-65%	233%	156%	517%

Fig. 6.10
Variances between budgets and actual results, expressed in both dollar amounts and as ratios, often help point to problems in a company's operations.

Tip

The formulas in figure 6.10 depend heavily on references to other worksheets. When you enter this sort of formula, your fingers are usually on the keyboard instead of moving the mouse. To save time, consider using Ctrl+Page Up and Ctrl+Page Down to move between the sheets that you need to reference in your formulas.

These variance analyses, useful as they are, do not present the full picture. For example, because the gross profit varies from month to month, Anderson cannot directly compare the actual-to-budget ratios for January with the actual-to-budget ratios for February: the basis differs across months. One way to make direct comparisons is to take ratios of the ratios (see fig. 6.11).

The formula for the figure of 178% in cell B4 of figure 6.11 is:

```
=Fig6.9!B18/Fig6.8!B17
```

("Fig6.9" in the formula is the name of the sheet that contains the numerator; "Fig6.8" is the name of the sheet that contains the denominator.) The numerator of this ratio is the percentage of January's actual gross profit accounted for by January's actual salaries paid. The denominator is the percentage of January's budgeted gross profit accounted for by January's budgeted salaries. Therefore, for the month of January, the actual salary expense ratio was nearly twice the budgeted salary expense ratio.

Fig. 6.11
New Way Tours variance ratios for the first half of 1996 put the percentages on a common footing.

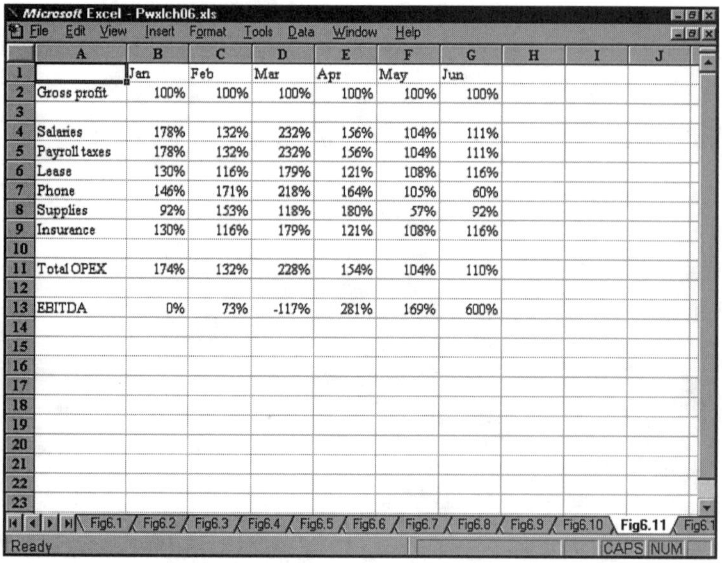

	A	B	C	D	E	F	G	H	I	J
1		Jan	Feb	Mar	Apr	May	Jun			
2	Gross profit	100%	100%	100%	100%	100%	100%			
3										
4	Salaries	178%	132%	232%	156%	104%	111%			
5	Payroll taxes	178%	132%	232%	156%	104%	111%			
6	Lease	130%	116%	179%	121%	108%	116%			
7	Phone	146%	171%	218%	164%	105%	60%			
8	Supplies	92%	153%	118%	180%	57%	92%			
9	Insurance	130%	116%	179%	121%	108%	116%			
10										
11	Total OPEX	174%	132%	228%	154%	104%	110%			
12										
13	EBITDA	0%	73%	-117%	281%	169%	600%			

This analysis places the variance for expenses into the context of the shifting gross profit figures, which are equalized by taking the ratio of the ratios. Notice that the ratio of the actual gross profit percentage to the budgeted gross profit percentage is, in each month, 100%. Thus, Anderson can tell that, regardless of the actual monthly gross profit, her firm's actual expense levels are running well ahead of its budgeted expense levels.

The case study on New Way Tours discussed one basic kind of variance analysis: actuals to budget. This sort of analysis is the one done most frequently, but there are other types of variance analysis that you can perform.

For example, you might analyze the differences between your year-to-date actuals and your current estimate. A *current estimate* is a type of budget. During the year, you revise and update your budget for the current year to take account of changes in the assumptions that you used to build your initial budget. It's useful, then, to do variance analysis on the year-to-date actuals with the current estimate.

It's also helpful to do variance analysis on year-to-date actuals with the actuals from the prior year. Yet another form of variance analysis involves a different sort of common-sizing: expressing a statement's data in terms of headcount.

Common-sizing by Headcount

Headcount, of course, refers to the number of people who are on the payroll at any given time. Particularly if you are in the midst of a downsizing or "rightsizing" situation, it is useful to common-size on the basis of headcount. Doing so does not result in the type of information shown by earlier figures in this chapter, where the basis was revenue or assets and the result was a percentage of revenue or assets. In contrast, common-sizing on the basis of headcount results in some number of dollars per employee (see fig. 6.12).

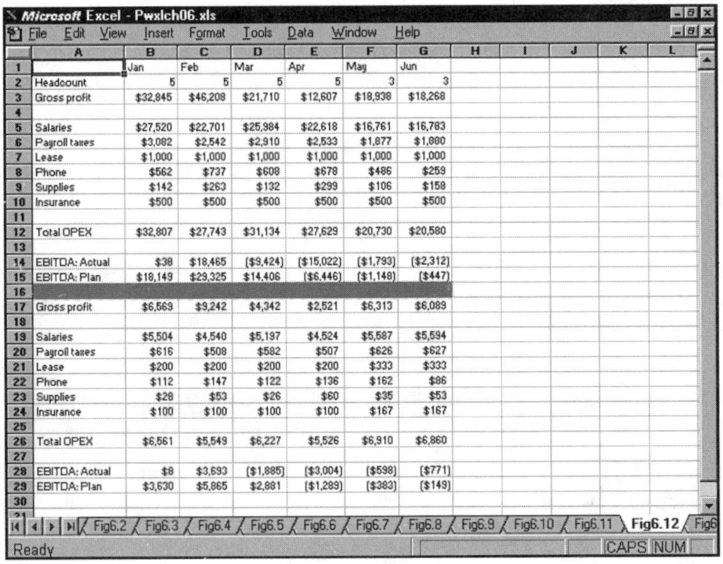

	A	B	C	D	E	F	G
1		Jan	Feb	Mar	Apr	May	Jun
2	Headcount	5	5	5	5	3	3
3	Gross profit	$32,845	$46,208	$21,710	$12,607	$18,938	$18,268
4							
5	Salaries	$27,520	$22,701	$25,984	$22,618	$16,761	$16,783
6	Payroll taxes	$3,082	$2,542	$2,910	$2,533	$1,877	$1,880
7	Lease	$1,000	$1,000	$1,000	$1,000	$1,000	$1,000
8	Phone	$562	$737	$608	$678	$486	$259
9	Supplies	$142	$263	$132	$299	$106	$158
10	Insurance	$500	$500	$500	$500	$500	$500
11							
12	Total OPEX	$32,807	$27,743	$31,134	$27,629	$20,730	$20,580
13							
14	EBITDA: Actual	$38	$18,465	($9,424)	($15,022)	($1,793)	($2,312)
15	EBITDA: Plan	$18,149	$29,325	$14,406	($6,446)	($1,148)	($447)
16							
17	Gross profit	$6,569	$9,242	$4,342	$2,521	$6,313	$6,089
18							
19	Salaries	$5,504	$4,540	$5,197	$4,524	$5,587	$5,594
20	Payroll taxes	$616	$508	$582	$507	$626	$627
21	Lease	$200	$200	$200	$200	$333	$333
22	Phone	$112	$147	$122	$136	$162	$86
23	Supplies	$28	$53	$26	$60	$35	$53
24	Insurance	$100	$100	$100	$100	$167	$167
25							
26	Total OPEX	$6,561	$5,549	$6,227	$5,526	$6,910	$6,860
27							
28	EBITDA: Actual	$8	$3,693	($1,885)	($3,004)	($598)	($771)
29	EBITDA: Plan	$3,630	$5,865	$2,881	($1,289)	($383)	($149)
30							

Fig. 6.12
New Way Tours actual results for 1996, common-sized by headcount, express operating expenses as dollars spent per employee.

Rows 17 through 29 of figure 6.12 show the actuals for January through June in rows 1 through 15, divided by the number of employees on payroll for each month (headcount, shown in row 2). This range makes it clear that the fixed expenses, such as those for the office lease and insurance, vary on a per-employee basis as the headcount changes. Other expenses, particularly salaries and payroll taxes, vary almost directly with headcount.

If gross profit and an operating income figure such as EBITDA are *not* sensitive to headcount, while such major expense classifications as salaries *are* sensitive, then there can be a compelling business reason to reduce the number of employees. For example, if New Way Tours can expect roughly the same level of revenue regardless of its headcount, Gena Anderson should give serious thought to reducing the number of employees.

Of course, doing so can have unanticipated consequences. It might be that, while increasing headcount does not increase gross profit, decreasing headcount below some minimum level results in poor customer service—which is guaranteed to reduce gross profit.

On the other hand, if headcount is directly related to gross profit, there might well be an argument for increasing headcount, particularly if the business uses some method of direct sales. The trick is to increase the number of salespeople, and hold steady the number of staff who do contribute only to expenses, not to gross profit. This process is tricky because, in most cases, the greater the gross profit, the larger the number of staff required to support after-sale processes.

Suppose, however, that Anderson believes that she can convert the responsibilities of three of her current full-time staff from both sales and staff functions to sales only. She also considers hiring one additional salesperson. She believes that if these employees are free to perform a sales role only, instead of both revenue-producing activities and support activities, each salesperson can generate an average of $13,138 per month instead of the current $6,569 per month. The remaining employees will devote 100 percent of their time to performing support activities. This scenario is shown in figure 6.13.

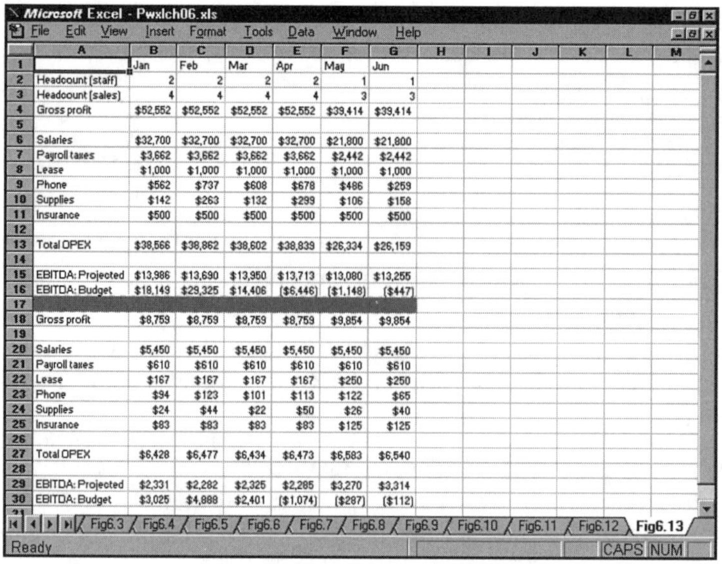

	A	B	C	D	E	F	G
1		Jan	Feb	Mar	Apr	May	Jun
2	Headcount (staff)	2	2	2	2	1	1
3	Headcount (sales)	4	4	4	4	3	3
4	Gross profit	$52,552	$52,552	$52,552	$52,552	$39,414	$39,414
5							
6	Salaries	$32,700	$32,700	$32,700	$32,700	$21,800	$21,800
7	Payroll taxes	$3,662	$3,662	$3,662	$3,662	$2,442	$2,442
8	Lease	$1,000	$1,000	$1,000	$1,000	$1,000	$1,000
9	Phone	$562	$737	$608	$678	$486	$259
10	Supplies	$142	$263	$132	$299	$106	$158
11	Insurance	$500	$500	$500	$500	$500	$500
12							
13	Total OPEX	$38,566	$38,862	$38,602	$38,839	$26,334	$26,159
14							
15	EBITDA: Projected	$13,986	$13,690	$13,950	$13,713	$13,080	$13,255
16	EBITDA: Budget	$18,149	$29,325	$14,406	($6,446)	($1,148)	($447)
17							
18	Gross profit	$8,759	$8,759	$8,759	$8,759	$9,854	$9,854
19							
20	Salaries	$5,450	$5,450	$5,450	$5,450	$5,450	$5,450
21	Payroll taxes	$610	$610	$610	$610	$610	$610
22	Lease	$167	$167	$167	$167	$250	$250
23	Phone	$94	$123	$101	$113	$122	$65
24	Supplies	$24	$44	$22	$50	$26	$40
25	Insurance	$83	$83	$83	$83	$125	$125
26							
27	Total OPEX	$6,428	$6,477	$6,434	$6,473	$6,583	$6,540
28							
29	EBITDA: Projected	$2,331	$2,282	$2,325	$2,285	$3,270	$3,314
30	EBITDA: Budget	$3,025	$4,888	$2,401	($1,074)	($287)	($112)

Fig. 6.13
New Way Tours 1996 projections common-sized by new headcount.

Anderson obtains the dollar figures for Gross Profit, in row 4 of figure 6.13, by multiplying the Sales headcount in row 3 by her assumed sales level of $13,138 per salesperson. She also assumes that her average salary per employee will be $5,450. Restated, these assumptions are:

- Both total gross profit and average gross profit are sensitive to the number of sales employees.

- Total salary expense is sensitive to the total number of employees, but average salary expense is constant.

The result, if Anderson's assumptions pay off, is that she can actually *increase* total headcount and cause New Way Tours' EBITDA to become positive, even during its traditionally money-losing summer months. The assumptions involved are optimistic—particularly the notion that making some employees full-time salespeople will double the per-employee gross profit. But even if the per-employee increase in gross profit is only 50 percent, the results would increase the profit in good months, and reduce the loss in bad months.

> **Note**
>
> This sort of headcount analysis is closely related to the concept of *leverage*, which is discussed in greater detail in chapter 14. The common ground between leverage and common-sizing on the basis of headcount is that you seek to keep certain costs constant as variable revenues increase.

In large corporations, common-size analysis on the basis of headcount is done frequently and is especially tricky. It often happens that one division reduces its headcount so as to decrease its expenses, hoping that as it does so its revenues will not suffer. It can also happen that the employees who leave that division find employment in another division of the same large corporation: usually, one that is not currently under pressure to reduce its expenses.

The net result is that, although one division might improve its profitability through a reduction in expenses, another division's profitability suffers because of an increase in expenses. Then, the corporation, considered as a whole, has probably not improved its profitability. However, it has managed to disrupt people's lives, increased levels of anxiety among those whose positions have been retained, and probably increased non-productive costs because overhead procedures usually change when people leave.

Therefore, when divisions report that they have reduced headcount and consequently increased their profitability, it is incumbent on them to estimate the effect of doing so on the corporation as a whole. Although this estimate is often a difficult task, it is a necessary ingredient of an accurate estimate of the effects of their analysis and consequent actions.

Summary

In this chapter, you have learned some of the basic techniques of statement analysis, including variance analysis and common sizing according to bases such as revenues, total assets, and headcount.

These are global techniques: that is, the results can serve to direct your attention to obstacles to your company's profitability, but they do not provide you as much specific information about problems as you might want. Chapter 7, "Ratio Analysis," discusses the particular ratios that you often want to calculate to obtain highly targeted information about your company's profitability and overall financial structure.

Chapter 7

Ratio Analysis

In earlier chapters of this book, you have learned about various indicators of a company's financial condition. Quantities and values such as current assets, inventory levels, sales, and accounts receivable all help you understand how much money a company has, how much it owes, and its profitability.

These numbers can be very informative if you happen to have intimate knowledge of the company itself. Suppose, for example, that you work for a company that today has $2 million worth of materials in its finished goods inventory. In that case, you probably know whether that's an acceptable figure; whether it's so low that the company will have difficulty delivering the products that it sells; or whether it's so high that the company might need to slow down its production rate. Because you are familiar with the company and its operations, you have a context to help interpret that $2 million figure.

But if you aren't familiar with the company, $2 million is just a number: it has no context to help you interpret it. Knowing that the company has $2 million worth of finished goods in stock tells you nothing about whether the company is doing very well, very poorly, or whether business is as usual.

However, if you also happened to know the amount of the company's current assets and current liabilities, you could quickly create a useful insight into the company's current financial situation. This formula:

```
(Current Assets - Inventory)/(Current Liabilities)
```

would tell you how liquid the company is in the short term. If the company's current assets are $4 million and its current liabilities are $1 million, the formula would return:

```
($4 million - $2 million)/($1 million) = 2
```

The company's quickly accessible assets are twice its short term liabilities: it is liquid. But if its current assets are $2.5 million, the formula would return:

```
($2.5 million - $2 million)/($1 million) = .5
```

The company's quickly accessible assets are only half its short term liabilities.

Depending on whether the value of that formula is 2 or .5, you would probably have a different attitude toward the company as a prospective employer. If the value is 2, you would be more confident that your paycheck wouldn't bounce. As a prospective stockholder, you would be more confident of receiving a dividend check if the value is 2. As the company's CEO, you would have a meeting with the production and sales managers if the value is .5, and the meeting would probably be a testy one.

Of course, the value of this ratio (which is called a *quick ratio*) does not depend solely on how well the company is managing its assets and liabilities. The ratio's value also depends on other considerations such as what business sector the company belongs to and how well that business sector is doing in the present economy. Your evaluation of the ratio's value would take these considerations into account, as well as how that ratio has behaved in the past: if the ratio has been constantly increasing, your confidence in the company's management and its financial structure would be greater than if it has been sliding for some time.

Ratios such as the quick ratio can tell you a great deal about a company's health, and relationships among ratios can help you locate sources of concern in the way a company is run. This chapter describes some of the most important ratios—those that are frequently published in financial reports and in commercially available data sources—as well as how to interpret them to determine a company's profit outlook.

Interpreting Industry Averages and Trends

Evaluating a ratio that describes a particular company in terms of the industry average for that ratio can be informative, but it can also be misleading. Consider one commonly reported indicator, the Price/Earnings (P/E) ratio.

Suppose that you know, from examining stock exchange tables in the newspaper or from some other source, that the P/E for a telephone company that serves your local area is 10. This means that stock in the company presently sells for 10 times its earnings. Perhaps you also know, by information obtained from a commercial service such as Standard & Poors, Moody's, or ValueLine, that the average P/E for the telecommunications industry is 15. At first glance, 10 looks like a good P/E, compared to the industry average: in terms of earnings, it is only two-thirds as expensive as other such stocks.

And 10 might be a good P/E ratio. However, there are various ways that this comparison can mislead you. For example, during the 1990s, the telecommunications industry is changing at least as fast and dramatically as it did during the 1980s, when the breakup of AT&T fostered the creation of many new companies, technologies, services, and products. Companies that once provided you with little more than basic telephone service have aggressively entered new fields such as data communications, wireless communications, cable TV, financial and other business services, and electronic advertising. They also have entered into partnerships with companies such as software developers and firms that provide the programming that you see on television and in theaters.

Some of these efforts will bear fruit in the form of higher earnings and some will result in losses for the firms involved. It might be that the telephone company with a P/E of 10 has refrained from investing in newer opportunities. Therefore, a larger portion of its revenues is available in the form of earnings than is the case with a telephone company that has aggressively invested in alternatives to its basic, historic revenue base. Greater earnings will tend to lower the P/E ratio.

The fact that a firm has a P/E that is lower than its industry average is not clear evidence that it is better managed than the other companies in that industry group. In fact, to continue the present example, you might find that this company is rather poorly managed if it turns out that other telephone companies do very well with their investment and partnering strategies.

The point is that industry groups are gross classifications. Just because a company is categorized in the "Telecommunications Industry" does not mean that its business strategies, product mix, and investments are directly commensurate with other companies in its category. Before you put much credence in the comparison of a financial ratio such as P/E with its industry average, you should be sure that the company is really managed and operated as are other firms in its classification.

But even if you are confident that you are comparing a ratio with an average that is derived from firms that are truly comparable, the question of accounting procedures comes into play. As was discussed in chapter 1 "Income Statements," there are ground rules that all companies must follow in computing their revenues, costs, expenses, earnings, and so on. But there is room for choices within the rules, and the rules operate differently in different cases.

For example, chapter 5 "Working Capital and Cash Flow Analysis," briefly discussed the effect that depreciation has on net income: you subtract depreciation, along with other expenses, from your gross profit to arrive at a net income figure. As you will see in chapter 16 "Fixed Assets," there is a variety of methods that you can use to compute depreciation, and these different methods usually return different figures. Different ways of figuring depreciation expense therefore result in different estimates of earnings.

You also saw, in chapter 3 "Valuing Inventories for the Balance Sheet," that there are different methods you can use to value inventories. The cost of goods sold is subtracted from sales to arrive at a figure for gross profit, and the cost of goods sold is often determined by this formula:

```
Cost of goods sold = Beginning Inventory + Inventory Purchases
    Ending Inventory
```

So, the method a firm uses to value its inventory has an effect on its gross profit, and therefore on the determination of its earnings.

In short, a financial ratio may not be commensurate among companies that are in the same line of business, because differences in accounting methods can bring about different results from computing the same ratio.

This sort of comparison of one company's ratio with that of an entire business sector is often termed *vertical* analysis. Another approach (termed, as you might expect, *horizontal* analysis) tracks financial ratios over time. Access to several years worth of information on, say, the P/E reported by a given company enables you to determine whether its P/E has been increasing, decreasing, or remaining stable.

Horizontal analysis minimizes many of the problems associated with vertical analysis. When you focus on the changes to a ratio reported by one company over time, there is less reason to be concerned about the effect of different accounting methods on the comparisons. Although a company may alter some of its methods from time to time, it is required to report any material changes in those methods. You are therefore better able to tell whether a substantial change in a financial ratio from one year to the next has been caused by a modification in accounting methods or by a change in the ways a company does business.

The major weakness of a strictly horizontal analysis is that it provides you no information about a *standard* for a given ratio. Suppose that you know that a retailer's inventory turns ratio has increased steadily from 8 per year to 10 turns per year over a five-year period. On the face of it, this is a cheery finding: the company has been moving goods through its retail outlets faster and faster over time. But if other, similar retailers average 15 turns per year, then although this company is improving it might not yet be managing its inventory as well as it should. A strictly horizontal analysis would not give you this information.

Neither a vertical nor a horizontal analysis of financial ratios is completely informative. Doing both types of analysis can be better than doing just one, and is certainly better than doing neither, but there are still ways that you can be misled by doing both. It is best if you do not regard financial ratios as absolute, objective measures of a company's performance, but rather as clues: pointers to questions that you would want to ask about a company's financial structure and business strategies.

To return to an earlier example, if a company reports a quick ratio of .8, it matters little whether the ratio has been steadily improving from .1 over a period of time. It also makes little difference that other, directly comparable companies report quick ratios that average .5. What does matter is that the company has greater current liabilities than it does current assets less inventory. Knowing this puts you in a position to ask *why* that situation exists, and the answers to that question might position you to take corrective action as a manager, or to make a more informed decision as a potential creditor or investor.

The remainder of this chapter discusses specific financial ratios: both their calculations and what questions you might ask as a result of calculating a ratio. By way of example, an income statement is shown in figures 7.1 and 7.2, and a balance sheet is shown in figures 7.3 and 7.4.

Fig. 7.1

The Income Statement for ratio analysis (Revenues and Expenses), contains information adapted from the Business Planner template.

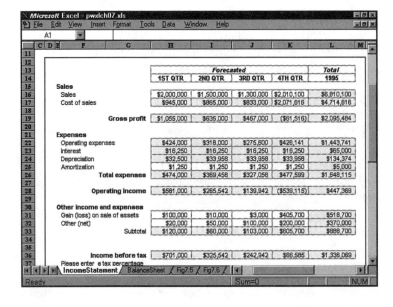

Fig. 7.2

The Income Statement data for ratio analysis (Tax, Distribution, and Supporting Information): the cost of sales plays a role in various financial ratios.

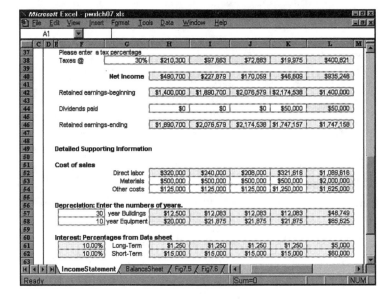

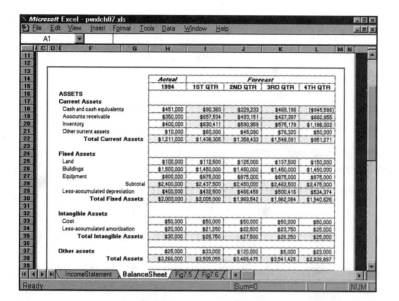

Fig. 7.3
The Balance Sheet data for ratio analysis (Assets section) are important for determining profitability ratios.

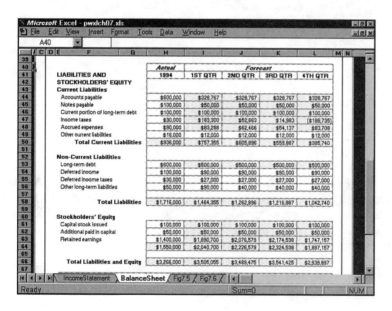

Fig. 7.4
The Balance Sheet data for ratio analysis (Liabilities and Equity section) are used to compute liquidity ratios.

Financial Statements and Statement Analysis

These figures, as well as the values that they display, are adapted from the Business Planner template that accompanies Excel 7. This template is described in detail in chapter 19 "The Business Planner." Although the Planner assumes that you will use it to forecast financial results, this chapter uses the Planner's data as though it were actual results for each of the four quarters of 1995. The data shown in figures 7.1 through 7.4 are used to compute each of the ratios discussed in the next several sections.

> **Tip**
>
> To open a new workbook based on the Business Planner, choose File, New. In the New dialog box, click the Spreadsheet Solutions tab and then choose the Business Planner template.

> **Tip**
>
> Did you note discrepancies between the data in figures 7.1 through 7.4 and the Business Planner's sample data? If so, you might want to modify the Planner's template. Early versions miscalculate the pre-tax income on the Income Statement worksheet (cells I36:K36). To correct this, copy the formula in H36 into cells I36:K36, and then re-save the template. The data in figures 7.1 through 7.4 are correct.

This chapter discusses 12 important financial ratios, listed in table 7.1. The ratios are usually thought of as belonging to four basic categories: profitability ratios, liquidity ratios, activity ratios, and leverage ratios:

Table 7.1 Ratios That Provide Insights Into a Company's Finances and Management Practices

Category	Ratio
Profitability ratios	Earnings Per Share Gross Profit Margin Net Profit Margin Return on Assets Return on Equity
Liquidity ratios	Current Ratio Quick Ratio
Activity ratios	Average Collection Period Inventory Turnover
Leverage ratios	Debt Ratio Equity Ratio Times Interest Earned

This is by no means an exhaustive list of the ratios that have been developed to help analyze a company's financial position and the way that it conducts business. It is, however, representative.

Analyzing Profitability Ratios

If you are considering investing money in a company, its profitability is a major concern. If the company intends to pay dividends to its stockholders, those dividends must come out of its profits. If the company hopes to increase its worth in the marketplace by enhancing or expanding its product line, then an important source of capital to make improvements is its profit margin. There are several different, but related, means of evaluating a company's profitability.

Finding and Evaluating Earnings Per Share

Depending on your financial objectives, you might consider investing in a company to obtain a steady return on your investment in the form of regular dividend payments, or to obtain a profit by owning the stock as the market value of its shares increases. These two objectives might both be met, but in practice they often are not. Companies frequently face a choicc of distributing income in the form of dividends, or retaining that income to invest in research, new products, and expanded operations. The hope, of course, is that the retention of income to invest in the company will subsequently increase its income, thus making the company more profitable and increasing the market value of its stock.

In either case, Earnings Per Share (EPS) is an important measure of the company's income. Its basic formula is:

```
EPS=Income available for common stock /
    Shares of common stock outstanding
```

EPS is usually a poor candidate for vertical analysis, because different companies always have different numbers of shares of stock outstanding. It *may* be a good candidate for horizontal analysis, if you have access both to information about the company's income and shares outstanding. With both these items, you can control for major fluctuations over time in shares outstanding. This sort of control is important: it is not unusual for a company to purchase its own stock on the open market to reduce the number of outstanding shares. So doing increases the value of the EPS ratio, perhaps making the stock appear a more attractive investment.

The Business Planner makes no provision for specifying the number of shares of stock outstanding, so you can assume for the purposes of these examples that there are 1,000 shares outstanding.

Tip

When you first open a workbook based on the Business Planner template, it contains almost no data. To populate the workbook, be sure that the Planner toolbar is visible, and click the Display Example/Remove Example toolbar button.

The EPS for this company at the end of each quarter in 1995 is shown in figure 7.5.

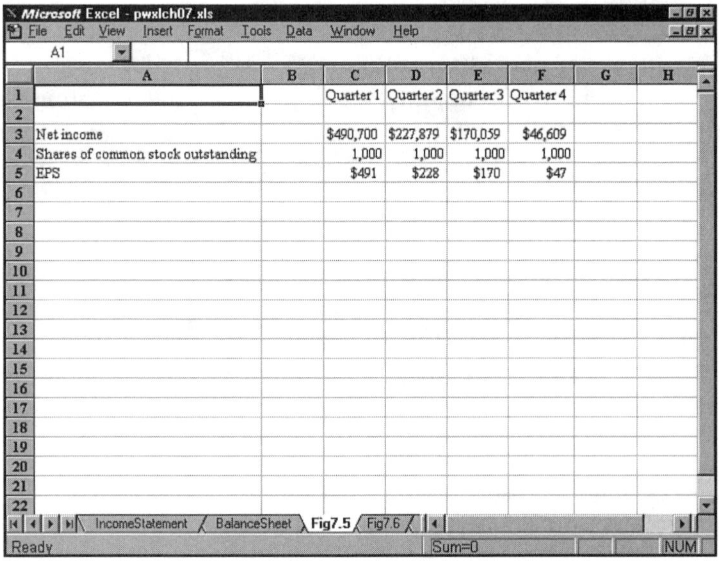

	A	B	C	D	E	F	G	H
1			Quarter 1	Quarter 2	Quarter 3	Quarter 4		
2								
3	Net income		$490,700	$227,879	$170,059	$46,609		
4	Shares of common stock outstanding		1,000	1,000	1,000	1,000		
5	EPS		$491	$228	$170	$47		

Fig. 7.5
EPS ratios during 1995 vary as net income drops.

Note that the EPS declines steadily throughout the year. Because, in this example, the number of shares outstanding is constant throughout the year, the EPS changes are due solely to changes in net income. The major impact to net income is the very small value of gross profit during the fourth quarter (see fig. 7.1, cell K19). In turn, that gross profit is due to the relatively large cost of sales during that quarter. The cost of sales is the sum of cells K52:K54 (shown in fig. 7.2).

Note that there is one very large "other" cost of $1,250,000 during the fourth quarter. As a prospective shareholder, you would want to know the reason for this cost, whether it will be recouped in the future, or whether it will repeat. Any extraordinarily large cost such as this will certainly impact the market value of the company's stock, and might well impact the company's ability to pay any dividends that you expect to receive.

Many companies issue at least two different kinds of stock: *common* and *preferred*. Preferred stock is issued under different conditions than common stock. Preferred stock is often callable at the company's discretion, it pays dividends at a different (usually, higher) rate per share, it might not carry voting privileges, and often has a higher priority than common stock as to the distribution of liquidated assets if the company goes out of business.

Calculating EPS for a company that has issued preferred stock introduces a slight complication. Because the company pays dividends on preferred stock before any distribution to shareholders of common stock, it is necessary to subtract these dividends from net income:

```
EPS= (Net Income - Preferred dividends) /
   Shares of common stock outstanding
```

Determining Gross Profit Margin

The gross profit margin is a basic ratio that measures the added value that the market places on a company's non-manufacturing activities. Its formula is:

```
Gross profit margin = (Sales - Cost of goods sold)/Sales
```

The gross profit margin using the Business Planner's data is shown in figure 7.6.

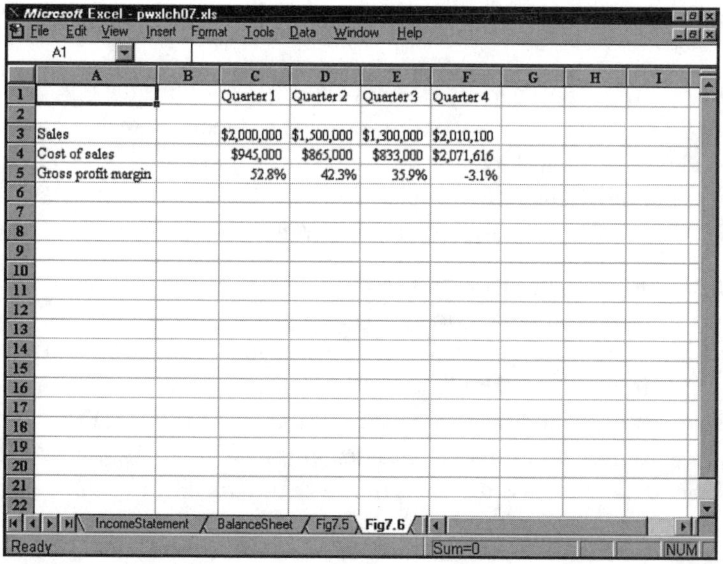

	A	B	C	D	E	F
1			Quarter 1	Quarter 2	Quarter 3	Quarter 4
2						
3	Sales		$2,000,000	$1,500,000	$1,300,000	$2,010,100
4	Cost of sales		$945,000	$865,000	$833,000	$2,071,616
5	Gross profit margin		52.8%	42.3%	35.9%	-3.1%

Fig. 7.6
The gross profit margin during the fourth quarter is negative due to the large cost of sales.

The formulas used to calculate the gross profit margins in figure 7.6 are as follows. The sales value for the first quarter, in cell C3, is returned by:

```
=IncomeStatement!1ST_QTR Sales
```

The cost of goods sold, in cell C4, is returned by:

```
=IncomeStatement!_1ST_QTR COGS
```

The range named COGS—Cost Of Goods Sold—in the Income Statement (refer to fig. 7.1) totals the Direct Labor, Materials and Other Costs (rows 52:54 in fig. 7.2). And the gross profit margin for the first quarter, in cell C5, is returned by:

```
=(C3-C4)/C3
```

Notice the use of named ranges in the formulas for cost of goods sold and for sales amounts. For example, the range named IncomeStatement!_1ST_QTR refers to cells H15:H62 on the Income Statement. The range named Sales refers to H16:L16 on the Income Statement. This fragment:

```
IncomeStatement!1ST_QTR Sales
```

uses the intersection operator, a blank character in the formula, to specify the cell where the two ranges intersect. In this case, that cell is H16, which contains the value of Sales during the first quarter. The same approach is used to obtain each quarter's value for the cost of goods sold.

The cost of goods sold is, clearly, an important component of the gross profit margin. It is usually calculated as the sum of the cost of materials the company purchases plus any labor involved in the manufacture of finished goods, plus associated overhead.

The gross profit margin depends heavily on the type of business in which a company is engaged. A service business, such as a financial services institution or a laundry, typically has little or no cost of goods sold. A manufacturing, wholesaling, or retailing company typically has a large cost of goods sold, with a gross profit margin that varies from 20 percent to 40 percent.

The gross profit margin measures the amount that customers are willing to pay for a company's product, over and above the company's cost for that product. As mentioned previously, this is the value that the company adds to that of the products it obtains from its suppliers. This margin can depend on the attractiveness of additional services, such as warranties, that the company provides. The gross profit margin also depends heavily on the ability of the sales force to persuade its customers of the value added by the company.

This added value is, of course, created by other costs such as operating expenses. In turn, these costs must be met largely by the gross profit on sales. If customers do not place sufficient value on whatever the company adds to its products, there will not be enough gross profit to pay for the associated costs. Therefore, the calculation of the gross profit margin helps to highlight the effectiveness of the company's sales strategies and sales management.

Determining Net Profit Margin

The net profit margin narrows the focus on profitability, and highlights not just the company's sales efforts, but also its ability to keep operating costs down, relative to sales. The formula generally used to determine the net profit margin is:

```
Net profit margin = Earnings after taxes / Sales
```

The net profit margin calculated from the Business Planner's data is shown in figure 7.7.

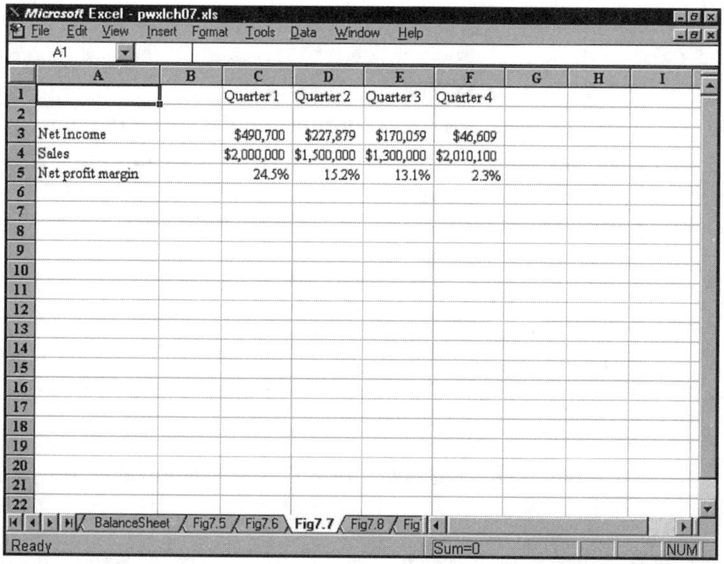

Fig. 7.7
The net profit margin, in contrast to the gross profit margin, takes expenses into account.

The earnings after taxes, in cell C3, is returned by this formula (for the first quarter):

```
=IncomeStatement!_1ST_QTR Net_income
```

As in the gross profit margin calculation, sales for the first quarter is returned in cell C4 by:

```
=IncomeStatement!_1ST_QTR Sales
```

And the quarter's net profit margin itself is returned in cell C5 by:

```
=C3/C4
```

Why does the net profit margin fall so dramatically from the first to the fourth quarters? One principal culprit is, again, the cost of sales. Notice in figure 7.2 that the materials expense is $500,000 per quarter. Even though sales fall by 25 percent from the first to the second quarter, and by 13 percent from the second to the third quarter, the company's production operations continue to consume a constant amount of materials during each quarter.

Another place to look when you see a discrepancy between gross profit margin and net profit margin is operating expenses. When the two margins covary closely, it suggests that management is doing a good job of reducing expenses when sales fall, and increasing expenses when necessary to support production and sales in better times.

Determining the Return on Assets

One of management's most important responsibilities is to bring about a profit by effective use of the resources it has at hand. One ratio that speaks to this question is return on assets. There are several ways to measure this return; one useful method is:

```
Return on assets = (Gross Profit - Operating Expense / Total assets)
```

This formula will return the percentage earnings for a company in terms of its total assets. The better the job that management does in managing its assets—the resources available to it—to bring about profits, the greater this percentage will be.

Figure 7.8 shows the return on total assets based on the Business Planner's data set.

The formula for Earnings Before Interest, Taxes, Depreciation and Amortization (EBITDA), cell C3 in figure 7.8, is:

```
=ANNUAL GrossProfit - ANNUAL OperatingExpense
```

This formula makes use of two range names that have been added to those supplied in the Business Planner: ANNUAL and OperatingExpense. ANNUAL refers to the total column in the Income Statement: column L. OperatingExpense refers to row 22 in the Income Statement. Refer to figure 7.1 to view these ranges.

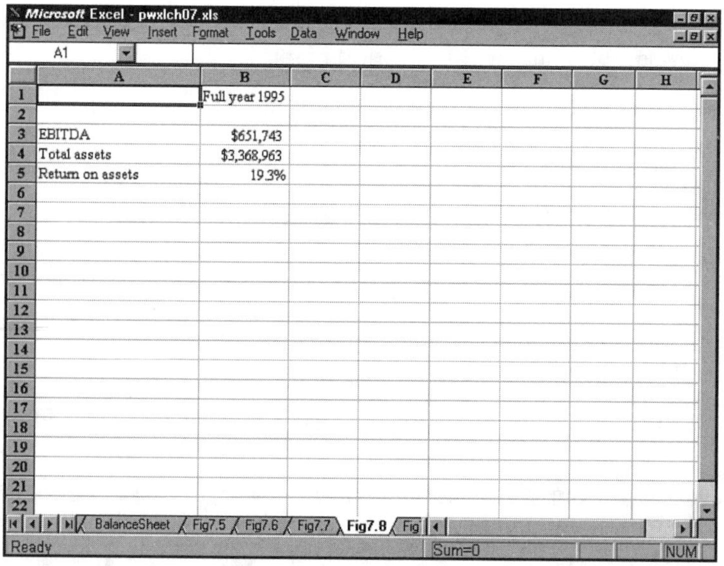

Fig. 7.8
The return on total
assets is usually
computed on an
annualized basis.

**Financial Statements
and Statement Analysis**

The formula uses the intersection operator (a blank space) between ANNUAL and GrossProfit to specify the cell where these two ranges intersect. Similarly, it uses the same operator to specify the cell where ANNUAL intersects OperatingExpense.

It's normal to calculate the return on total assets on an annual basis, rather than on a quarterly basis: therefore, the range named ANNUAL was added to the Income Statement and used to calculate the EBITDA for the full year. The total assets portion of the formula—its denominator—is usually computed by taking an average of the company's total assets for the period in question.

The formula for total assets, cell C4 in figure 7.8, is:

```
=AVERAGE(OFFSET(Total_Assets,0,1,1,4))
```

The Business Planner defines the range Total_Assets as referring to cells H38:L38 in its Balance Sheet (refer to figure 7.3). The first cell in this range, H38, contains the value of total assets for the prior year. Because this cell must be ignored when calculating the company's average quarterly total assets for the current year, Excel's OFFSET function is used.

This OFFSET specifies a range *within* Total_Assets (first argument) that is offset by 0 rows (second argument) and 1 column (third argument): that is, the offset range is right-shifted from Total_Assets by one column, so as to ignore its first cell (H38). It also specifies that the offset range is one row high (fourth argument) and 4 columns wide (fifth argument).

Finally, enclosing the OFFSET function within the AVERAGE function returns the average of the values within the offset range.

The return on total assets is calculated by means of:

```
=C3/C4
```

Determining the Return on Equity

Another, related profitability measure is the return on equity. Again, there are several ways to calculate this ratio; here, it is measured according to this formula:

```
Return on equity = Net income / Stockholder's equity
```

Figure 7.9 displays Return on Equity for the data in the Business Planner.

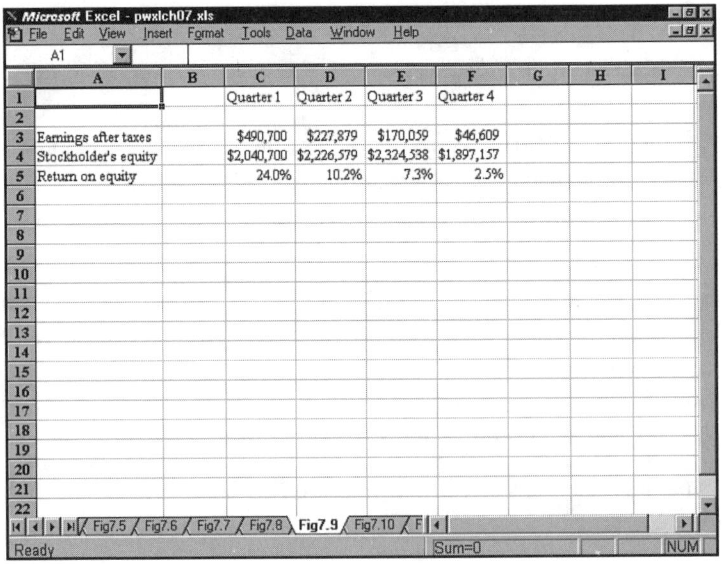

	A	B	C	D	E	F
1			Quarter 1	Quarter 2	Quarter 3	Quarter 4
2						
3	Earnings after taxes		$490,700	$227,879	$170,059	$46,609
4	Stockholder's equity		$2,040,700	$2,226,579	$2,324,538	$1,897,157
5	Return on equity		24.0%	10.2%	7.3%	2.5%

Fig. 7.9 You can compare return on equity with return on assets to infer how a company obtains the funds used to acquire assets.

The principal difference between the formula for return on assets and for return on equity is the use of equity rather than total assets in the denominator, and it is here that the technique of comparing ratios comes into play. By examining the difference between Return on Assets and Return on Equity, you can largely determine how the company is funding its operations.

Assets are acquired through two major sources: creditors (through borrowing) and stockholders (through retained earnings and capital contributions). Collectively, the retained earnings and capital contributions constitute the company's equity. When the value of the company's assets exceeds the value of its equity, you can expect that the difference is made up by some form of financial leverage: i.e., debt financing.

Therefore, if the Return on Equity ratio is much larger than the Return on Assets ratio, you can infer that the company has funded some portion of its operations through borrowing.

Analyzing Leverage Ratios

The term "leverage" means the purchase of assets with borrowed money. Chapter 14 "Planning Profits," goes into this subject in detail; for now, consider this example. Suppose that your company retails office supplies. When you receive an order for business cards, you pay one of your suppliers 50 percent of the revenue to print them for you. This is a variable cost: the more you sell, the greater your cost.

But if you purchase the necessary printing equipment, you could make the business cards yourself. So doing would turn a variable cost into a fixed cost: no matter how many cards you sell, the cost of printing them is fixed at however much you paid for the printing equipment. The more cards you sell, the greater your profit margin. This effect is termed *operating leverage*.

If you borrow money to acquire the printing equipment, you are using another type of leverage, termed *financial leverage*. The cost is still fixed at however much money you must pay, at regular intervals, to retire the loan. Again, the more cards you sell, the greater your profit margin. But if you do not sell enough cards to cover the loan payment, you could lose money. In that case, it might be difficult to find funds either to make the loan payments or to cover your other expenses. Your credit rating might fall, making it more costly for you to borrow other money.

Leverage is a financial tool that accelerates changes in income, both positive and negative. A company's creditors and investors are interested in how much leverage has been used to acquire assets. From the standpoint of creditors, a high degree of leverage represents risk because the company might not be able to repay a loan. From the investors' standpoint, if the return on assets is less than the cost of borrowing money to acquire assets, then the investment is unattractive. The investor could obtain a better return in different ways—one way would be to loan funds rather than to invest them in the company.

Two ratios that help you to measure leverage are the debt ratio and the debt-to-equity ratio.

Determining the Debt Ratio

The debt ratio is defined by this formula:

```
Debt ratio = Total debt / Total assets
```

Figure 7.10 shows the debt ratio calculated on the Business Planner's data set.

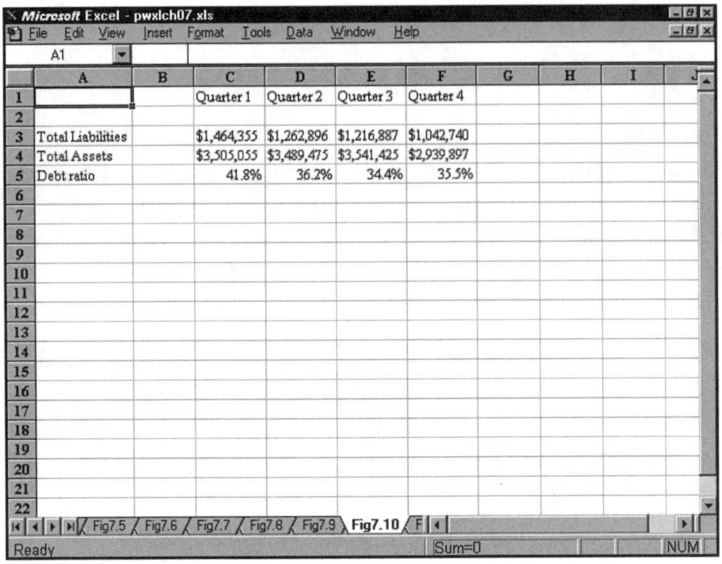

	Quarter 1	Quarter 2	Quarter 3	Quarter 4
Total Liabilities	$1,464,355	$1,262,896	$1,216,887	$1,042,740
Total Assets	$3,505,055	$3,489,475	$3,541,425	$2,939,897
Debt ratio	41.8%	36.2%	34.4%	35.5%

Fig. 7.10
The debt ratio indicates the company's use of financial leverage.

The formula used in cell C3 of figure 7.10 to return the total debt is:

```
=BalanceSheet!_1ST_QTR Total_Liabilities
```

Cell C4 of figure 7.10 returns the company's total assets for the first quarter, just as in figure 7.8, and cell C5 simply divides the total debt by the total assets.

Figure 7.8 shows that the company's return on assets falls rather sharply during the year. It is a healthy sign, then, that the company's debt ratio is also falling, although both stockholders and potential creditors would prefer to see the rate of decline in the debt ratio more closely match the decline in return on assets. As the return on assets falls, the net income available to make payments on debt also falls. This company should probably take action to retire some of its short-term debt, and the current portion of its long-term debt, as soon as possible.

Determining the Equity Ratio

The equity ratio is the opposite of the debt ratio. It is that portion of the company's assets financed by stockholders:

```
Equity ratio = Total equity / Total assets
```

In figure 7.11, the equity ratio and debt ratio in each quarter total to 100 percent. This is generally true of any enterprise: assets are acquired either through debt or through equity (investment plus retained earnings).

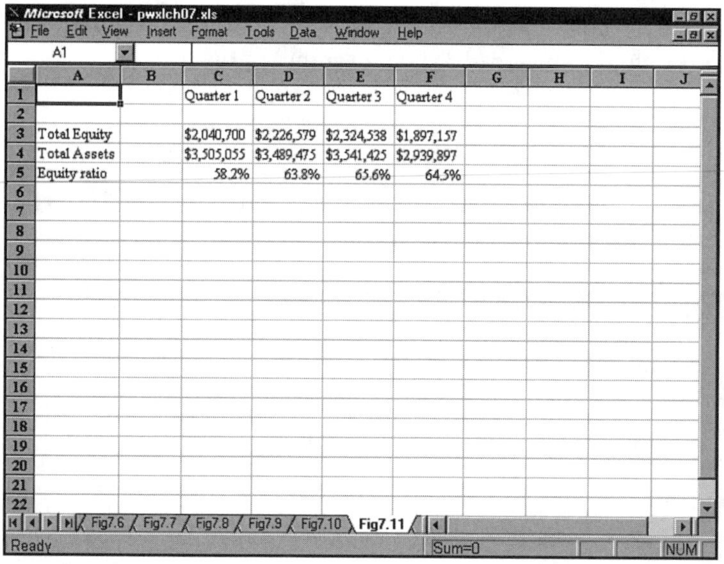

	A	B	C	D	E	F
1			Quarter 1	Quarter 2	Quarter 3	Quarter 4
2						
3	Total Equity		$2,040,700	$2,226,579	$2,324,538	$1,897,157
4	Total Assets		$3,505,055	$3,489,475	$3,541,425	$2,939,897
5	Equity ratio		58.2%	63.8%	65.6%	64.5%

Fig. 7.11
The equity ratio indicates the degree to which assets are acquired via capital contributions and retained earnings.

It is usually easier to acquire assets through debt than to acquire them through equity. There are certain obvious considerations: for example, you might need to acquire investment capital from many investors; whereas you might be able to borrow the required funds from just one creditor. Less obvious is the issue of priority.

By law, if a firm ceases operations, its creditors have the first claim on its assets to help repay the borrowed funds. Therefore, an investor's risk is somewhat higher than that of a creditor, and the effect is that stockholders tend to demand a greater return on their investment than a creditor does on its loan. The stockholder's demand for a return can take the form of dividend requirements or return on assets, each of which tend to increase the market value of their stock.

But there is no "always" in financial planning. Because investors usually require a higher return on their investment than do creditors, it might seem that debt is the preferred method of raising funds to acquire assets. Potential creditors, though, look at ratios such as the return on assets and the debt ratio. A high debt ratio (or, conversely, a low equity ratio) means that existing creditors have supplied a large portion of the company's assets, and that there is relatively little stockholder's equity to help absorb the risk.

Determining the Times Interest Earned Ratio

One measure frequently used by creditors to evaluate the risk involved in loaning money to a firm is the Times Interest Earned ratio. This is the number of times in a given period that a company earns enough income to cover its interest payments. A ratio of 5, for example, would mean that the amount of interest payments is earned 5 times over during that period.

The usual formula is:

```
Times Interest Earned = EBIT / Total interest payments
```

where EBIT stands for Earnings Before Interest and Taxes. The Times Interest Earned ratio for the Business Planner data is shown in figure 7.12.

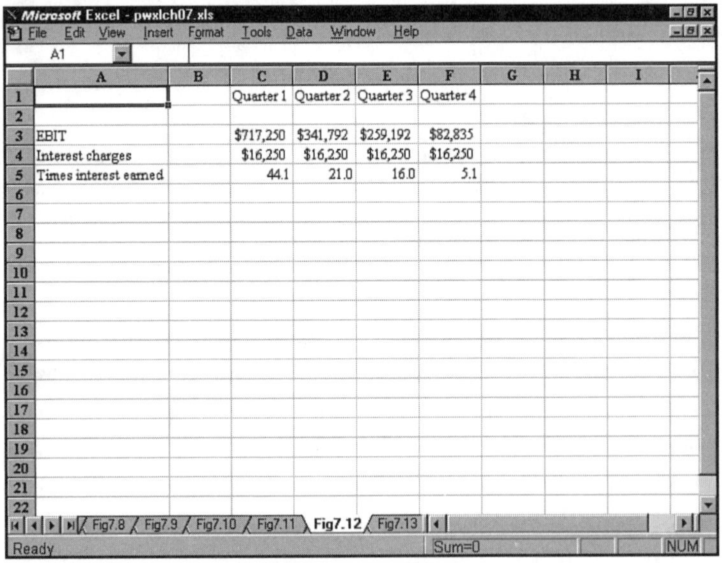

	A	B	C	D	E	F
1			Quarter 1	Quarter 2	Quarter 3	Quarter 4
2						
3	EBIT		$717,250	$341,792	$259,192	$82,835
4	Interest charges		$16,250	$16,250	$16,250	$16,250
5	Times interest earned		44.1	21.0	16.0	5.1

Fig. 7.12
The times interest earned ratio measures a company's ability to meet the cost of debt.

The formula used in cell C3 of figure 7.12 is:

```
=IncomeStatement!_1ST_QTR Net_income+IncomeStatement!_1ST_QTR
  Interest+IncomeStatement!_1ST_QTR Taxes
```

and the formula used to return the interest amount in cell C4 is:

```
=IncomeStatement!_1ST_QTR Interest
```

The Times Interest Earned ratio, in reality, seldom exceeds 10. A value of 44.1, such as that calculated in cell C5 of figure 7.12, is *very* high, although certainly not unheard of during a particularly good quarter. A value of 5.1, such as in cell F5 of figure 7.12, would usually be considered strong but within the normal range.

Notice that this is a measure of how deeply interest charges cut into a company's income. A ratio of 1, for example, would mean that the company earns enough income (after covering such costs as operating expenses and costs of sales) to cover only its interest charges. There would be no income remaining to pay income taxes (of course, in this case it's likely that there would be no income tax liability), to meet dividend requirements or to retain earnings for future investments.

Analyzing Liquidity Ratios

Creditors, as you might expect, are concerned by the issue of *liquidity*: a company's ability to meet its debts as they come due. As earlier chapters in this book have discussed, a company may have considerable total assets, but if those assets are difficult to convert to cash it is possible that the company might be unable to pay its creditors in a timely fashion. Creditors want their loans to be paid in the medium of cash, not in a medium such as inventory or factory equipment.

Two useful measures of a company's liquidity are the Current Ratio and the Quick Ratio.

Determining the Current Ratio

The current ratio compares a company's current assets (those that can be converted to cash during the current accounting period) to its current liabilities (those liabilities coming due during the same period). The usual formula is:

```
Current Ratio = Current Assets / Current Liabilities
```

The current ratio during each quarter for the Business Planner data is shown in figure 7.13.

Rows 3 and 4 in figure 7.13 simply refer to ranges named CurrentAssets (cells I22:L22 on the Balance Sheet) and CurrentLiabilities (cells I50:L50 on the Balance Sheet). The current ratio is simply the current assets divided by the current liabilities. The current ratio values in figure 7.13, ranging from 1.9 to 2.8, indicate that the company is in a strong position to meet its liabilities as they come due.

Fig. 7.13
The current ratio
measures the
company's ability
to repay the
principal amounts
of its liabilities.

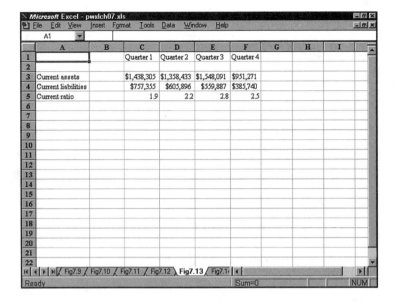

The current ratio is closely related to the concept of working capital, discussed in detail in chapter 5. Working capital is the *difference* between current assets and current liabilities.

Is a high current ratio good or bad? Certainly, from the creditor's standpoint, a high current ratio means that the company is well-placed to pay back its loans. Consider, though, the nature of the current assets: they consist mainly of cash and cash equivalents. Funds invested in these types of assets do not contribute strongly and actively to the creation of income. Therefore, from the standpoint of stockholders and management, a current ratio that is very high means that the company's assets are not being used to best advantage.

Determining the Quick Ratio

The quick ratio is a variant of the current ratio. It takes into account the fact that inventory, while it is a current asset, is not as liquid as cash or accounts receivable. Cash is completely liquid; accounts receivable can normally be converted to cash fairly quickly, by pressing for collection from the customer. But inventory cannot be converted to cash except by selling it. The quick ratio determines the relationship between quickly accessible current assets and current liabilities:

```
Quick Ratio = (Current Assets - Inventory) / Current Liabilities
```

Figure 7.14 shows the quarterly quick ratios based on the Business Planner data set.

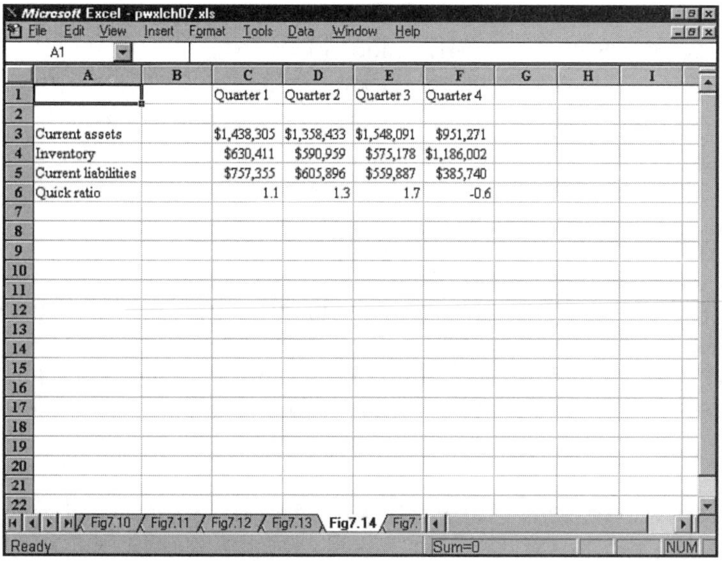

	A	B	C	D	E	F
1			Quarter 1	Quarter 2	Quarter 3	Quarter 4
2						
3	Current assets		$1,438,305	$1,358,433	$1,548,091	$951,271
4	Inventory		$630,411	$590,959	$575,178	$1,186,002
5	Current liabilities		$757,355	$605,896	$559,887	$385,740
6	Quick ratio		1.1	1.3	1.7	-0.6

Fig. 7.14
The quick ratio shows whether a company can meet its liabilities from quickly-accessible assets.

The negative quick ratio for the fourth quarter is caused by the extraordinarily large "other" cost of sales in cell K54 of the Income Statement, which contributes to a very large inventory valuation.

In practice, a quick ratio of 1.0 is normally considered adequate, with this caveat: the credit periods that the company offers its customers and those granted to the company by its creditor must be roughly equal. If revenues will stay in accounts receivable for as long as 90 days, but accounts payable are due within 30 days, a quick ratio of 1.0 will mean that accounts receivable cannot be converted to cash quickly enough to meet accounts payable.

It is possible for a company to manipulate the values of its current and quick ratios by taking certain actions toward the end of an accounting period such as a fiscal year. It might wait until the start of the next period to make purchases to its inventory, for example. Or, if its business is seasonal, it might choose a fiscal year that ends after its busy season, when inventories are usually low. As a potential creditor, you might want to examine the company's current and quick ratios on, for example, a quarterly basis.

Both a current and a quick ratio can also mislead you if the inventory figure does not represent the current replacement cost of the materials in inventory. As you learned from the discussion of inventories in chapter 3, there are various methods of valuing inventory. The LIFO method, in particular, can result in an inventory valuation that is much different from the inventory's current replacement value; this is because it assumes that the most recently acquired inventory is also the most recently sold.

If your actual costs to purchase materials are falling, for example, the LIFO method could result in an over-valuation of the existing inventory. This would tend to inflate the value of the current ratio, and to underestimate the value of the quick ratio if you calculate it by subtracting inventory from current assets, rather than summing cash and cash equivalents.

Analyzing Activity Ratios

There are various ratios that can give you insight into how well a company manages its operating and sales activities. One primary goal—perhaps, *the* primary goal—of these activities is to produce income through effective use of its resources. Two ways to measure this effectiveness are the Average Collection Period and the Inventory Turnover rate.

Determining the Average Collection Period

You can obtain a general estimate of the length of time it takes to receive payment for goods or services by calculating the Average Collection Period. One formula for this ratio is:

```
Average Collection Period = Accounts Receivable / (Credit Sales / Days)
```

where Days is the number of days in the period for which Accounts Receivable and Credit Sales accumulate. For an example based on the Business Planner data set, see figure 7.15.

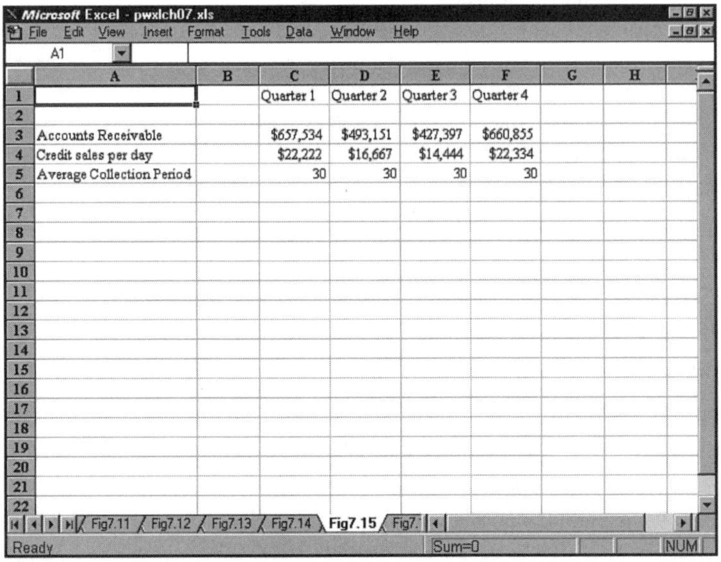

Fig. 7.15
The average collection period is an indicator of how well a company manages its accounts receivable.

The formula in cell C3 of figure 7.15, accounts receivable for the first quarter, is:

```
=BalanceSheet!_1ST_QTR AccountsReceivable
```

and for cell C4, credit sales per day, the formula is:

```
=IncomeStatement!_1ST_QTR Sales/90
```

(The assumption here is that all sales are credit sales.) Then, C4 contains simply the average day's worth of sales during the first quarter. Cell C5 is the ratio of cell C3 to cell C4. It measures the average number of days that any given sale remains in Accounts Receivable.

In this particular example, the average collection period is 30 during each quarter. This is because the Business Planner drives its estimate of Accounts Receivable on the basis of a constant that the user enters on its Data Sheet (see chapter 19 "The Business Planner," for a full discussion of this). The constant used by the Business Planner's data set is 30, which is why the formula for average collection period returns a constant value of 30 during each quarter.

You should interpret the average collection period in terms of the company's credit policies. If, for example, the company's policy as stated to its customers is that payment is to be received within two weeks, then an average collection period of 30 days indicates that collections are lagging. It may be that collection procedures need to be reviewed, or it is possible that one particularly large account is responsible for most of the collections in arrears. It is also possible that the qualifying procedures used by the sales force are not stringent enough.

> **Note**
>
> The calculation of the Average Collection Period assumes that credit sales are distributed roughly evenly during any given period. To the degree that the credit sales cluster at the end of the period, the Average Collection Period will return an inflated figure. If you obtain a result that appears too long (or too short), be sure to check whether the sales dates occur evenly throughout the period in question.

Regardless of the cause, if the average collection period is over-long, it means that the company is losing profit. The company is not converting cash due from customers into new assets that can, in turn, be used to generate new income.

Determining Inventory Turnover

No company wants to have too large an inventory (the sales force excepted: salespeople prefer to be able to tell their customers that they can obtain their purchase this afternoon). Goods that remain in inventory too long tie up the company's assets in idle stock, often incur carrying charges for the storage of the goods, and can become obsolete while awaiting sale.

Just-in-Time inventory procedures attempt to ensure that the company obtains its inventory no sooner than absolutely required in order to support its sales efforts. That is, of course, an unrealistic ideal, but by calculating the inventory turnover rate you can estimate how well a company is approaching the ideal.

The formula for the Inventory Turnover Ratio is:

```
Inventory Turnover = Cost of Goods Sold / Average Inventory
```

where the Average Inventory figure refers to the value of the inventory on any given day during the period during which the Cost of Goods Sold is calculated. Figure 7.16 shows the quarterly inventory turnover rate for the Business Planner's data set.

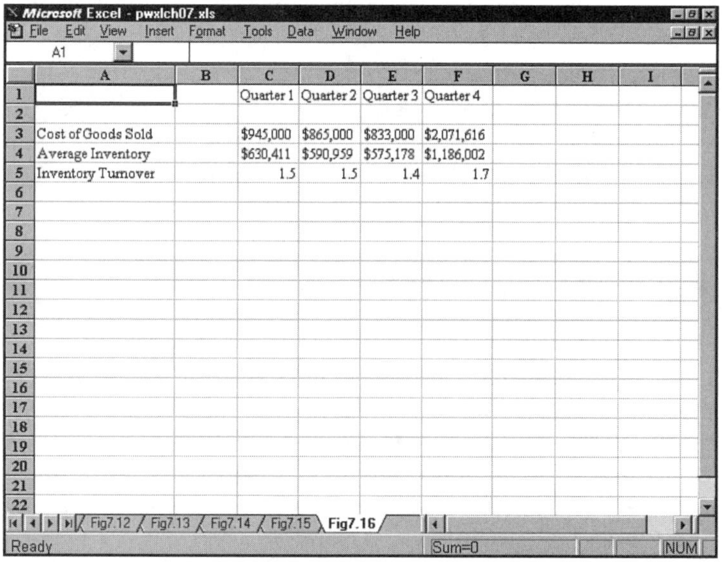

Fig. 7.16

The higher an inventory turnover rate, the more closely a company conforms to just-in-time procedures.

	A	B	C	D	E	F	G	H	I
1			Quarter 1	Quarter 2	Quarter 3	Quarter 4			
2									
3	Cost of Goods Sold		$945,000	$865,000	$833,000	$2,071,616			
4	Average Inventory		$630,411	$590,959	$575,178	$1,186,002			
5	Inventory Turnover		1.5	1.5	1.4	1.7			

Figure 7.16 suggests that this company's inventory is completely replaced around six times annually.

The figures for cost of goods sold and average inventory are taken directly from the Income Statement's cost of sales and the Balance Sheet's inventory levels. In a situation where you know only the beginning and ending inventory—for example, at the beginning and the ending of a period—you would use the average of the two levels: hence the term "average inventory."

An acceptable inventory turnover rate can be determined only by knowledge of a company's business sector. If you are in the business of wholesaling fresh produce, for example, you would probably require an annual turnover rate in the 50s: a much lower rate would mean that you were losing too much inventory to spoilage. But if you sell computing equipment, you could probably afford an annual turnover rate of around 3 or 4, because hardware does not spoil, nor does it become technologically obsolete more frequently than every few months.

Summary

This chapter has described some of the financial ratios that are important to understanding how, and how well, a company conducts its business. There are variations on virtually every ratio discussed here, and there are ratios that were not covered at all, but their principal forms follow the formulas illustrated.

Only occasionally can you calculate one of these indicators and gain immediate insight into a business operation. More frequently, it is necessary to know the sort of business that a company conducts, because the marketplace imposes different demands on different lines of business. Furthermore, you can usually understand one ratio by considering it in the context of another ratio (the debt ratio and the return on assets is a good example of one ratio providing the context for another).

Later chapters in this book (in particular, chapter 14 "Planning Profits" and chapter 20 "Using Financial Indicators") make extensive use of some of the ratios introduced here. Keep in mind that it's important to evaluate a financial ratio in terms of its trend over time, of a standard such as an industry average, and in light of other ratios that describe the company's operations and financial structure.

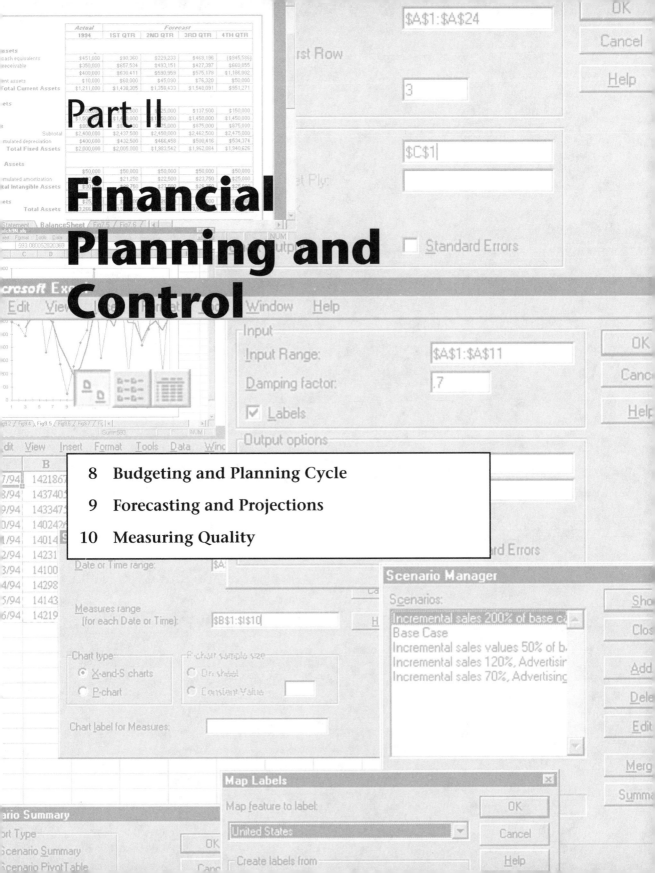

Part II

Financial Planning and Control

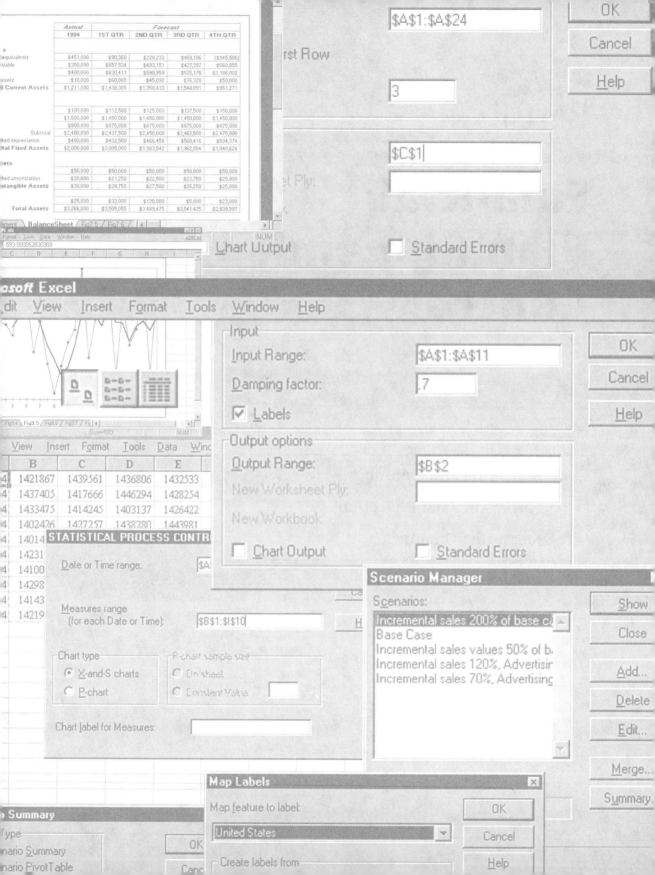

	Actual	Forecast			
	1994	1ST QTR	2ND QTR	3RD QTR	4TH QTR
s					
equivalents	$451,000	$90,360	$229,233	$469,196	($945,586)
vable	$350,000	$657,534	$493,151	$427,397	$660,855
ssets	$400,000	$630,411	$590,959	$575,178	$1,186,002
	$10,000	$60,000	$45,090	$76,320	$50,000
l Current Assets	$1,211,000	$1,438,305	$1,358,433	$1,548,091	$951,271
	$100,000	$112,500	$125,000	$137,500	$150,000
	$1,500,000	$1,450,000	$1,450,000	$1,450,000	$1,450,000
	$800,000	$875,000	$875,000	$875,000	$875,000
Subtotal	$2,400,000	$2,437,500	$2,450,000	$2,462,500	$2,475,000
ted depreciation	$400,000	$432,500	$466,458	$500,416	$534,374
tal Fixed Assets	$2,000,000	$2,005,000	$1,983,542	$1,962,084	$1,940,626
sets					
	$50,000	$50,000	$50,000	$50,000	$50,000
ted amortization	$20,000	$21,250	$22,500	$23,750	$25,000
tangible Assets	$30,000	$28,750	$27,500	$26,250	$25,000
	$25,000	$33,000	$120,000	$5,000	$23,000
Total Assets	$3,266,000	$3,505,055	$3,489,475	$3,541,425	$2,939,997

$A$1:$A$24

OK

Cancel

Help

rst Row

3

$C$1

et Ply:

Chart Output

Standard Errors

ment / BalanceSheet / Fig7.5 / Fig7.6 /

593.09005282035

osoft Excel

dit View Insert Format Tools Window Help

Fig9.4 / Fig9.5 / Fig9.6 / Fig9.7 / Fig

Sum=593

Input

Input Range: $A$1:$A$11

Damping factor: .7

☑ Labels

Output options

Output Range: $B$2

New Worksheet Ply:

New Workbook

☐ Chart Output   ☐ Standard Errors

OK

Cancel

Help

View	Insert	Format	Tools	Data	Wind
B	C	D	E	
1421867	1439561	1436806	1432533	
1437405	1417666	1446294	1428254	
1433475	1414245	1403137	1426422	
1402426	1427257	1438280	1443981	
14014				
14231				
14100				
14298				
14143				
14219				

STATISTICAL PROCESS CONTR

Date or Time range: $A

Measures range
(for each Date or Time): $B$1:$I$10

Chart type
○ X-and-S charts
○ P-chart

P-chart sample size
○ On sheet
○ Constant Value

Chart label for Measures:

Scenario Manager

Scenarios:

Incremental sales 200% of base c
Base Case
Incremental sales values 50% of b
Incremental sales 120%, Advertisir
Incremental sales 70%, Advertising

Show

Close

Add...

Delete

Edit...

Merge...

Summary...

Map Labels

Map feature to label:

United States

OK

Cancel

Help

Create labels from

o Summary

ype

nario Summary

nario PivotTable

OK

Canc

Chapter 8

Budgeting and Planning Cycle

Past operations have been the focus of this book up to this point. The income, balance sheet, and cash flow statements provide a picture of past performance. Understanding the past is, of course, very important, but planning for the future is also essential. This chapter provides an overview of financial planning and budgeting, and discusses how forecasts and projections form one basis for your planning. Chapter 9, "Forecasting and Projections," describes various forecasting techniques along with their Excel applications.

Textbooks prescribe elements for good business planning, such as mission statements, strategies, objectives, and tactics. These elements frequently focus on the customer's requirement for a quality product and for quality service. The prerequisite to these formal elements is to know where you're going and to know what you want to accomplish.

But inherent in that prerequisite is an understanding of how you want to reach your objective, and that involves understanding your profit picture. It's hard to ignore the profit motive in business planning. Very few people can afford to work or to invest without financial rewards. An entrepreneur may start a new business with this goal: "To provide customers with high quality bicycles and bicycle equipment at competitive rates that ultimately maximize profits." Most businesses try to strike a balance between meeting customers needs and the profit incentive.

The stated goal identifies the business's raison d'être: providing high quality bicycles. The business intends to sell, not to manufacture or rent, bicycles.

Furthermore, it intends to create profit by selling at competitive prices, rather than by selling specialized equipment to a small market segment of bicycle racers.

The process of business planning involves much more detail than these few concepts suggest. But they underscore that the foundation of good financial planning is good business planning. It's impossible to build meaningful financial plans without knowing what you want to accomplish and how you want to get there.

Creating Pro Forma Financial Statements

The goal of financial planning is to understand and project your financial future. Financial projections are used to evaluate and forecast business plans, to estimate future financing needs, and to establish internal operating budgets. Creating pro forma financial statements is a standard way to forecast a company's financial future. (A *pro forma* is simply a projection. A pro forma balance sheet, for example, projects assets and liabilities at the end of some future period.)

Pro forma statements build on the financial tools and concepts you've already learned about, such as income statements, balance sheets, and cash. There are many approaches to developing pro forma statements, ranging from back-of-the-envelope estimates to extensive computerized models which attempt to predict the future. Regardless of the approach, the goal is the same: to develop realistic and useful financial projections.

When developing pro forma statements, three important drivers should always be considered:

- *Historical relationships and trends*: sales commissions might normally have been 8 percent of revenue.

- *Information regarding future changes*: a competitor may be preparing to occupy a location two blocks away from yours.

- *Your business goals*: you intend to introduce a new product, or to reduce expenses by 5 percent.

There are many approaches to developing pro forma financial statements. The three drivers described here imply *horizontal* approaches: they focus on changes over time. Another class of *vertical* approaches focuses on industry groups.

For example, you might want to determine whether your cost of goods sold, as a percentage of net sales, is similar to other companies in your industry. Successful companies within an industry group often exhibit similar relationships between key indicators such as these. It can be useful to compare such a relationship, computed for your company, with the industry average. It would be discouraging to find that your cost-to-sales ratio is high, compared with the industry average, and it would probably prompt you to take action to lower costs.

Averages for key ratios within different industry groups are commercially available. The difficulty, of course, is that it might be misleading to compare your company to an industry average. Suppose that you work for a local telephone company. If you choose to compare your company's results to the industry averages for telecommunications firms, you will be comparing your results to those of cable TV firms, cellular communications firms, long-distance providers, firms that offer high-speed metropolitan area networks, and so on. Their financial structures are likely to be very different from yours, and any comparison could therefore mislead you. A vertical analysis can be enlightening, but it must be prepared with great care.

In contrast, a horizontal approach uses your own historic data as the point of comparison. In effect, your company acts as its own control group. While it requires every bit as much care as a vertical approach, it is relatively straight-forward, and the horizontal approach can be a very effective way to project financial results. The next section illustrates a horizontal analysis. The analysis is based on projections created by means of Percentage of Sales.

Forecasting by Percentage of Sales

The Percentage of Sales forecasting approach is based on the concept that many business activities, such as incurring certain expenses, acquiring assets, and assuming liabilities are directly tied to sales dollars. Without sales, a business would neither incur selling expenses nor generate accounts receivable. An increase in sales should result in additional cash in the bank, greater variable costs, higher income taxes, additional administrative expenses, and so on. Sales is a key driver of most other indicators. Therefore, it can be useful to base the projection of other indicators on the projection of sales.

The Percentage of Sales forecasting method entails several steps:

1. Analyze historical trends and financial relationships. It may be, for example, that variable costs have, over several years, averaged 7 percent of total sales.

2. Forecast the key driver, sales, through the next planning horizon—one year, for example.

3. Estimate future expenses and balances, based on their historical relationships to sales. If you project that sales will increase by 3 percent during the next year, it would be reasonable to project that sales commissions will also increase by 3 percent.

4. Prepare the pro forma financial statement using the projected sales and expenses.

Case Study: Cummins Printing

Cummins Printing is a small business that specializes in custom print runs of office stationery and catalogs. It has been in existence for three years, since Jim Cummins incorporated the company and acquired its assets partly through a bank loan and partly through funding that he supplied. Cummins Printing is preparing pro formas for 1995. It does so both to estimate its annual expenses and financial results for the next year, and to guide an operating decision it must make early in the year.

The first step is to review a company's existing financial statements for trends, patterns, and relationships. The statement and ratio analysis tools discussed in other chapters of this book make up the platform for the pro forma view. For example, figures 8.1 and 8.2 display the 1992–1994 income and balance sheet statements for the Cummins Printing Company.

Fig. 8.1

Cummins Printing income statement for 1992 through 1994.

	A	B	C	D	E	F	G	H
1	Cummins Printing							
2	Income statement for year ended:	12/31/92	12/31/93	12/31/94				
3								
4	Net sales	$349,595	$367,450	$389,864				
5	Cost of goods sold							
6	Inventory, 1/1	$122,904	$92,903	$113,120				
7	Purchases	$115,372	$141,137	$187,454				
8	Available for sale	$238,276	$234,040	$300,574				
9	Inventory, 12/31	$92,903	$113,120	$129,190				
10	Cost of goods sold	$145,373	$120,920	$171,384				
11	Gross profit	$204,222	$246,530	$218,480				
12	Expenses							
13	Advertising	$6,166	$5,915	$6,770				
14	Building lease	$8,750	$9,110	$9,544				
15	Depreciation: equipment	$4,194	$4,480	$4,536				
16	Insurance	$3,906	$3,754	$4,010				
17	Office supplies	$2,110	$2,680	$3,005				
18	Salaries	$62,378	$72,924	$94,347				
19	Telecommunications	$3,708	$5,507	$7,014				
20	Travel	$1,070	$6,310	$8,733				
21	Total expenses	$92,282	$110,680	$137,959				
22	Taxes	$27,985	$33,962	$20,130				
23	Net income	$83,955	$101,887	$60,391				
24								

Microsoft Excel - Pwxlch08.xls

File Edit View Insert Format Tools Data Window Help

Fig8.1 / Fig8.2 / Fig8.3 / Fig8.4 / Fig8.5 / Fig8.6 / Fig

Ready

CAPS NUM

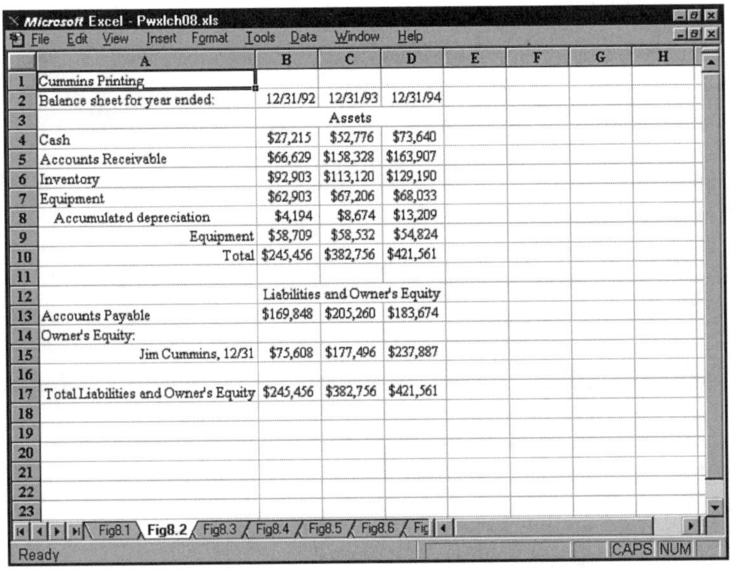

	A	B	C	D
1	Cummins Printing			
2	Balance sheet for year ended:	12/31/92	12/31/93	12/31/94
3			Assets	
4	Cash	$27,215	$52,776	$73,640
5	Accounts Receivable	$66,629	$158,328	$163,907
6	Inventory	$92,903	$113,120	$129,190
7	Equipment	$62,903	$67,206	$68,033
8	Accumulated depreciation	$4,194	$8,674	$13,209
9	Equipment	$58,709	$58,532	$54,824
10	Total	$245,456	$382,756	$421,561
11				
12		Liabilities and Owner's Equity		
13	Accounts Payable	$169,848	$205,260	$183,674
14	Owner's Equity:			
15	Jim Cummins, 12/31	$75,608	$177,496	$237,887
16				
17	Total Liabilities and Owner's Equity	$245,456	$382,756	$421,561

Fig. 8.2
Cummins Printing balance sheet for 1992 through 1994.

Cummins now needs to identify the financial trends, patterns, and relationships that flow from these worksheets. While there are many different analytical tools and indicators available, the key for budget planning is to focus on the key drivers of the business. Growth in revenues and increase in working capital are two examples of these drivers. Cummins Printing focuses on growth in revenue as the key driver, and uses percentage of sales as its principal indicator. Figure 8.3 displays the income statements from figure 8.1, along with a breakdown of components by sales. Each statement component is expressed not only in terms of raw dollars, but also as a percentage of sales. The assumption is that as sales dollars vary, other components such as inventory and most operating expenses should vary accordingly.

With so few data points (only three years worth of information on sales) it is unwise to project sales growth on the basis of prior data alone. For example, if you use an Excel method based on time snapshots, such as a moving average, or a regression-based method such as TREND or a chart trendline, you will get an answer but you should give it very little credence.

How can you tell what to believe? The issue is *generalizability*. When you do an analysis that seeks to project observed findings to an unobserved situation—such as next year's sales revenues—you make a logical assumption that the future will follow the past. If you have many data points in the analysis, then there can be much more justification for that assumption than if you have only a few. You can examine the baseline of the data and, perhaps, note that sales revenue in prior years does a good job of predicting the next year's revenue. But with a very short baseline such as three years, you can obtain an apparently reliable trend that turns out to be completely misleading.

In a situation such as the one depicted in figures 8.1 through 8.3, you should attempt to obtain additional evidence. For example:

- Do other indicators, such as local or national economic forecasts, support the notion that your business should continue to produce the results that you've observed?

- Is your competition gearing up or scaling back? Are they taking steps to acquire your customers?

- Are technological changes occurring that work for or against your line of business?

- What situations are your existing customers experiencing: do these situations suggest that they will continue to buy? And will they continue to buy from you?

- Are you preparing to discontinue or to introduce a new product line?

- What is the market trend for your product—declining or accelerating demand?

Fig. 8.3
Cummins expresses statement components as a percentage of sales as the first step in creating a pro forma.

	A	B	C	D	E	F	G	H
1	Cummins Printing							
2	Income statement for year ended:	12/31/92	12/31/93	12/31/94		Percentage of Sales		
3						3-yr Average	1994 Percent	
4	Net sales	$349,595	$367,450	$389,864		100.00%	100.00%	
5	Cost of goods sold							
6	Inventory, 1/1	$122,904	$92,903	$113,120		29.72%	29.02%	
7	Purchases	$115,372	$141,137	$187,454		40.11%	48.08%	
8	Available for sale	$238,276	$234,040	$300,574		69.82%	77.10%	
9	Inventory, 12/31	$92,903	$113,120	$129,190		30.28%	33.14%	
10	Cost of goods sold	$145,373	$120,920	$171,384		39.54%	43.96%	
11	Gross profit	$204,222	$246,530	$218,480		60.46%	56.04%	
12	Expenses							
13	Advertising	$6,166	$5,915	$6,770		1.70%	1.74%	
14	Building lease	$8,750	$9,110	$9,544		2.48%	2.45%	
15	Depreciation: equipment	$4,194	$4,480	$4,536		1.19%	1.16%	
16	Insurance	$3,906	$3,754	$4,010		1.05%	1.03%	
17	Office supplies	$2,110	$2,680	$3,005		0.70%	0.77%	
18	Salaries	$62,378	$72,924	$94,347		20.75%	24.20%	
19	Telecommunications	$3,708	$5,507	$7,014		1.47%	1.80%	
20	Travel	$1,070	$6,310	$8,733		1.46%	2.24%	
21	Total expenses	$92,282	$110,680	$137,959		30.80%	35.39%	
22	Taxes	$27,985	$33,962	$20,130		7.42%	5.16%	
23	Net income	$83,955	$101,887	$60,391		22.25%	15.49%	
24								

The answers to questions like these, combined with the actual results from prior years, leads Cummins Printing to the reasonable assumption that the growth in revenues for 1995 will be slightly weaker than that experienced during 1994. In particular, Cummins concludes that this decrease will be due to the combination of a larger customer base, a softer economy, and a new advertising campaign. Cummins projects that its 1995 revenue will be $411,696, a 5.6 percent increase over 1994.

The next step is to forecast expenses, based on their historical percentage of sales and applied to your projected 1995 revenue. This forecast is displayed in figure 8.4.

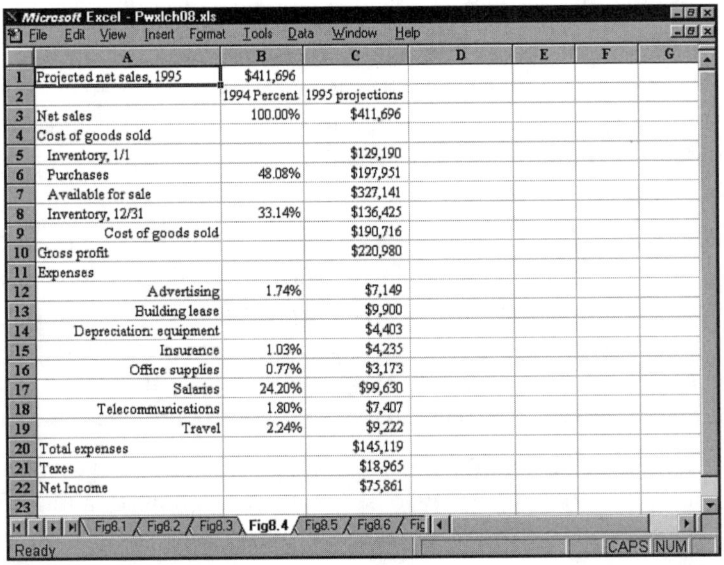

Fig. 8.4
Applying historical percentages to projected sales results in a pro forma budget for 1995.

Those components that are expected to vary with net sales have a percentage in column B. Other components, such as beginning inventory, lease payments, and depreciation, are given best estimates as of the end of the prior period.

The forecast is satisfying as far as it goes, but a disturbing trend emerges from the 1992–1994 income statements. Cummins Printing makes most of its revenues through custom print runs, which often require special paper stock. During the three years of its existence, Cummins has purchased stock for special uses in quantities larger than needed for a particular order. This was done to create lower variable costs, because larger purchases involved lower unit costs. There is also the hope that the customer would make a subsequent order that would require using the remainder of that stock purchase.

Unfortunately, this has not yet happened. Cummins Printing's inventory of paper goods has steadily increased over the three-year period, and has exceeded its growth in sales dollars. Notice in figure 8.3 that the end-of-year inventory has grown from $92,903 to $129,190 (an increase of almost 40 percent), whereas net sales has grown from $349,595 to $389,864 (an increase of about 11 percent). Figure 8.4 indicates that unless changes are made, inventory at the end of 1995 will be $136,425.

What impact would a change in purchasing procedures have on Cummins Printing's pro forma income statement and balance sheet for 1995?

Cummins knows that a significant proportion of its sales are linked to its ability to provide custom work for its customers. As much as 40 percent of its business has been due to its willingness to acquire the stock required for special jobs, to purchase stock in bulk, and to apply the unit cost savings to the price it charges its customers.

Cummins has no way of knowing when its existing customers will make further orders (allowing the company to work down the inventory it has acquired), but must assume that this will happen at some point. In the meantime, one option is to curtail new purchases to its inventory—so doing would slow the rate of increase of its inventory levels—until further orders from existing customers allow it to use the inventory it has already acquired.

Cummins needs to attract new customers. But if Cummins curtails new purchases to its inventory, its ability to perform custom production runs for new customers will suffer. Therefore, the process of working down the existing inventory to a more manageable level will certainly cause the level of new sales to decrease. Is this a sensible business decision?

Cummins explores the effect of reducing its purchase of stock by 50 percent during 1995, from the pro forma figure of $197,951 to $98,976. Net sales are expected to decrease, as a result, from a projected $411,696 to $247,018. Most expenses decrease proportionately, with the exceptions of the building lease and the equipment depreciation (these would not normally be expected to vary with net sales). The projected outcome is shown in figure 8.5 (the pro forma income statement) and 8.6 (the pro forma balance sheet).

Fig. 8.5
1995 pro forma income statement, based on curtailing inventory purchases, and resulting in lower net sales.

	A	B	C	D	E	F
1	Modified net sales, 1995	$247,018				
2		1994 Percent	1995 projections			
3	Net sales	100.00%	$247,018			
4	Cost of goods sold					
5	Inventory, 1/1		$129,190			
6	Purchases		$98,976			
7	Available for sale		$228,166			
8	Inventory, 12/31	33.14%	$81,855			
9	Cost of goods sold		$146,311			
10	Gross profit		$100,707			
11	Expenses					
12	Advertising	1.74%	$4,289			
13	Building lease		$9,544			
14	Depreciation: equipment		$4,403			
15	Insurance	1.03%	$2,541			
16	Office supplies	0.77%	$1,904			
17	Salaries	24.20%	$59,778			
18	Telecommunications	1.80%	$4,444			
19	Travel	2.24%	$5,533			
20	Total expenses		$92,436			
21	Taxes		$2,068			
22	Net Income		$6,203			

Fig. 8.6
The 1995 pro forma balance sheet. Column E reflects the effect of reduced sales on the company's worth.

	A	B	C	D	E	F	G	H
1	Cummins Printing							
2	Balance sheet for year ended:	12/31/92	12/31/93	12/31/94	12/31/95			
3			Assets					
4	Cash	$27,215	$52,776	$73,640	$91,397			
5	Accounts Receivable	$66,629	$158,328	$163,907	$155,621			
6	Inventory	$92,903	$113,120	$129,190	$81,855			
7	Equipment	$62,903	$67,206	$68,033	$68,033			
8	Accumulated depreciation	$4,194	$8,674	$13,209	$17,745			
9	Equipment	$58,709	$58,532	$54,824	$50,288			
10	Total	$245,456	$382,756	$421,561	$379,161			
11								
12			Liabilities and Owner's Equity					
13	Accounts Payable	$169,848	$205,260	$183,674	$135,071			
14	Owner's Equity:							
15	Jim Cummins, 12/31	$75,608	$177,496	$237,887	$244,090			
16								
17	Total Liabilities and Owner's Equity	$245,456	$382,756	$421,561	$379,161			
18								
19								
20								
21								
22								
23								

If stock purchases are cut in half, and if net sales consequently fall by 40 percent, net income will fall by $69,658, or 92 percent: a huge financial impact for any business. To reduce salaries in accordance with the reduction in net sales by 40 percent, one employee must be laid off: a major human factor for a small business.

All-in-all, the costs are just too great to justify the (undoubted) benefit to the inventory situation. This is as you might expect when an operational decision exerts such a powerful influence on the way a company does business with its customers.

Excel makes the analysis particularly easy—much easier than the business decision itself might be. The work is in setting up the worksheet that contains the historic data for the income statement and balance sheet. After that is done, the derivation of the percentages is easy and simple. For example, to create the 100 percent value shown in cell G4 of figure 8.3, you would enter this formula:

```
=D4/$D$4
```

Then, copy that formula and paste it into G6:G11 and into G13:G23. The absolute reference, $D$4, ensures that the denominator in the formula is always the value in cell D4, whereas the numerator in the formula changes according to where the formula is pasted. That is, the formula in G6 changes to D6/$D$4.

> **Tip**
>
> The F4 key gives you a convenient way to convert one reference style to another. If you use the mouse to create a formula, Excel uses the relative reference style (e.g., D4) by default. To convert the reference to D3 to the absolute reference style (e.g., $D$4), just highlight that portion of the formula in the Formula Bar and press F4. Pressing F4 repeatedly cycles the reference through mixed reference styles as well: D4, $D$4, D$4, $D4, and then back to D4. This is much more convenient than using the mouse or arrow keys to locate where the $ (dollar) sign should be placed.

To obtain the values shown in column F of figure 8.3, enter in cell F4 this formula:

```
=(B4+C4+D4)/($B$4+$C$4+$D$4)
```

Then, copy-and-paste it into F6:F11 and into F13:F23. Another version of this formula is:

```
=AVERAGE(B6/$B$4,C6/$C$4,D6/$D$4)
```

This latter version of the formula, once copied and pasted into other rows, assigns equal weight to each of the three years involved. The former version gives greater weight to a year in which, for example, the Advertising expense is high relative to net sales. Your choice of which version to use should be guided by whether you want the average to emphasize or restrain the effect of an unusual value.

After these formulas are set up, checking the effect of a change in net sales on such variables as expenses, net income, and owner's equity is simply a matter of changing the value of net sales. Because the remaining categories in the income statement and balance sheet depend directly on this value, Excel adjusts them accordingly.

Performing Sensitivity Analysis

After you have created your pro forma statements in Excel, you can use them to analyze different financial scenarios. Evaluating possible changes in your projected financial statements may help identify future risks or opportunities. The Cummins case study illustrated what might happen if sales declined by 40 percent. It did so by assuming that most costs would follow changes in net sales.

But it is also quite feasible to examine that assumption itself. You might want to understand the effect of lowering your cost of goods sold by 10 percent on your net income and cash forecast for the year. Or you might ask whether you could stay in business if one of your vendors raised its prices by 20 percent.

> **Tip**
>
> Excel provides the Scenario Manager to help you keep track of different assumptions in your pro formas. Chapter 13, "Creating a Sensitivity Analysis for a Business Case," discusses the use of the Scenario Manager in some depth.

For a single change to a pro forma, it is usually quicker to simply make a change to the critical cell instead of taking the time to deal with the Scenario Manager.

For example, you could change cell C6 in figure 8.4 from:

```
=ROUND(B6*$B$1,0)
```

which equals $197,951, to:

```
=ROUND(B6*$B$1*1.2,0)
```

which indicates projected purchases to inventory if the vendor raised its prices by 20 percent, to $237,541. The effect is to reduce net income from $75,861 to $36,271.

This adjustment can tell you much more than that your net income decreases by about $40,000. Another way of viewing the change in net income is to note that an increase in the cost of purchases to inventory results in a decrease of more than 52 percent (1 × $36,271/$75,861). This means that your net income tracks very closely with your vendor costs: your profit is virtually at the mercy of your vendors' pricing.

Moving from the Pro Forma to the Budget

A pro forma statement can be translated into financial budgets for the upcoming year. The pro forma statement is the forecast. Budgets are used to plan, coordinate, and control a company's operations. The budgeting time period is a matter of judgment. A business may develop annual, quarterly, or monthly budgets depending on such factors as its information needs, its sales patterns (for example, seasonal peaks and valleys versus a steady trend), its operational methods, and its financial structure.

Suppose that Cummins Printing wants to create a quarterly operating budget for 1995, based on its pro forma income statement for that year. The quarterly budget is shown in figure 8.7.

Fig. 8.7
The 1995 quarterly operating budget for Cummins Printing created from its pro forma.

Microsoft Excel - Pwxlch08.xls

	A	B	C	D	E	F
1		Total		Quarterly projections		
2		for 1995	Q1	Q2	Q3	Q4
3	Net sales	$411,696	$82,339	$164,679	$102,924	$61,754
4	Cost of goods sold					
5	Inventory, Start of Period	$129,190	$129,190	$119,723	$100,789	$88,955
6	Purchases	$98,976	$19,795	$39,590	$24,744	$14,846
7	Available for sale	$228,166	$148,985	$159,313	$125,533	$103,802
8	Inventory, End of Period	$81,855	$119,723	$100,789	$88,955	$81,855
9	Cost of goods sold	$146,311	$29,262	$58,524	$36,578	$21,947
10	Gross profit	$265,386	$53,077	$106,154	$66,346	$39,808
11	Expenses					
12	Advertising	$7,149	$1,430	$2,860	$1,787	$1,072
13	Building lease	$9,900	$2,475	$2,475	$2,475	$2,475
14	Depreciation: equipment	$4,403	$1,101	$1,101	$1,101	$1,101
15	Insurance	$4,235	$1,059	$1,059	$1,059	$1,059
16	Office supplies	$3,173	$635	$1,269	$793	$476
17	Salaries	$99,630	$19,926	$39,852	$24,908	$14,945
18	Telecommunications	$7,407	$1,481	$2,963	$1,852	$1,111
19	Travel	$9,222	$1,844	$3,689	$2,306	$1,383
20	Total expenses	$145,119	$29,951	$55,267	$36,280	$23,622
21	Taxes	$30,067	$5,782	$12,722	$7,517	$4,047
22	Net Income	$90,200	$17,345	$38,165	$22,550	$12,140
23						

Fig8.2 Fig8.3 Fig8.4 Fig8.5 Fig8.6 Fig8.7
Ready CAPS NUM

The quarterly budget follows the assumption in the pro forma that the main driver of expenses is the company's net sales. As it happens, revenues for this firm are moderately seasonal: historically, 20 percent of its sales have occurred during the first quarter, 40 percent during the second quarter, 25 percent during the third quarter, and 15 percent during the fourth quarter. To spread the annual projected net sales of $530,536 across the four quarters, it is necessary to make the following entries:

In cell C3:

```
=.2*B3
```

In cell D3:

```
=.4*B3
```

In cell E3:

```
=.25*B3
```

In cell F3:

```
=.15*B3
```

These formulas distribute the total projected revenue on a quarterly basis, based on net sales percentages for each quarter in prior years.

The inventory level at the start of each quarter is simply the inventory level at the end of the prior quarter.

Inventory purchases during each quarter are a function of both the total projected purchases for the year and the net sales for the quarter. The formula in cell C6 (inventory purchases during the first quarter) is:

```
=$B6*C$3/$B$3
```

The formula represents the amount of anticipated inventory purchases for the year (cell B6), prorated according to the ratio of net sales for the quarter (cell C3) to net sales for the year (cell B3). Due to the use of mixed references in the formula, copying and pasting from C6 into D6:F6 adjusts the reference to the quarterly net sales from C3 to D3, E3 and F3.

The inventory available for sale during each quarter is the sum of the inventory at the beginning of the quarter plus purchases during that quarter.

The projection for inventory at the end of the quarter is based on the amount that is available for sale, less the cost of goods sold. The cost of goods sold is, again, a function of net sales. For example, the formula in cell C9 is:

```
=$B9*C$3/$B$3
```

Then, the end-of-quarter inventory (cell C8) is projected by means of:

```
=C7-C9
```

The gross profit is estimated by subtracting the cost of goods sold from the net sales. For example, the gross profit for the first quarter is estimated by:

```
=C3-C9
```

Expenses for each quarter are estimated by prorating the annual expense according to the ratio of the quarter's net sales to the annual net sales. For example, the first quarter's advertising expense is estimated with this formula:

```
=$B12*C$3/$B$3
```

Financial Planning and Control

Again, due to the use of the mixed references, this formula can be copied and pasted into the remainder of the range C15:C19, and the cell precedents will adjust accordingly. Rows 13 and 14, which represent the cost of the building lease and depreciation, are assumed *not* to vary with net sales; instead, they are estimated on the basis of the most recent information available at the end of the prior period.

Total expenses are obtained by summing each quarter's expense categories, and taxes are estimated at 25 percent of operating income (gross profit less expenses). Net income is the gross profit less the total expenses, less taxes.

Now suppose that Cummins Printing wants to distribute its quarterly operations more evenly. Although the quarterly net sales will continue to be seasonal, it may be possible to obtain, during the first quarter, estimates from customers as to their probable orders during the second through fourth quarters. In that case, it may be possible to balance the quarterly workload more evenly, with consequent savings in overtime salary payments during the busy second quarter.

Cummins estimates that overtime payments during the year are roughly $10,000. Figure 8.8 displays the effect of distributing the workload evenly across quarters.

Fig. 8.8 1995 quarterly operating budget for Cummins Printing with workload adjustments to allocate salary costs evenly.

Microsoft Excel - Pwxlch08.xls

	A	B	C	D	E	F	G	H	I
1		Total	Quarterly projections				Modified		
2		for 1995	Q1	Q2	Q3	Q4	1995 totals		
3	Net sales	$411,696	$82,339	$164,679	$102,924	$61,754	$411,696		
4	Cost of goods sold								
5	Inventory, Start of Period	$129,190	$129,190	$124,672	$90,891	$79,058	$129,190		
6	Purchases	$98,976	$24,744	$24,744	$24,744	$24,744	$98,976		
7	Available for sale	$228,166	$153,934	$149,416	$115,635	$103,802	$228,166		
8	Inventory, End of Period	$81,855	$124,672	$90,891	$79,058	$81,855	$81,855		
9	Cost of goods sold	$146,311	$29,262	$58,524	$36,578	$21,947	$146,311		
10	Gross profit	$265,386	$53,077	$106,154	$66,346	$39,808	$265,386		
11	Expenses								
12	Advertising	$7,149	$1,430	$2,860	$1,787	$1,072	$7,149		
13	Building lease	$9,900	$2,475	$2,475	$2,475	$2,475	$9,900		
14	Depreciation: equipment	$4,403	$1,101	$1,101	$1,101	$1,101	$4,404		
15	Insurance	$4,235	$847	$1,694	$1,059	$635	$4,235		
16	Office supplies	$3,173	$635	$1,269	$793	$476	$3,173		
17	Salaries	$99,630	$22,500	$22,500	$22,500	$22,500	$90,000		
18	Telecommunications	$7,407	$1,481	$2,963	$1,852	$1,111	$7,407		
19	Travel	$9,222	$1,844	$3,689	$2,306	$1,383	$9,222		
20	Total expenses	$145,119	$32,313	$38,550	$33,873	$30,754	$135,490		
21	Taxes	$30,067	$5,191	$16,901	$8,118	$2,263	$32,474		
22	Net Income	$90,200	$15,573	$50,703	$24,355	$6,790	$97,422		
23									

Fig8.3 / Fig8.4 / Fig8.5 / Fig8.6 / Fig8.7 / Fig8.8

Ready CAPS NUM

Notice first that the purchases to inventory shown in figure 8.8 have been distributed evenly across the four quarters. This is due to the assumption that the workload will be constant, and therefore, additional inventory will be needed on a constant basis.

Second, the projection of annual salaries has been reduced from $99,630 to $90,000. This reflects the anticipated savings in overtime payments. Additionally, the quarterly salary payments are constant across quarters in figure 8.8. This is done by changing the formula in cell C17 to:

```
=$G17/4
```

The formula is copied and pasted into cells D17:F17.

Performing these adjustments has two principal effects:

- The annual net income increases by $7,223, as a result of savings in overtime salary payments.

- The net income becomes more variable across quarters. This is because the gross profit for any quarter remains the same, but the quarterly expenses are reduced—and, in the case of the second quarter, the expenses are reduced dramatically, by about 25 percent.

> **Note**
>
> Most of the calculations for the modified 1995 totals, shown in column G, are simply the sum of the quarterly amounts. The inventory calculations are different: Starting inventory is taken from the first quarter's starting inventory, and the ending inventory is taken from the end of the fourth quarter. The cost of goods available for sale is the sum of the beginning inventory and purchases. And the cost of goods sold is the cost of goods available for sale less the ending inventory.

This example illustrates how an operating budget can be used to help you plan and schedule your expenses to increase your profitability. Simply reducing expenses by balancing the workload more evenly has an obvious effect on net income.

Additionally, though, it may be useful to distribute the net income differently than is done by adhering rigidly to percentage of net sales as the only driver. Suppose that Cummins Printing has a large loan payment coming due at the end of the second quarter. By balancing the workload more evenly, net income at the end of the second quarter is increased from 62 percent of annual net income to 67 percent of annual net income. Cummins Printing may find it useful to have that additional amount of income earlier in the year to help it meet the loan payment.

This is by no means the only benefit you can realize by reworking a pro forma as an operating budget. For example, if a business projects that its revenue will increase by 10 percent during the next year, it may want to develop targets for each product line on a quarterly, or even a monthly basis. The entire increase might occur during the month of December. If so, this would very likely have significant implications for the business—December's cash balances, inventory levels, and staffing levels are among the business components that would be impacted. Budgeting, then, is the process of translating the pro forma statements into plans that help you manage your business and optimize your profits.

By comparing your actual results to the budget projections, you can determine whether you are on track to achieve your business goals and financial forecasts. Budget comparisons help you focus on areas of opportunity and concern. If vendor costs increase markedly, you might want to search for a new supplier. An increase in demand for a product may cause you to raise the sales price or alter inventory schedules. Thus, budgets can serve as real-time flags for your operational and financial decisions.

Fitting the Budget to the Business Plan

For large companies the planning cycle is extensive. Multi-year business plans are established by top management. Next, managers create operational plans to attain the strategic goals. Pro forma financial statements are then created to quantify and evaluate the plans. Lastly, budgets are developed from the pro forma statements.

Here are three types of budgets that are commonly used:

- *Operating budgets* track projected revenues and expenses to ensure that the projected net income level is achieved.

- *Cash budgets* project cash receipts and disbursements over a period of time. Cash budgets help determine whether it may be necessary to seek outside investment or some other form of external financing.

- *Capital budgets* detail the planned capital (or additions to fixed assets) projects during a designated period.

There are many pitfalls to the budgeting process. One trap is to spend too much time considering the effects of many different scenarios that involve minuscule differences. This can be cumbersome, and tends to add little of value to the analysis. Another trap is to allow budgeting concerns to supersede business goals: budgeting is a means, not an end. It's important to keep budgeting in perspective—used properly, budgets can provide a business a way to plan, coordinate, and monitor its operations. Done improperly, budgeting can waste time and shift your attention away from the bottom line.

Multiple year business plans and pro forma statements are extremely valuable when an endeavor requires more than one year of planning. The company might reasonably ask whether it should continue to invest its resources in a particular division, or it might need to know the anticipated revenue for a product over the next five years. The long range forecast often impacts operational and financial plans during the current year. Financial plans should extend over the most meaningful planning horizon for your business.

Summary

In this chapter, you have learned how to use historical information to project future revenues and expenses by means of the Percentage of Sales method. This process enables you to create pro forma income statements and balance sheets. Pro formas, in turn, enable you to examine the likely effects on your operations and profits if conditions change or if you modify some aspect of your revenues and expenses.

Operating budgets, which help you plan and manage the way you conduct your business, flow naturally from pro forma statements. You can use budgets to break down your operations and finances into meaningful time periods such as months and quarters. This gives you additional insight into how changes, whether planned or thrust on you, might affect your financial picture.

Key to the entire process is the quality of your projections. Chapter 9, "Forecasting and Projections," describes how to use Excel to generate the most accurate forecasts possible.

Chapter 9

Forecasting and Projections

In business, you often use forecasting to project revenues, so as to estimate what future receipts will be on the basis of past history. This puts you in a position to estimate other quantities, such as cost allocations and staffing, that you need to support the revenue stream.

Unfortunately, businesses often make an offhand effort at a revenue forecast, and ignore other ways to use forecasts in their planning. Using Excel, you can forecast many other variables, so long as you have a reasonable baseline to create a forecast. For example:

- If your business depends on telecommunications, you might want to forecast the bandwidth required to keep your users connected to remote computing facilities.

- If you manage a particular product line, you might want to forecast the number of units that you can expect to sell. This kind of forecast can help you determine the resources necessary to support activities such as installation, warehousing, and maintenance.

- If you manage customer service, it can be important to forecast the number of new customers you expect. The forecast may lead you to consider changing your staffing levels to meet changing needs.

In this chapter you will learn what you need in a baseline to create a useful forecast. You will also learn about different methods of using baseline data to create forecasts, their advantages and drawbacks, and how to choose among them.

Making Sure You Have a Good Baseline

A *baseline* is a set of numeric observations made over time. From the standpoint of forecasting, there are four important aspects to baselines:

- A baseline is ordered from the earliest observation to the most recent.

- All the time periods in the baseline are equally long. You should not intersperse daily observations with, for example, the average of three days observations. In practice, you can ignore slight deviations. February and March have different numbers of days, but the two or three day difference is usually ignored for baselines that contain monthly observations.

- The observations come from the same point within each time period. For example, with weekly data, you might want to make each observation on a Friday.

- Missing data are not allowed. Even one missing observation can throw off the forecasting equations. If a small fraction of your time series is missing, try replacing that data by estimating it.

If your baseline has these four characteristics, then your chances of getting a useful forecast are much better.

> **Tip**
>
> A reasonable and quick way to estimate missing data in a baseline is to take the average of the observations immediately before and after one that's missing. For example, if the value for cell A5 is missing, you could enter:
>
>   =AVERAGE(A4,A6)
>
> in cell A5.

Some of Excel's forecasting tools require that you arrange your baseline observations vertically, in columns. For consistency, the examples in this chapter use baselines in columns rather than rows.

On the Disk

In addition to the baseline itself, you also need a method to create a forecast. Excel provides three basic approaches to forecasting: moving averages, regression, and smoothing. This chapter also describes a fourth approach, Box-Jenkins. The *Business Analysis with Excel* companion disk contains a VBA module that enables you to perform the identification phase of Box-Jenkins forecasting.

Moving Average Forecasts

Moving averages are easy to use, but sometimes they are too simple to provide a useful forecast. Using this approach, the forecast at any period is just the average of several observations in the time series. For example, if you choose a three-month moving average, then the forecast for May would be the average of the observations for February, March, and April. If you choose to take a four-month moving average, then the forecast for May would be the average of January, February, March, and April.

This method is easy to compute, and it responds well to recent changes in the time series. Many time series respond more strongly to recent events than they do to long established patterns. Suppose, for example, that you are forecasting the sales volume of a mature product, one that has averaged 1,000 units per month for several years. If your company significantly downsizes its sales force, the average units sold per month would probably decline, at least for a few months.

If you were using the average sales volume for the last 24 months as your forecast for the next month, the forecast would probably overestimate the actual result. If, however, you calculated your forecast by using the average of only the last three months, your forecast would respond more quickly to the effect of downsizing the sales force. The forecast would lag behind the actual results for only a month or two. Figure 9.1 gives a visual example of this effect.

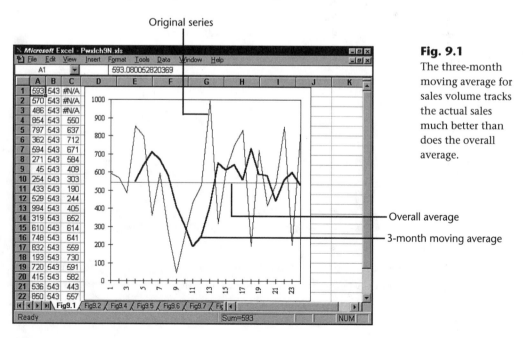

Fig. 9.1
The three-month moving average for sales volume tracks the actual sales much better than does the overall average.

II

Financial Planning
and Control

This effect occurs, of course, because with a three-month moving average, the three most recent months are each responsible for one-third of the forecast's value. With a 24-month average, the three most recent months are each responsible for only 1/24th of the forecast value.

Therefore, the smaller the number of observations involved in a moving average, the more quickly it responds to changes in the level of the baseline.

Case Study: Customer Service

You manage the customer service group for a software development firm. You receive an e-mail from one of your support staff that says she is getting phone calls from customers who are having a problem with one of your newer applications. You request her to track these calls over a two week period and report back to you.

The report that you receive has the daily number of calls that she has received concerning this product. You enter the data into an Excel worksheet, laid out as shown in cells A1:A10 of figure 9.2. To see whether there is any trend in the data, you create a moving average from the number of phone calls, as shown in cells B4:B10 of figure 9.2.

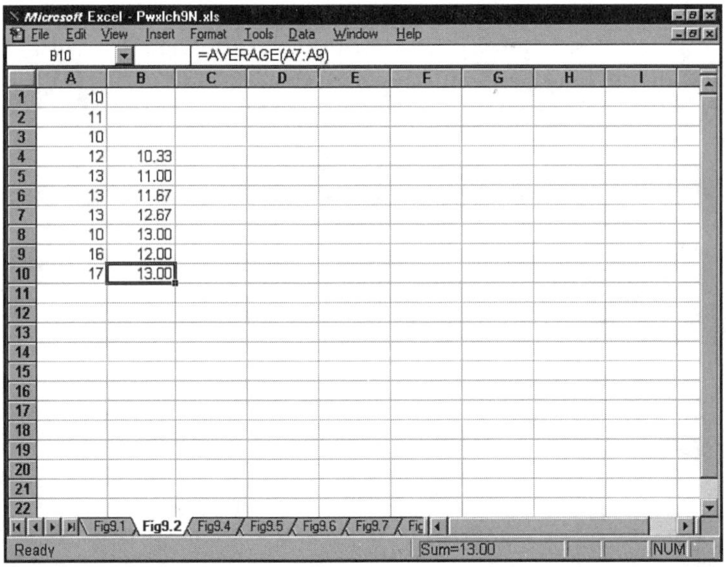

Fig. 9.2
Moving average forecasts entail the loss of some data at the beginning of the baseline period.

	A	B
1	10	
2	11	
3	10	
4	12	10.33
5	13	11.00
6	13	11.67
7	13	12.67
8	10	13.00
9	16	12.00
10	17	13.00

B10 =AVERAGE(A7:A9)

You decide to use a three-day moving average: a shorter moving average might not depict the trend well, and a much longer moving average would shorten the trend too much. One way to create a moving average in Excel is to enter the formula directly. To get the three-day moving average for the number of phone calls, you enter:

```
=AVERAGE(A1:A3)
```

in cell B4, and then autofill or copy-and-paste that formula into B5:B10, as shown in figure 9.2. The moving average does seem to be trending up, and you might decide to bring the situation to the attention of your company's product testing group.

> **Tip**
>
> To *autofill*, use your mouse pointer to drag the fill handle of a selected cell or range vertically or horizontally. The fill handle is the small square in the lower-right corner of the selection.

Creating Forecasts with the Moving Average Add-in

Another way to create a moving average is to use the Analysis ToolPak. You invoke this utility from the Tools menu by following these steps:

1. Have a worksheet active.

2. Choose Tools, Add-Ins.

3. Excel displays a dialog box with the available add-ins. Click the box labeled Analysis ToolPak - VBA, and choose OK.

4. If necessary, activate a worksheet that contains your baseline data.

5. At the bottom of the Tools menu, there is now a Data Analysis option. Choose Tools, Data Analysis.

6. Excel displays a dialog box containing the available data analysis functions. Scroll down the list box until you see Moving Average. Highlight that line, and then choose OK.

7. Excel displays a dialog box that prompts you for the Input Range, Interval, and Output Range, as shown in figure 9.3.

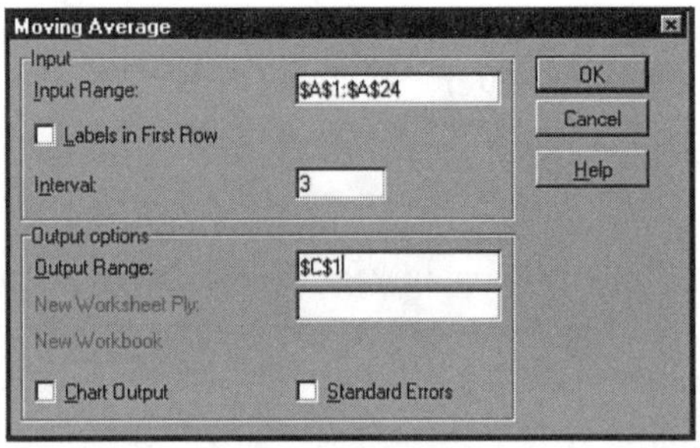

Fig. 9.3
The Moving
Average dialog box
lets you define a
period consisting
of the observa-
tions that go into
each average.

8. Click in the Input Range edit box, and either highlight your baseline
   data or type its reference.

9. Click in the Interval edit box, and enter the number of months that
   you want to include in the moving average.

10. Click in the Output Range edit box, and enter the address of the cell
    (or just click the cell) where you want the output to start.

11. Choose OK.

Excel fills in the formulas for the moving average on your behalf. The moving
averages begin with some #N/A values. There are as many #N/A values as the
interval you specified, minus one. This is because there isn't enough data to
calculate an average for those first few observations. Figure 9.4 shows the
results of using the moving average add-in on the same data as used in figure
9.1, with a 3-period Interval.

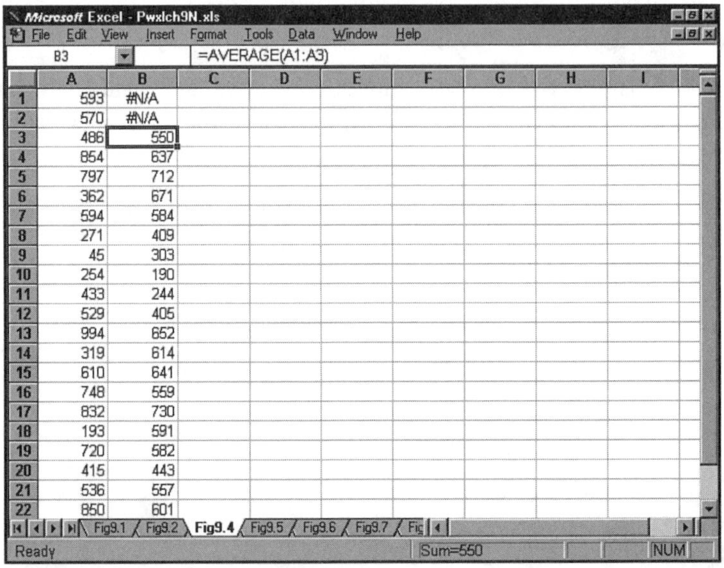

Fig. 9.4
Moving averages
smooth out shifts
in the underlying
baseline.

Dealing with the Formatting of Excel's Moving Average Calculations

It is standard to regard a moving average forecast as a forecast for the first period immediately following the last observation. For example, suppose that you create a three-month moving average of sales revenues, and that the final three observations in your baseline are for January, February, and March. The average of those three observations is usually regarded as the moving average forecast for April: the first period immediately following the last observation.

However, Excel's Moving Average add-in (and, as you will see in the next section, its Moving Average trendline) associate the forecast with the final observation in a given average. Compare, for example, figure 9.1, where the moving averages were created by entering formulas directly on the worksheet, and figure 9.4, which was created by the Moving Average add-in. Notice that each moving average in figure 9.4 is shifted up one position from its position in figure 9.1. This implies that 550, for example, the first moving average that is computed, is the forecast for the third period.

But it is illogical to regard a number as a forecast for a period that was used to calculate the forecast. The standard interpretation is that 550 is the forecast for the fourth period, not for the third period.

The best solution is to enter the formulas by hand. But another solution is as follows: After the Moving Average add-in has finished processing, select the values that it outputs and drag them all down by one row. Doing this will line up the forecasts with the periods that they are properly associated with.

> **Tip**
>
> If you choose to chart the output by checking the <u>C</u>hart Output checkbox in the Moving Average dialog box, the chart positions the forecasts as it does on the worksheet. After shifting the worksheet values down by one row, edit the chart's forecast series by clicking it and, in the formula bar, change the series' first row to the row that precedes it. For example, change =SERIES(Forecast,,Fig9.4!$B$2:$B$25,2) to =SERIES(Forecast,,Fig9.4!$B$1:$B$25,2).

Creating Moving Average Forecasts with Excel's Charts

You can trade speed for information by creating a chart that uses your baseline data to show a moving average trendline. This method is often faster, because it can take several seconds for Excel to load the Add-in Manager, and you can skip this step if you create a trendline on a chart.

The tradeoff is that the chart will not show the actual numeric values of the moving average. Further, it suffers from the defect already noted in the last section of this chapter: the forecast is displayed one time period too early. In this case, there is no workaround, because you cannot shift the location of a chart's trendline.

If you decide that you can live with these tradeoffs, you can create a moving average trendline by following these steps:

1. Highlight your baseline data.

2. Begin the Chart Wizard, either by clicking the button on the Standard or Chart toolbar, or by choosing Insert, Chart, As New Sheet. If you use the toolbar button, hold down the mouse button and drag through the part of the worksheet where you want the chart to appear.

3. In Step 1 of the Chart Wizard, verify the cell references to your baseline data, and click Next.

4. In Step 2, select the Line Chart, and click Next.

5. In Step 3, select a Line Chart subtype that includes both automatic lines and automatic markers such as subtype 1, 4, or 5. Click Next.

6. In Step 4, choose Data Series in Columns. If you have provided for x-axis labels or for a data series legend in the worksheet, set those options. Click Next.

7. In the final panel, set the Legend, Chart Title and Axis Titles options to the values that you want. Click Finish.

8. If you embedded the chart in the worksheet, double-click on the chart to open it for editing.

9. Click on the data series in the chart to highlight it, and choose Insert, Trendline.

10. On the Trendline Type tab, click the Moving Average box, and either type the periods you want in the edit box or use the spinner to change the number of periods. The period is the number of observations to include in any given moving average.

11. Choose OK.

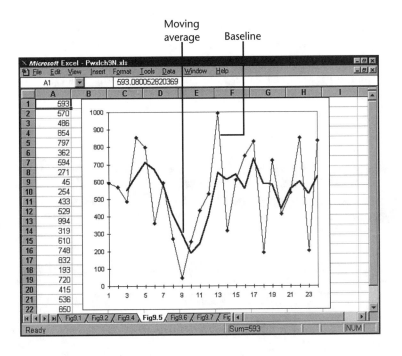

Moving
average   Baseline

Fig. 9.5
Because they are
based on prior
observations,
moving averages
tend to lag behind
movement in the
underlying
baselines.

When you are finished, you see the moving average trendline on the chart
(along with the actual observations) as shown in figure 9.5. The first few
moving averages on the trendline are missing, for the same reason that the
Moving Average add-in returns #N/A for the first few moving averages. A
moving average consisting of three prior observations cannot be calculated
until the third period has been observed.

Forecasting with Excel's Regression Functions

A simple moving average is a quick and dirty way to get a feel for the general
trend of a time series, but you're likely to want more than that. If you worked
through the examples for moving average forecasts, you probably noticed
that they don't give you a projection more than one period beyond the final
point in your baseline. You can get a projection further into the future by
using one of Excel's regression functions.

Each of the regression methods estimates the relationship between the actual
observations and some other variable. The other variable is often a measure of
when the observation was made. It could be the numeric position of each observation in the time series, or it could be the date when you made the observation.

Making Linear Forecasts: The TREND Function

The TREND worksheet function is the easiest way to create a regression forecast. Suppose that your observations are in A1:A10, and indicators such as the day of the month are in B1:B10, as in figure 9.6. Highlight cells C1:C10 and array-enter the following formula:

    =TREND(A1:A10,B1:B10)

to get the results in figure 9.6.

> **Tip**
>
> To array-enter a formula on a computer running Windows, use Ctrl+Shift and simultaneously press Enter.

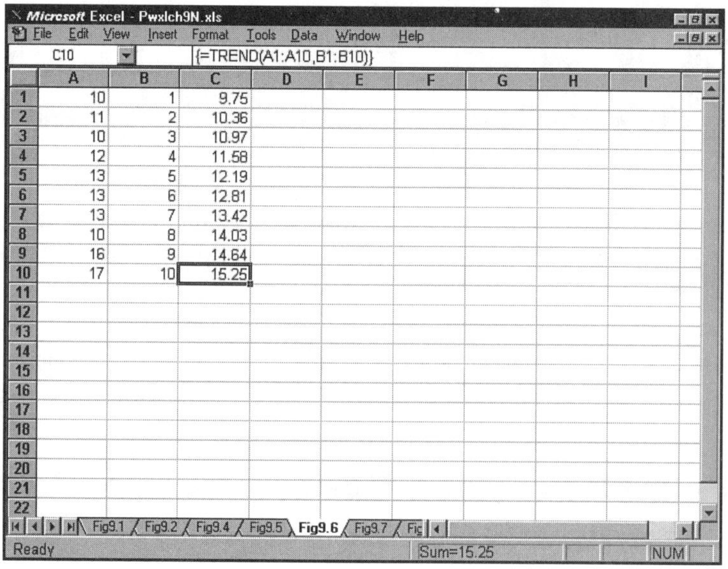

Fig. 9.6
The TREND function forecasts a baseline of observations on the basis of some other variable.

There are several points to notice about this forecasting method:

■ The same array formula returns each result in C1:C10. Hidden within the array-formula is a more complex expression. Here, the actual expanded formula is:

Cell C1: = 9.13 + .61 * 1

Cell C2: = 9.13 + .61 * 2

Cell C3: = 9.13 + .61 * 3

and so on. The value 9.13 is the *intercept* of the forecast line: that is, the value of the forecast at time zero. The value .61 is the *slope* of the forecast line: that is, the change in the value of the forecast for each change in the date of the observations.

■ Because the same intercept and slope values create each forecast value, the forecast doesn't reflect changes in the time series as they occur. For example, the series jumps between the eighth observation (10) and the ninth observation (16). The intercept and slope take account of this jump, but it affects *all* the forecast values. The jump affects the forecast at Time 2, even though Time 2 is six observations before the jump actually occurs.

■ In this example, TREND computes the forecast based on the relationship between the actual observations and the numbers 1 through 10, which could be the first ten days of the month or the first ten months of the year. Excel terms the first argument to the TREND function the *known-ys*, and the second argument the *known-xs*.

> **Tip**
>
> If you supply only the first argument, the known-ys, to TREND(), Excel assumes that the known-xs are a series beginning with 1 and ending with the number of known-y values that you specify. Assuming that the numbers 1 through 20 are in B1:B20, these two formulas are equivalent:
>
> =TREND(A1:A20)
>
> =TREND(A1:A20,B1:B20)

It was mentioned earlier that the regression approaches to forecasting let you make projections into the future. The regression forecast in figure 9.6 simply extended through the final actual observation. In practice, you normally want to forecast at least through the value of the next (and, so far, unobserved) point in the time series. Here is how to do that using TREND.

Using the same worksheet data as in figure 9.6, enter the number 11 in cell B11, and in cell C11 enter:

=TREND(A1:A10,B1:B10,B11)

Figure 9.7 shows additional syntax in the TREND function. The first argument, A1:A10, defines the baseline observations (the known ys). The second argument, B1:B10, defines the times when the baseline observations were made (the known xs). The value 11 in cell B11 is a *new x*, and it defines the time to associate with a projection.

Financial Planning and Control

Fig. 9.7

The TREND function forecasts beyond the end of the baseline by means of its *new-xs* argument.

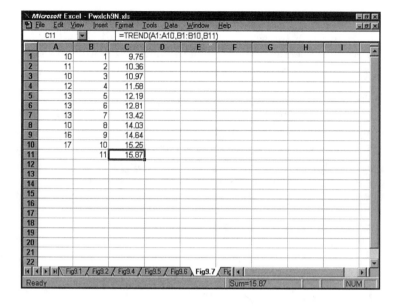

In effect, the formula says, "Given the relationship between the y-values in A1:A10 and the x-values in B1:B10, what y-value would result from a new x-value of 11?" Excel returns the value 15.87, which is a projection of the observed data into the as yet unobserved 11th time point.

> **Tip**
>
> You can forecast to dates later than just the next time point, by entering a larger value into cell B11. Suppose that the observations in A1:A10 were monthly sales volume for January through October 1995. Then the number 24 in B11 would specify the 24th month: December 1996. The TREND function would return 23.8. This is the projected sales volume for December 1996 on the basis of actual observations from January through October 1995.

You can project to more than one new time point at once. For example, enter the numbers 11 through 24 in cells B11:B24. Then, highlight cells C11:C24 and array-enter:

```
=TREND(A1:A10,B1:B10,B11:B24)
```

Excel returns, in C11:C24, its forecast for the 11th through 24th time points. It bases the forecast on the relationship between the baseline observations in A1:A10 and the baseline time points 1 through 10 in B1:B10.

Making Nonlinear Forecasts: The GROWTH Function

The TREND function creates forecasts based on a *linear* relationship between the observation and the time that the observation was made. Suppose that you chart the data as a line chart with the observations as the vertical axis and time as the horizontal axis. If the relationship is a linear one, the line on the chart is relatively straight, trending up or down, or it may be horizontal. That's your best clue that the relationship is linear, and that TREND is probably the best regression forecasting tool.

But if the line has a dramatic upward or downward curve to it, then the relationship is probably *nonlinear*. There are many kinds of data that change over time in a nonlinear way. Some examples of this data include new product sales, population growth, payments on debt principal, and per-unit profit margin. In cases where the relationship is nonlinear, Excel's GROWTH function can give you a better picture of the pattern than can the TREND function.

Case Study: Book Sales

The purchasing manager of a large mail order book club has just mailed a new catalog to the club's members. The catalog advertises a novel that is receiving very favorable reviews. The manager suspects that it will be necessary to order additional copies earlier than normal. To avoid being caught short, the manager starts to track weekly orders for the book, and records the sales shown in figure 9.8.

Figure 9.8 shows how both the actual data and the forecasts appear in a standard line chart. Because the line for the actuals curves upward, the decision is to forecast using the GROWTH function. As with TREND, the user can generate forecasts by simply providing new x-values. To forecast into weeks 11 through 13, enter those numbers in B12:B14, and array-enter the following GROWTH function in C2:C14:

```
=GROWTH(A2:A11,B2:B11,B2:B14)
```

Cells C12:C14 forecast the number of orders you can expect for the next three weeks, if the current growth pattern continues. It's necessary to temper such optimistic forecasts with some reality, though. When this sort of forecast projects orders that exceed the total book club membership, its probably time to back off the forecast.

Fig. 9.8
The GROWTH function can be useful in forecasting nonlinear baselines.

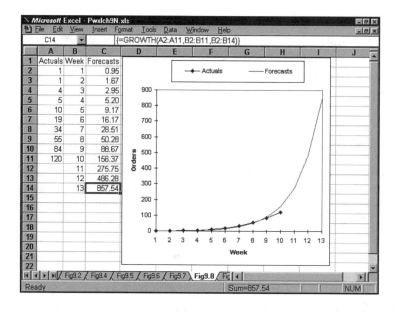

Tip

In cases that display this sort of explosive growth, you might find it more convenient to deal with the logarithms of the observations instead of the observations themselves. For example, you can show the exponential growth as a straight line by using a log scale for the charts vertical axis. Figure 9.9 shows how the book club data appear in a line chart where the scale of the vertical axis is in log values.

Fig. 9.9
The logarithmic chart of exponential growth in book sales can be easier to interpret than the standard line chart.

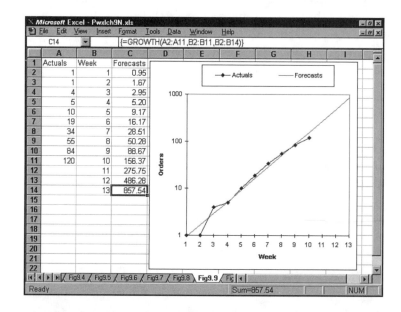

What if TREND instead of GROWTH were used on the book club data? In that case, because the known-xs are linear, TREND would return linear values. See figure 9.10: note that the TREND series in column C describes a straight line on the chart. Figure 9.10 shows the three series as a standard line chart. Clearly, the GROWTH line is a much better representation of the first ten observations than is the TREND line.

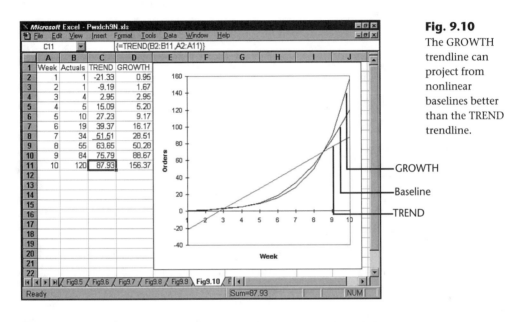

Fig. 9.10

The GROWTH trendline can project from nonlinear baselines better than the TREND trendline.

Nevertheless, there's nothing magical about GROWTH: it's simply a convenient way to return specifically logarithmic results. Natural logarithms do not describe all nonlinear series: you might want to project a quadratic (second order) trend, or even a cubic (third order) trend. You should often use TREND in these cases, because you can maintain better control over your projections.

Figure 9.11 shows an example of how to use the TREND function to return results identical to the GROWTH function. The array formula used in cells C2:C14 is:

=EXP(TREND(LN(B2:B11),A2:A11,A2:A14))

Fig. 9.11

You can use the TREND function in place of the GROWTH function to handle either nonlinear relationships of any type.

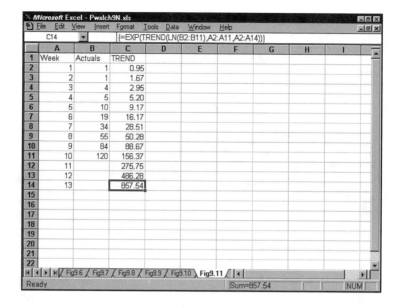

Note that these values are identical to the ones returned by GROWTH, and would describe the same curve on a line chart.

Many times you will want to use TREND instead of GROWTH, even if the baseline is nonlinear. GROWTH is a useful alternative to TREND when you have data that natural logarithms fit well.

Creating Regression Forecasts with Excel's Charts

At times, you just want to view a regression forecast on a chart, without putting the forecast values in the worksheet. You do so by using a chart trendline, in much the same way as you obtain a moving average forecast from a chart. Figure 9.12 displays baseline data and a chart with the baseline, trendline and forecasts.

To create the chart in figure 9.12, use the Chart Wizard to create a line chart of the baseline data in cells A2:A25. Double-click the chart to open it for editing, and click the data series on the chart to select it. Then:

1. Choose Insert, Trendline.

2. Choose Linear under Trend/Regression Type.

3. Click on the Options tab.

4. In the Forecast group box, either enter the number of Forward forecast periods you want, or use the spinner to specify the number of forecast periods.

5. If you want, click the Display Equation on Chart check box. Doing so will place the forecast equation (intercept and slope) as text on the chart. Excel's placement of the equation may obscure the charts data or trendline, or the equation may not be fully visible. You can select the equation by clicking on it and then dragging it to a new location.

6. Choose OK.

Unlike the Moving Averages trendline, a Linear trendline can return forecast values, and, if specified, it displays them on the chart.

Trendline

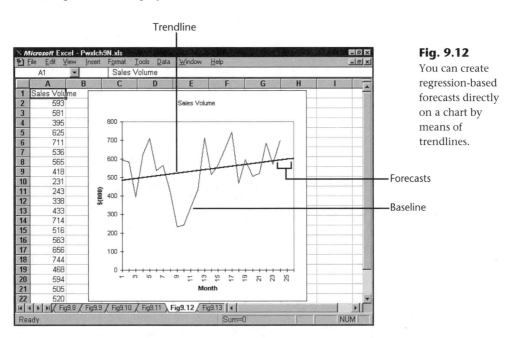

Fig. 9.12
You can create regression-based forecasts directly on a chart by means of trendlines.

Forecasts

Baseline

Forecasting with Excel's Smoothing Functions

Smoothing is a way to get your forecast to respond quickly to events that occur during the baseline period. Regression approaches such as TREND and GROWTH apply the same formula to all the forecast points, and getting a quick response to a shift in the level of the baseline becomes quite complex. Smoothing is a simple way around this problem.

Projecting with Smoothing

The fundamental idea behind the smoothing approach is that each new forecast is obtained in part by moving the *prior* forecast in a direction that would have improved the old forecast. Here's the basic equation:

$$F[t+1] = F[t] + a \times e[t]$$

where:

- t is the time period: e.g., Month 1, Month 2, etc.

- $F[t]$ is the forecast at time t, and $F[t+1]$ is the forecast at the time period immediately following time t

- a is the smoothing constant

- $e[t]$ is the error: the difference between the forecast for time t and the actual observation at time t

So a smoothing forecast is, in a sense, self-correcting. In words, each new forecast is the sum of the prior forecast, plus a correction factor that moves the new forecast in the direction that would have made the prior forecast more accurate.

Consider the example shown in figure 9.13

Fig. 9.13

The linear trendline forecast misses the baseline's step function, but the smoothing forecast tracks it.

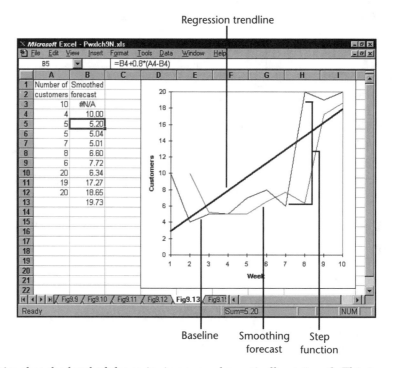

Notice that the level of the series increases dramatically at time 8. This is known as a *step* function. Smoothing is useful when there are large differences between levels of data in the time series. The linear trendline does not do a good job of reflecting the step increase that occurs between time 7 and time 8. It overestimates the level of the series through time 7, and it underestimates the series thereafter. But the smoothing forecast tracks the actual baseline fairly closely.

Using the Exponential Smoothing Add-in

The forecasting methods collectively known as smoothing handle the step function effect much better than regression methods do. Excel provides one such method directly with the Exponential Smoothing tool in the Analysis ToolPak.

The Exponential Smoothing tool creates forecasts that are identical to the one shown in figure 9.13. It uses a different but algebraically equivalent formula to calculate each forecast. Each component—prior observation and prior forecast— in each forecast is multiplied by a factor that represents the components contribution to the current forecast.

You can invoke the Exponential Smoothing tool by choosing Tools, Data Analysis after you have loaded the Analysis ToolPak.

Case Study: Rental Cars

Suppose that you operate a car rental agency in the Rocky Mountain region. As winter approaches, you start to track customer requests for vehicles with ski racks. After a few days of monitoring these requests, an early winter storm passes through the area and, as expected, the number of requests per day increases substantially. You would like to know, on the tenth day, how many cars equipped with ski racks you should arrange to make available on the eleventh day.

You enter the data for the first ten days in cells A1:A10 of a worksheet, and start Excels Exponential Smoothing add-in (see fig. 9.14).

Fig. 9.14
The Exponential Smoothing dialog box asks you for a damping factor, rather than a smoothing constant.

> **Note**
>
> The *damping factor* in the Smoothing dialog box and the *smoothing constant* mentioned in the prior section are related as follows:
>
> 1 – smoothing constant = damping factor
>
> Therefore, knowing the damping factor means that you also know the smoothing constant, and vice versa. Excel chooses to ask you for the damping factor.

You use A1:A12 as the Input Range, fill the Labels checkbox, use B1 as the Output Range, and .7 as the Damping factor. Excel returns the results shown in figure 9.15.

> **Tip**
>
> To forecast one time period beyond the end of the baseline, enter one extra row in the Smoothing dialog box's Input Range edit box.

Fig. 9.15
Car rental data with smoothed forecasts; notice the lag in the forecasts.

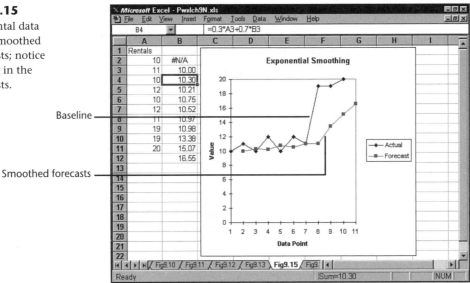

According to the smoothed forecast, the best estimate of the required number of cars with ski racks on day eleven is 16 or 17. This estimate reflects both the overall level of the baseline data and the increase in requests that occurred on the eighth day. The actual number needed on the eleventh day could drop by several units, as a result of anything from a change in weather conditions to an increase in airline fares. The smoothed forecast strikes a good balance between the recent surge in requests and the average number of requests for the entire 10-day period.

> **Note**
>
> Even though you might fill the Labels checkbox in the Smoothing dialog box, Excel does not show the label in the resulting chart.

Notice in figure 9.15 that the forecast increases on day 9, reflecting the increase in the baseline that occurs on day 8. Generally, simple smoothing approaches lag one step behind occurrences in the time series itself.

The smaller the damping factor, the more responsive the forecast is to recent observations. On the other hand, the larger the damping factor, the longer the forecasts will lag behind recent observations. This is useful if recent observations reflect random occurrences that do not alter the overall level of the time series for long.

Choosing a Smoothing Constant

You should avoid using a damping factor smaller than .7. If exponential smoothing appears to work *significantly* better with a larger smoothing constant, it is likely due to a substantial amount of autocorrelation in the time series.

Autocorrelation is an important concept in forecasting. It occurs when there is a dependency between observations that occur at a given time and observations that occur some number of time periods earlier. For example, if you pair up each observation with the observation that immediately precedes it, you can calculate the correlation between the two sets of data. If the correlation is strong—say, .5 or greater—then there is a substantial amount of autocorrelation in the time series.

> **Tip**
>
> You can use Excel's CORREL function to test for autocorrelation. Suppose that your baseline is in A1:A10. You might use:
>
>   =CORREL(A1:A9,A2:A10)
>
> to estimate the autocorrelation between each observation and its predecessor. If it is strong, then each observation depends largely on the value of the observation that immediately preceded it.

Another kind of autocorrelation has to do with seasonality in the series. In a time series that consists of months in a year, the observation in each February might be dependent on the prior February. In such cases, you should use seasonal smoothing (see the next section) or a Box-Jenkins model (see the section in this chapter titled "Using the Box-Jenkins ARIMA Approach: When Excel's Built-in Functions Won't Do").

Making Smoothed Forecasts Handle Seasonal Data

If you ever want to forecast sales, then you almost certainly need to account for seasonal trends. Sales data and related time series are frequently seasonal. For example, sales may spike at the beginning of the year and then return to a lower level until the next year.

This effect can be due to the nature of the product: the demand for parkas is lower during spring and summer than during fall and winter. It can also be due to fiscal years: buyers might increase their purchases at the point in the fiscal year when dollars are plentiful. In cases like these, the regression and simple smoothing methods may be inadequate to forecast a seasonal trend.

When a time series displays a seasonal trend, it is usually necessary to modify the smoothing formula. Instead of forecasting just on the basis of the prior observation, a seasonal forecast works on the basis of two components:

- A trend component, which represents any upward or downward drift in the baseline.

- A seasonal component, which represents any upward or downward spikes in the baseline that occur at regular intervals.

The seasonal smoothing process takes place in two phases: an initialization phase, which quantifies the magnitude of the trend and seasonal components, and a forecasting phase, which makes the projections based on those components. Consider the time series in figure 9.16.

The series in figure 9.16 has considerable seasonality. It trends up each August and down again each November. A forecast that used simple exponential smoothing would have some undesirable lag, because a current forecast is based only on the prior observation and the prior forecast. Therefore, a forecast of the surge in the series value that occurs each August would lag by a month each year. Figure 9.16 also shows the forecast based on the time series by means of simple exponential smoothing.

Seasonal smoothing takes account of this regularity in the data by looking back at the pattern in prior years. The current forecasts then reflect the prior pattern. This minimizes the lag from the prior observation to current forecast.

Figure 9.17 shows the same baseline as in figure 9.16, along with a seasonally smoothed forecast. There is still some lag, but not as much as with simple smoothing. Furthermore, because each forecast depends in part on an observation from a prior *year*, it is possible to extend the forecast further into the future than it is with simple smoothing.

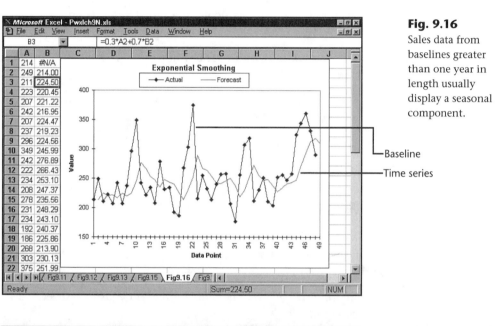

Fig. 9.16

Sales data from baselines greater than one year in length usually display a seasonal component.

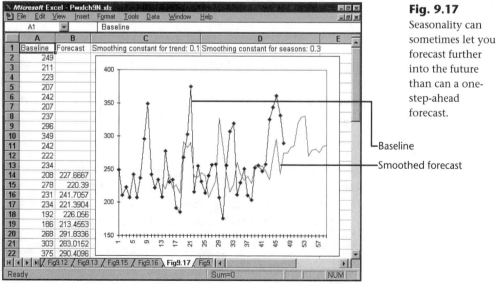

Fig. 9.17

Seasonality can sometimes let you forecast further into the future than can a one-step-ahead forecast.

II

Financial Planning and Control

Two smoothing constants are necessary for seasonal smoothing: one for any trend there may be in the series, and one for the seasonal component.

On the Disk

The *Business Analysis with Excel* companion disk that accompanies this book contains a file named Smooth.xls. The file contains a module, also named Smooth. The module contains a VBA macro, SeasonalSmooth. SeasonalSmooth performs seasonally smoothed forecasts on a baseline of observations. To run the macro, follow these steps:

1. Have a worksheet with your baseline open. The baseline should occupy a single column.

2. Open Smooth.xls, and switch back to the worksheet that contains your baseline observations.

3. From the Tools menu, select Macro.

4. In the Macro Name/Reference list box, select Smooth.xls!SeasonalSmooth.

5. Choose Run.

When you run that macro, a dialog box similar to the Exponential Smoothing dialog box appears on your screen, giving you the opportunity to identify:

■ An input range—your baseline—found on your worksheet in a single column.

■ The number of periods in each season. For example, if your input data consist of one observation for each month in the year, then the number of periods in each season (Spring, Summer, Fall, and Winter) would be 3. If your input data consists of one observation for each week in the month, then the number of periods in each season would be 4, if you consider that a month is a season, or 12, if you consider that a quarter is a season.

■ The number of seasons per calendar block. A calendar block is the period of time during which a seasonal cycle becomes complete. For example, if you are concerned with quarterly cycles, then the calendar block would likely be one year. If you are concerned with weekly cycles, then the calendar block might be one month.

■ The two smoothing constants: one for the trend, and one for the seasons. Both constants should be set to a fractional value between 0 and 1.

Using the Box-Jenkins ARIMA Approach: When Excel's Built-in Functions Won't Do

Box-Jenkins methods, often called *ARIMA* (for *AutoRegressive Integrated Moving Average*) models, have much broader scope than simple moving average, regression or smoothing forecasts, and they can often remove most of the drawbacks of the approaches discussed above.

However, Box-Jenkins methods are also much more complex, well beyond the scope of this book to cover in detail. This chapter discusses only the preliminary phase of these methods, the identification phase. Completing the identification phase helps you to decide whether to make your forecast using a program written specifically for Box-Jenkins, or whether you can choose a regression or smoothing approach that Excel supports directly.

The Disk that accompanies this book includes VBA code that will assist you in determining whether a Box-Jenkins model is necessary to forecast your time series properly.

On the Disk

Understanding ARIMA Basics

Suppose that you have a baseline of observations from which you want to make a forecast. Excel provides little in the way of guidance as to whether you should use a regression approach such as TREND or GROWTH, or a smoothing approach such as the Exponential Smoothing add-in, to create forecasts from your baseline. Many people choose one or the other on an *ad hoc* basis: they might be more familiar with one approach than with another, or they might want to save time by forecasting with a chart trendline, or they might simply flip a coin.

Box-Jenkins models provide you with a quantitative basis for deciding between regression and smoothing—and, carried to their conclusion, can apply both regression and smoothing simultaneously to create the best forecast. The process does this by examining the patterns of correlations in the baseline and returning information to you that suggests whether a regression approach (in ARIMA, AutoRegressive) or a smoothing approach (in ARIMA, Moving Average), or a combination, is optimal.

The Box-Jenkins identification phase, covered in this section, is a formal, rather than *ad hoc*, means of choosing an approach to forecasting. To understand this more fully, consider that a time series can have:

- *An autoregressive component.* Each observation is dependent on a prior observation (not necessarily the immediately prior observation). An example is revenue from leases, where the amount of revenue each month reflects the amount of revenue the prior month. This is very similar to the concept of autocorrelation, described above in the section on Choosing a Smoothing Constant.

- *A trend component.* The series level drifts regularly up or down over time. The term *integrated* refers (rather obscurely) to the computations that describe that trend numerically. An example is unit sales of a new product that is gaining market acceptance. Eventually the unit sales figures will become constant and the trend will disappear, but during the early phases there is often a clear, sometimes explosive trend.

- *A moving average component.* In the Box-Jenkins context this means that the series experiences random shocks over time. The effect of these shocks may linger in the level of the series after the shock itself has occurred.

These three components may exist separately or in combination in any time series. There are AR models, MA models, ARMA models, IMA models, ARIMA models, and so on. Furthermore, there may be seasonality in the series, leading to (for example) a series that has both a regular and a seasonal AR component, as well as a regular and a seasonal MA component.

With all these models from which to choose, how do you select the one that best fits your time series, and is thus the best one to use for forecasting? ARIMA jargon refers to this as the *identification* phase. Early in the analysis, charts called *correlograms* are created. These correlograms help identify what sort of forecasting model, if any, you should consider.

On the Disk

A Box-Jenkins module can be found in the file named ARIMA.xls on the *Business Analysis with Excel* companion disk. This module contains a macro named ARIMA, which creates correlograms for your time series. By examining the correlograms, you can determine whether you should use of one of the complete Box-Jenkins computer programs to complete the analysis, or whether you can use an Excel regression function or the Exponential Smoothing add-in. There are many programs available that perform complete Box-Jenkins analyses, such as SAS, SPSS and Systat.

To run the ARIMA macro, have a worksheet open that contains your baseline in a single column. Then, follow these steps:

1. Open ARIMA.xls, and switch back to the worksheet that contains your baseline observations.

2. Choose Tools, Macro

3. In the Macro Name/Reference list box, select ARIMA.

4. Choose Run.

The module displays a dialog box where you enter the address of your baseline data, whether to compute first differences, and how many lags you want to view for the autocorrelations. The remainder of this section describes the choices you have in the dialog box, and how to interpret the macros output.

You should not use Box-Jenkins models with fewer than 50 observations in the time series. It takes at least this many observations to model the data with any accuracy. In practice, it is usual to wait for well over 100 observations prior to starting the forecast process.

> **Tip**
>
> This recommendation is not limited to Box-Jenkins forecasts: it could and should be used for most forecasts using any regression method. Before you place much faith in a forecast using one of Excel's regression functions, use LINEST or LOGEST to determine the standard error of estimate for the regression (this is the value returned in the second column of the array's third row). If the standard error is large relative to the precision that you need, it's probably best to obtain a longer baseline before you proceed with a forecast.

In sum, before you decide to employ these methods with any real baseline data, be sure that you have enough data points for the task to be worthwhile.

Starting with Correlograms to Identify a Model

A *correlogram* displays correlation coefficients in graphic form, one for each lag in a time series. Figure 9.18 shows a correlogram for lags 1 through 20.

> **Note**
>
> The time series used in figures 9.18 through 9.23 are far too long to include here. You can find them in a workbook titled ARIMA Series.xls on the companion disk.

On the Disk

II

Financial Planning
and Control

Fig. 9.18

The correlogram for ACFs for lags 1 through 20: this could be either an AR or an ARMA process.

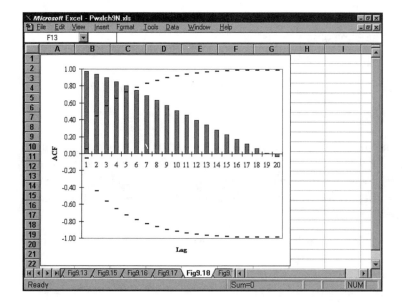

The ACF is the *autocorrelation function*, and is a type of correlation coefficient, akin to the autocorrelations discussed in "Choosing a Smoothing Constant" earlier in this chapter. The dashed lines show two standard errors of the ACFs. An ACF that extends above an upper dashed line, or one that extends below a lower dashed line, is statistically significant. Here, the ACFs gradually tail off. This pattern in the ACFs is typical of an autoregressive (AR) model.

The lags simply identify which data are used in the ACF. For example, consider the ACF at lag 1 in figure 9.18. It is the autocorrelation between the second through twentieth observations, and the first through nineteenth observations.

The second series, consisting of observations one through nineteen, lags one step behind the second through twentieth observations. Similarly, the ACF at lag 2 is based on the data in the third through twentieth observations and the first through eighteenth observations. The second set lags two steps behind the first set (see fig. 9.19).

	A	B	C	D	E	F	G	H	I
1	Original series			Lag 1:			Lag 2:		
2			2 - 20	1 - 19		3 - 20	1 - 18		
3	16		14	16		3	16		
4	14		3	14		5	14		
5	3		5	3		9	3		
6	5		9	5		15	5		
7	9		15	9		17	9		
8	15		17	15		1	15		
9	17		1	17		4	17		
10	1		4	1		9	1		
11	4		9	4		6	4		
12	9		6	9		19	9		
13	6		19	6		14	6		
14	19		14	19		15	19		
15	14		15	14		14	14		
16	15		14	15		1	15		
17	14		1	14		3	14		
18	1		3	1		11	1		
19	3		11	3		15	3		
20	11		15	11		3	11		
21	15		3	15					
22	3								

Fig. 9.19
Lags are relationships between different subsets of a time series.

Note

When a baseline has a trend—that is, when it has a pronounced upward or downward slope—it is often necessary to *difference* the observations. First-differencing usually removes the trend in the baseline, making it stationary—that is, roughly horizontal. The ACFs of a stationary baseline can be interpreted; the ACFs of an undifferenced baseline that has a trend are ambiguous.

The ARIMA macros dialog box has a check box for first-differencing. If your baseline has a pronounced slope, click the check box. ARIMA will then difference your baseline, removing the trend and making the ACFs interpretable.

Identifying Other Box-Jenkins Models

To identify a particular Box-Jenkins model, it is necessary to examine two correlograms: one for the ACF at different lags, and one for the PACF (partial autocorrelation function) at the same lags.

A PACF is conceptually similar to a partial correlation coefficient, which is the relationship between two variables after the effect of another variable or variables has been removed. For example, a partial correlation coefficient might measure the relationship between revenue and profit margin, after the effects of the number of salespeople and advertising costs have been removed from the relationship.

Similarly, a PACF at lag 4 would measure the relationship between, say, A5:A20 and A1:A16, after the effects of the intervening series have been removed.

Each Box-Jenkins model (AR, MA, IMA, ARIMA, and so on) has a distinctive signature in the pattern of the ACFs and PACFs in their correlograms. Figure 9.18 shows the ACF of an autoregressive series. It is characterized by either a gradual decline in the ACFs (as shown) and by a single spike in the PACF. For a baseline that displays this pattern of ACFs and PACFs, you could use an Excel regression technique, and regress the baseline onto itself, according to the location of the PACFs spike. For example, suppose that the spike were at lag 1. In that case, your known-ys would begin at the second observation in the baseline, and end at the end of the baseline. Your known-xs would begin at the start of the baseline, and end at its next-to-last observation.

Figure 9.20 shows the ACFs for a moving average process, and figure 9.21 shows its PACFs.

Fig. 9.20

ACFs of a moving average process: notice the single spike at lag 1.

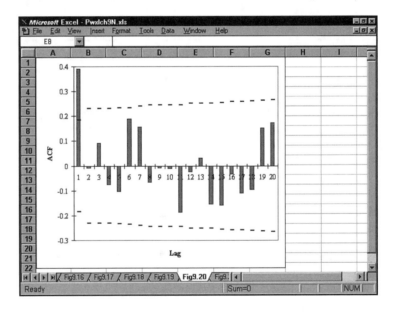

Notice the large, statistically significant ACF value at lag 1 in figure 9.20. (A value such as this is often termed a *spike* in a correlogram.) It is the only significant ACF in the correlogram.

Also notice that among the first six PACF values in figure 9.21, three are statistically significant and two just miss significance. This suggests that the PACFs are gradually dying out—in contrast to the single spike in the ACF correlogram in figure 9.20.

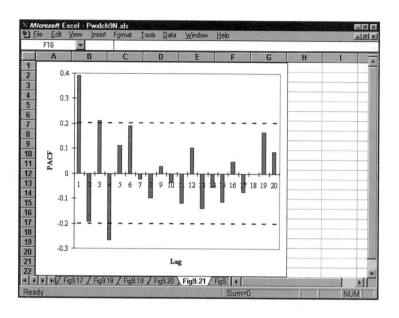

Fig. 9.21
PACFs of a moving average process: notice the gradual decline in the absolute magnitude of the PACFs.

This pattern—single spike in the ACF, gradual decline in the PACF—is characteristic of an MA process. If the ACFs spike is at lag 1, you can use Excel's Exponential Smoothing add-in with some confidence that it is the proper forecasting tool. If the single spike occurs at some other lag, you should resort to an application that provides specifically Box-Jenkins forecasting.

Figures 9.22 and 9.23 show the ACFs and the PACFs in the correlograms for a mixed process, one with both autoregressive and moving average (ARMA) components.

Notice the gradual decline in the ACFs in figure 9.22, as well as in the PACF in figure 9.23. This pattern in the correlograms is typical of a mixed, ARMA process. To forecast properly from this baseline, you would need to use an application that performs Box-Jenkins forecasting.

If your time series show any patterns similar to these when you run the Box-Jenkins add-in, you should consult a text that specifically covers Box-Jenkins models, and use one of the standard statistical programs that offer Box-Jenkins options. You are likely to get a much more accurate forecast of your data if you do so than if you use simple moving averages, regression, or exponential smoothing.

Financial Planning and Control

Fig. 9.22
ACFs of an autoregressive, moving average process gradually decline.

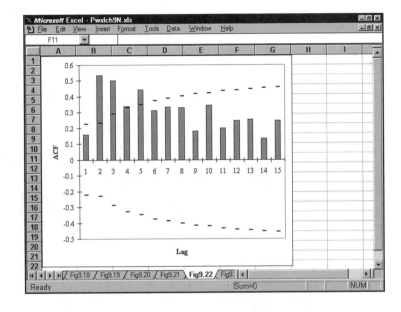

Fig. 9.23
PACFs of an autoregressive, moving average process, like its ACFs, gradually decline.

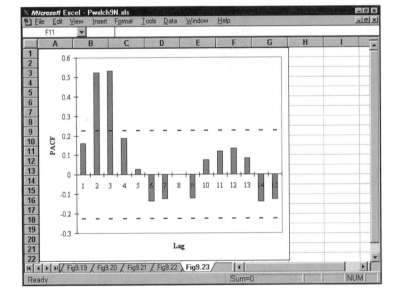

Summary

Forecasting can be trappy. To create a good forecast, you need a well-measured, well-defined baseline of data. You should use the suggestions made in this chapter to choose the most appropriate approach (moving average, regression, smoothing, or Box-Jenkins). At times, your baseline might not suggest an appropriate method, and you might need to wait for a longer baseline before you can be confident of your forecast.

Even if you feel you've done everything right, conditions have a way of changing unexpectedly—making your careful forecast look like a blind guess. Be sure to regard your forecasts with a healthy dose of skepticism. The more variables you have to work with, the more ways there are to view the future. Changes in one forecast can tip you off to the possibility that another forecast is about to change.

The methods described in this chapter are accurate ways to help you build your business plan. They can help you answer questions such as whether to anticipate an increase or a decrease in demand, whether price levels are rising or falling, and (perhaps more importantly) to what degree. Because the discussion has not explored the underlying theory of these approaches in great depth, you should consider studying a text (such as *Time Series Analysis, Forecasting and Control* by Box, G.E.P, and Jenkins, G.M.) devoted to the topic if you make many forecasts in the course of your work.

II

Financial Planning
and Control

Chapter 10

Measuring Quality

The 1980s and 1990s have taught American business that an emphasis on product quality is an important route toward profit. Other things being equal, a product with a reputation for high quality tends to sell more units than a product without that reputation. A product with good quality suffers fewer customer complaints, fewer free service calls, and fewer warranty repairs. Poor product quality goes directly to the bottom line in the form of lost profit.

It is also true that the quality of *operations* also drives profit margins. When customer service representatives spend too much time chatting with one customer, that means another customer is on hold, planning to buy someone else's product. When invoices are incorrect or sloppy, there is usually a delay in receipts. When the purchasing department orders unnecessary parts from a supplier, there is an unnecessary increase in carrying costs. When the quality of goods purchased is *too* high, the cost of the goods is probably also too high: zero-defect manufacturing is very expensive.

You can monitor each of these sorts of processes using Excel. The only other item you need is a source of data. This chapter describes how to use Excel to help you track and control these processes.

In this chapter, you learn to create and interpret statistical process control charts for both variables and attributes, create sampling plans to help you determine whether shipments of goods are acceptable, and decide whether a tested sample's defects are representative of those in its population.

Monitoring Through Statistical Process Control

The idea behind statistical process control (SPC) is that over a period of time you can take measurements on a process and determine whether that process is going out of control. Examples of process measurements include the following or virtually any other process that your company uses:

- Number of defective units in a manufacturing run

- Average number of defects in a unit

- Average diameter of a part that must meet a precise specification

- Average number of errors in an invoice

- Average length of time that customers remain on hold

- Average available capacity of a data communications circuit

The key phrases here are "over time," "average," and "out of control." *Over time* means that SPC depends on repeatedly and regularly measuring the process—daily, perhaps, or hourly or weekly. Your choice of how often to measure the process depends on how closely you want to monitor it.

If it is a constant process, one that is critical to your company's success, you might decide to monitor it hourly. This could happen if you were in the business of manufacturing ceramic tiles, and the color of the glaze as it leaves the kilns is a standard that is important to your customers.

Average means that SPC often depends on sampling several units at any given time. Suppose that you decide to monitor errors in invoices that your accounts receivable department prepares. It would be too costly and time consuming to examine every invoice. On the other hand, if you examine only one invoice per day you probably won't get a good estimate of the overall accuracy of the invoices.

In cases like these, SPC uses a random sample of the process, and it uses the average of that sample as an estimate of the process for that time period. You might decide to sample five invoices daily, and to use the average number of errors in that sample as the process estimate for that day.

On the other hand, you might use a 100 percent sample, in which case you would monitor every instance of the process. For example, this could occur in a manufacturing environment if you use a procedure that tests every unit as soon as assembly is complete.

Out of control means that SPC uses information not only about the average level of a process, but about its variability too. Suppose that you run the customer service department for a financial services company, and that 20 people answer your phones to take orders from your customers. You arrange to monitor the call length of 16 randomly-sampled calls per day, and learn that the average call length is two minutes and twenty seconds.

140 seconds for the average phone call seems satisfactory until you notice that 12 calls took less than a minute, and four calls took over six minutes each. You might decide that you need to learn why some calls take so long. (Are some of them personal calls? Is a representative putting callers on hold to look up something that he should have known?) You would not have known about the variations if you looked only at the average call length.

Using X-and-S Charts for Variables

SPC typically uses charts to depict the data in graphic form (see fig. 10.1).

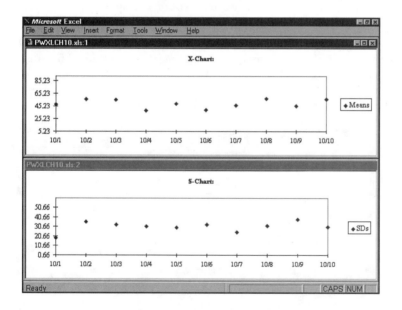

Fig. 10.1
These SPC x-and-s charts summarize the actual observations, but control limits are needed to interpret them properly.

There are two charts: one for the process average (the x-chart) and one for the process standard deviation (the s-chart).

> **Note**
>
> A *standard deviation* is a measure of how much individual scores vary around an average. Conceptually, it is similar to the range between the highest score and the lowest score. It is a more useful measure than the range, though. The range tells you only the difference between the two most extreme observations. The standard deviation takes all the scores into account in measuring how much variability there is in the group of scores.
>
> If you're not familiar with standard deviations, just keep in mind that a standard deviation, like a range, is a measure of variability. This book explains standard deviations more fully in chapter 15, "Investment Decisions Under Uncertainty."

Most SPC charts are laid out in a fashion similar to the ones shown in figure 10.1. The horizontal axis always shows the time (which hour, which day, which week, etc.) that a measurement was taken. The x-chart's vertical axis always represents the average measurement of a sample at a particular time. The s-chart's vertical axis always represents the standard deviation of the sample at a particular time. They are known as x-and-s charts because the statistical symbol for an average is *x*, and the statistical symbol for the standard deviation is *s*.

Figure 10.2 adds three refinements to the charts in figure 10.1.

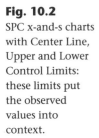

Fig. 10.2
SPC x-and-s charts with Center Line, Upper and Lower Control Limits: these limits put the observed values into context.

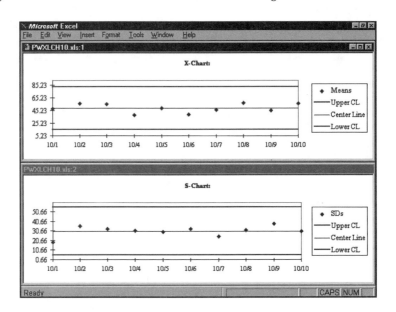

The charts in figure 10.2 have three horizontal lines that can help you understand the process. These horizontal lines are called the Upper Control Limit (UCL), the Center Line (CL), and the Lower Control Limit (LCL). For example:

- If too many points are either above the UCL or below the LCL, then something's wrong with the process.

- If a long series of points are between the CL and the UCL, or between the CL and the LCL, something may be wrong with the process.

- If a series of points are trending up toward the UCL, or down toward the LCL, something may be going wrong with the process.

You can see how useful this sort of information can be. It alerts you not only to the possibility that the process is out of control, but also to when it started going out of control. Knowing when might help you to pinpoint the cause of the problem: perhaps it always occurs during a staff change, such as at the end of a shift. Perhaps it occurs during a change from daylight savings time to standard time, which might interfere with people's sleep for a few days. Perhaps it's associated with drops in ambient temperature that cause the heating system to come on, introducing dust into a delicate manufacturing environment.

Whatever the cause, if you know that a problem has occurred as well as when it occurred then you are well on your way to identifying its cause.

The CL is a double-average. In an x-chart where each point represents a particular day, the observations for a given day are averaged to get the point for that day. Then, the averages for all the days are averaged to get the overall average: this is the CL for the x-chart. You create the CL for an s-chart in the same way, except that you start by calculating each day's standard deviation, and then average those standard deviations to get the CL for the s-chart.

On the Disk

The UCL and the LCL are a little more complicated. A UCL is usually three standard deviations above the CL, and an LCL is usually three standard deviations below the CL. (It's actually more complicated than that. The standard deviations are really standard errors, and the gamma distribution gets involved. Unless you're really interested, don't worry about it. If you are really interested, examine the SPC VBA module, SPC.XLS, on the disk that comes with this book—particularly the subroutine named EnterVariables( ).)

> **Note**
>
> While it is obviously impossible in many cases to actually *observe* a value below zero, SPC calculations sometimes result in a negative LCL value. Some texts replace a negative LCL with a zero value. To make it clear that UCLs and LCLs are equidistant from the center line, both SPC.XLS and the figures in this book allow for a negative LCL.

Due to the way that standard deviations behave, it is known that in the long run less than three-tenths of one percent of daily averages (.003) occurs above the UCL or below the LCL, *unless something unexpected is going on.*

So, in the normal course of events, you would expect to see about one observation in 300 that is outside either control limit. If you do find one or more observations outside the limits, it suggests that something might have happened to the process.

It's easy (and often correct) to conclude that observations occurring outside a control limit are "bad": consistency is usually a desirable trait for a process. More broadly, though, it means that something unusual has occurred. For example, suppose that you found an observation *below* a lower control limit on an s chart. This means that the variability among the individual observations made at that time is very low. Is that bad?

It's hard to tell and it depends on the nature of the process. It could mean that something changed in the way the observations are measured. Or, it could mean that all the observations were made on one machine, or one person, or any other process component, when the other samples were taken from multiple components. Or it could be one of the 300 cases that is expected, just by chance, to exceed a control limit.

Whatever the cause, the outcome might be "bad" or it might not: the main point is that something unusual has occurred that probably warrants closer attention.

Case Study: Manufacturing

Suppose that your company manufactures floppy disks, and that you are monitoring the disks' storage capacity. There are too many disks manufactured on a given day to test each of them, and you decide to test a random sample of eight disks from each day's production run. You measure the disks' storage capacity in bytes, and over a ten-day period you obtain the results shown in figure 10.3.

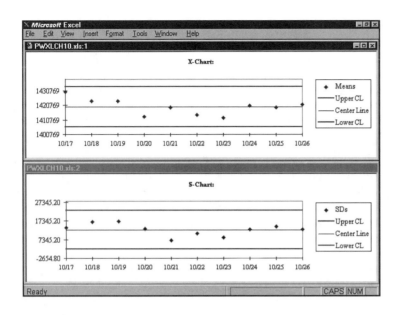

Fig. 10.3
The x-and-s charts for floppy disk storage capacity point to a process that's in control.

In figure 10.3, all appears to be fine. All of the points are between the UCL and the LCL on both the x-chart and the s-chart, there are no long runs above or below the CL, and there appears to be no trend in the values.

On the other hand, suppose that your SPC charts looked like those in figure 10.4.

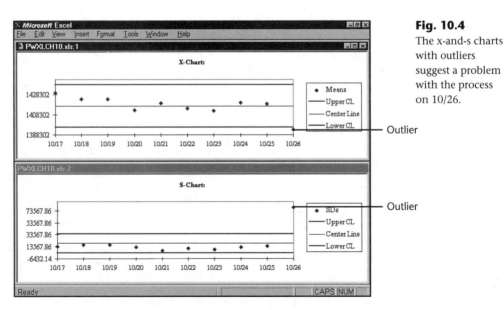

Fig. 10.4
The x-and-s charts with outliers suggest a problem with the process on 10/26.

II

Financial Planning and Control

In figure 10.4, the average capacity for floppy disks manufactured on 10/26 is below the LCL on the x-chart, and the standard deviation for the disks' capacity on 10/26 is well above the UCL on the s-chart. These two points are known as *outliers*, because they lie outside the charts' control limits.

What does this mean to you? Because the 10/26 average capacity dropped, there must be one or more disks on 10/26 that have relatively low storage capacity. The standard deviation for 10/26 is relatively high because the capacity of at least one disk was far from that day's average measured capacity. Thus, the variability in storage capacity among those disks is relatively large.

There are two possibilities:

- There was something unusual going on with the production process on 10/26/94.

- The average of the observations on 10/26/94 was one of the 300 expected, by chance, to diverge so far from the overall process average.

While it may be a chance finding, there is evidence that you should look into the production conditions on 10/26.

The observations used to create the charts in figure 10.4 are shown in table 10.1. Notice that the fourth measurement on 10/26 (boldface) is well below the level of all the other measurements, thus lowering the average and raising the standard deviation for that day.

Table 10.1 Data For Figure 10.4: Floppy Disk Storage Capacity							
Disk: 1 **Date**	**2**	**3**	**4**	**5**	**6**	**7**	**8**
10/17 1421970	1445852	1406897	1436859	1446271	1434959	1420128	1426424
10/18 1444357	1415618	1409933	1429544	1446601	1410771	1400657	1430475
10/19 1449892	1431635	1427423	1436118	1408108	1405997	1400926	1429746
10/20 1400088	1443116	1410786	1409694	1406425	1418465	1405021	1410238
10/21 1423175	1406126	1416449	1420671	1427192	1413840	1421505	1426484
10/22 1401442	1429202	1426506	1424363	1408183	1405559	1410345	1409108
10/23 1402426	1427257	1408280	1403981	1418220	1411746	1419280	1407419
10/24 1413475	1414245	1403137	1426422	1406381	1432664	1437300	1429160
10/25 1407405	1417666	1446294	1428254	1428110	1405154	1406399	1413903
10/26 1408183	1416470	1439869	**1200863**	1404776	1429217	1434428	1412609

Why is it necessary to look at both the x-chart and the s-chart? (See fig. 10.5.)

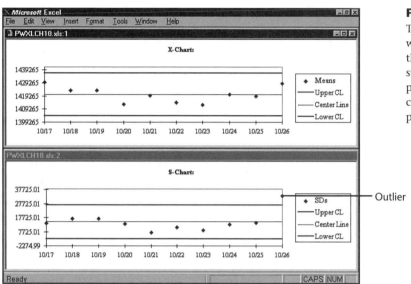

II

Financial Planning
and Control

Fig. 10.5
The x-and-s charts
with an outlier on
the s-chart *only*
suggest the
presence of
compensating
problems.

Here, there is nothing unusual about the x-chart, but the standard deviation on 10/26 is well above its UCL. The data for figure 10.5 are shown in table 10.2.

Table 10.2	Data For Figure 10.5: Floppy Disk Storage Capacity							
Disk: Date	1	2	3	4	5	6	7	8
10/17	1421970	1445852	1406897	1436859	1446271	1434959	1420128	1426424
10/18	1444357	1415618	1409933	1429544	1446601	1410771	1400657	1430475
10/19	1449892	1431635	1427423	1436118	1408108	1405997	1400926	1429746
10/20	1400088	1443116	1410786	1409694	1406425	1418465	1405021	1410238
10/21	1423175	1406126	1416449	1420671	1427192	1413840	1421505	1426484
10/22	1401442	1429202	1426506	1424363	1408183	1405559	1410345	1409108
10/23	1402426	1427257	1408280	1403981	1418220	1411746	1419280	1407419
10/24	1413475	1414245	1403137	1426422	1406381	1432664	1437300	1429160
10/25	1407405	1417666	1446294	1428254	1428110	1405154	1406399	1413903
10/26	**1361867**	1439561	1446806	1432533	1403855	**1473898**	1440723	1430756

Notice that the first and sixth measurements on 10/26 (in boldface) are, respectively, well below and well above the average. In the average observation for that day, the two measurements cancel one another out, but they increase the variability around the mean—thus increasing the standard deviation for that day. This is evidence that something unusual went on in the production process, resulting in less consistency in the disks' storage capacity. Again, the process for that day should be examined.

Even if neither the x-chart nor the s-chart contains outliers, you may find a trend that causes you to examine a process. (See fig. 10.6.)

Fig. 10.6
When x-and-s charts display a trend, it suggests problems in the process, even though there are no outliers.

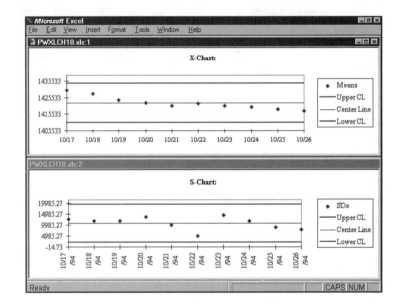

Here, the daily average capacity of the floppy disks is gradually but consistently declining. It is probable that the operating specification of some device or the quality of some raw material is progressively degrading.

You usually try to have the same number of observations in every sample. This is because the control limits on an SPC chart are sensitive to the sample size. If the sample size varied from sample to sample, so would the control limits. This would make it more difficult to determine whether the process was in control.

Creating P-charts for Dichotomies

Sometimes it is necessary to make a more general measurement of a unit than a variable such as the storage capacity of a floppy disk. There are, for example, many ways that a floppy disk can be unacceptable: it won't initialize, or there are too many bad clusters when it is formatted, or the write safe tab won't slide back and forth, and so forth.

Or, if you were monitoring the quality of invoices produced by an accounts receivable department, you might not be interested in exactly how an invoice falls short of being acceptable—just that it does. In cases such as this, you might want your measurement to be a dichotomy such as acceptable versus unacceptable (other terms used in quality control are conforming versus non-conforming and defective versus nondefective).

An SPC chart for this kind of analysis is based on the fraction of a sample that is nonconforming. For example, if you find that 5 invoices in a sample of 50 are unacceptable, then the fraction nonconforming is 0.1. This is the value that is shown on the chart. In quality control, this is usually termed a p-chart (for *proportion*), and it is analogous to an x-chart.

There is no analog for the s-chart when the measurement is a dichotomy. This is because the standard deviation for a dichotomy is completely represented by the fraction itself, and is defined as:

$$s = \text{SQRT}(p * (1-p))$$

where p is the fraction, and SQRT stands for the square root. For example, if the fraction is .2, then its standard deviation is:

$$\text{SQRT}(.2 * (1-.2)) = \text{SQRT}(.2 * .8) = \text{SQRT}(.16) = .4$$

Because knowing the fraction means that you automatically know the standard deviation, it is usual to create only the p-chart.

There are, though, a UCL, an LCL and a CL on a p-chart. The CL is the overall average fraction nonconforming for the process, just as the CL on an x-chart is the overall average of the process. The UCL and LCL are based on the overall fraction nonconforming: they represent three standard deviations above and below the CL. These standard deviations are calculated from the fraction nonconforming for the process, taking the sample size into account.

For example, if the overall fraction nonconforming is .2, and the size of each sample is 50, then the UCL is:

$$.2 + 3 * \text{SQRT}((.2 * (1-.2) / 50)) = .37$$

and the LCL is

$$.2 - 3 * \text{SQRT}((.2 * (1-.2) / 50)) = .03$$

II

Financial Planning
and Control

Fig. 10.7
P-charts for
conforming/
nonconforming
are not normally
accompanied by
an s-chart.

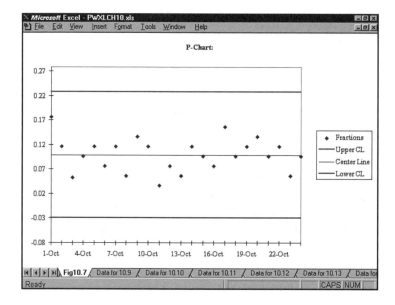

As with x-and-s charts, it is better to maintain a constant size for each sample, if possible, so that the UCL and LCL be constant for all samples. If it is not possible to maintain a constant sample size, there are transformations that you can apply to make the UCL and LCL constants. For information on these transformations, consult an advanced text on statistical process control.

Choosing the Sample Size

The size of the sample you take, for either an x-and-s or a p-chart, is important both to the accuracy of the average or fraction, and to the distance of the control limits from the center line. From that point of view, the larger the sample that you take, the better.

However, it is also true that the larger the sample you take, the greater the cost of quality control. This is particularly true of destructive testing, where the test makes an item unsalable. Suppose that you manufacture automobiles, and one quality test that you run is how well the front bumper stands up to a collision. It will be difficult to sell the cars that you have tested.

Therefore, you would like to take samples that are small enough to be affordable, but large enough to yield accurate estimates. One useful way to define an accurate estimate is that there is a 50 percent chance of detecting that a process has gone out of control.

A 50 percent chance may not seem too accurate, but keep in mind that you have multiple opportunities to detect the problem. Suppose that you are monitoring a process hourly. If the process goes out of control at, say, 10:15

a.m., then you have an opportunity to detect it at 11:00, 12:00, 1:00, and so on. The probability that the problem will remain undetected at, say, 2:00 p.m. is $.5 \times .5 \times .5 \times .5 = .0625$. You have nearly a 94 percent chance to detect that the process is out of control.

The above examples used samples of size 8 for x-and-s charts, and of size 50 for a p-chart. In combination with the process standard deviation, these sample sizes defined the location of the UCL and the LCL. You can, instead, turn it around and begin by defining the location of the UCL and the LCL. So doing determines the required sample size. In effect, you ask, "How large a sample do I need if I want the UCL to be at a given criterion?"

Suppose that the overall fraction nonconforming for a process is .1. You decide that a fraction nonconforming of .25 is unacceptable. You also decide that you want to have a 50 percent chance of detecting that the fraction nonconforming has increased from .1 to .25. If the process average increases to .25, then half the samples would be larger than .25, and half would be smaller. (This assumes that defects are distributed symmetrically around their average, which is the usual assumption in statistical process control.) In that case, you would have your desired 50 percent chance to detect a shift in the process average: 50 percent of the observations would exceed .25. You can set the UCL, three standard deviations above the CL, to equal the fraction nonconforming that you want to detect. The size of the change to detect is $.25 - .1 = .15$, and you can set up this equation:

$$.25 - .1 = .15 = 3 * \text{SQRT}((.1 * (1-.1) / N))$$

where N is the sample size. Rearranging this equation, you have:

$$N = (3/.15)^2 * .1 * (1-.1)$$

$$N = 36$$

or, more generally:

$$N = (s/d)^2 * p * (1-p)$$

where d is the size of the shift you want to detect, p is the fraction nonconforming, and s is the number of standard deviations above and below the CL for the UCL and LCL. Given that the UCL and LCL are three standard deviations above and below the CL, that the process average is .1, and that you want a 50 percent chance of detecting a shift from .1 to .25, you should take samples of 36 observations each. The Excel worksheet formula is:

```
= (3 / .15)^2 * .1 * .9
```

> **Note**
>
> Setting the probability of detecting a shift to 50% simplifies the equation that determines the necessary sample size. If you wanted to modify the probability to, say, 80%, you would need to determine or assume the shape of the distribution of defects, make reference to the resulting theoretical distribution, and add to the equation a term that represented the units of measurement associated with an increase of 30% (that is, 80% – 50%). For detailed information, consult an advanced text on statistical quality control.

On the Disk

Creating SPC Charts Using Excel

SPC charts are easy to create by using the VBA module *SPC Chart Maker* in the file named SPC.xls on the *Business Analysis with Excel* companion disk that accompanies this book.

> **Tip**
>
> The companion disk also contains a file named SPC.HLP. This file contains extensive help information for running the SPC.xls module. Be sure that you store SPC.xls and SPC.HLP in the same folder/subdirectory on your computer's main disk.

To create SPC charts, you will need a worksheet that contains data laid out as in tables 10.1 and 10.2. There should be a range of dates or times of day in a column, and a range of observations for each date or time in columns immediately to its right.The observations can be either several columns of variable measurements (such as floppy disk storage capacity) or one column of dichotomies (such as the fraction nonconforming). In the case of dichotomies, the module assumes that there is one column for the measurements. This is because it's easier for you to enter the fraction nonconforming than to enter several columns, each with a 1 or a 0 to indicate conforming/nonconforming.

When you have opened SPC.xls, a new item appears in the <u>D</u>ata menu: SP<u>C</u> Chart. With a worksheet active and laid out as described above, choose that item to begin SPC analysis. When you close SPC.xls, the SP<u>C</u> Chart item is removed from the <u>D</u>ata menu.

When you start the module, it shows a dialog box prompting you to enter the range that contains the times or dates, and the range that contains the actual observations. It also lets you select between x-and-s charts, for variables, and a p-chart, for dichotomies. If you select a p-chart, there is an edit box where you can enter the sample size if it is a constant number. If the sample size is not a constant, you can enter the size of each sample on your worksheet in a column to the right of and immediately adjacent to the fraction nonconforming. Figure 10.8 shows this dialog box.

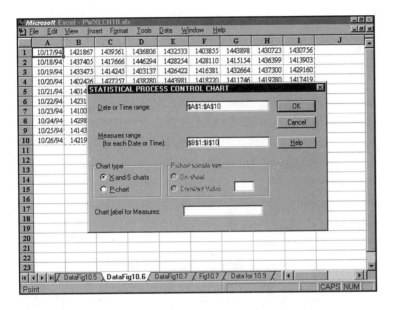

Fig. 10.8
The dialog box to create SPC charts lets you identify the required worksheet ranges and the type of charts you want to create.

The module performs the necessary calculations to create an x-chart and an s-chart. After you have run the module, to the right of your worksheet data you will find ranges that define the CL, the UCL and the LCL for each chart. You can examine the module code to determine exactly how the module has calculated the center line and the control limits in each case. The code that calculates these limits is found in subroutine EnterVariables( ) in SPC.xls.

Performing Acceptance Sampling

Acceptance sampling often enables you to reduce the cost of goods that you purchase. It can also enable you to control the costs you incur when a purchaser returns products to you due to defects.

You do not want to purchase materials, whether supplies or equipment, that are faulty. Nor do you want to offer defective goods for sale. However, it is normal for the purchaser and the seller of large amounts of merchandise to negotiate an acceptable fraction of that merchandise that may be defective.

Here's the reasoning. It is extremely expensive to produce any appreciable amount—one lot, say—of goods that has no defective units. To do so, the producer would have to perform 100 percent testing, because any less would run the risk of having at least one defective product in the lot. And, because testing itself is not perfect, a test result of 0 percent defective is not a guarantee that no defects exist. Furthermore, the producer would always bear the sunk cost of having manufactured the defective units.

The producer is presumably in business to make a profit. So as to cover the costs of attaining 0 percent defects, the producer would have to raise the selling price. You, as a purchaser, might then decide to purchase the goods elsewhere. But if you demand 0 percent defects from another producer, that producer also has to raise the selling price to meet your requirement.

If you, as the purchaser, can tolerate a relatively small percent defective in the lots that you purchase, you might be in a position to negotiate a lower price from your suppliers.

This is the "invisible hand" at work. Adam Smith's principle that optimum values result when participants in an economic activity act in their own self-interest.

Now consider it from the producer's viewpoint. Suppose that the contract that you, the producer, enter into with your customer allows you to make shipments that contain some small percentage of defective product. In that case, you could test a *sample* of the product that you ship, instead of the entire lot. Your testing costs therefore immediately drop. Your costs drop again when you consider that you do not have to bear the cost of returned, defective goods, if you have met the customer's criterion for an acceptable shipment. This puts you in a position to gently reduce your selling price, thus retaining the customer but still making a profit.

However, the moment that you enter the domain of sampling, you enter the domain of probability. Suppose that the contract with your customer calls for you to ship no more than 1 percent defective units. You test twenty units, and you find one defective. How likely is it that there are only 1 percent defective in your entire shipment? Put another way, how likely is it that any shipment from your inventory will exceed the 1 percent limit? How large a sample should you take? And if you start finding defects in the sample, when should you stop testing sample units?

Excel provides several functions that answer these questions, and the next sections explore them.

Charting the Operating Characteristic Curve

An operating characteristic curve shows how an agreement between buyer and vendor works out in practice. The curve in figure 10.9 is an example.

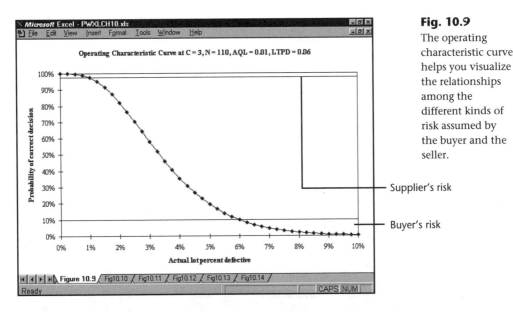

Fig. 10.9
The operating characteristic curve helps you visualize the relationships among the different kinds of risk assumed by the buyer and the seller.

The curve shows the probability that a lot will be acceptable (vertical axis) with different percents of defects (horizontal axis). Notice that, as you would expect, the lower the number of actual defects, the higher the probability that a lot will be accepted. Four factors define the curve:

- The acceptable quality level (AQL) of the supplier's goods. This is the worst percent of defects that the buyer is willing to accept *as a process average*.

- The lot tolerance percent defective (LTPD) of a given lot. This is the worst level of quality that the buyer is willing to accept *in a given shipment*.

- The amount of risk to the supplier that a good shipment will be rejected due to sampling error. The *distance between* the upper horizontal line and the 100% point in figure 10.9 represents this amount of risk.

- The amount of risk to the buyer that a bad shipment will be accepted due to sampling error. The lower horizontal line in figure 10.9 represents this amount of risk.

Taken together, these four factors can provide a great deal of information to the supplier and buyer:

- The operating characteristic curve itself

- The sample size necessary to keep both the supplier's risk and the buyer's risk acceptably low

- The maximum number of defects in a sample before a lot is rejected (usually termed C)

- The actual supplier's risk and the actual buyer's risk, at a specific sample size and a specific C

Figure 10.10 shows the curve for a an AQL of 1%, an LTPD of 3%, and supplier's risk of 5% and buyer's risk of 10%. The upper horizontal line represents the supplier's risk: the distance between this horizontal line and the top of the vertical axis indicates the probability that a good shipment will be rejected. The lower horizontal line represents the buyer's risk: the distance between this horizontal line and the bottom of the vertical axis indicates the probability that a bad shipment will be accepted.

Fig. 10.10

The steepness of operating characteristic curves usually depends largely on their sample sizes.

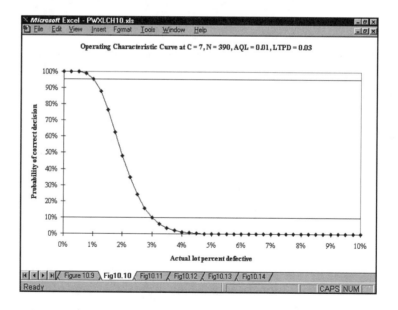

Also shown at the top of figure 10.10 is N, the sample size needed, and C, the maximum number of defects that you can find in a sample before concluding that the entire lot contains too many defects. Therefore, this operating characteristic curve tells you that you should sample 390 units. As you test those units, when and if you find as many as eight defective units, you can stop testing and conclude that the full lot contains too many defects.

> **Note**
>
> Excel offers a function, CRITBINOM, that returns a number similar to the C that this section discusses. It is normally different from C, because it takes into account only the supplier's risk or the buyer's risk. The procedures discussed here, and that are contained in the *Business Analysis with Excel* companion disk's VBA module, take both types of risk into account. Therefore, C is usually different from the value you would obtain if you used CRITBINOM.

On the Disk

The curve shown in figure 10.10, while steeper than the curve in figure 10.9, is not extremely steep. Generally, the larger the sample size, the more capable you are of discriminating between an acceptable and an unacceptable lot. Contrast figure 10.10 with figure 10.11, where the sample size is larger and the curve is steeper.

In figure 10.10, an increase in the actual defect rate from 2% to 3% is accompanied by a drop in the probability of acceptance from about 48% to 10%.

In figure 10.11, the increase in actual defect rate from 2% to 3% is accompanied by a drop in probability of acceptance from about 95% to 10%.

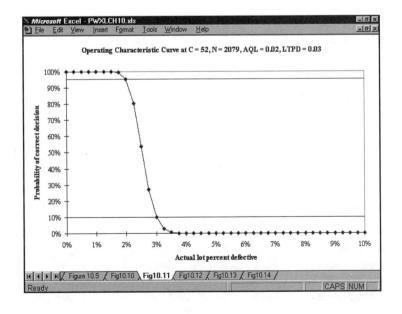

Fig. 10.11
The required sample size of an operating characteristic curve depends to some degree on the value of the AQL.

II

Financial Planning and Control

What causes the sample size to increase? The operating characteristic curve in figure 10.10 uses an AQL of 1%, whereas the curve in figure 10.11 uses an AQL of 2%. The companion disk's workbook, Operating Characteristic Curves.xls, that created these charts seeks the minimum sample size that satisfies all four criteria (AQL, LTPD, supplier's risk and buyer's risk). The smaller the AQL, the smaller the sample required. This is because the smaller the AQL, the fewer defects there are to find. Further, the smaller the AQL, the smaller the value of c that's required to determine whether the current lot is a bad one.

> **Tip**
>
> The VBA module named Derive Op Char Curve can be found in the file named Operating Characteristic Curves.xls on the companion disk. To run it, open that file and choose Tools, Macros. Select OC_Macro from the Macro list box, and choose Run.

So, when you change the AQL from, say, .01 to .02, you also change the necessary sample size from a smaller figure to a larger one. This effect can be quite pronounced: in the case of figures 10.10 and 10.11, the increase in sample size is from 390 to 2079.

LTPD also exerts an influence on the required sample size. Figure 10.12 shows the operating characteristic curve with the same inputs as 10.10, except that instead of an LTPD of 3 percent, it uses an LTPD of 4 percent.

Fig. 10.12
An operating characteristic curve with a smaller Lot Tolerance Percent Defective reduces the required sample size.

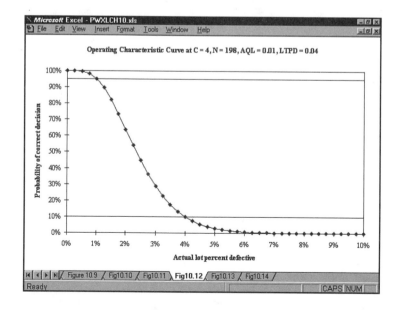

Modifications of supplier's risk and buyer's risk have relatively small effects on sample size. Figure 10.13 shows the effect of reducing the supplier's risk from 10% to 5%, and figure 10.14 shows the effect of reducing the buyer's risk from 10% to 5%.

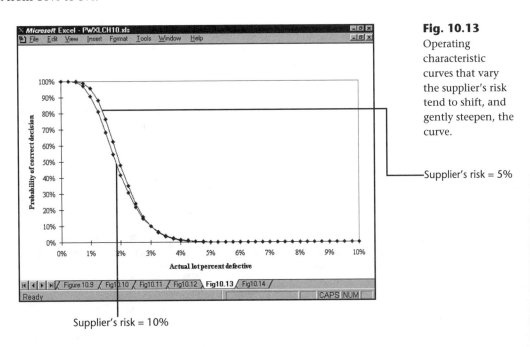

Fig. 10.13
Operating characteristic curves that vary the supplier's risk tend to shift, and gently steepen, the curve.

Supplier's risk = 5%

Supplier's risk = 10%

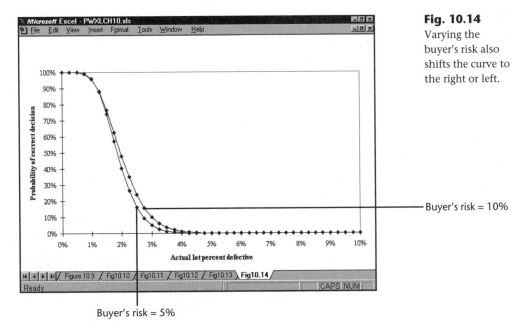

Fig. 10.14
Varying the buyer's risk also shifts the curve to the right or left.

Buyer's risk = 10%

Buyer's risk = 5%

II

Financial Planning and Control

Note that in all the cases discussed previously, if you want to lower the degree of risk, you need to increase the power of the testing to discriminate between a good lot and a bad lot. You increase the power of the testing by increasing the size of the sample. So doing causes the curve to steepen: the steepness of the curve is a visual guide to how well the testing will discriminate between lots that meet the criteria and lots that are substandard. And, of course, the better the discrimination, the better the degree of protection for both the buyer and the supplier.

On the Disk

Again, you can generate these curves by running the VBA macro OC_Curve in the file named Operating Characteristic Curves.xls, found on the *Business Analysis with Excel* companion disk that accompanies this book. When you do so, Excel will display a dialog box that prompts you to supply an AQL, an LTPD, a fraction that represents supplier's risk, and a fraction that represents buyer's risk. After you choose OK, Excel searches for the minimum sample size and C that satisfy these four criteria. A set of summary data are placed on a worksheet, and the curve is plotted on a separate chart sheet.

> **Tip**
>
> Depending on the input values that you choose, it can take the VBA code a long time to execute. Press the Esc key to halt a lengthy search.

You can use these curves and the associated summary data in negotiations between suppliers and buyers. As a buyer, you might be willing to increase your LTPD requirement slightly to reduce the required sample size. This would save the supplier some testing costs that could be reflected in the cost of the goods.

As a supplier, you might be willing to accept a slightly increased level of risk that a good shipment will be rejected due to sampling error. Accepting this additional risk would save sampling and testing costs, and you might be able to apply these savings to another negotiating point where you need additional bargaining room.

The operating characteristic curves discussed in this section are based on a single sample from a lot. There are other, more complex sampling plans that include double samples, multiple samples, and sequential samples. For further information, consult an advanced text on quality control.

Using Worksheet Functions for Quality Control

You can use Excel to help answer a variety of questions that occasionally arise in quality control situations. It's important to understand the nature of the tools that are available to you when such questions come up. Because statistical quality control is largely an exercise in probability—and in choosing the right tool in a given case—this chapter concludes with a discussion of some of these questions and how you can use Excel to answer them.

Sampling Units from a Finite Population

To this point statistical process control and acceptance sampling in terms of theoretically infinite populations have been discussed. There has been no limit to the size of the population of products that has been sampled to create x-and-s charts, p-charts or operating characteristic curves.

Things change some when you sample from a finite population. You have a finite population when you are interested only in a specific group, such as the items in a special production run, or your own company's sales staff, or customers' responses to a temporary price reduction.

When you sample from a finite population, it's usual to do so *without replacement*: that is, if you are going to sample two items, you select the first item, and then select the second item without putting the first item back into the pool. Suppose that you have a population of 10 items. The chance of selecting any given item at random is 1/10, or 10 percent. If, after selecting the item, you put it back into the pool, the chance of selecting any given item is still 10 percent. If, however, you do not return the item to the pool, the chance of selecting at random any given item as your second choice is 1/9, or 11 percent.

Case Study: Manufacturing

A customer wants you to manufacture 200 coffee cups with a glazing that differs substantially from the glazing of those that you normally make. This will be a special production run, and therefore the 200 cups constitute a finite population. Your agreement with the customer allows for a 5 percent defect rate.

You plan to sample 20 cups from your production run, and to reject the run if you find unacceptable imperfections in the glazing on more than 5 percent of the sample. That is, you will reject the run if the sample contains two or more defectives. What is the probability that your full run has met the 5 percent criterion if you find zero or one defective cup?

You answer this question with Excel's HYPGEOMDIST function. It takes four arguments:

- *The number of "successes" in the sample.* Here, that argument is zero or 1: the number of imperfect cups in your sample if you are to accept the production run.

- *The sample size.* Here, that argument is 20, the number of cups you sample.

- *The number of "successes" in the population.* Here, that argument is 10. If you tested all 200 cups, then the 5 percent criterion implies that not more than 10 would be imperfect.

- *The size of the population.* Here, that argument is 200, the number of special cups that you manufactured.

HYPGEOMDIST returns the probability that you would observe an exact number of successes, given the sample size, the successes in the population, and the population size. So, if you entered:

```
=HYPGEOMDIST(0,20,10,200)
```

then Excel would return .34. Therefore, there's a 34 percent probability of finding no imperfect cups in a sample of 20, when there are exactly 10 imperfect cups in the population of 200.

You also need to know the probability of finding exactly one defective cup in your sample, so you enter:

```
=HYPGEOMDIST(1,20,10,200)
```

Excel returns .40. Therefore, there's a 40 percent probability of finding exactly one imperfect cup in your sample. Together, these two probabilities add up to 74 percent. So it is more likely (74 percent) than not (100%–74% = 26%) that there are 10 imperfect cups in the full production run.

Tip

You can use an array constant in HYPGEOMDIST, and similar functions, to get the sum of the function's results. Instead of entering:

```
=HYPGEOMDIST(0,20,10,200)
```

and

```
=HYPGEOMDIST(1,20,10,200)
```

and summing the results, you can enter:

```
=SUM(HYPGEOMDIST({0,1},20,10,200))
```

This formula executes HYPGEOMDIST twice: once for the first element in the array {0,1} and once for the second element. It then adds the results together, and in this case it returns .74, or 74%.

Sampling Units from a Nonfinite Population

When you monitor a nonfinite population, you are interested in a larger group than when you monitor a finite population. For example, instead of testing a special, finite production run, you might be testing your normal, ongoing, nonfinite product line. If you were testing a new invoice format, you might try it for a week before deciding to adopt it; then, sampling for invoice accuracy would involve a finite population. On the other hand, if you were monitoring invoice accuracy as a normal procedure, you would probably consider your sample to be from a nonfinite population.

To make probability statements about a sample from a nonfinite population, you use Excel's NORMSINV function.

Case Study: Videotape Rentals

Suppose that you are in the business of renting videotapes to the public. After tapes have been viewed some number of times, their quality deteriorates to the point that you consider them to be defective. Furthermore, some customers own tape players that are defective, and they can ruin your videotapes.

You want to maintain an inventory of tapes that is at least 85 percent acceptable; you would really prefer 95 percent, but because you can't keep your customers' machines from damaging the rental tapes, you relax the criterion a little. Although you have a finite number of tapes on any given day, your inventory is constantly changing due to the acquisition of new tapes, and the removal of old ones. You therefore consider your population of tapes to be nonfinite.

Testing video tapes is a time-consuming process, and you would like to keep the sample as small as possible. A rule of thumb that works well in quality testing is to make sure both of these equations result in a number that is five or greater:

$$n * p$$

and

$$n * (p - 1)$$

where n is the sample size, and p is the probability of an acceptable unit in the population. If your tapes meet your criterion of 85% acceptable, p is .85. To make sure that both n * p and n * (p–1) are both greater than 5, you will need n, the sample size, to be at least 43. To keep the numbers easy to work with, you decide to take a sample of 50.

Note

The rule of thumb described above is due to the relationship between the binomial and the normal distributions. The sampling distribution of a binomial variable such as defective/acceptable is very close to a normal distribution when both n * p and n * (1-p) are greater than five.

You test the random sample of 50 tapes, finding three that are defective and 47 that are acceptable, so 94% of your sample are acceptable. What is the probability that at least 85% of your population of tapes are acceptable?

You decide that you want to make a correct decision about the defects in your population of tapes 95% of the time that you test samples. The following Excel formula returns the criterion that you need if you are to have that amount of protection (it is known as a *critical value*):

```
=NORMSINV(.95)
```

Excel returns 1.64. This critical value is the number that your test statistic needs to exceed if you are to make a correct decision.

Tip

NORMSINV( ) is easier and quicker to use than NORMINV( ). However, NORMINV( ) gives you greater control over the characteristics of the underlying distribution.

To get the test statistic itself, enter the Excel formula:

```
=(0.9-0.85)/SQRT(0.15*0.85/50)
```

which returns 1.78. The general formula is:

$$= (x-p)/SQRT(p * (p - 1)/n)$$

where x is the percent acceptable in the sample, p is the hypothetical percent acceptable in the population, n is the sample size, and the denominator is the standard deviation of p.

Because your test statistic of 1.78 exceeds your critical value of 1.64, you conclude that your inventory of tapes is at least 85 percent acceptable.

Sampling Defects in Units

This chapter has so far discussed one particular attribute: whether a unit is acceptable or defective. A related measure is the number of defects in a particular unit. For example, if you were concerned with the quality of the purchase orders that your company distributes, you might want a more detailed measure than acceptable/defective. It might be important to understand the frequency of occurrence of critical defects in the purchase orders (such as account number or ship-to address) versus minor defects (such as the spelling of the supplier's street address).

To make inferences about numbers of defects, as distinct from numbers of defective units, the Excel POISSON function is often useful.

Case Study: Forms

As the manager of the purchasing department for a large firm, you have noticed an unusual number of complaints that deliveries from suppliers have been late. Following up on some of the complaints, you find that some suppliers report that the deliveries have been delayed because of errors on the purchase orders relating to unit pricing, want-dates, model numbers, and contract references.

Because suppliers sometimes place inappropriate blame on buyers, you decide to examine a sample of purchase orders to see whether the overall rate of defects per form might be high enough to cause these delays.

You decide that an overall defect rate of .5 defects per purchase order is acceptable. If Purchase Order A is perfect and Purchase Order B has only one defect (therefore, the average rate is .5 defects per purchase order), there should be enough good information on B for the supplier to be able either to fill the order or to quickly resolve the incorrect information.

You also decide that you want to limit the likelihood of deciding that the average defect rate is one-half of one defect per order, when in fact it is some other number, to 5 percent.

You sample 10 purchase orders at random and examine them for inaccuracies. You find twelve instances of misinformation in the sample. Given this data, should you continue to believe that the average number of defects in all your purchase orders is .5?

Use Excel's POISSON function. Enter:

```
=1-POISSON(11,5,TRUE)
```

which returns .005. The first argument, 11, is 12–1: that is, the number of inaccuracies that you found, minus 1. The second argument, 5, is the number of inaccuracies that you would expect to find in ten purchase orders if the average number of inaccuracies were .5. The third argument, TRUE, specifies the cumulative form of the Poisson distribution: that is, the sum of the probability for zero inaccuracies, plus the probability for one inaccuracy, and so on.

You decided beforehand that the level of protection you wanted against an incorrect decision was 5%, or .05. Because .005 is less than .05, you reject your hypothesis that there are .5 errors per form among all your purchase orders. You probably need to make sure that your staff is properly trained on your new system, and that the system itself is operating as it was designed.

Summary

This chapter has described how to use Excel to create x-and-s statistical control charts and p-charts, to monitor the ongoing performance of systems. X-and-s charts are used for variables such as the capacity of floppy disks, the length of telephone calls, or the profit margin on daily sales. P-charts are used for attributes. For example, the percent of defective units such as manufactured goods, or forms that you can classify as either defective or acceptable. These statistical control charts enable you to judge the performance of a system over time.

Another topic in this chapter is operating characteristic curves. Studying these curves puts you in a position, as a supplier, to limit the risk that an entire shipment of goods will be rejected because the number of defective units in a sample is an overestimate of the entire shipment. As a purchaser, you can use operating characteristic curves to limit your risk of accepting an entire shipment of goods because the number of defective units in a sample is an underestimate of the entire shipment.

This chapter has also discussed three ways to estimate overall process quality on the basis of sampling:

- The overall rate of defective items in a finite population. You can estimate this rate using the HYPGEOMDIST function.

- The overall rate of defective items in a nonfinite population. Use the NORMSINV function to make this estimate.

- The overall rate of defects per unit. Use the POISSON function to determine whether your estimate of this overall rate is accurate.

Part III

Investment Decisions

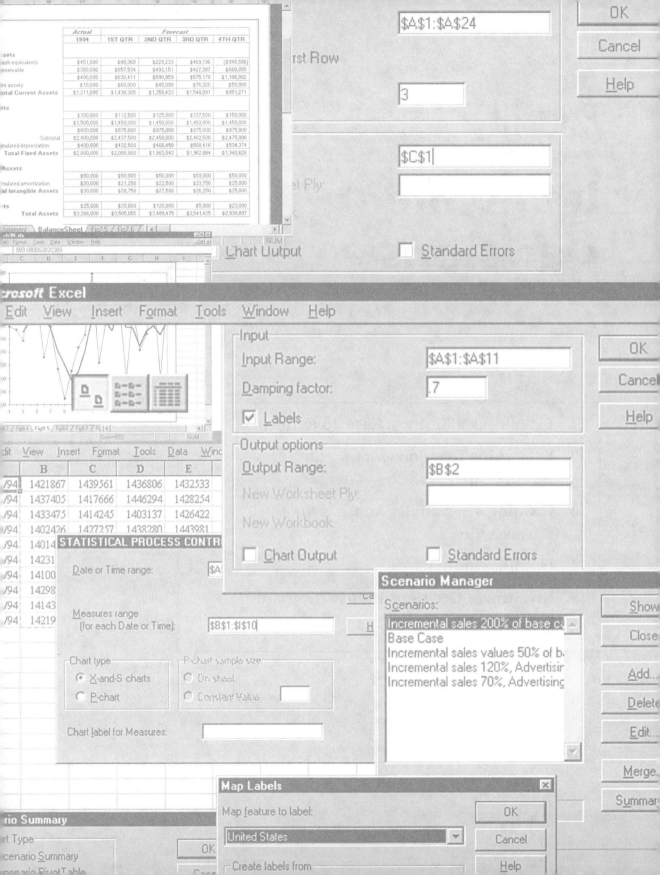

OK

Cancel

Help

$A$1:$A$24

rst Row

3

$C$1

et Ply

Chart Output   □ Standard Errors

	Actual		Forecast		
	1994	1ST QTR	2ND QTR	3RD QTR	4TH QTR
sets					
ash equivalents	$451,000	$90,360	$229,233	$469,196	($945,586)
eceivable	$350,000	$657,534	$490,151	$427,397	$660,855
	$400,000	$830,411	$590,959	$575,178	$1,186,002
nt assets	$10,000	$60,000	$45,090	$76,320	$50,000
tal Current Assets	$1,211,000	$1,438,305	$1,358,433	$1,548,091	$951,271
ts					
	$100,000	$112,500	$125,000	$137,500	$150,000
	$1,500,000	$1,450,000	$1,450,000	$1,450,000	$1,450,000
	$800,000	$875,000	$875,000	$875,000	$875,000
Subtotal	$2,400,000	$2,437,500	$2,450,000	$2,462,500	$2,475,000
nulated depreciation	$400,000	$432,500	$466,458	$500,416	$534,374
Total Fixed Assets	$2,000,000	$2,005,000	$1,983,542	$1,962,084	$1,940,626
Assets					
	$50,000	$50,000	$50,000	$50,000	$50,000
nulated amortization	$20,000	$21,250	$22,500	$23,750	$25,000
al Intangible Assets	$30,000	$28,750	$27,500	$26,250	$25,000
ts	$25,000	$33,000	$120,000	$5,000	$23,000
Total Assets	$3,266,000	$3,505,055	$3,489,475	$3,541,425	$2,939,897

tatement \ BalanceSheet / Fig7.5 / Fig7.6 / ◄

ch9N.xls

t Format Tools Data Window Help

593.08005282036?

| C | D | E | F | G | H | I |

crosoft Excel

Edit View Insert Format Tools Window Help

Fig9.4 / Fig9.5 / Fig9.6 / Fig9.7 / Fi ◄

Sum=593   NUM

dit View Insert Format Tools Data Wind

	B	C	D	E
/94	1421867	1439561	1436806	1432533
/94	1437405	1417666	1446294	1428254
/94	1433475	1414245	1403137	1426422
/94	1402426	1427257	1438280	1443981
/94	14014			
/94	14231			
/94	14100			
/94	14298			
/94	14143			
/94	14219			

Input

Input Range: $A$1:$A$11

Damping factor: .7

☑ Labels

Output options

Output Range: $B$2

New Worksheet Ply

New Workbook

□ Chart Output   □ Standard Errors

OK

Cancel

Help

STATISTICAL PROCESS CONTR

Date or Time range: $A

Measures range
(for each Date or Time): $B$1:$I$10

Chart type
◉ X-and-S charts
○ P-chart

P-chart sample size
○ On sheet
○ Constant value

Chart label for Measures:

Scenario Manager

Scenarios:

Incremental sales 200% of base c
Base Case
Incremental sales values 50% of b
Incremental sales 120%, Advertisir
Incremental sales 70%, Advertising

Show

Close

Add...

Delete

Edit...

Merge.

Summar

rio Summary

Map Labels   ⊠

Map feature to label: OK

United States   ▼   Cancel

Create labels from   Help

art Type

cenario Summary
cenario PivotTable

Chapter 11

Examining a Business Case: Investment

Business case analysis is one of the most valuable activities a finance organization can undertake to support management decision making. A business case can take any of a variety of forms, depending on the question that's been asked and the decision that needs support.

For example, a very basic question on the use of capital is "Should we lease a copy machine or should we buy one?" Although it may seem trivial, the answer to the question depends in part on an analysis of the cost effects of purchasing versus leasing. This is because there are tax implications to a capital expenditure that differ from those of an operating lease.

At the other end of the complexity spectrum, management might ask "Should we enter a new line of business?" A drastic decision such as this involves activities that include the following:

- Investing capital to purchase equipment
- Hiring new staff to operate the equipment
- Acquiring market research to quantify the potential costs and revenues
- Assessing cross-elasticities among product lines

Each of these involves costs: costs that must be taken into account when making the decision.

This chapter discusses these activities from two viewpoints: why they are important to making a good business decision, and how they flow quantitatively into an Excel workbook that supports the eventual decision.

Developing a Business Case

Most business case development is incremental. That is, the business case focuses on changes that would occur only if a company adopts a proposal. The business case emphasizes the relevant benefits of a proposed decision, such as:

- New revenues

- Larger market share

- Lower expenses

- Product diversification

The business case analysis also emphasizes the relevant costs of the proposal, such as:

- Incremental investment

- Additional operating expenses

- Additional taxes

- Losses to existing line of business

Typically, a business case does not include the costs of doing business as usual, because you usually regard these costs as fixed. You would incur the costs whether or not the business case was approved for implementation. For example, the costs of doing General Ledger accounting and the cost of paying rent for corporate headquarters would not change if you decide to lease a new copy machine. It is possible that these costs would not change even if you decide to expand your line of business.

Inthe first stage of business case analysis, you should undertake a qualitative review of all potential benefits and costs. The stakeholders within the firm (those on whom the business decision would have substantial impact) should participate in the review. This approach is similar to obtaining, from individual operating units, agreement on their annual budgets.

In large organizations, it frequently happens that the marketing or product management group offers up an idea for a new product. The proposal often defines an opportunity in terms of a customer need. The marketing group might have identified this need by means of focus groups, general awareness of the industry, or an understanding of the life cycle of current product sets—in short, any of a variety of subjective and objective indicators.

No analysis tool such as Excel can create a business case on your behalf. It can help you analyze the business decision, but before it can do so you must provide it with some quantitative basis. Therefore, the marketing or product groups proposal should usually frame its product description with several types of quantitative analysis. These analyses often include the product's market potential, the competitive environment and the plans to bring the product to market.

The proposal usually describes the product's market potential in terms of:

- *Its current size:* How many product units would the marketplace purchase if the product were available for sale today?

- *Its growth potential:* What is the forecast for additional sales during the life cycle of the product?

Normally, you make these estimates in terms of unit sales, and these unit sales projections form part of the basis for projecting new product revenue. To complete the projection, an analysis of the competitive environment is necessary, so as to translate unit sales estimates into dollars. In assessing the competitive environment, it's useful to understand the competition's:

- *Product alternatives*: Do they have products or options that compete directly with our new product?

- *Pricing:* Is it a single price? Is it tiered in some fashion? Can our product meet that pricing, and does it need to?

- *Costs:* What level of resources must they commit to the production and sale of their product? Do they have a technological edge that holds down their costs relative to ours?

- *Profitability:* Faced with price pressure from our product, is their product profitable enough that they would continue production and sales?

- *Competitive advantage:* What hurdles can they present to us in the way of market presence, name recognition, brand loyalty, long-term contracts with resellers, and so on.

Each of these considerations exerts an influence on the pricing that you plan for the product. Taken in combination with unit sales forecasts, it may then be possible to create a credible projection of revenue for the proposed product.

To complete the initial quantitative picture, you need to present Excel with information about the variable costs associated with bringing the new product to market. In particular, it's useful to assess the costs of:

III

Investment Decisions

- *Market research:* What basis is there to anticipate additional revenue from a new product? Is there evidence from prior product rollouts that the new product will generate new revenue? What about external sources of information, such as trade association data? How good is the evidence for the purpose of quantifying the added revenue? How much will it cost to obtain these data?

- *Distribution channels:* What are the costs, such as reseller discounts and warehousing, of getting the product to consumers?

- *Promotion and advertising:* How much must we pay different media to run our advertisements? How much will it cost to produce new brochures and other product literature? Should we purchase mailing lists?

- *Rollout and implementation:* Is it necessary to travel to meet with our distributors or salespeople? Should we offer special incentives to the distribution channel so that they will focus their efforts on selling this product? Does the distribution channel need any special training to understand the product's price structure, its market niche, and its competitive strengths and weaknesses?

- *Product cross-elasticities (any characteristics that are complementary to existing products):* To what degree is the proposed product likely to cut into the sales of existing product lines? Will this reduce existing revenue? By how much?

- *Objectives for market share and penetration:* Will the cost of attaining one more percentage point of market share outweigh the additional revenue? Does it cost more to fill the last seat in the airplane than the revenue earned from that ticket?

These kinds of questions are not just useful adjuncts to a product concept. Their answers are necessary to quantify the projected costs and revenues that are associated with the new product. The estimated costs and revenues form the quantitative basis for deciding whether to go ahead with the product development, or to pass on the opportunity.

So far, only marketing issues have been considered. In addition, there are operational and customer service costs that must be quantified to determine the new product's profit potential. The drivers of these costs include:

- *Technology:* Is the technology that is required to produce this product available, or must it be acquired? If it must be acquired, how much will it cost to purchase and maintain it? If existing capacity is available, what is the opportunity cost of exploiting it?

- *Systems:* Are appropriate methods and processes in place, or must they be developed? Such systems usually include sales support, product tracking, billing and collections, inventory management, and the software needed to manage them.

- *Implementation plans:* Are they feasible? Are the timelines reasonable and achievable for existing staff, or are there any incremental staffing requirements?

- *Training:* Do company personnel or customers require additional training in the production or use of the new product? If so, should training be developed in-house or obtained externally? How much will it cost in either case?

It's useful for a company to develop a formal process for business case development. After formal procedures are in place, they make it much easier to repeat when the company contemplates bringing new products to market. Furthermore, a formal and repeatable process can help you validate a business case currently under consideration against the results of earlier business cases.

All research and analysis should be documented. It can be difficult to take this step, particularly with research. Early on in the planning process, research is often anecdotal, non-replicable, and soft. Only later, perhaps not until well after product release, is sufficient hard data available to support decisions with real confidence. Documenting soft research data often seems futile, and this may be one reason it's so seldom done. But if you do not document it, it's very difficult to assess your business case after the fact, to determine the source of either a bad or a good decision.

Analysis is another matter. Particularly if you use the tools that Excel provides to document and audit your work, it's relatively painless to determine how you came to make a decision. As you develop your analysis worksheets, give names to your constants and your ranges. Fill in the summary information for the workbook. Add notes to cells. Create scenarios, and associate those scenarios with the names of the people who defined them.

Tip

Excel 7 has a new method for displaying cell notes. To view a note, simply move your mouse pointer over a cell that contains a note (you can identify such a cell by the red dot in the cell's upper-right corner). A box, similar to a ToolTip box, then displays the cell's note.

III

Investment Decisions

Once approved, the business case should stipulate how the company should measure results against the assumptions made in the business case. It is important to establish accountability early, and to track significant milestones. If it addresses these issues, the business case process can become an integral piece of the firm's strategic and tactical operations.

Developing the Excel Model

An Excel model for a business case synthesizes concepts and methods that you have already learned about in this book: income statement formation (chapter 1), the budget/planning cycle (chapter 8), forecasting (chapter 9), and cash flow analysis (chapter 5).

The first step in developing the Excel model is the creation of a pro-forma income statement. The pro-forma income statement takes into account the relevant benefits and relevant costs involved in the proposed course of action.

Case Study: A New Type of Automobile Tire

Your manufacturing company has been a market leader in the tire business for the last ten years. Other firms have imitated your product offering with some degree of success. Because you were first in the marketplace with a quality product, you occupy a dominant position.

Is life too comfortable at the tire factory? What would happen if you offered a new, enhanced automobile tire? This new tire would not replace your current product offering, but would offer additional safety, longer wear, and better performance for a somewhat higher price. As a result, some of your current distributors might migrate from a current tire to the new tire.

Offering this new tire would establish a new revenue stream for your company. Using the forecasting tools developed in chapter 9 along with some market research, you can identify the first benefit (shown in fig. 11.1) of this new product offering.

Fig. 11.1
The added value (the incremental margin) of the new automobile tire takes into account both the new tire's total sales and the old tire's lost sales.

Microsoft Excel - Pwxlch11.xls						
File Edit View Insert Format Tools Data Window Help						
A1	Enhanced Auto Tire B: Sales Forecast					

	A	B	C	D	E	F	G
1	Enhanced Auto Tire B: Sales Forecast						
2	Year:	1	2	3	4	5	6
3							
4	Total sales, Tire B	$100,000	$300,000	$400,000	$600,000	$1,000,000	$2,000,000
5	Cost of Goods Sold @ 50% of sales	$50,000	$150,000	$200,000	$300,000	$500,000	$1,000,000
6	Incremental sales margin, Tire B	$50,000	$150,000	$200,000	$300,000	$500,000	$1,000,000
7							
8							

Your marketing department has provided you with a total sales forecast for the new tire, shown in row 4 of figure 11.1. The range B4:G4 is named TotalSales; this is done by highlighting B4:G4, clicking the Name Box, and then typing the name TotalSales into the box.

Row 5 shows the cost of goods sold, and assumes that this cost will be 50 percent of revenue. This is calculated by highlighting B6:G6, and then typing this formula:

```
=0.5*TotalSales
```

Do not yet press Enter. Instead, hold down the Ctrl key and, while still holding it down, press Enter. Doing this causes the formula to be entered into each of the six highlighted cells. The formula takes advantage of Excels implicit intersection. Each column in row 6 is matched to its corresponding column in the range that's named TotalSales, and the value in that column is multiplied by .5.

> **Tip**
>
> A good way to think of an implicit intersection is that it is *implied* by a formula—usually, one that occupies more than one cell. In this case, the intersection is implied by the column where each instance of the formula exists and the row where the range TotalSales exists.

The cost of goods sold reflects only the purely variable costs of material and labor to produce the tire: that is, it does not include any cost allocations for overhead. Sometimes these variable costs are referred to as the direct cost of sales. Revenue, minus the associated cost of sales, is the sales margin—in this case, the incremental sales margin. This line item, shown in row 6 of figure 11.1, is linked to the main worksheet shown in figure 11.2.

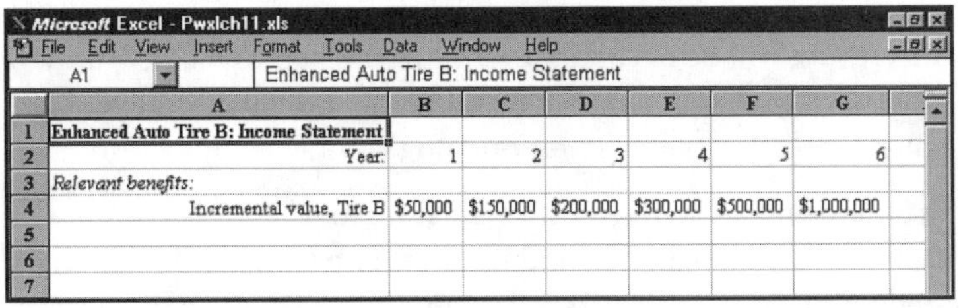

Fig. 11.2
The pro-forma income statement begins by identifying the relevant benefits—the incremental margin—of the new automobile tire.

You can easily make this linkage by means of the following steps:

1. In the Sales Forecast worksheet, name the range B6:G6 as IncrementalMargin.

2. In the same workbook, activate a worksheet that will become your pro-forma income statement.

3. To duplicate the information for the product's incremental value as shown in figure 11.2, highlight the range of cells from B4:G4.

4. Type the formula:

   ```
   =IncrementalMargin
   ```

   and enter it by using Ctrl+Enter.

Note

Again, the use of range names makes it easier to reuse data that you have already entered, to document your work, and to ensure that any changes you make in the data are reflected in dependent formulas. Suppose, for example, that at some later time you need to adjust the sales forecast. The combination of these formulas and the named ranges lets the adjustment migrate throughout the workbook into formulas that depend, either directly or indirectly, on the sales forecast.

After a qualitative review of this product offering with the stakeholders in your organization, you identify the following relevant costs:

- Some of the current distributors of the existing type of tire will prefer the safety and performance enhancements in the new tire. You can expect that they will stop buying your existing tire and convert their purchases to the new tire. An estimate of the lost gross margin of these lost sales is shown as Lost value, Tire A in figure 11.3.

- Advertising will be necessary to inform the public about your new product. The Advertising line in figure 11.3 quantifies the budget for an initial marketing blitz and for ongoing commercials.

- This new tire has characteristics (relating to its design, consumer market, types of targeted cars, and so on) that necessitate hiring a new product manager. This person specifically will oversee the new tires' product introduction and its future development and life cycle. The New Product Manager line in figure 11.3 shows the ongoing cost of this position.

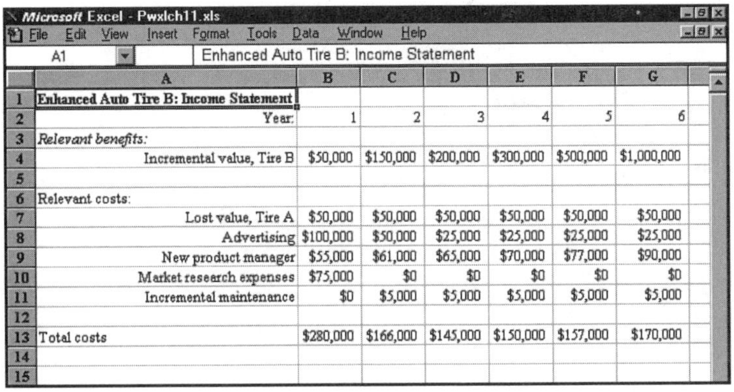

Fig. 11.3
The relevant costs in the pro-forma include only the costs that are directly attributable to the new product.

- The market research expenses needed to launch the product are directly related to the new tire itself, and are incremental to business as usual. The Market research expenses line shows this cost.

- New equipment is needed to produce the new tire. The maintenance on this new equipment will increase total maintenance expense for the company by about $5,000 per year. The Incremental maintenance line contains this cost. Notice that the firm does not begin to incur these maintenance costs until Year 2, after the equipment has been in use for one year.

A pro-forma income statement can now be constructed from the data you have entered so far. The income statement is shown in figure 11.4. The relevant costs are totaled in row 13 and subtracted from the new products' incremental value in row 4. The result, sometimes referred to as *EBITDA* and shown in row 15, constitutes the estimated earnings from the product before taking other indirect costs into consideration. As awkward an acronym as EBITDA is, it's easier than what it stands for: "Earnings Before Interest, Taxes, Depreciation, and Amortization."

Row 16 includes the cost of depreciation on the new production equipment as a line item in order to arrive at a pre-tax income figure (row 17). The cost of the equipment to be depreciated is $500,000, it will be depreciated over a ten year period, and its salvage value at the end of that period will be zero. The formula for depreciation cost is therefore:

```
=SLN(500000,0,10)
```

where the SLN function returns straight-line depreciation, 500000 is the cost of the equipment, 0 is its salvage value, and 10 is its useful life. You can enter this formula either in a single cell and copy it across the remaining cells, or in all six cells at once by means of Ctrl+Enter.

III

Investment Decisions

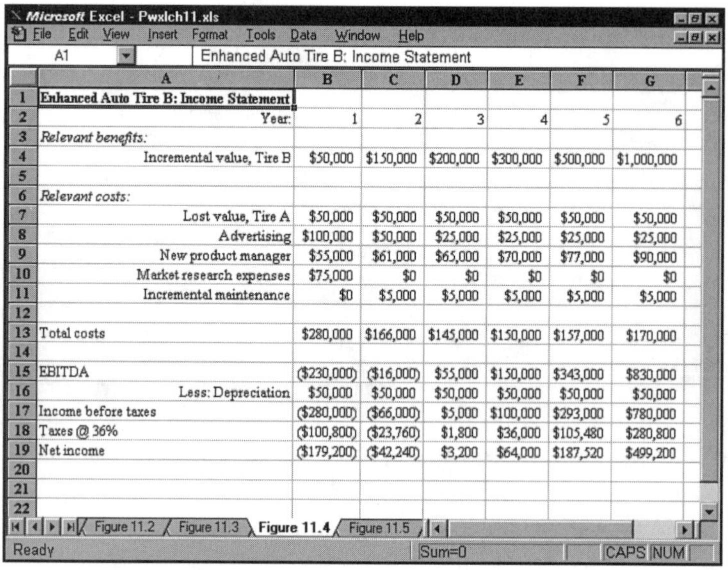

	A	B	C	D	E	F	G
1	Enhanced Auto Tire B: Income Statement						
2	Year:	1	2	3	4	5	6
3	*Relevant benefits:*						
4	Incremental value, Tire B	$50,000	$150,000	$200,000	$300,000	$500,000	$1,000,000
5							
6	*Relevant costs:*						
7	Lost value, Tire A	$50,000	$50,000	$50,000	$50,000	$50,000	$50,000
8	Advertising	$100,000	$50,000	$25,000	$25,000	$25,000	$25,000
9	New product manager	$55,000	$61,000	$65,000	$70,000	$77,000	$90,000
10	Market research expenses	$75,000	$0	$0	$0	$0	$0
11	Incremental maintenance	$0	$5,000	$5,000	$5,000	$5,000	$5,000
12							
13	Total costs	$280,000	$166,000	$145,000	$150,000	$157,000	$170,000
14							
15	EBITDA	($230,000)	($16,000)	$55,000	$150,000	$343,000	$830,000
16	Less: Depreciation	$50,000	$50,000	$50,000	$50,000	$50,000	$50,000
17	Income before taxes	($280,000)	($66,000)	$5,000	$100,000	$293,000	$780,000
18	Taxes @ 36%	($100,800)	($23,760)	$1,800	$36,000	$105,480	$280,800
19	Net income	($179,200)	($42,240)	$3,200	$64,000	$187,520	$499,200

Fig. 11.4
This pro-forma income statement arrives at a figure for net income by taking depreciation and income taxes into account.

It's good practice to use ranges or range names as the arguments to this formula. In this case, you have not yet entered the $500,000 cost of the equipment into the worksheet, so use the constant 500000 as the first argument to the SLN function. Ideally, you would revise this function after creating names that are associated with the equipment's cost, salvage value, and useful life:

```
=SLN(CapitalCost,Salvage,Life)
```

You can now calculate pre-tax income as, in this case, EBITDA minus depreciation:

1. Highlight cells B15:G15, and use the Name Box to name the range as EBITDA.
2. Highlight cells B16:G16 and name the range as Depreciation.
3. Highlight cells B17:G17. Type an equal sign (=).
4. Click the down arrow by the Name Box, and click the name EBITDA. Type a minus sign (–).
5. Click the down-arrow by the Name Box, and click the name Depreciation.
6. Press Ctrl+Enter.
7. While B17:G17 is still highlighted, click in the Name Box and give this range the name PreTaxIncome.

To calculate taxes, simply highlight cells B18:G18, and enter this formula:

```
=.36*PreTaxIncome
```

by using Ctrl+Enter. While B18:G18 is still highlighted, it's convenient to name the range as Taxes. Again, as a matter of general practice, you might want to create a constant named TaxRate, to avoid using a constant such as .36 in your formula for taxes.

Tip

Some accountants would (legitimately) quarrel with the projection of a negative income tax expense. Others would (also legitimately) find it a sensible usage, because early losses from a new operation can offset income from profitable operations, thus reducing the total tax expense. To keep this example simple (by avoiding reference to other, profitable operations), the negative figure is used here.

After figuring in taxes (row 18), net income (row 19) is calculated by subtracting taxes from income before taxes. The Net Income line is the end result of the income statement. It denotes the added (or *incremental*) income that the company can anticipate as a result of the combined revenues and costs due to offering a new product. However, net income is seldom identical to net cash flow. You will want to know the amount of cash that will flow into and out of the business each year if your company decides to proceed with bringing this new product to market.

To quantify the cash flow, it's necessary to extend the pro-forma income statement so that it becomes a cash flow statement. In this case, there are two additional items needed to derive annual cash flow from the income statement: the depreciation on the new equipment and its purchase price. Figure 11.5 shows these modifications.

Note

Again, to keep this example simple, factors due to working capital requirements (such as additional inventory and accounts receivable on incremental sales) have been omitted. If you have worked through chapter 5, "Working Capital and Cash Flow Analysis," you will find it straightforward to add these considerations to your pro-forma.

Begin by adding the depreciation expense from row 16 back into the statement in row 20 of figure 11.5. Row 17, which contains income before taxes, subtracts depreciation from EBITDA, and now that process is reversed in row 20.

III

Investment Decisions

	A	B	C	D	E	F	G
1	**Enhanced Auto Tire B: Cash Flow Statement**						
2	Year:	1	2	3	4	5	6
3	*Relevant benefits:*						
4	Incremental value, Tire B	$50,000	$150,000	$200,000	$300,000	$500,000	$1,000,000
5							
6	*Relevant costs:*						
7	Lost value, Tire A	$50,000	$50,000	$50,000	$50,000	$50,000	$50,000
8	Advertising	$100,000	$50,000	$25,000	$25,000	$25,000	$25,000
9	New product manager	$55,000	$61,000	$65,000	$70,000	$77,000	$90,000
10	Market research expenses	$75,000	$0	$0	$0	$0	$0
11	Incremental maintenance	$0	$5,000	$5,000	$5,000	$5,000	$5,000
12							
13	Total costs	$280,000	$166,000	$145,000	$150,000	$157,000	$170,000
14							
15	EBITDA	($230,000)	($16,000)	$55,000	$150,000	$343,000	$830,000
16	Less: Depreciation	$50,000	$50,000	$50,000	$50,000	$50,000	$50,000
17	Income before taxes	($280,000)	($66,000)	$5,000	$100,000	$293,000	$780,000
18	Taxes @ 36%	($100,800)	($23,760)	$1,800	$36,000	$105,480	$280,800
19	Net income	($179,200)	($42,240)	$3,200	$64,000	$187,520	$499,200
20	Plus: Depreciation	$50,000	$50,000	$50,000	$50,000	$50,000	$50,000
21	Minus: Investment	$500,000	$0	$0	$0	$0	$0
22	Net Cash Flow	($629,200)	$7,760	$53,200	$114,000	$237,520	$549,200

Fig. 11.5
Adding the depreciation back in, and accounting for the equipment expenditure, clarifies the actual cash flows for the new product.

Why deal with depreciation twice? Because depreciation is not an actual cash outlay. It is an accrued expense: to each time period, it assigns a portion of the loss in the value of the capital investment. As an *expense*, you can use it to reduce income, for the purpose of calculating tax liabilities. As a *non-cash* expense, it should not count against the net cash flow. Therefore, you can subtract it from pre-tax income for the purpose of calculating taxes, and add it back in for the purpose of estimating actual net cash flow.

As mentioned above, your company needs new machinery to produce the new product. It is necessary to retool some of the assembly line's production facilities that at present are dedicated to your current product. You require $500,000 in capital expenditures to accomplish the retooling, and this amount is shown in row 21.

As noted previously, this analysis assumes that the equipment has a useful life of 10 years, and that it has zero salvage value. In this case, you have decided to depreciate the equipment on a straight-line basis, as shown on the *Depreciation* lines (rows 16 and 20 of fig. 11.5).

Finally, the $500,000 capital investment in the new machinery is subtracted in row 21 to produce the net cash flow figure for the period (row 22). At this point, it would be wise to name cell B21 as CapitalCost and to replace the constant 500000 in the SLN depreciation function with that name.

By performing these steps, you will have taken what was originally a pro-forma income statement and extended it such that it is now a pro-forma cash flow statement.

Summary

The topics covered in this chapter constitute the basic inputs to a full business case. Chapters 12 and 13 explain how to analyze these inputs to determine whether the business case makes financial sense. So, while the process is by no means complete, by this point you have accomplished the following:

- Identified all the relevant benefits and costs of this business decision.

- Quantified all the relevant benefits and costs of the decision, and entered them in a workbook format.

- Merged the benefits and costs to construct a pro-forma income statement.

- Extended the pro-forma income statement so as to depict a pro-forma cash flow statement.

The result is a projection of the future cash flows that would result if the company embarked on this business venture.

How can management use this information? It should base its decision of whether to proceed with the new product on an analysis of the cash flow's current value to the business.

Put another way, investments must be made at the outset to implement the proposal. The company must provide funds for retooling, anticipate the loss of revenues from the current product, support promotional activities, hire more staff, and so on.

Are the anticipated returns adequate to justify these investments? Chapter 12 "Examining Decision Criteria for Business Analysis," discusses the additional financial concepts and indicators that assist in the decision-making process. It also demonstrates how you can use Excel to extend the pro-forma cash flow model, and how you can apply valuation tools to help determine whether a decision to implement the proposal is a sound one.

Chapter 12

Examining Decision Criteria for Business Analysis

Chapter 11 looked at the relevant facts surrounding a business case decision. If you worked your way through the case study, you constructed a pro forma income statement and a pro forma cash flow statement. These statements help you to describe the decision quantitatively. An important criterion to use in the evaluation of an income or cash flow statement is the discount factor.

The term *discounting* refers to the estimation of the present value of future cash flows. For example, every dollar you own today has a different value in the future. If you deposit $100 in a savings account that yields 5 percent annually, that $100 will be worth $105 in one year. Its future value is $105.

That future value depends on several issues, including length of time that you hold the money and rate of return you can obtain on the dollar. This chapter shows you how to take discounting into account in your income and cash flow statements. By doing so, you can make these statements more meaningful.

Specifically, Chapter 12 covers payback periods, discounted payback periods, and the concepts of future value, present value, and net present value.

Understanding Payback Periods

The *payback period* is the length of time between an initial investment and the recovery of the investment from its annual cash flow. Suppose, for example, that you purchase a store for $500,000. Taking into account the income from the store, your expenses and depreciation, and your taxes, it takes you 48 months to earn back the $500,000. The payback period for your investment is 48 months.

Figures 12.1 and 12.2 repeat the information in figure 11.5 of the prior chapter. This chapter describes how to extend that information to arrive at payback periods and associated decision criteria such as discounted cash flows.

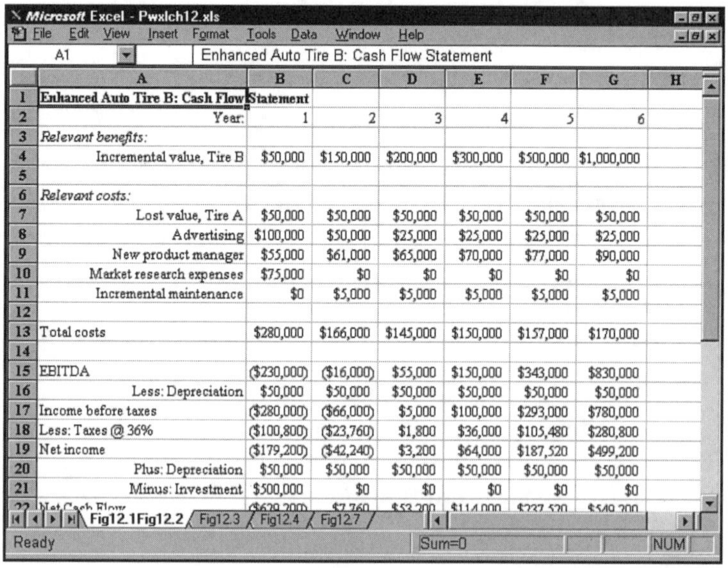

Fig. 12.1

The cash flow statements benefits and costs summarize the relevant business case inputs.

To make the calculations clearer, add a row labeled Cumulative Net Cash Flow to the cash flow statement that was developed in Chapter 11. To add the Cumulative Net Cash Flow row, follow these steps:

1. Highlight cells B22:G22.

2. Click in the Name box, type **NetCashFlow**, and press Enter. This name is needed to calculate the cumulative net cash flow.

3. Select cell A24, and enter the label **Cumulative Net Cash Flow**.

4. Select cell B24, and enter this formula:

```
=SUM(OFFSET(NetCashFlow,0,0,1,Year))
```

   5. Copy cell B24 and paste it into C24:G24, either by choosing Edit, Copy
   and Edit, Paste, or by dragging B24's fill handle into the C24:G24 range.

   6. Select the range B24:G24, click the Name box, type
   CumulativeNetCashFlow, and press Enter.

Refer to figure 12.2 for the result. The formula you entered in step 4 returns
the running total of the range NetCashFlow for each consecutive year.

The range named Year occupies cells B2:G2 on the worksheet, and has the
values 1 through 6. As you fill row 24 with its formula, the fifth argument of
the OFFSET function adjusts for each successive value of Year, so that 1 becomes 2, then 3, and so on. This argument specifies the number of columns
in NetCashFlow to return to the SUM function by way of OFFSET.

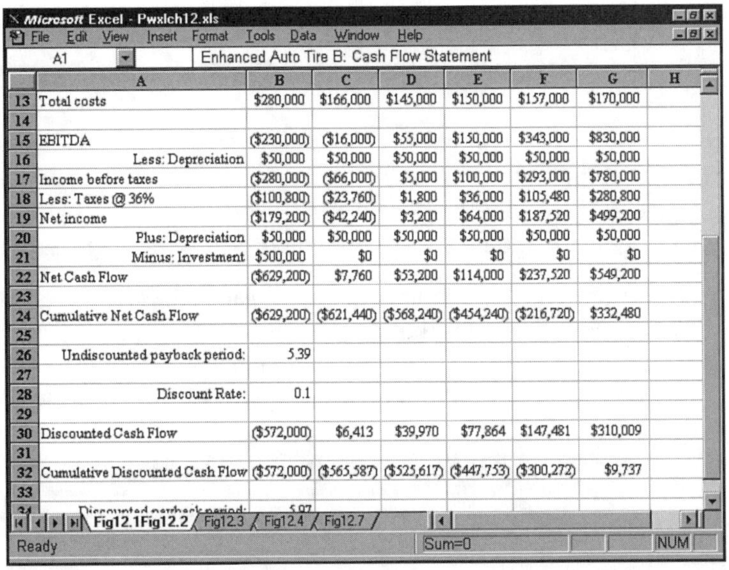

Fig. 12.2
The cash flow
statement's
adjustments take
account of
depreciation,
taxes, and capital
investment to
arrive at net cash
flows.

	A	B	C	D	E	F	G	H
13	Total costs	$280,000	$166,000	$145,000	$150,000	$157,000	$170,000	
14								
15	EBITDA	($230,000)	($16,000)	$55,000	$150,000	$343,000	$830,000	
16	Less: Depreciation	$50,000	$50,000	$50,000	$50,000	$50,000	$50,000	
17	Income before taxes	($280,000)	($66,000)	$5,000	$100,000	$293,000	$780,000	
18	Less: Taxes @ 36%	($100,800)	($23,760)	$1,800	$36,000	$105,480	$280,800	
19	Net income	($179,200)	($42,240)	$3,200	$64,000	$187,520	$499,200	
20	Plus: Depreciation	$50,000	$50,000	$50,000	$50,000	$50,000	$50,000	
21	Minus: Investment	$500,000	$0	$0	$0	$0	$0	
22	Net Cash Flow	($629,200)	$7,760	$53,200	$114,000	$237,520	$549,200	
23								
24	Cumulative Net Cash Flow	($629,200)	($621,440)	($568,240)	($454,240)	($216,720)	$332,480	
25								
26	Undiscounted payback period:	5.39						
27								
28	Discount Rate:	0.1						
29								
30	Discounted Cash Flow	($572,000)	$6,413	$39,970	$77,864	$147,481	$310,009	
31								
32	Cumulative Discounted Cash Flow	($572,000)	($565,587)	($525,617)	($447,753)	($300,272)	$9,737	
33								

Note

The OFFSET function returns a range that is shifted some number of rows or columns
from its first argument. For example:

   =OFFSET(A1,1,1,2,2)

returns the range B2:C3, which is shifted (or *offset*) down by one row and right by
one column from A1, and contains 2 rows and 2 columns.

III

Investment Decisions

So, because the first value of Year is 1, OFFSET returns just the first column of NetCashFlow to SUM in B24. In C24, the formula refers to the second value of Year, or 2, and OFFSET returns the first two columns of NetCashFlow to be added together by SUM. The result is a cumulative, summed value for NetCashFlow in the line labeled Cumulative Net Cash Flow.

By visually inspecting CumulativeNetCashFlow you can see that, sometime after five years, this project will have recouped the original investment for the company. It is at this point that CumulativeNetCashFlow changes from negative values to a positive value. This is the payback period for this example. However, you cannot as yet tell exactly when the payback period has ended. All you can tell so far is that the payback period ends sometime during the sixth year.

You can modify the worksheet to calculate the payback period exactly by array-entering the following formula:

```
=INDEX((Year-CumulativeNetCashFlowNetCashFlow),
    1,SUM(IF(CumulativeNetCashFlow<=0,1,0))+1)
```

which is shown in cell B26 of figure 12.2. This is a lengthy formula. As is the case with most complicated formulas, it is easier to understand if you break it up into segments, and enter those segments on your worksheet. Figure 12.3 shows these segments, and how they combine to return the payback period.

Row 1 in figure 12.3 shows the number of each year in the calculation of the payback period. Row 3 contains the net cash flow, and row 5 contains the cumulative net cash flow. Each of these rows is a named range, with the names Year, NetCashFlow, and CumulativeNetCashFlow, respectively.

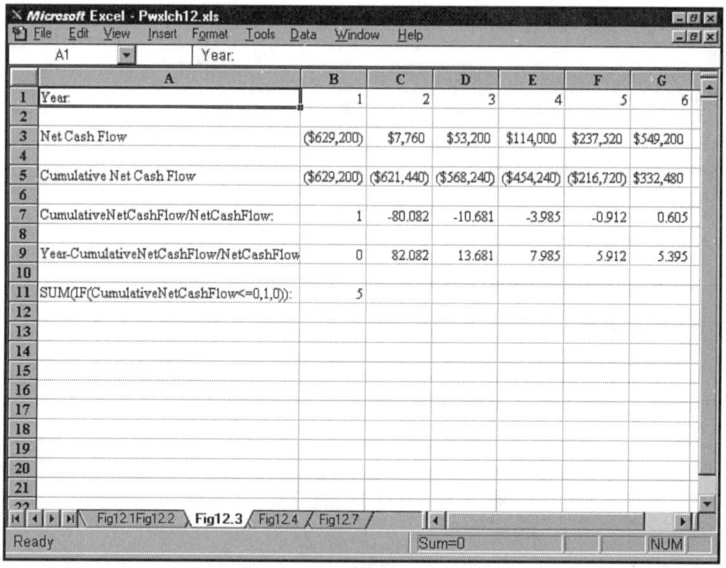

Fig. 12.3

All of these calculations are summarized in the single array formula in cell B26 of figure 12.2.

Tip

The three named ranges in figure 12.3 are not the same ranges as those with the same names in figures 12.1 and 12.2. In figure 12.3, the ranges are sheet level, and in the Define Name dialog box their names appear as, for example, Fig12.3!Year. The reference to the sheet where they are found distinguishes them from book level names, which are not qualified by a worksheet name. These sheet level names are used in formulas on the same sheet where they are defined, so the formulas do not need to qualify the names with the name of their worksheet.

Row 7 in figure 12.3 shows the ratio of each year's cumulative net cash flow to that year's net cash flow. To enter the formula, highlight B7:G7 and type:

```
=CumulativeNetCashFlow/NetCashFlow
```

Tip

If you use named ranges in formulas, the Name box makes it easier to enter the formulas. After selecting a cell, type the equal sign (=), then click the down arrow next to the Name box to display any defined names. Clicking on a name moves it into the formula bar. (Some long names might not fully appear in the Name box.)

Then, hold down Ctrl and press Enter. Holding down Ctrl enters the formula in each of the highlighted cells, taking advantage of the *implicit intersection*.

Note

The implicit intersection is an important feature of Excel. When you entered the cash flow ratios on row 7, using Ctrl+Enter, you specified that each individual value in the CumulativeNetCashFlow range be divided by its corresponding value in the NetCashFlow range. Excel automatically recognizes which values in each range correspond to one another. That is, cell 1 of CumulativeNetCashFlow is the intersection of that range's first row (here, its only row) with its first column. Similarly, cell 1 of NetCashFlow is the intersection of that range's first row (again, its only row) with its first column.

Notice that there is nothing in the formula that expresses which column of CumulativeNetCashFlow is to be divided by which column of NetCashFlow. Excel derives this information automatically, which is why it is termed an implicit intersection.

III

Investment Decisions

The ratio in row 7 of figure 12.3 has a particularly useful meaning for the year during which the payback period is complete. The ratio expresses the proportion of that year during which the cumulative net cash flow has exceeded the payback of the investment.

Notice that it is not until the end of year 6 that cumulative net cash flow becomes a positive number. The ratio of the cumulative net cash flow to the net cash flow for year 6 is $332,480/$549,200, or .605. If you assume that cash flows are evenly distributed throughout the year, then the initial investment has been recouped at about 40 percent (1–.605) of the way through year 6. Put another way, when 40 percent of year 6 has elapsed, the cumulative net cash flow reaches zero: therefore, the amount of the initial investments has been paid back.

Subtracting that ratio (.605) from the year number (6) results in 5.39: it will take about 5.4 years to pay back the initial expenses and capital investment. This calculation is shown for each of the six years in row 9 of figure 12.3. These cells contain this formula (again entered with Ctrl+Enter):

```
=Year-CumulativeNetCashFlow/NetCashFlow
```

How can you tell which of the values in row 9 represents the true payback period? Again, the payback period cannot have elapsed so long as the cumulative net cash flow is negative. Therefore, you want Excel to ignore all years until the cumulative net cash flow turns positive.

The following array formula (cell B11 in figure 12.3) assigns a 1 if the CumulativeNetCashFlow is less than or equal to 0, and assigns a 0 otherwise. By summing the 1s and 0s, the formula returns the number of years during which the cumulative net cash flow is less than or equal to zero:

```
=SUM(IF(CumulativeNetCashFlow<=0,1,0))
```

In this case, the array formula returns 5: the cumulative net cash flow is still negative at the end of year 5. Adding 1 to this result returns the first year during which the cumulative net cash flow is greater than 0:

```
=SUM(IF(CumulativeNetCashFlow<=0,1,0))+1
```

Finally, you are in a position to express all this with one *array* formula, in cell B26 of figure 12.2 and repeated here:

```
=INDEX((Year-CumulativeNetCashFlow/NetCashFlow),
    1,SUM(IF(CumulativeNetCashFlow<=0,1,0))+1)
```

The general syntax of the INDEX function is:

```
=INDEX(ARRAY,ROW,COLUMN)
```

Here, the ARRAY argument is the row of six values expressed by:

(Year–CumulativeNetCashFlow/NetCashFlow)

and shown as row 9 in figure 12.3. The ROW argument is 1, because there is only one row in the array. The COLUMN argument is the result of:

=SUM(IF(CumulativeNetCashFlow<=0,1,0))+1

which is the first year during which the cumulative net cash flow is positive, or 6.

The result of the full array formula is 5.39—the sixth column in the only row of the array of the ratios—which you can find in cell G9 of figure 12.3, and in cell B26 of figure 12.2.

Note

The approach outlined here returns the length of time required for the cumulative net cash flow to become a positive number *for the first time*. There are instances where additional investments must occur subsequent to the initial investment, and these subsequent investments can cause the cumulative net cash flow to become negative again, after it has initially become a positive number.

Thus, the undiscounted payback period for this series of cash flows is 5.39 years.

Understanding Future Value, Present Value, and Net Present Value

This analysis so far has not taken into account the time value of money. One dollar received today is worth more than one dollar received five years from today. But how much more? This would depend on the recipients' *expectations* about how much could be earned on that dollar received today, or what their expectations are for an adequate rate of return on that dollar.

Calculating Future Value

A dollar received today and invested in a financial instrument that yields 10 percent would be worth $1.10 after one year. $1.10 is the future value of your dollar given the time period for investment (one year) and the rate of return (10 percent). After five years, the future value of your dollar would be $1.61.

This value is:

$$\$1.00 \times 1.1 \times 1.1 \times 1.1 \times 1.1 \times 1.1 = \$1.61$$

or

$$\$1.00 \times 1.1^5 = \$1.61$$

Calculating Present Value

Conversely, what is today's value of a dollar to be received five years from now? You can calculate the present value of that dollar (again, assuming a rate of return of 10 percent) by means of:

$$\$1.00 \div 1.1 \div 1.1 \div 1.1 \div 1.1 \div 1.1 = \$0.62$$

or

$$\$1.00 / 1.1^5 = \$0.62$$

You can set up a formula in your worksheet that will compute present value discount factors, given a selected interest rate. You can then apply the discount factors to the period's cash flow. To do so, follow these steps as shown in figure 12.4, where rows 1 through 6 are taken from figure 12.2.

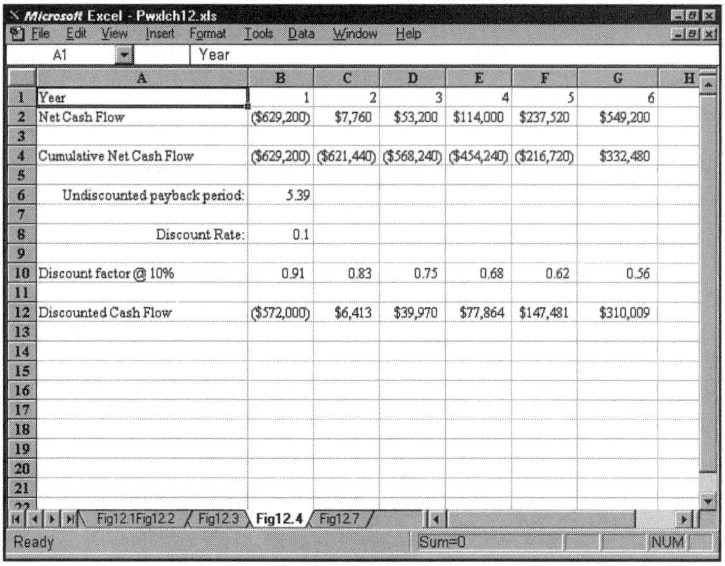

Fig. 12.4
The discounted cash flow takes into account the time value of money.

1. Select cell A8, and enter the label Discount Rate.

2. Select cell B8, and enter **.1**.

3. With B8 selected, click in the Name box and type **DiscountRate**. Press Enter. You have now created a range named DiscountRate, whose value is the number (.1) that you entered in cell B8.

4. Select cells B10:G10, and type this formula:

   ```
   =1/(1+DiscountRate)^Year
   ```

   Hold down Ctrl and press Enter to place the formula in all six highlighted cells.

5. With B10:G10 still highlighted, select Format, Cells and click the Number tab. Choose the 0.00 format from the dropdown list of Format Codes.

The result is as shown in figure 12.4.

Notice that the discount factor ranges from .91 at the end of the first year, to .83 at the end of the second year, to .56 at the end of the sixth year. This represents the value of a dollar that you have today at the end of one, two,..., six years. For each year, the number 1 is divided by 1 + DiscountRate (or 1.1) raised to the number of years that have elapsed.

Line 12 in figure 12.4, labeled Discounted Cash Flow, is the result of multiplying line 2 (NetCashFlow) by line 10 (the discount factor). This represents the discounted value of NetCashFlow: that is, the value in today's dollars of future annual cash flows.

For example, the NetCashFlow in year 6 is $549,200. The Discounted Cash Flow in year 6 is $310,009. This means that, under the assumption of an annual 10 percent rate, the funds needed to start producing the new product return $310,009 six years hence—taking into account that you could make 10 percent per year in an alternative investment.

Calculating Net Present Value

This discussion has described the discounting process in two steps: creating each year's discount factor, and multiplying that discount factor times the annual net cash flow. The discussion used these two steps to make what happens in the discounting process a little clearer. Excel provides a function, NPV (Net Present Value) that enables you to perform the discounting process with just one formula:

1. If you have already created the range name DiscountRate on the worksheet shown in figure 12.2, skip to step 4. Otherwise, highlight cell A28, and enter the label Discount Rate.

2. Select cell B28, and type **.1**.

3. With B28 still selected, click in the Name box, type **DiscountRate**, and press Enter.

4. Select cells B30:G30, and enter this formula:

   ```
   =NetCashFlow/(1+DiscountRate)^Year
   ```

   by holding down the Ctrl key as you press Enter.

5. With B30:G30 still selected, select Format, Cells and click the Number tab. Select the first Currency format from the dropdown list of Format Codes.

The result is the discounted cash flow and is shown in row 30 of figure 12.2.

Line 32 in figure 12.2, labeled Cumulative Discounted Cash Flow, is calculated in much the same way as CumulativeNetCashFlow is calculated. It shows the running total for each year of the *discounted* cash flows rather than the *undiscounted* cash flows. To obtain the cumulative discounted cash flow, highlight cells B32:G32 and array enter this formula:

```
=NPV(DiscountRate,OFFSET(NetCashFlow,0,0,1,Year))
```

The outer portion of this formula, initiated by NPV, returns the net present value of its arguments. The OFFSET component of this formula returns as many elements from the NetCashFlow range as are specified by the Year argument. For cell B32, Year is equal to 1, so OFFSET returns the first element of NetCashFlow. For cell C32, Year is equal to 2, so OFFSET returns the second element of NetCashFlow.

The cumulative discounted cash flow figure in year 6, $9,737, is the *net present value* of the cash flows for the 6-year period of this project. It is simply the sum of the discounted cash flows for the full 6-year life of the business case.

At this point, you can also add into your worksheet a payback calculation similar to the one that you developed for the undiscounted cash flows. In cell B34 of the worksheet shown in figure 12.2, enter the following array formula:

```
=INDEX((Year-CumulativeDiscountedCashFlow/
DiscountedCashFlow),1,SUM(IF(CumulativeNetCashFlow<=0,1,0))+1)
```

Notice that the payback period for the discounted cash flows is 5.97 years, instead of the payback period of 5.39 years for the undiscounted cash flows. This makes sense because actual dollars being paid back are worth less the farther into the future you go. Therefore, payback takes longer.

Shortening the Payback Period

It's an unfortunate but immutable fact of business life that, after you have gone through these careful calculations to derive payback periods based on both undiscounted and discounted cash flows, your Executive Director of Finance will say:

> "Smith, your analysis is close, but we have to keep the undiscounted payback to a maximum of five years. Go do it again."

Here's how to increase your bonus check:

> As you analyze the effects of costs on the payback period for offering a new automobile tire product, you see that there are several cost categories that you must take into account. Some costs, such as tax rates and the revenue that will be lost from discontinuing the old product, are beyond your company's control. Other costs, such as the initial capital investment of $500,000, the advertising budget, the product manager's salary, and the market research are all controllable.

> You need a way to simultaneously modify all the controllable costs so as to meet the newly imposed conditions for the payback periods. Other examples in this book have used Excel's Goal Seek function to adjust one value by changing another. This is a faster method to find a particular precedent value than is trial and error. However, Goal Seek limits you to just one changing cell. Furthermore, that changing cell cannot contain a formula: it must contain a value.

> You can use the Solver instead. The Solver is an add-in that comes with Excel, and, if you did a complete installation of Excel to your hard disk, then it is available to you. By using the Solver, you can modify more than one cell at once to get to a desired outcome. The changing cells do not need to contain values, but can contain formulas (although Solver converts the formulas to values if you save the Solver's solution at the end of the process).

III

Investment Decisions

To access Solver, follow these steps:

1. Choose <u>T</u>ools, Add-<u>I</u>ns from Excel's main menu.

2. If the check box for the Solver Add-in is empty, check it and then choose OK; otherwise, if the box is already checked, choose Cancel.

3. Excel works for a few moments loading the Solver add-in. When it has finished, Sol<u>v</u>er will be a new option in the <u>T</u>ools menu.

Note

If you cannot find the Solver add-in in the Add-ins dialog box, try choosing Browse to find SOLVER.XLA. It is normally found in the SOLVER folder of the LIBRARY folder under the folder where you have stored Excel. SOLVER.XLA may have inadvertently been moved to another location. If you cannot locate it, you will have to reinstall it from your distribution disks or CD; as you are setting the installation options, make sure that you request the installation of the Solver.

You want the Solver to change your controllable costs, but you need to give it some criteria to work with. For example, the Solver has no way of knowing *a priori* that you must pay the product manager a positive amount of money each year. Unconstrained, the Solver might suggest that you pay the product manager a negative amount of money to shorten the payback periods.

Because this is unacceptable, establish some minimum values. In cell H4, enter this formula:

```
=MIN(B4:G4)
```

Then copy that formula and paste it into cells H5 and H6. These cells will act as *constraints* on the solution that the Solver reaches. The formulas return the minimum values for advertising, the product manager's annual salary, and the market research expenses.

Highlight cell B22, which contains the undiscounted payback period. Then, choose <u>T</u>ools, Sol<u>v</u>er and complete the entries in the Solver Parameters dialog box as follows:

1. The S<u>e</u>t Target Cell box should contain $B$22. If it does not, click in that box and then highlight B22 on the worksheet.

2. Click the <u>V</u>alue option button, and enter 5 in the edit box to its right.

3. Click in the <u>B</u>y Changing Cells box, and on the worksheet highlight cells B4:G6. These cells contain the annual costs for advertising, the

product manager's salary, and market research. After B6 in the edit box, type a comma, and highlight cell B17, which contains the cost of the initial investment.

4. Click the Add button. In the Add Constraint dialog box, click in the Cell Reference box and then select cell H4 on the worksheet. H4 contains the minimum value of the annual advertising cost.

5. Click the down arrow next to the operator symbol, and select the >= operator.

6. Click in the Constraint box, and enter 0. The Add Constraint dialog box should appear as shown in figure 12.5

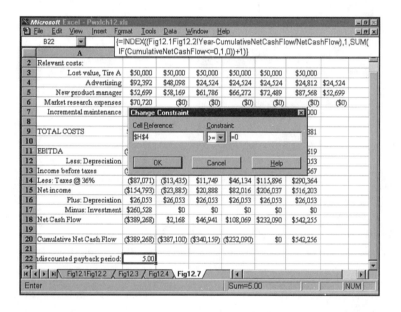

Fig. 12.5
Setting a constraint on advertising expenses prevents the Solver from changing them to negative values.

7. Choose Add.

8. Repeat steps 4 through 7 for cells H5, H6, and B17, to establish constraints for the product manager's salary, the market research expense, and the initial capital investment. Use a >= value of 250000 for the initial investment: although you may have to forego advertising, a product manager, and market research by means of zero costs, you cannot forego the initial investment entirely.

9. When you have finished entering cell B17 as a constraint, choose OK. This returns you to the Solver Parameters dialog box, which should appear as shown in figure 12.6.

Fig. 12.6

Using the Solver to optimize costs involves setting the target cell, the changing cells, and any necessary constraints.

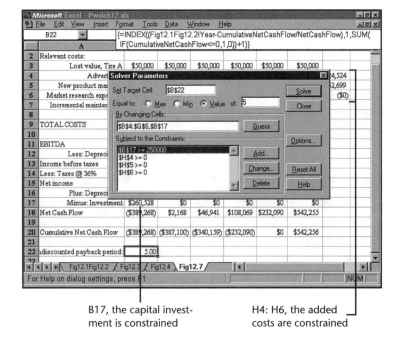

B17, the capital invest-
ment is constrained

H4: H6, the added
costs are constrained

10. Choose <u>S</u>olve.

The Solver now begins adjusting the various costs that you specified as changing cells in order to reach the value 5 for the undiscounted payback period (5 represents the *end* of Year 4). Because you specified 0 as the minimum allowable value for cells H4:H6 and B17 via the Add Constraints dialog box, the Solver will not attempt to establish a negative value in B4:G6 or in B17.

You can watch the Solver's progress in the Status Bar at the bottom of the worksheet. For each trial solution, you can see how far the Solver has progressed toward a solution that meets your specifications.

Eventually, the Solver presents the Solver Results dialog box. On occasion, the specifactions may make it impossible for the Solver to reach a solution, and the dialog box will let you know. With the example data, though, the Solver is able to shorten the undiscounted payback to period 5.

Because the Solver is capable of modifying a variety of cells to reach a specified result, there may be many ways to achieve that result. Therefore, it is useful to save the different solutions as *scenarios*. One of the scenarios that you should save contains the original values in your worksheet. To save it, click the <u>S</u>ave Scenario button in the Solver Results dialog box. The Save

Scenario dialog box appears, and you can type a descriptive name such as Shorter Payback in the Scenario Name edit box. Click OK to return to the Solver Results dialog box. Click the Restore Original Values radio button in the Solver Results dialog box, and choose OK.

As a result of this manipulation of values and saving them in a scenario, you have an easy way of going back and forth between your original input values, and the values that Solver found such that the undiscounted payback period is 5. Just choose Tools, Scenarios, highlight the name of the scenario that you want to view in the Scenarios list box, and choose Show. The Solver has saved the proper addresses and values for the changing cells into the scenario.

Figure 12.7 shows the changes to the advertising, product management, market research, and initial investment costs that the Solver made to shorten the undiscounted payback period.

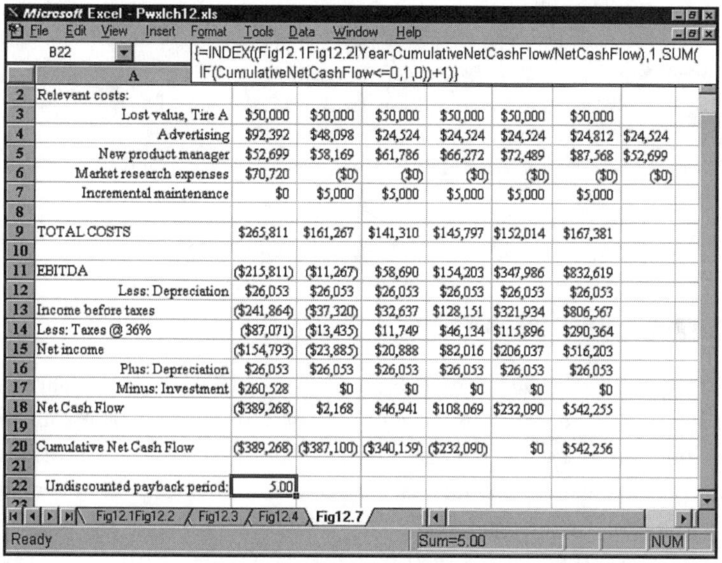

	A							
2	Relevant costs:							
3	Lost value, Tire A	$50,000	$50,000	$50,000	$50,000	$50,000	$50,000	
4	Advertising	$92,392	$48,098	$24,524	$24,524	$24,524	$24,812	$24,524
5	New product manager	$52,699	$58,169	$61,786	$66,272	$72,489	$87,568	$52,699
6	Market research expenses	$70,720	($0)	($0)	($0)	($0)	($0)	($0)
7	Incremental maintenance	$0	$5,000	$5,000	$5,000	$5,000	$5,000	
8								
9	TOTAL COSTS	$265,811	$161,267	$141,310	$145,797	$152,014	$167,381	
10								
11	EBITDA	($215,811)	($11,267)	$58,690	$154,203	$347,986	$832,619	
12	Less: Depreciation	$26,053	$26,053	$26,053	$26,053	$26,053	$26,053	
13	Income before taxes	($241,864)	($37,320)	$32,637	$128,151	$321,934	$806,567	
14	Less: Taxes @ 36%	($87,071)	($13,435)	$11,749	$46,134	$115,896	$290,364	
15	Net income	($154,793)	($23,885)	$20,888	$82,016	$206,037	$516,203	
16	Plus: Depreciation	$26,053	$26,053	$26,053	$26,053	$26,053	$26,053	
17	Minus: Investment	$260,528	$0	$0	$0	$0	$0	
18	Net Cash Flow	($389,268)	$2,168	$46,941	$108,069	$232,090	$542,255	
19								
20	Cumulative Net Cash Flow	($389,268)	($387,100)	($340,159)	($232,090)	$0	$542,256	
21								
22	Undiscounted payback period:	5.00						

Fig. 12.7 Controllable costs are reduced to shorten the payback period.

Notice that the cumulative net cash flow is now $0 at the end of the fifth year: therefore, the payback period is now exactly five years. The advertising, product management, and market research expenses have all been gently reduced. The initial investment cost has been drastically reduced, from $500,000 to $260,528. This is because it represents the greatest portion of the controllable costs. You might want to modify the Solver constraint on the initial investment, from a minimum of $250,000 to a somewhat higher value.

So doing could cause the other expense categories to drop unacceptably far, or it may make it impossible for the Solver to reach a solution that meets the required criteria. In that event, you might request additional guidance in setting the criteria, or you could report that the business case analysis suggests that the numbers do not support developing the new product.

> **Tip**
>
> When you try to change or delete a constraint in the Solver Parameters dialog box, you may occasionally receive an error message alerting you to a Type Mismatch, an internal error, or insufficient memory. Assuming that you do have enough memory available, this is generally due to the use of a named cell in a constraint, and represents a bug in the Solver.
>
> For example, if you have specified the constraint that cell A10 must be greater than 0, and if you have given cell A10 the name DiscountRate, the Solver shows that constraint as DiscountRate > 0: i.e., the Solver uses the cells name. To change or delete that constraint without encountering an error message, return first to the worksheet and choose Insert, Name, Define. Select the name and choose Delete to remove the cells name. Then, start the Solver again: you should be able to change or delete the constraint, which is now based on the cell's address.

Good luck with that bonus.

Summary

In this chapter, you have learned about payback periods, which quantify the length of time required to break even on an investment. The concepts of future value, present value, and net present value set the stage for discounted payback periods, which can vary as the value of money changes over time. And you have learned how to use a very powerful add-in, the Solver, to optimize a variety of input values so as to achieve an outcome that you specify.

Each of these concepts and tools plays a part in developing a business case that conforms to your decision criteria. This chapter has also described how to save different combinations of input values in scenarios, so that you can revisit them and eventually select the best combination to achieve your plan's objectives. The next chapter takes up the topic of sensitivity analysis, which enables you to quantify the magnitude of changes to the case's outcomes as you manipulate changes to its inputs.

Chapter 13

Creating a Sensitivity Analysis for a Business Case

A business case is fundamentally a snapshot of a set of assumptions surrounding a business activity that your firm is considering. Some of these assumptions can be made with a relatively high degree of confidence; others are little more than educated guesses. A well prepared business case recognizes that there is imprecision in at least some of its inputs.

The business case should document the logic behind the numbers, and should also test the sensitivity of its results to variations in its input assumptions. Put another way, suppose that a business case assumes that a company can obtain a loan at 9 percent. In that case, according to the business case, the company can expect profits to increase by 12 percent. The business case should also report the expected profit increase if the company obtains a loan at other interest rates. By varying the input assumption (here, interest rate) decision makers can determine how *sensitive* certain measures (here, profits) are to changes in assumptions.

When you first construct a particular business case, you normally undertake a qualitative review of all the potential drivers of costs and benefits. As discussed in chapters 11 and 12, you then attempt to quantify those drivers— to attach credible numbers to them. After constructing the basic framework and reviewing its output, you have an opportunity to review each one of those drivers. This review enables you to determine your level of confidence in their accuracy; remember, the drivers are variables that can be anything from hard data to vague estimates.

In some cases, the accuracy of your estimate matters little. In other cases, an apparently minor change to an estimate has a profound effect on the outcome. Sensitivity analysis enables you to calculate the importance of a particular assumption. This puts you in a position to focus on the accuracy of the critical drivers, and to disregard drivers that have little effect on the outcome. If a critical driver is very difficult to estimate with great confidence, it will be equally difficult to place much faith in the results of the business analysis.

Excel provides several ways to manage and manipulate these drivers. One, scenario management, helps you to manage the inputs to your business case. Using scenarios, you can alter different assumptions about decision drivers such as the discount rate, or the cost of capital.

An additional Excel function that gives you more insight into your business case's outcomes is the IRR (the *internal rate of return*). And by using Excel's Goal Seek function, you can enhance the usefulness of a sensitivity analysis.

This chapter covers each of these topics in detail.

Managing Scenarios

Chapters 11 and 12 explained how to construct a base business case. During the initial construction process, the tendency is to be neither optimistic nor pessimistic about the initial inputs: these estimates are starting points, and should lie within the range of best guesses. After constructing the basic business case, it's useful to continue with a sensitivity analysis—an examination of each input variable, and the assignment of best case, worst case, and base case values to each.

Scenario management is the process of examining individual variables, and assigning ranges of values to them. Each combination of values results in a different view, or *scenario*. Decision makers can then focus their attention on each scenario, and assess the sensitivity of the most likely outcome (the base case) to changes in the assumptions that underlie the business opportunity.

The input variables involved in the automobile tire enhancement decision case, developed in chapters 11 and 12, include the following:

- Incremental sales volume

- Lost sales (sales substitution)

- Cost of goods sold for incremental sales

- Cost of goods sold for lost sales

- Advertising

- New product manager salaries and benefits

- Market research expense

- Retooling capital required

- Incremental maintenance required

A quick scan of this list makes it evident that the two items in which you would have the lowest level of confidence are the incremental sales volume and the volume of lost sales. (Lost sales represent the purchases that current customers would make in the absence of a new product. It is expected that some of these lost sales would be converted to purchases of the new product when it is introduced).

You normally have a greater degree of confidence in your estimates of the other input variables, because they involve controllable costs. For example, you expect to have an accurate estimate of the factors that influence the cost of goods sold. These line items include both labor and material costs. You can often exert considerable control over these by entering into long-term purchasing agreements for material, and long-term wage agreements for labor. Often, these agreements are in place at the time that you undertake the sensitivity analysis.

You can also estimate retooling capital, and the associated incremental maintenance, with a high degree of certainty. You can obtain quotations from vendors for the required equipment, and ensure that the quotes will remain firm during the process of evaluating the business case.

You can estimate the costs associated with hiring a new product manager with some precision. You can, for example, investigate the current job market conditions that define the salary requirements for such a position. You would also check the salaries and benefits offered for similar positions within your company.

Market research is also a controllable expense. It is your source of information on the degree of lost sales you should expect. You might decide to spend very little on market research, and just guess at the level of lost sales; or, you could spend millions of dollars on focus groups and test marketing. Because the volume of lost sales is a critical input variable, you might use the $75,000 initially budgeted for market research as a minimum amount. You could

III

Investment Decisions

retain the option to consider additional research expenses if, after reviewing preliminary research results, you have little confidence in their estimate of lost sales.

Advertising expenses are also under your control. Assume that, historically, sales of this product have had a strong positive correlation with the dollar level of advertising. Varying the advertising expenditures would have a measurable impact on sales volumes; in turn, sales have a corresponding impact on profitability. Of course, there is a level of advertising expenditure at which the law of diminishing returns begins to apply (that is, a point of market saturation). For present purposes, assume that the market research would identify this ceiling.

That leaves incremental sales volume as the remaining input variable that is neither under your direct control nor open to accurate estimation. To determine how sensitive the business case is to both underestimates and overestimates of incremental sales, it is useful to create scenarios that specify different conditions, such as:

- Incremental sales volumes are doubled

- Incremental sales volumes are halved

- Advertising expense is doubled, causing incremental sales volumes to increase by 20 percent

- Advertising expense is halved, causing incremental sales volumes to decline by 30 percent

> **Note**
>
> These conditions, such as double the incremental sales and half the advertising expenses, are just examples. In your own situation, you would doubtless be concerned about other variables in addition to advertising and incremental sales. Further, you would want to identify a *relevant range* for each variable. Depending on the particular business case, other upper and lower limits would apply: for example, plus and minus 15 percent of the base case's incremental sales assumption.

In the preceding list, the first two scenarios give management both an optimistic and pessimistic view of the opportunity, considering large variations in incremental sales volume only. The second two scenarios enable you to analyze the profitability impact of modifications to the advertising plan, as mediated by fluctuations in incremental sales.

The base case is the starting point for the sensitivity analysis (see fig. 13.1).

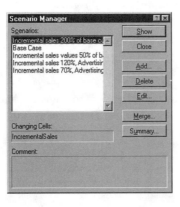

	A	B	C	D	E	F	G	H
1	Year:	1	2	3	4	5	6	
2								
3	Relevant benefits:							
4	Incremental sales, Tire B	$50,000	$150,000	$200,000	$300,000	$500,000	$1,000,000	
5								
6	TOTAL BENEFITS	$50,000	$150,000	$200,000	$300,000	$500,000	$1,000,000	
7								
8	Relevant costs:							
9	Lost value, Tire A	$50,000	$50,000	$50,000	$50,000	$50,000	$50,000	
10	Advertising	$100,000	$50,000	$25,000	$25,000	$25,000	$25,000	
11	New product manager	$55,000	$61,000	$65,000	$70,000	$77,000	$90,000	
12	Market research expenses	$75,000	$0	$0	$0	$0	$0	
13	Incremental maintenance	$0	$5,000	$5,000	$5,000	$5,000	$5,000	
14								
15	TOTAL COSTS	$280,000	$166,000	$145,000	$150,000	$157,000	$170,000	
16								
17	Earnings before interest, taxes,							
18	depreciation and amortization	($230,000)	($16,000)	$55,000	$150,000	$343,000	$830,000	
19								
20	Less: Depreciation	$50,000	$50,000	$50,000	$50,000	$50,000	$50,000	
21	Income before taxes	($280,000)	($66,000)	$5,000	$100,000	$293,000	$780,000	
22	Less: Taxes @ 36%	($100,800)	($23,760)	$1,800	$36,000	$105,480	$280,800	
23	Net income	($179,200)	($42,240)	$3,200	$64,000	$187,520	$499,200	

Fig. 13.1
The base case analysis of automobile tire enhancement decision depicts only one possible outcome.

Using Excel, you can document each scenario by means of the Scenario Manager. With the Base Case sheet chosen, take these steps:

1. Choose Tools, Scenarios. The Scenario Manager dialog box appears as shown in figure 13.2.

Fig. 13.2
You can manipulate scenarios in several different ways by means of the Scenario Manager.

III

2. Choose Add. The Add Scenario dialog box appears as shown in figure 13.3.

Fig. 13.3
Scenarios enable
you to store
several different
sets of values for
the same
worksheet.

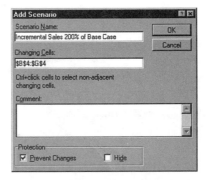

3. In the Scenario <u>N</u>ame edit box, type a descriptive name for the new scenario. In this case, type **Incremental Sales 200% of Base Case**.

4. Click the Changing <u>C</u>ells edit box.

5. Either highlight on the worksheet, or type into the Changing <u>C</u>ells edit box, the address of the cells that contain the input assumption that you are varying. In this case, the input is Incremental Sales, shown in cells $B$4:$G$4 of figure 13.1.

6. You can, if you want, click in the C<u>o</u>mment edit box and enter lengthier information about the scenario than you entered in the Scenario <u>N</u>ame edit box.

7. Check the <u>P</u>revent Changes checkbox if you want to protect the scenario from modification (even by you). You can also check the Hi<u>d</u>e checkbox to prevent the scenario's name from appearing in the Scenario Manager dialog box.

> **Tip**
>
> Neither the <u>P</u>revent Changes nor the Hi<u>d</u>e option has an effect unless the worksheet is protected by means of <u>T</u>ools, <u>P</u>rotection, <u>P</u>rotect Sheet. If the worksheet is protected and you check <u>P</u>revent Changes, the <u>E</u>dit and the <u>D</u>elete buttons on the Scenario Manager dialog box are dimmed. If the worksheet is protected and you check Hi<u>d</u>e, the <u>E</u>dit and <u>D</u>elete buttons are available but the scenario name is missing from the S<u>c</u>enarios list box.

8. Choose OK. The Scenario Values dialog box appears as shown in figure 13.4. In this case, you would change the "50000" entry in cell $B$4 to "=50000*2", the "150000" entry in $C$4 to "=150000*2", and so on, doubling the existing value of each cell.

> **Note**
>
> Although you enter formulas for the changing cells, Excel will convert these formulas to values when it creates the scenario.

> **Tip**
>
> All the scenarios developed in this chapter can be found in the workbook for chapter 13 on the *Business Analysis with Excel* companion disk.

On the Disk

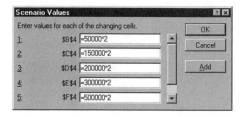

Fig. 13.4
These values are saved under the scenario's name after you add the scenario to the worksheet.

9. Choose OK. The Scenario Manager dialog box appears again. Choose Show to activate the worksheet and show the values for the scenario highlighted in the Scenarios list box or Close to activate the worksheet with its Base Case values.

In the Scenario Manager dialog box, you can also choose Add (which displays the Add Scenario dialog box so that you can add another scenario), Delete a scenario, Edit a scenario, Merge the scenarios from other worksheets or workbooks into the list of available scenarios for the active worksheet, and create a Summary of the available scenarios.

You now have a scenario that represents the optimistic input assumption that incremental sales will be twice as great as those represented in the Base Case. You should also create a scenario that represents a pessimistic input assumption: that incremental sales will be half those of the Base Case.

To create this pessimistic scenario, first ensure that the worksheet shows the Base Case values (Select Tools, Scenarios, highlight Base Case in the Scenarios list box, and choose Show). Then, repeat steps 1 through 9 shown previously, except:

■ In step 3, type **Incremental Sales 50% of Base Case** as a scenario name.

III

Investment Decisions

■ In step 8, enter values for each Changing Cell that are half those of the Base Case. Change the "50000" entry for cell $B$4 to "=50000/2", the "150000" entry for $C$4 to "=150000/2", and so on through cell $G$4.

You now have a Base Case scenario, an optimistic scenario, and a pessimistic scenario associated with the worksheet. The latter two scenarios assume that the market research was wrong, and that with no additional effort the sales of the new automobile tire will be either double the Base Case values or, sadly, half the Base Case values.

There are two more scenarios to consider, in which you change the cost of the Advertising expense. While the optimistic and pessimistic scenarios assume that incremental sales will differ from the Base Case even though you use Base Case Advertising levels, you should also assume that changing the Advertising expenditure will change the level of incremental sales.

First, assume that you will double the Base Case Advertising budget, and that this additional expenditure will increase incremental sales by 20 percent. To create this scenario, repeat steps 1 through 9 shown previously, except:

■ In step 3, type **Incremental Sales 120%, Advertising 200% of Base Case** as a scenario name.

■ In step 5, begin by highlighting cells $B$4:$G$4. Then, hold down the Ctrl key and highlight cells $B$10:$G$10. This enables you to change both the Incremental sales values and the Advertising budget values.

■ In step 8, enter values for cells $B$4:$G$4 that are 1.2 times the Base Case values. Change the "50000" entry for cell $B$4 to "=50000*1.2", the "150000" entry for $C$4 to "=150000*1.2", and so on through cell $G$4. For cells $B$10:$G$10, double the Advertising budget by changing the "100000" value in $B$10 to "=100000*2", the "50000" value in $C$10 to "=50000*2", and so on through cell $G$10.

Then, assume that you will cut the Base Case Advertising budget by 50 percent, and that this additional expenditure will decrease incremental sales by 20 percent. To create this scenario, repeat steps 1 through 9 shown previously, except:

■ In step 3, type **Incremental Sales 70%, Advertising 50% of Base Case** as a scenario name.

■ In step 5, begin by highlighting cells $B$4:$G$4. Then, hold down the Ctrl key and highlight cells $B$10:$G$10. This enables you to change both the incremental sales values and the Advertising budget values.

■ In step 8, enter values for cells $B$4:$G$4 that are .7 times the Base Case values. Change the "50000" entry for cell $B$4 to "=50000*.7", the "150000" entry for $C$4 to "=150000*.7", and so on through cell $G$4. For cells $B$10:$G$10, halve the Advertising budget by changing the "100000" value in $B$10 to "=100000/2", the "50000" value in $C$10 to "=50000/2", and so on through cell $G$10.

This completes the preparation of individual scenarios that reflect different input assumptions. It is useful to summarize the results of these scenarios on one worksheet. You can do this by selecting Tools, Scenarios and clicking the Summary button. The Scenario Summary dialog box appears (see fig. 13.5).

Fig. 13.5
Summarizing the results of the worksheet's scenarios.

The Scenario Summary dialog box proposes default result cells to show in the summary. You can add to these if you want more results. When you choose OK, Excel creates a new worksheet in the active workbook that contains a summary of the scenarios available to the active worksheet. See figure 13.6 for an example.

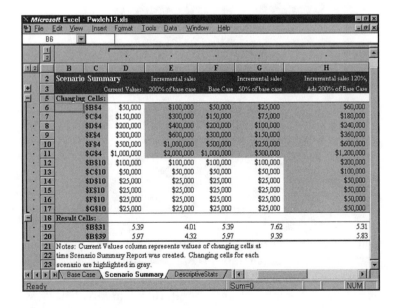

Fig. 13.6
Summary of the five scenarios for the sensitivity analysis.

III

Investment Decisions

The information in this summary is useful in itself, because it displays the discounted and undiscounted payback periods for each of the scenarios. However, it does not give you a direct measure of the variability in the payback periods caused by modifying the input assumptions.

The input assumptions that you have specified for the various scenarios constitute a *sample*—a nonrandom and nonrepresentative sample, to be sure, but a sample nonetheless—of the possible outcomes. To bracket the payback period with minimum and maximum expectations, you can use Excel's Analysis ToolPak. To do so, follow these steps:

1. Display the worksheet that contains the scenario summary.

2. Choose Tools, Data Analysis. If the Data Analysis option is not visible in the Tools menu, complete step 3; otherwise, continue with step 4.

3. Choose Tools, Add-Ins. In the Add-Ins dialog box, check the Analysis ToolPak - VBA item in the Add-Ins Available list box. Choose OK. If the Analysis ToolPak - VBA item does not appear in the list box, you will have to run the Excel Setup and select the ToolPak as an installation option.

4. Select Descriptive Statistics from the Analysis Tools list box in the Data Analysis dialog box, and choose OK. The Descriptive Statistics dialog box appears, as shown in figure 13.7.

Fig. 13.7
Descriptive statistics add another dimension to a sensitivity analysis.

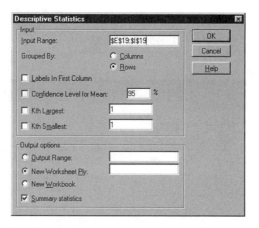

5. Click in the Input Range edit box and highlight the cells on the Summary Sheet that contain one row of the result cells. In this example, the result cells $B$31 and $B$39 in the Base Case worksheet are shown in rows 19 and 20 of the Summary Sheet. Highlight $E$19:$I$19, which contain the undiscounted payback periods for the five scenarios.

6. Click the Rows option button.

7. Check the Summary Statistics checkbox, and choose OK.

A new worksheet is added to the active workbook, containing 14 statistics that describe your sample of undiscounted payback periods (see fig. 13.8).

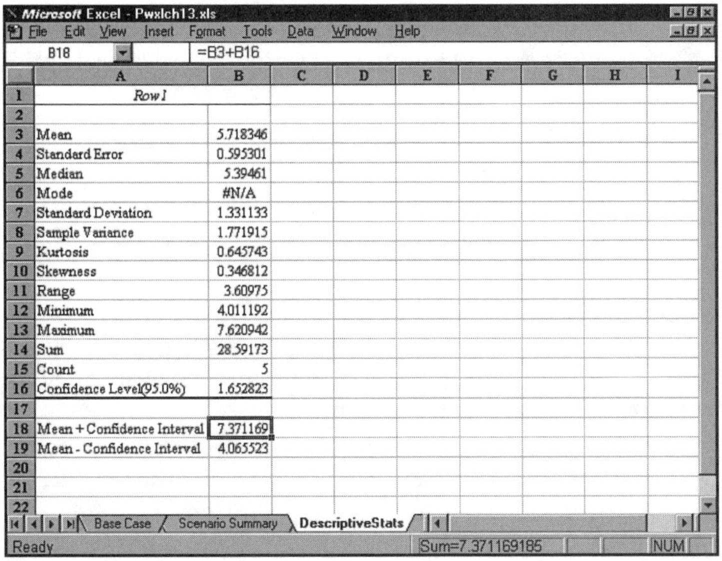

Fig. 13.8
Descriptive statistics summarize the variability and central tendency of undiscounted payback periods for five scenarios.

It is useful to examine these, particularly the mean, range, maximum, and minimum values, to better understand how the undiscounted payback period could vary as a function of your different input assumptions. But to get a better picture of your expectancy for the undiscounted payback period, select a blank cell and enter:

    =B3+B16

Select another blank cell and enter:

    =B3-B16

These formulas are shown in cells B18 and B19 of figure 13.8. They identify the upper and lower values of a 95 percent confidence interval around the mean undiscounted payback period. If, heaven forbid, you were to repeat this sensitivity analysis 100 times, using input assumptions similar but not equal to the input assumptions used here, then 95 of the 100 sensitivity analyses would have a 95 percent confidence interval that captures the best expectancy of the mean undiscounted payback period.

III

Investment Decisions

It is more rational to assume that this sensitivity analysis is one of the hypothetical 95 whose confidence interval captures the best expectancy than it is to assume that this analysis is one of the 5 that do not. Therefore, it is reasonable to assume that the undiscounted payback period will be between 4.1 and 7.4 years.

> **Note**
>
> Because the payback periods were not created randomly but systematically, this discussion is not truly accurate in a statistical sense. However, it is a useful way to estimate the potential variability in the results of the sensitivity analysis.

You can repeat this analysis for the discounted payback period by repeating steps 1 through 7 shown previously, except that you would highlight $E$20:$I$20 in step 5.

Decision makers can now examine the Summary Sheet and the results of the Descriptive Statistics analysis, and make a subjective judgment about the risk of undertaking this product enhancement. If, for example, an undiscounted payback period of 7.5 years (the maximum payback period with 95 percent confidence) is regarded as too long, you might decide either to repeat the sensitivity analysis with reasonable, but less radical, input assumptions. If you can make your input assumptions neither less pessimistic nor less optimistic, you might decide that the risk is too great to undertake the project at all.

Measuring Profit

To this point, the complexity of the sensitivity analysis has been minimized by considering only one measure of profit: payback period. There are other measures that you can use, and each of these alternatives provides another point of view on your profit. These include the Internal Rate of Return, the Modified Internal Rate of Return, and the Profitability Index.

Calculating Internal Rate of Return

Given the assumptions used in the Base Case, it is apparent that introducing a new product will generate more than a 10 percent return on the funds that the project requires. This is easy to determine from the net present value of the project. Taking the discount rate (10 percent) into account, the project returns a positive net present value: therefore, the company has positive earnings compared to the 10 percent alternative.

But how much better than the 10 percent discount rate does the investment perform? Asked differently, what discount rate would cause the net present value to be zero? Excel's IRR function answers that question, and figure 13.9 shows the result returned by IRR for the Base Case in cell B43.

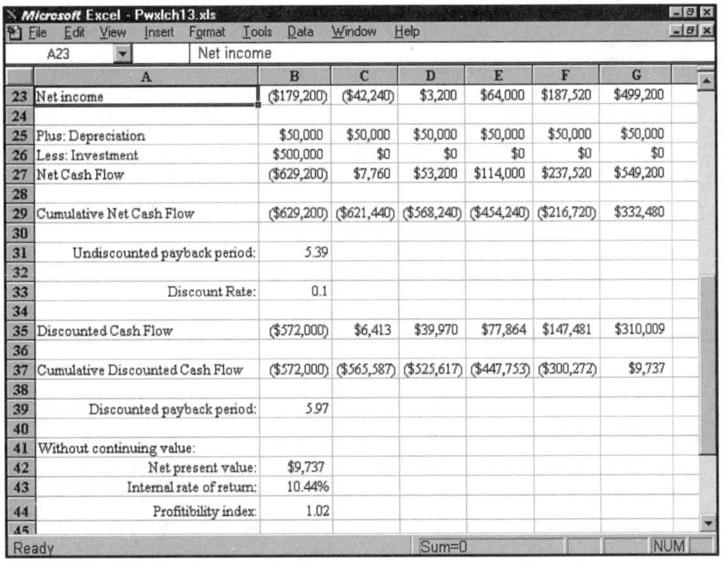
Microsoft Excel - Pwxlch13.xls

File Edit View Insert Format Tools Data Window Help

A23 | Net income

	A	B	C	D	E	F	G
23	Net income	($179,200)	($42,240)	$3,200	$64,000	$187,520	$499,200
24							
25	Plus: Depreciation	$50,000	$50,000	$50,000	$50,000	$50,000	$50,000
26	Less: Investment	$500,000	$0	$0	$0	$0	$0
27	Net Cash Flow	($629,200)	$7,760	$53,200	$114,000	$237,520	$549,200
28							
29	Cumulative Net Cash Flow	($629,200)	($621,440)	($568,240)	($454,240)	($216,720)	$332,480
30							
31	Undiscounted payback period:	5.39					
32							
33	Discount Rate:	0.1					
34							
35	Discounted Cash Flow	($572,000)	$6,413	$39,970	$77,864	$147,481	$310,009
36							
37	Cumulative Discounted Cash Flow	($572,000)	($565,587)	($525,617)	($447,753)	($300,272)	$9,737
38							
39	Discounted payback period:	5.97					
40							
41	Without continuing value:						
42	Net present value:	$9,737					
43	Internal rate of return:	10.44%					
44	Profitibility index:	1.02					
45							

Ready | Sum=0 | NUM

Fig. 13.9
You can use various financial indicators to summarize the results of different scenarios in different ways.

Excel gives 10.44 percent as the internal rate of return for the project's Base Case. As compared to the discount factor of 10 percent, this is not a spectacular increase, but it is useful.

Again: put differently, if the discount factor were 10.44 percent instead of 10 percent, the net present value of the funds required for the new product would be zero. IRR returns a value greater than the 10 percent assumed by the discount rate. Therefore, this business case represents a more attractive use of the funds than a 10 percent alternative investment.

The formula that returns the 10.44 percent figure in cell B43 is:

```
=IRR(NetCashFlow,DiscountRate)
```

The first argument, NetCashFlow, represents the values that IRR uses to determine the rate of return. Notice that the result of 10.44 percent reflects the return on values *prior* to applying the discount factor of 10 percent.

> **Note**
>
> You may be able to infer from this discussion that you would not want to apply IRR to *discounted* cash flows. To do so would be to ask what discount rate would return a net present value of zero on cash flows that have already been discounted.

The second argument, .1, is simply an assist that you can give Excel. Excel calculates the internal rate of return by an iterative method, and it gives up (returning #NUM!) if it cannot reach a meaningful result within 20 iterations. By providing a second argument that is fairly close to what you guess the internal rate of return might be, you give IRR a head start on its iterations. This makes it a little more likely that you will get a usable result. If you do not supply the second argument, Excel uses a default value of .1.

Note that at least one of the values in the first argument must be positive and at least one must be negative: otherwise, IRR returns the #NUM! error value. In the Base Case, net cash flow conforms to this requirement: there is only one change in sign (negative to positive) in the series of cash flows.

> **Note**
>
> Use caution if the series of cash flows you use as the first argument to IRR changes sign more than once. There is one distinct IRR for each change in sign in the series. In most of the cases where the sign changes more than once, there is only one IRR that makes sense. But if you do not supply a reasonable initial guess as IRR's second argument, it is possible that IRR will iterate to an unacceptable value.

Calculating Profitability Indices

Discounted payback, net present value, and internal rate of return are all indicators of the profitability of a business case. They can be used as tools that help a company decide which projects to undertake. The company may have decision criteria specifying, for example, that a project must have a payback period of no more than five years, or that it must have an internal rate of return greater than 15 percent, to be considered for implementation.

But in all likelihood, there is a limit to the amount of investment that a firm is willing or able to undertake during a given time period. If a company is presented with two projects, both with net present values of $500,000, which project is the right one to select? In a case such as this, it may be useful to calculate a profitability index.

A *profitability index* is simply a comparison of the present value of the inflows that result from an investment to the value of the investment amount itself. The present value of the inflows is the net present value of the project, with the initial investment added back. To calculate a profitability index, two values are required: the project's net present value and its initial investment.

In the worksheet for figure 13.9, two named ranges have been established:

- NetPresentValue represents cell B42, the net present value of the cash flows given the discount rate.

- InitialInvestment represents cell B27: the funds that would initially be committed to the project.

The formula for the profitability index shown in cell B44 of figure 13.9 is:

```
=(NetPresentValue + ABS(InitialInvestment))/ ABS(InitialInvestment)
```

(The ABS function converts a negative value to a positive value.) In words, the formula adds the project's net present value to the value of the first year's investment, and divides the sum by the value of the first year's investment. It is a way of expressing the project's value as a function of the initial investment amount: expressed in this way, for every dollar invested at inception, the project returns $1.02

The profitability index is useful for ranking projects that have similar internal rates of return or net present values, but that require very different initial investment amounts.

Estimating the Continuing Value

The impact of a decision made today often has effects that last beyond the study life of a business case. In evaluating a startup business opportunity, for example, you can review the financials of a forward-looking, ten-year business planning horizon (as done in the tire enhancement case). Such an analysis, however, would be missing a critical element: after ten years, the business would have some sort of value in the marketplace. How can you incorporate this value into the discounted cash flow analysis?

The concept of continuing value attempts to quantify this element. It assigns a future value to the startup opportunity. It then discounts that value back to the present (the decision point) to be incorporated into the net present value of the decision that is under consideration.

Not all business cases should necessarily incorporate continuing value into their framework. For example, suppose that a computer software manufacturer announced that it would make major changes to a popular operating system in three years. And suppose that another company prepares a business case that involves improvements to software that requires the current operating system. In that event, the business case would look at no more than three years of cash flow, and would not incorporate any continuing value estimates.

Figure 13.10 shows an estimate of continuing value in cell B46, and uses a common method of estimating continuing value: as a multiple of after tax cash flows. The formula used for continuing value is:

```
=G27/DiscountRate
```

where cell G27 contains the net cash flow during the final year of the Base Case.

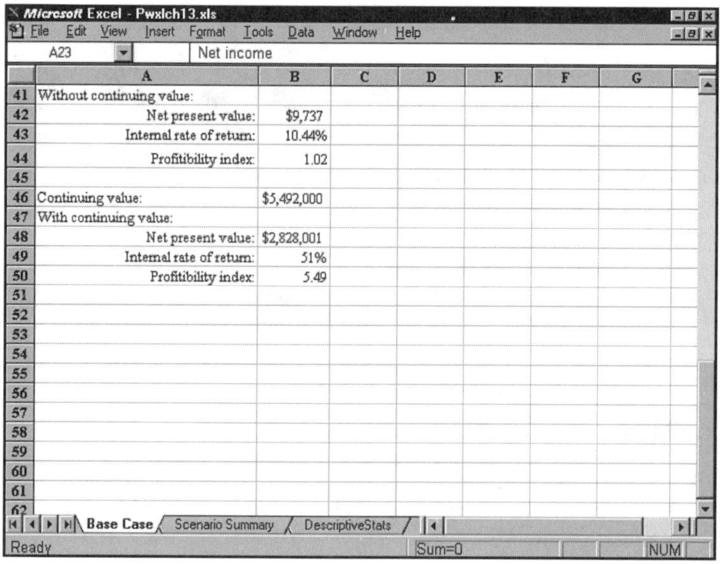

Fig. 13.10

Establishing a continuing value extends your business case to the point that the product is well established.

		A	B	C	D	E	F	G
41	Without continuing value:							
42		Net present value:	$9,737					
43		Internal rate of return:	10.44%					
44		Profitibility index:	1.02					
45								
46	Continuing value:		$5,492,000					
47	With continuing value:							
48		Net present value:	$2,828,001					
49		Internal rate of return:	51%					
50		Profitibility index:	5.49					

Cell A23: Net income

Sheet tabs: Base Case / Scenario Summary / DescriptiveStats

Dividing the basis of $549,000 by the discount rate of 10 percent results in a continuing value of $5,492,000, measured as a net cash flow. In effect, this assigns a multiple of 10 to after tax cash flows. It is one possible answer to this question: What value would you place on a business that generates $549,200 after taxes, if your target return rate is 10 percent?

Figure 13.10 also shows several other values that follow from the continuing value. The cumulative net cash flow, discounted cash flow, and cumulative discounted cash flow can be extended to take the continuing value into account. Now you can calculate another set of indicators that include net present value, internal rate of return, and the profitability index (cells B48:B50 of figure 13.10). The indicators reference the cash flows that incorporate the continuing value of the project.

It's convenient to establish two new names on the worksheet: NetCashFlowContinuingValue, that extends the NetCashFlow name to include the continuing value figure, and ContinuingValueNPV, that represents the net present value of the project under the continuing value assumption. To establish these names do the following:

1. Select the cell that contains the continuing value formula (in figure 13.10, this is cell B46).

2. Click in the Name Box and type **ContinuingValueNPV**. Then, press Enter.

3. Click in the Name Box and highlight the NetCashFlow name. This selects the NetCashFlow range.

4. Hold down the Ctrl key and click cell B46, which contains the continuing value figure. This creates a multiple selection, consisting of the existing NetCashFlow range plus the cell that contains the continuing value.

5. Click in the Name Box and type **NetCashFlowContinuingValue**.

The formulas for the indicators are:

For net present value, in cell B48:

```
=NPV(DiscountRate, NetCashFlowContinuingValue)
```

For internal rate of return, in cell B49:

```
=IRR(NetCashFlowContinuingValue,.1)
```

For the profitability index, in cell B50:

```
=(ContinuingValueNPV + ABS(InitialInvestment))/ABS(Initial Investment)
```

This puts you in a position to compare profitability indicators during the period covered by the business case with indicators that assess the project beyond the business case's horizon. And, using the techniques for sensitivity analysis discussed earlier in this chapter, you can compare these indicators under different sets of input assumptions.

III

Investment Decisions

Varying the Discount Rate Input

One input assumption that can exert a major influence on your profitability is the discount rate. Chapter 14, "Planning Profits," discusses in some detail how the relationship between fixed costs and variable costs, and the amount of debt financing a company uses, impacts profitability. If a company borrows funds to obtain fixed cost assets, then the discount rate—the cost of borrowing funds—has effects on profitability that go well beyond the interest charges.

How sensitive are the financial indicators to changes in the size of the discount factor? Figures 13.11 through 13.13 recapitulate the indicators that result from the base case assumptions.

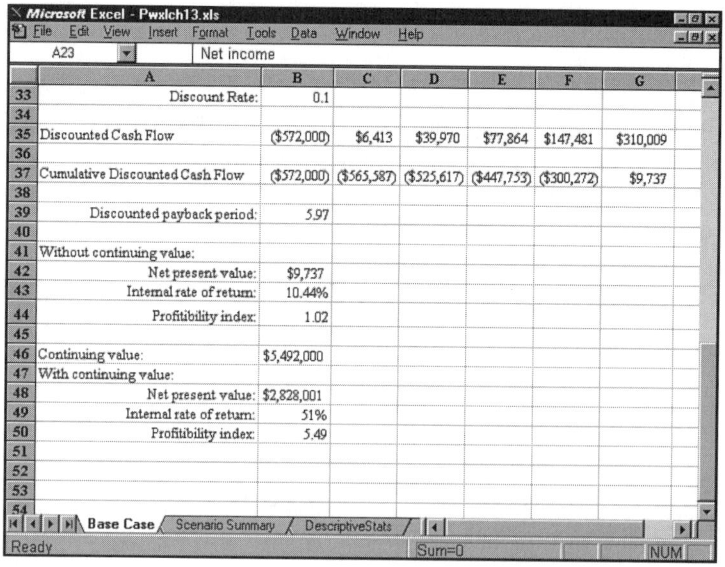

Fig. 13.11

Indicators with discount rate of 10 percent: this is identical to the base case.

The IRR results are the same in each figure for the Without Continuing Value analysis. This is because they are independent of the choice of discount rate: they measure the rate of return of the investment.

Net present value, however, uses the discount rate to adjust the value of the future cash flows back to the value of money at the present time. This quantifies how many dollars this project would generate over and above the cost of capital.

The profitability index also varies as a function of the discount rate. This is because it is a function of both the net present value of an investment and the actual dollar investment amount.

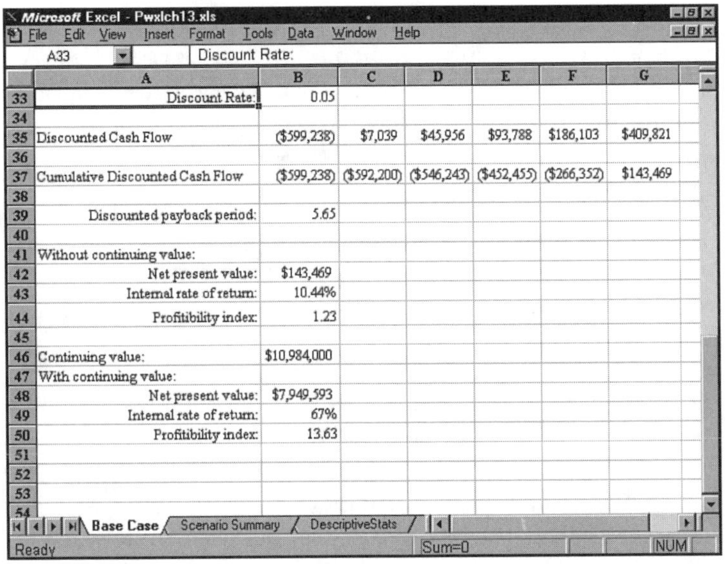

	A	B	C	D	E	F	G
33	Discount Rate:	0.05					
34							
35	Discounted Cash Flow	($599,238)	$7,039	$45,956	$93,788	$186,103	$409,821
36							
37	Cumulative Discounted Cash Flow	($599,238)	($592,200)	($546,243)	($452,455)	($266,352)	$143,469
38							
39	Discounted payback period:	5.65					
40							
41	Without continuing value:						
42	Net present value:	$143,469					
43	Internal rate of return:	10.44%					
44	Profitibility index:	1.23					
45							
46	Continuing value:	$10,984,000					
47	With continuing value:						
48	Net present value:	$7,949,593					
49	Internal rate of return:	67%					
50	Profitibility index:	13.63					
51							
52							
53							

Fig. 13.12
Indicators with discount rate of 5 percent: the business case is much more attractive than with a discount rate of 10 percent.

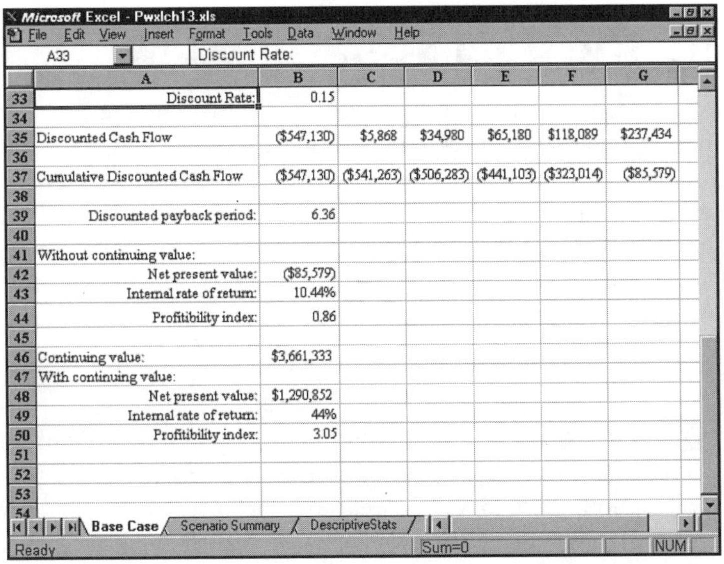

	A	B	C	D	E	F	G
33	Discount Rate:	0.15					
34							
35	Discounted Cash Flow	($547,130)	$5,868	$34,980	$65,180	$118,089	$237,434
36							
37	Cumulative Discounted Cash Flow	($547,130)	($541,263)	($506,283)	($441,103)	($323,014)	($85,579)
38							
39	Discounted payback period:	6.36					
40							
41	Without continuing value:						
42	Net present value:	($85,579)					
43	Internal rate of return:	10.44%					
44	Profitibility index:	0.86					
45							
46	Continuing value:	$3,661,333					
47	With continuing value:						
48	Net present value:	$1,290,852					
49	Internal rate of return:	44%					
50	Profitibility index:	3.05					
51							
52							
53							

Fig. 13.13
Indicators with discount rate of 15 percent: an alternative investment that returns 15 percent would be much more attractive.

These same sensitivities hold for the indicators that include continuing value. In addition, the IRR indicator is sensitive to changes in the discount rate, because the formula for computing continuing value uses the discount rate in its calculation.

The analysis depicted in figures 13.11 through 13.13 tells you that you can be comfortable with the discount rate you have chosen for the project. A discount rate should reflect, at a minimum, a firm's weighted cost of capital. This rate can vary from year to year as a firm undergoes changes in its capital structure.

Using this minimum value as a benchmark enables you to adjust the rate upward so as to consider the relative risk of the project, over and above normal business operations. In the Base Case example, enhancing the current product line does not represent a substantial deviation from the firm's core business: the enhancement is simply a newer version of an existing product.

However, if the business case involved the development of a new product that is substantially different from the firm's current operations (for example, if the product were hubcaps instead of tires), it would be wise to employ a higher discount rate than the one used for existing operations. Doing so would reflect the greater risk involved in developing an entirely new product line.

Using the Goal Seek Function

When you perform a sensitivity analysis, you usually try to identify the value of an input variable that is necessary to produce a specific output. For example, it may be useful to quantify the level of incremental sales required for this project to break even, or the level that is required to produce a 15 percent internal rate of return. Rather than using the trial and error method of changing the sales inputs and visually inspecting the relevant outputs, you can use Excel's Goal Seek function.

Goal Seek is similar to the Solver, in that it backtracks to an input value (the Changing Cell) that satisfies a result value which depends on the input value. Goal Seek is easier to use than the Solver, however, and it often finds the optimal input value faster than does the Solver. (This is because the Solver offers more options than does Goal Seek, and the Solver can modify more than one Changing Cell.) Furthermore, because Goal Seek is a built-in capability, there is no need to install it. Because the Solver is an add-in, you must install it before you can use it.

You can use the Goal Seek function when you want to find an input value that generates the answer you want in a formula cell. To find the level of sales required to break even, for example, the formula cell would contain the net present value, and you would want the NPV function to return a zero value (which represents a break-even figure).

Because the Goal Seek function adjusts the value in *one* cell that is a precedent to the formula cell, you need to make an adjustment to the Base Case worksheet. Refer to figure 13.1, where the relevant cells appear. Treating Year 1 as an anchor point, notice that each subsequent year's sales is a multiple of the Year 1 sales. You can then express sales for Years 2 through 6 as a function of Year 1 sales:

In cell C6, enter: =B6*3

In cell D6, enter: =B6*4

In cell E6, enter: =B6*6

In cell F6, enter: =B6*10

In cell G6, enter: =B6*20

These changes make the values of sales in Years 2 through 6 dependent on the value in cell B6. Now, even though net present value depends on sales values for all six years, you can use the single Changing Cell B6 in Goal Seek to answer a variety of questions. For example: What level of incremental sales would be required for this project to break even? To answer that question, follow these steps:

1. Select cell B42, which contains the NPV function.

2. Choose Tools, Goal Seek. The Goal Seek dialog box appears as shown in figure 13.14.

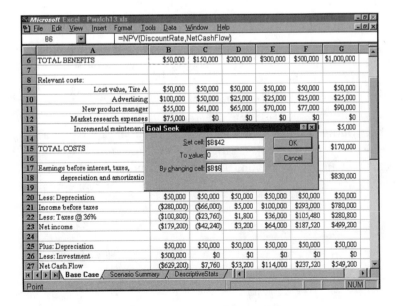

Fig. 13.14

You can use Goal Seek to modify a business case's inputs and determine their effect on its results.

3. The Set cell box should already contain the reference B42; if not, select that cell on the worksheet.

4. Click in the To value box, and enter 0 (zero).

5. Click in the By changing cell box, and highlight worksheet cell B6 (or simply type B6 in the box).

6. Choose OK.

Goal Seek returns a value for Year 1 sales. Because you changed the values for Years 2 through 6 to formulas that depend on Year 1, their values also change. The result is the incremental sales required for the project to break even—that is, to have a net present value of zero.

What level of incremental sales would be required for this project to return a 15 percent internal rate of return? Simply repeat steps 1 through 6 shown previously, but begin by selecting the cell that contains the IRR function, and specify in step 4 that the To value is to be .15.

Summary

When sensitivity scenarios are included in a business case package, management obtains a better overall feel for the project under review. The analyst who constructs the business case also has the opportunity to answer pertinent "what if" questions proactively. It provides multiple points of view on a project, and enables the review team to focus on the business drivers that have the most significant impact on potential outcomes.

In this chapter, you have learned how to use Excel's Scenario Manager to establish and examine the effect of variances in the input assumptions of a business case, as well as how to establish upper and lower limits on the sensitivity of the business case's outputs. You have extended your understanding of profitability indicators to different ways of measuring the rate of return, and have learned a quicker (although less powerful) means of optimizing a value by means of Goal Seek. Chapter 14, "Planning Profits," examines the effect that changing the relationship between your fixed and variable costs, as well as the effect of borrowing, on the profitability of your enterprise.

Chapter 14

Planning Profits

The concepts of *operating leverage* and *financial leverage* are key to an accurate analysis of a company's value. A firm is said to be leveraged whenever it incurs either fixed operating costs (operating leverage) or fixed capital costs (financial leverage). More specifically, a firm's degree of *operating leverage* is the extent to which its operations involve fixed operating expenses such as fixed manufacturing costs, fixed selling costs, and fixed administrative costs.

A firm's degree of *financial leverage* is the extent to which that firm finances its assets by borrowing. More specifically, financial leverage is the extent to which a firm's Return on Assets exceeds the cost of financing those assets by means of debt. The firm expects that the leverage acquired by borrowing will bring it earnings that will exceed the fixed costs of the assets and of the sources of funds. The firm expects that these added earnings will increase the amount of returns to shareholders.

In the business environment of the 1990s, it is almost impossible for a firm to succeed financially without using some form of leverage. Firms commonly use leverage as a tool to help bolster their financial position and operating condition (for example, their return to stockholders).

However, with increased leverage comes increased risk. If your company chooses to be highly leveraged, it must be willing to accept the risk that the downside losses will be as great as its upside profits. This can easily occur if a firm's sales volume is not large enough to cover its fixed operating expenses and the required interest payments on its debt.

You can find plenty of examples of this phenomenon in a stack of annual reports from the 1980s. Within that stack you can find several companies that were highly leveraged. Tracking these firms through the 1990s, you would see trends depicting peaks and troughs: the positive and the negative impacts of using leverage to operate a business. Many firms were acquired via "leveraged buyouts," where the funds needed to make the acquisition were themselves borrowed (hence the term "leveraged").

The likelihood of experiencing these kinds of swings is one reason that managers, analysts, and stockholders must apply the concepts of operating and financial leverage to accurately analyze a firm's overall value and financial health.

An additional concept that is useful in interpreting the risks due to operating leverage and financial leverage is *business risk*. Business risk is the inherent uncertainty of doing business. It represents the risk that a company assumes by the nature of the products it manufactures and sells, its position in the marketplace, its pricing structure—in short, all the fundamental aspects involved in the creation of profitable revenues. Assuming a higher degree of operating or financial leverage is seldom risky when the business risk is very low. But if the business risk itself is high, then increasing the degree of either type of leverage compounds the risk.

Analyzing Operating Leverage

Operating leverage is the extent to which a firm's operations involve fixed operating expenses. Managers can define the degree of operating leverage they want the firm to incur, based on the choices they make regarding fixed expenses. They can, for example, acquire new equipment that increases automation and reduces variable labor expenses. Alternatively, they can choose to maintain their variable labor expenses. Other things being equal, the more automated equipment a firm acquires through capital investment, the higher its operating leverage will be.

Case Study: Business Forms

You own a small company that prints business forms such as invoices, letterheads, envelopes, and business cards. At present, your variable operating costs are $0.03 per card to print a box of 500 business cards, which you sell for $35.00.

One of your employees suggests that, if you purchase a personal computer and a modem, your customers could send their own designs for business cards to you electronically. This would save you the cost of doing the design and layout of the cards for each order.

You review some recent orders and find that you paid an employee an average of $3.00 per order to do the design and layout. So your costs and profit per order are as follows:

- Variable $0.03 per card for 500 cards = $15.00

- Fixed design and layout per box = $3.00

- Total cost per box: $18.00

- Operating income per box: $17.00

If you can remove the cost of design and layout, your total costs will drop from $18.00 to $15.00 per order and your operating income per box will increase from $17.00 to $20.00.

On the other hand, purchasing a computer and a modem will cost $1,400. This will introduce a new, fixed cost to the production of the cards. You will have to sell 70 boxes of business cards (70 boxes * $20.00 profit) to cover the cost of the equipment—that is, to break even on the investment.

You should base your decision on how dependable your business card orders are. Suppose that you have a steady stream of around 60 orders per month. In that case, you break even on the investment in a little over a month, and after that you show an additional $3.00 profit for every order. That added profit is the result of *leveraging* your capital investment.

Now suppose that your business card orders are not so dependable. Most of your business depends on the patronage of one large account. When its business is good, and it is hiring and promoting staff, you receive frequent orders from it for business cards. But when its business is not so good, you can go for several months with only a few orders.

If the timing of your investment in the computer coincides with a drop in orders for business cards, the computer could sit idle for several months. There will be little profit to cover its cost, the break-even point will be pushed well into the future, and you will have lost the opportunity to invest the $1,400 in some other manner, such as advertising. The leverage is actually working against you.

Of course, there are other considerations you must take into account. You would want to consider how many of your customers have the inclination and equipment to send their own designs to you, whether they would demand a price break if they do so, maintenance on the computer, and so on. Business decisions are seldom clear-cut.

So, operating leverage cuts both ways. A good decision can increase your profitability dramatically, once you have broken even on the fixed cost. Bad timing can cut your profitability dramatically if it takes longer than anticipated to break even on the investment.

Case Study: Comparing the Degree of Operating Leverage

For a more detailed example, consider three different hardware stores whose operations are identical in all respects, except for the decisions they have made regarding their variable and fixed expenses:

- Store A has decided to incur the lowest fixed and highest variable costs of the three stores. It has little in the way of special equipment, and relies heavily on the experience and knowledge of its salespeople. At this store, sales commissions are relatively high.

- Store B has decided to incur fixed costs that are higher than that of Store A, but to keep its variable costs lower than Store A. This store has invested a moderate amount of money in paint-mixing equipment that enables a salesperson to match paint samples automatically. It believes that reliance on this equipment allows it to hire salespeople who are less experienced; its sales staff therefore does not earn as much as that at Store A.

- Store C has decided to incur the highest fixed and lowest variable costs of the three. It has invested heavily in equipment that not only matches paint samples exactly, but mixes paints automatically to produce a gallon of matching paint. Its salespeople need no special knowledge, and receive lower commissions than the sales staffs at Store A and Store B.

Figures 14.1, 14.2, and 14.3 display an analysis of each store's sales and Earnings Before Interest and Taxes (EBIT) for a given quantity of sales at their existing fixed costs, variable costs, and unit sales rates.

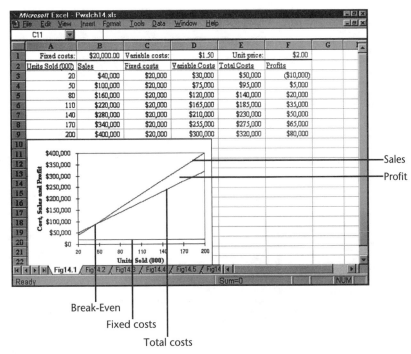

Fig. 14.1
Store A breaks
even quickly, but
has relatively low
profit growth after
break-even.

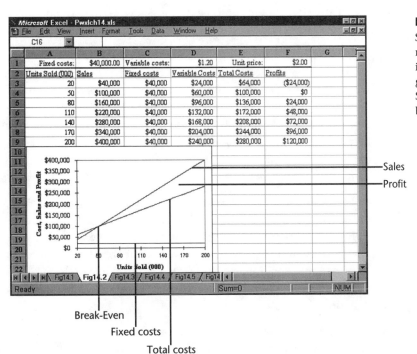

Fig. 14.2
Store B breaks even
more slowly, but
its profitability
grows faster than
Store A after
break-even.

III

Investment Decisions

Fig. 14.3
Store C breaks
even most slowly,
but experiences
fast profit growth
thereafter.

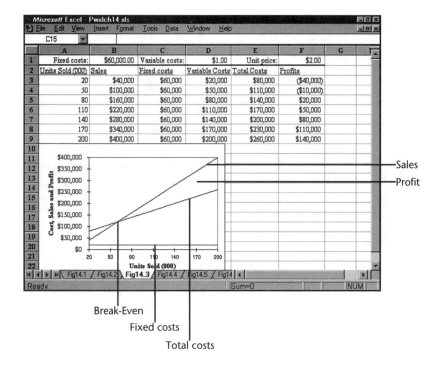

Break-Even

Fixed costs

Total costs

Figures 14.1 through 14.3 make some trends evident. These trends are consequences of each store's decision as to the relationship between its variable costs and its fixed costs:

- Store A, which has the lowest fixed cost and the highest per unit cost, will break even faster than Store B and Store C. However, once the break-even point has been met and as the level of production increases, Store A's EBIT will not be as great as either Store B's or Store C's. This is because Store A has the highest per unit sales cost. No matter how many gallons of paint it sells, it incurs the same, relatively high sales commission on each sale.

- Store B, which has fixed costs that fall between Store A and Store B, breaks even slower than Store A but faster than Store C. Once it reaches its break-even point, it is more profitable than Store A because its unit sales cost is lower than Store A. However, after breaking even on its paint-matching equipment, Store B is less profitable, in terms of EBIT, than Store C as sales increase: it pays its sales staff a higher commission than does Store C.

- Store C, which has the highest fixed costs and the lowest per unit sales cost, breaks even more slowly than the other two stores. But after the break-even point has been reached, Store C's EBIT rises faster than either Store A or Store B because of its low sales commission rates.

Figure 14.4 summarizes these trends. It shows the profitability of each store across its range of units sold. This reflects the different operating leverage involved at each store.

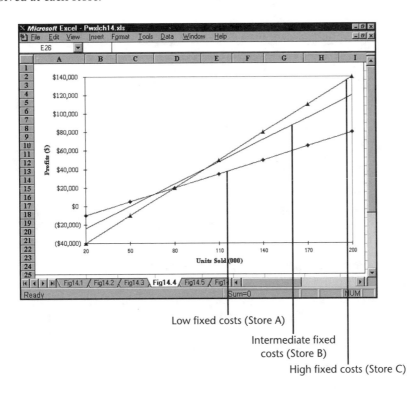

Fig. 14.4
Comparison of profitability of three stores with different degrees of operating leverage.

Low fixed costs (Store A)

Intermediate fixed costs (Store B)

High fixed costs (Store C)

Another way to understand how operating leverage impacts your company's profitability is by calculating the Degree of Operating Leverage (DOL):

```
DOL = Units*(Price-Variable Cost)/(Units*(Price-Variable Cost)-Fixed Cost)
```

or, equivalently:

```
DOL = Contribution Margin/(Contribution Margin - Fixed Cost)
```

(Chapter 20, "Contribution and Margin Analysis," discusses contribution margins in detail.) Using the data for the three hardware stores, one can calculate the DOL at the point where unit sales are 120,000:

Store A, for example, has a DOL of 1.5 with unit sales of 120,000:

```
DOL =120,000*($2.00-$1.50)/(120,000*($2.00-$1.50)-$20,000)
DOL = 1.5
```

These calculations quantify the data shown in figure 14.5. The numbers indicate that the EBIT of the companies that have the greatest operating leverage are also the most sensitive to changes in sales volume.

Fig. 14.5

The Degree of Operating Leverage accelerates EBIT as unit sales increase.

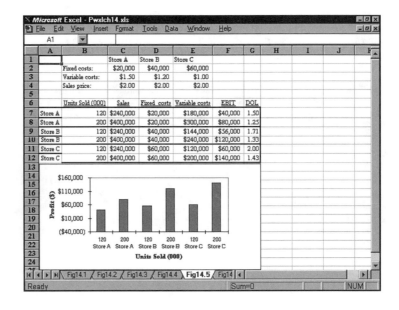

Each store sells the same number of units: 120,000 or 200,000. Each store sells them for the same price: $2.00 per unit. But because the stores differ in their fixed and variable costs, they also differ in their EBIT. For Store A, a 67% increase in unit sales from 120,000 to 200,000 results in a (67% * 1.5 DOL) or 100% increase in EBIT. For Store B, a 67% increase in unit sales results in a (67% * 1.7 DOL) or 114% increase in EBIT. And Store C experiences a (67% * 2.0 DOL) or 133% increase in EBIT. So, the higher the DOL, the greater the EBIT as unit sales increase.

Expressed in raw dollar amounts, an increase in unit sales from 120,000 to 200,000 means an increase in profits of $40,000 for Store A, $64,000 for Store B, and $80,000 for Store C.

However, the calculated DOL will be the same on the downside. So for every decrease in sales volume, each firm's DOL will cause an unwanted decrease in EBIT corresponding to the desired increase in EBIT (see fig. 14.6).

The DOL gives managers a great deal of information for setting operating targets and planning profitability. For example, you would want to make operating leverage decisions based on your knowledge of how your sales volume fluctuates. If your company experiences large swings in sales volume throughout the year, it would be much riskier to maintain a high degree of leverage than it would be if your company has a predictable, steady stream of sales.

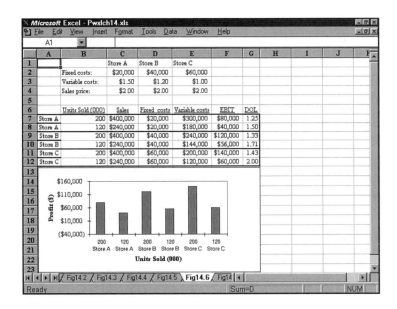

Fig. 14.6
The Degree of Operating Leverage accelerates loss of profit as unit sales decline.

Case Study: Coffee Sales

Java Man is a small business that sells specialty coffee drinks at office buildings. Each morning and afternoon, trucks arrive at offices' front entrances, and the office employees purchase various drinks, from latte to espresso. The business is profitable, but Java Man's offices are located to the north of town, where rents are less expensive, and the principal sales area is south of town. This means that the trucks must drive crosstown four times each day.

The cost of transportation to and from the sales area, plus the power demands of the trucks' coffee brewing equipment, are a significant portion of the variable costs. Java Man could reduce the amount of driving—and, therefore, the variable costs—if it moves the offices much closer to the sales area.

Java Man presently has fixed costs of $10,000 per month. The lease of a new office, closer to the sales area, would cost an additional $2,200 per month. This would increase the fixed costs to $12,200 per month (see fig. 14.7).

Although the lease of new offices would increase the fixed costs, a careful estimate of the potential savings in gasoline and vehicle maintenance indicates that Java Man could reduce the variable costs from $0.60 per unit to $0.35 per unit. Total sales are unlikely to increase as a result of the move, but the savings in variable costs could increase the annual profit from $82,986 to $88,302. This is a 6.4% growth in profit margin: not an insignificant amount (see fig. 14.8).

III

Investment Decisions

Fig. 14.7

Profit analysis for the lease of existing offices by Java Man, Inc.

Microsoft Excel - Pwxlch14.xls

D4 | =D3/(D3-SUM(D8:D19))

	A	B	C	D	E	F	G
1	Units sold per month	20,000	Unit variable costs	$0.60			
2	Average unit sales price	$2.20	Current fixed costs	$10,000			
3			Contribution margin	$202,986			
4			DOL	2.45			
5							
6				Fixed	Variable		
7	1994 sales month	Units	Sales	costs	Costs	EBIT	
8	January	6,582	$14,480	$10,000	$3,949	$531	
9	February	11,121	$24,466	$10,000	$6,673	$7,794	
10	March	14,178	$31,192	$10,000	$8,507	$12,685	
11	April	13,692	$30,122	$10,000	$8,215	$11,907	
12	May	11,597	$25,513	$10,000	$6,958	$8,555	
13	June	9,599	$21,118	$10,000	$5,759	$5,358	
14	July	9,913	$21,809	$10,000	$5,948	$5,861	
15	August	10,926	$24,037	$10,000	$6,556	$7,482	
16	September	14,349	$31,568	$10,000	$8,609	$12,958	
17	October	12,965	$28,523	$10,000	$7,779	$10,744	
18	November	6,972	$15,338	$10,000	$4,183	$1,155	
19	December	4,972	$10,938	$10,000	$2,983	($2,045)	
20							
21					Sum:	$82,986	
22					Standard Deviation:	$4,963	

Fig14.3 / Fig14.4 / Fig14.5 / Fig14.6 / **Fig14.7** / Fig14

Ready | Sum=2.45 | NUM

Fig. 14.8

Profit analysis for the lease of new offices by Java Man, Inc.: variable costs fall and Degree of Operating Leverage increases.

Microsoft Excel - Pwxlch14.xls

D4 | =D3/(D3-SUM(D8:D19))

	A	B	C	D	E	F	G
1	Units sold per month	20,000	Unit variable costs	$0.35			
2	Average unit sales price	$2.20	Current fixed costs	$10,000			
3	Additional monthly lease		Contribution margin	$234,702			
4	payment, new offices:	$2,200	DOL	2.66			
5	Projected fixed costs:	$12,200					
6				Fixed	Variable		
7	1994 sales month	Units	Sales	costs	Costs	EBIT	
8	January	6,582	$14,480	$12,200	$2,304	($23.30)	
9	February	11,121	$24,466	$12,200	$3,892	$8,374	
10	March	14,178	$31,192	$12,200	$4,962	$14,029	
11	April	13,692	$30,122	$12,200	$4,792	$13,130	
12	May	11,597	$25,513	$12,200	$4,059	$9,254	
13	June	9,599	$21,118	$12,200	$3,360	$5,558	
14	July	9,913	$21,809	$12,200	$3,470	$6,139	
15	August	10,926	$24,037	$12,200	$3,824	$8,013	
16	September	14,349	$31,568	$12,200	$5,022	$14,346	
17	October	12,965	$28,523	$12,200	$4,538	$11,785	
18	November	6,972	$15,338	$12,200	$2,440	$698	
19	December	4,972	$10,938	$12,200	$1,740	($3,002)	
20							
21					Sum:	$88,302	
22					Standard Deviation:	$5,738	

Fig14.4 / Fig14.5 / Fig14.6 / Fig14.7 / **Fig14.8** / Fig14

Ready | Sum=2.66 | NUM

But look at the change in the variability of the profit from month to month. From November through January, when it is much more difficult to lure office workers out into the cold to purchase coffee, Java Man barely breaks even. In fact, in December of 1994, the business lost money.

Figure 14.8 indicates that by moving some of the expenses from the category of variable costs to that of fixed costs, Java Man increases total annual earnings but the variability of the earnings from month to month also increases. Although the company earns more during the spring and fall by reducing the variable costs, it loses more during the winter months because it must continue to meet its higher fixed costs.

This increase in variability is reflected in the month-to-month standard deviation of earnings, which is shown both in figures 14.7 and 14.8 directly under the annual sum of earnings. The current cost structure results in a standard deviation of $4,963, but the projected cost structure has a month-to-month standard deviation of $5,738. (To learn more about the meaning and use of standard deviations, which measure the amount of variability in a set of numbers, see chapter 15, "Investment Decisions Under Uncertainty.")

The increase in variability is also reflected in the Java Man's DOL. As shown in cell D4 of figures 14.7 and 14.8, the DOL would increase from 2.45 to 2.66 as a result of increasing fixed costs and decreasing variable costs. Both the DOL and the business risk would increase if Java Man moved its offices.

Tip

The DOLs calculated in figures 14.7 and 14.8 use the *contribution margin* to shorten the formulas. The contribution margin is defined as revenues less total variable costs.

If Java Man has plenty of money in the bank to meet unexpected expenses, such as major repairs to its trucks or the trucks' coffee brewers, then the acceptance of greater fixed costs may make good financial as well as operational sense.

But if Java Man's owners frequently take profits out of the business, so that it has relatively little in the way of resources to cushion the impact of unexpected expenses, it might be unwise to add to its fixed costs. Where will the money come from to repair a truck that breaks down at the end of January?

Managers can use the DOL to plan not only their operations, as was done in the Java Man case study, but also their net income and their pricing. It is useful to perform sensitivity analysis around sales volume levels, and around adjustments to both fixed and variable expenses. (For a detailed example of sensitivity analysis see chapter 13, "Creating a Sensitivity Analysis for a Business Case.")

III

Investment Decisions

> **Note**
>
> Variability in profit levels, whether measured as EBIT, operating income, or net income does not *necessarily* increase the level of business risk as the DOL increases. If the variability is predictable—if the timing and size of the swings can be forecast with confidence—then a company can anticipate and allow for them in its budgets.

Planning by Using the DOL

In January, for example, the managers of Firms A, B, and C might set out their annual operations and profit targets by means of the following assumptions:

- We want to increase our sales volume from 120,000 to 200,000.

- Our market research leads us to believe that to sell an additional 80,000 units we must lower our unit sales price from $2.00 to $1.70.

- Neither total fixed costs nor unit variable costs will change during this year.

Based on these assumptions, the change in net operating income for each firm would be as shown in figure 14.9.

Fig. 14.9

Changes to net operating income with higher unit sales and lower sales prices.

	A	B Unit Sales	C Unit Price	D Total Sales	E Fixed Costs	F Unit variable costs	G Total variable costs	H Net operating income	I Increase in net income
5	Firm A	120,000	$2.00	$240,000	$20,000	$1.50	$180,000	$40,000	
6		200,000	$1.70	$340,000	$20,000	$1.50	$300,000	$20,000	($20,000)
8	Firm B	120,000	$2.00	$240,000	$40,000	$1.20	$144,000	$56,000	
9		200,000	$1.70	$340,000	$40,000	$1.20	$240,000	$60,000	$4,000
11	Firm C	120,000	$2.00	$240,000	$60,000	$1.00	$120,000	$60,000	
12		200,000	$1.70	$340,000	$60,000	$1.00	$200,000	$80,000	$20,000

As before, Firm C has a higher DOL than either Firms A or B. Although the managers of Firm C believe that this works to their advantage, they should also perform the same analysis on the downside. If, despite reducing their unit sales price, their total sales remain at 120,000 instead of increasing to 200,000, the reduction in unit price would reduce profits by $36,000 instead of increasing them by $20,000. It is for this reason that companies with a high degree of leverage must be confident that their sales volumes will not fall. Otherwise, they run a significant risk of missing their profit objectives.

Performing an analysis of the impacts that leverage can have on a firm's profitability is essential to a clear picture of the risk a company has decided to take on. However, the DOL is only one of the indicators that a manager, shareholder, or creditor uses to measure the value and risk to a firm's financial health. Another important measure is a company's degree of financial leverage.

Analyzing Financial Leverage

Financial leverage is the extent to which a company finances the acquisition of its assets by means of debt: that is, a company that borrows money to acquire assets engages financial leverage. This type of leverage is a critical component in the measurement of the financial health and value of a company. It helps managers, analysts, stockholders, as well as long and short-term creditors distinguish between a firm's level of business risk and the financial risk that the firm has assumed.

In contrast, financial risk is the additional exposure, above and beyond business risk, that a firm incurs by using financial leverage: that is, the debt that the firm assumes by financing the acquisition of its assets.

Suppose, for example, that you decide to start a business that offers training classes in the design of databases and the use of database management systems. Your business risk consists of factors such as the desirability of the training, the number of people who might want it, the number of other firms that offer similar training classes, the market share of the database management systems that you choose to focus on, and the quality and price of your service relative to that of your competition.

If you obtain a loan to finance the purchase of computer workstations for your clients to use during training, you have assumed an additional financial risk, beyond your business risk: the possibility that your firm will be unable to repay that loan from its earnings.

III

Investment Decisions

It is useful to separate business from financial risk to make decisions pertaining to financial leverage. One way to focus on financial risk is to analyze a firm's financial structure: that is, the way that the firm has gone about financing its assets. Part of a company's overall financial structure is its capital structure. The company's capital structure is the combination of various forms of debt and equity that are used to finance its assets.

A thorough understanding of the debt that your company has assumed significantly enhances your ability to make good decisions about acquiring new debt. As a creditor, it is essential to understand a borrower's capital structure in order to measure the risk of making a loan, and to determine whether the interest rate is in line with that risk.

The acquisition of additional debt, of course, changes a company's degree of financial leverage, and therefore new debt can have either a beneficial *or* a detrimental impact on the evaluations made by creditors and stockholders.

Suppose that you can obtain a loan at 9 percent interest to finance the acquisition of new computer workstations. If the return on the assets represented by the new workstations is 12 percent, you will have *leveraged* the loan, to your benefit. But if the return on this equipment turns out to be only 6 percent, the leverage works against you: you will pay more in interest than you will earn from the asset.

Clearly, financial leverage is an important indicator to investors (should I buy this stock?), to managers (will this decision get me a promotion or a pink slip?), to stockholders (should I sell or stand pat?) and to creditors (can they repay this loan?). There are several financial leverage ratios that help you analyze a company's capital structure. These ratios include the Debt Ratio and the Times Interest Earned ratio.

The ratios provide managers, analysts, investors, and creditors with useful indications of how financial leverage impacts the level of financial risk a company has assumed. The ratio information is critical for determining the stability, and even the solvency, of a company.

Determining the Debt Ratio

The Debt Ratio is the ratio of total debt to total assets. (Another term for the Debt Ratio is the *Leverage Factor*.) Figure 14.10 calculates the Debt Ratio of three firms that are identical in all respects except for the amount of debt that they have assumed.

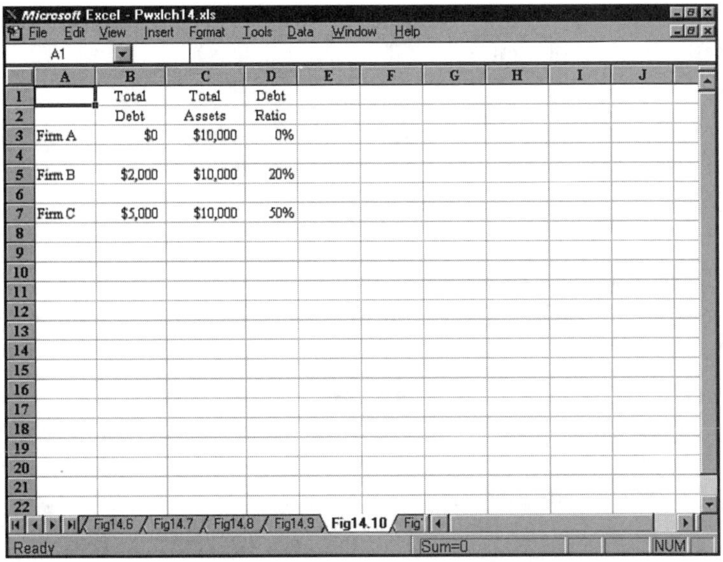

	Total Debt	Total Assets	Debt Ratio
Firm A	$0	$10,000	0%
Firm B	$2,000	$10,000	20%
Firm C	$5,000	$10,000	50%

Fig. 14.10
The Debt Ratio is one way of measuring financial leverage.

The Debt Ratio measures the proportion of a firm's total assets that are financed, both short-term and long-term, by means of creditors' funds. Managers, analysts, shareholders, and creditors use the Debt Ratio as one indicator of how much risk a firm is carrying.

For example, a company's value is in large measure a function of the value of its assets. If a firm has a high debt ratio, then a high proportion of its assets has been financed by means of debt. This implies that the company must spend a greater proportion of its earnings to pay off those debts, instead of reinvesting its earnings in the company.

On the other hand, a company with a low debt ratio has used its equity to acquire assets. This implies that it requires a smaller proportion of its earnings to retire debt, and the company can make more dollars available for reinvestment and dividends.

A firm's debt ratio is also a useful indicator of how well it will weather difficult financial times. For example, if a company with a high debt ratio suffers significant earnings losses, it will be hard pressed to continue operations and simultaneously pay off its debts. But a company with a low debt ratio is in a much better position to continue operations if earnings decrease, because it will not need to use its earnings for debt retirement.

In figure 14.10, Firm C has the highest debt ratio. This implies that if the firm were to experience a recessionary period, the cash flow it generates may not be sufficient to meet principal and interest payments on the debt acquired. In this example, the Debt Ratio indicates that Firm C is at the greatest financial risk.

> **Note**
>
> The Equity Ratio, discussed in chapter 7, "Ratio Analysis," is the opposite of the Debt Ratio. It returns the ratio of a firm's equity to its assets. The higher the Equity Ratio, the lower a firm's financial leverage.

Determining the Times Interest Earned Ratio

Times Interest Earned refers to the number of times that interest payments are covered by a firm's earnings. It is calculated by dividing the EBIT by interest charges: that is, the income that is available for the payment of interest, divided by the interest expense. Thus, the Times Interest Earned ratio indicates the extent to which a firm's current earnings are able to meet current interest payments out of net operating income or EBIT. Figure 14.11 shows possible Times Interest Earned ratios for three firms.

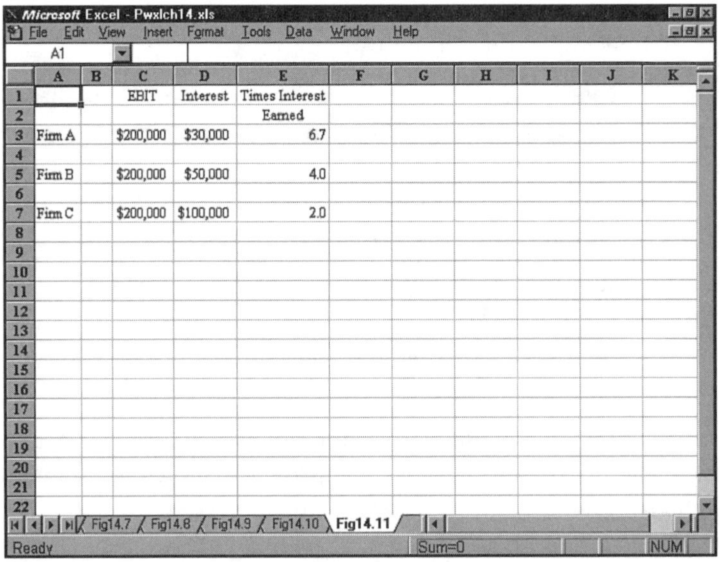

Fig. 14.11
The Times Interest Earned Ratio measures a company's ability to meet its interest payments.

	A	B	C	D	E	F	G	H	I	J	K
1			EBIT	Interest	Times Interest						
2					Earned						
3	Firm A		$200,000	$30,000	6.7						
4											
5	Firm B		$200,000	$50,000	4.0						
6											
7	Firm C		$200,000	$100,000	2.0						

The Times Interest Earned ratios in figure 14.11 indicate that Firm A, because it has relatively low debt, uses a lower proportion of its earnings to cover interest payments. Firm B covers annual interest payments four times at its current earnings level, and Firm C covers annual interest payments two times at its current earnings level.

Firm C runs a greater risk of financial difficulty than the other two firms. This is because it must cover interest payments before applying earnings to any other purpose, such as reinvestment.

Summary

In the business environment of the 1990s, operating and financial leverage are important ingredients in determining the success or demise of many companies. Firms acquire leverage to bolster their financial positions, thus increasing shareholder value. However, with increased leverage comes increased risk. Managers, analysts, shareholders, and creditors must be very clear about the implications of the risks associated with a firm's operating and financial leverage to make investment decisions. Knowing these implications brings their decisions in line with their desired levels of risk.

III

Investment Decisions

Chapter 15

Investment Decisions Under Uncertainty

It is often the case that you have dependable information at hand to help you make business decisions. You might know, for example, how much you must pay in interest charges for a loan that will enable you to retool a manufacturing operation or hire an employee who can perform a critical role for your company.

It also very frequently happens that you must make a decision without access to firm information. In this case, if you are fortunate, you can look to historical data or acquire new empirical information that bears, even if indirectly, on your decision. The appropriate analysis of the data can put you in a position to make probability statements about different courses of action: for example, if we pursue Course A, the likelihood that we'll achieve an additional 10 percent profit is 95 percent. If we pursue Course B, achieving an additional 10 percent profit has a probability of only 45 percent.

Being able to make statements like that with confidence can be very useful when you are confronted with an investment decision that depends on uncertain conditions. This chapter explores the use of information about variability in data to help you make such statements. There are three concepts, and associated Excel tools, that are fundamental to this sort of decision making: standard deviations, confidence intervals, and multiple regression analysis.

Standard Deviations

A *standard deviation* is a measure that expresses how much different numbers vary. It is one important method of determining the spread of different numbers across the range of values that the numbers are able to take. For example, and as a practical matter, the age of individual human beings can range from 0 to 90. But the ages of 500 high school students spread across the possible range of values differently than do the ages of 500 college students.

Suppose that you are interested in analyzing the commissions that you are paying salespeople who work for your firm. After you have determined this total amount, it is natural to inquire about the average, or mean, commission earned by the salespeople. This is easy to obtain by dividing the number of salespeople into the total commissions paid.

The average commission is a measure of the central tendency of the individual observations—the amount that each individual earns in commission. It is a point on the scale of commission payments that lies somewhere between the smallest commission and the largest commission.

In contrast, the standard deviation is a distance along that same scale. Like the range, which is the distance between the smallest and largest commissions, the standard deviation is a distance, and is a measure of how the individual amounts vary.

For example, suppose that you find the average annual commission is $15,000. You also find (by calculations described later in this section) that the standard deviation of these commissions is $6,000. In that case, the individual commissions vary from one another more than if you found that the standard deviation was $1,000.

Why is this kind of information useful? One reason—and there are many—is that it immediately gives you information about the performance of your sales force. It turns out, for example, that about two-thirds of the individual observations lie one standard deviation above and below the mean.

In this example, where the average annual commission was $15,000, you might take a very different view of the performance of the sales force if the standard deviation were $1,000 than if it were $6,000. If about two thirds of the sales force makes between $14,000 (mean – 1 standard deviation, or $15,000 – $1,000) and $16,000 (mean + 1 standard deviation, or $15,000 + $1,000), then most salespeople are performing at roughly the same level.

On the other hand, if you found that the standard deviation is $6,000, then about two thirds of the sales force is earning between $9,000 (mean – 1 standard deviation, or $15,000 – $6,000) and $21,000 (mean + 1 standard deviation, or $15,000 + $6,000) in commissions. You might then conclude that most salespeople are performing very differently, and you might want to investigate the reasons for those differences.

It can help to view these concepts visually. Figures 15.1 and 15.2 display these two situations.

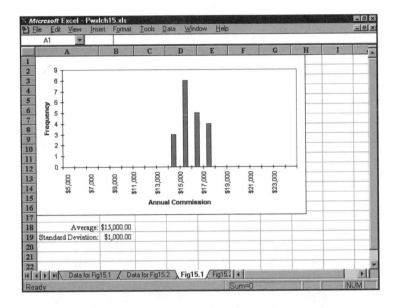

Fig. 15.1
A smaller standard deviation means that the observations cluster around their average.

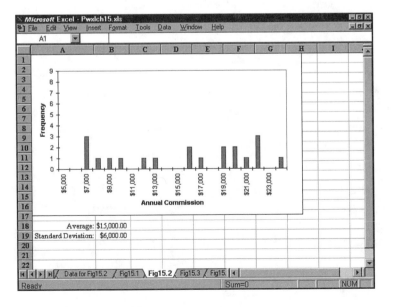

Fig. 15.2
A larger standard deviation means that the observations are more dispersed around their average.

III

Investment Decisions

In both figures 15.1 and 15.2, the horizontal x-axis shows different values of annual commissions—for example, $16,000. The vertical y-axis shows a count of the number of observations in each category. Notice that the observations are less spread out, left to right, in figure 15.1 than in figure 15.2. This is as you would expect, given the relative sizes of the standard deviations in each figure.

The formula for a standard deviation is not as intuitively obvious as is the formula for an average. The definitional form of the formula is:

```
Standard deviation = √ Σ(X-μ)²/n
```

where $\Sigma(X-\mu)^2$ means to take each number (X), subtract from it the average of the numbers (μ), square that difference, and then take the sum of the squared differences. /n means to divide that sum by n, or the number of observations. Finally, take the square root of the result of the division.

Fortunately, Excel provides a worksheet function for the standard deviation. Suppose, for example, that you have twenty observations in A1:A20. To get the standard deviation of these observations, the Excel formula is:

```
=STDEV(A1:A20)
```

Unfortunately, it's not quite that simple, because there's more than one *kind* of standard deviation. The standard deviation, as defined above, is a *biased* statistic when you apply it to a sample. If the twenty numbers in A1:A20 are a sample from a larger population, then the definitional formula for the standard deviation underestimates the standard deviation of the full population. Applied to a sample, the proper formula is:

```
Standard deviation = √ Σ(X-μ)²/(n-1)
```

Notice that the denominator of the ratio is now (n–1): the number of observations minus 1.

Therefore, Excel actually provides two functions for a standard deviation: one if your data constitute a sample, and another if your data consititute the entire population of interest. If a sample, you should use the STDEV function. If a population, use the STDEVP function instead:

```
=STDEVP(A1:A20)
```

where the P at the end of the function name is a mnemonic for Population. STDEV uses (n–1) in the denominator, whereas STDEVP uses n in the denominator.

> **Tip**
>
> Be very cautious when you use STDEV or STDEVP on data whose magnitude is either very large (on the order of, say, 10^5 or greater) or very small (say, 10^{-5} or smaller). With such data, rounding errors can occur in any PC application, not just Excel, because of the effect of squaring the differences between the observations and their mean. If you work with data such as this, you might consider re-scaling the numbers before applying STDEV or STDEVP, and interpreting their results in terms of the rescaling.

There are many other uses for the standard deviation than discussed here. This is particularly true in the area of inferential statistics, which help you make inferences about a population on the basis of a sample. For example, chapters 9 and 10 in this book make extensive use of standard deviations in statistical process control and of standard errors (a type of standard deviation; see this chapters section on multiple regression) in forecasting.

Understanding Confidence Intervals

In many investment situations, it is either too expensive or completely impossible to acquire all the information that would allow you to make a decision with 100 percent confidence. Then, the best that you can do is to obtain a sample of the information. With the sample in hand, you can calculate a statistic that you hope is a close approximation of the value you would calculate if you had access to the entire information set. You can measure the closeness of the approximation by means of confidence intervals.

A *confidence interval* is a bracket around a sample statistic such as the mean. It expresses an interval in terms of both an upper and a lower bound, within which you can have some level of confidence that the population value exists.

Using Confidence Intervals in a Market Research Situation

Your company is considering the acquisition of a new retail store, and foot traffic past the stores location is, for you, an important measure of its desirability. Each day for two weeks, you arrange to count the number of people who walk past the location. This constitutes a sample from the population of all possible days that you might own the store.

III

Investment Decisions

You take the average of each daily observation, which turns out to be 403. How accurate is this average, obtained from a sample, as an estimate of the number of people who would walk past the site on *any* given day?

On the Disk

A confidence interval around the mean value of 403 helps answer this question. The raw data and analysis are shown in figure 15.3, and you can also find them on the *Business Analysis with Excel* companion disk.

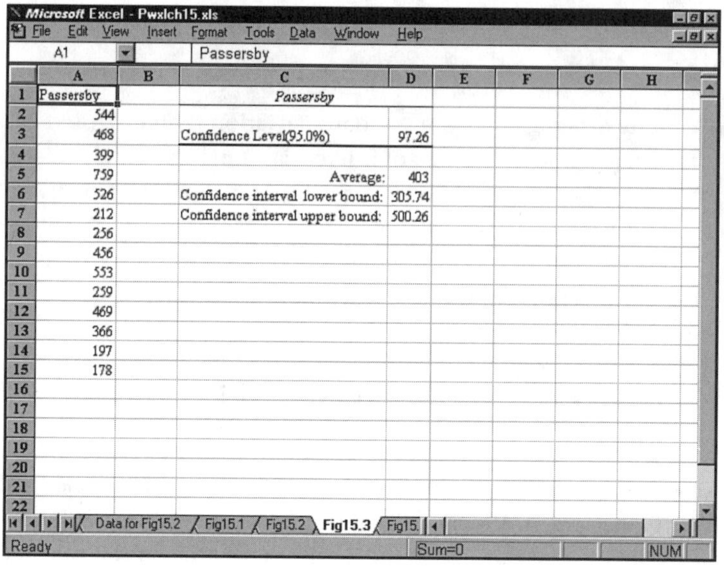

Fig. 15.3
A confidence interval around a sample mean helps you locate the mean of the population.

	A	B	C	D	E	F	G	H
1	Passersby		Passersby					
2	544							
3	468		Confidence Level(95.0%)	97.26				
4	399							
5	759		Average:	403				
6	526		Confidence interval lower bound:	305.74				
7	212		Confidence interval upper bound:	500.26				
8	256							
9	456							
10	553							
11	259							
12	469							
13	366							
14	197							
15	178							

To obtain this analysis, take the following steps:

1. Choose Tools, Add-Ins.

2. Check the Analysis ToolPak - VBA checkbox. If you do not see this option in the Add-Ins dialog box, you need to run Add/Remove Programs in the Windows 95 Control Panel. Be sure to specify that Setup should install the Analysis ToolPak add-in.

3. Choose OK.

4. After the add-in manager has finished processing, choose Tools, Data Analysis.

5. Choose Descriptive Statistics from the Analysis Tools list box.

6. Choose OK.

7. With the flashing cursor in the Input Range edit box, highlight cells A1:A15.

8. Check the Labels in First Row checkbox, and ensure that the Confidence Level for Mean is set to 95%.

9. Click the Output Range radio button. Ensure that the flashing cursor is in the Output Range edit box, and then enter (or select) $C$1.

10. Choose OK.

For these data, the Descriptive Statistics tool returns a confidence level of 97.26. You can add this number to the mean, and also subtract it from the mean, to obtain a confidence interval of 305.74 to 500.26. To do so, follow these steps, which assume that the confidence level of 97.26 appears in cell D3:

1. In some blank cell, enter:

```
=AVERAGE(A2:A15)+D3
```

This returns the confidence interval's upper bound.

2. In another cell, enter:

```
=AVERAGE(A2:A15)-D3
```

to return the confidence interval's lower bound.

What does this interval mean? If you repeated your experiment 100 times, you would have 100 two-week means and associated confidence intervals. 95 of the confidence intervals would capture the population mean: that is, the true population mean would lie between the intervals lower bound and its upper bound. Five of the confidence intervals would *not* span the true population mean.

It is more rational to assume that the actual experiment is one of the 95 (hypothetical) experiments whose confidence intervals do capture the population mean, than it is to assume that this is one of the five experiments that do not. Therefore, you make the rational assumption that the true number of people walking past this site on any given day is somewhere between 306 and 500.

It's up to you to decide whether this is a precise enough estimate for your purposes, and whether the average is large enough to make it an attractive site.

For example, you might take a formal approach to this experiment and specify *beforehand* that you will consider this site if there is an average of 520 people who walk by it on any given day. After collecting and analyzing the information, you find that the confidence interval's upper limit is 500. Therefore, you can conclude with 95 percent assurance that this site does not meet your criterion: the confidence interval does not capture the average number of 520 that you require.

III

Investment Decisions

Refining Confidence Intervals

Several factors are involved in the calculation of a confidence interval. One is the standard deviation of the observations: you can't do much about this, because it's based on the data that you observe.

Another is the confidence level that you specify in the Descriptive Statistics analysis tool, and here you can exercise some control. The greater the confidence level that you specify, the larger the confidence interval. Of course, there's a tradeoff involved: you can make the interval smaller by specifying, say, 90 percent as a confidence level. But while this reduces the size of the interval, it also reduces the confidence that you can place in the estimate.

The surest way to narrow the interval and yet retain an acceptable degree of confidence is to increase the sample size. By taking three weeks of observations, rather than two weeks, you might be able to narrow the confidence interval to, say, 353 to 453. You might find this interval to be a precise enough basis for your decision of whether to acquire the location.

Although increasing the sample size is your best bet to reduce the size of a confidence interval, it is not guaranteed to do so. It is possible that an increase in the sample size will cause an increase in the standard deviation. This is virtually certain to happen if the additional observations that you obtain are quite low or quite high relative to the mean of the original sample.

The meaning of a confidence interval is one that many people misinterpret. It is easy to think, the probability is 95 percent that this confidence interval captures the true population mean, but this is an false conclusion. Either the interval captures the mean or it does not: so, the probability that it captures the mean is either 1 or 0. However, 95 percent of confidence intervals *will* capture the mean, and it would be illogical to believe that this is one of the five percent that fail to do so.

Using Regression Analysis in Decision Making

Regression analysis is an extremely powerful tool that can help you make sense of much larger amounts of data than were used in the case study on confidence intervals earlier in this chapter. It is a technique thats fundamental for exploring and understanding relationships among variables, and you can use it to guide decisions about everything from operations to finance and from sales commissions to marketing.

Excel provides good support for regression analysis. There are 15 worksheet functions that bear directly on regression analysis, and other capabilities such as the Regression add-in, menu items such as Edit, Fill, Series, Linear, and trendlines on charts that make certain regression computations more convenient.

Regressing One Variable Onto Another

Suppose that you are considering an increase in your advertising budget for a particular product to increase your company's unit sales for that product. You're concerned, though, that you will not sell enough additional units to justify the increased cost of advertising, and this would depress your earnings. In this case, you would be interested in the relationship between your company's advertising budget for each product and the number of unit sales of those products. Can you estimate the effect of an increase in advertising on unit sales?

Yes, if you have the data necessary to do a regression analysis. In the 1990s, many—perhaps most—stores have point-of-sale terminals that can capture information about product sold, sales price, date, and location sold, and (if the customer pays by credit card) about the customer. Operations, marketing, and finance groups have learned to mine the resulting databases for insight into how best to distribute, price, and sell their companies' products.

Figure 15.4 shows two variables, advertising budget and unit sales, for 18 different models of a product sold by a company. The figure also shows an XY chart that summarizes the relationship between advertising budget and unit sales.

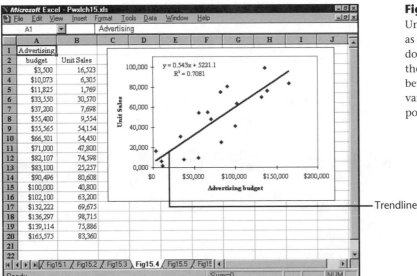

Fig. 15.4

Unit sales increase as advertising dollars increase: the relationship between the variables is positive.

The data that underlie the chart in figure 15.4 are in the chapter 15 workbook on the companion disk. To create the embedded chart shown in figure 15.4, open the workbook, activate the data worksheet and follow these steps:

1. Highlight the data in A3:B20.

2. Choose Insert, Chart, or click the Chart Wizard button. If you use Insert, Chart, select On This Sheet.

3. While holding down the mouse button, drag across the worksheet to establish a location for an embedded chart. Release the mouse button.

4. In Step 1 of the Chart Wizard, verify that the Range edit box contains the address of the data you want to chart. Click Next.

5. In Step 2 of the Chart Wizard, click the XY (Scatter) chart option. Click Next.

6. In Step 3 of the Chart Wizard, click the first (markers only) chart format option. Click Next.

7. In Step 4 of the Chart Wizard, make sure that the Data Series in Columns radio button is selected, and that the spinner for X-data columns is set to 1. Click Next.

8. In Step 5 of the Chart Wizard, add a legend and axis titles, and click Finish.

9. After the chart has appeared in your worksheet, double-click on it to open it for editing. The chart border changes to a diagonally hatched pattern.

10. Click on any of the series' markers to select the series. Choose Insert, Trendline, and click the Type tab if necessary. Choose the Linear regression type.

11. Click the Options tab, and check the Display Equation on Chart and the Display R-squared Value on Chart checkboxes. Choose OK.

> **Tip**
>
> If your columns of data have header rows that contain labels, you can use the header rows in the charts legend by identifying them as such in Step 4 of the Chart Wizard.

What can you learn from the information in figure 15.4? It's clear that as advertising dollars increase, so do unit sales. The trendline (the straight line that runs from the chart's lower-left corner to its upper-right corner) emphasizes that the budgets and the unit sales grow jointly.

The chart also contains this equation:

```
y = 0.543x + 5221.1
```

This is the *regression equation* for the data in the worksheet. It expresses numerically the relationship between dollars spent on advertising these products and their unit sales volume. In the equation, *y* stands for unit sales and *x* stands for advertising dollars. It gives you the best estimate of the unit sales volume, y, given any value of advertising dollars, x.

This does not mean that you can estimate unit sales precisely, given knowledge of advertising dollars. For example, plug the value of $55,400 advertising dollars into the equation as x, and it returns 35,302 units sold. Notice that $55,400 is one of the actual observations in figure 15.4, but the units sold for that product is 9,554. To repeat: regression gives you the best estimate (35,302 units) on the basis of the data at hand, not a precise prediction.

> **Note**
>
> If you use the values in the chart's regression equation to predict a y-value, you are likely to obtain a slightly different value than if you use a worksheet function. This is because the intercept and slope in a chart's regression equation are rounded to fit in the chart.

Continuing with the downside of regression analysis, it's important to understand that regression expresses an *association* between or among variables. This is different than *causation*, which means that manipulating one variable necessarily results in a change to another variable.

You could, for example, plug the value $200,000 into the regression equation and get 113,818 as the estimated number of units sold. That does not necessarily mean that spending $200,000 to advertise a product would result in the sale of 113,818 units (although it certainly might do so). There are many reasons other than amount of advertising budget for unit sales to vary, and these other reasons (for example, unit sales price) are not represented in the regression equation.

Furthermore, even if the relationship between variables is a causal one, you have no way to know for sure the direction of the causation. It is entirely plausible that as unit sales increase, the marketing department has increased that product's advertising budget—thus, unit sales may have driven spending on advertisements, instead of the other way around.

III

Investment Decisions

There are two terms in the right side of this regression equation. The number 0.543 is called the *slope*, and the number 5221.1 is called the *intercept*. The slope is simply a measure of the steepness of the trendline: the higher the number that measures the slope, the more steep is the trendline. The slope might be a negative number, and in that case the trendline would run from the upper-left corner of the chart to the lower-right corner. If you were to chart unit price against unit sales, for example, you would be likely to get a trendline with a negative slope: the higher the unit price, the lower the number of unit sales.

The intercept indicates where the trendline crosses the y (that is, the vertical) axis. In this case, it is 5221.1. One way to interpret this number is to state, "If we spend zero dollars on advertising a product, we estimate that we will sell about 5220 units."

The chart also shows a statistic called R^2, pronounced "R squared." This statistic is absolutely fundamental to regression analysis (R stands for regression). It expresses the proportion of the variance in y (here, unit sales) associated with the variance in x (here, advertising dollars).

> **Tip**
>
> The variance is the square of the standard deviation. Like the standard deviation, it is a measure of the degree to which individual scores are dispersed about their mean. But while the standard deviation can be thought of as a distance, the variance can be thought of as an area: the square of a distance. It's often useful to keep this in mind when considering the relationship between variables, as in figure 15.5.

Assume for the moment that there is a causal relationship between advertising dollars and unit sales (this is not a necessary assumption, but it makes understanding this concept more straightforward). When you change a product's advertising budget, then, its unit sales change. When the product's unit sales change, the variance of unit sales for all products changes. To prove this to yourself, enter some numbers in an Excel worksheet—say, in A1:A5. Then, enter this formula in another cell:

```
=VAR(A1:A5)
```

Now, when you change any number in A1:A5, you will see that the value returned by the formula also changes. As you change the values in A1:A5, you are exerting a causal influence on their variance.

The R^2 shown in figure 15.4 is .7081, which means that about 71 percent of the variability in unit sales is associated with variability in advertising dollars. Figure 15.5 illustrates this relationship.

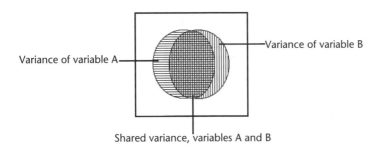

Variance of variable A

Variance of variable B

Shared variance, variables A and B

Fig. 15.5
The overlapping areas indicate shared variance: changes in the values of one variable are associated with changes in the values of the other variable.

Why R *squared*? Because R^2 is the square of the correlation coefficient. If you entered, on figure 15.4's worksheet, the formula:

```
=CORREL(A3:A20,B3:B20)^2
```

it would return .7081: the same as the R^2 for these data.

Using Excel charts and trendline options is the most visually appealing and informative way to examine the relationship between two variables, but there are other worksheet functions that are quicker and sometimes more convenient. Referring again to the data in figure 15.4:

- This worksheet formula uses the RSQ function to return R^2 just as does the chart trendline option:

  ```
  =RSQ(B3:B20,A3:A20)
  ```

- You can get the intercept for the equation by means of:

  ```
  =INTERCEPT(B3:B20,A3:A20)
  ```

- The slope of the regression equation is available from:

  ```
  =SLOPE(B3:B20,A3:A20)
  ```

- If you want both the slope and intercept from one function, select a 2-cell range consisting of one row and two columns, and array enter:

  ```
  =LINEST(B3:B20,A3:A20)
  ```

Why bother with these functions when the chart trendline options are so convenient? One reason is that you might want to include the values returned by the functions in a report, or use them with other utilities such as the Scenario Manager or the Solver. And it will become apparent in the next section that worksheet functions like LINEST are much more powerful than anything you can display with a trendline option.

III

Investment Decisions

Regressing One Variable Onto Several Other Variables

Suppose that, besides increasing advertising dollars for a product, you are considering lowering its unit sales price. Again, you might look to the data on all your product lines for guidance. Figure 15.6 shows, in addition to the advertising budget and unit sales, the sales price for 18 different models of a product.

Fig. 15.6

Unit sales increase as advertising dollars increase and sales price decreases.

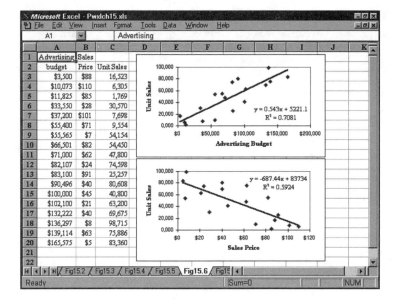

What is the best estimate of the *combined* effect of changing the advertising budget and the sales price on units sold? Neither chart's regression equation answers this question.

To answer it, it's necessary to resort to the worksheet function LINEST. LINEST is capable of analyzing the relationship between a variable such as units sold (sometimes called a *criterion* variable or *dependent* variable) on the one hand, and multiple variables such as advertising dollars and sales price (sometimes called *predictor* variables or *independent* variables) on the other. Figure 15.7 shows LINEST in this context.

The range E9:G13 contains the LINEST function, which in this case is array-entered as:

```
=LINEST(C3:C20,A3:B20,TRUE,TRUE)
```

The result of the function is rich in information. First, it provides the best-estimate multiple regression equation to predict units sold from the combination of advertising dollars and sales price. The equation is:

```
y = 36842.9715 + (.3818 * x1) + (-358.4634 * x2)
```

where y represents units sold, x1 represents advertising dollars, and x2 represents sales price.

Notice first that there are three terms to the right of the equal sign in the equation. The first, 36842.9715, is the intercept, as it is in two-variable regression. The second and third terms contain .3818 and –358.4634. These are no longer slopes, because there is only one regression line to consider and one straight line can't have two different slopes. They are, instead, termed *regression coefficients*. They are coefficients that you can multiply times a value for advertising dollars and a value for sales price, to predict units sold.

Also notice that LINEST does not return the regression coefficients in the same order as the predictor variables on the worksheet. That is, the first coefficient (–358.4634) applies to the second predictor variable, Sales Price (found in B3:B20). The second coefficient (.3818) applies to the first predictor variable, Advertising Budget (found in A3:A20). This is an inconvenience in the

LINEST function, and there is no way around it: the order that LINEST returns the coefficients is always the reverse of the order of the arguments that refer to the worksheet ranges.

What else does the LINEST function tell you? The value 0.8068, in the third row and first column of the LINEST results, is the R^2 between units sold and the best combination of advertising budget and sales price. When you optimally combine sales price and advertising budget by means of the regression equation, you get a new variable that shares 80.68% of its variance with units sold.

Figure 15.7 shows this new variable in cells I3:I20. The formula in cell I3 is:

```
=$G$9+($E$9*B3)+($F$9*A3)
```

This formula is copied-and-pasted into cells I4:I20. Finally, this formula is entered in cell G17:

```
=RSQ(C3:C20,I3:I20)
```

Recall that the RSQ function returns the R^2 between two variables: the percent of variance that they have in common. In this case, it returns 0.8068, which is identical to the value returned in cell E11 by the LINEST function.

More importantly, 0.8068 is larger than .7081, which is the R^2 between units sold and advertising dollars alone. This means that by combining advertising dollars and sales price as predictor variables, you can explain an additional 10% (80.68% – 70.81%) of the variability in unit sales.

What of the second row in the LINEST results, cells E10:G10 in figure 15.7? These speak to the statistical significance, or the dependability, of the regression coefficients. They are the standard errors of the regression coefficients and the intercept. A standard error is a kind of standard deviation. If you divide each regression coefficient by its standard error, you get whats known as a *t-statistic*. For example, using the data shown in cells F9 and F10 of figure 15.7:

```
=.3818/.0936
```

```
=4.0799
```

This means that .3818 is slightly more than four standard errors away from zero. Four standard errors is a considerable distance. (Until and unless you've had a fair amount of experience working with standard deviations and standard errors, it's difficult to know that intuitively, and for now it's okay to take the statement at face value.) You can use Excel's TDIST function to determine whether you think it's statistically significant. For example, you could enter this formula on the worksheet:

```
=TDIST(F9/F10,15,1)
```

which returns .0005. Taking the formula's components one-by-one:

- F9/F10 is the ratio of the regression coefficient for advertising dollars to its standard error. Again, this is the t-statistic, whose value is 4.0799.

- 15 is the number of degrees of freedom for the t-statistic. It is the number of observations, minus the number of terms in the equation. Here, there are 18 observations in the data set (A3:C20). There are three terms in the equation (one intercept and two regression coefficients), so the degrees of freedom is 18 –3 = 15. It is the same as the value returned by the LINEST function in the second column of its fourth row (see cell F12 in fig. 15.7).

- 1 is the number of tails to reference in the t-distribution. This book does not go into sufficient detail about the directionality of statistical hypotheses to fully explain this argument to the TDIST function. However, you can use this as a rule of thumb: if you expect, before you look at the data, a positive (or a negative) relationship between a predictor variable and a criterion variable, use 1 as TDISTs third argument. If you don't know whether to expect a positive or a negative relationship, use 2 as TDISTs third argument. Here, it's reasonable to expect a positive relationship between advertising dollars and unit sales (the more you advertise, the more you sell), so 1 is used.

- The TDIST function itself, given its three arguments, returns the probability of observing a ratio of the regression coefficient to its standard error as large as this one, if the regression coefficient for all such products were really zero. For these data, the probability is .0005 (or 5 chances in 10,000) of getting a t-statistic of 4.08 if the population regression coefficient were really zero.

Why do you care whether the regression coefficient is significantly different from zero? Consider the implication of a regression coefficient whose value is zero. If you multiply zero times all the values of the associated predictor variable, as you would in the regression equation, you add nothing—zero—to the predicted value of the criterion variable. Therefore, the predictor variable would be of no use to you.

III

Investment Decisions

Tip

Excel's TDIST function requires a value greater than or equal to zero as its first argument; it returns #NUM! if its first argument is negative. You can get a negative ratio of the coefficient to its standard error if the coefficient itself is negative (a standard error or a standard deviation can never be negative). A negative regression coefficient can be every bit as informative as a positive one: the coefficient's sign is just a matter of whether the relationship is direct (as with advertising dollars and units sold) or inverse (as with sales price and units sold).

The significance level of a regression coefficient is unrelated to the direction of the relationship between the predictor and the criterion variables. Therefore, to get around TDIST's insistence on a positive value for its first argument, use Excel's ABS function, which returns the absolute value of a number. For example:

=TDIST(ABS(E9/E10),15,1)

If all this seems like a lot of work to you (array-entering LINEST, accounting for the order of the regression coefficients in LINESTs results, noting the R^2 value, getting the degrees of freedom, getting the ratio of the coefficients to their standard errors, using TDIST correctly), it should. Fortunately, Excel's Regression add-in provides a shortcut: it returns all this information, and more, from your choices in just one dialog box. Figure 15.8 shows the results of running the Regression add-in on the data in figure 15.7.

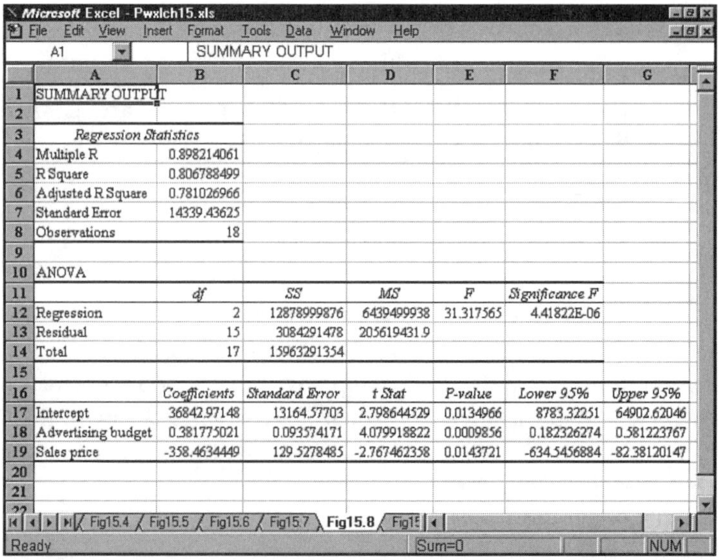

Fig. 15.8
The Regression add-in automates much of the work involved in a multiple regression analysis.

	A	B	C	D	E	F	G
1	SUMMARY OUTPUT						
2							
3	*Regression Statistics*						
4	Multiple R	0.898214061					
5	R Square	0.806788499					
6	Adjusted R Square	0.781026966					
7	Standard Error	14339.43625					
8	Observations	18					
9							
10	ANOVA						
11		*df*	*SS*	*MS*	*F*	*Significance F*	
12	Regression	2	12878999876	6439499938	31.317565	4.41822E-06	
13	Residual	15	3084291478	205619431.9			
14	Total	17	15963291354				
15							
16		*Coefficients*	*Standard Error*	*t Stat*	*P-value*	*Lower 95%*	*Upper 95%*
17	Intercept	36842.97148	13164.57703	2.798644529	0.0134966	8783.32251	64902.62046
18	Advertising budget	0.381775021	0.093574171	4.079918822	0.0009856	0.182326274	0.581223767
19	Sales price	-358.4634449	129.5278485	-2.767462358	0.0143721	-634.5456884	-82.38120147
20							
21							

On the Disk

To obtain this analysis, verify that you have loaded the Analysis ToolPak - VBA via <u>T</u>ools, Add-<u>I</u>ns. The workbook that contains the data in figure 15.7 can be found on the companion disk. Open that workbook and follow these steps with the worksheet containing the data for figure 15.7 active:

1. Choose <u>T</u>ools, <u>D</u>ata Analysis.

2. Choose Regression from the <u>A</u>nalysis Tools list box.

3. Choose OK. The dialog box shown in figure 15.9 appears.

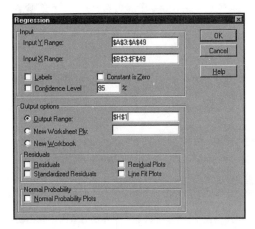

Fig. 15.9
With the Regression add-in dialog box you can specify just a few options to obtain a complete multiple regression analysis.

4. With the flashing cursor in the Input <u>Y</u> Range edit box, highlight cells C3:C20 or type the address directly in the edit box.

5. Click in the Input <u>X</u> Range edit box, and highlight cells A3:B20 or type the address.

6. Ensure that the Con<u>f</u>idence Level edit box contains 95, and that the New Worksheet <u>P</u>ly option button is selected. (There's nothing magic about these settings: they are simply the ones used to create figure 15.8.)

7. Choose OK.

There's plenty of useful information in the Regression output, even though no special options such as residual analysis were used. For example, figure 15.8s cell B5 shows the R^2 between the units sold and the combination of advertising dollars and sales price. It also shows the multiple R, which is of course the square root of R^2, in B4. The multiple R is a correlation coefficient, and expresses the correlation between units sold and the derived combination of the predictor variables.

III

Investment Decisions

The adjusted R^2, shown in cell B6, takes into account the number of observations and the number of predictor variables. In multiple regression analysis, when the number of observations is small, relative to the number of predictor variables, the R^2 tends to be biased upward. The adjusted R^2 informs you what value you would expect to obtain in another sample of data, one that was much larger than the current one. If this example had been based on, say, 100 observations, then the adjusted R^2 would have been only trivially different from the observed R^2.

Tip

The formula for the adjusted R^2 is:

$$1 - (1 - R^2) \times ((N\text{–}1)/(N\text{–}k\text{–}1))$$

where N is the number of observations and k is the number of x (predictor) variables.

A discussion of the ANOVA (Analysis Of Variance) table is beyond the scope of this book, and would add little to the object of this analysis, the regression coefficients. If you are interested in more information about ANOVA, consult an intermediate text on statistical analysis.

The third section of figure 15.8 provides detailed information about the terms in the regression equation. The intercept and coefficients are reported, as are their standard errors, and are identical to those returned by LINEST. The Regression add-in, however, returns them in the same order as they exist on the worksheet.

The add-in also returns the t-statistic for the intercept and for each regression coefficient: recall that this is the ratio of each term to its standard error. For example, cell D18 in figure 15.8 reports the t-statistic for sales price as 4.079918822. This is the same value as is shown in figure 15.7, cell G18, which is 4.0799 (the apparent difference between the two values is due to the display format characteristics).

The P-values reported by the add-in are different than those shown in figure 15.7. There, cell G19 reports the results of the TDIST function for advertising dollars as 0.0005, whereas the add-in reports it as 0.00098559. The reason for the difference is in the third argument to TDIST, which specifies using a one- or two-tailed test. The analysis in figure 15.7 used a one-tailed test, because the direction of the relationship between the predictor and the criterion was known (or, at least, strongly suspected) before the data were examined.

However, the Regression add-in has no way of knowing or suspecting the direction of the relationship prior to performing the analysis. Therefore, it is programmed to supply a two-tailed test. If you were to enter this formula:

```
=TDIST(F9/F10,15,2)
```

on the worksheet shown in figure 15.7, it would return 0.00098559, just as does the Regression add-in.

Finally, the add-in reports the upper and lower limits to a 95 percent confidence interval around the intercept and each coefficient (see the section on confidence intervals earlier in this chapter for a fuller explanation of their interpretation). Notice that none of the three confidence intervals spans zero: this is as you would expect, because the p-values are each significant beyond the 5 percent level. If a p-value were .05 or greater, the 95% confidence interval for that term would span zero.

So, you can conclude with 95 percent confidence that the intercept and regression coefficients are non-zero: that the predictor variables add information meaningfully to the regression equation, and that you can predict unit sales from advertising dollars and sales price with reasonable accuracy.

Predicting With Multiple Regression

After you have verified that a meaningful relationship exists between a criterion variable and a set of predictor variables, how do you go about predicting the outcome of modifying the value of one or more of the predictors? More concretely, what unit sales would you expect for a product whose advertising budget is $200,000 and whose unit sales price was $10?

The most intuitive method is simply to apply the multiple regression equation, with the values for the predictor variables inserted. In this case, you would use:

```
=36842.97+(.3818*200000)+(-358.4634*10)
```

```
=109613.34
```

If you sold 109,613 units at $10 each, your revenues would be over $1 million, and this might be a good investment. (However, there are plenty of other tests for the quality of an investment discussed in chapters 11, 12, and 13 on business case development; this is only one preliminary test you might make when you are uncertain of the investments outcome.)

A slightly easier method of applying the multiple regression equation is to use Excel's TREND function. It is *much* easier to use TREND when there are many predictor values that you want to manipulate. TREND calculates the regression equation as does LINEST, and optionally applies that equation to new predictor values, returning the values you would obtain if you entered the multiple regression formula itself.

For example, suppose that you enter the value 200000 in cell A21 and the value 10 in cell B21 in the worksheet shown in figure 15.8. If you then entered this formula:

```
=TREND(C3:C20,A3:B20,A21:B21)
```

it would return 109613.34, just as does the explicit entry of the multiple regression equation. In the TREND equation, C3:C20 is the address of the range containing the criterion variable, A3:B20 is the address of the range containing the predictor variables, and A21:B21 is the address of the range containing the new predictor variable values that you want to apply.

This may not seem much easier than entering the regression equation explicitly, but what if you had 20 pairs of new values to test? If these new values were in A21:B40, you could array-enter this formula in a one-column by 20 row range:

```
=TREND(C3:C20,A3:B20,A21:B40)
```

and in that way obtain all 20 predicted values with one array formula.

Case Study: Improving Profit Margin

As product manager for a manufacturer of frames for eyeglasses, you manage a product line comprised of 47 different frames. One of your primary responsibilities is to maximize the profit margin returned by your individual products.

You have just completed a survey of the retail outlets that market your frames. The survey collected a variety of information about the products, and included variables such as retail price, perceived quality of the frames, and satisfaction with the warranty terms that you extend to the resellers.

Your product line includes everything from conservatively-designed frames that do little but function well to so-called designer frames that are inexpensive to manufacture but are perceived as stylish by the customer. You also have at hand information on your profit margin for each product, the total of your fixed and variable manufacturing costs, and the share of your total product line achieved by each frame.

Each of these variables could be related in some way to your profit margin. For example:

■ A higher average retail price charged by the outlets might mean that you could increase the price you charge them.

■ It may be that the greater the perceived quality of the frames, the more you can charge for them; or, it may be that the greater their actual quality, the more it costs to manufacture them.

■ The more that each type of frame contributes to your overall sales, the more popular it is likely to be, and, perhaps, the more you could charge the retail outlets.

■ The better the warranty terms, the more it costs you in product replacements, thus reducing your margin.

■ And, of course, the more it costs you to manufacture the frames, the lower your profit margin.

How, if at all, can you manipulate any or all of these variables to boost profit margins? The price that you charge the retail outlets is under your control, but if you raise some prices you run the risk that the outlets will promote the less expensive frames; or, worse, will promote frames made by your competitors. You could modify your manufacturing operations in a way that would reduce the quality of the product, and therefore make it less expensive to produce. But then the retail outlets might demand a price reduction. There is little you can do about the popularity of a given frame, but if it is a powerful driver of profit margin you might decide to do nothing about the other variables: any action you take is likely to entail some cost, to no benefit. You might modify the warranty terms or retool your manufacturing operation to reduce costs, but would doing so materially increase your profit margin?

The data that you have collected are shown in part in figure 15.10. The full data set can be found on the companion disk.

On the Disk

You run the Regression add-in on the data, using product margin as the y-range and the remaining variables as the x-range. You obtain the results shown in figure 15.11.

Fig. 15.10

A partial listing of the product data for the multiple regression analysis shown in figure 15.11.

	A	B	C	D	E	F
1	Profit	Product	Warranty	Retail	Unit	Component
2	Margin	Quality	Terms	Price	Cost	Share
3	0.99%	1.22	1.24	$130	$35.19	2.08%
4	1.21%	1.45	1.54	$104	$80.00	1.09%
5	2.07%	1.90	1.31	$100	$23.31	2.28%
6	2.14%	2.53	1.36	$164	$80.00	1.44%
7	3.05%	3.41	2.65	$119	$80.00	1.75%
8	3.87%	1.96	1.63	$126	$68.84	1.54%
9	4.78%	2.71	1.66	$128	$80.00	0.47%
10	5.45%	1.76	1.40	$142	$30.32	2.51%
11	5.55%	2.09	2.61	$165	$80.00	2.81%
12	6.42%	1.10	2.42	$124	$32.94	0.59%
13	6.51%	3.62	3.50	$109	$28.56	0.64%
14	6.95%	3.53	1.29	$129	$78.75	1.73%
15	7.24%	2.09	2.44	$165	$38.63	1.83%
16	7.45%	1.54	2.60	$119	$48.67	0.76%
17	8.88%	2.41	2.11	$164	$40.83	0.14%
18	10.08%	3.64	2.06	$146	$80.00	3.53%
19	10.25%	2.61	1.85	$159	$80.00	2.13%
20	10.81%	2.62	2.28	$157	$80.00	3.86%
21	11.09%	3.29	4.07	$178	$80.00	1.28%
22	11.64%	1.24	1.84	$138	$31.20	4.25%

Fig. 15.11

The multiple regression analysis of product data for eyeglass frames forms the basis for avoiding a useless change in pricing and operations.

SUMMARY OUTPUT

Regression Statistics	
Multiple R	0.71684266
R Square	0.51386340
Adjusted R Square	0.45457845
Standard Error	0.04694102
Observations	47

ANOVA

	df	SS	MS	F	Significance F
Regression	5	0.09549447	0.01909889	8.66768713	0.00001137
Residual	41	0.09034183	0.00220346		
Total	46	0.18583630			

	Coefficients	Standard Error	t Stat	P-value	Lower 95%	Upper 95%
Intercept	-0.11895439	0.04970656	-2.39313270	0.02136750	-0.21933887	-0.01856990
Product Quality	0.02980053	0.00767474	3.88293909	0.00036802	0.01430108	0.04529998
Warranty Terms	0.00693261	0.00889049	0.77977789	0.44000000	-0.01102212	0.02488734
Retail Price	0.00119016	0.00039374	3.02269683	0.00430578	0.00039498	0.00198534
Unit Cost	-0.00083227	0.00033930	-2.45288035	0.01851416	-0.00151751	-0.00014703
Component Share	0.63455512	0.59762352	1.06179743	0.29454224	-0.57237072	1.84148096

You notice, first, that there is variation in profit margin that is associated with variation in the predictor variables. The amount of variation is around 50 percent: the multiple R^2 (labeled *R Square* by the Regression add-in) is .51 and the adjusted R^2 is .4546. The difference between the observed R^2 value and the adjusted value is not so great that you would conclude that you have either too many predictors or too few observations. 50 percent is a useful amount of shared variance. It's not perfect, but at least there's a substantial amount of variation in profit margin that is associated with variation in the predictor variables.

Turning your attention to the analysis of the regression coefficients, you see that product quality, retail price, and unit cost are all significantly related to profit margin at the 95 percent confidence level. The p-values for the t-tests of each variable are lower than .05, and the 95 percent confidence intervals do not span zero.

The coefficients for product quality and retail price are positive, so the relationships are direct: for example, the higher the retail price, the higher the profit margin. The coefficient for unit cost is, as expected, negative: the higher the unit cost, the lower the profit margin.

This suggests, then, that there might be room to raise the price that you charge your retailers, given the average retail prices that they charge. There might also be an opportunity to modify your manufacturing operations, simultaneously reducing the product quality a bit and lowering your unit production costs.

Keep in mind, though, that these data come from a snapshot sample, not from a true experimental design in which you purposely manipulate the independent variables and note the effect of doing so on the dependent variable. The results are suggestive, and its reasonable to hypothesize that changes in the predictors will influence the criterion variable. But without evidence from a true experiment, it's very dangerous to adopt a firm conclusion that changing a predictor will *necessarily* cause a change in the criterion.

Before you undertake such possibly drastic measures as raising prices or modifying your manufacturing operations, you should estimate the effect of doing so on your present results. At present, for example, you have one product that has a profit margin of 10.25 percent. Its unit cost is $80 and its perceived quality is 2.61. What would happen if you were to find a way to reduce its unit cost to, say, $20 and if the perceived quality of the eyeglass frame therefore fell from 2.61 to 1.30?

Begin by copying its predictor values (cells B19:F19 of figure 15.10) to a blank range such as G19:K19. Change the unit cost in that range from $80 to $20, and the value of perceived quality from 2.61 to 1.30. Selecting another blank cell, enter this formula:

```
=TREND(A3:A49,B3:F49,G19:K19)
```

The result is 11.84 percent, about 1.5 percent greater than 10.25 percent, your current profit margin for that product. This is not a dramatic increase, certainly not one that should convince you to invest money in drastic changes to your manufacturing operations or the price you charge your retailers.

Summary

In this chapter you have learned how to use information about the variability in an indicator to make decisions about investment options when you do not have perfect information at your disposal. In particular, confidence intervals can help you to bracket the likely outcome by means of worst- and best-cases, which gives you a range within which you can make your decision.

You have also learned how to use the powerful multiple regression technique to analyze data and to estimate the potential effect of a change in such variables as pricing, quality and component share on an important outcome like profit margin. Excel provides convenient and powerful tools to assist you in these analyses, but it's necessary to understand the meaning of the results so you can apply them sensibly.

Chapter 16

Fixed Assets

Your company probably owns various tangible assets that it uses to produce revenue. These assets might include, among others, buildings, land, manufacturing equipment such as molds, office equipment such as computers, and transportation equipment such as trucks.

Together, these assets are known as *fixed assets*. Your financial statements and reports may also refer to them as *plant and equipment* or *property, plant, and equipment*. In contrast to supplies, these assets are regarded as long-lasting. In contrast to intangible assets such as trademarks, fixed assets have an objective value. And in contrast to goods, such as an inventory of products that your company manufactures, fixed assets are not intended for resale.

Of course, categorizing an asset depends not only on the asset itself but on your line of business. If your company resells computers, you would usually regard a computer component as a unit of inventory. But if your company uses computers to help sell real estate, you would regard the same computer component as a fixed asset.

There are two principal ways that the way you treat fixed assets contributes to your company's profitability and worth: the determination of its original cost and the determination of its current value. This chapter explores these two processes in detail.

Determining Original Cost

If you acquire a new fixed asset—a telephone system, for example, or a new building—you need to account for that asset in your books. The asset's value contributes to your company's worth on its balance sheet. Furthermore, it's likely that you obtain the fixed asset to help you produce revenue over time, and you need to be able to match the asset's cost to the revenue it helps to produce. Therefore, it can be critically important to value the asset accurately if you are to understand your company's worth and profitability.

Among the issues involved in determining an asset's original cost are the choice of which costs to include, which assets to treat as capital expenses, and whether to use the actual expenditure or its replacement value as the cost of the asset.

Choosing Costs

Suppose that you purchase a new computer to help you run your business, expecting that this computer will contribute to the creation of revenue over a period of several years. Figure 16.1 shows the costs involved in acquiring the computer.

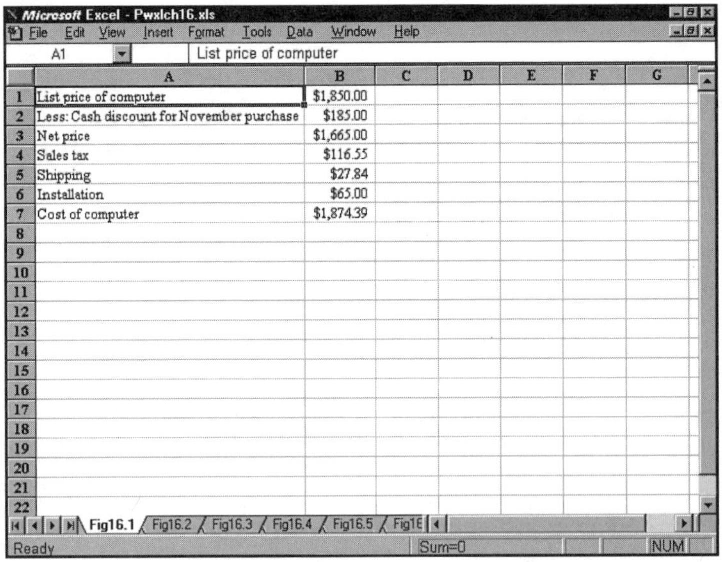

Fig. 16.1

Fixed asset acquisition costs involve more than just the list price of the asset.

The main portion of the expenditure is, of course, the computer's list price. But the list price does not represent the actual cost of the equipment. Suppose that the supplier is trying to clear its inventory of this particular model, and offers a cash discount of 10 percent if a purchase is made before the end of November. You take advantage of this offer, reducing the basic price from $1,850 to $1,665. A sales tax of 7 percent applies, increasing the cost by $116.55. Shipping adds an additional $27.84, and you pay a local firm $65 to install the computer, its software, and its connection to your company's local area network.

These additional costs are not really part of the computer itself. Shouldn't you treat them as expenses for the month of November? No—you should normally treat them as part of the cost of the fixed asset. The reason is once again due to the basic principle of matching costs to revenues.

The computer will presumably remain in service for several years, and will contribute to the generation of your revenue during that time. The ancillary costs are necessary aspects of putting the equipment into service: you could not use the computer to generate revenue unless you have paid the sales tax on it, have it shipped to your place of business, and arrange for its installation. Therefore, these costs should be matched to revenue generated not only this month, not only this year, but generated during the entire useful life of the equipment.

If you allocated the costs to expenses for the current period, you would understate your income for that period and overstate it for subsequent periods. All the costs associated with the acquisition of the equipment should be included in its valuation and, via the depreciation process, allocated against revenue during all the periods that the equipment retains a value.

Are there any other costs that you should apply to the computer's valuation? Possibly: it depends on whether the costs are reasonable and necessary for its use. Suppose that you erroneously told the firm that installs the computer that your local area network is Token Ring, when in fact it is an Ethernet. The technician must make a special trip to obtain different equipment, and charges you extra for this trip. That extra charge is not a reasonable and necessary cost, and should not be included as part of the depreciable cost of the asset.

Choosing Assets

Companies frequently acquire equipment that has a useful life that extends over several accounting periods, but that they hesitate to treat as fixed assets. Items such as staplers, postage scales, beverage carafes, and inexpensive office decor all tend to be long-lasting and have an objective value. But the effort the company will make to account for their depreciation usually costs more than the benefit derived from the additional accuracy of accounting for the assets.

Therefore, it is useful to have a company policy that establishes a minimum cost (for example, $500) for an item before it is treated as a capital expense. Items that cost less are treated as current expenses, even though they are tangible, continue in use over more than one accounting period, and in theory represent fixed assets.

III

Investment Decisions

Choosing Between Actual Cost and Replacement Cost

Depending on the nature of the fixed asset, as well as on the way that you put it into service, you might need to use the replacement or market value of the asset to determine its cost. If you contribute an asset to the business as capital, this choice can become important. (Generally Accepted Accounting Principles state that other assets are to be valued at their historical costs.)

Suppose that you own a house that cost you $150,000 to purchase, and that after living in it for some time you convert it to a rental property. For your own business purposes, it might be necessary to value the house at its current market value, which could be $175,000, $125,000, or virtually any other figure.

In some cases such as this, the Lower of Cost or Market principle can come into play. This principle, which can apply to inventory valuation as well as to the valuation of fixed assets, states that an item should be valued at either the price you paid for it, or the current market value of an identical item: whichever is lower.

However, this principle does not apply in all cases. You should consult an accountant to determine whether to use an assets actual cost, its replacement cost, or the lower of its actual cost or its market value.

The choice of the appropriate valuation method affects both your company's worth on the balance sheet and its earnings on the income statement. Clearly, the greater the asset's valuation, the greater the company's worth. But furthermore, as you depreciate the asset over its useful life, you will be showing some portion of its cost as an expense attributable to each accounting period.

The greater the cost of the asset, then, the greater the depreciation expense for any given period of time. Other things being equal, the greater the depreciation expense, the lower your reported income and the lower your income-tax liability.

This is fine in theory, but in practice it can be very difficult to determine either a replacement cost or a market cost—and the two are not necessarily the same. Suppose that you want to determine the replacement cost of a personal computer, two years into its useful life. Because two years have passed since you acquired the asset, the technology has changed, and it could (and probably would) be extremely difficult to obtain a price on a computer that is both new and directly comparable to the one you own.

Even if you were able to find several replacement sources for an asset, it could be very difficult to determine the market price. When many sources exist for a product, it is likely that their prices vary. Deciding when to stop searching for additional pricing information, which price to adopt as an estimate of market value, whether to average several values as your estimate, and so on can take an amount of effort that is not commensurate with the benefits that you might derive.

Your choices as to valuing an asset are of course restricted by the income tax laws and regulations, and for this reason it is recommended that you consult an accountant or tax lawyer for advice on how to value any significant asset. You should be aware, though, of how establishing a cost for an asset has implications both for the valuation of a company and for its reported income.

Depreciating Assets

Depreciation, in accordance with the accrual principle, influences the timing of your company's earnings by matching revenues and costs. It is the means by which a company can spread the cost of an asset over its expected useful life. In other words, *depreciation* is the allocation of prior expenditures to future time periods, so as to match revenues and expenses.

Typically, you make the cash outlay to purchase an asset during the first year of the asset's useful life. The cash outlay itself is not reflected in the depreciation line of an income statement. Depreciation does not represent a cash outlay: it is a noncash charge that you use to match the first year's expenditure with the subsequent flow of revenue.

Suppose that you match the entire cost of an asset to the earnings shown in the income statement for the year you make the purchase. Your operating income for that year would then be lower than if you spread the cost over the asset's useful life. Furthermore, the following years of the asset's useful life would get a free ride. The asset will contribute to revenue generation, but the income statements in subsequent years would not reflect the associated expense.

Depreciation enables you to properly match the first year's expenditure to subsequent revenue (see fig. 16.2).

Fig. 16.2

The straight line method results in an equal amount of depreciation during each period.

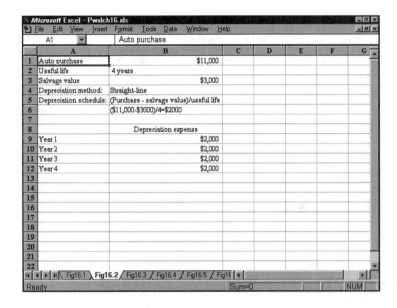

Suppose that your company purchases a vehicle to pick up materials from your suppliers and to deliver products to your customers. Figure 16.2 shows how the vehicle depreciates over a four-year period, which here is considered to be the asset's useful life. At the end of that period, the vehicle still has a *salvage* value: say, $3,000. The salvage value is subtracted from the purchase cost to obtain the amount that is depreciated: $8,000. The expense in each of the four years is therefore $2,000. By spreading the expense over the asset's useful life (instead of taking the entire expense during the first year) you can more accurately match the expense to the revenue the vehicle will help to produce.

If this company sold $20,000 annually in goods and services, the impact to operating profit would be substantial. During Year 1, without depreciation, earnings would be $20,000 – $8,000, or $12,000. During Year 1, with depreciation, earnings would be $20,000 – $2,000, or $18,000. The difference between the two calculations is $6,000, or 30% of the company's annual revenue.

Four items are needed to determine the annual amount of depreciation:

- The asset's useful life

- The asset's original cost

- The asset's salvage value (its value at the end of its useful life)

- The depreciation method employed

There are two general methods of allocating an asset's cost over its useful life: *straight-line depreciation* and *accelerated depreciation*. Under the straight-line method, you depreciate the asset by a constant amount each year, as shown in figure 16.2.

The second general method of depreciation is actually a family of techniques, together known as accelerated depreciation. Each accelerated technique charges more depreciation in the early years of an asset's life and less in later years. Accelerated depreciation does not enable a company to take more depreciation in total, but simply alters the timing of the depreciation.

The basic rationale for accelerated depreciation is the recognition that when an asset is new, it tends to operate more efficiently than after it has been in service for several accounting periods. The presumption is that when the asset operates at a high level of efficiency, its contribution to the creation of revenue is greater than after its efficiency has declined. The timing of the acquisition expense—the depreciation—should reflect the asset's contribution to revenue creation. Therefore, more depreciation should be recognized earlier, and less later, during the asset's useful life.

This rationale is, of course, rather disingenuous. One effect of accelerated depreciation is to increase reported expenses, and thus to decrease reported income, during the early periods of an asset's useful life. In turn, this has the effect of reducing income taxes early on. If you suspect a political rationale for accelerated depreciation in addition to a rationale based on the matching principle, your suspicion is probably correct.

Excel offers several different methods to calculate depreciation. These are shown in figures 16.3 through 16.9.

Using Straight-line Depreciation

Straight-line is the simplest method to calculate an asset's depreciation. It is the cost of the asset, less its salvage value, divided by its number of years of useful life.

Excel's SLN function returns the amount of depreciation taken each year using the straight-line method. It requires three arguments: the asset's cost, its salvage value, and its useful life. Figure 16.3 shows these values (in named ranges on the worksheet), and the formula used in cells B6:B10 is:

On the Disk

```
=SLN(Cost,Salvage,Life)
```

The SLN function is the simplest of Excel's depreciation methods. It takes only three arguments, but gives you very little control over the amount of depreciation that occurs during any given accounting period.

Fig. 16.3

The total amount of depreciation taken over time, using straight-line depreciation, describes a straight line.

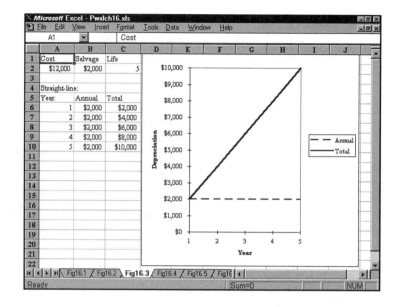

Using Declining Balance Depreciation

Figure 16.4 shows depreciation calculated by the *declining balance* (DB) method, one of the accelerated depreciation techniques.

Fig. 16.4

Depreciation using DB calculates depreciation based on the remaining, undepreciated value of the asset.

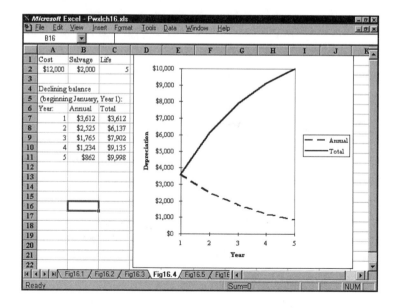

Excel's DB function returns the amount of depreciation taken each year using the declining balance method. This method calculates the depreciation each year according to the current value of the asset. (In contrast, the straight-line method uses the original value of the asset to return each year's depreciation.) The range B6:B10 in figure 16.4 contains this array-formula:

```
=DB(Cost,Salvage,Life,Year)
```

The ranges named Cost, Salvage, and Life are the same as in figure 16.3. The DB function requires one more argument than SLN. DB's fourth argument is the period for which it calculates the amount of depreciation. For clarity, that argument has been named Year, although Excel refers to it as Period. In figure 16.4, Year actually refers to the named range A7:A11.

On the Disk

Notice that there is a different amount of depreciation that is taken during each year. In this example, the amount of depreciation taken in each period is almost exactly 70% of the amount taken during the prior period.

There is nothing special about 70%: the ratio of the current period's depreciation to that of the prior period depends on the asset's original cost and the number of periods in its useful life. However, this ratio is always a constant figure with the DB function.

Also notice the slight inaccuracy induced by the DB function: the sum of the depreciation is $9,998 instead of $10,000. This is due to the fact that DB calculates a constant rate that it uses to obtain the depreciation in all periods following the first period. This constant factor is limited to three significant digits, which results in small rounding errors. See this chapter's section titled "Correcting Rounding Errors" for a method to correct these inaccuracies.

Declining Balance Depreciation, Incomplete Year

Figure 16.5 introduces a wrinkle to the DB function. DB can take a fifth argument, an optional one termed Month. By specifying this argument, you can take account of the fact that a purchase may have been made, not in the first month of the year, but well into the year. Figure 16.5 assumes that the purchase has been made at the end of June, and that depreciation begins in July.

Notice that the amount of depreciation during the first year is less than that in the second year. This reflects the fact that revenues have been matched to the cost of the asset during the second six months of the first year. It was during the second six months, not the full twelve months, that the asset was available to help produce revenue.

III

Investment Decisions

Fig. 16.5

When an asset is put into use part-way through a period, the matching principle states that depreciation should begin at that time.

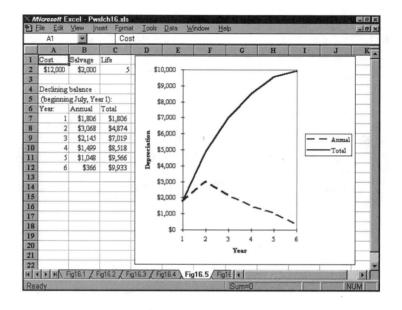

The formula used in cells B7:B12 of figure 16.5 is:

```
=DB(Cost,Salvage,Life,Year,6)
```

where 6 represents the number of months during which depreciation will be taken in Year 1 (July through December).

Also notice that figure 16.5 shows six years, not five as in figure 16.4. This is because the five years during which depreciation is taken begin halfway through Year 1 and end halfway into Year 6.

Correcting Rounding Errors

On the Disk

The inaccuracy induced by rounding error in the DB function is somewhat more severe in figure 16.5 than in 16.4. Here is a method to eliminate the rounding error in both cases. It assumes that you have set up your worksheet as shown in figures 16.4 and 16.5 (or that you use the worksheets containing these figures, found in this chapter's workbook on the companion disk), with the appropriate named cells and ranges (Cost, Salvage, and Life):

1. In some empty cell such as A15, enter this formula:

   ```
   =1-((Salvage/Cost)^(1/Life))
   ```

2. With A15 selected, choose <u>E</u>dit, <u>C</u>opy. Then, choose <u>E</u>dit, Paste <u>S</u>pecial and check the <u>V</u>alues radio button in the Paste Special dialog box. This converts the formula to a value. (It is necessary to have a value in this cell because you will be using it as the <u>c</u>hanging cell for the Goal Seek

command in step 8, and Goal Seek requires that the changing cell contain a value, not a formula.) Choose OK.

3. Name cell A15 as Rate: with A15 still selected, click in the Name Box, type *Rate*, and press Enter.

4. In another empty cell such as A17, enter this formula:

```
=Cost*Rate*12/12
```

where you would use 12/12 for 12 months of depreciation in the first year (thus, depreciation begins in the first month, as in figure 16.4). Or, you could use 6/12 for 6 months of depreciation in the first year (thus, depreciation begins in the seventh month, as in figure 16.5).

5. In A18, enter this formula:

```
=(Cost-SUM($A$17:A17))*Rate
```

> ### Tip
>
> The formula shown in step 5 uses a combination of an absolute reference ($A$17) and a relative reference (A17). This is a standard and useful technique to create a running total. As the formula is copied or dragged into other cells, the absolute reference does not change, but the relative reference does.

Copy this formula, and paste it into cells A19:A21. The formula in A21 should now be:

```
=(Cost-SUM($A$17:A20))*Rate
```

6. In cell A22, enter this formula:

```
=((Cost-SUM(A17:A21))*Rate*(12))/12
```

for depreciation starting in January, or

```
=((Cost-SUM(A17:A21))*Rate*(6))/12
```

for depreciation starting in July.

7. In cell A23, enter this formula:

```
=SUM(A17:A22)
```

8. With cell A23 selected, choose Tools, Goal Seek. The Set cell will be A23.

9. In the To value box, enter 10000 (or whatever the difference is between the asset's cost and its salvage value).

III

Investment Decisions

10. In the By changing cell box, enter A15, or highlight cell A15 after clicking in the By changing cell box.

11. Choose OK.

The Goal Seek tool now adjusts the value of Rate, in cell A15, so that the sum of the depreciation taken equals the difference between the cost of the asset and its salvage value. In essence, you will have duplicated the DB function, but without its errors of rounding.

Using Double Declining Balance Depreciation

Figure 16.6 shows how you can accelerate depreciation even faster than with the declining balance method. It shows the results of using Excel's DDB (double declining balance) function.

Fig. 16.6

Depreciation using DDB (double declining balance) causes faster depreciation: compare with figures 16.4 and 16.5.

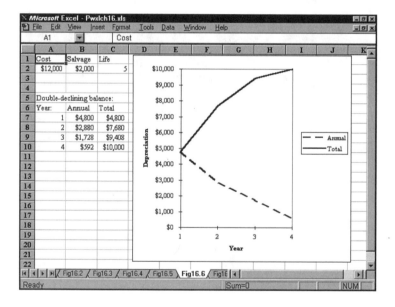

The DDB function used for the data in figure 16.6 is:

```
=DDB(Cost,Salvage,Life,Year,2)
```

Double declining balance doubles the rate that you would depreciate an asset under the straight-line method, and applies that rate to the original cost minus the sum of prior depreciation amounts.

Excel's DDB function allows you to use a value other than 2 as its fifth argument. If, for example, you did not want to double the straight-line rate per period, but instead use 1.5 times that rate, you could enter:

```
=DDB(Cost,Salvage,Life,Year,1.5)
```

Using Variable Declining Balance Depreciation

The *variable declining balance* function (VDB) is the most flexible (and the most complex) of Excel's depreciation functions. VDB's general syntax is:

```
=VDB(Cost,Salvage,Life,StartPeriod,EndPeriod,Factor,NoSwitch)
```

The Cost, Salvage, and Life arguments operate in exactly the same way as with the other depreciation functions. The Factor argument operates as it does in the DDB function: the larger the Factor argument, the faster that depreciation accumulates.

The StartPeriod and EndPeriod arguments enable you to focus on a particular time period during the asset's useful life. For example, to obtain the depreciation on an asset during the first year of a five-year Life, you could use this formula:

On the Disk

```
=VDB(Cost,Salvage,5,0,1,Factor,NoSwitch)
```

where using a StartPeriod of 0 and a StopPeriod of 1 specifies a span of time from when the asset is first placed in service until the end of the first period. Similarly,

```
=VDB(Cost,Salvage,5,0,.5,Factor,NoSwitch)
```

returns the depreciation on the asset during the first half of the first period. And this formula:

```
=VDB(Cost,Salvage,5,1,3,Factor,NoSwitch)
```

returns the *total* depreciation on the asset that occurs during the second and third periods of its 5-period life.

The NoSwitch argument is a little convoluted. Suppose that you specify a depreciation factor low enough that the asset does not fully depreciate to its salvage value during its useful life. Figure 16.7 illustrates this situation.

Fig. 16.7

Depreciation using VDB (variable declining balance): NoSwitch is FALSE, so Excel switches to straight-line depreciation.

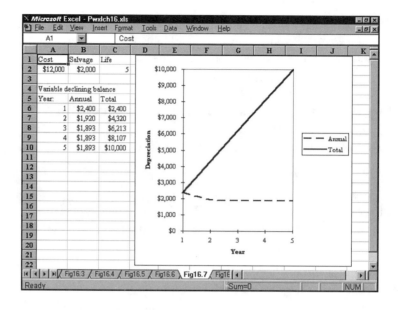

The array-formula used to return the annual depreciation amounts shown in figure 16.7 is:

```
=VDB(Cost, Salvage, Life, Year-1, Year,1,FALSE)
```

The depreciation factor is 1, and the NoSwitch argument is FALSE. Setting the NoSwitch argument to FALSE means that VDB switches to straight-line depreciation in the event that, and when, the straight-line depreciation for that period would be greater than the depreciation under declining balance. In figure 16.7, the total accumulated depreciation over the five years of the asset's useful life is $8,068. This situation arises because the depreciation factor, 1, is so low that depreciation does not accumulate fast enough to fully depreciate the asset to its salvage value during five periods.

Note

Excel 7's help file information for the VDB function is worded poorly. The explanation in this section is the correct one.

Tip

Recall that accelerated depreciation methods depreciate faster early on than does the straight-line method. This means that they depreciate more slowly toward the *end* of the asset's useful life. Setting NoSwitch to FALSE causes VDB to use straight-line depreciation at the point that straight-line begins to depreciate faster than VDB.

This can occur when tax accounting regulations for a particular type of asset limit your accelerated depreciation factor to a relatively low value, given your estimate of the asset's useful life.

If you set the NoSwitch argument to TRUE, the VDB function *does not* switch to straight-line depreciation (see fig. 16.8).

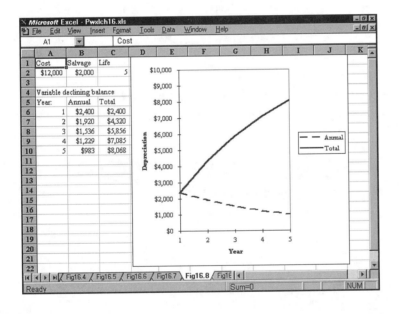

Fig. 16.8
Depreciation using VDB (variable declining balance): NoSwitch is TRUE, so VDB does not switch to the straight-line method.

The array-formula used to return the depreciation in figure 16.8 is:

```
=VDB(Cost, Salvage, Life, Year-1, Year,1,TRUE)
```

On the Disk

Notice that, with NoSwitch set to TRUE, VDB continues to return smaller depreciation amounts in each period. The result is that the asset is not depreciated to its salvage value at the end of the final period. VDB would, however, fully depreciate the asset if the depreciation factor were, say, 2 instead of 1—in fact, it would depreciate the asset by the end of the fourth period.

III

Investment Decisions

Setting the NoSwitch argument to FALSE, as in figure 16.7, causes the VDB function to return constant, straight-line depreciation values for periods three through five ($1,893). As has been discussed, one effect of this is to fully depreciate the asset to its salvage value by the end of the fifth period. Notice that the total depreciation by the end of the fifth period is $10,000, which is the difference between the asset's cost ($12,000) and its salvage value ($2,000).

Another effect of setting NoSwitch to FALSE is to increase the amount of depreciation taken in period 3: $1,893 in figure 16.7 versus $1,596 in figure 16.8.

Tip

You can replicate VDB explicitly with simple worksheet formulas. For any period, VDB is: =MIN(Cost-Salvage-TotalSoFar),BookValue*Factor/Life) where TotalSoFar is the total depreciation taken in prior periods and BookValue is Cost-TotalSoFar.

Using Sum-of-Years'-Digits Depreciation

Yet another method of accelerated depreciation, sum-of-years'-digits, is shown in figure 16.9.

Fig. 16.9
The SYD (sum-of-years'-digits) method is easy to understand, but gives you little control in situations such as mid-year asset purchases.

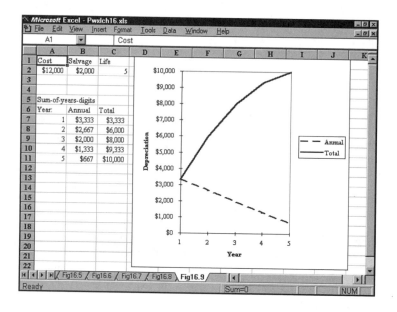

This method, which is used in Excel's SYD function, sums the number of years of the asset's useful life. For example, if the useful life is five years, the sum would be 1 + 2 + 3 + 4 + 5 = 15. Each year, this sum is divided into the *remaining* years of useful life. For example, during the first year, the fraction would be 4/15; during the second year, the fraction would be 3/15, and so on. The appropriate fraction for each year is multiplied by the difference between the asset's cost and its salvage value, to compute each year's depreciation expense.

Thus, in figure 16.9, $2,000 will be taken in depreciation during the third period. At the beginning of period 3, there are three periods remaining in the asset's useful life (period 3, period 4 and period 5). Three remaining periods divided by the sum of the years' digits is 3/15, or 20%. The difference between the cost and the salvage value is $12,000 – $2,000, or $10,000. Twenty percent of $10,000 is $2,000.

Summary

This chapter has discussed the process of valuing fixed assets—usually defined as a company's property, plant, and equipment—for the purposes of determining the company's worth as well as its income for an accounting period.

An asset contributes to the creation of a company's revenue during the time that it is in service. The principle of matching expenses to revenue over time suggests that some portion of the expense involved in acquiring the asset be attributed to the revenue created during an accounting period. This is done by means of depreciation: even though the entire cash outlay for the asset usually occurs during the first accounting period, this expense is distributed across the useful life of the asset.

Excel offers five methods of calculating depreciation: straight-line, declining balance, double declining balance, variable declining balance and sum-of-the-years'-digits. The latter four methods adopt an accelerated approach, under which more depreciation is allocated early during an asset's useful life, and less is allocated later.

With all these methods at hand to determine depreciation, how do you select the appropriate method? The tax laws allow you to use different methods depending on the type of asset that you are depreciating. It's wise to check with your accountant to determine which method you should use for a particular kind of asset.

III

Investment Decisions

> **Note**
>
> It is not required that a company use the same method of depreciation for tax purposes as it does for purposes such as internal planning or external reporting. Many businesses use an accelerated method in figuring their taxes, and straight-line depreciation when presenting financial information to, say, a bank.

The depreciation method that you choose has an impact on the earnings that you show for a given period. If you depreciate quickly, early profits tend to be understated: you expense more depreciation early on and therefore reduce the earnings for those periods. If you depreciate slowly, early profits tend to be overstated because you do not expense as much in earlier time periods as you would if you accelerated the depreciation.

This chapter concludes Part III, "Investment Decisions." Part IV, "Sales and Marketing," begins with a discussion of how to use Excel 7's new mapping tool to help make marketing decisions.

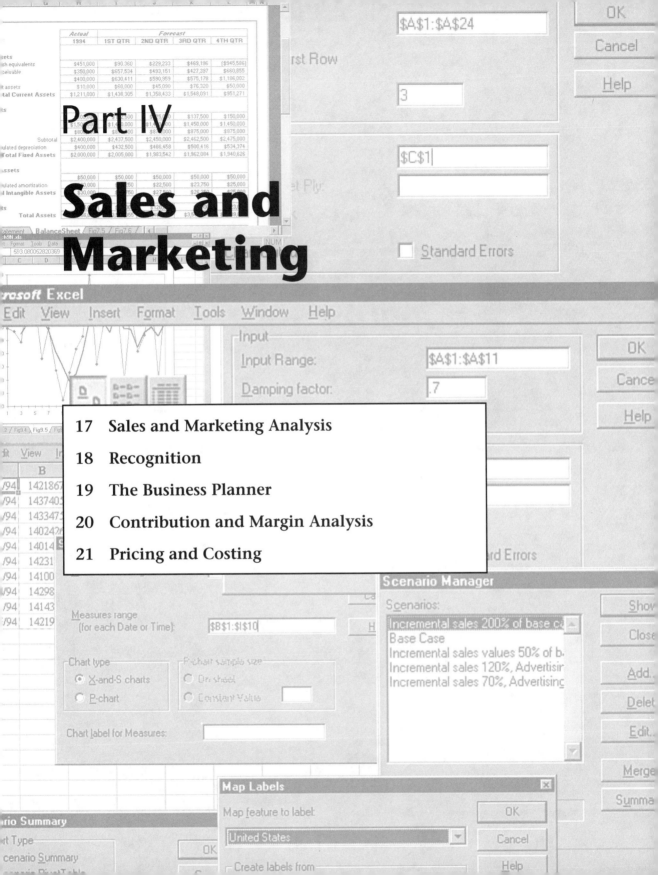

Part IV

Sales and Marketing

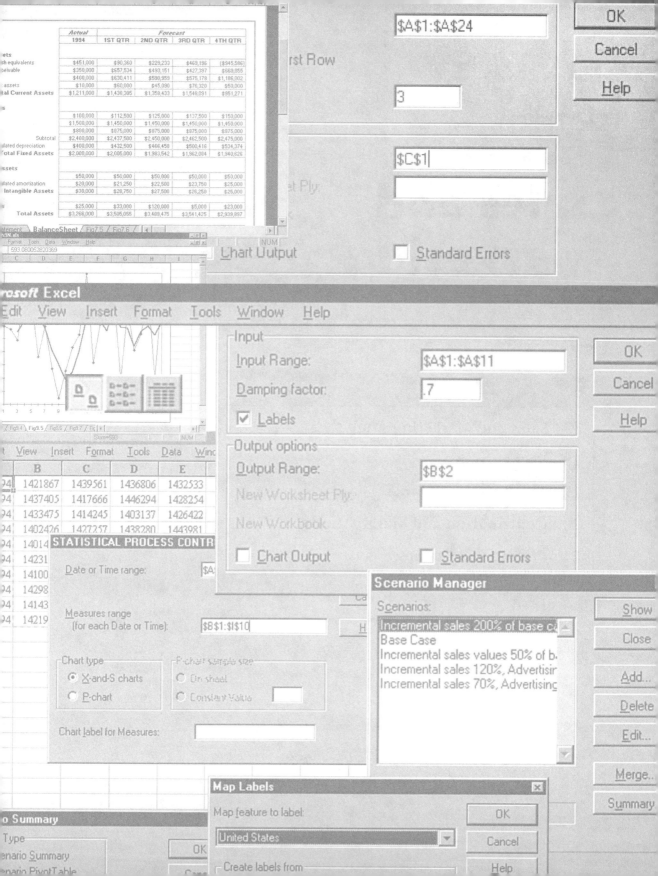

Chapter 17

Sales and Marketing Analysis

Excel has long offered a variety of tools that can help you analyze data about your profitability: among them, capabilities like Pivot Tables that summarize data descriptively, statistical functions like the Regression tool that analyze data inferentially, and charts that display descriptive data along with trendlines that provide inferential information.

In version 7, Excel provides an additional tool that can help you analyze data *geographically*, maps. By using this tool, you can put a map in your worksheet that displays information about data such as revenues, numbers of customers, percentage of earnings—any type of information that might vary on a geographical basis.

This tool is obviously useful for tasks such as creating visuals in reports. However, coupled with other capabilities in Excel, it is also useful for analysis: in particular, for understanding the results of an analysis by viewing them graphically.

Raw numbers seldom carry the impact of charts, maps, and graphs. By using Excel's Data Map, you can better understand the implications of geographic analyses that you do. This chapter describes how to use this tool, some of the traps involved with its usage, and techniques for using it efficiently. It also illustrates how to use the Data Map, a demographics file that accompanies version 7, the Analysis ToolPak and an add-in supplied on the *Business Analysis with Excel* companion disk that accompanies this book so as to perform an inferential analysis of sales revenues.

On the Disk

Understanding Mapping Requirements

You might have already experimented with Excel's Data Map, and discovered several aspects that are either undocumented or covered only briefly in its Help information. If not, this section might save you some time and grief.

When you first create a map in an Excel worksheet, you will notice that the operation takes a relatively long time. Also, saving and opening a workbook that contains a map are lengthy operations. This is largely because the files that support the maps—files that contain formatting information and data about different map elements—control the display of information in the map. Therefore, various housekeeping functions must occur during the open and close operations.

Note

When you first start Excel 7 after installing it, you should see the Map button on the Standard toolbar: it looks like a globe, and by default is located between the Chart Wizard and the Drawing buttons. If you do not find it on the Standard toolbar, you might need to reinstall Excel by running the Setup routine again, making sure that you choose to install all mapping options.

If you do see a button in that position on the Standard Toolbar, but it is blank, choose View, Toolbars and click the Reset button. If you installed version 7 without removing an earlier version of Excel, there might be a conflict in the files that control the appearance of the toolbars.

The process of creating the map is similar to that of creating a chart. You need a range of data on a worksheet that consists of at least one column. The one required column must contain geographic data of some sort: the name of states or countries, for example, or a list of ZIP codes. You may use *only one* column that contains geographic data. Usually, though, you will have more than one column to map. The additional columns can contain data that you want to include on the map, such as revenues or number of sales.

After you have a range of data on the worksheet, highlight it and click the Map button. This causes Excel to draw the map, as an embedded picture on the worksheet.

There are some key differences and similarities between the process of creating a map and that of creating a chart:

- After clicking the Map button, the mouse pointer changes to a crosshair. Excel waits for you to drag in the worksheet to specify the location and size of the map. This process is the same as that of creating an embedded chart; however, unlike charts, there is no provision for creating a map on its own sheet.

- Like charts, your data may be in noncontiguous ranges (for example, you could have names of states in column A and sales data in column C). Unlike charts, though, the Data Map requires that your data be in *columns*. All your geographic information must be in one column, and all your other information must be in another column or columns. Charts allow you to have one data series in one row, and another series in another row.

- Like charts, you must highlight the entire range that you want to appear on the map.

- Like charts, the columns in your highlighted range may have titles, such as "State," "Country," and "Revenues." If you choose to use column titles, then the title of the column that contains the geographic information must be recognizable as a geographic category. It cannot be a mnemonic or an abbreviation such as "Geocode."

   If you omit column titles, Excel attempts to match the geographic data you have provided with one of the mapping databases it has available. However, when you omit column titles, your variables (for example, "Revenues") are not labeled as such on the map; instead, Excel uses default labels such as "Column C."

- Unlike charts, clicking the Map button does not start a Wizard which poses questions and options for you to respond to. Instead, a series of messages appear, informing you of Excel's progress in creating the map, and possibly asking you to choose among options for map templates.

- Unlike charts, your "category" variable—usually, the geographic data such as state name—need not be in the leftmost column. The column containing the geographic data may be anywhere in your highlighted range. (The Chart Wizard makes the default assumption that your category, or x-axis, variable is in the leftmost column or topmost row.)

The combination of a pivot table with a map can be particularly powerful. Suppose that on a worksheet you have a variety of measurements for different geographic areas: for example, monthly total sales commissions in each of several states. You could create a pivot table that sums the sales commission in each state, displaying the annual sum on a state-by-state basis. After the pivot table appears on the worksheet, you could highlight the columns in the pivot table and map the information.

Note, though, that you would have to specify in the Pivot Table Wizard that "state" is a row variable. If you do so, each different value of "state" appears in a different row of the same column, and this conforms to the Data Map's requirement for the layout of the data: that each *variable* appear in a separate column. If you specify that "state" is a column variable, each *value* of "state" appears in a separate column of the same row, and the Data Map will force you to choose one, and only one, of those columns.

Creating a Map

With this as background, consider the worksheet displayed in figure 17.1.

Fig. 17.1

Sample sales data and map created by Excel 7's new Data Map.

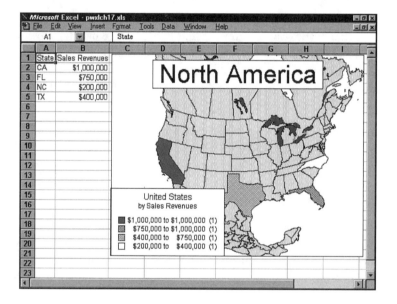

Notice that the geographic data, in column A, consists of abbreviations of state names. You can use abbreviations rather than state names (if you can remember the abbreviation for, say, Arizona) or you can type the full state name (if you spell and type accurately).

You can also use postal ZIP codes as your geographic data. If you do so, however, be sure to enter the ZIP codes as text: Excel will not recognize the ZIP codes as such if you enter them as numbers. To enter ZIP codes as text, precede each ZIP code with a single quotation mark.

> **Tip**
>
> If you have so many ZIP codes to map that it is inconvenient to type a single quotation mark before each one, there's a shortcut. Highlight the ZIP code range and choose Format, Cells to format the range as text.

The map shown in figure 17.1 was created this way:

1. Highlight the range A1:B5.

2. Click the Map button. The mouse pointer changes to crosshairs.

3. Drag in the worksheet to establish the location and size of the map.

4. When you release the mouse button, Excel begins to create the map.

During the process of creating the map, Excel determines that there is more than one template available that contains the states contained in A2:A5. (A template is simply a map that is included with Excel 7. The template has data that describe for example, where state boundaries are and other default formatting information.) One template contains all 50 states in their actual orientation, and another template displays Alaska and Hawaii as insets. Choose whichever you want; the map in figure 17.1 was created using the former template.

Notice the map's legend. It displays the shading used for each of the four states named in cells A2:A5. You can arrange for this kind of legend by taking these steps:

1. Double-click the map to open it for editing. Excel's main menu is replaced by the menu for data maps.

2. Choose Tools, Options. The dialog box shown in figure 17.2 appears.

3. Clear the Compact Legends by Default checkbox.

4. Choose OK.

The next time you create a map, Excel will use a verbose legend, such as is shown in figure 17.1. You can also change the format of a legend in an active map by double-clicking on the legend, and changing the status of the Use Compact Format checkbox in the Edit Legend dialog box.

Fig. 17.2
The Data Map
Options dialog
box lets you speed
up map creation,
set a map's metric,
and control the
size of map
legends.

Notice also the shading—the patterns—in the four states on the map and in the legend. Unlike the patterns used in the various areas of charts, the shading patterns in maps are not under your control. Each time you add another data point to the original worksheet range, another shading pattern becomes available to the value shading on the map.

Using the Map Toolbar

When you have created the map, a new toolbar appears. You can find it in figure 17.2 directly below the main map menu. It contains buttons to change the mouse pointer to an arrow that you use to select objects in the map, to zoom in and out, to insert labels and text, and so on. Each button of course has a ToolTip associated with it; simply position your mouse pointer over the button to see a brief description of its function.

> **Tip**
>
> If you do not see a ToolTip, close the map by clicking in some worksheet cell. Choose View, Toolbars and check the Show Tooltips checkbox. Then, double-click on the map to reopen it and move your mouse pointer over each button in the Data Map toolbar to see its function.

When you have clicked some of these buttons, you must then click somewhere on the map to complete the button's function. For example, clicking the Zoom In button does not by itself increase the size of the map within its frame. To do so, you must first click the button and then click within the map. Other buttons that behave in this fashion are the Select Objects (arrow) button, the Zoom Out button, the Grabber (hand) button, the Map Labels button, the text button, and the Custom Pin Map button.

An interesting and useful feature of the Map Labels button (immediately to the right of the Grabber button) is that it displays labels on the map as you move your mouse pointer over a geographic area included in your worksheet range. Using the data shown in figures 17.1 and 17.2, for example, clicking the Map Labels button would bring up the Map Labels dialog box (see fig. 17.3).

Fig. 17.3
Use the Map Labels dialog box to choose shading that distinguishes categories or values.

Suppose that you click the Map Feature Names radio button, and choose OK. If you now place your mouse pointer over, say, Texas, a box appears temporarily that displays "TX." If you place the mouse pointer over a map element that is not included in the original data range, the box displays Excel's name for that element. For example, using the map in figure 17.3, placing the pointer over Oregon displays "OREGON."

If, on the other hand, you choose the Values From option button, placing your mouse pointer over Texas would cause the box to display the value associated with Texas, which is $400,000. If you click your mouse button at this point, the temporary label will be attached to the map itself.

Using the Data Map Control

The button on the extreme right of the map toolbar toggles the Data Map Control on and off. This Control appears in figure 17.4.

The Data Map Control enables you to change the formatting of your map. It contains three main elements: column buttons (labeled Count of State and Sales Revenues in figure 17.3), six format buttons found at the left of the control, and a format box in the lower-right quadrant of the control. You drag the column and format buttons into and out of the format box to change the formatting in your map.

The map in figures 17.1 through 17.4 uses value shading: that is, the shading of each state named in worksheet cells A2:A5 is based on its associated value in cells B2:B5. To change the shading option from value shading to category shading, you would position your mouse pointer over the category shading button (the format button in the first row, second column of the format button group). Your mouse pointer changes to a drawer pull. Hold down the mouse button and drag the format button to the right, over the existing value shading button in the format box. When you release the mouse button, the map changes from shading that represents values to shading that represents categories.

You can show categories and values on the map at the same time by using either the dot density button (format buttons, second row, first column) or the graduated symbol button (format buttons, second row, second column). To do so:

1. Position your mouse pointer over the Sales Revenue column button. Hold down the mouse button and drag the column button into the format box.

2. Usually, the dot density button will automatically appear in the format box. If it does not, drag the dot density button into the format box, just to the left of the new Sales Revenue column button.

Fig. 17.4
The Data Map Control dialog box is the key to structuring most of the features on your map.

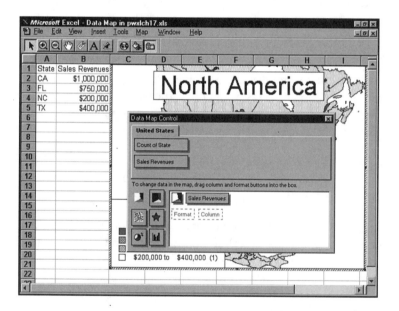

The map now has both category shading and dot density shading, and a legend for each type of shading. The effect is shown in figure 17.5.

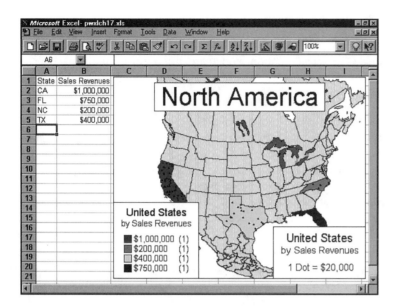

Fig. 17.5
You can combine category shading and dot density to distinguish both categories and values simultaneously.

The greater the number of dots in a geographic area, the greater its associated value.

Using the Demographic Data File

Version 7 of Excel also comes with a file named Mapstats.xls. This is a workbook file that contains information about different map elements. For example, Mapstats.xls has a worksheet named USA. That worksheet has demographic information on each of fifty states, including the following variables:

- Population for 1990, 1994, and projected for 1999

- 1990, 1994, and 1999 population by sex

- 1994 population by age group, and by age group by sex

- 1994 population by ethnicity

- Number of households during 1990, 1994, and 1999, and average household size

- Median household income, and number of households with income under $25,000, from $25,000 to $49,000, and over $50,000

- Total number of businesses and total employment

The file also contains worksheets with data for world countries, for Canadian provinces, Mexican states, European countries, the United Kingdom, and Australia. (The specific data provided are different for each worksheet.)

> **Note**
>
> The Help information in early versions of Excel 7 states that the Mapstats.xls file is installed in the directory path \Windows\Msapps\Datamap\Data. However, these versions installed the Mapstats.xls file in \Program Files\Common Files\Microsoft Shared\Datamap\Data (in DOSspeak, the path is \Progra~1\Common~1\Micros~1 \Datamap\Data). You might need to use Tools, Find, Files or Folders in the Windows Explorer to locate Mapstats.xls.

The full range of data in each worksheet is referred to by a global name. This makes it easy to jump to a particular data set by selecting its name from the Name box.

How can all the information in Mapstats.xls help you? It enables you to put business data into context. Suppose that you are in charge of sales for a large company with territories in 27 states. You have defined five regional sales territories, each containing several states, and each run by a regional sales manager.

You are preparing to analyze regional performance for the year that has just ended. The basic data appear in figure 17.6.

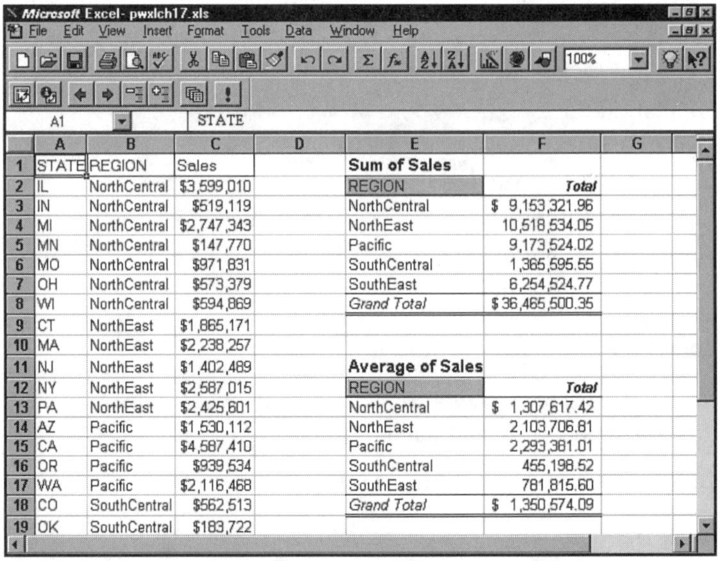

	A	B	C	D	E	F
1	STATE	REGION	Sales		Sum of Sales	
2	IL	NorthCentral	$3,599,010		REGION	Total
3	IN	NorthCentral	$519,119		NorthCentral	$ 9,153,321.96
4	MI	NorthCentral	$2,747,343		NorthEast	10,518,534.05
5	MN	NorthCentral	$147,770		Pacific	9,173,524.02
6	MO	NorthCentral	$971,831		SouthCentral	1,365,595.55
7	OH	NorthCentral	$573,379		SouthEast	6,254,524.77
8	WI	NorthCentral	$594,869		Grand Total	$ 36,465,500.35
9	CT	NorthEast	$1,865,171			
10	MA	NorthEast	$2,238,257			
11	NJ	NorthEast	$1,402,489		Average of Sales	
12	NY	NorthEast	$2,587,015		REGION	Total
13	PA	NorthEast	$2,425,601		NorthCentral	$ 1,307,617.42
14	AZ	Pacific	$1,530,112		NorthEast	2,103,706.81
15	CA	Pacific	$4,587,410		Pacific	2,293,381.01
16	OR	Pacific	$939,534		SouthCentral	455,198.52
17	WA	Pacific	$2,116,468		SouthEast	781,815.60
18	CO	SouthCentral	$562,513		Grand Total	$ 1,350,574.09
19	OK	SouthCentral	$183,722			

Fig. 17.6
A pivot table is a useful method to summarize data before creating a map.

The total sales for the year, within each state, are shown in column C of figure 17.6. As a first step in your analysis, you create a pivot table that shows the total sales for each region. This pivot table appears in cells E1:F8 of figure 17.6.

> **Tip**
>
> The pivot table in figure 17.6 is formatted to show the total sales values as currency. When you initially create a pivot table, the value field is displayed in General format. If you want to apply some other format such as Currency, you can highlight the appropriate cells and use Format, Cells to apply that format.
>
> However, if you subsequently modify the pivot table by pivoting it or by changing its calculation method from, say, Sum to Average, the formatting reverts to General.
>
> To apply a format that follows the Data Field as the table pivots, as you change the calculation method, or as you make some other change to the pivot table, first highlight one of the table's Data Field values. Choose Data, Pivot Table Field, and click Number. You will see the standard Number format dialog box. Select a format and then choose OK. Setting the format in this way lets you modify the pivot table without having to re-apply the format that you want.

After creating the pivot table in figure 17.6, you note that the South Central region has contributed relatively little to your company's revenues this year. However, there are fewer states in that region than in other regions, and to obtain a fairer comparison your next step is to create another pivot table that calculates the average revenue per state in each region. This pivot table is also shown in figure 17.6, in cells E11:F18.

Even correcting for the number of states in each region by displaying the sales data as an average across states, the South Central region still appears to have performed relatively poorly during the year.

(Note, by the way, that the summary information in the final row of the Average Sales pivot table, in cells E18:F18, contains a misleading label. The "Grand Total" designation in cell E18 is not the total of the average sales per state, but rather is the overall average of all the states' sales, without regard to region.)

As your company's Director of Sales, should you take some reorganizational action that changes the way that regional sales management handles its responsibilities in the South Central region? If you do so, what about the Southeast region, whose average sale per state is also well below the overall average per state? Perhaps a sweeping overhaul of the sales organization is required.

Understanding the Analysis of Variance

Before taking any drastic steps, you decide to investigate a little further. It's possible that the differences among the regions are random and unreliable. If the results that you see are not consistent, it would be unwise to make major organizational changes: the sales results might be entirely different next year, even if you make no changes in the way the regions are managed. How can you test whether these results are reliable?

One way is to use the ANOVA tool included with Excel's Analysis ToolPak. *ANOVA* stands for *Analysis of Variance*, and is a statistical technique for testing the differences among averages. (If you have just two averages to test, as you would if you had only two sales regions, you would use the T-test tool in the Analysis ToolPak, or the TTEST worksheet function. You normally use the ANOVA tool when you have more than two averages to compare.)

To access Excel's ANOVA tool, it's necessary to install it by following these steps:

1. Choose Tools, Add-Ins.

2. Check the checkbox labeled Analysis ToolPak - VBA in the Add-Ins Available list box. If this checkbox does not appear in the list box, you will need to run Setup again, making sure to install the ToolPak add-in.

3. Choose OK.

After the Analysis ToolPak has been installed, a new item appears in the Tools menu: Data Analysis. This item gives you access to a variety of financial, statistical, and engineering analysis functions and tools.

To perform the ANOVA analysis, you need to organize your data in a particular fashion, one that is required by the ANOVA add-in. Figure 17.7 displays the required data format.

Notice that the data for each of the five regions is now in a separate column, with the region's name in the first row. Figure 17.7 also shows the ANOVA: Single Factor dialog box, in which you enter information that defines the analysis. To bring up this dialog box, choose Tools, Data Analysis from the menu, highlight the Anova: Single Factor item in the Analysis Tools list box, and choose OK.

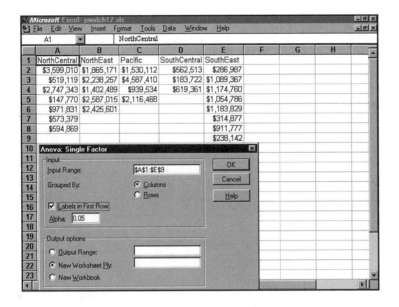

Fig. 17.7
Each value of the factor in a Single Factor ANOVA must appear in a different column or different row.

In the dialog box, make sure that the following items are chosen or filled in:

- Click in the Input Range edit box, and highlight the worksheet range A1:E9.

- Make sure that the Columns option button is selected.

- Make sure that the Labels in First Row checkbox is checked.

- You can leave the Alpha edit box with its default value of 0.05, or change it to some other decimal value between 0 and 1 if you want. The default is a conventional but arbitrary value in the testing of statistical significance. If you choose to change it, be sure that you understand the implications of doing so: for further information, consult any intermediate level statistics textbook.

- If you want the analysis output to appear on the currently selected worksheet, select the Output Range option button. If you want it to appear on a new worksheet, select the New Worksheet Ply option button, and for a new workbook, select the New Workbook option button.

Tip

If you change the default selection in the Output options group box, be sure to enter the Range or Ply information carefully. When you select a different option button, the focus in the dialog box returns to the Input Range edit box, and you do not want to enter, say, the output range address in the Input Range box.

When you have finished entering the information in the dialog box choose OK. The output shown in figure 17.8 appears. (Depending on the width of your worksheet's columns, you might see a different number of decimals in the output.)

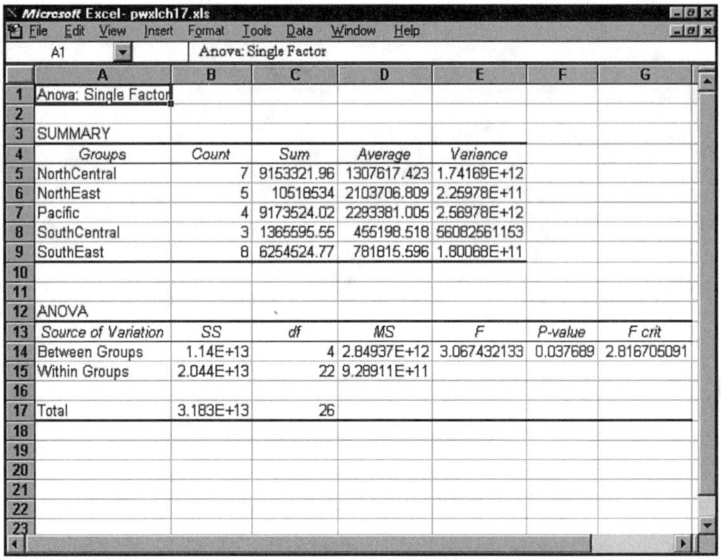
Microsoft Excel- pwxlch17.xls
File Edit View Insert Format Tools Data Window Help
A1 Anova: Single Factor

	A	B	C	D	E	F	G
1	Anova: Single Factor						
2							
3	SUMMARY						
4	Groups	Count	Sum	Average	Variance		
5	NorthCentral	7	9153321.96	1307617.423	1.74169E+12		
6	NorthEast	5	10518534	2103706.809	2.25978E+11		
7	Pacific	4	9173524.02	2293381.005	2.56978E+12		
8	SouthCentral	3	1365595.55	455198.518	56082561153		
9	SouthEast	8	6254524.77	781815.596	1.80068E+11		
10							
11							
12	ANOVA						
13	Source of Variation	SS	df	MS	F	P-value	F crit
14	Between Groups	1.14E+13	4	2.84937E+12	3.067432133	0.037689	2.816705091
15	Within Groups	2.044E+13	22	9.28911E+11			
16							
17	Total	3.183E+13	26				
18							
19							
20							
21							
22							
23							

Fig. 17.8 The ANOVA helps you determine whether differences among averages are dependable.

The first portion of the ANOVA results, in cells A3:E9, are simply a report of descriptive statistics for each region: the count of observations, and the sum, average, and variance of sales in the region.

The second portion, in cells A13:G17, contains the inferential information: that is, the data that address the question of the reliability of the observed sales results. The key finding is in cell F14, the P-value (Probability-value), and its interpretation is a little convoluted.

Suppose that you were to measure the sales results in each of the five regional territories over a period of many years. Also suppose that there is *no real difference* in average sales among the regions during that time. Under the assumption of no real difference in average sales, what is the likelihood that you would observe differences as large as the ones in the current year's data—differences that can be attributed solely to chance?

After all, there's a multitude of random factors that affect sales results. Temporary fluctuations in consumer confidence, turnover in sales personnel and changes in their assignments, modifications to a product line, redefined commission plans, changes in technology, and various other events both within and beyond your control all affect sales figures. What you are after is an answer to this question: Given that there is some randomness in the system, are the differences in sales results among my sales regions systematic or entirely random?

ANOVA enables you to assess the probability of observing the differences as large as those you observed under the assumption that the observed differences are due to chance conditions. In this case, that probability level, or p-value, is .0376 (fig. 17.8, cell F14). That is, the likelihood that you would observe differences this large by chance is less than 4 percent It's more rational to conclude that the differences are real, reliable, and consistent (a 96 percent probability) than it is to conclude that they are random (a 4 percent probability).

Before you reassign your regional sales managers, though, you decide to take another, closer look, and it's here that the information in Mapstats.xls comes into play.

Understanding the Analysis of Covariance

You have already accounted for the fact that the different regions have different numbers of states by examining the average number of sales dollars contributed by each region. Doing so gave you a clearer picture of sales results than just examining total sales results for each region. However, the five regions have different demographics and economic conditions: each state has a different population size, and also has a different median income level. These are nonrandom marketplace differences that almost surely have an effect on your sales results in any given state.

You can control for these differences in demographics by an extension to ANOVA, termed ANCOVA—the *Analysis of Covariance*. Because variables such as population size and median income have an effect on sales levels, they *covary* with sales: changes in one variable are associated with changes in another variable. You would, for example, expect that a state with a larger population would return a higher level of sales. You have access to these data in the Mapstats.xls workbook.

By performing an ANCOVA, you are asking whether you would observe differences in sales results as large as these *if each region had the same population and median income*. ANCOVA allows you to equate each region in terms of the population and median income of the states that compose it. Then, given that all five regions had the same value on these two variables, would the differences in sales results shrink, increase or stay the same?

(Of course, ANCOVA does not care what variables you use to equate the sales regions: the preceding paragraph cites population and median income only as an example of how you can use the technique with the data in the Mapstats.xls file.)

Excel does not provide an ANCOVA tool as it does an ANOVA tool. On the *Business Analysis with Excel* companion disk that accompanies this book, however, you will find an add-in named ANCOVA.xla. By installing it by choosing of Tools, Add-Ins, just as you do with the ANOVA tool, you will be able to perform Analysis of Covariance. Copy ANCOVA.xla and ANCOVA.hlp onto your main disk drive, and install ANCOVA.xla as an add-in. When you have done so, a new menu item, ANCOVA, appears at the bottom of the Data menu.

The ANCOVA add-in extends the capability of the ANOVA tool in ways other than illustrated here. For example, there are actually three ANOVA tools that accompany Excel: the other two allow you to analyze not just one variable such as Region, but another independent variable as well. The limit, however, is two independent variables. The ANCOVA add-in allows for as many independent variables as you choose to define (within limits: see the ANCOVA Help file for more information).

Furthermore, the ANOVA tools require that there be an equal number of observations in each cell. The ANCOVA add-in allows you to have unequal numbers of observations. And, unlike the two-factor ANOVA tools, ANCOVA accounts properly for missing data.

Additionally, the ANCOVA add-in does not require that you rearrange your worksheet data as does the ANOVA add-in. To run ANCOVA on the sales and region data, taking into account the states' population sizes and median incomes, the data can be laid out as shown in figure 17.9.

You can, of course, put demographic data found in Mapstats.xls into any worksheet by opening Mapstats.xls, selecting the range of demographic data that you want, copying it, and then pasting it into your own worksheet.

When you choose the ANCOVA item from the Data menu, the General Linear Model dialog box (also shown in fig. 17.9) appears. To analyze the data in figure 17.9, click in the Range of dependent variable edit box and highlight cells E1:E28. Click in the Range of independent variables edit box, and highlight cells B1:D28. Check the Labels in first row checkbox, and choose OK.

The Independent Variable Definition dialog box appears (see fig. 17.10).

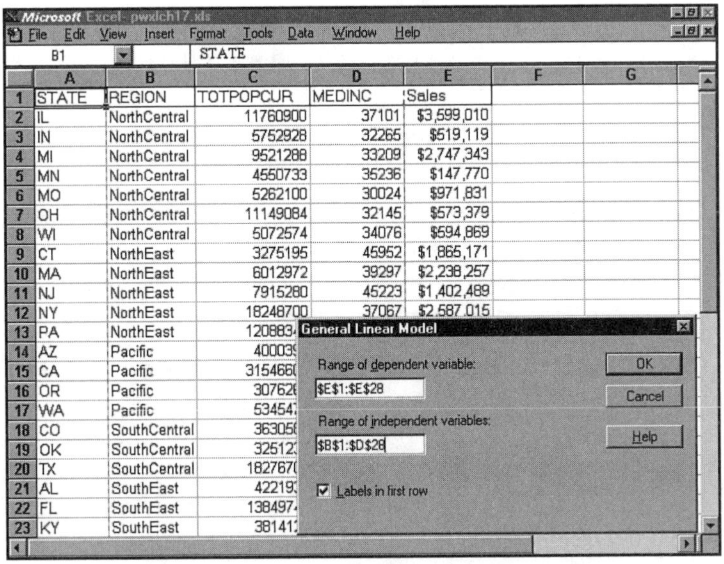

Fig. 17.9
Annual sales, population, and income data by region, arranged for ANCOVA.

Fig. 17.10
ANCOVA's Independent Variable Definition dialog box lets you identify variables as either factors or covariates.

The Independent Variable list box names the independent variables chosen in the General Linear Model list box. Each independent variable may be either a factor or a covariate.

A *factor* is a variable whose values are categories: ANCOVA tests the differences in the dependent variable—sales—according to its average for each value of the factor. A *covariate* is a continuous numeric variable—here, total current population and median income from the Mapstats.xls file—that is used to adjust the dependent variable as though each region started with the same population size and median income.

Highlight the variable name REGION in the list box. Notice that the Factor option button is already selected. Click the Define this variable button. An "(F)" appears after the variable name REGION in the list box, indicating that you have defined it as a factor.

Highlight the variable named TOTPOPCUR in the list box (this variable represents each state's total current population) and select the Covariate option button. Then click the Define this variable button. A "(C)" appears after the variable name in the list box, indicating that you have defined it as a covariate. Also define the variable MEDINC (median income) as a covariate.

Notice that the p to remove covariate by factor interaction edit box becomes available as soon as you define the TOTPOPCUR variable as a covariate. This box is dimmed until at least one variable has been defined as a factor, and at least one has been defined as a covariate.

When ANCOVA goes through the process of equating each region with each other region as to its states' populations and median incomes, it assumes that the correlation between sales and population (and between sales and income) is the same within each region. The value in the p to remove covariate by factor interaction edit box provides ANCOVA with a means to test this assumption. If the test indicates that the assumption is valid, ANCOVA proceeds normally and makes the necessary adjustments. If the test indicates that the assumption is not valid, ANCOVA does *not* make adjustments, but returns, in its output range, information about the covariate that violated the assumption.

The *lower* the value that you enter in this edit box, the *more likely* that the test will regard as valid the assumption of equal correlations between the covariates and the dependent variable. For the purposes of this example, leave the value in the edit box at its default value of zero.

Finally, choose OK in the Independent Variable Definition dialog box. ANCOVA's Remove Effects from Design dialog box then appears. This dialog box is provided in case you want to omit any effects from the analysis. In many cases—although not in this example—ANCOVA generates interactions among independent variables as possible sources of variation in the dependent variable, in addition to the independent variables that you have already specified. This dialog box allows you to delete any such variables from the analysis if your hypothesis suggests that they are unimportant.

For the purposes of this example, do not choose any variables in the list box. After you choose OK, the results shown in figure 17.11 appear in a new worksheet.

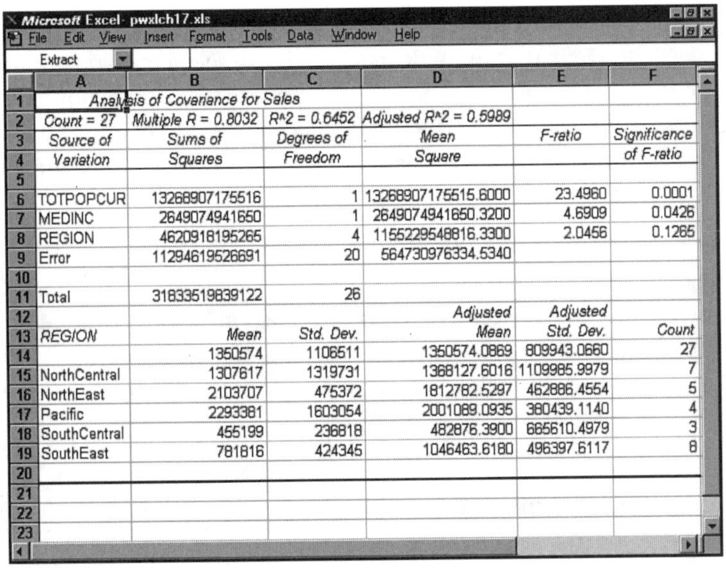

	A	B	C	D	E	F
1	Analysis of Covariance for Sales					
2	Count = 27	Multiple R = 0.8032	R^2 = 0.6452	Adjusted R^2 = 0.5989		
3	Source of	Sums of	Degrees of	Mean	F-ratio	Significance
4	Variation	Squares	Freedom	Square		of F-ratio
5						
6	TOTPOPCUR	13268907175516	1	13268907175515.6000	23.4960	0.0001
7	MEDINC	2649074941650	1	2649074941650.3200	4.6909	0.0426
8	REGION	4620918195265	4	1155229548816.3300	2.0456	0.1265
9	Error	11294619526691	20	564730976334.5340		
10						
11	Total	31833519839122	26			
12				Adjusted	Adjusted	
13	REGION	Mean	Std. Dev.	Mean	Std. Dev.	Count
14		1350574	1106511	1350574.0869	809943.0660	27
15	NorthCentral	1307617	1319731	1368127.6016	1109985.9979	7
16	NorthEast	2103707	475372	1812782.5297	462886.4554	5
17	Pacific	2293381	1603054	2001089.0935	380439.1140	4
18	SouthCentral	455199	236818	482876.3900	665610.4979	3
19	SouthEast	781816	424345	1046463.6180	496397.6117	8
20						
21						
22						
23						

Fig. 17.11
The Analysis of Covariance results for the regional sales data suggest that regional differences might not be dependable.

In the results shown in figure 17.11, the inferential portion of the analysis appears in the range A1:F11. Again, the key value for this analysis is in cell F8. It is 0.1265, and (although labeled "Significance of F-ratio") it has the same meaning as the "P-value" shown in figure 17.8.

Recall that, in the ANOVA analysis shown in figure 17.8, the p-value was .0376: less than 4 percent of the time would you observe differences in regional sales averages as large as these, if the differences were random occurrences. This finding led you to believe that the differences among the regions were consistent and reliable.

The ANCOVA results present a different picture. By taking into account the pre-existing differences in the sales regions as to population size and median income, it returns a p-value (or significance level) of .1265. In other words, it states that you would observe differences as large as these almost 13 percent of the time if the differences were due to chance.

Even so, it is still more rational to conclude that the differences are nonrandom and systematic (an 87 percent chance) than to conclude that they are due to chance (a 13 percent chance). However, taking into account the inevitable disruption to your sales organization if you were to make major changes in its staffing, functions, or structure, you might conclude that the chance that these results are random is too great to justify the disruption.

Or, you might not reach that conclusion. The interpretation of a significance level is a subjective matter: it all depends on how great a risk you are willing to accept that you are really observing a random result. One major purpose of techniques such as ANOVA and ANCOVA, however, is to quantify the risk for you. After the degree of risk has been measured, you are in a position to evaluate it.

Another major purpose of ANCOVA in this example, as discussed at the beginning of this section, is to adjust the values of the sales variable in such a way as to equate each region with each other region as to their population values and their median incomes. The section of the analysis shown in cells A12:F19 provides additional information about these adjustments.

(The third major purpose of ANCOVA is that it creates a more sensitive statistical analysis than does ANOVA. Discussion of this effect is beyond the scope of this book; for more information, consult an intermediate to advanced statistical textbook.)

Cells B14:C14 contain the overall average and standard deviation of sales, across all regions. Cells B15:C19 contain the average and standard deviation of sales for each region.

Cells D15:E19 contain the *adjusted* averages and standard deviations for each region (due to the mathematics of ANCOVA, the adjusted overall averages and standard deviations are the same as the observed averages and standard deviations).

Notice that the regions whose observed sales values were *below* the overall average sales level have been adjusted up; regions whose observed sales values were *above* the overall average sales level have been adjusted down. For example, the South Central region's observed average sales is $455,199. This value is below the overall average of $1,350,574. Its adjusted average sales value is $482,876.

In sum, after differences in population and income among the states that comprise the regions have been taken into account, their differences in adjusted average sales are less exaggerated. Again, there *may* be less reason for you to take action with respect to your regional sales management.

Displaying the Observed and Adjusted Values Geographically

It remains to convert the numeric results of the analysis to a visual format. To do so, it's necessary to convert the layout of the data to a form usable by Excel's Data Map (see fig. 17.12).

	A	B	C	D	E	F	G	H
1	REGION	STATE	Observed Mean	Adjusted Mean				
2	NorthCentral	IL	1307617.4225	1368127.6016				
3	NorthCentral	IN	1307617.4225	1368127.6016				
4	NorthCentral	MI	1307617.4225	1368127.6016				
5	NorthCentral	MN	1307617.4225	1368127.6016				
6	NorthCentral	MO	1307617.4225	1368127.6016				
7	NorthCentral	OH	1307617.4225	1368127.6016				
8	NorthCentral	WI	1307617.4225	1368127.6016				
9	NorthEast	CT	2103706.8090	1812782.5297				
10	NorthEast	MA	2103706.8090	1812782.5297				
11	NorthEast	NJ	2103706.8090	1812782.5297				
12	NorthEast	NY	2103706.8090	1812782.5297				
13	NorthEast	PA	2103706.8090	1812782.5297				
14	Pacific	AZ	2293381.0055	2001089.0935				
15	Pacific	CA	2293381.0055	2001089.0935				
16	Pacific	OR	2293381.0055	2001089.0935				
17	Pacific	WA	2293381.0055	2001089.0935				
18	SouthCentral	CO	455198.5180	482876.3900				
19	SouthCentral	OK	455198.5180	482876.3900				
20	SouthCentral	TX	455198.5180	482876.3900				
21	SouthEast	AL	781815.5961	1046463.6180				
22	SouthEast	FL	781815.5961	1046463.6180				
23	SouthEast	KY	781815.5961	1046463.6180				

Fig. 17.12
Analysis of Covariance results laid out for mapping: each state in a given region has the same observed and adjusted mean.

There are four columns displayed in figure 17.12: Region, State, Observed Mean, and Adjusted Mean (*mean* is simply another term for *average*). Of these, only the latter three are used to create a map.

There is no generally accepted meaning for the term "region," and Excel would not be able to interpret it as a legitimate geographic location: it is included in the worksheet only to help keep straight which state belongs to which region.

The geographic information that defines where to draw the data is the State variable. Each state belongs to a region, and each region has only one value for average observed sales and for average adjusted sales. Therefore, each state in a given region has the same value for observed sales and adjusted sales: the average value for the region to which the state belongs.

The map is created by highlighting the cells in the range B1:D28 and clicking the Map button on the Standard toolbar. After the mouse pointer turns to crosshairs, drag in the worksheet to locate and size the map.

> ## Tip
>
> You cannot drag in *another* worksheet to create the map. If your data are located in, say, Sheet1, you must create the map in Sheet1. However, after Excel has finished drawing the map and returned control to you, you can click in some worksheet cell to close the map. Click on the map once to select it, choose Edit, Cut, switch to another worksheet, and choose Edit, Paste. This places the map on another worksheet, just as though you had originally located it there.

The resulting map is shown in figure 17.13. During the process of creating the map, and if there is a choice, Excel displays a dialog box asking the user to specify which map template to use. The map in figure 17.13 is based on the template named "United States (AK & HI Inset) in US with AK & HI Insets."

Fig. 17.13

Default map formats often require that you rearrange them by hand in order to view the information properly.

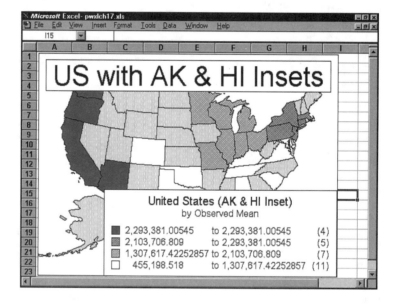

There are a number of adjustments that are needed to make the map more useful.

(Your map's legends might appear different from those shown in figure 17.13. If so, double-click on a legend to display the Edit Legend dialog box, and clear the Use Compact Format checkbox.)

If, when Excel returns control to you, you do not see the Data Map Control on the screen, click the Show/Hide Data Map Control button at the right-hand end of the Data Map toolbar (this toolbar appears only if you have opened an existing map for editing by double-clicking the map: you cannot display it by using Underline{V}iew, Underline{T}oolbars).

The first task is to remove the map's main title, US with AK and HI Insets. After you have double-clicked the map, click on the main title and press the Delete key.

Next, change the value shading to category shading. Notice that, by default, only the first data series ("Observed Mean") has been mapped, and value shading is used as the default format to represent it. Using value shading, though, it may not be possible to display each geographic category, when there are different numbers of observations in each category. Notice that the legend displays only four categories, and that only four levels of shading appear in the map.

This is because the levels are defined by their value *ranges*: because there are five categories, there is one range from the first category's value to the second category's value, another range from the second category's value to the third category's value, and so on. There are then, by definition, fewer ranges than categories.

In this situation, while you cannot specify more levels of shading than the number of ranges, you can specify fewer. To do so:

1. With a map containing value shading open for editing, choose Underline{M}ap, Underline{V}alue Shading Options from the menu.

2. The Value Shading Options dialog box appears (see fig. 17.14).

3. In the Number of value ranges edit box, type a number smaller than the one that is displayed. Alternatively, you can click the down-arrow button to the right of the edit box to display a dropdown list of values. Select a smaller number from that list.

4. Choose OK.

However, because the data contain five categories (regions) it's desirable to use category shading, instead of value shading. To change this option, use the Data Map Control:

1. There is one pair of buttons already in the format box. One is the Value Shading format button, paired with a column button for Observed Mean.

2. Position your mouse pointer over the Category Shading button in the group of format buttons to the left of the format box. The Category Shading button is in the first row, second column.

3. Hold your mouse button down, and drag the Category Shading button on top of the Value Shading button in the format box. This changes the option for the format of the Observed Mean from Value to Category Shading.

4. The five different regions appear on the map, distinguished by five different colors, and replacing the four different patterns that represented the four levels of values.

Fig. 17.14

The Value Shading Options dialog box lets you define shading categories by a count of items, or to the spread of their values.

The next step is to include the Adjusted Mean variable in the map. Again using the Data Map Control, position your mouse pointer over the Adjusted Mean column button, and drag it into the format box, just below the Observed Mean column button. When you release the mouse button, the Dot Density button automatically appears next to the Adjusted Mean button.

After moving the Adjusted Mean variable into the map, dots appear in each mapped state that represent the value of the Adjusted Mean: the greater the mean, the more dots (and, thus, the greater their density) in each state. Also, a new legend appears in the map. There are now two legends: one that represents the Category Shading, and one that represents the Dot Density.

You are now through with the Data Map Control, and to recapture some space on your screen you can close it by clicking its Close button, in the Control's upper-right corner.

The legends might obscure the mapped information, and if so, you will want to move and resize them. They are shown in figure 7.16 in the map frame's lower-left and lower-right corners. To move the legends:

1. With the map open for editing, click on a legend. Its border thickens and darkens.

2. Position your mouse pointer over the legend, press your mouse button and drag the legend to the position you want it to occupy.

3. After you release the mouse button, the legend remains selected. You can resize it by moving your mouse pointer over one of its corners. Your mouse pointer changes to a diagonal, double-headed arrow.

4. Hold down the mouse button and drag up and right or down and left to resize the legend box.

The Category Shading legend uses formats that match those of the numbers on the source worksheet. In this case, it displays four significant digits, and this is more precision than is needed. To reduce the number of digits—or to change the legend entries entirely—use the Edit Legend and Edit Legend Entry dialog boxes, shown in figure 17.15.

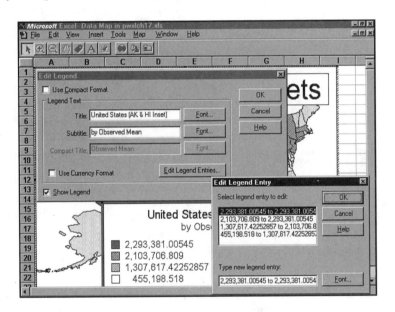

Fig. 17.15
The Edit Legend and Edit Legend Entry dialog boxes help you control the legend's appearance on the map.

To activate the Edit Legend dialog box, double-click on a legend. To activate the Edit Legend Entry dialog box, click the Edit Legend Entries button in the Edit Legend dialog box.

Notice that you can also use the Edit Legend dialog box to change the font used for the legend's Title and its Subtitle.

After you have made these changes to the original, your map should appear as in figure 17.16.

Tip

If you want to reformat all the entries in a legend, you must edit each of them. There is no provision to choose a particular format to apply to all entries.

Fig. 17.16

Analysis of Covariance results shown in map form: Regional differences are not as great as they originally appeared.

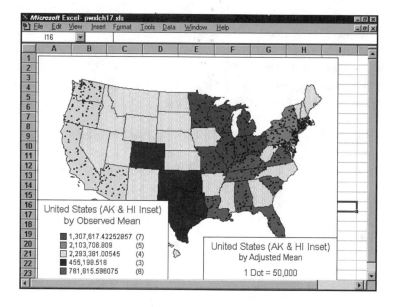

Because this book is printed in black and white, it might be difficult for you to discern in figure 17.16 the effect of the colored patterns used to distinguish the five regional categories.

On a color monitor, however, it is possible to see the results of adjusting each region's average sales on the basis of the population and median income in each state in the region. The Category Shading legend shows the values for the Observed Mean regional sales values, and the dot density in a region suggests the value of the Adjusted Means. A little study will clarify what you could expect of your regional sales management if their territories each started on an equal demographic and economic footing.

Summary

This chapter has provided you an introduction to the use of Excel version 7's new Data Map. Be aware that there are many aspects to this tool that are not documented in its Help files. While this chapter has discussed many of those aspects, you are encouraged to experiment with Excel's data maps so as to understand the functionality even better.

You can use these maps to obtain a more complete insight to patterns in your data. It is frequently the case that business data vary on a geographic basis, and strictly numeric reports can obscure these relationships. Given that you have data that is associated with a geographic variable, it is every bit as important to view the data in a map as it is to view nongeographic results in a chart.

The chapter has also provided you a very brief introduction to the Analysis of Variance and the Analysis of Covariance. These are extremely valuable tools for understanding the results that your business achieves. You can, for example, also use them to help distinguish among the revenues, margins, or earnings returned by different product lines.

If you decide to employ these tools at all extensively for financial analysis, be sure to study a statistics textbook first. Many such texts devote hundreds of pages to explaining the requirements, assumptions and uses of ANOVA and ANCOVA; indeed, several textbooks are devoted to nothing but these techniques. To extract maximum value from using them, you should take the time to study more information about them than this chapter has been able to present.

The results of these analyses can also be represented in mapping formats—again, assuming that the data are associated with geographic variables. It's useful to do so, to better understand the meaning of the adjustments they make to your variables of interest.

This chapter has been concerned primarily with the analysis and depiction of revenues. Chapter 18, "Recognition," continues the theme by discussing how businesses recognize and realize their revenues.

Chapter 18

Recognition

This book has had much to say about the matching principle: timing the occurrence of costs so as to match them with the occurrence of revenues. Depreciation, for example, is one way of doing so, by recording a portion of an asset's cost during the period that it helps to generate revenue. The entire basis for calculating profit, and determining how and why you make it, is the matching principle and its corollary, accrual.

The other side of the coin has not been discussed: timing the occurrence of revenues to match them with the occurrence of costs. *Recognition* and *realization* are two closely related concepts that help you match revenues to costs.

Revenue Recognition in Theory

Most companies use accrual as the basis of their accounting systems. Again, ;*accrual* means that when a company transacts business involving the receipt of revenue for a service or a product, it records the transaction when the transaction occurs. This can be, and often is, at a different time than when the revenue is actually in hand in the form of, say, a check.

Accrual-based accounting can make it more difficult to accurately report revenue, because there are normally differences between the date of the transaction and the date that payment is received. It's important, then, to have standard procedures and rules in place so that this accuracy can be maintained, even if it is more difficult to do so.

The Financial Accounting Standards Board (FASB) promulgates these guidelines as Generally Accepted Accounting Principles, or GAAP. One rationale for these rules is to help companies better understand how to use the theory of accrual-based accounting, as it applies to revenue recognition and realization. Most of the procedures that this chapter describes are based on GAAP.

It's common to assume that the processes of realizing and recognizing revenue are one and the same. For accounting purposes, this is not always the case:

- *Recognition* is the act of recording revenue in the accounting records and reporting it in the financial statements.

- *Realization* is a more abstract process, used to determine when revenue should be recognized. Realization, applied to recognition, brings the issue of timing into the picture.

More formally, FASB has defined realization as the occurrence of an event that reduces uncertainty about future cash flows. Such an event makes the decision to recognize revenue objectively justifiable. When applied to GAAP, the following criteria are used to determine when you should treat revenue as realized:

- When you can determine the amount of the revenue, and when you know its timing, on an objective basis

- When the earning process is virtually complete

These are the two fundamental criteria that most people use to decide that revenue has been realized. GAAP has further defined the timing of revenue recognition by means of these guidelines:

- When the item to be recognized meets the definition of an element of financial statements

- When the item has a relevant attribute, measurable with sufficient reliability

- When information about the item can make a difference to a participant in the decision-making process

- When information about the item to be recognized is objective

Accountants can be very picky. In most cases, these latter four guidelines make little difference to you. Your business normally provides a product or service in return for a cash payment, whether you actually receive the payment now or at a later time. Cash is an element used in financial statements, has a reliably measurable quantity, makes a difference to you, and has a value that different people can agree on.

Nevertheless, there are situations in which you would want to consider these guidelines. Suppose that your firm enters into an informal arrangement with another company to perform services for one another. The two firms agree that they will do so as long as the arrangement is mutually satisfactory, and that no cash payments need change hands during that time.

Under an agreement like this, it's unlikely that all four of the additional criteria would be met. If not, then you should neither realize nor recognize any revenue.

In summary, you should realize revenue—that is, decide that it is time to recognize it—and recognize it in the income statement when the particular event, critical to the earning of revenue, has occurred. Furthermore, you should do so when you can objectively measure the amount and timing of the revenue that you will receive.

For example, suppose that a bicycle shop sells a bicycle, but the buyer has not yet taken possession of it. The recognition of the sale takes place when the bicycle is sold, not when the buyer picks it up. The critical event is the sale of the bicycle, not the act of riding it away.

The Earning Process

The process of earning revenue has a great deal to do with when revenue recognition occurs. Consider two major industries: manufacturing and merchandising. These two industries have very different earning processes, but from the standpoint of recognizing revenue, they are quite similar.

A manufacturing firm acquires materials for production, makes the finished product from the materials, sells it to a wholesaler, a retailer or end user, and finally collects payment for the product. The sale and the collection of the payment might occur simultaneously. They might also occur over a long period of time, if the manufacturer and the customer have negotiated conditions for a long-term receivable.

The earning process for a merchandiser differs from that of a manufacturer in that the merchandiser acquires inventory, holds it for an indeterminate period, perhaps rotates it back to the manufacturer under an exchange agreement, advertises it, and so on. Although their operating activities are very different, their earning processes are identical.

Both a manufacturer and a merchandiser produce something: a manufacturer produces goods, and a merchandiser produces sales. Both assume that as their level of production grows, their level of income will also grow (see fig. 18.1).

Figure 18.1 suggests a parallel assumption: that over time, costs grow along with revenues. It's easy to see how either a manufacturer or a merchandiser can incur costs during its production cycle. It's not quite so easy to see how it can be generating revenue—how it can be realizing and recognizing it—before a sale is actually completed. And yet the matching principle requires that it associates revenues with costs as they occur.

Fig. 18.1

Revenue recognition over time: it's normal to recognize revenue when the product is sold, not when payment is received.

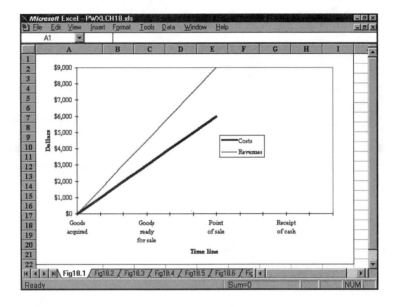

To understand how this can happen, consider that there are four different times in the process of moving from production to sales when a company might recognize revenue:

- During production
- At the completion of production
- At the point of sale
- During the cash collection process

In practice, revenue is almost always recognized at the point of sale. However, there are a few exceptional cases when it might be necessary to recognize revenue either before the sale or subsequent to it. The remainder of this chapter describes each of the points in time that revenue can be recognized, along with the reasons for recognizing revenue at that point.

> **Note**
>
> Although the discussion proceeds from the earliest time (during production) to the latest time (subsequent to sale), keep in mind that recognizing revenue before or after the point of sale is the exceptional case.

Recognizing Revenue During Production

Some companies engage in long-term projects, in which the production of goods extends over several accounting periods. It's usually a straightforward process to assign those costs to the period in which they are incurred. But should any revenue be recognized during the course of production? And if so, how?

For example, suppose that it takes a prime contractor several years to complete construction of a major highway. Should the contractor recognize any portion of the expected revenue while the highway is under construction? So doing would help investors to better understand the revenue, cost, and profit implications of the contractor's current activities.

Therefore, the contractor should recognize some revenue during the construction period. If the contractor can make a reasonable determination of the amount and the timing of revenue, or if the earning process is virtually complete, then some portion of the revenue can and should be recognized during the construction process.

So, at least some revenue should be recognized prior to the completion of the project. How should the contractor determine the timing and the amount of revenue to recognize?

There are two ways to account for revenue recognition when long-term projects are in progress. These are the *percentage of completion* method and the *completed contract* method.

Using the Percentage of Completion Method

To determine how much revenue the contractor should recognize during any given period in a long-term contract, the contractor needs to know or estimate four quantities:

- The total price of the contract—that is, the price that the buyer will pay

- The total cost that the contractor will incur during the life of the construction project

- The cost that the contractor incurred during the current accounting period

- The percentage of the project that has been completed

Using the percentage of completion method, the contractor would estimate the total cost, the total price and the current cost for the production that is in progress.

There are various convenient ways to determine the portion of the project that has been completed to date, but each is based on costs expended. For example, before the project begins, the contractor estimates the number of labor hours that will be needed to complete the project. This estimate is used as a base to determine the percentage of completion at a given point in time (see fig. 18.2).

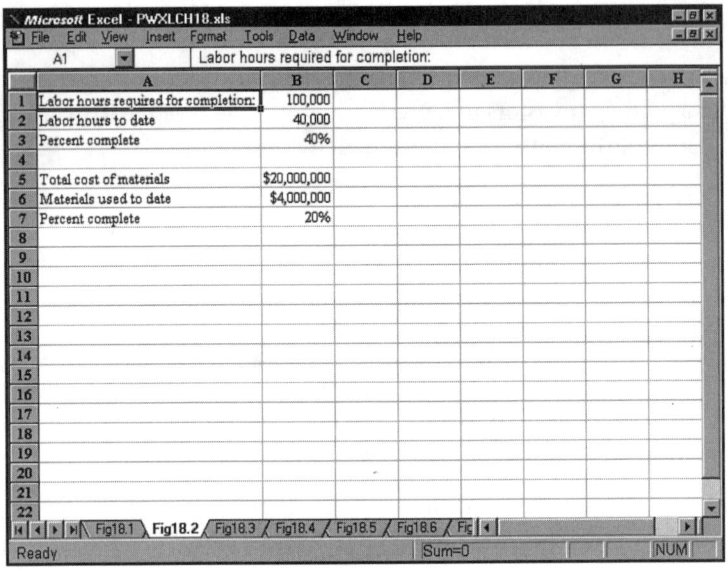

Fig. 18.2
Determining percentage of project completion is one way to estimate costs and revenues while work is in progress.

Suppose that the contractor estimates that a total of 100,000 labor hours will be needed to complete the project. After the first year, 40,000 labor hours have actually been used, so it's reasonable to estimate that 40 percent of the project is complete.

Or, another contractor could compare the costs that have been incurred through the current date to the total estimated construction costs. For example, given an estimate of $20,000,000 in materials needed to complete the project and a first year cost of $4,000,000, the percentage of completion would be 20 percent.

For the purpose of revenue recognition, the contractor applies the percentage of completion method at the end of each accounting period. The total contract price is compared to the estimated total contract cost to determine the estimated total income.

For example, suppose that a contractor wins a bid for a four-year building construction project, with a total price of $20,000,000 and with estimated total costs of $16,000,000. The estimated income from project completion is therefore $4,000,000 (see fig. 18.3).

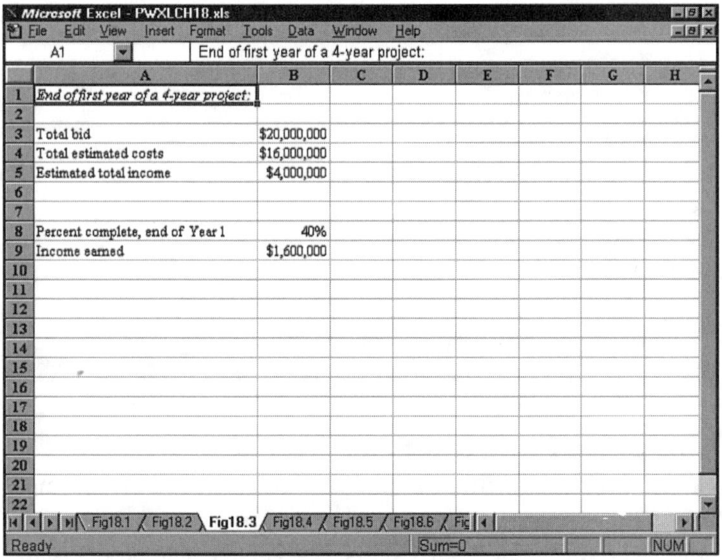

	A	B
1	*End of first year of a 4-year project:*	
2		
3	Total bid	$20,000,000
4	Total estimated costs	$16,000,000
5	Estimated total income	$4,000,000
6		
7		
8	Percent complete, end of Year 1	40%
9	Income earned	$1,600,000

Fig. 18.3
The percentage of project completion can be different than the percentage of time elapsed.

At the end of the first year, using one of the methods to measure percentage of completion, the contractor determines that the project is 40 percent complete, $8,000,000 should be recognized as revenue. Further, $1,600,000 should be recognized as income.

Now suppose that due to bad weather during the final year of the contract, progress slows, and only 90 percent of the project is complete after 48 months. The contractor estimates revenue *through* year four at 90% * $20,000,000 = $18,000,000, and subtracts the revenue that has already been recognized. So in this example, at the end of year four the total income to be recognized would be calculated as $18,000,000. Prior revenues of, say, $14,000,000 are subtracted, so revenues for year four are $18,000,000 – $14,000,000, or $4,000,000 (see fig. 18.4).

Fig. 18.4
It's important to re-estimate revenues as a project nears completion: both revenues and income may have been over-recognized.

	A	B	C	D	E	F	G	H	I
1	End of Year 4:								
2									
3	Total bid	$20,000,000							
4	Total estimated costs	$16,000,000							
5	Estimated total income	$4,000,000							
6									
7	Percent complete,								
8	end of Year 4	90%							
9	Total revenue earned	$18,000,000							
10									
11	Less revenues earned								
12	through Year 3	$14,000,000							
13									
14	Revenue, Year 4	$4,000,000							
15									
16	Total income earned	$3,600,000							
17									
18	Less income earned								
19	through Year 3	$2,800,000							
20									
21	Income, Year 4	$800,000							
22									

The Completed-contract Method

The completed-contract method should be used when you cannot make reasonable estimates concerning the percentage of project completion. Using this method, revenue recognition occurs when deliverable products are transferred from seller to buyer once the project has been completed. Until this time, however, no revenue should be recognized.

In the highway construction example, if the contractor cannot make a reasonable estimate of either the total cost or total revenue, it might be appropriate to use the completed-contract method. Then, the contractor would recognize the entire $30,000,000 revenue, $20,000,000 in costs, and $10,000,000 in gross profit in the final year of the project. By that point, it should be possible to determine these amounts with reasonable accuracy.

Recognizing Revenue at Completion of Production

For certain types of commodities, such as agricultural products and some precious metals, it is best to recognize revenue when production is complete. To recognize revenue when production has been completed, it is necessary to meet the following criteria:

- The product is sold in a market with a reasonably assured selling price.
- The costs of selling and distributing the product are not significant and can be reasonably estimated.
- Production is considered the most critical event in the earning process, not the sale itself.

For example, the most critical event in a wheat farmer's earning process is the harvesting of the grain, not the act of selling the grain. This is because the grain price has already been determined by the marketplace. In fact, in the commodities markets, options to buy or sell at a certain price are often negotiated well in advance of the actual production of the commodity.

Once again, the recognition of revenue using the completion of production method, as distinct from its recognition using some other method, is purely a timing issue. For example, suppose that a farmer harvests grain in late 1995, sells 75 percent of the harvest in 1995, and sells the remainder in 1996. According to the completion of production method, the total value of the farmer's harvest would be recognized in 1995. Using the point of sale method, 75 percent would be recognized in 1995 and 25 percent in 1996 (see fig. 18.5).

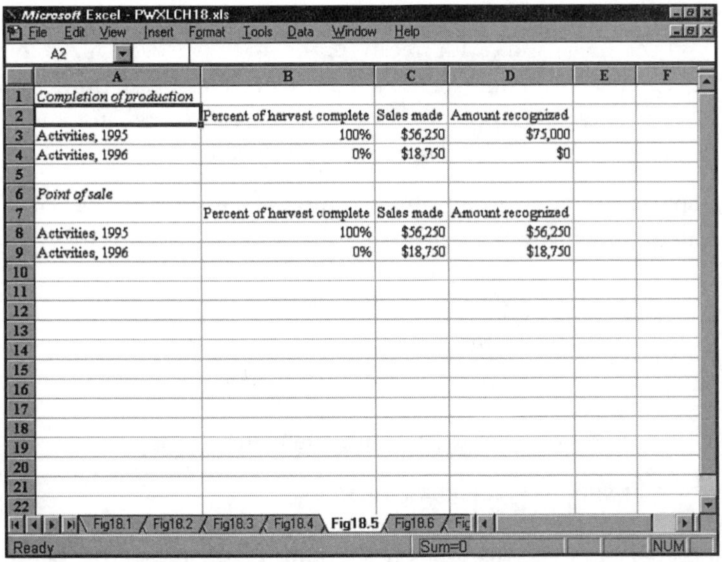

	A	B	C	D
1	*Completion of production*			
2		Percent of harvest complete	Sales made	Amount recognized
3	Activities, 1995	100%	$56,250	$75,000
4	Activities, 1996	0%	$18,750	$0
5				
6	*Point of sale*			
7		Percent of harvest complete	Sales made	Amount recognized
8	Activities, 1995	100%	$56,250	$56,250
9	Activities, 1996	0%	$18,750	$18,750

Fig. 18.5
Assigning revenue to accounting periods at completion of production can cause full recognition prior to the point of sale.

Of course, the total revenue recognized is the same using both the completion of production and the point of sale methods. Using completion of production, the producer might recognize $75,000 in 1995. Using the point of sale method, the producer might recognize $56,250 in 1995 and $18,750 in 1996. The difference lies in *when* the revenue is recognized.

Recognizing Revenue with the Point of Sale Method

Without a sale a company would not generate revenue, and for many businesses the sale itself is the most important part of the entire earning process. It is for this reason that most companies use the point of sale as the point of revenue recognition. As a rule of thumb, a sale takes place when one or more of the following events takes place:

- Ownership of goods is transferred to a buyer

- Services are performed

- Asset services (such as apartment rentals) have been provided

Revenue recognition at the point of sale is the most intuitive method, and can be the least complicated of the possible methods of recognizing revenue. A sale has been made and cash is received; the revenue is recognized immediately because there is no uncertainty about the timing of cash flows. Point of sale also represents the completion of the earning process because the merchandise has been physically transferred to the buyer.

While apparently simple, recognizing revenue at the point of sale can be complicated by factors such as these:

- Sales made on credit

- Trade and cash discounts

- Uncollectible accounts

- Costs related to the sale that are incurred after the date of sale

- Return privileges on merchandise sold

Each of these factors can snap the direct connection between the point of sale and the recognition of revenue, making it necessary to accrue costs or revenues into some later period. Their effects, and how to resolve them, are discussed in the next section.

Making Sales on Credit

When you make a sale on credit, you record the revenue from the sale net of any discounts, and at the value of the merchandise at the time of the sale.

For example, assume that your store sells a sweater in April to a customer who uses a credit card to make the purchase. The price of the sweater at the time of the purchase is $56. Your store is offering a discount of 10 percent from list during April (see fig. 18.6).

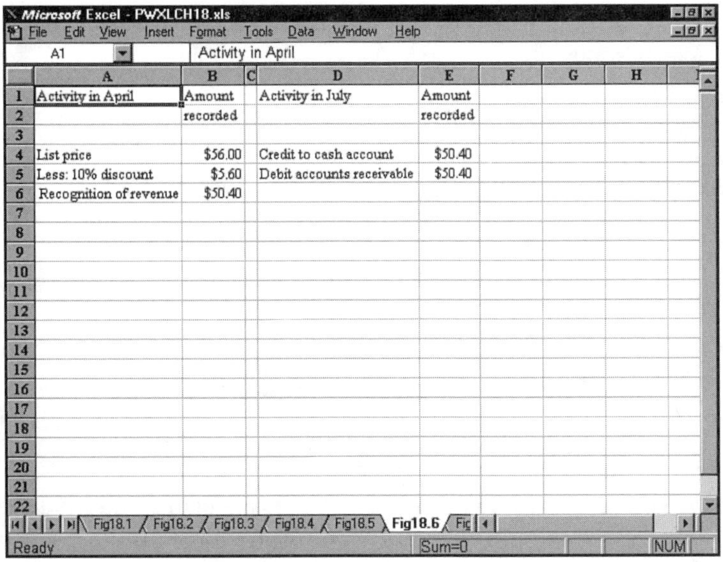

IV

Sales and Marketing

	A	B	C	D	E	F	G	H
1	Activity in April	Amount		Activity in July	Amount			
2		recorded			recorded			
3								
4	List price	$56.00		Credit to cash account	$50.40			
5	Less: 10% discount	$5.60		Debit accounts receivable	$50.40			
6	Recognition of revenue	$50.40						

Fig. 18.6
Recognizing net income from a credit sale occurs when the sale is made; additional postings occur when payment is made.

The buyer puts the purchase on a credit card and does not pay it off until three months from the time of purchase. Based on the criteria described above, the sale would be recorded for $50.40 in revenue: the present value at the time of sale of $56 less the 10 percent purchase discount.

When a business deals with credit sales, it is normal to establish a special kind of account called a *contra-revenue* account. There are different kinds of contra accounts, such as contra-liability and contra-asset (for example, depreciation is one kind of contra-asset account, because it continually reduces the value of depreciable assets). You use a contra-revenue account to allow for uncollectible sales.

Not all consumers pay off their credit debts, so the seller must make estimates for those credit sales that will never be collected to present a true picture of actual cash flows. Usually, this is done by using historical data: for example, you might find that over the past five years, it has proved impossible or impractical to collect 3 percent of the apparent revenue from your credit sales. Figure 18.7 depicts this situation.

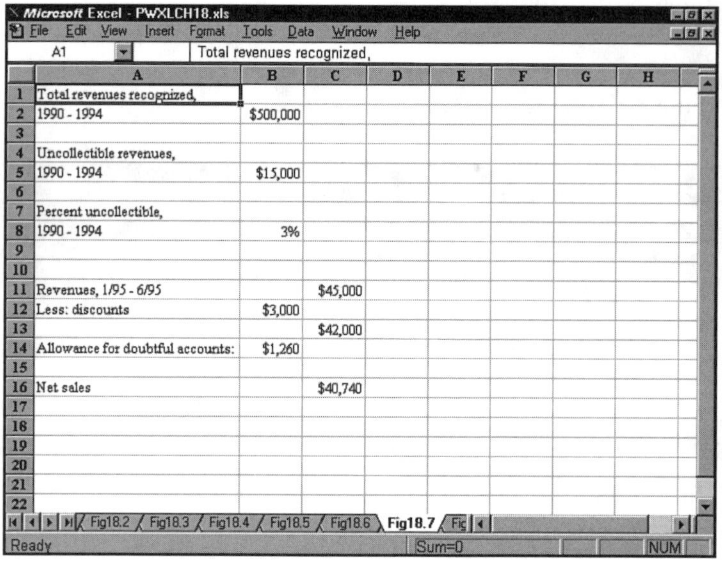

	A	B	C
1	Total revenues recognized,		
2	1990 - 1994	$500,000	
3			
4	Uncollectible revenues,		
5	1990 - 1994	$15,000	
6			
7	Percent uncollectible,		
8	1990 - 1994	3%	
9			
10			
11	Revenues, 1/95 - 6/95		$45,000
12	Less: discounts	$3,000	
13			$42,000
14	Allowance for doubtful accounts:	$1,260	
15			
16	Net sales		$40,740

Fig. 18.7
Accounting for doubtful collectibles by means of a contra account helps to prevent the overestimation of revenue.

Therefore, you might use a contra-revenue account to allow for the sales during the current period that turn out to be uncollectible. You would record 3 percent of the current period's sales in the contra account, and use it as an offset to Sales (along with other offsets such as Sales Discounts) to arrive at a Net Sales figure for the period.

Incurring Costs After the Point of Sale

Using the point of sale method, even though revenue is recognized at the time of the sale, it does not necessarily follow that the earning process is complete. In some cases, you incur costs associated with selling a product after the sale itself has been made. However, you need to estimate and accrue these costs as of the time of the sale.

For example, if you sell cameras, you will very likely include a warranty as a part of the sale. According to accrual accounting, the cost of servicing that warranty must be estimated and recognized and accrued at the time of sale. In this way, revenues and associated expenses are recorded at the same time.

Allowing for Returns Privileges

In some types of sales, the buyer can return the item for various reasons. In fact, in many states, the buyer can even cancel a sale made somewhere other than the seller's normal place of business, without citing a reason of any sort. (This applies principally to door-to-door sales.)

For revenue recognition purposes, the seller needs to make some assumptions about how much revenue might be returned to the customer, and include this assumption in the amount of revenue that is recognized. Just as with uncollectible credit sales, an allowance for expected returns should be used, at the date of sale, as a contra-revenue account in order to properly measure the expected cash flows resulting from the sale.

Recognizing Revenue During the Cash Collection Process

As mentioned before, there are certain criteria that must be met before revenue can be recognized at the point of sale. It was also mentioned that complications occur when you recognize revenue at the point of sale, and when those sales are made on credit. In some cases the complications due to credit sales are so great that the collection of the amounts due for those sales become highly uncertain. In that case, revenues should not be recognized at the point of sale.

This is the sort of situation that might call for the application of the concepts and methods for recognizing revenue during the cash collection process. There are two ways to do so: the installment method and the cost recovery method.

Using the Installment Method

If the criteria for point of sale revenue recognition have been met, you would simply recognize the revenue for installment sales at the point of sale.

However, if the criteria are not met (for example, the collection period on credit sales extends well beyond the normal time in which a credit sale should be paid, and there is no reasonable basis for estimating uncollectibles), then you might use the installment method to recognize the revenues associated with these sales. The basis for the installment method is that gross profit on the sale of the goods in question is deferred. Recognition occurs over time, as the cash is collected.

For example, suppose that a company sells stereos on a deferred payment plan. The total sales price for a stereo is $500, and the plan requires a $100 down payment, with the remaining payments to be made over the next 10 months. Each of the stereos sold costs $400 to produce. You can calculate the amount of revenue to be recognized under the installment method as follows:

$$\text{Gross Profit Percentage} = (\text{Sales} - \text{Cost of Goods Sold})/$$
$$\text{Sales} = (\$500 - \$400)/\$500 = 20\%$$

So, in this example, each time that additional cash is collected over the 10-month period, 20% of the cash would represent profit and the remaining 80% of cash would be used to recover costs. If the remaining $400 in sales is collected over the 10-month period, the company receives $40 each month.

Twenty percent of the $40, or $8, is recognized as gross profit and $32 would be used to recover costs of producing the stereo. These calculations are shown in figure 18.8.

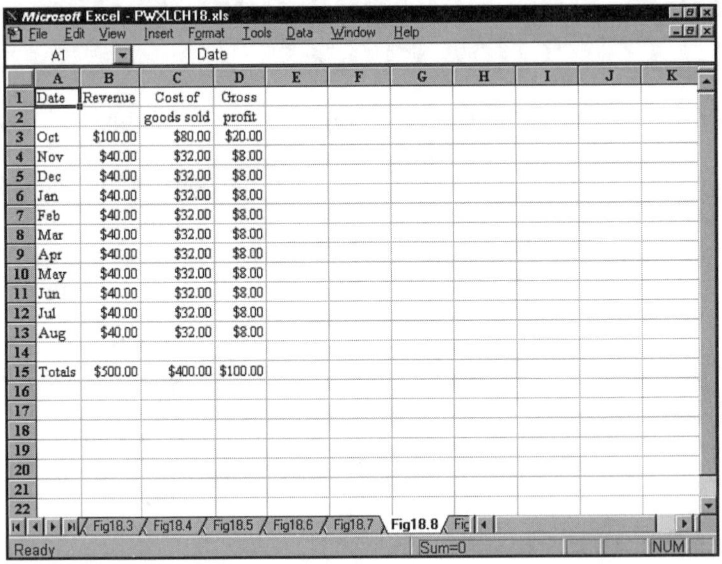

Fig. 18.8
Recognizing revenues using the installment method pushes recognition past the point of sale.

	A	B	C	D
1	Date	Revenue	Cost of	Gross
2			goods sold	profit
3	Oct	$100.00	$80.00	$20.00
4	Nov	$40.00	$32.00	$8.00
5	Dec	$40.00	$32.00	$8.00
6	Jan	$40.00	$32.00	$8.00
7	Feb	$40.00	$32.00	$8.00
8	Mar	$40.00	$32.00	$8.00
9	Apr	$40.00	$32.00	$8.00
10	May	$40.00	$32.00	$8.00
11	Jun	$40.00	$32.00	$8.00
12	Jul	$40.00	$32.00	$8.00
13	Aug	$40.00	$32.00	$8.00
14				
15	Totals	$500.00	$400.00	$100.00

> **Note**
>
> Although the installment method is not used frequently in the preparation of financial statements, it is sometimes used in the preparation of income tax records. By deferring the recognition of income until it is actually in hand, a company might be able to adjust its tax liability to its benefit.

Using the Cost Recovery Method

Under the cost recovery method, no revenue is recognized on credit sales until the cost of the product sold has been fully recovered by cash collections. When enough cash has been collected to recover the costs, any remaining cash collections are reported as income in the period in which they are collected.

To continue the example given above, if a stereo was sold in October of 1995 with a $100 down payment and $300 additional was received by April of 1996, the $400 cost of the stereo would then have been recovered. Using the cost recovery method, therefore, all cash collected from May to June 1996 would be recognized as income during the remaining two months (see fig. 18.9).

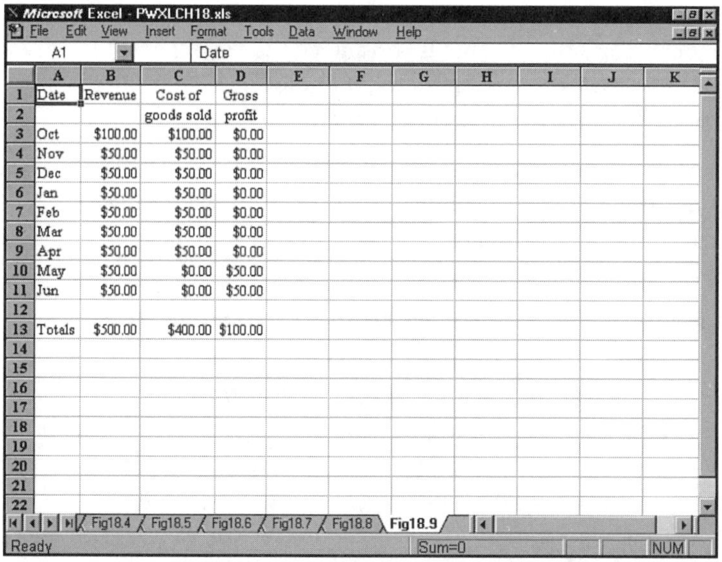

Date	Revenue	Cost of goods sold	Gross profit
Oct	$100.00	$100.00	$0.00
Nov	$50.00	$50.00	$0.00
Dec	$50.00	$50.00	$0.00
Jan	$50.00	$50.00	$0.00
Feb	$50.00	$50.00	$0.00
Mar	$50.00	$50.00	$0.00
Apr	$50.00	$50.00	$0.00
May	$50.00	$0.00	$50.00
Jun	$50.00	$0.00	$50.00
Totals	$500.00	$400.00	$100.00

Fig. 18.9
Distributing recognition by means of the cost recovery method

This method is occasionally used when there is a great deal of uncertainty surrounding the profitability associated with a new venture or contract.

Recognizing Revenue in Different Industries

Although the methods of revenue recognition are standard across all industries, industries differ as to the methods they use to implement recognition.

Recognizing Revenue in Service Industries

Revenue recognition in service industries is composed of four different methods. These four methods are described here:

- The *specific performance method* occurs when performance of a service consists of a single act. Under this method, revenue is recognized when the service has been completed.

- The *proportional performance method* occurs when several similar acts are performed. Under this method, revenue is recognized as it is under the percentage of completion method.

- The *completed performance method* occurs when more than one act is required and the final act is considered the critical event in the earning process. Under this method, the revenue recognition process is similar to the completed production method.

- The *collection method* is used when there is a great deal of uncertainty surrounding the collectibility of revenue. Under this method, revenue is recognized only when cash collection has been made.

Recognizing Revenue in Manufacturing Industries

Manufacturing industries operate on the same basis for revenue recognition as do service industries. The primary difference is that a large portion of manufacturing operates on long-term contracts. As described previously, the methods specific to long-term projects include the percentage of completion and completed contract methods.

Understanding the Impact of Revenue Recognition Methods

No matter which method of revenue recognition you use, the eventual, total amount of recorded revenue should be the same. What differs is the time at which the revenue is recognized. The timing of revenue recognition carries significant implications for different aspects of your business. For example, if your firm's primary activity is sales, then the timing of revenue recognition can become critical both to you and to your employees.

Suppose that you compensate your employees by means of commissions, and that commissions are paid when revenue is recognized. If, as is very likely, you recognize revenue on a point of sale basis, then your employees have an advantage. This is because you must pay them their commissions no matter when you actually receive the cash payment from the customer.

On the other hand, if you recognize revenue only at the completion of a contract, you will have the advantage because you will not have to pay commissions on earnings not yet recognized. You might have received payment, but you can defer the commission expense until the contract is complete.

There are various ways to structure sales commission plans, and many companies structure their plans so as to benefit both the company and the employee. One deceptively straightforward plan is to pay 40 percent of the commission at the point of sale, and to pay the remaining 60 percent at the time payment is actually made. Notice that, depending on the recognition method you use, you could record the cost of the full commission amount as of the point of sale, and defer the actual cash payment of 60 percent of the commission until you receive the full amount due from the customer.

Summary

Under accrual-based accounting, the realization and the recognition of revenue are critical to determining a company's financial position at any given time. In this chapter, you have seen how different circumstances can alter this timing.

Normally, you will find it both necessary and expedient to recognize revenue at the point of sale, along with its associated costs and the profit that results. However, the critical event that produces the revenue is not always the sale itself, or a project that generates revenue extends over a very long period of time, or certain subsequent events make it difficult to determine the revenue amount as the sale occurs. In such cases, it can be necessary to alter the timing of the recognition.

Chapter 19

The Business Planner

Excel 7 includes a spreadsheet template called Business Planner. You can use it to help create the three forms that are fundamental for profitability management: the balance sheet, the income statement, and the cash flow statement.

While the format that the Business Planner uses may not precisely suit your needs, it's a fine starting point. Because it's a template, you can base new workbooks on its structure and tailor them to your own uses. Many of the necessary relationships among the forms are already built into it. It emphasizes forecasting: that is, you are expected to input some basic assumptions about sales volume, cost percentages, inventory levels, and so on. The Planner then applies hundreds of formulas to those inputs so as to generate an overview of a company's worth, income, and cash position.

After you have created a starting point with your inputs, you can examine their effect on the company's financial position. You can also modify certain key results, displayed on the Planner's charts, to determine what changes in your inputs are needed to achieve a given set of goals.

Earlier chapters in this book have discussed in some detail the uses of balance sheets, income statements, and cash flow statements, as well as the variety of formats that they can take on. This chapter shows how the three interact: in particular, how changes in one can, and usually do, exert an influence on the other two.

Exploring the Business Planner

The Business Planner template itself is located in the Templates folder, within whatever folder you have chosen to store Excel 7. It is not necessary to open the template itself, however. To access it, choose File, New. When you do so, the New dialog box shown in figure 19.1 appears. Click the Spreadsheet Solutions tab.

Fig. 19.1
The New File dialog box lets you choose the template you want to use.

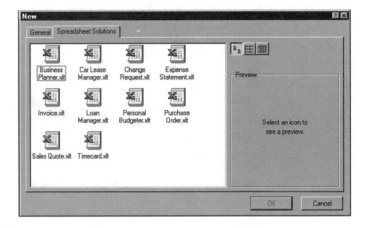

Tip

The New File dialog box does not appear when you click the New file icon on Excel's Standard toolbar: to reach it, you must use File, New.

When you double-click the Business Planner.xlt template, Excel opens a new file named Business Planner 1 that is based on the template. It contains all the sheets, formatting, formulas, tools, and scenarios that the template contains.

The main purpose of the Business Planner is to enable you to forecast financial results during each of four quarters of a year. Each worksheet has a column for each quarter. Some of the cells in a quarter's column are intended for you to enter data, while other cells contain formulas that depend on the data you enter. The cells that contain formulas are shaded; the cells where you are to enter data are not shaded.

The new file will first display the Data Sheet, where you enter many of your inputs. You will also see the Planner toolbar, which contains buttons that let you quickly do the following:

■ Zoom the size of the used part of the sheet to fit entirely in the active window, or return to a higher zoom level.

- Hide or display cell tips (if hidden, the red note indicator in the upper-right corner of the cell is suppressed).

- Add or change a cell note

- Jump to a Help topic for the Planner template

- Display or remove sample data. Clicking this button loads or removes the data that is supplied as a scenario.

- Split the window into panes at the active cell, and freeze the panes. If a window already contains panes created by this button, clicking the button removes them.

- Display the Windows 95 Calculator accessory

Figure 19.2 shows the location of these buttons. If you do not see the Planner's toolbar when you open the workbook, choose <u>V</u>iew, <u>T</u>oolbars, and check the Planner checkbox in the <u>T</u>oolbars list box.

A workbook opened by using the Business Planner template contains several sheets:

- The *Customize Your Planner* sheet lets you embed a logo and provides for the entry of information, such as company name and phone number. The logo and other information will appear on all other worksheets in the book. This sheet appears in figure 19.2.

> **Tip**
>
> To view the Customize Your Planner sheet, click the Customize button on any Planner sheet.

> **Note**
>
> When you open a workbook based on the Business Planner and load the sample data, you might see figures that do not correspond to some of the figures in this chapter. To make them correspond, change the value of cell G15 in the data sheet from an "S" to a "C". This change causes the workbook to treat the data as pertaining to a C-corporation instead of an S-corporation. See the section titled "Specifying the Type of Corporation" for more information.

Fig. 19.2

The Customize Your Planner worksheet lets you specify information that appears on all worksheets in the book.

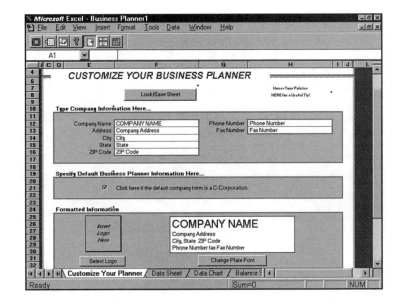

- The *Data Sheet* provides for the entry of selected operating data such as Days Sales in Accounts Receivable, expense data such as Direct Labor as % of Sales, and financing data such as amount of Short-term and Long-term Debt.

  In the case of the operating and expense data, there is a column for each of four quarters.

  The other worksheets in the workbook make both direct and indirect use of the data you enter in the Data Sheet. This is *not* the only location in the workbook where it is necessary for you to enter your inputs, but it does contain most of the basic information.

- The *Data Chart* (see fig. 19.3) displays in a column chart the operating data that you enter in the Data Sheet. After you have completed the entry of all inputs in the workbook, you can resize the columns in the Data Chart. Doing so changes the operating data in the Data Sheet. In turn, this causes any formula in the workbook that depends on the Data Sheet's operating data to recalculate.

For example, you might drag the Days Materials Cost in Inventory column down, to reflect your intention to move raw materials through your production system more quickly. This would have the effect of reducing your inventory assets as shown on the Balance Sheet. See the section on "Forecasting with the Charts" for more information on carrying out this process.

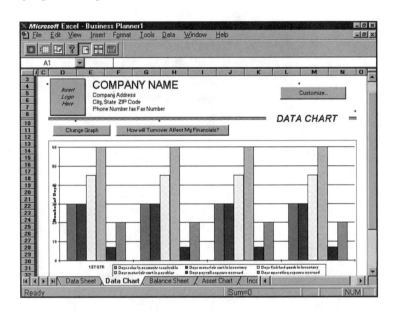

Fig. 19.3
The Data Chart helps you do "what-if" analysis on operating data.

- The *Balance Sheet* contains standard information on assets and liabilities. The changes in the assets and liabilities across the forecast year's four quarters are shown here.

- The *Asset Chart* (see fig. 19.4) displays, for each quarter, the three main classes of assets from the Balance Sheet: Current Assets, Fixed Assets, and Intangible Assets. Each column represents the total of these three asset classes.

- The *Income Statement* lists, for each quarter, information on sales, expenses, and income, along with supporting documentation from the Data Sheet.

Fig. 19.4

The Asset Chart tracks the flow of assets over time.

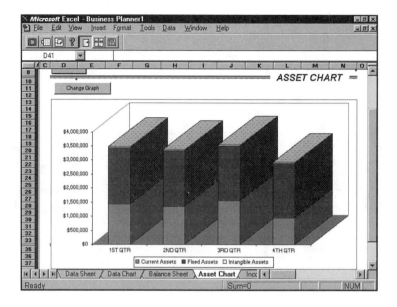

The *Income Chart* (see fig. 19.5) displays, for each quarter, the calculated Sales, Gross Profit, Expenses, and Income Before Taxes, taken from the Income Statement.

Fig. 19.5

The Income Chart shows the relationships among revenues and expenses.

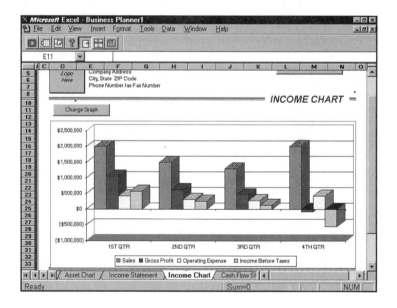

- The *Cash Flow Sheet* is completely dependent on data in the other worksheets in the workbook. Based on these data, it calculates working capital due to operations, operating activities, asset transactions, and financing transactions. As has been noted in prior chapters, a comparison of the Cash Flow Sheet with the Income Statement and Balance Sheet enables you to assess the financial health of a company that, on paper, is both profitable and asset-rich.

- The *Macros* sheet contains VBA routines that drive your interaction with the workbook. If you want to customize certain aspects of that interaction, this sheet is the place to do it. It is a hidden sheet, and you will therefore not be able to see it when you first open a workbook based on the Business Planner template. The next section provides instructions for making the Planner's macro sheets visible.

- The *Credits* and *Lock* macro sheets are also hidden when you first open the workbook. The Credits sheet contains a dialog box that is not called by the Macros sheet. The Lock sheet contains a dialog box that is called if you click the Lock/Save Sheet button on the Customize Your Planner worksheet.

Opening the Macro Sheet

If you want to make changes to the VBA subroutines and functions that are provided with a Business Planner workbook, you will need to unhide the Macros sheet. To make all the sheets visible, choose Insert, Macro, and select Module. This will insert a new VBA module sheet into the workbook. Place this code in the module:

```
Sub MakeAllSheetsVisible()
Dim SheetInBook As Variant
For Each SheetInBook In ThisWorkbook.Sheets
    SheetInBook.Visible = True
Next SheetInBook
End Sub
```

Choose Tools, Macro, and highlight MakeAllSheetsVisible in the Macro Name/Reference list box. Click Run to invoke the macro. After a few seconds, you will find three new sheet tabs: Macros, Credits, and Lock.

As long as the Macros tab is visible, you will get error messages if you move among the workbook tabs or take certain other actions. Therefore, after making any custom modifications, you should rehide the Macros sheet. Using the same process described for creating and running the MakeAllSheetsVisible procedure, run this VBA code:

```
Sub HideMacroSheets()
With ThisWorkbook
        .Sheets("Macros").Visible = xlVeryHidden
        .Sheets("Credits").Visible = xlVeryHidden
        .Sheets("Lock").Visible = xlVeryHidden
End With
End Sub
```

Installing the Main Scenario

This chapter uses the sample data supplied with the Business Planner to illustrate examples. If you want to populate a workbook with the sample data, you can use either the Planner toolbar or the Scenario Manager.

After opening a new workbook based on the Business Planner template, click the Display Example / Remove Example button on the Planner toolbar. This will place the sample data in the workbook.

If you have used an existing workbook based on the Business Planner template for a while, you might want to save the information that you have entered as a scenario. You can do so, and retrieve the supplied sample data, by using the Scenario Manager.

To save your own data as a scenario, choose Tools, Scenarios and click Add. Supply a name for your scenario in the Scenario Name box, and choose OK. Change any changing cell values you want in the Scenario Values dialog box, and then choose OK. Excel returns you to the Scenario Manager dialog box. You can also highlight "sample 1" in the Scenarios list box, and click Show. Doing this brings the supplied sample data into the workbook.

Forecasting with the Charts

All Excel charts contain values that are linked to their supporting worksheets: what you see in the chart is a graphical representation of numeric values in the worksheet. When you change a value in a supporting worksheet, the appearance of the chart changes accordingly.

It is also possible to turn this around: by changing the appearance of the data in the chart, you change the numeric value in the supporting worksheet. This is true only of certain chart types, including bar, column, line, stacked, pie, doughnut, and XY charts. The chart must be a two-dimensional chart type.

Of the three charts provided with a Business Planner workbook, only the Data Chart is, by default, structured to allow you to change the values by means of the chart itself. The Data Chart is a two-dimensional column chart, whereas the Asset Chart and the Income Chart are three-dimensional column charts. (You can, of course, change the latter two charts to a two-dimensional type if you want to use them to modify data values. To do so, choose the Change Graph button, which displays other chart formats.)

It can be useful to change underlying data in this way if you want immediate visual confirmation of the effect on other, dependent values of changing one precedent data value. To see this in action, take these steps:

1. Open a business planner workbook.

2. Choose Window, New Window. After the new workbook window has appeared on your screen, choose Window, Arrange. In the Arrange Windows dialog box, choose the Vertical button, and check the Windows of Active Workbook checkbox. You should now see the two windows simultaneously.

3. Select the workbook window on the right of your screen and select the Asset Chart sheet tab. Using the scroll bars, move within the sheet until you can see the Asset Chart columns that represent the fourth quarter.

4. Select the workbook window on the left of your screen and select the Data Chart sheet tab. Scroll within the sheet until you can see the Data Chart columns that represent the fourth quarter.

5. Double-click the Data Chart in the left workbook window. This opens the chart so that you can edit it. When you have more than one window open, as you should at present, double-clicking a chart opens yet another window that contains the chart object. Move and resize this new window until you can see the entire right-hand window containing the Asset Chart.

6. Look at the Data Chart legend to identify the fourth-quarter column that represents the Data Sheet variable called Days Materials Cost in Payables. Single-click this column. A marker appears in the center of each column associated with that data series.

7. Single-click the column once again. Handles appear at each corner of the column that you clicked, and a data marker appears in the center of the column's top edge. The left, Data Chart window should now appear as shown in figure 19.6.

> **Tip**
>
> Make the two single-clicks in steps 6 and 7 rather slow. If they occur too close together, Excel interprets them as one double-click instead of two single-clicks, and brings up the Format Object dialog box.

Fig. 19.6

Preparing to adjust worksheet values by means of a chart.

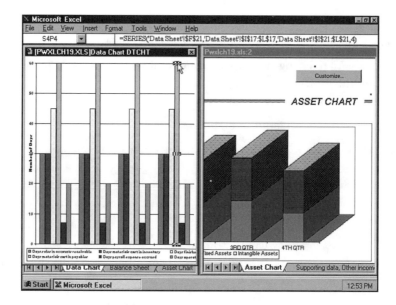

8. Position your mouse pointer over the data marker at the top of the column, and hold down the left mouse button. When you do so, the mouse pointer becomes a double-headed arrow, and the column's border changes to dashed lines.

9. Drag the data marker nearly to the bottom of the y-axis scale. Notice that as you do so, the column height changes to follow the data marker. If you watch the Name Box as you drag the marker, you will see the current value of the underlying cell change.

10. Release the mouse button, and watch the fourth-quarter column in the Asset Chart in the right-hand window. Note that when you use the Data Chart column to reduce the value of Days Materials Cost in Payables, the value of the total assets changes in the Asset Chart.

Why do the total assets for the fourth quarter change when you change the Days Materials Cost in Payables for the fourth quarter? It's a circuitous route:

Days Materials Cost in Payables for the fourth quarter is cell L21 on the Data Sheet. It has one directly dependent cell: L44 in the Balance Sheet, which is Accounts Payable under Current Liabilities. In the sample data, the only source of Accounts Payable is the cost of Materials for a given quarter, found on the Income Statement in cell K53 for specifically the fourth quarter.

> **Tip**
>
> The Business Planner contains a large number of named, single-cell ranges. When you select one of these cells, the Name Box shows the name of the cell rather than its A1- or R1C1-style address. Furthermore, the default worksheet options in the workbook suppress the normal row and column headers. This can make it difficult to determine exactly where you are in a worksheet.
>
> To quickly display the A1- or R1C1-style address of such a cell, whether or not in the Business Planner, hold down the left mouse button after selecting the cell. You will see the Name Box display the cell's address as long as you are holding down the mouse button.
>
> You can also use Tools, Options and fill the Row and Column Headers checkbox in the View tab.

The worksheet formula for Accounts Payable in the fourth quarter (Balance Sheet cell L44) is:

```
=ROUND(('Income Statement'!K53/(365*0.25))*'Data Sheet'!L21,0)
```

or, substituting values for references:

```
=ROUND((500000/(365*0.25))*60,0)
```

and removing the syntax for the ROUND function, which simply drops the fractional portion of the cell's value:

```
=500000/(365*0.25))*60
```

This formula first divides the cost of materials for the quarter by one-fourth of 365, or the number of days in one-fourth of a year. The result, about $5,480, is the number of dollars expended on materials on any given day during the quarter. In turn, this is multiplied by 60, the Days Materials Cost in Payables. That is, $328,767 of the $500,000 purchased is in Accounts Payable at the end of the quarter.

The Cash item for the fourth quarter, cell L18 on the Balance Sheet, accumulates many items on the Balance Sheet. Among them are the Accounts Payable at the end of the third quarter and Accounts Payable at the end of the fourth quarter. Accounts Payable at the end of the fourth quarter is *added* to Cash, and Accounts Payable at the end of the third quarter is *subtracted* from Cash.

The logic is that if Accounts Payable for any quarter is less than Accounts Payable for the prior quarter, cash must have been expended to pay the account down.

Therefore, a reduction in Accounts Payable at the end of the fourth quarter means that a smaller number is added to the Cash account. As a result, the value of Current Assets declines—as does the value of Total Assets.

The next several sections of this chapter deal in detail with the items on the Data Sheet, Balance Sheet, Income Statement, and Cash Flow Sheet. Many of the relationships among these worksheets are variations on the pattern of the Data Sheet and the Balance Sheet, discussed in this section. You will find it useful to make sure that you have traced this example, using a Business Planner file, and that you have thought it through conceptually, before you begin the remainder of this chapter.

Understanding the Data Sheet

The Data Sheet contains many of the inputs that you supply to create the necessary formula values in the workbook's other sheets. Figure 19.7 shows the Data Sheet populated with the Business Planner's sample data.

Fig. 19.7

The Data Sheet is where you enter basic information about expenses as a percentage of sales, and about operating data as number of days' worth of various quantities.

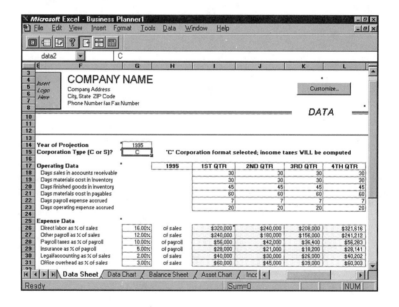

There are several sections to this sheet, including operating data, expense data, financing data, and information that identifies the year that will be forecast and the type of corporation involved.

Specifying the Type of Corporation

Use cell G15 in the Data Sheet to specify the type of corporation described in the Business Planner: normally, you would enter either a "C" or an "S." The income tax laws and regulations treat an S-corporation differently than they do a C-corporation. There are methods of tax treatment available to an S-corporation that are not available to a C-corporation. (Consult your lawyer or accountant for advice on the type of corporation you should create, or if you do not know which type of corporation your company has elected.) This is the reason that the Business Planner automatically estimates income taxes if you specify a C-corporation in the Data Sheet, and does not do so if you specify an S-corporation.

For example, examine cell H38 in the Income Statement (see fig. 19.8).

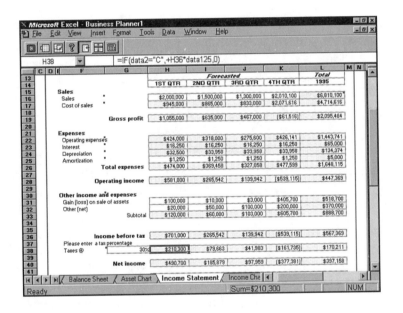

Fig. 19.8
Tax liability information in the Income Statement depends on whether you specify "C" as the type of corporation on the Data Sheet.

Cell H38's formula is:

```
=IF(data2="C",+H36*data125,0)
```

The range named data2 is cell G15 on the Data Sheet. If you have entered a "C" in that cell, you have specified a C-corporation. The range named data125 is cell G38 on the Income Statement, and contains the applicable tax rate.

> **Tip**
>
> Notice that names such as "data2" and "data125" are not useful means of documenting a worksheet. When you are choosing a name, consider using names such as "TypeOfCorporation" and "TaxRate."

So, the effect of this formula is to apply the tax rate in data125 to the Income Before Taxes (cell H36 of the Income Statement) if data2 contains a "C," and to return a zero otherwise. The zero value does not necessarily mean that no taxes apply—although that might well be the case—but that, in the case of an S-corporation, calculating the corporate income tax requires much more information than the workbook contains.

Entering the Operating Data

There are six categories of operating data that you should enter in the Data Sheet, from Days Sales in Accounts Receivable to Days Operating Expense Accrued (refer to fig. 19.7). Each category requires four entries: one for each of the forecast year's quarters. To completely specify each of these categories, you will need to enter data in cells I18:L23 of the Data Sheet.

Each entry serves to allocate certain amounts in the Business Planner's other worksheets. For example, consider cells I19:L19 and I20:L20, which contain the number of Days Material Costs in Inventory and Days Finished Goods in Inventory. The sample data set specifies 30 days and 45 days, respectively, for these two categories.

Materials refers to the raw materials that a company obtains to support its operations. To a manufacturing company, materials might mean steel, chemicals, or glass. To a merchandising company, materials might mean goods that it will retail to its customers. *Finished goods* refers to the result of a company's production activities. The value of finished goods includes the materials used to produce them, as well as the cost of the direct labor required and any factory overhead (such as the cost of electricity) that is expended as a result of the production process.

Days Material Costs in Inventory means the number of days worth of material costs that are in the inventory at the end of the quarter.

Similarly, Days Finished Goods in Inventory means the number of days worth of finished goods that are in the inventory at the end of the quarter.

The Balance Sheet makes use of this information in cells I20:L20, which contain inventory dollar amounts for each quarter. Cell I20 in the Balance Sheet contains this formula (which is then extended into cells J20:L20):

```
=ROUND(((('Income Statement'!H53/(365*0.25))*'Data
    Sheet'!I19)+((SUM('Income Statement'!H52:H54)/(365*0.25))*'Data
    Sheet'!I20),0)
```

Begin with this fragment from the formula:

```
('Income Statement'!H53/(365*0.25))
```

Cell H53 on the Income Statement contains the dollar amount of materials used in the production of the goods sold during the forecast year's first quarter. The sample data give this amount as $500,000—it is an entered value, rather than a calculated formula. So, the preceding fragment divides the $500,000 by the 91 days in a calendar quarter, so as to return the average cost of materials on any given day in a quarter.

Expand the fragment:

```
(('Income Statement'!H53/(365*0.25))*'Data Sheet'!I19)
```

This multiplies the previous result by the Days Material Costs in Inventory for the first quarter, cell I19 in the Data Sheet, which the sample data specifies as 30. The result, $164,384, indicates that at the end of the quarter the company has $164,384 worth of materials in its inventory: materials that have not yet been converted to finished goods. This is, in other words, 30 days worth of the average daily usage of materials.

The next fragment in cell I20 of the Balance Sheet is:

```
SUM('Income Statement'!H52:H54)/(365*0.25)
```

The sum of the Income Statement's cells H52:H54 includes the total Cost of Sales for the first quarter: Direct Labor, Materials, and Other Costs (for a manufacturing firm, Other Costs typically refers to factory overhead). Again, this fragment converts the total Cost of Sales ($945,000 in the sample data) to a daily average.

Expand the fragment:

```
(SUM('Income Statement'!H52:H54)/(365*0.25))*'Data Sheet'!I20
```

The daily average Cost of Sales is multiplied by the value in cell I20 of the Data Sheet, Days Finished Goods in Inventory. As noted previously, the cost of finished goods is typically the cost of the labor involved in production, the cost of the materials used, and the cost of the associated overhead.

Multiplying the average daily total cost of these three categories by Days Finished Goods in Inventory returns the value of finished goods in inventory at the end of the quarter ($466,027 using the sample data).

Finally, the complete formula in cell I20 of the Balance Sheet:

```
=ROUND((('Income Statement'!H53/(365*0.25))*'Data
    Sheet'!I19)+((SUM('Income Statement'!H52:H54)/(365*0.25))*'Data
    Sheet'!I20),0)
```

adds the value of materials at the end of the quarter to the value of finished goods at the end of the quarter, and rounds that total to eliminate fractions of a dollar. This amount represents the value of the company's inventory at the calendar quarter's end.

The Days Materials Cost in Payables, Days Materials Cost in Inventory, and Days Finished Goods in Inventory have been examined. The remaining operating data categories function in much the same way:

- The Income Statement's Sales data (cells H16:K16) is divided by the number of days in each quarter, and multiplied by Days Sales in Accounts Receivable to return the Balance Sheet's Accounts Receivable (cells I19:L19).

- The Data Sheet's Direct Labor and Other Payroll Expenses (cells I26:L27) are divided by the number of days in each quarter, and multiplied by Days Payroll Expense Accrued to return a portion of the Balance Sheet's Accrued Expenses (cells I48:L48).

- The Data Sheet's Payroll Taxes, Insurance, Legal and Office Overhead expenses (cells I28:L31) are divided by the number of days in each quarter, and multiplied by Days Operating Expense Accrued to complete the Balance Sheet's Accrued Expenses.

Entering the Expense Data

Chapter 8, "Budgeting and Planning Cycle," discussed the notion that many types of costs and income track sales volumes very closely. Net income, for example, normally departs from sales volume only as a result of discounts and returns. Similarly, you can expect that payroll costs will increase as sales grow, and that in the long run they will decrease as sales fall.

The Business Planner makes use of these relationships in its estimation of expense data. There are six expense categories in the Data Sheet that are based either directly or indirectly on sales volume:

- Direct labor as % of sales

- Other payroll as % of sales

- Payroll taxes as % of payroll

- Insurance as % of payroll

- Legal/accounting as % of sales

- Office overhead as % of sales

The assumption is that each of these categories is driven by sales volumes (refer to fig. 19.7). This is a reasonable assumption in most cases. Certainly, both direct labor and other payroll normally bear a close relationship to sales volumes. Legal/accounting and office overhead do not track sales volumes quite as well. Knowing that your company will soon be involved in litigation, for example, could cause you to modify the assumption by changing the formulas that depend on the Legal/accounting percentage.

The Payroll taxes and Insurance categories refer to payroll, rather than to sales, mainly as a matter of convenience. When you incur payroll taxes such as FICA, they are based directly on payroll amounts, and you can obtain the appropriate percentage from the state and Federal forms. Similarly, because it is based on payroll, the Insurance category refers principally to the employer's portion of expenses such as unemployment insurance. There is no particular reason to believe that insurance on plant and equipment tracks payroll well, so you should estimate the cost of this insurance elsewhere, such as in Other Income and Expenses on the Income Statement.

You will have to estimate the percentage for each expense category on the basis of either historical information or special knowledge. For example, you might know that for the past five years, Direct Labor has averaged 19 percent of sales, and you might see no reason to believe that this relationship will change next year. Or, your accountant might notify you that the Federal unemployment tax rate will increase by 0.2 percent next year.

Each of these six estimates applies directly to the dollar amounts on the Data Sheet, in cells I26:L31. The calculation of the dollar amounts for each expense category is straightforward. For example, the estimate of Direct Labor costs for the first quarter (cell I26) is returned by:

```
='Income Statement'!H16*$G26
```

Cell H16 on the Income Statement contains your estimate of sales volume for the first quarter, and cell G26 on the Data Sheet contains your estimate of the ratio of Direct Labor to Sales. On this basis, then, the Business Planner estimates your first quarter Direct Labor expenses as the percentage you enter on the Data Sheet, multiplied by the amount you enter for first quarter sales.

The costs associated with Other Payroll, Legal/Accounting, and Office Overhead are computed in a similar fashion.

The estimate of Payroll Taxes for the first quarter (cell I28 on the Data Sheet) is returned by:

```
=SUM(I$26:I$27)*$G28
```

where cells I26:I27 contain the Direct Labor and Other Payroll costs, respectively. Because these amounts depend directly on sales volume, the formula could refer to sales volume instead of to payroll. As noted above, referring to payroll instead of to sales volume is principally a matter of convenience in entering the correct percentage.

The estimate of Insurance for the first quarter (cell I29 in the Data sheet) works just like the estimate of Payroll Taxes, except that the Insurance percentage of payroll is used instead of the Payroll Tax percentage of payroll.

The dollar amounts for the expense categories support items on the Balance Sheet and Income Statement. For example, Accrued Expenses on the Balance Sheet is the sum of:

- Direct Labor and Other Payroll in conjunction with Days Payroll Expense Accrued, plus

- Payroll Taxes, Insurance, Legal/Accounting and Office Overhead in conjunction with Days Operating Expense Accrued

This calculation is examined in more detail in the section "Understanding the Balance Sheet" later in this chapter.

Entering the Financing Data

The Financing Data section of the Data Sheet is shown in figure 19.9.

In this section of the Data Sheet, enter information that pertains to amounts borrowed from lenders, capital stock issued, additional capital invested, and depreciation accumulated from prior periods. As noted in the cell tips for short- and long-term debt, the following rules apply:

- Long-term debt includes obligations that are payable over a term greater than one fiscal year.

- The current portion of long-term debt is the amount that is payable during the current fiscal year. The long-term portion of long-term debt is the amount that is payable subsequent to the current fiscal year.

- Short-term debt includes obligations that are payable during the current fiscal year: of course, short-term debt has no long-term portion.

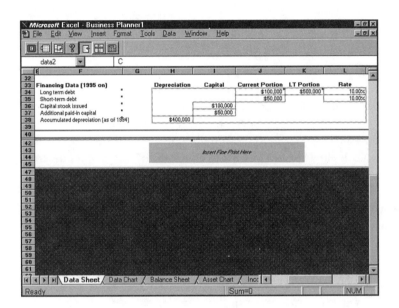

Fig. 19.9

Enter information about how the company acquires funds through debt and investment in the Financing Data section of the Business Planner's Data Sheet.

These amounts, including capital and depreciation, are linked directly to the corresponding areas of the Balance Sheet. Accumulated Depreciation is used on the Balance Sheet as an offset to Fixed Assets (see Balance Sheet cell H29, fig. 19.10).

The remaining financing data appear in the Balance Sheet under the heading of Liabilities and Stockholders' Equity for a C-corporation (the heading uses the term Owners' Equity for other than a C-corporation). See figure 19.11. The short-term debt from the Data Sheet shows up in the Balance Sheet as Notes Payable. The Data Sheet's Additional Paid-in Capital appears on the Balance Sheet as Additional Capital Invested. The Data Sheet's Long Term Portion of Long Term Debt is labeled Long Term Debt on the Balance Sheet.

The interest rates on the Data Sheet, one for Long Term and one for Short Term Debt, are linked to the Income Statement in the section labeled Detailed Supporting Information. See "Understanding the Income Statement" later in this chapter for a detailed discussion.

Understanding the Balance Sheet

Just as depicted in chapters 2, 3, and 4, the Balance Sheet in the Business Planner contains two main sections: Assets and Liabilities and Stockholders' (Owners') Equity. These two sections must, of course, balance with one another. The final, summary section of the Balance Sheet provides a convenient means of determining if they do—and, if they do not, by how much they are out of balance. This summary section also helps you determine whether the Cash and Cash Equivalents line on the Balance Sheet agrees with the Cash Flow Sheet.

The Balance Sheet is the most complex of the four main worksheets in the Business Planner: it is linked to each of the other three main worksheets. It receives data from the Data Sheet, from the Income Statement and from the Cash Flow Sheet, and it passes information to both the Income Statement and the Cash Flow Sheet. The next two sections of this chapter describe these relationships in detail.

Determining the Company's Assets

The Asset portion of the Balance Sheet is shown in figure 19.10.

Fig. 19.10

The Business Planner's Balance Sheet (Assets section) calculates assets on the basis of information you provide in the Data Sheet and the Income Statement.

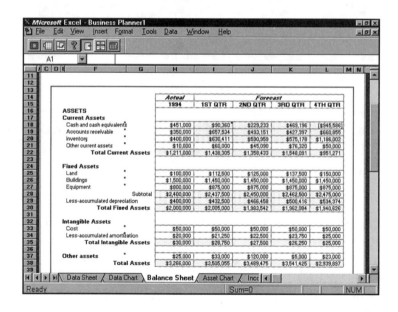

		Actual	Forecast			
		1994	1ST QTR	2ND QTR	3RD QTR	4TH QTR
ASSETS						
Current Assets						
Cash and cash equivalents		$451,000	$90,360	$229,233	$469,196	($945,586)
Accounts receivable		$350,000	$657,534	$493,151	$427,397	$660,955
Inventory		$400,000	$630,411	$590,959	$575,178	$1,186,002
Other current assets		$10,000	$60,000	$45,090	$76,320	$50,000
Total Current Assets		$1,211,000	$1,438,305	$1,358,433	$1,548,091	$951,271
Fixed Assets						
Land		$100,000	$112,500	$125,000	$137,500	$150,000
Buildings		$1,500,000	$1,450,000	$1,450,000	$1,450,000	$1,450,000
Equipment		$800,000	$875,000	$875,000	$875,000	$875,000
Subtotal		$2,400,000	$2,437,500	$2,450,000	$2,462,500	$2,475,000
Less-accumulated depreciation		$400,000	$432,500	$466,458	$500,416	$534,374
Total Fixed Assets		$2,000,000	$2,005,000	$1,983,542	$1,962,084	$1,940,626
Intangible Assets						
Cost		$50,000	$50,000	$50,000	$50,000	$50,000
Less-accumulated amortization		$20,000	$21,250	$22,500	$23,750	$25,000
Total Intangible Assets		$30,000	$28,750	$27,500	$26,250	$25,000
Other assets		$25,000	$33,000	$120,000	$5,000	$23,000
Total Assets		$3,266,000	$3,505,055	$3,489,475	$3,541,425	$2,939,897

The company's assets are categorized as Current Assets, Fixed Assets, Intangible Assets, and Other Assets. Current Assets begins with Cash and Cash Equivalents, which is by far the most complicated of the asset categories: it contains 90 components. For example, the formula for Cash and Cash Equivalents in the second quarter is:

```
=IF(ISERR(ROUND(I18+I19+I20+I21+I25+I26+I27+I33+I37+J44+J45+J46+J47+J48+J49
+J53+J54+J55+J56-J19-J20-J21-J25-J26-J27-J33-J37-I44-I45-I46-I47-I48-I49-I53-
I54-I55-I56+J63-I63+'Income Statement'!I24+'Income Statement'!I25+J61-
I61+J62-I62,0)),"",ROUND(I18+I19+I20+I21+I25+I26+I27+I33+I37+J44+J45+J46+J47
+J48+J49+J53+J54+J55+J56-J19-J20-J21-J25-J26-J27-J33-J37-I44-I45-I46-I47-I48-
I49-I53-I54-I55-I56+J63-I63+'Income Statement'!I24+'Income
Statement'!I25+J61-I61+J62-I62,0))
```

It may be more evident to you, as you examine a formula such as this, why you should give the cells and ranges in your worksheets meaningful names.

The first half of the formula tests whether the addition and subtraction of its components results in an error. This would occur if one or more of the components itself returned an Excel error value such as #VALUE! or #NUM!. In that event, the formula would return a null value, represented in the formula by the consecutive double quotation marks ("").

If the addition and subtraction do not return an error value, the formula returns the result itself. That's a little more manageable:

```
ROUND(I18+I19+I20+I21+I25+I26+I27+I33+I37+J44+J45+J46+J47+J48+J49+J53+J54+J55
+J56-J19-J20-J21-J25-J26-J27-J33-J37-I44-I45-I46-I47-I48-I49-I53-I54-I55-
I56+J63-I63+'Income Statement'!I24+'Income Statement'!I25+J61-I61+J62-I62,0)
```

but it's still unwieldy, so break it up into fragments. This fragment:

```
I18+I19+I20+I21
```

is the sum of the prior quarter's current assets: Cash and Cash Equivalents, Accounts Receivable, Inventory, and Other Current Assets.

The next fragment:

```
I25+I26+I27
```

is the sum of the prior quarter's fixed assets, including land, buildings, and equipment. Why add fixed assets to a current asset category? Bear with it—it will become clear shortly.

This fragment:

```
I33+I37
```

returns the sum of intangible assets and other assets.

So far, the formula has taken into account the valuation of various assets at the end of the prior quarter. Because the cell addresses now refer to Column J instead of Column I, you can tell that the formula now begins to take the current quarter into account with this fragment:

```
J44+J45+J46+J47+J48+J49
```

This is the sum of the current quarter's current liabilities: Accounts Payable, Notes Payable, Current Portion of Long-term Debt, Income Taxes, Accrued Expenses, and Other Current Liabilities. (See fig. 19.11 which displays the Liabilities portion of the Balance Sheet.)

The Cash and Cash Equivalents line on the Balance Sheet (to which this formula belongs) is a means of accumulating differences from one quarter to the next in different asset and liability accounts. Notice, for example, that in the fragment above the value of cell J45 is added in. That value is the amount of Notes Payable during the second quarter.

Later on in the formula, the value of cell I45 is subtracted. The joint effect of +J45 and –I45 is to accumulate the difference between Notes Payable for the second quarter and Notes Payable for the first quarter.

Suppose that I45 contained $10,000 and J45 contained $25,000. In that case, the company would have borrowed an additional $15,000 sometime during the second quarter. When the formula adds the $25,000 in J45 and subtracts the $10,000 in I45, it accumulates the difference of $15,000—the additional amount borrowed—into the Cash account.

Or, suppose that I45 contained $25,000 and J45 contained $10,000. This indicates that the company would have paid off $15,000 in debt during the second quarter. By adding $10,000 and subtracting $25,000, the formula reduces the Cash account by the amount of debt that was paid off.

The next fragment:

```
J53+J54+J55+J56
```

represents the sum of the current quarter's Long-term Debt, Deferred Income, Deferred Income Taxes, and Other Long-term Liabilities. Later in the formula, their corresponding values from the prior quarter are subtracted. The effect is the same as for adding the current quarter's current liabilities and subtracting the prior quarter's current liabilities.

The next fragment begins the adjustment process:

```
-J19-J20-J21
```

by subtracting from current assets the value of the current quarter's Accounts Receivable, Inventory, and Other Current Assets. Recall that, previously, the formula added the value of these assets from the prior quarter. Now, by subtracting their values for the *current* quarter, the formula evaluates the difference between the two time periods. For example, when inventory decreases from the prior to the current quarter, it is converted into a positive cash flow by means of selling finished goods to customers, and the cash category increases accordingly.

On the other hand, when inventory increases from the prior to the current quarter, more materials have been purchased than have been sold. The assets represented by Cash and Cash Equivalents are used to acquire that extra inventory, and the cash category drops in value by the corresponding amount.

The formula returns to the issue of fixed assets with this fragment:

```
-J25-J26-J27
```

which represent the value of land, buildings, and equipment, and it is now possible to explain what fixed assets are doing in a current asset calculation. Earlier, the formula added in the value of fixed assets from the prior quarter; now, it subtracts the value of the fixed assets in the current quarter. A positive change in their valuation (similar to a change in the valuation of Current Liabilities shown previously) normally means that additional land, buildings, or equipment have been acquired. The resources expended on the acquisition come from the Cash and Cash Equivalents category, so it is decreased by the corresponding amount.

Alternatively, if the valuation of the equipment is smaller in the current period than in the former period, it might be because the company has sold a building for less than the value it carried on its books. Nevertheless, the company realizes some proceeds from the sale, and it is this amount that is credited to the Cash and Cash Equivalents category. The loss represented by the difference in the asset's book value and its sales price shows up in the Fixed Assets category; any payment received from the transaction appears as cash.

Similarly, this fragment:

```
-J33-J37
```

adjusts the Cash and Cash Equivalents category by subtracting the current quarter's Intangible Assets and Other Assets, to account for any change in their valuation from the prior to the current quarter.

Recall that, earlier, the formula added in the current quarter's Current Liabilities. The formula now subtracts the prior quarter's Current Liabilities by means of this fragment:

```
-I44-I45-I46-I47-I48-I49
```

to take account of changes in Current Liabilities from quarter to quarter. If, for example, Accounts Payable contains a larger amount in the current quarter than in the prior quarter, then there is a corresponding increase in Cash and Cash Equivalents. But if the value of Accounts Payable is smaller in the current quarter than in the prior quarter, the Cash and Cash Equivalents value drops accordingly.

In the same fashion, the formula adjusts for the prior quarter's Non-current Liabilities via this fragment:

```
-I53-I54-I55-I56
```

The distribution of earnings, usually as dividends, is accounted for by taking the difference between the current and prior quarters' earnings:

```
+J63-I63
```

These earnings are referred to on the Income Statement as "retained" if the company is a C-corporation, and as "undistributed" otherwise. As these earnings grow from the prior quarter to the current quarter, and if no payments are made from the earnings to the stockholders, the Cash and Cash Equivalents category increases.

This fragment:

```
+'Income Statement'!I24+'Income Statement'!I25
```

represents an action that causes considerable confusion over the issue of depreciation. It adds to the Cash and Cash Equivalents category the prior quarter's Depreciation and Amortization amounts. Yet, depreciation is not cash. As an asset gets older, a company does not have more cash as a result.

Recall from chapter 16 "Fixed Assets," that the reason to depreciate an asset is to distribute its cost over the periods during which it is in service. According to the matching principle, this enables the business to account for the asset's usefulness during the time that it contributes to the business's profitability. Considered in that light, depreciation represents an expired cost. At the same time, it is necessary to distribute the payment for that asset over the same time period, and adding the prior quarter's depreciation to the current quarter's Cash and Cash Equivalents category is a means of doing that. In a sense, the process of adding depreciation to this category represents the act of borrowing from the period in which the asset was actually acquired.

You will see, in the discussion of Fixed Assets, later in this section, how adding depreciation to this category is compensated by subtracting depreciation from Fixed Assets.

The formula for Cash and Cash Equivalents during the second quarter is completed by this fragment:

```
+J61-I61+J62-I62
```

which adds in the current quarter's Capital Stock Issued and Additional Capital Invested, and subtracts the prior quarter's valuation of these amounts. Thus, as investments increase from quarter to quarter, the Cash and Cash Equivalents category also increases.

To summarize this very long and complex formula, you can recast it in terms of names rather than cell addresses. The Cash and Cash Equivalents for a quarter is:

```
Cash and Cash Equivalent Assets (prior quarter) plus:

Non-cash Assets(prior quarter) minus Non-cash Assets(current
    quarter) plus:

Liabilities(current quarter) minus Liabilities(prior quarter) plus:

Earnings(current quarter) minus Earnings(prior quarter) plus:

Depreciation and amortization(prior quarter) plus:

Capital stock and investment(current quarter) minus Capital stock
    and investment(prior quarter)
```

After trudging through all the components of the formula for Cash and Cash Equivalents, the remaining formulas in the Balance Sheet (indeed, in the entire Business Planner workbook) will be easy for you. Here's the formula for Accounts Receivable at the end of the second quarter:

```
=ROUND(('Income Statement'!I16/(365*0.25))*'Data Sheet'!J18,0)
```

Cell I16 on the Income Statement contains your estimate of sales volume for the second quarter. Recall from the discussion of the Data Sheet that Accounts Receivable is estimated by using Days Sales in Accounts Receivable, a value that you provide in Data Sheet cell J18. The sample data give 30 days as the latter estimate, and $1,500,000 as the second quarter sales. So this formula evaluates to:

```
=ROUND((1500000/(365*0.25))*30,0)
```

or $493,151. In words, divide the quarter's sales by the number of days in a quarter, and multiply by the number of days worth of sales that are still in Accounts Receivable at the end of the quarter.

The formula for Inventory is very similar to the Accounts Receivable formula:

```
=ROUND((('Income Statement'!I53/(365*0.25))*'Data
    Sheet'!J19)+((SUM('Income Statement'!I52:I54)/(365*0.25))*'Data
    Sheet'!J20),0)
```

Cell I53 on the Income Statement contains your estimate of the cost of materials purchased during the prior quarter; the sample data provide a $500,000 estimate. Cell J19 in the Data Sheet contains your estimate of Days Materials Cost in Inventory; the sample data estimate this value as 30.

Cells I52:I54 on the Income Statement contain the costs of Direct Labor, Materials (again), and Other Costs involved in the creation of finished goods. Cell J20 on the Data Sheet contains Days Finished Goods in Inventory. Using the sample data, the formula for Inventory on the Balance Sheet evaluates to:

```
=ROUND(((500000/(365*0.25))*30)+((865000/(365*0.25))*45),0)
```

or $590,959. Again, the materials cost for the quarter is prorated to a daily average and then multiplied by the number of days worth of materials in inventory at the end of the quarter. Then, the total cost of finished goods is prorated and multiplied by the number of days worth of finished goods in inventory at the end of the quarter. These two quantities are summed, to return the inventory valuation at the end of the quarter.

Other Current Assets, a value that you enter, consists of assets not identified elsewhere that you can convert to cash (a) within a short period of time, and (b) without conflicting with your normal business operations.

Total Current Assets is simply the sum of Cash and Cash Equivalents, Acccounts Receivable, Inventory and Other Current Assets.

The Fixed Assets category is composed mainly of values that you enter for Land, Buildings and Equipment. The sum of these asset values is adjusted by subtracting Accumulated Depreciation. Its formula for the second quarter (in cell J29 on the Balance Sheet) is:

```
=I29+SUM('Income Statement'!I57:I58)
```

Cell I29 contains the accumulated depreciation through the end of the prior quarter. Cells I57:I58 on the Income Statement contain the second quarter's depreciation on buildings and equipment (land, by the way, is not considered depreciable, so there is no provision in the Business Planner for depreciating it).

It is here that balancing takes place to account for including the prior quarter's depreciation in the Cash and Cash Equivalents category. As described previously, the latter formula adds cell I24 from the Income Statement. That cell is the sum of Income Statement cells I57:I58, depreciation on buildings and equipment. At this point, that amount is subtracted from the valuation of Fixed Assets, with the result that the net effect of depreciation on Total Assets is zero. However, and although it has no effect on Total Assets, it does modify both the Current Asset and Fixed Asset valuations. Among other results and analyses, these are important for the determination of various operating ratios discussed in Chapter 7, "Ratio Analysis."

Total Fixed Assets is, of course, the sum of the valuation of land, buildings and equipment, less the accumulated depreciation.

Intangible Assets includes any other assets (labeled "Cost" on the Balance Sheet) that have no physical basis, and accumulated amortization. The other assets might include items such as a copyright or goodwill, and their values are normally very difficult to quantify. The amortization of these assets is, in concept, similar to the depreciation of a tangible asset: over time, the value of the intangible asset is written off to current period's expense. To reflect this reduction in value, Total Intangible Assets is the result of subtracting Accumulated Amortization from the intangible assets' cost.

The Other Assets category is another value that you enter. This category might include an asset such as prepaid insurance or the advance payment of rental fees.

The final portion of the Assets section of the Balance Sheet is Total Assets. For each quarter, these cells simply return the total of Current Assets, Fixed Assets, Intangible Assets and Other Assets.

Determining the Company's Liabilities and Equity

The second section of the Business Planner's Balance Sheet concerns the company's liabilities and stockholders' (owners') equity. Using the sample data, it is shown in figure 19.11.

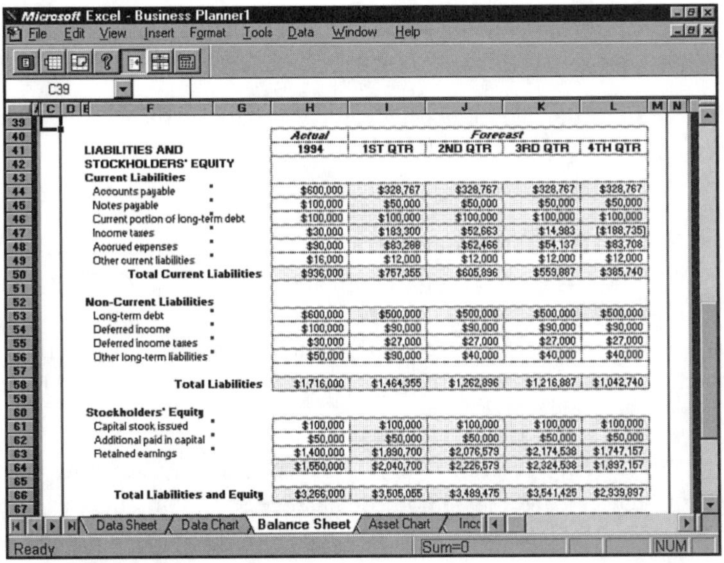

	Actual	Forecast			
LIABILITIES AND STOCKHOLDERS' EQUITY	1994	1ST QTR	2ND QTR	3RD QTR	4TH QTR
Current Liabilities					
Accounts payable	$600,000	$328,767	$328,767	$328,767	$328,767
Notes payable	$100,000	$50,000	$50,000	$50,000	$50,000
Current portion of long-term debt	$100,000	$100,000	$100,000	$100,000	$100,000
Income taxes	$30,000	$183,300	$52,663	$14,983	($188,735)
Accrued expenses	$90,000	$83,288	$62,466	$54,137	$83,708
Other current liabilities	$16,000	$12,000	$12,000	$12,000	$12,000
Total Current Liabilities	$936,000	$757,355	$605,896	$559,887	$385,740
Non-Current Liabilities					
Long-term debt	$600,000	$500,000	$500,000	$500,000	$500,000
Deferred income	$100,000	$90,000	$90,000	$90,000	$90,000
Deferred income taxes	$30,000	$27,000	$27,000	$27,000	$27,000
Other long-term liabilities	$50,000	$90,000	$40,000	$40,000	$40,000
Total Liabilities	$1,716,000	$1,464,355	$1,262,896	$1,216,887	$1,042,740
Stockholders' Equity					
Capital stock issued	$100,000	$100,000	$100,000	$100,000	$100,000
Additional paid in capital	$50,000	$50,000	$50,000	$50,000	$50,000
Retained earnings	$1,400,000	$1,890,700	$2,076,579	$2,174,538	$1,747,157
	$1,550,000	$2,040,700	$2,226,579	$2,324,538	$1,897,157
Total Liabilities and Equity	$3,266,000	$3,505,055	$3,489,475	$3,541,425	$2,939,897

Fig. 19.11
The Business Planner's Balance Sheet (Liabilities and Equity section) accumulates information about existing liabilities and the company's equity position.

Just as the company's assets are classified as current, fixed and intangible, the company's liabilities are classified as either current or non-current. Many of the entries in the liabilities section are either data that you enter yourself or are linked to cells in the Data Sheet where you have entered data.

The first current liability is Accounts Payable. Its formula, for cell J44 (second quarter) is:

```
=ROUND(('Income Statement'!I53/(365*0.25))*'Data Sheet'!J21,0)
```

This formula follows a familiar pattern, established in the Assets section. Cell I53 on the Income Statement is the cost of materials for the second quarter. That amount is prorated for the number of days in a quarter, and multiplied by Days Materials Cost in Payables, Data Sheet cell J21, for the current quarter.

Notes Payable for the second quarter, cell J45 on the Balance Sheet, links directly to the Data Sheet:

```
='Data Sheet'!J35
```

This is the amount of short-term debt that you have entered in the Data Sheet.

Current Portion of Long-term Debt for the second quarter, cell J46 on the Balance Sheet, links directly to the Data Sheet:

```
='Data Sheet'!J34
```

which is the value that you enter for the portion of long-term debt that is payable during the current fiscal year.

Income Taxes for the second quarter, cell J47 on the Balance Sheet, contains this formula:

```
=IF($H68="Y",ROUND(('Income Statement'!I38-J55),0),0)
```

Cell H68 looks to the range named data2, cell G15 on the Data Sheet, which should contain a "C" for a C-corporation, and returns a "Y" if G15 contains a "C". So, if the company is *not* a C-corporation, the Balance Sheet's cell J47 returns a zero. Otherwise, if the company *is* a C-corporation, the formula returns the difference between the Income Statement's cell I38 and J55 on the Balance Sheet.

I38 on the Income Statement contains the corporate taxes attributable to the current quarter's income. J55 on the Balance Sheet contains the current quarter's deferred income taxes. The Income Tax liability is, therefore, the difference between the payable taxes and the taxes that the company is deferring to some future period.

Accrued Expenses, cell J48 on the Balance Sheet, contains this formula:

```
=ROUND(((('Data Sheet'!J26+'Data Sheet'!J27)/(365*0.25))*'Data
    Sheet'!J22)+((SUM('Data Sheet'!J28:J31))/(365*0.25))*'Data
    Sheet'!J23,0)
```

Cells J26 and J27 on the Data Sheet contain the Direct Labor and Other Payroll expenses for the current quarter. These are summed, prorated for the number of days in a quarter, and multiplied by the Days Payroll Expense Accrued at the end of the quarter (Data Sheet cell J22).

Cells J28:J31 on the Data Sheet contain Payroll Taxes, Insurance, Legal/Accounting, and Office Overhead expenses for the current quarter. Again, these are summed, prorated and multiplied by Days Operating Expense Accrued (Data Sheet cell J23).

These two amounts are then summed to return the Accrued Expenses for the current quarter.

Other Current Liabilities is a value that you enter yourself, and of course includes liabilities not accounted for in the other categories under Current Liabilities. An example is unearned revenue: money that you have been paid for work that you have not yet performed. Because you must perform the work at some future time, this unearned revenue is regarded as a current liability.

Total Current Liabilities is, of course, the sum of each current liability category for the quarter.

Moving to the Non-current Liabilities section of the Balance Sheet, the first entry is Long-term Debt. This is linked to cell K34 of the Data Sheet, the Long-term portion of Long-term Debt (recall that there is a current portion of Long-term debt: that portion that is payable during the current fiscal year).

The remaining information in Non-current Liabilities consists of data that you enter yourself: Deferred Income, Deferred Income Taxes and Other Long Term Liabilities. Total Liabilities is the sum of these items, plus the Long-term portion of the Long-Term Debt.

The next section of the Balance Sheet details the Equity held in the company by owners or stockholders. That category consists of Capital Stock Issued, Additional Paid In Capital (for an entity other than a C-corporation, this is termed Additional Capital Invested) and Retained Earnings (for an entity other than a C-corporation, this is termed Undistributed Earnings).

Capital Stock Issued links directly to cell I36 on the Data Sheet, which is where you enter the figure for the par value of Capital Stock. Additional Paid In Capital (Additional Capital Invested) links directly to cell I37 on the Data Sheet; again, this is a figure that you enter.

Retained (Undistributed) Earnings links to the Income Statement, cell I46 for the second quarter. As will be discussed in the next section, this is the company's earnings for the quarter, less any dividends paid (C-corporation) or distributions to the owners of, for example, an S-corporation).

The final entry in the Liabilities and Equity section totals all liabilities and equity categories. It is compared to Total Assets in the summary section of the Balance Sheet to ensure that the assets and liabilities are in balance.

Determining Whether the Assets and Liabilities Balance

The final section of the Balance Sheet tests the equality of the company's assets, on one hand, and its liabilities and equity, on the other. It also compares the Cash and Cash Equivalents category of the Assets section to the cash position reported by the Cash Flow Sheet.

Cell H68 simply recaps the information in cell G15 of the Data Sheet: it returns a "Y" if G15 contains a "C," and an "N" otherwise.

The Cash Balance Positive Or (Negative) line depends on the value of Cash and Cash Equivalents (Balance Sheet cells H18:L18): if this is a positive number, the corresponding column for the Cash Balance test returns "Positive," and otherwise it returns "Negative."

The Amount Sheet is Out-of-Balance line returns the difference between Total Assets and Total Liabilities and Equity. Cell J70, for example, tests the equality of assets and liabilities for the second quarter by means of this formula:

```
=J38-J66
```

which is Total Assets minus Total Liabilities and Equity. Therefore, a positive number in this cell means that the Balance Sheet calculates greater Assets than Liabilities and Equity. Any non-zero number in the Amount Sheet is Out-of-Balance line means that an error exists somewhere in the workbook, and you should track down its source before you put any credence in the amounts reported and forecast.

Other than making entries in cells that already contain formulas, there aren't many ways that you can enter data in the Business Planner such that the Balance Sheet would show an out-of-balance condition after all the data has been entered. But there are some ways you can bring this situation about.

For example, suppose that you were to adjust the Accumulated Depreciation amount in the Data Sheet. The sample data provides a value of $400,000 as the starting value for Accumulated Depreciation, and if you change this by $1 to $400,001 you will find that the Balance Sheet's Total Assets and Total Liabilities and Equity are out of balance by $1. As noted previously, Accumulated Depreciation acts as an offset to Fixed Assets, and therefore adding $1 to it reduces Total Assets by $1.

However, this action does not cause an offsetting adjustment in Total Liabilities and Equity. To bring the Balance Sheet back into balance, you would need to make a corresponding reduction in a liability or equity account—in this case, you would probably reduce the initial value of Undistributed (Retained) earnings by $1.

The Amount Cash Flow Out-of-Balance line compares the current quarter's Cash and Cash Equivalents value to the Cash at End of Period from the Cash Flow Sheet. Again, these two numbers will be equal if the Business Planner is in balance. This chapter discusses how the Business Planner derives the Cash at End of Period value, in the section "Understanding the Cash Flow Sheet."

As noted at the beginning of this section, the Balance Sheet is the most complex of the sheets in the Business Planner. If you have followed the discussion of the flow of information into and out of the Balance Sheet, you are well placed to understand the Income Statement and Cash Flow Sheet.

Understanding the Income Statement

It's useful to consider the Income Statement as consisting of two parts: the first main section contains information about sources and amounts of revenue and expenses, and the second main section contains information about the tax and distribution consequences, plus standard supporting information.

Determining Revenue and Expenses

The revenue and expense portion of the Income Statement is repeated for convenience in figure 19.12.

The Income Statement contains some information that you enter yourself, some that comes from the Data Sheet, and some that comes from the Balance Sheet. One range of information that you enter yourself, Sales, is particularly important. Recall that virtually all the expense information recorded on the Balance Sheet is calculated as a percentage of Sales, using percentages that you enter on the Data Sheet. In turn, these expense figures are used by the Cash Flow Sheet to forecast the company's cash position at the end of each quarter.

Fig. 19.12

The Business Planner's Income Statement (Sales and Expenses) applies the Percentage of Sales approach to estimate quarterly operating expenses.

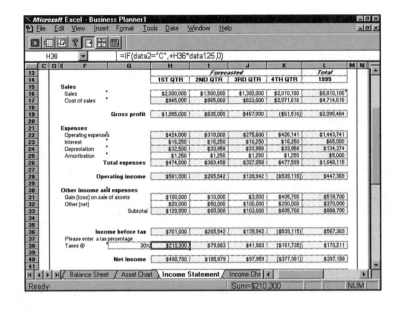

Therefore, it is important to estimate both the total sales volume for the forecast year, and the sales volume during each quarter, as accurately as possible. Suppose, for example, that at the end of the second quarter you have a major payment on a loan coming due. Suppose further that your sales are seasonal, with most of the annual revenue occurring during the third and fourth quarters. If you estimate quarterly sales simply by dividing estimated annual sales by 4, you will probably over-estimate the sales volume for the second quarter. The result will be that your forecast cash position for the end of the second quarter will be higher than it should be—when the end of the second quarter comes around, you might even find that your cash balance has a negative instead of the forecast positive value.

Chapter 9, "Forecasting and Projections," discusses the process of estimating future values on the basis of historic values. Use the Excel procedures and tools described there to assign sales volumes for each quarter as accurately as possible.

Following the Sales range, the Income Statement calculates the Cost of Sales by summing figures for Direct Labor, Materials and Other Costs (cells H52:L54 on the Income Statement; see fig. 19.14). Cost of Sales is subtracted from Sales to return the Gross Profit in cells H19:L19.

The Expenses section of the Income Statement (cells H22:L26) calculates Operating Expenses, Interest and Depreciation. You enter quarterly Amortization expenses in H26:K26.

Operating Expenses for each quarter are determined by a link to the Data Sheet. For example, Operating Expenses for the second quarter are calculated by this formula:

```
=SUM('Data Sheet'!J27:J31)
```

Cells J27:J31 on the Data Sheet are Other Payroll, Payroll Taxes, Insurance, Legal/accounting, and Office Overhead for the second quarter. Notice that this range does not include Direct Labor, which has already found its way into the Income Statement by means of the calculation of Cost of Sales, and has been subtracted from Sales as part of the Gross Profit calculation.

Total Expenses, in cells H26:L26 on the Income Statement, sums these operating expenses. Then, Operating Income (cells H28:L28) is found by subtracting Operating Expenses from Gross Profit. Other Income and Expenses, cells H31:K32 on the Income Statement, is a range where you enter the effect of transactions not included in the Sales and Expenses sections of theworksheet. Usually, any values that you enter here would be transactions that are not part of the company's normal line of business. As the note for cell F30 states, you should exercise great care in determining these amounts; furthermore, you should be careful of how they contribute to the Income Before Tax range, in cells H36:L36. These transactions may or may not produce taxable income, and you should consult your accountant or tax lawyer before deciding how they should be treated for the purpose of reporting income.

Note also that cells H31:K31, Gain (Loss) on Sale of Assets, and cells H32:K32, Other (net), both represent net amounts for a given quarter. If you have transactions to record in these ranges, it's useful to add a worksheet to the Business Planner where you can record any individual transactions and their amounts. Then, create links to the net amounts of those transactions in H31:K32. To do so, follow these steps:

1. Select the sheet in the Business Planner workbook before which you want to put a supporting sheet.

2. Choose Insert, Worksheet.

3. On the new worksheet, enter the amounts of the individual transactions.

4. Activate the Income Statement. Select one of the cells in the Other Income and Expenses range.

5. Type the following formula fragment:

   =SUM(

   and then activate the new worksheet by selecting its sheet tab.

6. Using the mouse pointer, select the cells in the new worksheet that contain the transaction amounts that you want to sum.

7. Press Enter.

See figure 19.13 for an illustration of the result of this process.

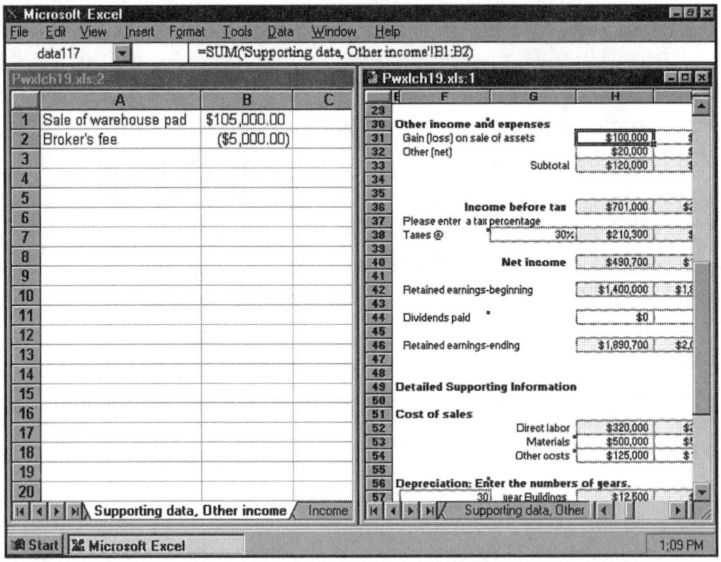

Fig. 19.13

Using a supporting worksheet to provide values for Other Income and Expenses.

Note

As distributed, the Business Planner template calculates cell H36, Income Before Taxes for the first quarter, as H28 + H33. This is the sum of Operating Income and Other Income and Expenses. However, it calculates I36, Income Before Taxes for the second quarter, as I19 – I26. This is Gross Profit minus Total Expenses. The third and fourth quarter calculations, in J36:K36, follow the pattern for I36.

The result is that, for the second through fourth quarters, Income Before Taxes equals Operating Income, and does not take Other Income and Expenses into account.

Unless Other Income and Expenses have no income tax implications during the second through fourth quarters, you should copy the formula in H36 into I36:K36.

Determining Tax Consequences, Distribution Consequences and Supporting Information

The second part of the Income Statement returns information about payable taxes, how (if at all) earnings are distributed to owners or shareholders, and about some pertinent details that are usually included in Income Statements (see fig. 19.14).

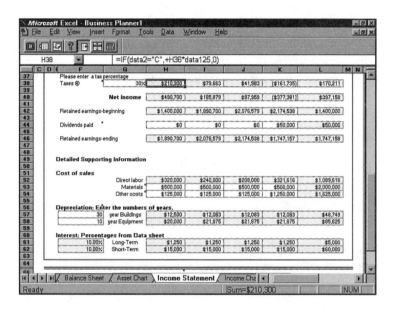

Fig. 19.14
The Business Planner's Income Statement (Distribution and Supporting Information) determines the company's earnings, which are then moved to the Balance Sheet.

In cell G38 of the Income Statement, enter the rate at which the company is taxed. Doing so has no effect if you do not define the company as a C-corporation in cell G15 on the Data Sheet. For example, the formula for taxes payable in the second quarter (Income Statement cell I38) is:

```
=IF(data2="C",+I36*data125,0)
```

The range named data2 is cell G15 on the Data Sheet, where you define the type of corporation. The range named data125 is cell G38 on the Income Statement, where you enter the tax rate. If the value in data2 is "C", this formula returns the product of Income Before Tax for the second quarter (cell I36 on the Income Statement) and the tax rate. Otherwise, the formula returns zero.

The next line on the Income Statement, Net Income, is the result of subtracting the payable taxes from Income Before Tax.

The section that pertains to the distribution of earnings begins with Retained Earnings - Beginning (or, if the company is not defined as a C-corporation, the label is Undistributed Earnings - Beginning). The corresponding cells, H42:K42, link to the Balance Sheet by means of this formula (which applies to the second quarter):

```
='Balance Sheet'!I63
```

Cell I63 on the Balance Sheet is Retained Earnings at the end of the first quarter. Cell I63 itself is linked to cell H46 on the Income Statement: Retained Earnings - Ending for the first quarter.

The amount of Retained Earnings that is subsequently distributed to stockholders (or the amount of Undistributed Earnings that is subsequently distributed to owners) is entered in Income Statement cells H44:K44. These amounts are subtracted from Retained Earnings to return Retained Earnings - Ending in cells H46:K46.

So the flow of information for Retained (Undistributed) Earnings is as follows:

1. The user enters an initial value for Retained Earnings at the end of the prior year in cell H63 of the Balance Sheet.

2. Cell H42 on the Income Statement, Retained Earnings - Beginning for the first quarter, links to the initial value entered in step 1.

3. Earnings that are distributed during or at the end of the first quarter are entered in cell H44 of the Income Statement.

4. Distributed earnings for the first quarter are subtracted from Retained Earnings - Beginning for the first quarter, and the current quarter's net income is added in, to produce Retained Earnings - Ending for the first quarter in cell H46 of the Income Statement.

5. Cell I63 on the Balance Sheet is linked to Retained Earnings - Ending for the first quarter on the Income Statement.

6. Cell I42 on the Income Statement, Retained Earnings - Beginning for the second quarter, links to cell I63 on the Balance Sheet, Retained Earnings at the end of the first quarter.

This process continues through the end of the fourth quarter.

Note that Retained Earnings for the full forecast year, in cell L42 of the Income Statement, also links to cell H63 on the Balance Sheet: Retained Earnings at the beginning of the year is identical to Retained Earnings at the beginning of the first quarter.

The final section of the Income Statement, Detailed Supporting Information, summarizes key data for Cost of Sales, Depreciation and Interest paid.

The Direct Labor portion of Cost of Sales comes directly from the Direct Labor section of the Data Sheet, and indirectly from the Sales section of the Income Statement. Recall that the Data Sheet multiplies the estimated sales for the quarter by the figure entered for Direct Labor as % of Sales. The result of this multiplication appears in the Direct Labor line within the Cost of Sales section.

It is also in the Cost of Sales section that the user enters the estimates for the amount of Materials that will be consumed during each quarter of the forecast year, as well as Other Costs (such as factory overhead) to be included in the Cost of Sales.

The next section, Depreciation, calculates the amount of depreciation that applies to each quarter during the forecast year. The Business Planner uses the straight-line method of depreciation in this calculation. For example, depreciation for the second quarter on buildings (cell I57 on the Income Statement) contains this formula:

```
=IF(ISERR(ROUND(SLN('Balance Sheet'!I26,0,$F$57)/
    4,0)),0,ROUND(SLN('Balance Sheet'!I26,0,$F$57)/4,0))
```

The formula first tests whether its intended result contains any errors: for example, whether cell I26 on the Balance Sheet (the value of the fixed asset for buildings) is itself an error value such as #VAL! or #NUM!, or whether the use of Excel's SLN( ) function returns an error when applied to its arguments. (See chapter 16, "Fixed Assets," for a discussion of SLN( ) and the straight-line method of depreciation. There is no reason that you could not choose some other method of depreciation, such as DB( ) or DDB( ), that is appropriate to the particular asset, to return the depreciation amount.)

If an error value does result, the formula returns a zero. Otherwise, it returns the depreciation on buildings for the full forecast year, divided by 4 to distribute it evenly across four quarters. If you choose to use some other method of depreciation, you could define its Periods argument so that it contains the number of quarters of the asset's life: then, you can eliminate the division by 4.

Notice that the use of the SLN( ) function here assumes that the salvage value of the buildings is zero. Also notice that the function takes as an argument the value in cell F57 of the Income Statement. This is the number of periods over which the asset is to be depreciated. Cells F57 and F58 are where the user enters the useful life of the buildings and of the equipment, respectively.

> **Tip**
>
> The Business Planner assumes that all equipment has the same useful life—probably, an unrealistic assumption. It also assumes that all buildings have the same useful life—possibly, an unrealistic assumption. You could use Goal Seek with SLN as the Set cell, an estimate of its Periods argument as the By changing cell, and your current total quarterly equipment depreciation as the To value. This would return a value for cell F57 that would result in the proper depreciation amount for each quarter.

Interest payable during a given quarter, cells H61:K62 on the Income Statement, depends in part on cells F61 and F62. These contain the interest rates that apply to Short-term and Long-term debt, and link to the Data Sheet cells where these rates are originally entered (cells L34 and L35 in the Data Sheet's Financing section).

> **Note**
>
> The Business Planner template reverses the labels in cells G61 and G62 of the Income Statement. To correct this, enter "Short-Term" in cell G61, and "Long-Term" in cell G62.

Income Statement cells H61:K61, the values for Short-term interest payments, multiply the short-term interest rate by the values for Notes Payable (cells I45:L45 on the Balance Sheet). In turn, these Notes Payable cells each link to cell J35 on the Data Sheet, where the user enters the full amount of short-term debt. The Income Statement's Short-term interest payment formula for the second quarter is:

```
=$F$61*'Balance Sheet'!J45/4
```

Notice that the formula divides the result of the multiplication by 4, to distribute the annual payment across each of the four quarters.

Income Statement cells H62:K62, the values for Long-term interest payments, multiply the long-term interest rate by sum of the values for Long-term debt (current portion) and Long-term debt (non-current portion). These values are obtained from rows 46 and 53 on the Balance Sheet, which in turn are linked to cells J34 and K34 on the Data Sheet where they are originally entered by the user. For example, the Income Statement's Long-term interest payment formula for the second quarter is:

```
=$F$62*('Balance Sheet'!J53+'Balance Sheet'!J46)/4
```

Again, notice that the formula divides the annual payment amount by four to return the amount payable during each quarter.

Understanding the Cash Flow Sheet

The final worksheet in the Business Planner template is the Cash Flow Sheet. This sheet collects information from the Balance Sheet and Income Statement and uses it to calculate the company's cash position at the end of each quarter of the forecast year.

There are no cells in the Cash Flow Sheet where you must enter information. All cells are either dependent on another worksheet, or return the results of calculations that are based on those links.

The Cash Flow Sheet contains five main sections:

- Cash from Operations

- Cash Provided or Used by Operating Activities

- Increases or Decreases from Investment Transactions

- Increases or Decreases from Financing Transactions

- Cash flow summary

Determining Cash Flow from Operations and Operating Activities

Figure 19.15 shows the first two sections of the Cash Flow Sheet.

The Cash from Operations section begins by taking Net Income, or Net Income after Tax, from the Income Statement and displaying it as Net Earnings (Loss). For example, the formula for Net Earnings (Loss) for the second quarter is:

```
=IF('Balance Sheet'!H68="y",ROUND('Income
    Statement'!I40,0),ROUND('Income Statement'!I36,0))
```

The formula begins by checking cell H68 on the Balance Sheet for a "Y" value (Excel does not distinguish between upper- and lowercase letters when it tests the equality of two text values). H68 on the Balance Sheet contains a "Y" if the company has been defined as a C-corporation on the Data Sheet. So, for a C-corporation, this formula returns the value in cell I40 of the Income Statement, which contains income after tax. For other than a C-corporation, this formula returns the value in cell I36 of the income statement, or before tax income: often, but not always, the pre-tax income is the same as after tax income for a company that is not a C-corporation.

Fig. 19.15

The Business Planner's Cash Flow Sheet shows whether the accrual method masks any problems with the company's cash availability.

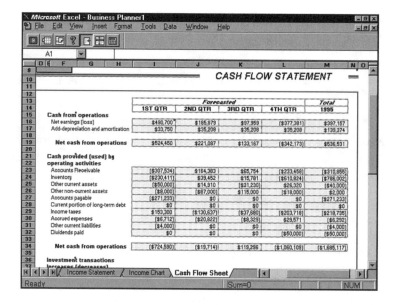

Tip

Because the Income Statement already has the logic to deal with the treatment of income taxes, the logic in the Cash Flow sheet is redundant. It's best to avoid this sort of redundancy, because if you subsequently need to modify the logic, you must remember to modify it everywhere it appears. In this case, the Cash Flow sheet could simply pick up the net income from the Income Statement, regardless of the type of corporation.

The next line, Add-Depreciation and Amortization, returns the value of depreciation and amortization values to the cash category. The value of Net Earnings for the quarter depends, as just discussed, on the value of income shown on the Income Statement. For the purposes of the Income Statement, depreciation is subtracted from Gross Profit to arrive at a figure for Operating Income.

However, the depreciation expense that was subtracted is a *non-cash* expense: even though it was used to reduce the measured income for the quarter, it had no effect on the company's cash position. The same is true of the amortization expense. Therefore, the Cash Flow Sheet adds the depreciation and amortization amounts back to the reported income, to obtain the figure for Net Cash from Operations. The formula for the Depreciation and Amortization cell for the second quarter is:

```
=ROUND('Income Statement'!I24+'Income Statement'!I25,0)
```

This formula picks up the depreciation and amortization amounts from the Income Statement. Then, the formula for Operating Income in the second quarter is:

```
=ROUND(SUM(J16:J17),0)
```

or the sum of Net Income plus Depreciation and Amortization.

The next section on the Cash Flow Sheet is Cash Provided (Used) by Operating Activities. Its first entry is Accounts Receivable. This is the difference between Accounts Receivable at the end of the prior quarter and Accounts Receivable at the end of the current quarter. For example, the impact of the difference in Accounts Receivable on cash at the end of the first quarter is shown in cell I23 of the Cash Flow Sheet:

```
=ROUND('Balance Sheet'!H19-'Balance Sheet'!I19,0)
```

Cell H19 on the Balance Sheet is $350,000, and cell I19 is $657,534, so the formula returns ($307,534). Because the size of Accounts Receivable grew from the end of the prior year to the end of the first quarter in the current year, there is an impact on cash. Some of the Sales that have been made during the first quarter, which contribute to measured income, have not yet been paid for by quarter's end. Therefore, the apparent cash value of first quarter sales must be reduced by the amount of Accounts Receivable that the company is still carrying.

In contrast, notice that Accounts Receivable increases the cash balance during the second quarter: its value, the difference between Accounts Receivable at the end of the first and the end of the second quarters, is $164,383. This is because Accounts Receivable decreased during that quarter, and the receivable amounts were converted to cash as customers paid for their purchases.

The same is true for three other items in the Cash Provided (Used) by Operating Activities section: Inventory, Other Current Assets, and Other Non-current Assets. As is the case with Accounts Receivable, these items subtract the corresponding amount on the Balance Sheet for the current quarter from the amount for the prior quarter. A positive difference represents a gain for the company's cash position, and a negative difference represents a decrease in cash.

Thus, subtracting the Inventory valuation at the end of the second quarter from the Inventory valuation at the end of the first quarter (cell J24 on the Cash Flow Sheet) returns a value of $39,452: Inventory valuation decreased from the end of the first quarter to the end of the second quarter. The effect of this decrease in inventory is to convert into cash those assets that were tied up in goods.

As you might expect, this relationship is reversed for the remaining items in the Cash Provided (Used) by Operating Activities section:

- Accounts Payable

- Current Portion of Long-term Debt

- Income Taxes

- Accrued Expenses

- Other Current Liabilities

- Dividends Paid (Distributions to Shareholders)

Any of these six items that increases from the end of the prior quarter to the end of the current quarter constitutes a decrease in the company's cash position.

For example, cell I27 on the Cash Flow Sheet contains the change in Accounts Payable from the end of the prior year to the end of the first quarter of the current year. Its formula is:

```
=ROUND('Balance Sheet'!I44-'Balance Sheet'!H44,0)
```

In contrast to the formula for Accounts Receivable, which subtracts the value for the current quarter from the value for the prior quarter, this formula subtracts the value for the prior quarter from the value for the current quarter.

In this case, Accounts Payable at the end of the prior year (Balance Sheet cell H44) was $600,000, and at the end of the first quarter (Balance Sheet cell I44) it was $328,767. The difference, ($271,233), is negative because the formula calls for $600,000 to be subtracted from $328,767. Reducing Accounts Payable by paying creditors reduces the company's cash position.

The final entry in the Cash Provided (Used) by Operating Activities section is Dividends Paid (or, if the company is not a C-corporation, Distributions to Shareholders). These cells are linked to the corresponding information in the Income Statement; for example, the formula for the first quarter is:

```
=ROUND('Income Statement'!H44*-1,0)
```

Any distribution shown on the Income Statement is multiplied by –1 to convert it to a negative value, because a distribution has the effect of reducing the company's cash position.

> **Note**
>
> A more typical treatment would be to classify dividends as a financing item, rather than as an operating item.

Row 34 on the Cash Flow Sheet, labeled Net Cash from Operations, would be more effectively labeled Net Cash from Operating Activities. It is simply the sum of each of the items in the Cash Provided (Used) by Operating Activities section.

Determining Cash Flow from Investments and Financing Transactions

The remainder of the Cash Flow Sheet is shown in figure 19.16.

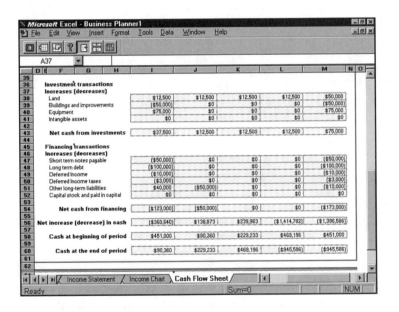

Fig. 19.16
The Business Planner's Cash Flow Sheet: check Cash at End of Period to determine whether liquidity problems exist.

The net cash change due to investments is due to any quarter-to-quarter changes in Land, Buildings, Equipment, and Intangible Assets. For example, the effect of Land investments on cash for the second quarter (Cash Flow Sheet cell J38) is $12,500. This value is obtained from the formula:

```
=ROUND('Balance Sheet'!J25-'Balance Sheet'!I25,0)
```

which subtracts the value of Land investments at the end of the first quarter from their value at the end of the second quarter. Using the sample data, this represents an increase of $12,500, from $112,500 to $125,000. Notice that this is *not* intended to represent an increase in the market value of the land; rather, it represents the flow of capital out of cash, and invested in land, during the second quarter.

A change in the value of an asset due to market valuation does not immediately affect the company's cash position. Eventually, however, such a profit on a fixed asset finds its way into the Cash Flow Statement.

You would recognize the effect of, say, inflation on the value of the investment when it is sold. Then, that profit is recorded on the Income Statement, as a Gain (Loss) on Sale of Assets, where it contributes to Income before Tax. Income, adjusted for any payable taxes, forms the basis for the Cash Flow Sheet's Net Earnings category.

The Cash Flow Statement sums the value of the changes in investments to arrive at the Net Cash for Investments. This value is subtracted from the company's Cash from Operations and Cash from Operating Activities in the calculation of Net Increase (Decrease) in Cash. An increase in investments brings about a decrease in the company's cash position; a decrease in investments brings about an increase in the company's cash position.

The final source of changes in the company's cash balance is Financing Transactions, which include:

- Short Term Notes Payable

- Long Term Debt

- Deferred Income

- Deferred Income Taxes

- Other Long-Term Liabilities

- Capital Invested

When the company acquires cash via financing, its cash balance increases, as does its debt. The formulas for these six financing categories subtract the prior quarter's debt from the current quarter's debt to arrive at the amount by which the available cash has increased by acquiring debt. For example, the formula for Short Term Notes Payable during the first quarter (cell I47 on the Cash Flow Sheet) is:

```
=ROUND('Balance Sheet'!I45-'Balance Sheet'!H45,0)
```

which is the difference between the current quarter's Notes Payable ($50,000) and the prior quarter's Notes Payable ($100,000). The company paid off the difference between these amounts, $50,000, during the first quarter. This transaction decreased the company's cash position by $50,000.

Similarly, the values on the Balance Sheet for Other Long-Term Liabilities are $50,000 at the end of the prior year, $90,000 at the end of the first quarter of the forecast year, and $40,000 at the end of the second quarter. The company acquires an additional $40,000 in Other Long-Term Liabilities during the first quarter ($50,000 + $40,000 = $90,000), and retires $50,000 in Other Long-Term Liabilities during the second quarter ($90,000 – $40,000 = $50,000).

These transactions appear in the Cash Flow Sheet as changes in the company's cash position: the acquisition of the liability increases its cash, and the retirement of the liability decreases its cash. The effects of these quarter-to-quarter changes are summed in the line labeled Net Cash from Financing.

Finally, the four sources of change to the company's cash position are combined in Net Increase (Decrease) in Cash. For example, the formula for the second quarter (cell J56 on the Cash Flow Sheet) is:

    =ROUND(J19+J34-J43+J54,0)

which returns $349,173. This is the company's Cash from Operations, plus its Cash from Operating Activities, less its Cash from Investment Transactions, plus its Cash from Financing Transactions.

The Cash at Beginning of Period is obtained from the Balance Sheet's Cash and Cash Equivalents. This value is added to Net Increase (Decrease) in Cash to arrive at Cash at End of Period. Finally, the Balance Sheet subtracts Cash at End of Period from Cash and Cash Equivalents to determine the amount that the Cash Flow Sheet is out of balance (refer to fig. 19.11).

Tracing Unexpected Values

Using the sample data, notice that the Cash at End of Period for the fourth quarter is ($945,586): for the first time during the forecast year, the company actually has a negative cash balance. What is the source of this problem?

Glancing over Column L, which summarizes cash flow information for the fourth quarter, notice that the value for Net Earnings is ($377,381), and the value for Inventory is ($610,824). These large, negative values seem to be good places to start the search for the source of the cash flow problem.

Net Earnings links to after-tax income on the Income Statement. Switching to the Income Statement and examining the after-tax income shows that a pre-tax income of ($539,115) is mitigated by a negative tax liability. The negative pre-tax income is the Gross Profit minus Total Expenses. Recall that the expenses are driven by the Percentage of Sales method. Because forecast Sales for the fourth quarter are higher than in any other quarter, the forecast expenses are relatively high also. However, the Cost of Sales is quite high during the fourth quarter, leading to a negative Gross Profit.

Details on the Cost of Sales for the fourth quarter are found in cells K52:K54. Examining those values, notice that the value for Other Costs, cell K54, is $1,250,000: this is $1,125,000 higher than the Other Costs for quarters 1 through 3. These values also contribute to the Inventory valuation for the fourth quarter on the Cost Flow Sheet.

Try reducing the estimate for Other Costs from $1,250,000 to $125,000. Doing so changes the Cash at End of Period in the fourth quarter from ($945,586) to $734,208.

As a user, if you track down an unexpected result in the Business Planner in this way, you might find that its source is a typing error—something easily fixed—or that its source is an assumption that you cannot afford to make. If your plans for the forecast year had included the extra $1,125,000 in Other Costs, you would either have to accept a negative cash flow during the fourth quarter or find some means of offsetting this cost. This other means might be an increase in Sales, or perhaps a major reduction in Operating Expenses, resulting from the added cost.

Summary

Prior chapters in this book have discussed balance sheets, income statements, and cash flow statements, but they have not emphasized the relationships among them. In this chapter, you have seen how the three types of reports interact to support one another's results, and to help you ensure that your estimates are accurate and sensible.

You have also seen how prior chapters on forecasting, on fixed asset depreciation, and on budgeting and planning can help you use the Business Planner template to forecast financial results based on varying inputs.

Chapter 20, "Contribution and Margin Analysis," gives you the Excel tools needed to analyze these financial results, and to look more deeply into the relationships among the outcomes provided by the Business Planner.

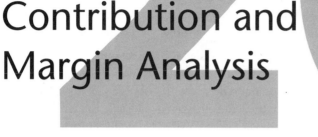

Chapter 20

Contribution and Margin Analysis

The key to successfully operating a business is having the right information to make your decisions. This concept may appear elementary, but it can be one of the greatest strategic and operational obstacles your company faces.

As any person who reads or analyzes financial statements knows, there are more financial indicators available than are needed. The trick is to choose the indicators that have the greatest relevance to your financial goals.

Management accounting as a profession concerns itself with the internal operations and drivers of business performance. One of its primary tools is contribution and breakeven analysis, which uses financial indicators such as:

- *Contribution margin.* This is usually defined as the sales revenue less the variable costs of production.

- *Unit contribution.* This is the margin contributed by each unit sold.

- *Break-even point.* This is the point in the sales process at which the revenues equal the costs of production.

These indicators enable you to make decisions about how you can:

- Increase product profitability

- Manage your product sales mix

- Optimize your resources to hold your costs down and raise your profits

These decisions often involve making assumptions about the profitability, resources, and product mix. You can test the assumptions by considering what effect they have on variables such as unit contribution.

For example, suppose that you manage a product whose contribution margin is $1 million per year. If your company is to meet its targeted profit for next year, you must assume that you can raise your product's contribution margin by 10 percent to $1.1 million. What options could you exercise that would cause your product to return an additional $100,000 profit?

To guide you in a search for your options, you could refer back to a contribution margin analysis and, perhaps, a unit contribution analysis. These analyses spell out the factors that tend to hold your revenues down and that keep your costs up. By examining these factors, you may be able to determine which costs, sales prices, and volume levels you can modify so as to achieve your assumed $1.1 million target.

This chapter explores the relationships among these variables. It shows you how to use Excel to identify which inputs you can modify to meet your goals.

Calculating the Contribution Margin

All firms have costs that are directly associated with their products or services. One of the most powerful means of understanding and controlling those costs is *contribution margin* analysis. The contribution margin itself is calculated by subtracting the variable costs required to manufacture the product from the revenue achieved by selling that product.

Variable costs are those that change as production levels rise and fall: the cost of raw materials is a variable cost. *Fixed costs* are those that do not change along with differences in production levels: the cost of salaried workers is a fixed cost. (The next section discusses this distinction in more detail.)

In practice, the definition of the contribution margin is often expanded to "revenue minus directly traceable costs." This is because it can be extremely difficult to distinguish between some fixed and variable costs. But these directly traceable costs should include all those that are variable.

Case Study: Producing Compact Discs

Discography, Inc. produces CD-ROMs. To make the CDs, it costs Discography:

- $5 per CD for the materials used in the CD itself

- $1 per CD for the packaging materials (the jewel box, the paper insert, and the plastic wrapping)

- $0.50 per CD for the factory employees

for a total production cost of $6.50 per CD. The contribution margin therefore would be calculated as shown in figure 20.1.

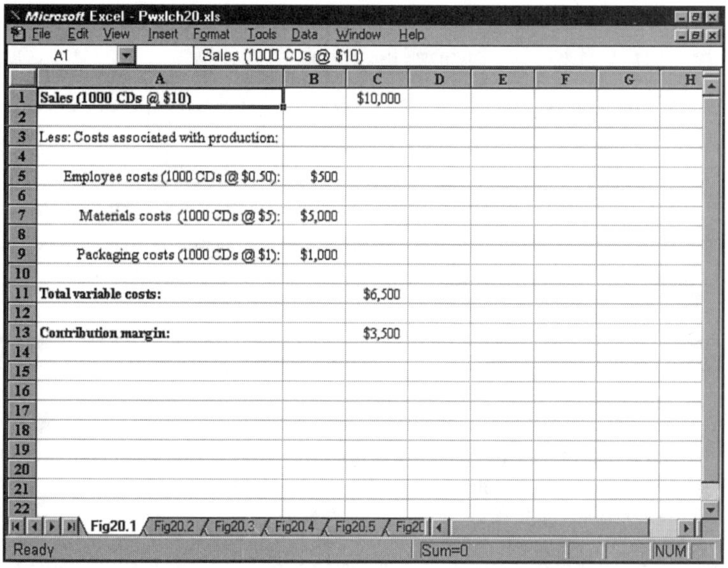

	A	B	C
1	**Sales (1000 CDs @ $10)**		$10,000
2			
3	Less: Costs associated with production:		
4			
5	Employee costs (1000 CDs @ $0.50):	$500	
6			
7	Materials costs (1000 CDs @ $5):	$5,000	
8			
9	Packaging costs (1000 CDs @ $1):	$1,000	
10			
11	**Total variable costs:**		$6,500
12			
13	**Contribution margin:**		$3,500

Fig. 20.1
The contribution margin is defined as revenues less varible costs.

The $6.50 per unit in costs required to make each CD is called a variable cost. Remember, variable costs are the costs that vary with the level of production. When production goes down, variable costs decrease, and when production goes up, variable costs increase.

Besides variable costs, Discography also has fixed costs. Fixed costs do not vary with the level of production. For example, rent paid for a building, legal fees, and business insurance are usually the same regardless of how many CDs it makes. In contrast, when Discography makes more CDs, the total amount that it pays for materials such as blank CDs increases: it is a variable cost.

In practice, and even when you can separate variable from fixed costs, the distinction between them is not quite as crisp as this. Consider, for example, the $0.50 per CD that Discography pays its employees. There are several ways that Discography can incur that cost:

- The employee is paid by the CD and (perhaps due to a negotiated contract) the payment cannot be changed. If that is the payment arrangement, the payment is a variable cost: the more CDs produced, the more the employee is paid.

■ The employee receives a fixed wage, regardless of the number of CDs produced, and the $0.50 per CD is just a long-term average. In this case, the employee represents a fixed cost. Unless you negotiate payment terms that are based directly on production, you should not include this cost in the contribution margin analysis.

■ The employee is paid by the CD, but the payment changes according to how many CDs are made. Up to 1,000 CDs made per day, you pay the employee $0.50 per CD, but you pay $0.60 per CD for anything over 1,000 CDs made. This is a *semi-variable* cost. A semi-variable cost changes with the number of units, but the change is not precisely *proportional* to the number of units.

Note

Semi-variable costs are often *step functions*. A step function is one that changes suddenly when a variable reaches a certain threshold. In this example, when the production level reaches the threshold of 1,000 CDs, the employee cost jumps from $0.50 per unit to $0.60 per unit.

Up to 1,000 CDs, the ratio of total employee cost to units made is exactly $0.50. After 1,000 CDs, the ratio is exactly $0.60. But across the full range of production (say, from 0 to 10,000 CDs produced) the ratio is inexact: it depends on the number produced.

Figure 20.2 shows an example of how you might account for a semi-variable cost: in this case, an employee makes $0.50 for each CD sold up to and including 1,000 CDs per day, $0.60 per CD for 1,000 to 2,000, and so on.

Notice the IF statements in cells F3:F8:

```
=IF(SalesLevel>CDsMade,MIN(1000,(SalesLevel-CDsMade))*UnitCost,0)
```

This formula uses three named ranges:

■ SalesLevel refers to cell B1.

■ CDsMade refers to cells D3:D8.

■ UnitCost refers to cells E3:E8.

The MIN function appears in the formula because no more than 1,000 units should be counted for any level of CDsMade. In the figure example, SalesLevel is 4510. For the 4000 level of CDsMade, SalesLevel–CDsMade = 510, and this amount is multiplied by the corresponding UnitCost of $0.90 to return $51.00.

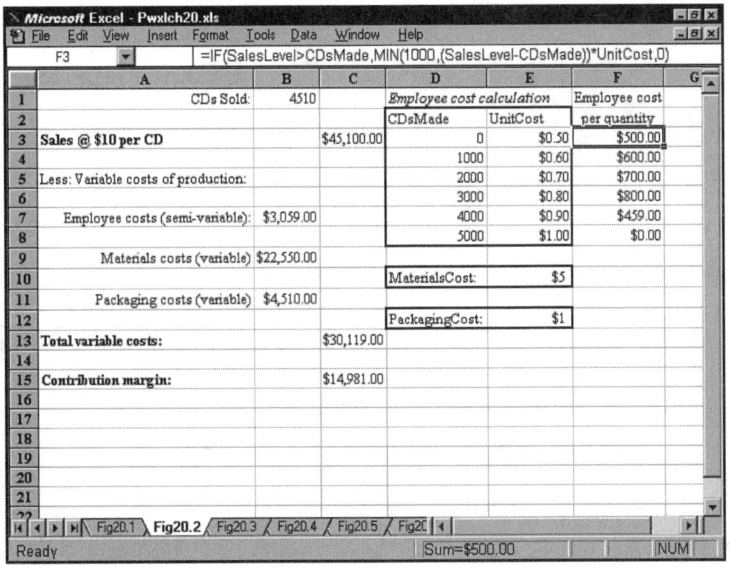

Fig. 20.2
Calculating semi-variable costs in a contribution margin analysis: employee costs are purely variable within a quantity range, but describe a step function across ranges.

In contrast, at the 3000 level of CDsMade, SalesLevel–CDsMade = 1510. But this is too many units to count: 1000 is the maximum number of units to count for any given level. Therefore, the formula makes use of the MIN function to return the smaller of 1000, or the difference between SalesLevel and CDsMade.

The smaller of those two values (1000, or SalesLevel–CDsMade), is multiplied by the corresponding UnitCost to return the cost of the CDs made at that level of production.

Finally, SalesLevel can be less than any given level of CDsMade. In the figure example, 4510 is less than 5000, so no units should be counted for that level. The IF function returns 0 in that case.

Using Unit Contribution

The analysis of contribution margin in the case study of CD production involved total variable costs and total revenues. You can also break the information down to a per unit and percent of sales basis. This gives you a different perspective on the relationship between your costs and revenues. To continue the Discography example, consider the same information from a different perspective shown in figure 20.3.

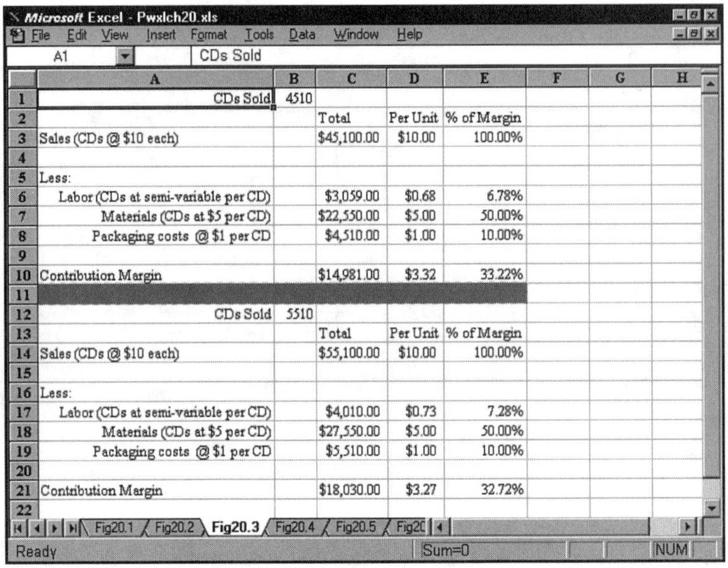

	A	B	C	D	E
1	CDs Sold	4510			
2			Total	Per Unit	% of Margin
3	Sales (CDs @ $10 each)		$45,100.00	$10.00	100.00%
4					
5	Less:				
6	Labor (CDs at semi-variable per CD)		$3,059.00	$0.68	6.78%
7	Materials (CDs at $5 per CD)		$22,550.00	$5.00	50.00%
8	Packaging costs @ $1 per CD		$4,510.00	$1.00	10.00%
9					
10	Contribution Margin		$14,981.00	$3.32	33.22%
11					
12	CDs Sold	5510			
13			Total	Per Unit	% of Margin
14	Sales (CDs @ $10 each)		$55,100.00	$10.00	100.00%
15					
16	Less:				
17	Labor (CDs at semi-variable per CD)		$4,010.00	$0.73	7.28%
18	Materials (CDs at $5 per CD)		$27,550.00	$5.00	50.00%
19	Packaging costs @ $1 per CD		$5,510.00	$1.00	10.00%
20					
21	Contribution Margin		$18,030.00	$3.27	32.72%
22					

Fig. 20.3
You can derive a greater level of detail by breaking down the total cost information to a per unit and percent of sales analysis.

The detailed per unit and percent of margin information gives you a better idea of:

- The product's individual contribution to total revenue
- The source of the greatest percentage of variable costs
- The relationships among the magnitudes of the variable costs

The detail that you obtain from this type of analysis is valuable information because it gives you the tools you need to make decisions that maximize your profits. Figure 20.3, for example, makes it clear. Suppose that Discography wants to increase the contribution margin from 33.22% to 35%. By analyzing the information shown previously, Discography notices that if it can lower the cost of its materials from $5.00 per CD to $4.82 per CD, it can increase the contribution margin to 35%. One way of doing so might be by using a different supplier. Lowering the cost of materials will decrease the direct material cost to 48.2% of total costs. This enables Discography to achieve its desired margin of 35%.

In summary, a contribution margin analysis provides the following advantages when you must make operational decisions:

- The analysis helps you decide what price to charge for your product. For example, if you want an additional $10 contribution margin on every unit you sell, you will have to either increase your price by $10 or reduce your unit variable costs by $10.

- The analysis helps you control those costs that are directly related to manufacturing the product. For example, if you are currently using a vendor who charges $50 per each 10 units of materials, you may be able to find a vendor that charges $45, and yet obtain the same quality that your current vendor offers.

- The analysis helps you understand the relationships among the volume of products produced and sold, their costs, and your profits. This is especially useful in the case of semi-variable costs, which are usually difficult to account for without doing the formal analysis.

Creating an Operating Income Statement

Once created, an Excel worksheet can make performing a contribution analysis very easy. The first thing you should do is create your Operating Income Statement on a worksheet. The worksheet contains your Sales, Variable Cost, and volume information on a total, per unit, and percent of margin basis. This portion of the worksheet contains the values that depend on unit pricing (see fig. 20.4).

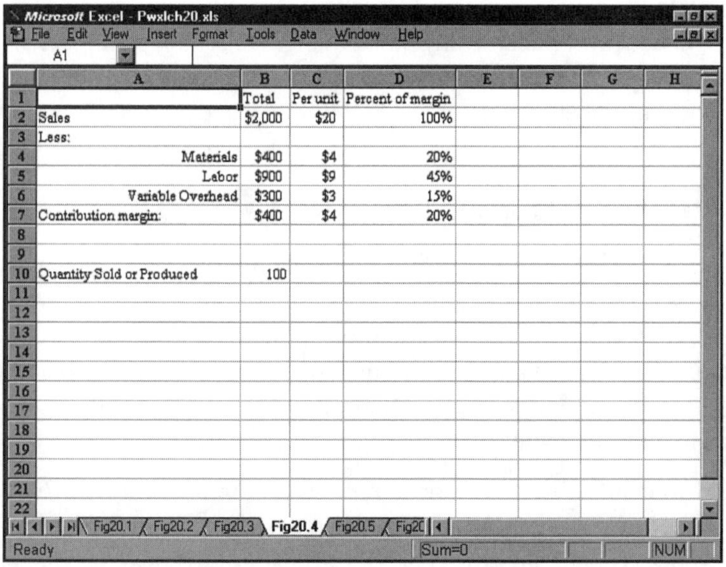

	A	B	C	D
1		Total	Per unit	Percent of margin
2	Sales	$2,000	$20	100%
3	Less:			
4	Materials	$400	$4	20%
5	Labor	$900	$9	45%
6	Variable Overhead	$300	$3	15%
7	Contribution margin:	$400	$4	20%
10	Quantity Sold or Produced	100		

Fig. 20.4
An operating income statement should detail the product's sales price, variable costs, and quantities.

Fig. 20.5
Excel formulas for Operating Income Statement.

The formulas used to create the information in figure 20.4 are shown in figure 20.5.

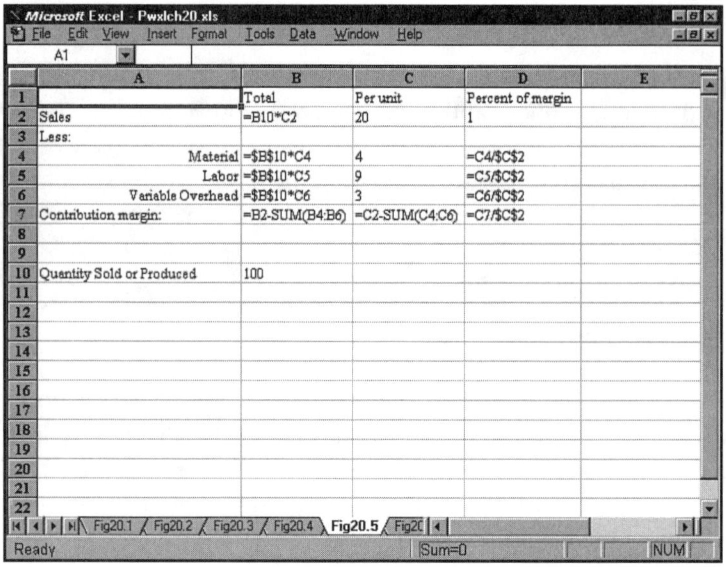

	A	B	C	D	E
1		Total	Per unit	Percent of margin	
2	Sales	=B10*C2	20	1	
3	Less:				
4	Material	=$B$10*C4	4	=C4/$C$2	
5	Labor	=$B$10*C5	9	=C5/$C$2	
6	Variable Overhead	=$B$10*C6	3	=C6/$C$2	
7	Contribution margin:	=B2-SUM(B4:B6)	=C2-SUM(C4:C6)	=C7/$C$2	
8					
9					
10	Quantity Sold or Produced	100			

By separating your price, cost, and quantity information from your Operating Income Statement, you can easily make changes to selling prices, costs, and quantities. These changes will be reflected in the Operating Income Statement, and will therefore raise or lower your calculated contribution margin.

Finding the Break-Even Point

One of the key benefits of the information acquired from management accounting is the ability to perform a cost/volume/profit analysis. Creating this analysis is nothing more than the manipulation of the information derived from your contribution analysis. In this way, you can determine the optimal production volume and sales price that will enable you to maximize your profits and minimize your costs.

One way to manipulate your contribution margin to perform a cost/volume/profit analysis is to calculate the Break-Even point. This is the point where total revenues equal total expenses, both fixed and variable. Thus, the Break-Even point is the point at which total revenues equals total costs:

Total Revenues	=	Total Costs
(Price * Quantity)	=	(Fixed Costs + (Variable Costs * Quantity)

Break-Even information allows you to plan for the level of sales that you need to cover your total costs. It also provides you with information on the level of sales that will be necessary to achieve your desired level of profitability.

There are several ways to calculate the Break-Even point. Each calculation method provides you with a different slant, and your choice should depend on your information requirements. The Break-Even calculations include Break-Even in units, Break-Even in dollars, and Break-Even with an expected level of profit.

Calculating Break-Even in Units

Break-Even in units is the number of units that must be sold at current price levels to cover fixed and variable costs. The Break-Even point measured in units is:

Break-Even point (units) = Total fixed costs/(Unit Sales Price – Unit Variable costs)

Calculating the Break-Even point in units is most useful when managers need to analyze current or projected volume levels. You might know, for example, that with your current sales force you can expect to sell 10 units per month. By calculating Break-Even in units, you can determine whether your company can be profitable at 10 units sold per month. If your company cannot be profitable at that level, you might decide that you need to add sales staff.

Suppose that total fixed costs are $50, unit sales price is $20 and unit variable costs are $15. You can calculate the Break-Even point in units by means of this formula:

Break-Even point (units) = $50 / ($20 – $15)

The result is 10. Therefore, the company needs to sell 10 units during the period when the fixed costs are incurred to break even. With this information, you can manipulate the pricing and costs to calculate the number of units that need to be sold to break even.

Or, you might find it useful to turn this relationship around. Suppose that you know that your total fixed costs will increase by $10 per month, from $50 to $60. You do not want to change your unit sales price, and your unit variable costs will not change. How many units must you sell to break even?

Begin by rearranging the formula for Break-Even point in units, as follows:

Total Fixed Costs = Break-Even point (units) * (Sales Price – Unit Variable Costs)

You can use Excel's Goal Seek function to quickly determine your new Break-Even point in units. See figure 20.6 for a sample worksheet layout.

Fig. 20.6
Using Goal Seek to find a new Break-Even point.

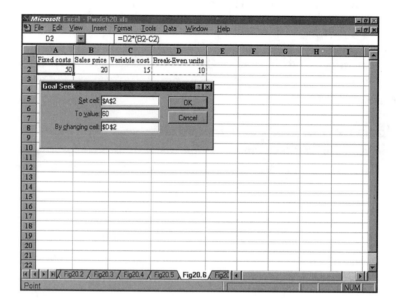

Cell A2 contains this formula:

```
=D2*(B2-C2)
```

Cells B1 through D1 contain the values shown (not formulas). Follow these steps:

1. Select cell A2, and choose Goal Seek from the Tools menu. The reference to cell A2 appears in the Set Cell box.

2. Click in the To value box, and enter the number **60**. This is the new total fixed costs.

3. Click in the By changing cell box and then click cell D2.

4. Choose OK.

Goal Seek now changes the value in cell D2 until the value in cell A2 equals 60. The result is 12: the number of units you must sell to cover the new total fixed costs.

Calculating Break-Even in Sales

Break-Even in Sales is the number of dollars of sales revenue that are needed to cover fixed and variable costs. There are several ways to calculate

Break-Even in sales. Each provides the same result, but each method uses slightly different inputs. One method is:

Break-Even in Sales = (Break-Even Units * Unit Sales Price)

Suppose that the Break-Even units is 10 and the unit sales price is $20. These data result in Break-Even in sales dollars of $200:

```
$200 = (10 * $20)
```

Here, you already know how many units you need to sell so as to break even, and you simply multiply that by the price of each unit.

Another formula that you can use if you haven't yet calculated Break-Even units is:

Break-Even in Sales = Total Fixed Costs / ((Unit Sales Price – Unit Variable Costs) / Unit Sales Price)

Here, the total fixed costs is $50, unit sales price is $20, and unit variable costs is $10. The data result in:

```
$200 = $50 / (($20 - $15)/ $20)
$200 = $50 / ($5 / $20 )
$200 = $50 / .25
```

In this case, you find your profit per unit ($20 – $15 = $5) and divide by the unit sales price: $5 / $20, or .25. This is the proportion of unit sales price that is profit over and above your variable costs. Dividing the additional costs that you need to cover, your total fixed costs, by that profit proportion results in the sales dollars needed to meet total costs.

A third approach is:

Break-Even in Sales = (Break-Even Units * Unit Variable Cost) + Total Fixed Costs

or, where Break-Even Units is 10, Unit Variable Cost is 15, and total Fixed Costs is $50:

```
$200 = (10 * $15) + $50
$200 = $150 + 50
```

This formula simply determines the Total Variable Cost for Break-Even units, and adds to that the Total Fixed Cost.

In each case, you find that you need $200 in sales to break even.

Break-Even as measured in sales dollars will provide you with valuable information regarding how much sales revenue is required to cover your operating costs. It can give you an understanding of how aggressively you must market your product to meet your operating costs. It also gives you some indication of how efficiently you are using your resources. For example, if your sales expectations are higher than the Break-Even point, and yet you are just meeting it, you may need to reevaluate how efficiently you are using the resources that are available to you.

> ### Tip
>
> In practice, it is easiest to set up one formula that involves each component as a named cell reference. The formula might be:
>
> = Units * (Unit Price – Unit Cost) – Fixed Costs
>
> Then, you can use Goal Seek to set the value of the formula to zero (the Break-Even point) by varying any one of the formula's precedent cells.

Calculating Break-Even in Sales Dollars with an Expected Level of Profit

Break-Even in sales dollars represents the sales revenue needed to cover fixed and variable costs, and still return a profit at the level that you require. Conceptually, this is similar to treating profit as a cost. You need to meet your fixed costs, and you need to meet your variable costs; you simply consider that profit is another cost category that you need to meet.

You can calculate Break-Even in sales dollars by using this formula:

$$\text{Break-Even in Sales Dollars} = \text{Variable Costs} + \text{Fixed Costs} + \text{Expected Profit}$$

Suppose that a company wants to make a $5 profit on every unit it sells. The Variable Cost is $15 per unit, 10 units are sold, the Fixed Costs total $50, and the expected profit is $5 per unit. Then, the formula that provides the Break-Even point in terms of sales dollars is:

$$\text{Break-Even} = (\text{Unit Variable Cost} * \text{Units}) + \text{Fixed Costs} + (\text{Expected Profit} * \text{Units})$$

```
= ($15 * 10) + $50 + ($5 * 10)
= $250
```

and the company's Break-Even point, measured in sales dollars, is $250 for 10 units with a profit of $5 per unit.

Charting the Break-Even Point

Besides using equations to perform a Break-Even analysis, a graphic depiction of your Break-Even point is another valuable tool to analyze your Cost/Volume/Profit relationship. Figures 20.7 through 20.9 display graphs that depict the elements of a Cost/Volume/Profit analysis.

Figure 20.7 shows a company's fixed costs by way of a straight line, at $50, regardless of sales volume.

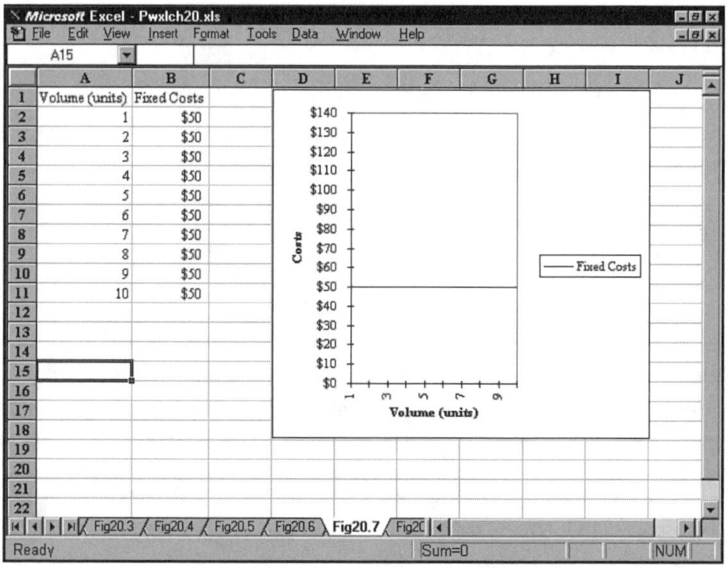

Fig. 20.7
Fixed costs are constant across the relevant range of production.

To create this chart from the data shown by figure 20.7 in cells A1:B11, follow these steps:

1. Select the range that contains the data.

2. Click the Chart Wizard button on the main toolbar. Or, choose Insert, Chart, and select On this sheet from the cascading menu.

3. The cursor will change to crosshairs with a depiction of a column chart below and right of the crosshairs. Place the crosshairs where you want the upper-left corner of your chart on the worksheet. Holding down the mouse button, drag right and down until you have outlined the location where you want your chart. Then, release the mouse button.

4. Step 1 of the Chart Wizard allows you to confirm or change the range address of the cells that you want to chart. Choose Next.

5. Step 2 of the Chart Wizard displays 15 different chart types from which to choose. Click the Line chart type, and then choose Next.

6. Click format 2 in Step 3 of the Chart Wizard, and choose Next.

7. In Step 4 of the Chart Wizard, enter the number of columns to use for Category (X) Labels. Either click the spinner until the spin box contains 1, or type **1** directly in the Use First...Columns for Category (X) Labels box. Set Use First...Rows for Legend Text to 1.

8. In Step 5 of the Chart Wizard, type **Volume (Units)** in the Category (X) box. Type **Costs** in the Value (Y) box. Choose Finish.

9. After Excel has drawn the chart on your worksheet, double-click the chart. This opens the chart for editing. (In versions of Excel prior to 5.0, double-clicking an embedded chart expanded it to full-screen size.)

10. Click on the (automatic) title at the top of the chart. Press the Delete key, or choose Clear from the Edit menu, and select All from the cascading menu.

11. Click inside the chart's plot area. Move your cursor to the handle at the center of the top border of the plot area. Your cursor changes to a double arrow. Hold down the mouse button, and drag the top border toward the top of the chart. Release the mouse button

12. Click the value axis. Choose Selected Axis...from the Format menu. If necessary, click the Scale tab at the top of the Format Axis dialog box. Type **140** in the Maximum edit box, and type 10 in the Major Unit edit box. Choose OK.

13. Click somewhere in the worksheet outside the embedded chart to deselect it.

You can create the charts shown in figures 20.8 and 20.9 by taking similar steps. Figure 20.8 illustrates how variable costs increase as production volume increases.

Figure 20.9 represents the relationship between Total Costs and Total Sales at different levels of production. The figure illustrates the quantity at which Loss, Break-Even, and Profit are achieved. Below 10 units on the X-axis, the company loses money because the unit profit has yet to make up for the fixed costs. At 10 units, there is exactly enough unit profit to cover fixed costs, and the Total Sales equals Total Costs. Above 10 units, the company is making a profit at the rate of $5 per unit over 10.

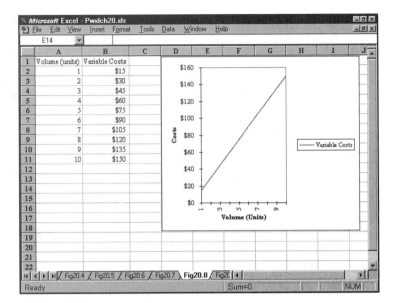

Fig. 20.8
Variable costs increase as production levels increase.

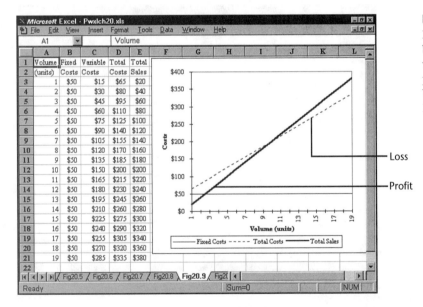

Fig. 20.9
Relationships between costs, volume, and profit: Profit begins at the Break-Even point.

The graphical representation of a company's current cost/volume/profit relationship gives you an effective tool for determining what adjustments you need to make to volume, cost, or both so as to increase your profit level. Relationships among these variables can become extremely complex, especially when several different products are involved. When you are dealing with a complicated situation, it is usually easier to make sense of the relationships by viewing them on a chart, rather than by gazing at a table of raw numbers.

Making Assumptions in Contribution Analysis

The analysis of contribution margin, Break-Even points, and the relationships among costs, volume, and profit makes some assumptions that must be met before you can fully trust the results of the analysis. The assumptions that follow are particularly important.

Linear Relationships

Contribution margin analysis assumes that revenues and expenses are linear across the relevant range of volume. Suppose that you offer volume discounts to your customers. In that case, when you sell more goods, each additional, incremental sale generates less revenue per unit than when you sell fewer units. The revenue line would be similar to that in figure 20.10. Notice that it is no longer straight (*linear*), but that it increases more slowly as volume increases (*curvilinear*).

Fig. 20.10
Volume discounts can cause non-linear revenue growth.

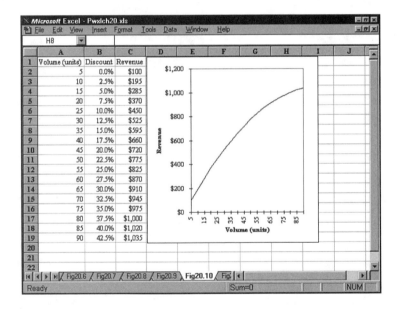

Or suppose that you take advantage of volume discounts from your suppliers—in that case, the more supplies you buy, the less you pay in unit costs. The contribution margin line might be similar to that in figure 20.11.

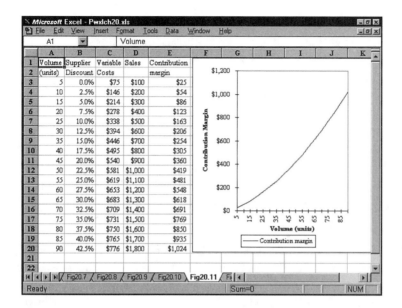

Fig. 20.11
Purchase discounts
can cause non-
linear increases in
the contribution
margin.

IV

Sales and Marketing

Assignment of Costs

Contribution margin analysis assumes that you can accurately divide expenses between fixed and variable costs. In most cases you will be able to assign an expense to one category or another. For example, up to the point that you need to acquire additional space, your monthly office lease is fixed regardless of how many units you sell. In some cases, however, it can be difficult to decide whether to treat a particular expense as fixed or variable. In particular, it can be difficult to assign an expense that bears a relationship to volume but not necessarily a direct, one-to-one relationship.

An example is your monthly long-distance phone bill. Unless your sales are restricted to your local phoning area, it is likely that the more you sell, the higher your bill will be. But some of those long-distance calls probably have nothing to do with incremental sales volume.

The accuracy of your analysis of contribution margin and Break-Even will depend on how accurately you can assign a portion of the long distance charges to fixed costs vs. variable costs.

Constant Sales Mix

The analysis assumes that the sales mix is constant: that, from one period to the next, your total sales are based on the same percent of each product line. Sales mix is discussed in greater detail in the section, "Determining Sales Mix," but here note that different products usually have different cost and profit structures. If the sales mix changes so that, overall, either costs or contribution margins also change, then the Break-Even points will vary.

Constant Inventory

The analysis assumes that inventories do not change in Break-Even computations. Inventory costs can change over time, or as your sales volume rises and falls, for a variety of reasons: the overall inventory level might rise due to slowing sales or fall with increasing sales, or the mix of inventory for different product lines might change (creating a change in the mix of both fixed and variable costs), or the carrying costs might change. Any of these can bring about a change in your Break-Even points.

Worker Productivity

The analysis assumes that worker productivity does not change. If, at a constant rate of pay, your workers begin to produce more product per period of time, then the structure of your variable costs will change: the Break-Even points will drop, and the product's contribution margin will rise. Conversely, if your workers begin to produce less per period of time, due perhaps to illness or procedural changes, variable costs will increase, as will your Break-Even points.

Determining Sales Mix

More often than not, a company manufactures, or offers for sale, more than one product line. In these cases, you should consider the sales and costs value of *each* of those product lines as you analyze the company's sales value as a whole.

For example, suppose that a company sells three product lines. besides the vases, the ceramics company also produces and sells figurines and frames. A side-by-side analysis of each of these products' price and cost information is a valuable way to analyze each product's impact on the bottom line. For a sample analysis, see figure 20.12.

A sales mix analysis helps you analyze the relative value of the products in your current sales mix. You can determine which of your products provides the greatest contribution to your company's total sales. Suppose that your company produces an over-the-counter medicine in three different package sizes: 8-ounce, 6-ounce, and 4-ounce.

Figure 20.12 shows that it costs twice as much to make figurines as it does to make vases ($30 per unit versus $15 per unit), and 1.25 times as much to make figurines as it does to make frames ($30 per unit versus $24 per unit).

However, the contribution margin from selling figurines is four times greater than from selling vases ($200 versus $50), and more than 3 times greater than from selling frames ($200 versus $60).

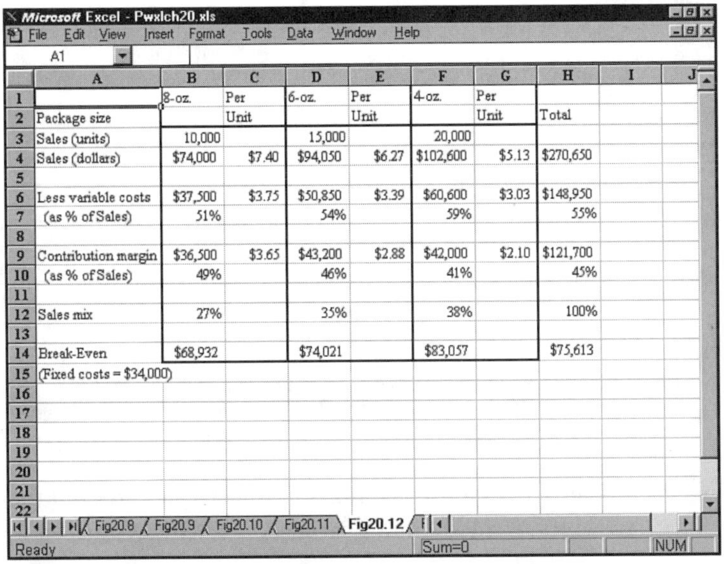

Fig. 20.12
The sales mix analysis focuses on contribution margins for each type of product sold.

	A	B	C	D	E	F	G	H	I	J
1		8-oz.	Per	6-oz.	Per	4-oz.	Per			
2	Package size		Unit		Unit		Unit	Total		
3	Sales (units)	10,000		15,000		20,000				
4	Sales (dollars)	$74,000	$7.40	$94,050	$6.27	$102,600	$5.13	$270,650		
5										
6	Less variable costs	$37,500	$3.75	$50,850	$3.39	$60,600	$3.03	$148,950		
7	(as % of Sales)	51%		54%		59%		55%		
8										
9	Contribution margin	$36,500	$3.65	$43,200	$2.88	$42,000	$2.10	$121,700		
10	(as % of Sales)	49%		46%		41%		45%		
11										
12	Sales mix	27%		35%		38%		100%		
13										
14	Break-Even	$68,932		$74,021		$83,057		$75,613		
15	(Fixed costs = $34,000)									

Figure 20.12 shows that the variable costs to make the 8-ounce package are 1.10 times greater than to make the 6-ounce package ($3.75 per unit versus $3.39 per unit), and 1.24 times greater than the 4-ounce package ($3.75 per unit versus $3.03 per unit). However, the contribution margin from selling the 8-ounce package is 1.27 times greater than from selling the 6-ounce package ($3.65 versus $2.88), and 1.74 times greater than from selling the 4-ounce package ($3.65 versus $2.10).

The difference in contribution margin is due to the fact that variable costs are only 51% of the selling price for the 8-ounce package, whereas they are 54% of the selling price for the 6-ounce package and 59% of the selling price for the 4-ounce package. So even though it costs more to make the larger package, the sales price of the 8-ounce package is high enough to recover more of its variable costs than does the sales price of the other sizes.

This type of analysis is valuable in helping you determine which products you want to market most actively, which products (if any) you should discontinue, and which products you wish to keep but at a reduced level of production. For example, if you focused sales and production efforts on the larger sizes, and de-emphasized the 4-ounce size, your total profit might appear as in figure 20.13.

Fig. 20.13

A redistribution of product types within the sales mix can increase profitability.

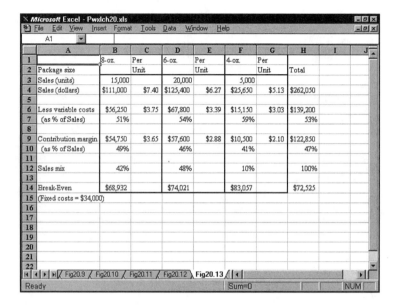

	A	B	C	D	E	F	G	H	I	J
1		8-oz.	Per	6-oz.	Per	4-oz.	Per			
2	Package size		Unit		Unit		Unit	Total		
3	Sales (units)	15,000		20,000		5,000				
4	Sales (dollars)	$111,000	$7.40	$125,400	$6.27	$25,650	$5.13	$262,050		
5										
6	Less variable costs	$56,250	$3.75	$67,800	$3.39	$15,150	$3.03	$139,200		
7	(as % of Sales)	51%		54%		59%		53%		
8										
9	Contribution margin	$54,750	$3.65	$57,600	$2.88	$10,500	$2.10	$122,850		
10	(as % of Sales)	49%		46%		41%		47%		
11										
12	Sales mix	42%		48%		10%		100%		
13										
14	Break-Even	$68,932		$74,021		$83,057		$72,525		
15	(Fixed costs = $34,000)									

In figure 20.13, sales and production efforts have been shifted from the 4-ounce package to the 8- and 6-ounce packages. The effect has been to decrease sales of the 4-ounce package by 15,000 units, and to increase sales of the 8-ounce package and 6-ounce package by 5,000 each. The total sales revenue has dropped by $8,600, but the total contribution margin has increased by $1,150.

This result, of course, is achieved by selling more of the higher-profit products and fewer of the lower-profit products. And while it is obvious that doing so will increase profit, it is useful to carry out this sort of analysis: both to quantify the potential results and to focus attention not just on the revenues but on the contribution margins as well.

The previous analysis is a very basic snapshot of the impacts that are associated with discontinuing a product line. In addition, you should also consider such issues as:

■ The incremental costs of discontinuing a product line—for example, the value of an existing contract to purchase the materials used.

■ The ease of shifting resources to a different product line—for example, can those employees who produce one product also produce another product with no additional training?

There can be a variety of reasons that you might want to change the sales mix. An obvious one is that discontinuing a low-margin product can create additional profit. Another is that discontinuing a product that is out of line with the company's long-range strategic goals might outweigh the associated incremental costs. In either case, the best decision is probably to change your sales mix to achieve your profit target and strategic goals.

Achieving the optimum sales mix is a more difficult task in reality than it is in a book. Nevertheless, it is wise to monitor your sales mix closely. The wrong mix can prevent your company from being profitable. Using the tools that have been presented in this chapter, and extending them to your actual line of business, will help you achieve the optimum sales mix for your company's expectations, both short- and long-term.

Analyzing Segment Margin

Suppose that a ceramics company has three divisions: household ceramics, ceramic tiles, and ceramic conductors. It may be that each division uses a different physical plant, employs different operating and sales staff, has a different overhead structure, and so on.

If so, the divisions' fixed costs are likely to differ. An analysis of segment margin—so called because each division is termed a segment—is primarily an extension of contribution margin analysis for products to segments. You can determine the segment margin by deducting the direct fixed costs from the segment's contribution margin, as shown in figure 20.14.

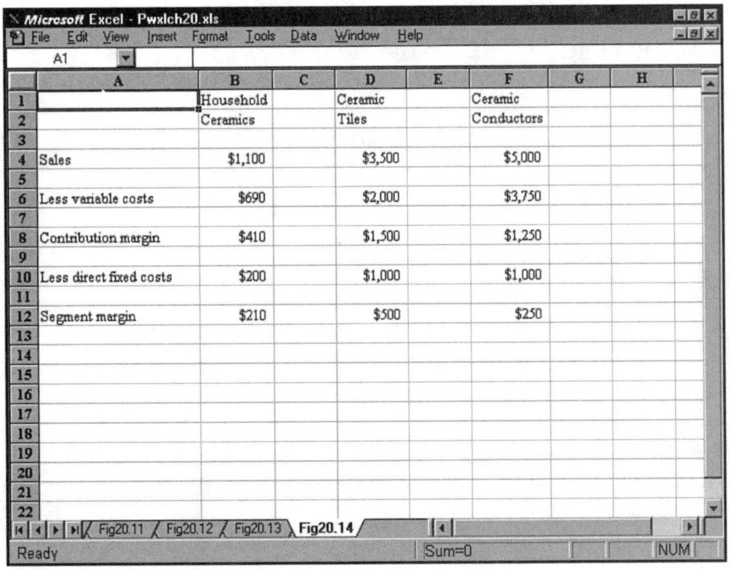

	B	D	F
	Household Ceramics	Ceramic Tiles	Ceramic Conductors
Sales	$1,100	$3,500	$5,000
Less variable costs	$690	$2,000	$3,750
Contribution margin	$410	$1,500	$1,250
Less direct fixed costs	$200	$1,000	$1,000
Segment margin	$210	$500	$250

Fig. 20.14
A segment margin analysis can shed light on the profitability of product lines that incur different fixed costs.

Unlike a contribution margin analysis, which focuses on short-term impacts, the segment margin can help you understand a segment's long-term profitability. It gives you information on how much revenue is available after a segment has covered all its direct costs. The remaining revenue can be used to cover the common costs incurred by the total company, and any extra represents the segment's contribution to the company's total net income.

By deducting direct fixed costs from the segment's contribution margin, you have a better picture of each segment's contribution to the cost/volume/profit relationship for the company as a whole.

Summary

This chapter has discussed several important tools that can help you understand how your company's profit picture is structured:

- The Contribution Margin analysis gives you a snapshot of how a particular product is performing, in terms of both its variable costs (which increase with each additional unit produced) and its contribution margin (sales revenue less variable costs).

- The Unit Contribution analysis puts you in a position to consider the profitability of a given product in greater detail.

- The Break-Even point in sales tells you how much revenue you must generate to cover both your products' variable costs as well as your fixed costs. This may imply that you need to lower your costs, increase your sales price, or increase the number of units sold.

- The Break-Even point in units tells you how many units you need to sell to cover your fixed and variable costs. You may find that you need to increase sales staff to reach the Break-Even point in units. This can be a complex decision when increasing staff leads to a concomitant increase in fixed costs.

- The Sales Mix analysis helps you understand how your product lines combine to result in a profit or loss. It can help pinpoint which products are performing best, and where you may need to make adjustments to costs so as to lift the performance of a given product.

- The Segment analysis gives you a broader perspective on a company with several divisions, each with its own set of products. You would typically use this sort of analysis to gain a longer-term understanding of the source of a company's profits.

Chapter 21

Pricing and Costing

The issues of how much it costs your company to produce a product, and how much you can sell it for, go directly to the question of whether the business operates at a loss or makes a profit. Costs and prices are intimately related, and this chapter goes into some detail concerning ways to analyze that relationship.

Although neither costs nor prices are under your complete control, you can exercise some influence on both. As to costs, there are many methods of cost control: from reducing the company's payroll to lowering inventory levels to exerting greater control over travel and lodging expenses.

As to prices, another, truly wicked variable enters the equation: competition. A competitor intent on capturing some of your market share, or on forcing you into a precarious position in the marketplace, can usually do so by cutting its prices for products comparable to yours. Yes, selling on the basis of features and quality, and engaging in so-called "relationship selling," can mitigate the impact of a head-on assault on price structures. But in the long run, even the most skilled sales force cannot make up for a dramatic price disadvantage.

There are, though, some techniques that put you in a position to better understand the relationship between your costs and the prices you charge for your products. By understanding these relationships, you are often able to make adjustments in cost components without having to resort to measures that disrupt your business's operations. In turn, these adjustments often have an effect on how you price your products.

"Buy low and sell high" is one of those deceptively simple adages that are both true and totally useless: How low is low? As the next section shows, that depends on the costs that are fixed and the costs that are variable.

Using Absorption and Contribution Costing

Two of the most important methods of determining costs are absorption and contribution costing. Although they can yield very different results, there is only one major difference between the two approaches: absorption costing allocates certain production costs between the total cost of goods sold and the ending inventory, while contribution costing allocates those production costs entirely to the cost of goods sold.

The result is that the income for a period can be different, depending on which method is used. The specific reasons are discussed in the two sections that follow.

Understanding Absorption Costing

A problem arises in determining profitability when, at the end of a period, you have some quantity of goods that remain in your ending inventory. Because you normally have some goods on hand at all times, including at the end of a period, this is the typical situation. The difficulty stems from the fact that your valuation of inventories includes both variable and fixed costs.

Case Study: QuickData Modems

QuickData Modems, Inc. is a subsidiary of a large electronics manufacturer. QuickData purchases modems from another subsidiary (DataPump, Inc., which is discussed later in this chapter). QuickData then puts its own logo on the modems, and sells them at a lower price than the manufacturing subsidiary, DataPump. It keeps its own costs lower by offering a much more restricted product warranty than does DataPump.

QuickData's production process therefore consists of placing its logo on each product and preparing the product for sale (for example, putting a disk with software in a box along with the modem itself). Its production costs involve the cost of purchasing the modem from the manufacturing subsidiary, stamping the logo on the modem, and boxing the product.

Figure 21.1 shows some basic operating data and an (incomplete) income statement for QuickData for the first quarter of 1995.

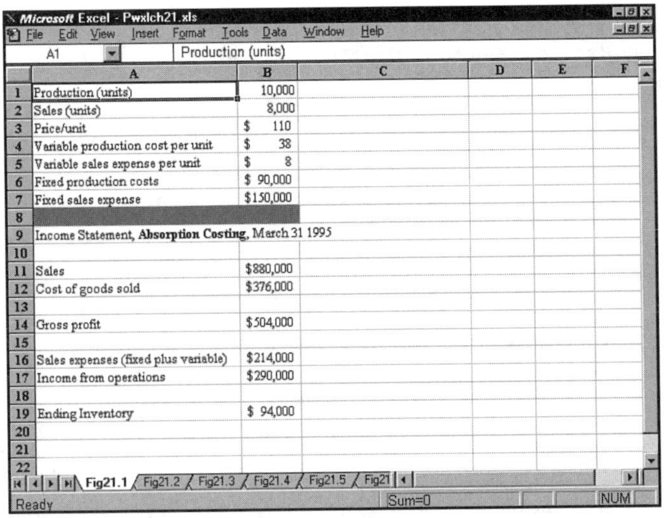
Microsoft Excel - Pwxlch21.xls

	A	B	C	D	E	F
1	Production (units)	10,000				
2	Sales (units)	8,000				
3	Price/unit	$ 110				
4	Variable production cost per unit	$ 38				
5	Variable sales expense per unit	$ 8				
6	Fixed production costs	$ 90,000				
7	Fixed sales expense	$150,000				
8						
9	Income Statement, **Absorption Costing**, March 31 1995					
10						
11	Sales	$880,000				
12	Cost of goods sold	$376,000				
13						
14	Gross profit	$504,000				
15						
16	Sales expenses (fixed plus variable)	$214,000				
17	Income from operations	$290,000				
18						
19	Ending Inventory	$ 94,000				
20						
21						
22						

Fig. 21.1
Under absorption costing, some production costs are allocated to the value of the ending inventory.

QuickData prepares 10,000 modems for sale during the first quarter, and sells 8,000 of them for $110 each. The *variable* production cost of each modem is $38. Additionally, QuickData has *fixed* production costs of $90,000 per quarter that it must meet, regardless of how many modems it produces—1 modem or 100,000 of them.

Note

The purpose of this case study is to focus on the different effects of fixed and variable costs on the valuation of finished goods. To keep the example clear, it is assumed that QuickData has no beginning inventory at the start of the period. By the end of the case study, you will see how two different approaches to costing lead to two different valuations of the ending inventory—which is, of course, the beginning inventory for the next period.

When you understand how the approaches lead to two different valuations of the ending inventory, you will be better placed to understand how they affect the value of the beginning inventory for the next period.

There are also both variable and fixed sales expenses. The variable sales expense is $8 per modem, and this amount includes the sales force's commission as well as a provision for fulfilling the restricted product warranty. The fixed sales costs include such items as the production of product brochures and the salaries paid to the sales force.

By selling 8,000 modems at $110 each during the first quarter, QuickData realizes revenue in the amount of $880,000. To arrive at its gross profit, QuickData computes its cost of goods sold as:

```
=UnitsSold*(VarProductionCost+(FixProductionCost/UnitsMade))
```

or, using actual values:

```
=8000*(38+(90000/10000))
```

which is $376,000. Notice that this is the sum of the number of units sold (8,000) times the sum of the variable production cost ($38) and the average fixed production costs of each unit that was made.

8,000 × ($90,000/10,000) equals $72,000, which is 80 percent of the $90,000 in fixed production costs: the portion that can be allocated to the 8,000 modems that were sold.

The gross profit, sales less cost of goods sold, is $504,000. The fixed sales costs and the variable sales costs are calculated by:

```
=UnitsSold*VarSalesExpense+FixSalesExpense
```

or, again using actual values:

```
=8000*8+150000
```

which returns $214,000.

The income from operations is therefore $290,000 ($504,00 – $214,000). This is simply the difference between the gross profit on the modems and the expenses associated with the sales process.

QuickData sells 8,000 of the 10,000 units it produces during the quarter. The remaining 2,000 units constitute its ending inventory, which is calculated as:

```
=(UnitsMade-UnitsSold)*(VarProductionCost+(FixProductionCost/UnitsMade))
```

Again, this formula multiplies the units remaining in inventory (10,000 – 8,000 = 2,000) times the sum of their variable production costs and the average fixed production costs for all units made.

2,000 × ($90,000/10,000) equals $18,000, which is 20 percent of the fixed production costs: the portion that can be allocated to the 2,000 modems that went unsold. This is the remaining 20 percent of the fixed production costs that were not allocated to the 8,000 modems that were sold. The result of the full formula is $94,000, which is the total value of QuickData's inventory at the end of the first quarter.

Notice that neither the fixed nor the variable sales expense is involved in the valuation of the ending inventory: because these 2,000 modems have not yet been sold, the expenses of selling them have not yet been incurred.

At the end of the second quarter, QuickData prepares another income statement (see fig. 21.2).

	A	B	C	D	E
	Microsoft Excel - Pwxlch21.xls				
	File Edit View Insert Format Tools Data Window Help				
	A1		Starting inventory (units)		
1	Starting inventory (units)	2,000			
2	Production (units)	11,000	Beginning inventory	$ 94,000	
3	Sales (units)	8,000	Variable production costs	$418,000	
4	Price/unit	$ 110	Fixed production costs, 2nd quarter	$ 90,000	
5	Variable production cost per unit	$ 38	Available for sale (13,000 units)		$602,000
6	Variable sales expense per unit	$ 8	Unit production cost	$ 46.18	
7	Fixed production costs	$ 90,000	Units on hand, end of quarter	5,000	
8	Fixed sales expense	$150,000	Ending inventory, FIFO basis	$230,909	
9			Cost of goods sold		$371,091
10	Income Statement, **Absorption Costing**, June 30 1995				
11					
12	Sales	$880,000			
13	Cost of goods sold	$371,091			
14					
15	Gross profit	$508,909			
16					
17	Sales expenses (fixed plus variable)	$214,000			
18	Income from operations	$294,909			
19					
20	Ending Inventory	$230,909			
21					
22					

Fig21.1 \ **Fig21.2** / Fig21.3 / Fig21.4 / Fig21.5 / Fig21
Ready   Sum=0   NUM

Fig. 21.2
Absorption costing causes operating income to vary with production levels.

Comparing the two income statements in figures 21.1 and 21.2, notice that:

- The number of units sold has not changed.

- The sales price has not changed.

- Neither the fixed production cost nor the fixed sales expenses has changed.

- Neither the per unit variable production cost nor the per unit variable sales expense has changed.

- The number of modems produced has increased from 10,000 during the first quarter to 11,000 during the second quarter.

- The net income from operations has increased from $290,000 in the first quarter to $294,909 in the second quarter.

You might not have expected this. When the number of units sold, the selling price, and the costs and expenses are constant, as they are here, you would intuitively expect that the net income would also be constant.

Instead, the only change in the basic inputs is that the number of units produced has increased. Therefore, *a different proportion of the fixed production costs is allocated to the cost of goods sold.* A larger proportion of the $90,000 in fixed production costs—which do not vary as the number of units produced rises or falls—has been allocated to the ending inventory, and a smaller proportion has been allocated to the cost of goods sold. When the cost of goods sold falls, the gross profit increases, as does the net income from operations.

From the standpoint of management, this is an unwelcome development. A manager for QuickData would want net income to vary as a function of sales quantities and prices, minus costs and expenses. Instead, using the approach displayed in figures 21.1 and 21.2, net income has varied as a function of production.

For that reason, QuickData might not want to use this approach to support its decision-making process. (It is termed the *absorption* approach to costing. This term is used because the fixed production costs are absorbed partly by the goods sold and partly by the goods that remain in inventory at the end of the period.) A more informative approach would be one that allows QuickData to estimate income independent of changes in the volume of products that it produces.

To get a better feel for what happens with absorption costing, consider some of the additional information shown in figure 21.2, focusing on the range of cells C2:E9.

The cost of goods sold is calculated by an algorithm used in several other chapters of this book: Cost of Goods Sold = Beginning Inventory plus Production less Ending Inventory. The beginning inventory for the second quarter, $94,000, is simply the value of the first quarter's ending inventory.

To that beginning inventory is added the total variable production costs of $418,000, which is returned by:

```
=UnitsMade*VarProductionCost
```

or 8,000 * $38. The beginning inventory, plus the variable production costs, totals to $512,000. Adding in the $90,000 in fixed production costs gives a total value of goods available for sale of $602,000 (cell D5).

The Unit Production Cost, found in cell D6, is found by adding the total variable production costs of $418,000 plus the fixed production cost of

$90,000, and dividing by the number of units produced (11,000). This distributes both the variable and fixed production costs across the 11,000 units, and returns $46.18 as the total cost of producing a single unit.

By multiplying the Unit Production Cost times the ending inventory of 5,000 units, QuickData can establish a total value for its ending inventory: 5,000 units times $46.18 is $230,909. The first-in, first-out (FIFO) method is used in this method of inventory valuation (see chapter 3 for a discussion of the various methods of inventory valuation, including FIFO).

Finally, QuickData can arrive at a figure for cost of goods sold during the second quarter. The figure of $371,091 in cell D9 is just the cost of goods available for sale, $602,000, less the ending inventory of $230,091.

Notice that part of the fixed production costs of $90,000 appears in the valuation of the ending inventory. The Unit Production Cost includes a per-unit fixed production cost, and is used to value the 5,000 units that remain in inventory at the end of the quarter. And because the cost of goods sold depends partly on the valuation of the ending inventory, it includes the remaining portion of the fixed production costs.

Another way to look at it is to start with the beginning inventory, instead of starting with the ending inventory (see fig. 21.3).

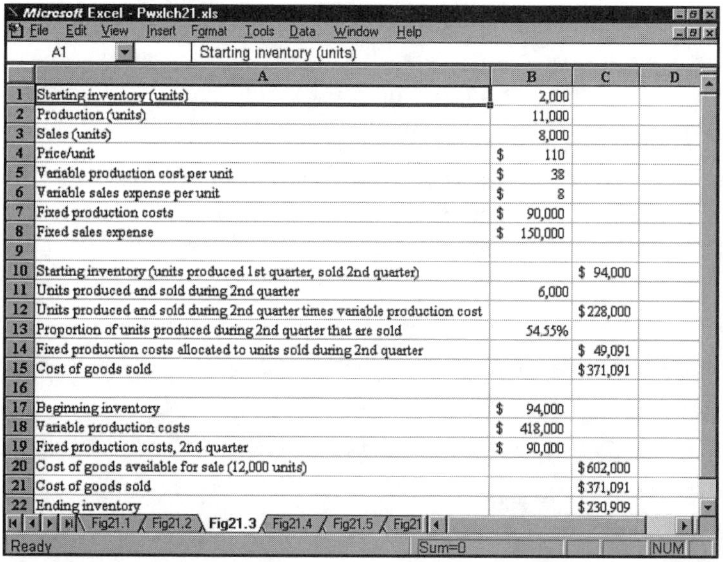

Fig. 21.3
With absorption costing, fixed costs are allocated according to the ratio of units sold to units produced.

	A	B	C	D
	A1	Starting inventory (units)		
1	Starting inventory (units)	2,000		
2	Production (units)	11,000		
3	Sales (units)	8,000		
4	Price/unit	$ 110		
5	Variable production cost per unit	$ 38		
6	Variable sales expense per unit	$ 8		
7	Fixed production costs	$ 90,000		
8	Fixed sales expense	$ 150,000		
9				
10	Starting inventory (units produced 1st quarter, sold 2nd quarter)		$ 94,000	
11	Units produced and sold during 2nd quarter	6,000		
12	Units produced and sold during 2nd quarter times variable production cost		$ 228,000	
13	Proportion of units produced during 2nd quarter that are sold	54.55%		
14	Fixed production costs allocated to units sold during 2nd quarter		$ 49,091	
15	Cost of goods sold		$ 371,091	
16				
17	Beginning inventory	$ 94,000		
18	Variable production costs	$ 418,000		
19	Fixed production costs, 2nd quarter	$ 90,000		
20	Cost of goods available for sale (12,000 units)		$ 602,000	
21	Cost of goods sold		$ 371,091	
22	Ending inventory		$ 230,909	

Because FIFO is the valuation method used, the assumption is that the first 2,000 of the 8,000 modems sold come from the beginning inventory; its cost is $94,000.

To that $94,000, add the total variable cost of the other 6,000 modems sold: 6,000 times $38 is $228,000. The third component in the cost of goods sold is the proportion of fixed production costs that are allocated to the 6,000 newly-produced modems: 6,000 divided by 11,000 (54.55%) times $90,000 is $49,091. The total of the ending inventory, plus the variable costs of production of 6,000 modems, plus the sold goods' share of $90,000, is $371,091.

And because the cost of the goods available for sale is $602,000, the ending inventory is $230,909: $602,000 – $371,091 = $230,909. However you go about calculating the cost of goods sold and the cost of the ending inventory, a portion of the fixed costs of production appears in each quantity. *The portion of the fixed production costs that is attributable to either quantity depends on the ratio of number of units sold to the number of units remaining in inventory at the end of the period.* This is the reason that a change in units produced causes a change in net income, even though the number of units sold remains constant.

Understanding Contribution Costing

Contribution costing (also known as *variable costing*) adopts a different point of view toward the allocation of fixed production costs. Instead of allocating these costs in part to goods that are sold and in part to goods that remain in inventory, this approach allocates the entire amount of fixed production costs to the cost of goods sold. Figure 21.4 shows how this works.

Compare figure 21.4 with figure 21.1 for QuickData's first quarter income statement under the absorption approach. The first major difference is in the calculation of the cost of goods sold. Using contribution costing, the cost of goods sold is:

```
=UnitsSold*VarProductionCosts
```

which is 8,000 times $38, or $304,000. The absorption approach included in this figure a portion of the fixed production costs.

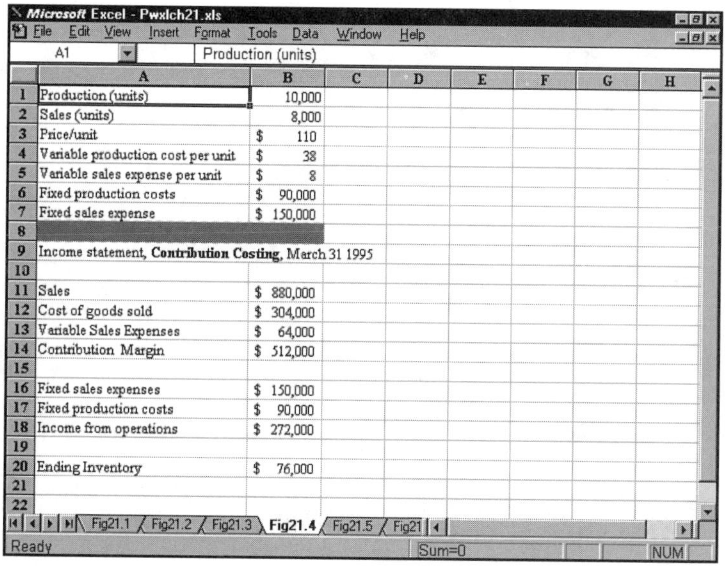

Fig. 21.4
Contribution costing allocates all fixed costs to the products that are sold.

IV

Sales and Marketing

The variable sales expense is entered in cell B13 as:

```
=UnitsSold*VarSalesExpense
```

which returns $64,000. When the cost of goods sold and the variable sales expense are subtracted from the sales figure of $880,000, the result is the product's *contribution margin* (hence the term "contribution costing").

Then, just as under the absorption approach, the fixed sales expenses are entered. But in contrast to the absorption approach, the *total* fixed production costs are entered into the computation: they are subtracted from the contribution margin to return the income from operations, in cell B18, of $272,000.

Notice that this is $18,000 less than the $290,000 income from operations reported in figure 21.1. The reason is that in the latter figure, 20% (2,000 modems in ending inventory divided by 10,000 modems produced) of the fixed production costs were allocated to the ending inventory. Twenty percent of the $90,000 fixed production costs is $18,000, which, using the contribution approach, is charged to income instead of to ending inventory.

Compare the income statement in figure 21.4 with the one shown in figure 21.5, for the second quarter of 1995.

Fig. 21.5

Contribution costing makes income independent of production quantities.

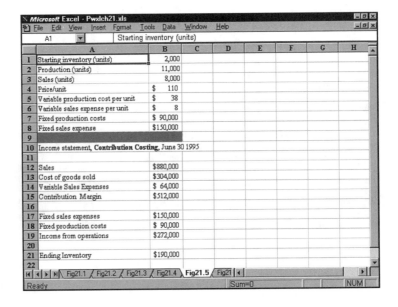

	A	B	C
1	Starting inventory (units)	2,000	
2	Production (units)	11,000	
3	Sales (units)	8,000	
4	Price/unit	$ 110	
5	Variable production cost per unit	$ 38	
6	Variable sales expense per unit	$ 8	
7	Fixed production costs	$ 90,000	
8	Fixed sales expense	$150,000	
9			
10	Income statement, **Contribution Costing**, June 30 1995		
11			
12	Sales	$880,000	
13	Cost of goods sold	$304,000	
14	Variable Sales Expenses	$ 64,000	
15	Contribution Margin	$512,000	
16			
17	Fixed sales expenses	$150,000	
18	Fixed production costs	$ 90,000	
19	Income from operations	$272,000	
20			
21	Ending Inventory	$190,000	
22			

All the input information in figure 21.5 for the second quarter is the same as figure 21.4, which shows the income statement, also under contribution costing, for the first quarter. However, and in contrast to absorption costing, notice that the income from operations is the same in the second quarter as in the first quarter. This is because, despite the fact that production has increased from the first to the second quarter, sales, cost, and expense data have remained constant.

This is the desirable effect of contribution costing: income is a function of sales, not production. From a management viewpoint, it is more efficient to analyze the effect of changes in pricing, expenses and quantities sold on a variable that responds directly to those inputs, than it is to perform an analysis on a variable that also responds to production levels.

Of course, there is a consequence for ending inventory. Notice, under contribution costing, that income from production is $272,000 for the first quarter, which is $18,000 less than income for production for the first quarter under absorption costing. Furthermore, the first quarter's ending inventory under the contribution approach is $76,000 versus $94,000 at the end of the first quarter under the absorption approach: again, a difference of $18,000.

The $18,000 in costs that appeared in ending inventory under the absorption approach is shifted to a current period expense under the contribution approach. This has the simultaneous effect of both reducing the valuation of ending inventory and reducing the income from operations by $18,000 each.

Note

Because of the way that it values inventories, the contribution approach is not normally used to prepare income statements and balance sheets that are used outside the company—for example, by potential creditors and investors. The contribution approach tends to undervalue inventories because it omits a portion of fixed production costs from their valuation, and it tends to understate income because it charges the full amount of fixed production costs for a period against the contribution margin.

Therefore, although it's a useful tool for internal planning and analysis purposes, the contribution approach is not normally used for external reporting.

It should not surprise you that the matching principle appears in a discussion of the relative merits of absorption costing versus contribution costing. According to this principle, costs should be matched with the revenues that they help to produce, during the period that the costs were incurred and the revenue occurred.

Absorption costing causes the costs associated with the production of products to remain with those products until they are sold. It is proper to show those costs after they have been recovered: when a product that remains in one period's ending inventory is sold during a subsequent period.

Equally, it is reasonable to argue that fixed costs of production represent the cost of being able to produce a product in the first place. Without incurring those costs, a company would be unable to produce *any* product. Therefore, these costs should not be regarded as attributable to one collection of goods or another—not some to goods sold and some to ending inventory—but as a cost of the period in which they were incurred. In that case, these costs should be fully charged to the period, not distributed among the products that were manufactured and either sold or remain in inventory.

These are philosophical positions, though, and are rendered moot by the dictum that absorption costing should normally be used for external reporting purposes. For internal planning purposes, in which you want to investigate the relationships among costs, volume of sales, and profitability, you are of course free to use any method of analysis that you and your company approve.

Applying the Contribution Approach to a Pricing Decision

How can a contribution analysis of a product line help you decide how best to set its sales price? Suppose that QuickData's income statement for the first quarter is as shown in figure 21.6.

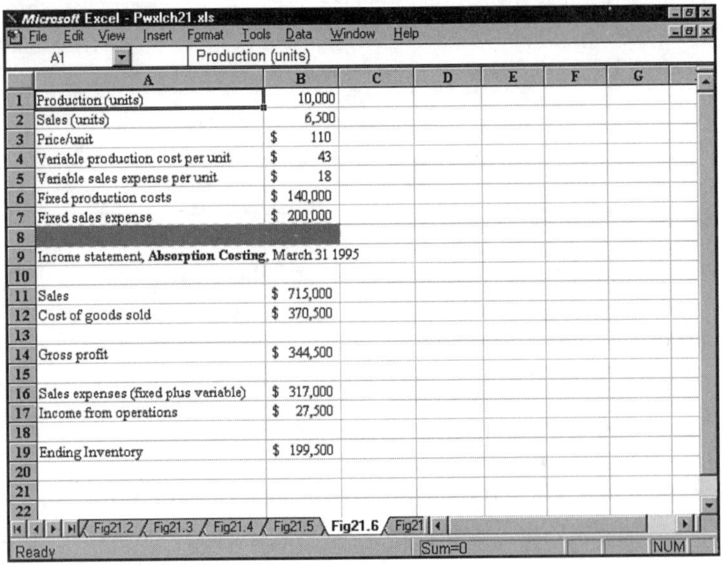

	A	B
1	Production (units)	10,000
2	Sales (units)	6,500
3	Price/unit	$ 110
4	Variable production cost per unit	$ 43
5	Variable sales expense per unit	$ 18
6	Fixed production costs	$ 140,000
7	Fixed sales expense	$ 200,000
8		
9	Income statement, **Absorption Costing**, March 31 1995	
10		
11	Sales	$ 715,000
12	Cost of goods sold	$ 370,500
13		
14	Gross profit	$ 344,500
15		
16	Sales expenses (fixed plus variable)	$ 317,000
17	Income from operations	$ 27,500
18		
19	Ending Inventory	$ 199,500

Fig. 21.6 Absorption costing makes it difficult to arrive at cost-volume-profit decisions.

This income statement, which uses absorption costing, depicts QuickData as not doing quite so well as suggested in earlier figures in this chapter. All of QuickData's costs and expenses have been increased, and the quarter's unit sales have been decreased to 6,500. As a result, the income from operations has fallen to $27,500.

QuickData's management wants to know how changes in the sales price for its modems, or changes in the quantities that it sells, might affect its net income from operations. As a first step, QuickData prepares an income statement in a contribution costing format (see fig. 21.7).

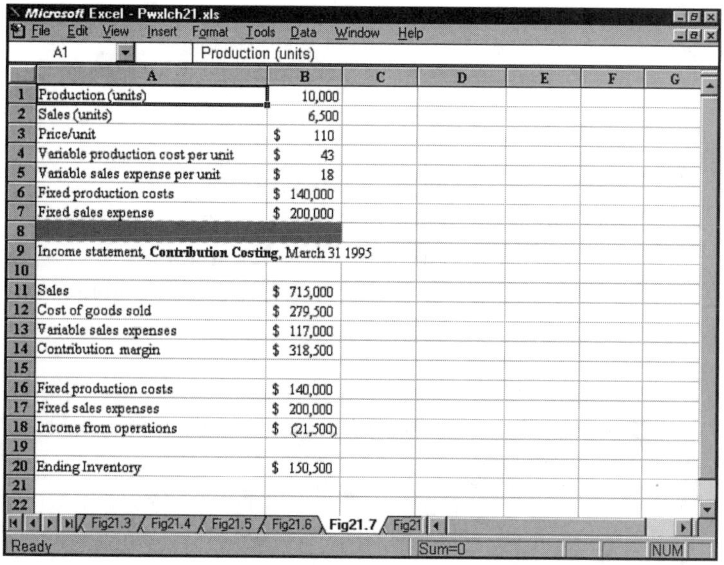

Microsoft Excel - Pwxlch21.xls

A1 | Production (units)

	A	B
1	Production (units)	10,000
2	Sales (units)	6,500
3	Price/unit	$ 110
4	Variable production cost per unit	$ 43
5	Variable sales expense per unit	$ 18
6	Fixed production costs	$ 140,000
7	Fixed sales expense	$ 200,000
8		
9	Income statement, **Contribution Costing**, March 31 1995	
10		
11	Sales	$ 715,000
12	Cost of goods sold	$ 279,500
13	Variable sales expenses	$ 117,000
14	Contribution margin	$ 318,500
15		
16	Fixed production costs	$ 140,000
17	Fixed sales expenses	$ 200,000
18	Income from operations	$ (21,500)
19		
20	Ending Inventory	$ 150,500
21		
22		

Fig. 21.7
With contribution costing, the relationships between pricing, costing and sales volumes become more clear.

The first feature to notice in this contribution analysis is that QuickData's operating income from this product is actually negative. When QuickData deducts the entire amount of the fixed production costs, $140,000, from the contribution margin—instead of allocating the fixed production costs in part to the ending inventory—the net income becomes a loss of $21,500.

Using the contribution approach, QuickData's management can isolate the effect of changes in sales quantities and pricing on income from operations. Recall that under the absorption approach, income is in part a function of production levels and costs. But when you use the contribution approach instead, the act of varying production volume has no effect on the net income attributable to the product. Therefore, if management can find the proper mix of sales price and quantity sold, it can be confident that the product will remain profitable regardless of changes that might occur in the production volumes.

If QuickData's management wants to focus solely on sales price, it can use Excel's Goal Seek function to determine its break-even point for income. To do so using the worksheet in figure 21.7, follow these steps:

1. Select cell B18.

2. Choose Tools, Goal Seek. In the Goal Seek dialog box, the Set Cell edit box is selected and contains B18.

3. Click in the To value edit box, and enter 0 (zero).

4. Click in the By changing cell edit box, and click in cell B3 on the worksheet.

5. Choose OK.

Cell B18, Income from operations, will now equal $0—on your computer, it may display as ($0) due to an infinitesimal error of rounding. Cell B3 will now equal $113.31. This is the price that QuickData must charge to arrive at a break-even point (see fig. 21.8, which uses a format including two decimal points so as to display cell B3 properly).

Fig. 21.8
Break-even points are easier to find using contribution costing.

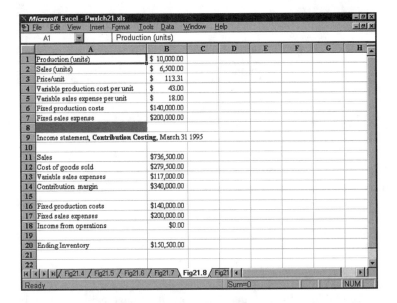

Tip

If QuickData's management wants to increase its income from operations beyond the break-even point, and yet to allow both price and sales quantities to fluctuate, it could use the Solver rather than the Goal Seek function. The Solver is able to modify several inputs simultaneously, whereas Goal Seek is restricted to one input variable (in this example, sales price).

Using Contribution Analysis for New Products

Several figures used in the section on contribution costing show that the contribution margin is calculated by subtracting a product's variable costs from its revenue. For example, in figure 21.8, the contribution margin is $340,000. This is the result of subtracting the cost of goods sold ($279,500) and variable sales expenses ($117,000) from the sales figure of $736,500. The cost of goods sold is returned by this formula:

```
=UnitsSold*VarProductionCost
```

So the contribution margin is obtained by the combination of sales revenue, variable sales expenses and the variable production cost. This in fact defines the contribution margin: it is the difference between sales revenue and variable costs and expenses. No fixed costs enter into the equation.

This method of segregating variable costs from fixed costs to determine contribution margin can be very useful in other situations, such as deciding whether to bring a new offering into your product set. Suppose, for example, that DataPump, Inc. currently manufactures two kinds of modems: a 9,600 bps (bits per second) and a 14,400 bps model. DataPump needs to decide whether to begin the manufacture of a new, 28,800 bps model. The company makes the preliminary calculations shown in figure 21.9, using the contribution approach.

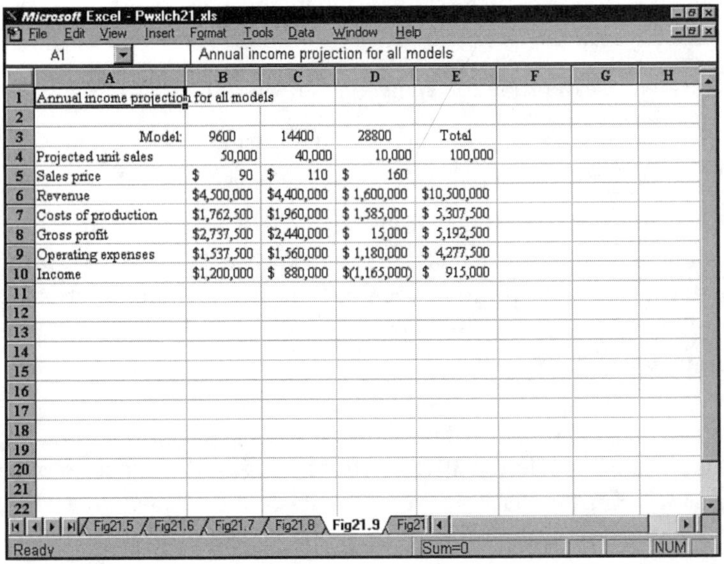

	A	B	C	D	E
1	Annual income projection for all models				
2					
3	Model:	9600	14400	28800	Total
4	Projected unit sales	50,000	40,000	10,000	100,000
5	Sales price	$ 90	$ 110	$ 160	
6	Revenue	$4,500,000	$4,400,000	$ 1,600,000	$10,500,000
7	Costs of production	$1,762,500	$1,960,000	$ 1,585,000	$ 5,307,500
8	Gross profit	$2,737,500	$2,440,000	$ 15,000	$ 5,192,500
9	Operating expenses	$1,537,500	$1,560,000	$ 1,180,000	$ 4,277,500
10	Income	$1,200,000	$ 880,000	$(1,165,000)	$ 915,000

Fig. 21.9
This initial view of a new product line suggests that it would lose money.

This analysis suggests that the outlook for a new model is poor. The actual revenue, cost and expense results for the existing 9,600 and 14,400 models are shown in columns B and C. These data indicate that the existing models are doing reasonably well in the marketplace.

DataPump's management believes that certain of the costs of producing the proposed modem can be shared among all three models. They also believe that some operating expenses can be kept to a minimum because a portion of the marketplace will seek out the new model due to its greater speed. The modem's higher speed will, it is hoped, help to reduce the amount of time and money required for the sales force to market the product effectively.

Even so, the projections for the proposed new model are not good. The projected revenue of $1,600,000 is just enough to cover the costs of production, with $15,000 to spare. And when the operating expenses associated with the new model are figured in, the 28,800 bps model will actually lose over a million dollars per year.

What if the projected sales quantity of 10,000 units is too conservative—that is, what if the new model proves popular enough that DataPump can sell 20,000 or 30,000 units?

The analysis in figure 21.9 cannot answer that question. Some of the cost of production is fixed, as are some of the operating expenses. These fixed dollar amounts would not change if more units were produced and sold. On the other hand, some of the costs and expenses are variable, and would increase as production and sales increase. To estimate the effect of greater sales, it's necessary to break the costs and expenses into fixed and variable categories.

The first step in extending the analysis is shown in figure 21.10.

For each model, the analysis estimates four dollar amounts: fixed production and sales amounts, and variable production and sales amounts.

The key word in the prior sentence is "estimates." In practice, it is often very difficult to determine the actual costs and expenses that are fixed versus those that are variable. It can be even more difficult to allocate these dollar amounts to different products. Suppose, for example, that DataPump's customers purchase both the 9600 and 14400 models. The cost of sales calls made by DataPump's sales force must somehow be allocated between the two models to arrive at a variable sales expense for the 9600 model and one for the 14400 model. To do so with a reasonable degree of accuracy, DataPump management must undertake a careful analysis of customer purchasing records and compare it to sales expense reports. Even so, the analyst will have to exercise judgment in allocating expenses to different products.

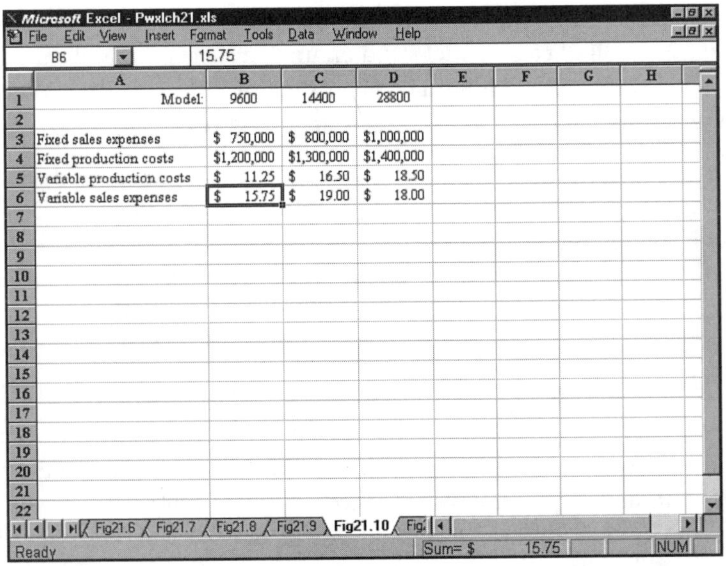

	A	B	C	D
1	Model:	9600	14400	28800
2				
3	Fixed sales expenses	$ 750,000	$ 800,000	$1,000,000
4	Fixed production costs	$1,200,000	$1,300,000	$1,400,000
5	Variable production costs	$ 11.25	$ 16.50	$ 18.50
6	Variable sales expenses	$ 15.75	$ 19.00	$ 18.00

Fig. 21.10
Accurate cost and expense breakdowns can be very difficult to achieve, but are necessary components of pricing analysis.

The process is not easy, but it is feasible and this discussion assumes that the costs and expenses shown in figure 21.10 are reasonably accurate. The next step is to use the cost analysis to create a contribution analysis (see fig. 21.11).

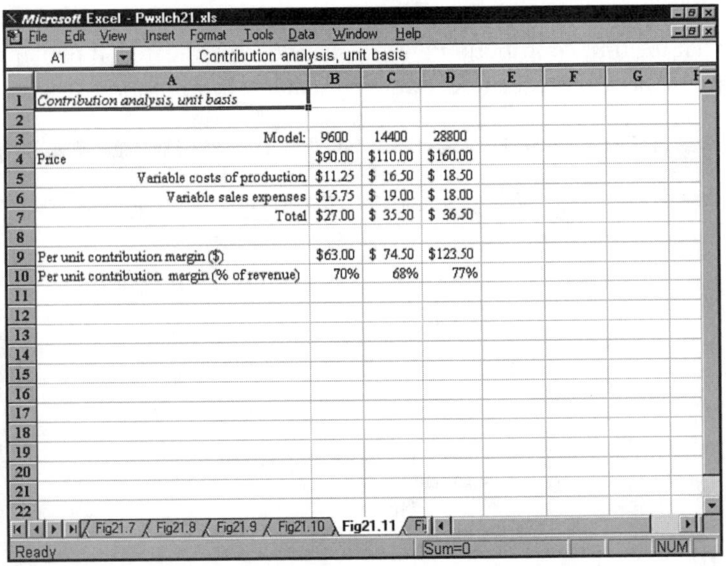

	A	B	C	D
1	*Contribution analysis, unit basis*			
2				
3	Model:	9600	14400	28800
4	Price	$90.00	$110.00	$160.00
5	Variable costs of production	$11.25	$ 16.50	$ 18.50
6	Variable sales expenses	$15.75	$ 19.00	$ 18.00
7	Total	$27.00	$ 35.50	$ 36.50
8				
9	Per unit contribution margin ($)	$63.00	$ 74.50	$123.50
10	Per unit contribution margin (% of revenue)	70%	68%	77%

Fig. 21.11
A product contribution analysis puts the new product in a different light.

The amounts shown in figure 21.11 are based on unit revenue—the sales price for one unit of each model—and on unit variable costs and expenses. Keep in mind that the definition of a contribution margin is the product's revenue, less its associated variable costs and expenses.

The situation starts to become a little clearer. Because DataPump can share some variable production costs among the three models, the incremental cost of producing each model 28800 can be held down. Further, the estimate of the variable sales expense of each model 28800 is actually lower than that of the model 14400. However, these amounts are no more than educated guesses on the part of the manufacturing department and of sales management, and the decision maker must interpret the analysis in that context.

Nevertheless, if the estimates are even reasonably accurate, the contribution margin for the proposed model is impressive. The proposed model is expected, before taking fixed costs into account, to contribute over three quarters of its sales price to gross profit. Again, only variable costs are used, in conjunction with sales revenue, to arrive at the contribution margin. DataPump's management can therefore estimate which costs will rise—and by how much—as production and sales volumes increase. The remaining, fixed costs should remain stable, and DataPump can get a better picture of how adding the new model to its product set will affect its net income from operations.

Now that the unit contribution margins have been estimated, it remains to determine the net income under different volume assumptions (see fig. 21.12).

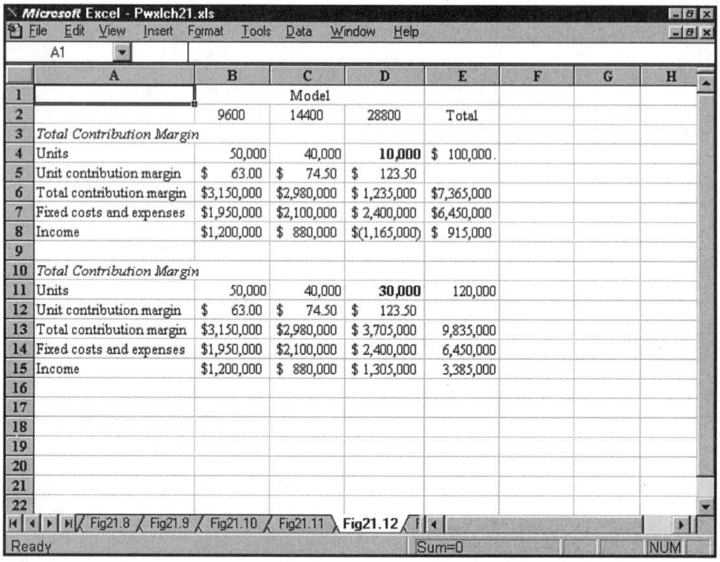

Fig. 21.12
An aggregate contribution analysis makes clear the relationship of sales volume to operating income.

	A	B	C	D	E	F	G	H
			Model					
2		9600	14400	28800	Total			
3	*Total Contribution Margin*							
4	Units	50,000	40,000	10,000	$ 100,000.			
5	Unit contribution margin	$ 63.00	$ 74.50	$ 123.50				
6	Total contribution margin	$3,150,000	$2,980,000	$ 1,235,000	$7,365,000			
7	Fixed costs and expenses	$1,950,000	$2,100,000	$ 2,400,000	$6,450,000			
8	Income	$1,200,000	$ 880,000	$(1,165,000)	$ 915,000			
9								
10	*Total Contribution Margin*							
11	Units	50,000	40,000	30,000	120,000			
12	Unit contribution margin	$ 63.00	$ 74.50	$ 123.50				
13	Total contribution margin	$3,150,000	$2,980,000	$ 3,705,000	9,835,000			
14	Fixed costs and expenses	$1,950,000	$2,100,000	$ 2,400,000	6,450,000			
15	Income	$1,200,000	$ 880,000	$ 1,305,000	3,385,000			

Figure 21.12 shows the effect of two different assumptions about sales volume: the range D4:D8 contains the estimated outcomes if 10,000 units (cell D4, in boldface) of the proposed model are sold, and D11:D15 contains the estimates given a sales volume of 30,000 units (cell D11, also in boldface).

As was the case in figure 21.9, the new model shows a net loss of $1,165,000 (cell D8) if DataPump sells 10,000 units. This is due largely to the fixed costs and expenses that are associated with producing and selling any number of units, from 1 to 100,000.

However, if DataPump sells 30,000 units, it stands to increase its income by $1,305,000 (cell D15). As the DataPump sells more and more units, the contribution margin grows, concomitant with the sales volume. But the fixed category remains fixed, and detracts—on a relative basis—less and less from the product's contribution margin.

Thus, this analysis suggests that should DataPump be able to sell more than the 10,000 units initially assumed, it will begin to make money on the product (19,433 units is the break-even point).

You have probably noticed several qualifications and caveats in this discussion. Predicting the future is a risky undertaking, fraught with uncertainties and unknowns. Not only does the analysis model itself involve many assumptions, but the realities of the marketplace can change during the period for which the company makes its projections. Here is a summary of the assumptions, both explicit and implicit, that the analysis makes:

- It is possible to distinguish fixed production costs from variable production costs.

- It is possible to distinguish fixed sales expenses from variable sales expenses.

- It is possible to allocate these costs and expenses accurately to the product lines in question.

- It is possible to estimate the number of units that the company will actually produce and sell.

- The fixed costs and expenses actually remain fixed across the probable range of units produced and sold. Although for clarity it is assumed that these amounts are constant across a very broad range of quantities, in practice there are usually breakpoints: for example, when a company must acquire new equipment to keep pace with increased production levels.

Even though it might seem difficult to justify this set of assumptions, you will find that you generally have a good sense of their validity, and therefore of the projections.

There is one more major assumption remaining: that the introduction of the new product will have no effect on the sales of the existing products. It is necessary to test this assumption, and the next section describes how to do so.

Estimating the Effect of Cross-elasticity

When a company introduces a new product, it is likely that the product will compete to some degree with products that it already produces and sells. This is termed *cross-elasticity*: the tendency of similar products to draw sales from one another, instead of expanding market penetration, due to their functional similarities.

There are many reasons that a company might want or need to introduce a new product. It might be necessary to do so because its customers demand it, because technological advances make the new product feasible, to maintain the marketplace's perception of the company, or—most typically—because the competition has introduced its own version.

If the new product is so clearly superior to existing products that very few customers would continue to purchase from the current product lines, it is often best to simply discontinue the existing products. However, if there are real differences in function, appearance, or cost, it is often sensible to introduce a new product and continue to offer the existing lines.

What effect might the introduction of DataPump's model 28800 have, both on the company's overall profitability and on the individual products? See figure 21.13.

The analysis in figure 21.13 depends on DataPump's ability to estimate the quantity of sales of an existing product that will be lost to the new product. Ideally, DataPump is in a position to test market the new product in a restricted market: restricted, to hold down the cost of actually performing the test.

If it can undertake a market test, DataPump will be able to observe the effect of the product introduction in one area on the sales of its existing modems. The company can then compare the outcomes in the test market to the outcomes in a control market. It should not focus simply on the test market, because other influences might be at work.

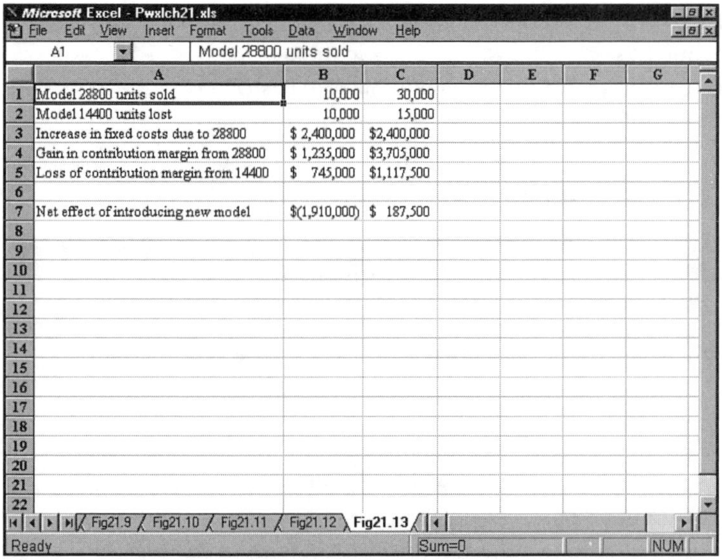

Fig. 21.13
It's necessary to account for cross-elasticity when a new model is similar to existing models.

	A	B	C
1	Model 28800 units sold	10,000	30,000
2	Model 14400 units lost	10,000	15,000
3	Increase in fixed costs due to 28800	$ 2,400,000	$2,400,000
4	Gain in contribution margin from 28800	$ 1,235,000	$3,705,000
5	Loss of contribution margin from 14400	$ 745,000	$1,117,500
6			
7	Net effect of introducing new model	$(1,910,000)	$ 187,500

Suppose, for example, that a national, commercial bulletin-board service happened to drop its charges for 14,400 bps connections at the same time that DataPump's market test is occurring. This might encourage some users to purchase new 14,400 modems, but there might be no similar motivation for them to purchase 28,800 modems.

In that case, the market for 14,400 modems might remain strong, and the effect of introducing the 28,800 model could be masked. But by comparing the test market results with a control market, where DataPump does not introduce the 28,800 model, it is possible to isolate the effect of the 28,800 on sales of the 14,400: in other words, the cross-elasticity of the two products.

For one reason or another, it might not be feasible to conduct a market test (for example, DataPump might not market on a geographic basis and thus could not control where its new product is sold). In that case, a typical alternative is to ask the sales force to estimate the degree of loss in the existing product that would come about as a result of the introduction of a new product. This approach is not, of course, as satisfying as conducting an empirical trial, but a carefully conducted survey of the sales force can be reasonably informative.

Assume, then, that DataPump has by one means or another been able to estimate how many sales in its existing 14,400 product it will lose to its new, 28,800 product. Figure 21.13 estimates financial outcomes under two scenarios: column B describes what will happen should each of 10,000 customers purchase DataPump's 28,800 model instead of its 14,400 model. Column C describes what will happen if 30,000 customers purchase the 28,800: 15,000 customers purchase the 28,800 instead of the 14,400, and 15,000 new customers purchase the 28,800. The latter 15,000 customers represent new sales, not losses to the model 14,400 product.

> **Tip**
>
> You can also use the procedures described in chapter 13, "Sensitivity Analysis," to test various outcomes under different cross-elasticity assumptions.

If DataPump's customers purchase the 28,800 model rather than the 14,400 model (column B), DataPump will lose nearly $2,000,000 in income. This is due to assuming $2,400,000 in fixed costs, at a level of sales that fails to generate sufficient contribution margin ($1,235,000) to cover those costs, and at a level that reduces the contribution margin for the 14,400 model ($745,000). The latter amount is returned by this formula:

```
=Fig21.12!C5*B2
```

where the amount represented by the reference to Fig21.12!C5 is the 14,400 model's unit contribution margin. Multiplied by the amount in cell B2, the model 14400 units that are lost to the model 28800, this is the contribution margin that DataPump loses to its new model.

The loss of $1,910,000 shown in cell B7 is returned by:

```
=B4-B3-B5
```

which is simply the margin gained from the 28800 model, less the fixed costs due to the 28800 model, less the contribution margin lost from the 14400 model.

In contrast, if DataPump sells 30,000 units of the model 28800, suffering a loss of 15,000 units of the model 14400, it can expect to increase its net income by $187,500. However, in the context of the fixed costs it must assume to produce any appreciable number of the 28800, this increase in margin appears negligible. On the basis of this financial analysis alone, it would be unlikely that DataPump's management would opt to introduce the new product.

Suppose that DataPump decides that it needs to increase its net income by at least $1,000,000 to justify the risk to its existing product line and the additional fixed costs that it would have to undertake. DataPump can try the effect of raising the sales price of the model 28800, so as to increase its contribution margin (see fig. 21.14).

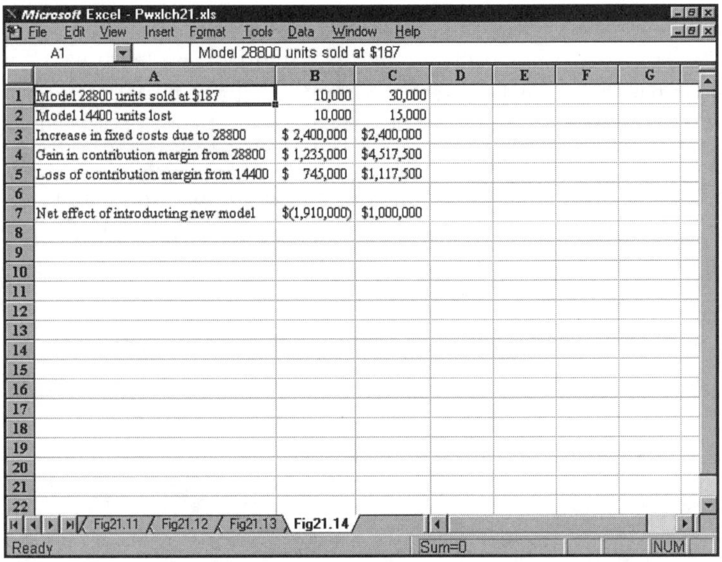

	A	B	C
1	Model 28800 units sold at $187	10,000	30,000
2	Model 14400 units lost	10,000	15,000
3	Increase in fixed costs due to 28800	$ 2,400,000	$2,400,000
4	Gain in contribution margin from 28800	$ 1,235,000	$4,517,500
5	Loss of contribution margin from 14400	$ 745,000	$1,117,500
6			
7	Net effect of introducting new model	$(1,910,000)	$1,000,000

Fig. 21.14
It's often necessary to revisit pricing decisions when two products or models share common characteristics.

By raising the proposed sales price of the model 28800 from $160 to about $187, the net effect of introducing the model is a $1,000,000 increase in income. Separating the 28800 from the 14400 by an additional $27 in sales price would certainly mitigate its cross-elasticity with the existing product lines, and it might be that the number of model 14400 sales lost would be less than the estimated 15,000.

However, raising the sales price would also tend to reduce the number of sales of the model 28800. DataPump must be convinced that the features in the 28800 are superior to its existing products by a similar margin: one that is wide enough to justify in the new customer's mind this additional cost.

Summary

This chapter has discussed the effect of the relationship between fixed costs and variable costs on your income from operations. There is a complex interplay among these costs, the price that you charge for your products and the product quantities that you produce.

The absorption approach to costing allocates the fixed costs of production between goods that are sold and goods that remain in inventory at the end of an accounting period. This approach is used for external reporting purposes, because it more accurately estimates the value of the inventory asset as well as the income earned during the period.

The contribution approach to costing assigns the total fixed costs of production to the goods that are sold. While this assignment understates the value of the company's inventory asset as well as its income, it makes the income for a period insensitive to variations in levels of production (a useful effect for cost-volume-profit planning). The contribution approach is also useful for determining the potential profitability of a new product under alternative pricing structures, and for assessing the impact on profitability of a product's cross-elasticity with other product lines.

Appendix

What's on the Disk

The disk included with this book contains all the worksheets that are depicted in the book's figures. This makes it easy for you to re-create the business analyses that are described in the text. It also contains several special VBA modules that you can use to automate some business analyses such as forecasting and quality control.

Moving Files to Your Hard Disk

Follow these steps to extract the files from the *Business Analysis with Excel* companion disk.

1. Place the disk into your floppy drive.

2. Copy the BUSAEXCL file to the root directory of your hard drive.

3. Click the START/Run: button in Windows 95.

4. Type *x*:\BUSAEXCL (where *x* is the letter you designate for your hard drive) and click OK.

5. After the files are done extracting, close the MSDOS window. You should now have a directory on your hard drive called BUSAEXCL with all the files from the disk.

Each file on the disk corresponds to a chapter in the book. The files are saved as workbooks, with individual worksheets that have the same names as a chapter's figures. So, to obtain the data shown in figure 9.2 in Chapter 9, just open the file named Chap09.xls and activate the worksheet named Fig9.2.

The only figures that do not have associated worksheets on the disk are the figures that display nothing other than an Excel dialog box.

VBA Modules and Subroutines

The disk also contains several VBA files that automate the creation of forecasts, quality control charts, and sales and marketing analysis.

Forecasting Modules

Chapter 9, "Forecasting and Projections," describes how to use Excel to make forecasts of variables such as revenues and product demand. It also describes how to extend Excel's built-in functions to make your forecasts more accurate. These extensions depend on VBA modules that you can find on the disk in the folder named *Chap09*:

- *Smooth.xls* contains code that you can use to extend Excel's Exponential Smoothing add-in to take account of seasonality in a baseline, so as to make annual forecasts more accurate.

- *ARIMA.xls* contains code that you can use to determine whether a Box-Jenkins analysis would provide a better forecast than Excel's functions and tools will make. This module displays ARIMA correlograms that help to identify the proper Box-Jenkins model.

Quality Control Modules

Chapter 10 describes various ways that you can perform quality control analyses using Excel, including statistical process control (SPC) charts. On the disk, in the folder named *Chap10*, there is a VBA module that creates SPC charts for you, named *SPC.xls*. The folder also contains an extensive Help file, named *SPC.hlp*. The VBA module creates SPC charts for both variables (x-and-s charts) and attributes (p-charts).

Sales and Marketing Analysis

Chapter 17 describes how to use an intermediate statistical technique, Analysis of Covariance, to fairly contrast sales results from different sales territories. On the disk, in the folder named *Chap17*, there is a VBA module that performs this analysis for you, named *ANCOVA.xla*. The folder also contains an extensive Help file, named *ANCOVA.hlp*. The VBA module extends the capabilities of Excel Analysis ToolPak, which contains three Analysis of Variance add-ins. Going beyond the capabilities of the add-ins, ANCOVA.xla also handles multiple covariates, a larger number of factors, and unequal cell sizes.

Instructions for installing and running each of these VBA modules are located in the appropriate chapter of *Business Analysis with Excel*.

Glossary

3-D reference   A reference to a range that spans more than one worksheet in a workbook. A reference to the range A1:D4 is *not* a 3-D reference. A reference to the range Sheet1:Sheet5!A1:D4 is a 3-D reference. Only certain Excel functions can make use of 3-D references: for example, =SUM(Sheet1:Sheet5!A1:D4) is legal, but =MMULT(Sheet1:Sheet5!A1:D4,F1:I4) is not.

Absolute reference   An absolute reference contains a dollar sign ($) before its row component and before its column component. $A$1 is an example of an absolute reference. If you enter =$A$1 in cell C1, and then copy the formula in C1 to cell D1, the formula in both C1 and D1 will be =$A$1. The reference is *absolute*, and will not change, regardless of where you might copy it. Compare with *relative reference* and *mixed reference*.

Absorption costing   Also called Full costing. A method of assigning both the variable and fixed costs of production to the goods produced on a pro-rata basis, and regardless of whether the goods are sold during the current period. Compare with *Contribution costing*.

Accelerated depreciation   Any of a variety of methods of calculating depreciation that do not necessarily assign an equal amount of depreciation to an asset during each period of its useful life. Declining balance and variable declining balance are two examples of accelerated depreciation.

Acceptable Quality Level   Used in acceptance sampling. The lowest proportion of non-defective goods that a buyer considers an acceptable average for the supplier's production process. Compare with *Lot Tolerance Percent Defective*.

Accounts payable   Amounts that a business has agreed to pay its suppliers for items purchased on credit.

Accounts receivable   Amounts owed to a business for products and services purchased on credit.

Accrual accounting Recording revenue when it is earned and expenses when they are incurred. It is coincidental if this is the same period that cash is collected from customers or paid to suppliers.

Actual cost The price paid to a supplier for an asset. Compare with *replacement cost.*

Adjusted trial balance A balance of accounts, struck at the end of an accounting period, that includes adjusting entries.

Adjusting entry An entry to an account, made at the end of an accounting period, that records any account activity that is not driven by an actual business transaction. Examples include depreciation, accrued salaries, and interest due for the period.

Aging approach A method of estimating the amount in Accounts Receivable that might never be collected. Under this approach, open accounts are classified according to the length of time that they are past due, and a different percentage of each category is treated as doubtful. Compare with *Percentage of Sales approach.*

Analysis of Covariance A statistical method for putting groups on an equal footing as to existing variables, prior to testing the reliability of differences in their average values on another variable.

Analysis of Variance A statistical method for determining the likelihood that differences among the averages of groups of numbers are reliable.

Argument A value or a variable that is used by a function (or, in VBA, by a procedure). For example, in the formula =SUM(1,2,3), the numbers 1, 2, and 3 are all arguments to the SUM function.

Autocorrelation function (ACF) A measure, used in ARIMA analysis, of the degree to which the current observation is dependent on a prior observation. Given that observations are recorded in the worksheet range A1:A20, a close approximation to a lag-1 ACF can be found by =CORREL(A2:A20,A1:A19), and lag-2 ACF by =CORREL(A3:A20,A1:A18).

Autoregressive Integrated Moving Average (ARIMA) Also known as Box-Jenkins analysis. A method used in forecasting that combines the advantages of regression approaches with moving-average and smoothing approaches to forecasting.

Array formula A special kind of formula in Excel. To enter a formula as an array formula, type it as usual but instead of pressing Enter, simultaneously hold down Ctrl and Shift as you press Enter. You will be able to tell that Excel has accepted it as an array formula if you see a pair of curly braces {} surrounding the formula in the Formula Bar. Do not try to enter the braces from the keyboard: this would indicate a text entry to Excel. Array formulas are required in certain worksheet functions such as LINEST() and MMULT(), and in these cases you must highlight a range of cells that corresponds to the functions requirements before you array-enter the formula. They are also required when one or more of their arguments consist of arrays that do not already exist on the worksheet, but instead are calculated by the formula.

Asset   Anything of value that a business owns and that contributes to its ability to make a profit.

Average collection period   The average length of time it takes to recover costs and earn profit on credit sales. The usual formula is Accounts Receivable divided by the ratio of sales made on credit to the number of days in the period. The longer the Average Collection Period, the longer the company does not have access to its assets for reinvestment.

Average cost   A method of inventory valuation that assigns a value to each unit in the inventory that is the average of the cost of all units in inventory.

Balance sheet   A financial statement that summarizes a business's assets in one section, and its liabilities and owner's equity in the other. The totals of the two sections should equal one another, that is, they should be in balance.

Block   A group of VBA statements that is initiated and terminated by certain keywords. For example, statements between an If condition and an End If statement are a block. Similarly, statements between a With statement and an End With statement are a block.

Break-even point   The date that the costs of an investment are fully recovered by the income it produces.

Collection   In VBA, a group of Objects. For example, the Worksheets collection consists of a group of Worksheet objects.

Common sizing   The conversion of the numbers in a financial statement from dollar amounts to another metric. This is often done by dividing each dollar amount by total sales for the period: in this way, each entry in the statement represents a percentage of sales. Different divisors, such as headcount and total assets, can be used for different analysis purposes.

Confidence interval   The size of the range between a minimum and a maximum value, such that some proportion of the averages of repeated samples from a population are expected to fall within the range. That proportion is the probability, or confidence, level associated with the interval. Therefore, a 95 percent confidence interval around a sample average is expected to capture 95 of 100 averages from *other* samples.

Continuing value   An estimate of the total value of an investment after some specified period of time. This estimate is often based on the value of an alternative investment that would return the same cash flow as the existing investment.

Contra account   A type of ledger account established to accumulate amounts that work against other accounts. For example, a contra-revenue account, such as Sales Returns or Uncollectible Accounts, is used as an offset to Sales to calculate Net Sales.

Contribution costing   Also called Variable costing. A method of assigning all the fixed costs of production to the goods sold during the current period. Compare with *Absorption costing*.

Contribution margin   The revenue created by the sale of a single product unit, less the variable costs associated with its production.

Control Limits   Values used in statistical process control that help define whether a process is in control. Usually, control limits are set at three standard deviations above and below the average value of the process.

Control variable   A variable that defines the number of times a Loop executes. For example, the For statement `For Counter = 1 to 10` causes the subsequent statements to execute 10 times. The Control Variable is `Counter`.

Correlogram   A graph, used in ARIMA analysis, of the correlations of observations with observations that occurred earlier in the baseline. Correlograms are used in the identification phase of an ARIMA analysis to help specify a model (AR, MA, IMA, etc.) for the data.

Cost of goods available for sale   The sum of the value of a period's beginning inventory, plus the value of goods produced (or acquired for resale) during the period.

Cost of Goods Sold (COGS)   The cost to a company of the acquisition and manufacture of the products that it sells. The components of Cost of Goods Sold include the cost of raw materials, any labor costs involved in manufacture or other preparation for sale, and any overhead associated with production. It is usually most convenient to determine the Cost of Goods Sold by subtracting the value of the Ending Inventory from the Cost of Goods Available for Sale. On the Income Statement, the Cost of Goods Sold is subtracted from Sales (or from Net Sales, if goods have been returned by the customer) to find Gross Profit. Compare with *Cost of goods available for sale.*

Cost/Volume/Profit analysis   Analyses of the relationships among the costs paid to produce or acquire goods, the number of such goods, and the profit obtained from their sale. Particularly important in these analyses are the understanding of the relative effects of fixed and variable costs, and the product's contribution margin.

Credits   The right-hand side of a T-account.

Cross-elasticity   The functional similarity of different products offered by a business. Products that are cross-elastic tend to cut into one another's sales.

Current assets   Cash, plus assets that a business can convert into cash, usually within the current period, in the course of conducting its normal operations.

Current liabilities   Debts or obligations to creditors and suppliers that must be satisfied within the current period.

Current Ratio   A measure of a company's ability to meet its current liabilities from its current assets. Current assets include inventory; compare with the *Quick Ratio*, which subtracts inventory from current assets.

Date serial number   In Excel, each possible day is assigned a different serial number. In Excel for Windows, the default system assigns serial number 1 to January 1, 1900, the serial number 2 to January 2, 1900, and so on. Optionally, you can use the 1904 date system (choose Tools, Options, and select the Calculation tab), under which serial number 1 is assigned to January 2, 1904.

Debits   The left-hand side of a T-account.

Debt Ratio   The ratio of a company's total debt to its total assets. From a creditor's standpoint, the lower the debt ratio the better.

Declining balance   A method of depreciation that bases the amount of depreciation of an asset for the current period on the value of the asset at the end of the prior period.

Depreciation   The loss in the value of an asset (typically, buildings and equipment) that occurs through its use in the production of revenue. This loss in value is recognized periodically, as the asset ages. Excel supports several methods of calculating depreciation, including straight-line, declining balance, and sum-of-year's-digits.

Dim statement   The typical method of declaring a VBA variable. You can use the Dim statement to name the variable, to declare it as a specific type such as String or Integer, to declare it as an array of values, and (if an array) to define the bounds of its dimensions.

Discount factor   The factor used to determine the future value of a given present value, or the present value of a given future value.

Discounted payback period   The length of time required to recover the cost of an investment, taking into account losses in the investment's value due to discounting.

Double Precision   A variable type. A VBA variable declared as Double occupies 64 bits of memory, and is therefore more precise than a Single Precision variable, which occupies only 32 bits of memory. Compare with *Single Precision*.

Double-entry accounting   The method of accounting under which every business transaction appears as a debit to one account and as a credit to another account.

Earnings per share (EPS) Ratio   A company's earnings (usually defined as its net income less an allowance for preferred dividends), divided by the number of shares of common stock outstanding. EPS is a measure of the attractiveness of an investment by a common stockholder.

EBITDA   Earnings Before Interest, Taxes, Depreciation, and Amortization. This figure is frequently used in financial analysis because it represents a company's earnings due to its normal business operations, undiluted by ancillary obligations.

Equity Ratio   The complement of the Debt Ratio. The ratio of a company's total equity to its total assets, and thus the portion of the company's asset base that has been acquired through investment rather than through borrowing.

First-in, First-out (FIFO)   A method of inventory valuation that assumes that the value of the goods which were sold from inventory during the period is the value of the goods acquired earliest. Compare with *LIFO* and *Average Cost*.

Fixed assets   Assets that, in contrast to consumable supplies, are long-lasting, and that have an objective value.

Fixed costs   Costs of conducting operations that are the same regardless of how many products are produced or services rendered. Compare with *variable costs.*

Future value   The value at some future time of an investment made today: its original value plus whatever amount the investment earns between today and some date in the future.

General Journal   A journal that contains, usually in chronological order, records of business transactions that do not belong in any of the Special Journals that a company has established. It is usually reserved for exceptional transactions, such as a one-time bonus to an employee; whereas a Special Journal is reserved for frequently occurring transactions such as weekly salary payments or cash sales. Compare with *Special Journal.*

General ledger   A grouping of all the accounts that pertain the to operation of a business, showing the debits and credits that apply to each account. Detailed information about very active accounts, such as Cash Receipts, Accounts Payable, and Accounts Receivable, are maintained in Subsidiary ledgers, and their total debits and total credits are transferred to the associated account in the General ledger.

Generally Accepted Accounting Principles (GAAP)   Methods used in accounting that help ensure accurate financial reporting, and that help make possible accurate comparisons of the results reported by one business entity with those reported by another.

Global names   Also known as book-level names. A global name belongs to the workbook, and can be used in functions or formulas in any workbook sheet. Costs is an example of a global name; to be a local name, it would have to contain the name of a specific sheet, such as Sheet1!Costs. When you define a name using the Name Box, instead of with Insert, Name, Define, you create a global name. Compare with *Local names.*

Gross Profit Margin   A measure of a company's profitability before operating expenses are taken into account. It is usually calculated by subtracting the Cost of Goods Sold from Sales, and dividing the result by Sales. This returns Gross Profit as a Percentage of Sales.

Horizontal Analysis   The comparison of a company's financial results with its own, prior results. Compare with *Vertical Analysis.*

Implicit intersection The intersection of a row and a column that is implied by a formula, rather than explicitly defined in the formula. If cells A1:E1 constitute a range named Prices, you could enter, using the key combination Ctrl+Enter, into cells A2:E2 the formula =Prices*.06 to return the sales tax. This formula implies that cell A2 should use the value in cell A1, cell B2 should use the value in cell B1, and so on. It implies an intersection between the first row and the column that contains a particular value.

Income statement A report of the changes in the financial position of a business during an accounting period, usually composed of a summary of its revenues, less the cost of goods sold, less operating expenses, less other expenses such as taxes, resulting in an estimate of earnings. Income statements used for external reporting must follow GAAP guidelines and rules, but income statements used for internal planning may take any of a variety of forms that help the user focus on a particular product, operation, or business strategy.

Intercept The y-axis value of a line at the point that its value on the x-axis is zero. Combined with knowledge of the line's slope, the intercept helps to forecast an unknown y-value given its known x-value.

Internal rate of return (IRR) A measure of the profitability of an investment based on a series of cash flows generated by the investment. IRR is the discount rate that causes the net present value of an investment to be zero.

Inventory profit The profit that can be created simply by holding goods in inventory as their replacement price increases due to changes in market conditions.

Just In Time (JIT) An approach to inventory management that calls for goods required for production or resale to be obtained no earlier than absolutely necessary.

Last-in, First-out (LIFO) A method of inventory valuation that assumes that the value of the goods which were sold from inventory during the period is the value of the goods acquired most recently. Compare with *FIFO* and *Average Cost*.

Liability A debt incurred by a business: thus, a claim by a creditor against the businesss assets.

Local names Also known as sheet-level names. A local name belongs only to the sheet where it is defined, and contains the name of the sheet as part of its name. For example, Sheet1!Expenses is a local name: it might be defined as =Sheet1!A1:D4. On Sheet1, you can use formulas that refer to Expenses, such as =SUM(Expenses). But unless Sheet2 also contains the name Sheet2!Expenses, you could not use =SUM(Expenses) on Sheet2, because an unqualified local name is not accessible from another sheet. Instead, on Sheet2 you would have to use =SUM(Sheet1!Expenses). Local names enable you to use the same name, qualified by the name of its sheet, in more than one sheet in a workbook. Compare with *Global names*.

Long-term note payable   An obligation to a creditor that must be satisfied at some point following the end of the current accounting period.

Loop   A series of VBA or Excel 4 macro language statements that execute repetitively. The loop can be under the control of a For statement, in which case the statements usually execute a fixed number of times. It can also be under the control of a Do statement; if so, the statements usually execute until some Boolean condition changes. Or, it can be under the control of a For Each statement; then, the statements execute once for each member of a collection, such as for each worksheet in a workbook.

Lot Tolerance Percent Defective   The lowest level of non-defective products that a buyer is willing to accept in an individual lot. Compare with *Acceptable Quality Level*.

Matching principle   A basic principle of accrual accounting: revenues should be matched with the expenses that helped to produce them.

Method   In VBA, an action that can be performed on an Object. For example, the Range object has the Delete method: you would use that method to delete a worksheet range.

Mixed Reference   A mixed reference is a combination of an absolute and a relative reference. It has a dollar sign before either its row component or its column component. $A1 and A$1 are examples of mixed references. If you enter =$A1 in cell C1, and copy it to cell D1, the reference will not change, but if you copy it from C1 to C2, the formula will change to =$A2. On the other hand, if you enter =A$1 in cell C1, and copy it to cell D1, the reference will change to =B$1, but if you copy it from C1 to C2, the formula will not change. Compare with *absolute reference* and *relative reference*.

Moving average   A method used in forecasting under which the variation of individual observations from a long-term trend is suppressed by converting each forecast into an average of several prior observations.

Named range   A range of cells that is assigned a name, usually by means of the Name Box, or by means of Insert, Name, Define or Insert, Name, Create. After you have assigned a name to a range, you can use the name in place of the range's address in formulas. This makes the structure and function of a worksheet much easier to understand. For example, suppose that cells A1:A12 are given the name MonthlySales. It is easier to understand the intent of the formula =SUM(MonthlySales) than it is to understand the intent of =SUM(A1:A12).

Net present value   The value of an investment as of today, less its loss in value due to discounting.

Net Profit Margin   A measure of a company's profitability after taxes and operating expenses are taken into account. After subtracting Cost of Goods Sold, operating expenses, and taxes from Sales, the result is divided by Sales. This expresses net profit—the amount available for distribution or reinvestment—as a percentage of the company's sales.

Object   In VBA, a structure in a workbook, such as a worksheet, a menu bar or a range (Excel itself, the Application, is also an object). Objects belong to collections (you can, for example, think of a workbook as a collection of worksheets). Objects have Methods and Properties.

Object variable   In VBA, a variable that stands in for an object such as a worksheet range. Object variables are assigned to the objects that they represent by means of the Set statement.

Operating Characteristic Curve   A curve used in acceptance sampling that provides a visual representation of the effects of requirements as to quality that are imposed by the buyer and by the nature of the production process.

Option Explicit   An option that can be set at the beginning of a VBA module sheet. Using this option means that you cannot use a variable name before you have declared it, usually with a Dim statement. If you omit this option from your VBA module, you can declare variables implicitly, simply by using their names. Because variables that are declared implicitly are, by default, Variant variables (and which occupy a relatively large amount of memory) and because it's easy to misspell a variable's name (which would simply create a new variable), it's recommended that you use Option Explicit except in *very* short VBA programs.

Owner's equity The difference between a company's total assets and its total liabilities. The sum of the amounts that the owner(s) invested in the business, plus any profits that the business has retained.

Passing a variable In VBA, the process of making a variable that is available to a calling procedure (a sub or a function) accessible to a called procedure. The called procedure might change the value of that variable, and subsequently pass the changed value back to the calling procedure.

Payback period The time required to recover the cost of an investment from the value (usually, the cash) generated by the investment.

Percentage of completion A method of determining how much revenue to recognize during any given period of a multi-period contract, usually based on the portion of total costs that have been expended.

Percentage of Sales A method of estimating items in an Income Statement. Most such items are driven by the dollar amount of sales in a given period, and it's often possible to establish that, for example, Salaries have historically been 35 percent of Sales. Then, it is possible to estimate Salaries for the upcoming period by first estimating Sales and calculating 35 percent of that estimate. The Percentage of Sales approach is also sometimes used to estimate the amount of past due Accounts Receivable that will never be collected.

Periodic inventory system A method of inventory valuation under which inventory is counted and valued at the end of an accounting period. This method is normally used by businesses that deal in a high unit volume of products whose unit value is relatively low.

Perpetual inventory system A method of inventory valuation under which the value, and the quantity on hand, of each inventory unit is known and can be recorded as frequently as desired. This method is normally used by businesses that deal with a relatively small number of units, each with a relatively high value.

Post To move transaction information, initially recorded chronologically in a journal, to the appropriate account in a ledger.

Prepaid expenses Amounts paid for goods and services prior to the time that the expense is actually incurred. An example is an insurance policy that is purchased at the beginning of the year, and that provides protection throughout the year. The expense is incurred as protection expires; the prepaid expense is the amount originally paid for the policy.

Present value   The value today of an amount you will receive at some future time. For example, present value is the amount you would have to invest in a financial instrument so that the instrument would be worth $1,000 one year from today.

Price-earnings (P/E) ratio   The ratio of the market price of one share of a company's stock to its per-share earnings. Generally, the lower the P/E ratio, the better the stock is as an investment. A company's earnings are usually a good measure of its value, and the smaller the price you must pay for that value, the better the investment.

Pro forma   A projection or forecast based on a financial statement. A pro forma income statement, for example, might project next year's revenues, costs, and expenses.

Profitability index   A measure that compares the profitability of investments that have equivalent rates of return, but that require different initial investment amounts.

Property   An aspect of an Object. For example, a worksheet Button object has the Height property, which defines how tall the button is.

Quick Ratio   A company's current assets less its inventory, divided by its current liabilities. This ratio tests a company's ability to meet its current obligations without having to liquidate its inventory.

R-squared   A measure of how well a regression equation predicts one variable on the basis of another variable or variables. R-squared can vary from 0.0 to 1.0; the closer it is to 1.0, the better the prediction.

Range   A group of cells on a worksheet, such as A1:D4. Technically, a single cell is itself a range, but in normal usage the term range means more than one contiguous cell.

Recognition   The recording of revenue in accounting records and financial statements. This occurs when you objectively know its amount, when you objectively know when it will occur, and when the earning process is virtually complete.

RefersTo property   Whatever an Excel name represents. Most often this is the address of a worksheet range, as entered in the Refers To edit box in the Define Name dialog box. It can also be a constant value if the name represents a constant.

Regression equation   An equation that can be used to predict an unknown value from known values. Excel uses the LINEST function to analyze the relationships among two or more variables and to return a set of coefficients that define the equation. For example, you could use LINEST to analyze the relationship between Year (1971, 1972, ..., 1995) and revenues for each year. By applying the equation to the value 1996, you can predict the revenues you would expect to have for 1996.

Relative reference   A relative reference contains no dollar signs ($). A1:D4 is an example of a relative reference. Suppose that you enter =SUM(A1:D4) in cell F1. If you then copy the formula in cell F1 to cell G1, the reference adjusts to =SUM(B1:E4). The reference remains *relative* to the location of the formula that uses it. Compare with *absolute reference* and *mixed reference*.

Replacement cost   The cost of replacing an existing asset. This is sometimes used in place of Actual Cost as a means of valuing the asset.

Return on Assets (ROA)   A measure of how well a company uses its resources to create earnings. One common formula for ROA divides EBITDA by total assets. Compare with *Return on Equity*.

Return on Equity (ROE)   A measure of a company's ability to create earnings, as a function of its equity. The usual formula is net income divided by stockholder equity. By comparing ROA with ROE, you can infer how a company tends to raise money: through debt financing or through new investment.

Revenue   The price paid by customers for a business's goods and services.

Sales mix   The manner in which different products are combined to create a product line.

Salvage value   The value of an asset at the end of its depreciable life.

Seasonality   The tendency of sales to increase during certain seasons and to decrease at other times of the year. The sale of winter apparel tends to be seasonal. Certain forecasting methods can account for and project seasonal variations in sales levels.

Semivariable costs   Costs of operations that do not increase on a one-to-one basis with each additional product that is produced, but that increase markedly as certain production thresholds are reached. Compare with *variable costs* and *fixed costs*.

Sensitivity Analysis   An analysis that examines the effects of changing different inputs, such as advertising expenses or depreciation method, on selected results, such as revenue or earnings.

Set statement   A VBA statement that causes an object, such as a range of cells on a worksheet, to be assigned to a VBA variable. For example:

Set CurrentRange = ActiveSheet.Range(Cells(1,1),Cells(5,5))

Short-term note payable   A debt that must be satisfied during the current accounting period.

Single Precision   A variable type. A VBA variable declared as Single occupies 32 bits of memory. It is less precise than a Double Precision variable for very large or very small numbers. However, it also occupies less memory than a Double Precision variable. If you need to declare a variable that takes on fractional values, or if its possible values are outside the permitted range for Long Integer, and if the variable could be an array, consider using Single Precision instead of Double Precision. However, if the variable would not be an array, the extra memory used by Double Precision is insignificant. Compare with *Double Precision*.

Slope   The change in the level of a line on its y-axis value as a function of a change in the level of the line on its x-axis. Combined with information about the lines Intercept, the slope can be used in regression approaches to forecasting to predict an unknown y-value, given knowledge of the associated x-value.

Smoothing   A type of forecasting technique that uses, for the current forecast, a combination of the prior observation and the error involved in the prior forecast.

Special Journal   Analogous to a subsidiary ledger, a Special Journal provides a place to record frequently occuring business transactions. This allows the General Journal to function as a place to record infrequently occurring transactions. In this way, similar transactions can be segregated into one location for easy reference.

Standard deviation   A measure of how far different values in a set of numbers vary from their average. In a normal distribution of values, you expect to find about 68 percent of the values within one standard deviation on either side of the average, about 95 percent within two standard deviations on either side of the average, and about 99.7 percent of the values within three standard deviations on either side of the average.

Starting inventory   The value of the goods on hand at the beginning of an accounting period, equal to the value of inventory at the end of the prior accounting period.

Statistical process control (SPC)   A method of determining if the results of a process, such as a production line, are in conformance with their specifications. If the process is not in control, SPC can also point to the time when it began to go out of control.

Straight-line depreciation   A method of calculating depreciation that divides the difference between an asset's original and final values by the number of periods that the asset is in service.

Subsidiary ledger   A representation of all the transactions that occur in a given account during an accounting period. A subsidiary ledger maintains the detail information about the account; its debit and credit totals are transferred to the associated account in the General ledger.

Sum-of-years'-digits   A method of accelerated depreciation that assigns an amount of depreciation based on the number of periods (years) that an asset has been in service, and factored against the asset's original value.

T-account   A format for displaying the debits and credits to an account, so called because the horizontal line under the column headings and the vertical line between the columns forms a "T."

Times Interest Earned   The ratio of a company's earnings before interest and taxes to its total interest payments. A measure of the company's ability to meet its periodic interest payments from its earnings.

Trend   In forecasting and time series analysis, the tendency of data values to increase or decrease over time. A trend might be linear, in which case it describes a straight line. Other frequently occurring, nonlinear trends include quadratic trends (one change of direction over the course of the time series) and cubic trends (two changes in direction over the course of the time series).

Turns Ratio   The number of times during a period that there is complete turnover in a company's inventory. The usual formula is Cost of Goods Sold divided by Average Inventory. Generally, the higher the Turns Ratio, the better: goods that remain in inventory too long tie up the company's resources and often incur storage expenses as well as loss of value.

Unearned revenue   Revenue that must be recognized during a period because it has been received from a customer, but that has not as yet been earned (and therefore has no associated expense during the current period).

Union   In Excel, the combination of two different ranges such that they are treated as one.

User-defined function   A function created by the user in either VBA code or in the Excel 4 macro language. You can enter a user-defined function in a worksheet cell, just as you enter a built-in worksheet function such as SUM( ). In VBA, a user-defined function is identified with the keyword Function, rather than with the keyword Sub. Within the body of the function's code, a value must be assigned to the function's name. A user-defined function can only return a value: it cannot perform other actions such as inserting a row or formatting a range.

Variable costs   Costs that increase as the number of goods produced or services rendered increase. Compare with *Fixed costs*.

Variable declining balance   An accelerated depreciation method that increases the speed with which an asset is depreciated, beyond that provided by declining balance depreciation.

Variable type   The type of a variable defines what sorts of values it may take on. A variables type is usually declared in a Dim statement. If a variable is declared as, for example, Integer, it cannot take on either the value Fred (which is a string) or 3.1416 (which has a decimal component). See *Variant*.

Variance Analysis   The comparison of an actual, financial result with an expected result. A company might have a negotiated contract with a supplier to purchase materials at a standard cost. If the actual amount of payment for the materials differs from the standard cost, the difference represents a variance. Other, similar comparisons include analyzing the differences between budgeted amounts and actual expenditures. The term is similar to Analysis of Variance but the two types of analysis are used for completely different purposes.

Variant   A type of variable in VBA. A variant variable, in contrast to other variable types, can take on any value, such as an integer, a decimal value, text, or a logical value. Declaring a variable as Variant is also a useful way to assign the values in a worksheet range to a VBA array.

VBA   Visual Basic, Applications Edition. You can use the VBA language to write programs (macros) that Excel executes.

Vertical Analysis   The comparison of a company's financial results with those of other companies in the same industry grouping. Compare with *Horizontal Analysis*.

Weighted Average   An average of a set of numbers such that certain numbers receive a greater weight than do other numbers. The formula =SUM(12*{1,2,3},4,5,6)/6 is a weighted average, because the numbers 1, 2, and 3 are weighted by a factor of 12, and the numbers 4, 5, and 6 are not weighted.

With statement and block   The With statement initiates a With block; the End With statement terminates the With block. Inside the block, you can refer to methods or properties of the object named in the With statement, and yet not have to qualify the method or property by referring again to the object.

Working capital   The difference between current assets and current liabilities: the amount of resources a business has on hand to support its operations.

Index

Y

y-axis values
    intercept, 536
    slope, 542

Z

zero amounts, suppressing,
  124
ZIP codes (geographic data),
  392

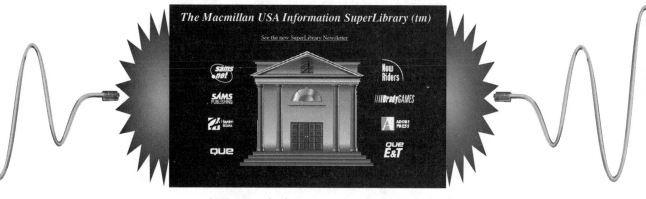

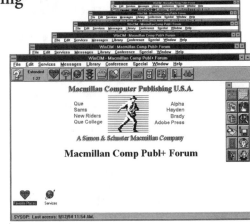

Complete and Return this Card
for a *FREE* Computer Book Catalog

Thank you for purchasing this book! You have purchased a superior computer book written expressly for your needs. To continue to provide the kind of up-to-date, pertinent coverage you've come to expect from us, we need to hear from you. Please take a minute to complete and return this self-addressed, postage-paid form. In return, we'll send you a free catalog of all our computer books on topics ranging from word processing to programming and the internet.

Mr. ☐   Mrs. ☐   Ms. ☐   Dr. ☐

Name (first) ☐☐☐☐☐☐☐☐☐☐☐☐ (M.I.) ☐ (last) ☐☐☐☐☐☐☐☐☐☐☐☐☐☐☐☐

Address ☐☐☐☐☐☐☐☐☐☐☐☐☐☐☐☐☐☐☐☐☐☐☐☐☐☐☐☐☐☐☐

City ☐☐☐☐☐☐☐☐☐☐☐☐☐☐ State ☐☐ Zip ☐☐☐☐☐ ☐☐☐☐

Phone ☐☐☐ ☐☐☐ ☐☐☐☐ Fax ☐☐☐ ☐☐☐ ☐☐☐☐

Company Name ☐☐☐☐☐☐☐☐☐☐☐☐☐☐☐☐☐☐☐☐☐☐☐☐☐

E-mail address ☐☐☐☐☐☐☐☐☐☐☐☐☐☐☐☐☐☐☐☐☐☐☐☐☐

1. Please check at least (3) influencing factors for purchasing this book.

Front or back cover information on book ☐
Special approach to the content ☐
Completeness of content ☐
Author's reputation ☐
Publisher's reputation ☐
Book cover design or layout ☐
Index or table of contents of book ☐
Price of book ☐
Special effects, graphics, illustrations ☐
Other (Please specify): _____ ☐

2. How did you first learn about this book?

Saw in Macmillan Computer Publishing catalog ☐
Recommended by store personnel ☐
Saw the book on bookshelf at store ☐
Recommended by a friend ☐
Received advertisement in the mail ☐
Saw an advertisement in: _____ ☐
Read book review in: _____ ☐
Other (Please specify): _____ ☐

3. How many computer books have you purchased in the last six months?

This book only ☐   3 to 5 books ☐
Books ☐   More than 5 ☐

4. Where did you purchase this book?

Bookstore ☐
Computer Store ☐
Consumer Electronics Store ☐
Department Store ☐
Office Club ☐
Warehouse Club ☐
Mail Order ☐
Direct from Publisher ☐
Internet site ☐
Other (Please specify): _____ ☐

5. How long have you been using a computer?

☐ Less than 6 months   ☐ 6 months to a year
☐ 1 to 3 years   ☐ More than 3 years

6. What is your level of experience with personal computers and with the subject of this book?

	With PCs	With subject of book
New	☐	☐
Casual	☐	☐
Accomplished	☐	☐
Expert	☐	☐

Source Code ISBN: 0-7897-0382-3

7. Which of the following best describes your job title?

Administrative Assistant .... ☐
Coordinator .... ☐
Manager/Supervisor .... ☐
Director .... ☐
Vice President .... ☐
President/CEO/COO .... ☐
Lawyer/Doctor/Medical Professional .... ☐
Teacher/Educator/Trainer .... ☐
Engineer/Technician .... ☐
Consultant .... ☐
Not employed/Student/Retired .... ☐
Other (Please specify): _____ ☐

8. Which of the following best describes the area of the company your job title falls under?

Accounting .... ☐
Engineering .... ☐
Manufacturing .... ☐
Operations .... ☐
Marketing .... ☐
Sales .... ☐
Other (Please specify): _____ ☐

Comments: _____
_____
_____

9. What is your age?

Under 20 .... ☐
21-29 .... ☐
30-39 .... ☐
40-49 .... ☐
50-59 .... ☐
60-over .... ☐

10. Are you:

Male .... ☐
Female .... ☐

11. Which computer publications do you read regularly? (Please list)

_____
_____
_____
_____
_____
_____
_____
_____
_____

Fold here and scotch-tape to ma

Licensing Agreement

By opening this package, you are agreeing to be bound by the following: